THE BLUEJACKET'S MANUAL

25TH EDITION

TITLES IN THE SERIES

THE U.S. NAVAL INSTITUTE
BLUE & GOLD PROFESSIONAL LIBRARY

For more than 100 years, U.S. Navy professionals have counted on specialized books published by the Naval Institute Press to prepare them for their responsibilities as they advance in their careers and to serve as ready references and refreshers when needed. From the days of coal-fired battleships to the era of unmanned aerial vehicles and laser weaponry, such perennials as *The Bluejacket's Manual* and the *Watch Officer's Guide* have guided generations of Sailors through the complex challenges of naval service. As these books are updated and new ones are added to the list, they will carry the distinctive mark of the Blue & Gold Professional Library series to remind and reassure their users that they have been prepared by naval professionals and meet the exacting standards that Sailors have long expected from the U.S. Naval Institute.

BLUE & GOLD
PROFESSIONAL LIBRARY

THE BLUEJACKET'S MANUAL

25TH EDITION

THOMAS J. CUTLER

EXECUTIVE EDITOR
Master Chief Petty Officer Mark T. Hacala, USN (Ret.)

ASSOCIATE EDITORS
Lieutenant Brian Corcoran, JAGC, USN
Senior Chief Petty Officer Phillip Laxton, USN
Petty Officer First Class Daniel Richard, USN
Senior Chief Petty Officer Terry Schmalgemeir, USN (Ret.)

ASSISTANT EDITORS
Petty Officer First Class Gabrielle Blake, USN
Petty Officer Second Class Bruno Calderon, USN
Petty Officer First Class Abby Cannon, USN
Petty Officer Second Class Jessica Carroll, USN
Petty Officer First Class Mario Delgadogonzalez, USN
Petty Officer First Class Lucien Gauthier, USN
Petty Officer First Class Lauren Jones, USN
Petty Officer First Class Ajhourni McClain, USN
Chief Petty Officer Han Peng, USN
Petty Officer First Class Lashia White-Wilson, USN

NAVAL INSTITUTE PRESS
ANNAPOLIS, MARYLAND

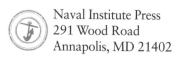

Naval Institute Press
291 Wood Road
Annapolis, MD 21402

© 2017 by the United States Naval Institute

ISBN: 978-1-61251-974-6 (hardcover)
ISBN: 978-1-61251-975-3 (paperback)
ISBN: 978-1-61251-976-0 (eBook)

⁕ Figures 2.2, 2.7, 3.2, 3.5, 6.16, 11.3, 11.4, 12.1, 12.2, 12.3, 12.4, 12.5, 12.6, 12.7, 12.8, 12.9, 12.10, 12.11, 12.12, 13.2, 13.3, 13.4, 14.5, 15.2, 15.3, 15.4, 15.5, 15.6, 15.7, 15.9, 17.2, 17.3, 17.4, 17.11, 20.1, 20.2, 20.3, and 20.4 created by Jim Caiella.

⁕ Figure 16.2 created by Chris Robinson.

⁕ TABS Figure 10-a-15 is U.S. Navy photo courtesy of General Dynamics NASSCO/Released.

⁕ All other images are officially released Navy Department photos or are from the U.S. Naval Institute photo archive.

⊗ Print editions meet the requirements of ANSI/NISO z39.48-1992 (Permanence of Paper). Printed in the United States of America.

25 24 23 22 21 20 19 18   9 8 7 6 5 4

THE NAVY ETHOS

We are the United States Navy, our nation's
sea power—ready guardians of peace,
victorious in war.

❧

We are professional sailors and civilians—
a diverse and agile force exemplifying the
highest standards of service to our nation,
at home and abroad, at sea and ashore.

❧

Integrity is the foundation of our conduct;
respect for others is fundamental to our character;
decisive leadership is crucial to our success.

❧

We are a team, disciplined and well-prepared,
committed to mission accomplishment.
We do not waver in our dedication and
accountability to our shipmates and families.

❧

We are patriots, forged by the Navy's core
values of honor, courage and commitment.
In times of war and peace, our actions reflect
our proud heritage and tradition.

❧

We defend our nation and prevail in the face of
adversity with strength, determination, and dignity.

❧

We are the United States Navy.

CONTENTS

ILLUSTRATIONS

ILLUSTRATIONS IN CHAPTERS

HOW TO USE THIS BOOK

The first part of the book consists of "**Chapters**" that provide introductions and basic explanations that Sailors new to the Navy will find most helpful.

The second part consists of "**Tabs**" that deal with specifics—often mere tables—that seasoned Sailors will find useful for reference purposes.

Also included are **Appendices** that contain general reference information. See the Table of Contents for lists of the above.

QUICK TAB INDEX

SUBJECT	TAB
3M Periodicity Codes	11-B
Addressing Military Personnel	5-A
Aircraft, Identifying Military	16-B
Anchor Chain Identification System	12-C
Anchoring Commands	12-D
Awards, Precedence	6-I
Awards, Wearing	6-H
Bells, Ship's	13-D
Blocks and Tackles	12-E

SUBJECT	TAB
Boat Customs and Etiquette	12-F
Classes of Fire	15-B
Classifications of Ships	10-B
Coast Guard Officer Shoulder Boards and Sleeve Markings	6-E
Code of Conduct	4-A
Conditions of Readiness (Cruising)	13-B
Conditions of Readiness (Material)	15-A
Core Values of the U.S. Navy	1-B
Correspondence (Letter Format)	19-C
Cruising Conditions	13-B
DOD Organization	8-A
Electronics Designation System	17-C
Enlisted Rank Devices of the Other Armed Services	6-B
Fire, Classes	15-B
Flag, Folding	3-A
Flags, Signal and Pennants	20-E
Folding the Flag	3-A
Force Protection Conditions	9-A
Forms of Address in the Armed Services	5-A
FPCONs	9-A
General Orders of a Sentry	13-A
General Rates	5-C
Identifying Military Aircraft	16-B
Joint Electronics Type Designation System	17-C
Letter Format	19-C
Line and Staff Corps Devices	6-G
Line-Handling Commands	12-B

SUBJECT	TAB
Material Conditions of Readiness	15-A
MC Systems	20-A
Message Format	19-D
Mooring Line Configurations and Terms	12-A
Morse Code	20-D
Naval Aircraft, Types	16-A
Naval Weapons, Types	17-B
Navy Enlisted Sleeve Markings	6-A
Navy Officer Shoulder Boards and Sleeve Markings	6-D
Navy Organization	8-A
Navy Publications	19-A
Navy Time	1-C
Officer Collar, Cap, and Shoulder Rank Devices	6-C
Organization, DOD	8-A
Organization, Navy	8-A
Pay Grades	5-A
Phonetic Alphabet	20-C
Precedence of Awards	6-I
Prowords, Radiotelephone	20-G
Publications	19-A
Radiotelephone Prowords	20-G
Ranks and Rates	5-A
Ratings	5-B
Sailor's Creed	1-A
Semaphore Signaling System	20-F
Sentry Orders	13-A
Ship Type Classifications	10-B
Ship's Bells	13-D

SUBJECT	TAB
Shipboard Compartment Identification	11-A
Ships and Craft	10-A
Signal Flags and Pennants	20-E
Small Arms, Proper Use	17-D
Sound-Powered Communications System	20-B
SSIC	19-B
Standard Subject Identification Codes	19-B
Time	1-C
Time Zones of the World	19-E
Warfare and Qualification Insignia	6-J
Warrant Officer Rank Devices	6-F
Watch Structure	13-C
Weapons	17-B
Weapons Designation Systems	17-A
Wearing of Awards	6-H

BLUEJACKET'S MANUAL (BJM) WEBSITE

www.usni.org/BlueAndGoldProfessionalBooks/TheBluejacketsManual

This website is provided by the U.S. Naval Institute to keep this manual up to date and to provide supplementary material. Checking this site periodically will keep the information in your BJM up to date and accurate.

If you find errors in your BJM, or if something needs to be updated, please visit the site or send an email to BluejacketsManual@usni.org with recommended changes. After verification, suggested modifications or corrections or updates will be posted on this website—**with or without your name as you prefer.**

ACKNOWLEDGMENTS

First I must acknowledge the contributions of the "BJM25 Crew" (see "Introduction"). Without them, this book would be impossible. It would take another volume to acknowledge all that each individual contributed, and one risks inadvertently diminishing the contributions of others when singling out a few among the many, so I must reluctantly refrain from saying many things that reside in my heart about the contributions of those whose names appear on the title page of this book. I hope that I have somehow assured each of them of my heartfelt gratitude for the many things they did.

In addition to the assistance provided by my "shipmates" in the BJM25 Crew, there are a number of individuals who also assisted in myriad ways. Again, limited space dictates that I cannot provide details, but I am very grateful to (in alphabetical order) Mary Acosta, Jessica Anderson, Art Athens, Jake Bebber, Heidi Blough, Nathan Christensen, Denis Clift, Jim Dolbow, Michael Good, Jonathon Hoppe, Janis Jorgensen, JD Kristenson, David Kupper, Inge Lockwood, Jehanne Moharram, Glenn Moyer, Christopher Robinson, Maryam Rostamian, David Smiley, Gary Thompson, and Jesse-LaRou Walsh. In the Navy, we have a long tradition of "pulling together" that stems from the hoisting of sails and continues today with the handling of mooring lines and the like. These individuals have indeed "pulled together" to help safely moor this ship and I cannot thank them enough.

There are two individuals who must be acknowledged for their outstanding work in areas outside of content. I have long been in awe of those unsung heroes of the book publishing process who do the behind-the-scenes editing that does much to make writers into *authors*; but it is no exaggeration to say that Emily Bakely, who managed the production process of this book, is unsurpassed in the amount of industry, talent, and dedication that she brings to every project she takes on. She improves every book exponentially through her "above and beyond" determination to make every book the best it can possibly be.

And words truly elude me in attempting to describe the talent, hard work, and cooperation that Jim Caiella brought to many of the new illustrations appearing in this twenty-fifth edition. Jim was incredibly responsive to my every request, no matter if it was tedious tweaking or starting from scratch. Jim's "can-do" spirit is compatible with those standards that have made our Sailors the finest in the world.

INTRODUCTION

I doubt that Lieutenant Ridley McLean had any idea that his book would become an American institution—lasting for much more than a century—when he wrote the first edition of *The Bluejacket's Manual* in 1902. Recognizing that young men entering the Navy had no source of information to introduce them to their new profession, he created this book to serve as a useful reference and to help them adjust to this strange new seafaring/military world with its strange culture, different language, and demanding ways.

Since Lieutenant McLean's day, the Navy has grown from fledgling sea power to master of the world's oceans, and both technology and American culture have changed in ways probably unimaginable in his day. Many new terms have been added (and many retained) to that strange lexicon of the sea. Although the term "Bluejacket" is less often used today than "Sailor," the original name has been retained out of respect for tradition (something the Navy has always valued highly). American Bluejackets themselves have evolved in many ways, and a comparison of the "tones" of the 1902 edition and this one is quite apparent. Today's Sailors are more informed and very often more educated than Sailors of yesteryear. They are volunteers—something that was not always true—and they are more unique in American society than they ever were before.

While *The Bluejacket's Manual* has evolved (through more than twenty revisions), its original purpose has remained steadfastly on course. Like its predecessors, this new edition makes no attempt to be a comprehensive textbook on all things naval—to do so today would require a multivolume set that would defy practicality—but it continues to serve two very important purposes. First, it serves as a primer that introduces new recruits to their Navy and helps them make the transition from civilian to Sailor. Second, it serves as a handy reference that Sailors can rely on as a ready source of basic information as they continue their service, whether for only one "hitch" or for an entire career. To that end, I have reorganized this twenty-fifth edition to reflect those dual purposes. Explained in more detail in the "How to Use This Book" section, readers will find that the first part of the book serves the "primer" purpose using traditional chapters and the second part uses "Tabs" to serve as reference material.

"BJM25 CREW"

A book of this size and importance could not (and *should not*) be assembled by only one person. There are too many varied topics covered, and much of the material periodically changes. Consequently, at the very beginning of this revision, I assembled a team of editors who voluntarily contributed their time and expertise to assist me in many ways in the writing of this book. We called ourselves the "BJM25 Crew" and enjoyed a wonderful working relationship over the many months that it has taken to complete the project. I am completely confident in them—if there are errors in this book, they are mine—and am in awe of their willingness to invest their valuable time knowing that the only rewards would be the pride that comes with having their names on the title page and the knowledge that they had contributed to the twenty-fifth edition of a book that has been serving Sailors for more than a century.

My debt to the "BJM25 Crew" is large indeed.

BJM WEBSITE

Another change to this twenty-fifth edition reflects the availability and volatility of information in these modern times. Things change rapidly today as technology advances and procedures evolve. This is compensated by the availability of information, most notably by the Internet. But a major drawback to the Internet is that information residing there is of varying quality—some of it out-of-date and some simply wrong.

Taking advantage of the timeliness afforded by the Internet, while ensuring accuracy and dependability, the Naval Institute is providing a *Bluejacket's Manual* companion website that can be accessed at **www.usni .org/BlueAndGoldProfessionalBooks/TheBluejacketsManual.** The primary purpose is to provide updates and corrections so that your manual is current and accurate, but the site also includes supplementary material, such as additional resources and items of related interest. In the latter category, readers visiting the website will find a PDF of the original 1902 edition of *The Bluejacket's Manual* and a listing of the revised editions that have appeared over the years.

READER PARTICIPATION

Because it is in the best interests of all concerned that this manual be kept up to date, *readers are encouraged* to submit recommended changes to:

> The Bluejacket's Manual
> U.S. Naval Institute
> 291 Wood Road
> Annapolis, Maryland 21409
> -or-
> **BluejacketsManual@usni.org**

DIFFERENCES FROM OLDER EDITIONS

Collectors of earlier editions of *The Bluejacket's Manual* and some older readers may note that the title of the last several editions is slightly different from what it was for many years prior. It has been slightly modified by moving the apostrophe in *Bluejackets'* from the plural possessive to the singular possessive—that is, *Bluejacket's*—position. This change was made because the original 1902 edition was entitled *The Bluejacket's Manual.* For reasons unknown today, the title was changed to *The Bluejackets' Manual* sometime after World War I and remained that way for many decades. A return to the original makes sense not only for traditional reasons but because the singular possessive is more appropriate to the personal nature of this book.

Another noticeable change is that since I have been writing this book, I have chosen to abandon the rather stilted language that comes with the third person; I choose to speak directly to the Sailor by frequently using the second person.

Ridley McLean is no longer the author of this book, and much of what is now in these pages would be wholly unfamiliar to him, but it is a testimony to the Navy's heritage and its traditions that he would be fully comfortable with many of the terms, customs, and ceremonies that have endured for more than a century. *The Bluejacket's Manual* has played an important role in the preservation of our naval heritage as well as serving as a reference book and as the introduction to the Navy that Lieutenant McLean intended.

ONE

WELCOME ABOARD

Welcome aboard! These words carry a world of significance. They mean that you have made one of the biggest decisions a person can—you have volunteered to enlist in the United States Navy. By raising your right hand and taking the oath of enlistment, you have become a member of one of the most important military services in the world and joined one of the biggest businesses in the United States. Not only have you proved your understanding of citizenship by offering your services to your country, but you have also taken the first step toward an exciting and rewarding career should you choose to remain in the Navy.

If you are not already familiar with names like John Paul Jones, Stephen Decatur, Doris Miller, William F. Halsey, Grace Hopper, and Marvin Shields, you soon will be. And you will likely feel honored to be serving, as they once did, in the same United States Navy.

Today's Navy is a massive and complex organization, a far cry from the makeshift fleet that opposed the British in the Revolutionary War. Hundreds of ships, thousands of aircraft, hundreds of thousands of people, and an annual budget in the billions of dollars go together to make the U.S. Navy a powerful and important component of the American defense establishment, playing a vital role in maintaining our national security, deterring potential enemies, protecting us against our adversaries in time of war, and supporting our foreign policy in peacetime. Through its exercise of sea power, the Navy ensures freedom of the seas so that merchant ships can bring us the vital raw materials we import from abroad, like petroleum, rubber, sugar, and aluminum. Sea power makes it possible for us to use the oceans when and where our national interests require it, and denies our enemies that same freedom. Sea power permits us to take the fight to the enemy when that is required, rather than waiting for the enemy to attack us in our homeland.

As a Sailor you are a part of all that—a vital part, for the ships and aircraft of the Navy are only as good as the people who operate them.

Because the Navy is both a military service and a sea service, to make the transition from civilian to Sailor you must learn the ways of both.

FIRST ENLISTMENT

Your introduction to the Navy probably started at your hometown recruiting station, with interviews and processing conducted by a Navy recruiter. He or she was specially trained to compare your desires and your qualifications with the needs of the Navy to establish the terms of your service. Your "contract" with the Navy is officially called an enlistment, but you might hear it described informally as a "hitch." It began when you took the oath of enlistment, and it will last from two to six years, depending upon the terms agreed upon by you and your recruiter.

"Boot Camp"

All recruits begin their naval careers in what is officially called Recruit Training Command (RTC), but is more traditionally referred to as "Boot Camp." Although you may have relatives who once trained at boot camps in other parts of the country, currently the Navy is operating only one RTC, located at the Naval Station (NAVSTA) in Great Lakes, Illinois. This 1,628-acre training facility, on the shore of Lake Michigan about forty miles north of Chicago, has been training Sailors since July 1911. During World War II, nearly a million Sailors were trained there.

You and the other recruits will make the transition from civilian to military life in the time you will spend at RTC. Nearly every minute of every day will be filled with military drills, physical training, hands-on experiences, and a busy schedule of drills and classes on naval history, traditions, customs, operations, and regulations. At first you will probably find the transition challenging and a bit disconcerting—you will have completely changed your environment, diet, sleep patterns, climate, clothes, and companions—but within a relatively short period, you will make the necessary adjustments and find a great deal of pride to replace your initial anxiety.

[1.1] As an American Sailor, you are a vital part of the world's most powerful Navy.

[1.2] A large group taking the oath of enlistment in Chicago

[1.3] Recruit Training Command, also known as "Boot Camp"

FIRST WEEKS IN THE NAVY

From the moment you arrive at RTC, the process of "Sailorization" begins, giving you the knowledge, capabilities, and attitudes necessary to be able to effectively participate in the defense of this nation and all it stands for as a valuable member of the United States Navy. It is a transformation that is not simple or easy, but it is one that has been accomplished by many before you and it is one you will not regret. Even those who remain in the Navy for only one enlistment often recall their time in the service as one of the most important times in their lives. And it all begins at RTC.

P-Days

The day of arrival at RTC is called receipt day, when your initial processing begins. The next five days will be your processing days (P-Days). The procedures may vary from time to time but in general begin like this: Report in; turn in orders; draw your bedding and bunk assignment for your first night aboard; begin learning how to be a Sailor.

Haircuts

Every recruit will get a haircut, and chances are, it will be different from what you are used to. While male recruits won't get their heads shaved, the barber won't leave enough hair to comb either. Female recruits must get special haircuts to conform to Navy standards. Later, at your first duty station, you will have more choice in hairstyle, but you will still have to conform to Navy Regulations.

Medical Examinations

As a Sailor, you will have to be in excellent health and good physical condition to perform your duties properly. Navy medical personnel will examine you from head to toe, run blood tests and urinalysis, take X-rays, and give you a series of inoculations—the works! If you need dental work, it will be done as well.

Clothing Issue

At first you will receive an initial clothing issue that includes enough uniform clothing to make you look like a Sailor and to allow you to perform your duties while in boot camp. Eventually you will receive a complete outfit, called a "seabag," worth hundreds of dollars and a source of great pride.

NEX Card

You will not need money while in boot camp. You will be issued a Navy Exchange (NEX) card to be used in the Navy Exchange for toilet articles, sewing kits, shoeshine gear, notebooks, and pens and pencils. The total cost will be deducted from your pay.

ID Card

You will be issued a Common Access Card (CAC), a "smart" card about the size of a credit card, which is the standard Armed Forces of the United States Identification Card—"ID card"—that identifies you as a member of the armed forces. While it is unique to you and in your possession, it remains government property and must be returned when you are discharged. Altering it, damaging it, counterfeiting it, or using it in an unauthorized manner (such as lending your card to someone or borrowing another person's card) can result in serious disciplinary action.

Your card shows your name and the date your enlistment expires. Carry it at all times. Besides granting you access to ships, Navy Exchanges, and other government installations, it will identify you as one protected by the provisions of the Geneva Convention should you become a prisoner of war.

If you lose your card, you must report it immediately and you will have to sign a statement detailing the circumstances of the loss.

BOOT CAMP ROUTINE

Soon after reporting in, you will be placed in a division and will meet the people you'll be with for the coming weeks, and you will be assigned a division number and introduced to your recruit division commanders (RDCs), who will guide you through the Sailorization process. Upon completion of your P-Days, you will move into your barracks (named after a Navy ship). Then, during a formal commissioning ceremony, an officer will welcome you, give a brief talk on the history and mission of the Navy, and present a division flag (called a "guidon"—pronounced "guide-on") bearing your division number.

Recruit Division Commander

Each division, usually about eighty-four recruits, is taken through training by its RDCs—outstanding chiefs and petty officers who are intimately familiar with instructional techniques, principles of leadership, and administrative procedures. The RDCs will instruct you in military and physical drills and show you how to keep yourself, your clothing, equipment, and barracks in smart, shipshape condition. While at boot camp, your RDCs are the most important people in the Navy. Keep in mind that your RDCs once went through recruit training just like you; by now, they have many years of naval experience. Follow your RDCs' example and you'll make a good start toward a successful time in the Navy.

Chain of Command

The Navy is organized like a pyramid, with the President of the United States at the top as commander in chief of the armed forces. There are many levels below the president leading eventually to you. This is known as the chain of command. Just as you must follow the orders and guidance of your RDCs, they must, likewise, follow the orders and guidance of the ship's leading chief petty officer, and he or she must follow those of the ship's officer, and so on. Your chain of command will change somewhat each time you report to a new duty station, but while you are at RTC, your chain of command is as follows:

> President of the United States (Commander in Chief)
> Secretary of Defense
> Secretary of the Navy
> Chief of Naval Operations
> Chief of Naval Personnel
> Commander, Naval Education and Training Command
> Commander, Naval Service Training Command (NSTC)
> Commanding Officer RTC
> Executive Officer RTC
> Military Training Director
> Department Head (Fleet Commander)
> Fleet Leading Chief Petty Officer
> Ship's Officer
> Ship's Leading Chief Petty Officer
> Recruit Division Commanders (RDC)
> Recruits (You)

Because you are new to the Navy, you will start out at the bottom of the pyramid, but time, training, experience, hard work, and the right attitude will change that. Keep in mind that everyone in the Navy began at the bottom, and your immediate seniors were once recruits like you.

Daily Routine

Nearly everything you do at boot camp is designed to prepare you for service in the Navy. In ships, submarines, aircraft squadrons, Seabee battalions, and naval stations throughout the world, the daily routine is prescribed by a bulletin called the "Plan of the Day" or, more commonly, the POD. At RTC, the daily routine appears as a schedule on the compartment bulletin board. It issues the special orders for the day, gives the hours of meals, inspections, parades, and other events. Using the master training schedule as their guide, your RDCs will post the information you need to get through each day. Once you leave boot camp, it will be your responsibility to read the POD each day to find out what uniform to wear, what special events are taking place, and so on.

Back to School

You have a lot to learn in order to make the transition from civilian to Sailor. Much of your time will be spent in classrooms. A typical day of instruction includes multiple fifty-minute periods with ten-minute breaks between periods. Many topics will be covered, such as grooming standards, educational benefits, aircraft familiarization, military discipline, and survival at sea.

Some of your classroom training will be augmented by hands-on training, which will give you the opportunity to work with actual equipment and simulate real conditions. Examples of this kind of training are firefighting, seamanship, chemical, biological, and radiological (CBR) defense, and survival at sea techniques where you will actually fight a fire, work with lines and deck equipment, put on a gas mask in a gas chamber, and learn to stay afloat using your clothing as a life preserver.

Few jobs in the Navy are completely independent, so a great deal of emphasis is placed upon teamwork during your training at RTC. Military drill (such as marching) is one way that you and your fellow recruits will learn the importance of instant response to orders and the value of group precision. Later on—when you are helping to launch and recover aircraft on the flight deck of an aircraft carrier, or rescuing a shipmate from the sea, or taking a nuclear submarine into the depths of the ocean—you will fully understand and appreciate the importance of such training.

Training at RTC—which includes such things as the meticulous folding and precise stowage of clothing—may sometimes be seen as nitpicky or unnecessary, but in the highly technical, sometimes dangerous, and often unique surroundings you will find in the Navy, attention to detail can make the difference between success and failure, survival and disaster, victory and defeat. Everything you do in boot camp has a purpose, and the overall mission of RTC is to make you ready for the challenges and opportunities that await you in the U.S. Navy.

Boot Camp Life

Not all of your time at RTC will be spent in training. There will be administrative periods during which you will make pay arrangements, be fitted for uniforms, complete your medical and dental work, and make known your desires for future assignment. Based upon your Armed Services Vocational Aptitude Battery (ASVAB) test scores and your classification interviews, the initial path of your Navy career will be determined.

While at boot camp you will be given the opportunity to attend religious services of your choosing. Chaplains are available for pastoral counseling and religious education. Recruit choirs are organized and often sing at the services.

Because of the tight schedule and the great number of recruits in training, you cannot receive telephone calls while at RTC, but on specified occasions, with permission from your RDC, you will be permitted to make a few outgoing calls.

Visitors are not permitted during training, but you will be permitted to have guests attend your graduation review. Information about this will be provided for you to send home.

You will be paid at least twice while at RTC, but once you graduate you (and every other member of the Navy) will be paid twice a month. You will be paid by electronic transfer of funds through the direct deposit system to the banking institution of your choice.

Competition

The Navy relies upon competition as a means of enhancing readiness and promoting pride. Individual Sailors compete with other Sailors for promotions, and ships and aircraft squadrons compete with each other using appropriate exercises to measure readiness in gunnery, engineering, safety, communications, and other important areas. While at boot camp, your division will compete for awards in athletic skills, scholastic achievement, military drill, inspections, and overall excellence.

Special flags are awarded to divisions in recognition of their achievements, and at the graduation ceremony a number of individuals are selected to receive outstanding recruit awards. Honor graduates will be designated and other recruits will receive special recognition. If you give your best, you may well be among those recognized.

Battle Stations

Near the end of your training at boot camp, you and your fellow recruits will participate in a large-scale exercise called "Battle Stations," which will place you in a realistic scenario designed to test what you have learned at RTC. You will simulate handling emergencies such as the kind you might encounter while serving in the Navy and learn how to function as part of a team while demonstrating your endurance. This physically, mentally, and emotionally demanding exercise will test your abilities in such events as fighting a fire, preparing for an approaching hurricane, conducting a search-and-rescue operation, transporting an injured shipmate, defending a position using small arms, abandoning ship, and so on. After success-fully completing this "final exam," your achievement will be recognized by replacing your recruit cap with the Navy ballcap you will wear in the fleet.

Core Values and the Sailor's Creed

Underlying all the training you will receive at RTC is a focus on self-respect, respect for others, and the core values of honor, courage, and commitment. These are not just words but interrelated concepts that you must take to heart to guide you in virtually everything you do as a Sailor. Before you make a decision or do something, you must consider whether your action will reflect a loss of honor, a failure of courage, or a lack of commitment. If it does, then you should not do it. You should keep in mind that honor includes the honor of your nation and your Navy as well as your own, and that maintaining honor will often require courage and commitment. You should also remember that courage can be physical or moral—sometimes you have to make a decision that is not easy and may not result in you get-ting what you want, but because it is the right thing to do, you must find the courage to do it. And you must be committed to doing what you know is right, what is honorable, what is courageous.

These core values are embodied in the "Sailor's Creed," which you and all recruits will be expected to memorize and to live by for as long as you are in the U.S. Navy. (See TAB 1-A: The Sailor's Creed and TAB 1-B: The Core Values of the United States Navy.)

FROM CIVILIAN TO SAILOR

The ways of the Navy are often very different from what you were used to in civilian life. In boot camp you will take the first steps toward becom-ing a Sailor. You will be introduced to the many differences between civilian life and Navy life, and for the rest of your time in the Navy, whether you stay for only one enlistment or have a thirty-year career, those differences will become second nature to you.

Navy Terminology

Just as doctors, lawyers, baseball players, engineers, artists, and police officers have their own language when communicating within their professions, the Navy too has its own special terminology. Doctors speak of contusions and hemostats, baseball players have their own meanings for "in the alley" or "ahead in the count," and police officers use special words like "perp" and "SWAT." In the Navy, special terms include helm, anchor, leeward, port, starboard, aft, bitts, chocks, and bollards for nautical equipment and concepts. Everyday items also take on new names in the Navy, where bathrooms are heads, floors are decks, walls are bulkheads, stairways are ladders, and drinking fountains are scuttlebutts. You go topside instead of upstairs and below instead of downstairs. (See **Appendix A: Navy Terms and Abbreviations** for more.) Many of these terms will seem strange to you at first, but you will get used to them and will soon be using them naturally. Remember that many of these terms come from a long history of seafaring and nautical traditions. By using them, you are identifying yourself as a member of a unique and very special group.

The Navy also uses short abbreviations (also known as acronyms) in place of long titles, such as OOD for officer of the deck, QMOW for quartermaster of the watch, and USW for undersea warfare.

The terms "Navy" and "naval" bear some explanation. "Navy" when used as a noun and capitalized (as in "the Navy defends the nation") is understood to refer to the U.S. Navy specifically, unless coupled with a different national modifier (as in "the Italian Navy was much smaller than the Royal Navy"). When not capitalized, it is a more general term (as in "a navy can be effective at defending commerce"). The term "naval" is an adjective that can be used to describe things pertaining to navies (as in "naval weapon systems are usually more complicated than those associated with field artillery units") and can also be understood to include the Marine Corps (as in "American naval forces handled the amphibious assault with efficiency"), but "Navy" is understood to mean only that service (as in "members of the Navy Reserve supplement active duty personnel in maintaining the nation's readiness along with the nation's other armed forces").

People Terminology

In earlier times—before the United States of America changed the world with its successful democracy—if you were born into the so-called nobility and entered military service, you would become an officer, and as a result of good performance (or often because of whom you knew), you could aspire to reach the levels of command and perhaps go beyond to achieve the highest ranks of general or admiral. If you were of so-called common birth, your only choice was to enter the army or navy as a foot soldier or deck hand, and while you could be promoted, there was a ceiling you could never penetrate because of your social class.

In the United States of America, even though our Army and Navy were modeled after the armies and navies of Europe, this class system was obviously not going to work in a democracy. Various means of keeping this basic system but tailoring it to American ideals were tried—including the election of officers—but what eventually evolved was a system based primarily upon education. Although not quite this neat and simple, a reasonable way to look at the system that evolved, and is still basically in effect today, is to think of officers as those individuals who enter the service with college degrees already completed and to think of enlisted as those who enter the service without a degree. There are numerous exceptions and variations to this "rule" and those lines are blurring today for a variety of reasons, but it is still a reasonably accurate way to understand the system. Another way of looking at this system that is not entirely accurate but may be helpful in understanding the differences is to think of enlisted and officers as roughly equivalent to labor and management, respectively.

Keep in mind that there are many exceptions to this simple pattern I have described. One exception is that a person may enter the service with a college degree but may prefer to be enlisted rather than become an officer. Another exception is that some young men and women who have demonstrated the appropriate potential may receive appointments to the U.S. Naval Academy, in which case they will enter the service without a college degree but will earn one at the Academy and become officers upon graduation. There are also many ways that enlisted Sailors can become officers partway through their career.

One other thing to keep in mind is that enlisted Sailors who demonstrate exceptional knowledge and capability are sometimes promoted to "warrant officer," which places them in a pay grade between officers and enlisted personnel.

People who enlist in the Navy are generically called "enlistees" or "enlisted personnel" and serve specifically contracted periods of time called "enlistments." Another term that is sometimes used—and gives its name to this book—is "Bluejacket" and refers specifically to enlisted personnel.

People who enter the Navy as officers (or later become officers) are referred to generically as "officers" and are said to be "commissioned." Their commissions come from the President of the United States and are open-ended in time, ending only when the officer resigns, or is retired, or is dismissed from the service. Although officers do not sign on for specific enlistments as enlistees do, they do often incur periods of obligated service—as "payback" for going to the Naval Academy or flight school, for example—that prevent them from resigning before that obligation is met.

People who are selected to become warrant officers from the enlisted ranks are often called "warrants" but are also included in the generic term "officers."

Although there are different terms used to distinguish officers and enlisted, all people serving in the Navy on active duty or in the Navy Reserve are known as "Sailors," just as all members of the Marine Corps are referred to as "Marines," regardless of their rank.

The Secretary of the Navy has directed that the terms "Marine" and "Sailor" should be capitalized. Not everyone adheres to that practice (including some newspapers and book publishers), so don't be surprised (or offended) if you see these terms used without capitalization.

Today, you can never go wrong calling anyone in a Navy uniform a "Sailor," but this was not always the case. In the past, the term "sailor" was often used to describe only enlisted people. In more recent times, Sailor applies to all Navy personnel in uniform—although you may encounter a "dinosaur" who still makes the old distinction.

In older books and articles about the Navy, you may see the phrase "officers and men" used when describing a ship's crew or a list of casualties, etc. This is no longer appropriate in today's Navy.

One holdover remains, although it may eventually go away: when making a distinction between enlisted and officer personnel, the term "enlisted Sailor" (or "enlisted sailor") is sometimes used, but "officer Sailor" is not. So you may encounter something like, "Many enlisted Sailors were there, but not many officers attended the seminar."

Dates and Time

You will find that in the Navy even dates and times are stated differently. Dates are expressed in a day-month-year format (e.g., 11 October 2001 or 30AUG99) instead of the civilian month-day-year format you are probably used to.

Time is referred to by the twenty-four-hour clock. Hours of the day are numbered from one to twenty-four and spoken in very specific ways. Never say "thirteen hundred hours." While this is acceptable practice in the Army and Air Force, the word "hours" is not used in the Navy. Just say "thirteen hundred."

See TAB 1-C: Navy Time for more information on the Navy's way of telling time.

Liberty and Leave

Even time off from your job is referred to differently in the Navy. At the end of a normal work day when your ship is in port or if you are stationed ashore, you may be allowed to leave the ship or station to spend some time doing what you enjoy (such as going to a movie, visiting local friends, eating at a restaurant, or going home to your family if they live nearby). This time off is called "liberty," and may last until the next morning, or for an entire weekend, or it may end at midnight or some other designated time, depending upon the circumstances. Liberty overseas when your ship is visiting a foreign port is one of the great advantages of being in the Navy. Most people would have to spend thousands of dollars to take a trip to Italy or Japan, but as a Sailor you may find yourself visiting such places as part of your job.

What would be called a vacation in the civilian world is called "leave" in the Navy. If you want some time off to go back to your hometown to visit friends and relatives, you must submit a request, using the chain of command, specifying the exact days you want to be away. Of course, you cannot take leave whenever you feel like it. You will be an important member of the crew of your ship or station, so your absence will have to be carefully planned in order to keep things running smoothly while you are gone. Do not make airline reservations or other firm plans until your leave request has been approved.

Everyone in the Navy earns leave at the rate of 2½ days per month (or thirty days per year). If you do not use all of your leave in a year, you may carry what is left over to the next year. There is a limit, however. The maximum you may carry over from one year to the next is sixty days.

Occasionally, a death in the family or some other serious consideration will require you to need leave in a hurry. This is called emergency leave, and the procedures are, of course, different from those of routine leave requests. Tell your family that the best way to get you home in an emergency is to notify the American Red Cross, which, after verifying the situation, will immediately notify the Navy.

While in boot camp, you will not be granted any routine leave or liberty until you have completed your training.

Ceremonies
There are many special ceremonies in the Navy that are different from civilian life. You encountered your first one when you took your oath of enlistment. Morning and evening colors are ceremonies you will quickly become familiar with while at RTC. Just before leaving boot camp you will participate in a special pass-in-review ceremony that includes a full parade and the presentation of special awards to outstanding recruits and divisions. Later in your Navy experience you may participate in other special ceremonies, such as a ship commissioning, a change-of-command ceremony, or a special awards presentation ceremony.

ORDERS
Before you know it, recruit training will be over. And it won't be long before you are a seaman apprentice instead of a recruit, with two stripes on your sleeve and higher pay. Some of your shipmates, those who went through training with you, may go with you to your next assignment; some you will never see again; others you may meet years later at some far-off duty station or aboard one of the Navy's many ships.

Training
Because the Navy is a very complex organization that is frequently leading the way in adopting new technologies, and because advancement is one of the goals the Navy has in mind for you, training is an almost constant part of Navy life. Recruit training is just the first step. After boot camp you will go to apprenticeship training or to a Class "A" school. After that, you may receive still more schooling. Later in your career you will probably

[**1.4**] You will participate in a special pass-in-review ceremony near the end of your training at Boot Camp.

go to other schools for advanced training. Even when you are doing your job aboard your ship or station, on-the-job training will frequently be a part of your routine.

All formal training in the Navy comes under the control of the Naval Education and Training Command (NETC), which is headquartered in Pensacola, Florida. NETC plans and directs training programs for several hundred activities, everything from basic recruit training to postgraduate instruction for officers.

APPRENTICESHIP TRAINING

If you have not been slated for a Class "A" school, you will attend a course called apprenticeship training. Upon completion of the course, you will be ordered to your first ship or duty station.

CLASS "A" SCHOOL

If you were selected for a Class "A" school, you will be going there after graduation from RTC. In Class "A" school you will receive specialized training that will prepare you for a specific occupational specialty. For example, you might receive specialty training in weapons or in the culinary arts. Successful completion of this training will give you the knowledge and skills necessary to do your job and will enhance your chances for promotion.

Transfers

Once your new duty assignment has been made and you have received your official orders, it will be time for you to check out of your old duty station and move yourself and your belongings to the new location. Sometimes a transfer can be as simple as walking across a street or a pier. Other transfers can involve moving you and your spouse and children halfway around the world. The Navy will provide you a great deal of assistance in making the transfer as smooth as possible, but you must also do your part to ensure a smooth transition.

DEPARTING

Make certain when you are checking out of your old duty station that you understand all the details outlined in the orders. If they authorize DELREP (delay in reporting) to count as leave, make certain you know the date on which you must report to the new station. Sailors are normally authorized to use up to thirty days of their personal leave between duty stations. If you have any questions at all, ask the person managing your transfer before you leave; this may save you a lot of trouble later.

If you have a spouse or children who will be going with you to your new duty assignment, it is a good idea to contact the local housing office at your new duty station to get housing information. The housing office can also give you information about the area you will be moving to, including schools for your children, employment opportunities for your spouse, special needs programs, and health care facilities.

Make certain that you file a change of address form at your old duty station so that your mail can catch up to you.

EN ROUTE

While you are on your way to your new duty station, you may encounter some problems. For example, if you are assigned to a ship, you may get to the port where she is supposed to be only to find that she got under way the day before because an airliner went down off the coast and the ship is needed for rescue operations. There may be no way to join the ship until she returns from the rescue operation. What do you do?

Remember, it's all one Navy, and no matter where you are you can find someone to help. Always keep your orders, records, and pay accounts with you, not in your baggage, which may be lost. With them, you can obtain further transportation if needed and draw some of your pay if you are running out of money. If you are in an area where there are no Navy facilities, Army and Air Force personnel can help you with these matters as well.

The Navy will assign you a sponsor—someone who has been at your new command for some time and can help you settle in. As soon as you get your orders, make contact with your new command and ask who your sponsor is so that he or she can begin helping you.

If you are in doubt as to the location of your new duty station when you arrive in the area, check in with the Navy Shore Patrol or look in the local telephone directory under "U.S. Government" to find some naval activity where you can obtain help. Most areas have a local Navy or other armed forces recruiting station, and they can help you find your new station.

If you have dependents (spouse and/or children) with you, get them settled into a temporary lodging facility (a hotel, a motel, or a Navy Lodge if one is available) before reporting to your new duty assignment. Navy Lodge facilities are often limited, so make your reservations as soon as your travel arrangements are complete.

REPORTING

When reporting to your new duty station, be in complete and proper uniform. Because you are going to be making a first impression and you want it to be a good one, look your sharpest and present yourself well when you report.

Be sure you have all your necessary gear with you; the ship may get under way the same day you report, and what you check in with could very well be all you will have for a while. Also keep in mind that you will have only a limited amount of space to store your personal belongings, so bringing large items like computers, and even oversized luggage, can cause you problems.

Hand your orders to the watch, either at the main gate or the quarterdeck, so that they can be endorsed and stamped with the time and date of reporting, and you can be logged in.

As soon as is practical, deliver your original orders and records to the personnel office. You certainly want to be paid on time, so turn in a copy of your orders to the disbursing office.

Whether you are going to a destroyer, an aircraft carrier, a submarine, a naval air station, a supply depot, or a Navy medical facility, you will be a vital part of the world's greatest navy. Whether you plan on making the Navy your career or are just trying it out for one enlistment, your performance of duty at this first duty station will have an important effect on the rest of your life. And keep in mind that it will also have an important effect on the effectiveness of this greatest of all navies and on the defense of your nation.

TWO

MILITARY DRILL

or the first century and a half of our nation's existence, the ability to protect American lives and interests around the world was accomplished by landing parties composed of Navy and Marine Corps personnel. Virtually every Sailor had to know the essentials of infantry tactics and fighting on land as thoroughly as his shipboard duties. This heritage remains with us today in the form of close order drill.

As much as the uniform, close order drill is at the very core of one's identity as a Sailor. It is a cornerstone of military discipline, professionalism, and leadership. Throughout your service in the Navy, you will participate in military formations for events ranging from the routine, like morning muster, to the exceptional, like ceremonies to honor individuals or commands. The need to execute close order drill with snap and precision will be a skill that will not disappear after recruit training.

Close order drill also teaches the practice of obeying orders immediately and exactly upon command. It visibly demonstrates leadership and followership, and it reinforces the concepts of unit cohesion and teamwork.

Some of the basics of close order drill will be discussed in this chapter, but the Navy's standard for close order drill is the *Marine Corps Drill and Ceremonies Manual* (MCO P5060.20), a descendant of the joint Navy-Marine publications governing landing party operations.

FORMATIONS

Various kinds of formations are used for different purposes throughout the Navy. Some, like Navy construction battalions, follow the basic structure of a Marine Corps unit:

Squad—A unit formed in a single rank, typically 8–13 personnel
Platoon—Two or more squads
Company—Two or more platoons
Battalion—Two or more companies
Regiment—Two or more battalions

In other naval activities, you may come across terms to denote partial units or small groups assembled for a specific task or purpose, like "detail" or "section."

At the Naval Academy, the midshipmen are organized into a "brigade," which is further subdivided into two regiments of three battalions, each with five companies.

"Division," as used in the Navy, is a shipboard work unit (subordinate to a "department") and not actually a military unit for drill purposes, although its personnel are often formed for daily musters. To avoid confusion, you should know that for a land military unit—such as in the Army—a "division" is composed of several regiments and has thousands of personnel.

At times aboard ship, you will likely be part of military formations used for morning quarters, for personnel inspections, to welcome dignitaries, and for many other reasons.

The two basic structures of all military formations are "ranks" (in which personnel are lined up side by side) and "files" (in which personnel are uniformly lined up one behind the other). There can be a single rank or a single file, or they can be combined.

In a formation with several ranks and files, the front rank is referred to as simply the front or first rank. Subsequent ranks are called the second rank, third rank, and so on. There are a number of other terms associated with formations that you should know:

Guide. In a formation, someone must serve as the reference point on which the others align themselves. This person is called "the guide." In a single file, the guide must be the person in the very front because it would be impossible for you to guide on an individual behind you (unless you have the proverbial "eyes in the back of your head"). In a single rank, the guide is usually (though not always) on the extreme right of the line. In a formation with several ranks and files, the guide is usually the person on the extreme right of the front rank.

[**2.1**] A military formation on a ship

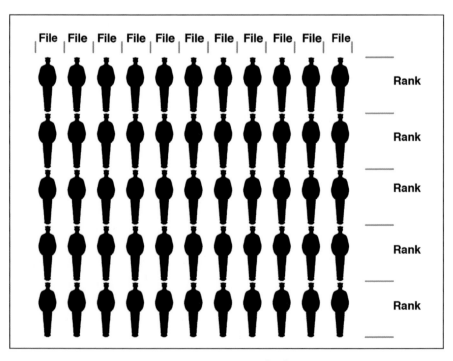

[**2.2**] Ranks and files

Interval. The lateral space between individuals who are standing on the same line in a rank, from shoulder to shoulder, is called the interval. "Normal interval" is one arm's length. Close interval is the horizontal distance between shoulder and elbow when the left hand is placed on the left hip. This is used when space is limited and is determined by the individuals in the rank placing their left hand on their hip, fingertips down, then closing up to the elbows.

Distance. The space between ranks, which is 40 inches from the chest of a person in one rank to the back of the person directly in front.

Commands

The difference between a command and an order is in timing. Both must be carried out if given by a superior in a military organization, but a command is to be carried out at a precise moment, whereas an order need not be instantaneously executed. For example, if your recruit division commander in boot camp calls "Attention on deck" because the base commander has just entered the auditorium to deliver an address, this is a command, and you must jump to your feet and assume the position of attention the instant you hear the words. If you are standing watch as a messenger aboard ship and the OOD tells you to sweep down the quarterdeck, this is an order, and while you certainly would not dawdle in carrying out the OOD's instructions, you would not be expected to begin sweeping instantaneously.

In close order drill, there are four types of commands.

Preparatory Command. Alerts the unit to an upcoming change in direction, position, or posture such as "*Forward*," "*Right*," or "*Parade*." (In our discussion, they are indicated by italics.)

Command of Execution. This command tells the unit to execute the order, such as "MARCH" or "FACE." (In our discussion, they are indicated by capitalizing all letters.)

Combined Commands. In combined commands, the preparatory command and command of execution are combined, such as "AT EASE" and "FALL OUT." (These are also indicated by capitalizing all letters.)

Supplementary Commands. Supplementary commands are used after a preparatory command and before the command of execution to direct subordinate units to act individually, such as "*Column of Files, <u>From the Right</u>*, MARCH." (Here, underlined.)

To Cancel a Command. If an order was given in error, the person giving the commands will call, "AS YOU WERE." Personnel in the unit resume their former position. For example, "*Second Squad, forward* . . . AS YOU WERE." The members of second squad would do nothing in this case, remaining as they were before the command began.

Using this system, the preparatory command serves to warn you what is coming so that when you hear the command of execution, you will be able to carry it out instantaneously. No two military drill commands begin with the same preparatory command, so once you have learned the various commands you will know what is coming every time you hear a preparatory command. For example, the command to get the members of a squad moving along together is "*Forward* . . . MARCH." The word "forward" is the preparatory command, and because this command is the only one that begins with the word "forward," all members of the squad know that the next word they hear will be the command of execution "MARCH," and they will all begin marching the instant they hear it. This method ensures the precision that is essential in military drill.

When giving military drill commands, you should always speak in a firm tone loud enough to be heard by everyone under your command. You should also develop the habit of giving the preparatory command, pausing briefly to allow everyone time to anticipate what is coming, and then giving the command of execution with emphasis.

Sometimes the preparatory command will be preceded by the name or title of the group concerned, for example, "First Division" or "Third Squad" or "Platoon," etc. This is especially important for avoiding confusion if there are a number of groups in the vicinity.

The cadence of commands should be that of quick time, whether stationary or while marching. The pause between the preparatory command and the command of execution should be one count while stationary, or one step between the two commands marching.

Most of the military drill commands you will encounter in the Navy are listed and explained below.

FORMING THE UNIT

Unit leaders should direct their units to begin forming by indicating where they are to form and at what interval. Once a unit is in place and its leader is ready to commence, he or she will bring the unit to attention by using one of the following two commands.

If the unit has been directed to form at normal interval, the (combined) command is:

"FALL IN"

If the unit has been directed to form at close interval, the combined command is:

"AT CLOSE INTERVAL, FALL IN"

(Note: "Fall in" in either form is the correct command to bring a unit to attention at the beginning of a formation. It should not be used to direct people to begin falling into ranks.)

DRESSING THE UNIT

"Dressing" refers to properly aligning the formation. To dress the unit, the leader will give the appropriate command with the direction of dress and the interval used.

If dressing the unit at normal interval, the command is:

"Dress Right (or Left) . . . DRESS"

- On the command "DRESS," everyone except the person at the extreme right of each squad smartly turns his or her head to the right, 90 degrees over the shoulder, looks, and aligns him- or herself.
- At the same time, all except the last individual on the left provide the appropriate interval by smartly raising their left arms to shoulder height and in line with their bodies. Fingers are extended and joined, thumb along the forefinger, palm down.
- Each person aligns his or her shoulder to the fingertips of the individual to his or her right.

➡ When dressing to the left, the alignment and eyes are to the left and the right arm is extended. The unit leader may come to the end of the squad and direct individuals forward or backward.

In some cases—such as when space is limited—a "close interval" may be ordered. The proper command is:

"At Close Interval, Dress Right (or Left) . . . DRESS"

➡ On the command "DRESS," all except the person at the extreme right of each squad smartly turn their heads to the right, 90 degrees over the shoulder, looks, and align themselves.

➡ At the same time, all except the last individual on the left provide the appropriate interval by placing the heel of their left hand on their hip with the elbow in line with their body. Fingers are extended and joined and pointing down.

➡ Individuals adjust the interval by moving by very short steps until their right arms are touching the left elbows of the individuals to their left. When dressing to the left, the alignment and eyes are to the left and the right elbow is extended.

To end the dressing sequence, the command is:

"Ready, FRONT"

➡ On the command "FRONT," all will look to the front and return their arms to the position of attention (see below). This is executed with precision, but the arm is not to make noise by striking the thigh.

To align individual files or a column, the command is:

"COVER"

➡ At this command, members move as necessary to place themselves directly behind the person in front of them, still maintaining a 40-inch distance.

[**2.3**] Members of the U.S. Navy Ceremonial Guard Drill Team formed up at "close interval"

DISMISSING THE FORMATION

If the formation is permanently disbanded, the command is:

"DISMISSED."

➡ This signals the end of the formation. Everyone will break ranks and go about his or her business.

BASIC COMMANDS

Once you are in a formation, you will need to know a number of basic commands. The position of attention is the basic military position from which most other drill movements are executed.

To bring the formation to attention from any position of rest, the command is:

"ATTENTION"

➡ Smartly bring your left heel against the right.

➡ Turn your feet out equally to form an angle of 45 degrees. Keep your heels on the same line and touching.

➡ Your legs should be straight, but not stiff at the knees. In other words, *do not lock your knees*—keep them flexed slightly forward—to prevent the restriction of your blood-flow, which can cause you to pass out.

➡ Your arms should be straight, but not stiff at the elbows; thumbs along the trouser seams, palms facing inward toward your legs, and fingers joined in their natural curl.

➡ Look straight ahead. Keep your mouth closed and your chin pulled in slightly.

➡ Keep your head and body erect. Keep your hips and shoulders level and your chest lifted.

➡ (To achieve this posture, try this: with your feet and hands in the position of attention, raise your shoulders an inch or so, gently rotate them in an arc upward and backward, and let them drop downward. This will straighten your back and bring your chest out in the manner described above. Practice this posture, as it will enable you to stand at attention for longer periods of time without the discomfort experienced when slouching.)

➡ Stand still and do not talk.

There are four positions of rest: Parade Rest, At Ease, Rest, and Fall Out.

"Parade . . . REST"

➡ On the command of execution "REST," move the left foot smartly 12 inches to the left of the right foot.

➡ At the same time, clasp your hands behind the back. Your left hand is placed just below the belt and your right hand is placed inside the left. The thumb of your right hand lightly grasps the thumb of the left. All fingers are extended and joined with the palms to the rear.

➡ The elbows will be in line with the body. You must remain silent and not move.

➡ Again, do not lock your knees—keep them flexed slightly forward—to avoid passing out.

➡ The only command that may be given after "Parade, REST" is "Attention."

[**2.4**] A member of the U.S. Navy's elite drill team at "attention" in front of the *Lone Sailor* statue at the Navy Memorial in Washington, D.C.

[**2.5**] Sailors at "parade rest"

"AT EASE"

➡ On this combined command, you may move any part of your body (such as stretching or looking about) except your right foot (this marks your place in the formation). You may not talk.

"REST"

➡ At the command, you may move and talk; however, you must keep your right foot in place just as when at ease. The only command you may receive while at rest is "ATTENTION."

"FALL OUT"

➡ When this command is given, everyone breaks ranks but remains nearby or proceeds to a predetermined area. When the command "fall in" is given, everyone should return to his or her original position in the formation and stand at attention.

SALUTING

When part of close-order drill, saluting is executed on the command:

"Hand . . . SALUTE"

➡ Raise your right hand smartly in the most direct manner until the tip of your forefinger touches the lower part of your cover above and slightly right of your right eye.
➡ Your fingers should be extended straight and joined with the thumb along the forefinger (not sticking out).
➡ You should be able to peripherally see your entire palm when looking straight ahead.
➡ Your upper arm should be parallel with the deck with your elbow nearly in line with your body (but slightly forward) and your forearm at a 45-degree angle.
➡ Your wrist and hand should be straight, a continuation of the line made by your forearm.

[2.6] A Navy Drill Team Sailor demonstrates the proper way to execute a "hand salute."

To terminate the salute, the command is:

"Ready, TWO"

➡ Return to the position of attention. Move your hand smartly in the most direct manner back to its normal position by your side. NEVER flick or chop the hand forward, but bring it down completely to your side in one unbroken motion.
(Note: If you are not armed and the command "*Present* . . . ARMS" is given, you should execute the hand salute on the command "ARMS." Stay at that position until the command "*Ready* . . . TWO" or "*Order* . . . ARMS" is given.)

(Note: Saluting is covered in more detail in **Chapter 3: Navy Customs, Courtesies, and Ceremonies.**)

FACING MOVEMENTS

Facing movements are used to turn everyone in the formation to face in a different direction.

To face right or left, the command is:

"Right (Left) . . . FACE"

➡ "Right, FACE" is a two-count movement. On the command "FACE," execute the first count by raising your left heel and right toe slightly. Turn to the right on your right heel and left toe. Keep your left leg straight but not stiff.

➡ The second count is executed by bringing the left foot smartly beside the right and stand at attention. "Left, FACE" is executed in the same manner substituting left for right and right for left.

To face to the rear, the command is:

"About . . . FACE"

➡ "About ... FACE" is a two-count movement. At the command "About," shift your weight to your left leg without noticeable movement.

➡ At the command "FACE," execute the first count by placing the tip of your right toe half a foot length behind and slightly to the left of your heel. Do not change the position of your left foot. Rest your weight evenly on the left heel and the ball of the right foot.

➡ Execute count two by turning smartly to the right until facing rear. The turn is made on the left heel and ball of the right foot.

➡ The knees remain straight but not locked during the movement. Your thumbs remain on the seams of your trousers.

➡ If properly executed, you will be at the position of attention facing in the opposite direction.

MARCHING COMMANDS

Military formations are sometimes moved, either to get from one place to another or to put on a parade or what is called a "pass in review." It will help to remember that all movements except "Right step" begin with the left foot.

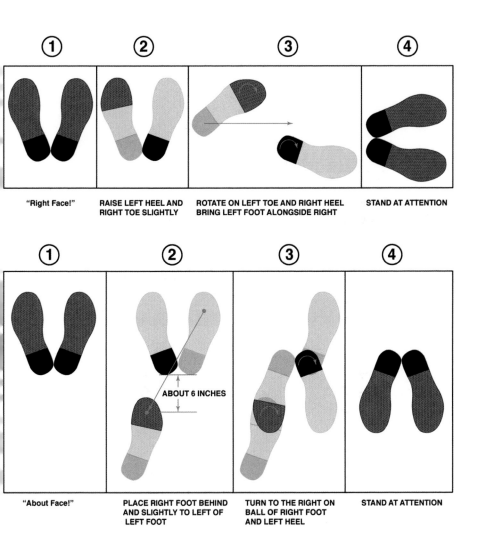

①	②	③	④
"Right Face!"	RAISE LEFT HEEL AND RIGHT TOE SLIGHTLY	ROTATE ON LEFT TOE AND RIGHT HEEL BRING LEFT FOOT ALONGSIDE RIGHT	STAND AT ATTENTION

①	②	③	④
"About Face!"	PLACE RIGHT FOOT BEHIND AND SLIGHTLY TO LEFT OF LEFT FOOT	TURN TO THE RIGHT ON BALL OF RIGHT FOOT AND LEFT HEEL	STAND AT ATTENTION

ABOUT 6 INCHES

[**2.7**] "Right face" and "about face" diagrammed

[2.8] Beginning an "about face"

[2.9] When done correctly, military marching is an impressive sight. Here, the U.S. Navy Ceremonial Guard marches in the parade celebrating the fifty-seventh presidential inauguration.

To commence marching to the front, the command is:

"Forward . . . MARCH"

- At the preparatory command "Forward," shift the weight of your body to the right leg.
- At the command of execution "MARCH," step off smartly with the left foot and continue marching with 30-inch steps taken straight forward without stiffness or exaggeration.
- Swing your arms easily in their natural arcs, 6 inches straight to the front and 3 inches to the rear. Do not exaggerate movements.
- Continue marching straight ahead until another command is given.

To stop the unit, the command is:

"HALT"

- The preparatory command is the name of the unit ("Detail," "Squad," "Platoon," etc.) followed by the command of execution "HALT."
- You can give the command of execution as either foot strikes the deck. If you give it on the left foot, each squad member will take one more step with the right foot and then bring up the left foot to stop alongside the right foot, so that all motion stops and everyone is standing at attention.

To take half steps, the command is:

"Half Step . . . MARCH"

- Begin taking steps of 15 inches instead of the normal 30 inches. To resume the full step from half step, the command is "Forward, MARCH."

To side step, the command is:

"Right (or Left) Step . . . MARCH"

- At the command "MARCH," move your right foot 12 inches to the right. Then place the left foot beside the right, keeping your left knee straight. Repeat until the command "HALT" is given. To step to the left, follow the same procedure in opposite form.

→ "Right (left) step" is ordered from a halt and for short distances only.

To step backward (used for short distances only and always ordered from a halt position) the command is:

"Back Step . . . MARCH"

→ At the command "MARCH," take steps of 15 inches straight to the rear until ordered to halt.

To march in place, the command is:

"Mark Time . . . MARCH"

To perform flanking movements (facing an entire unit to the left or right while marching) the command is:

"By the Right (Left) Flank . . . MARCH"

→ For a right flanking movement, the command "MARCH" will be given when your right foot hits the ground. Take another step with your left foot. Turn to the right on the ball of the left foot. At the same time, step off 30 inches in the new direction with the right foot.

→ "Left Flank" is executed in the opposite fashion of "Right Flank."

To march the unit to the rear for a short distance, the command is:

"To the Rear . . . MARCH"

→ The command of execution "MARCH" is given when the right foot strikes the deck. On the command "MARCH," take one more step. Turn about to the right on the balls of both feet and immediately step off to the rear with your left foot. This is done without loss of cadence. When turning, the feet should be about 15 inches apart.

➡ When marching to the rear, the only movement that can be given is another "To the Rear, MARCH" in order to bring the individual or unit back to its' original front.

To change a column's direction of march, the command of execution is given on the foot in the direction of the turn. The command is:

"Column Right (Left) . . . MARCH"

➡ On the command "MARCH," the leading member of the squad on the right takes one more 30-inch step to the front and then pivots 90 degrees to the right on the ball of the left foot. He/she then takes one 30-inch step in the new direction before beginning to half step.

➡ At the same time, the leading members of the other squads pivot less than 90 degrees to the right in an amount appropriate to partially make the turn (45 degrees for the squad immediately to the left the first squad, less for the next squad, etc.). They step in this new direction until they are on line with the new line of march (normally two and four steps, respectively) and then execute a second pivot (45 degrees for the second squad, less for the third, and so on).

➡ They then begin to half step as soon as they are aligned with the leading member of the inside squad. When all members of the same rank have come abreast, everyone in that rank resumes a full step.

➡ All successive ranks execute the same pivot movements on the same points and in the same way as those ahead of them.

➡ "Column Left" is executed in the opposite fashion of "Column Right."

To march while not at attention, the command is:

"Route step . . . MARCH"

➡ After "MARCH," you are no longer required to march in cadence, but must keep interval and distance. You may talk, but in a low voice. To return to marching at attention, the command will be, "ATTENTION," upon which you must resume cadence and cease talking.

Although close order drill is no longer a part of the battlefield, it remains an essential component of military culture that promotes good leadership and followership as well as instilling a strong sense of discipline that is essential to military efficiency. It can, in an indirect way, contribute to survivability in a dangerous situation. And it is a point of pride that can contribute to unit cohesion and pride. You should embrace it as one of the many things that makes being a Sailor special.

THREE

NAVY CUSTOMS, COURTESIES, AND CEREMONIES

A naval ceremony should follow the long established rules for its execution carefully and exactly. Such attention to detail honors those who, long before us, established the ritual, and all those who, past, present, and future, take part in that ceremony.

—*Fleet Admiral Chester Nimitz*

A major difference between civilian life and life in the Navy is the use of standard practices to mark specific kinds of events. Whether in the daily interactions you will have with senior personnel or in career milestones of an individual or ship, the Navy has developed routine procedures to acknowledge the occasion. These actions fall into the three interrelated categories of customs, courtesies, and ceremonies.

> *Customs* usually have no formal regulations or laws governing them but are universally recognized and practiced actions. For example, there is no directive stating that recipients of the Medal of Honor are saluted, but everyone from seaman to admiral would salute this individual regardless of rank or current military status.
>
> *Courtesies* are formal means of paying respect to personnel of senior rank or position. This does not mean to say that one person is better than another. Instead, it means that you recognize that another

has been given a greater responsibility and authority by the service. Even captains have to salute admirals, and even admirals have to salute the president. The Navy's success in peace and war depends on good order and discipline, and courtesies provide an important reminder that all play their part within a professional military organization.

Ceremonies are official rituals that honor individual or unit achievements or noteworthy occurrences. Their sequences of events are usually prescribed by very specific instructions or regulations. These observances, whether a large formal ceremony such as a change of command or a smaller personal one like a reenlistment, will become some of the most memorable events in your naval career.

As a Sailor, your ability to know and observe customs, render courtesies, and perform your role in Navy ceremonies will be a visible indicator of your military bearing and professionalism to all who observe you.

THE SALUTE

The hand salute is perhaps the most widely known military ritual throughout the world. Its origins are uncertain, but the salute probably evolved from one of several practices or from a combination of them. The act of armored medieval knights raising their visors to recognize whether another knight was a friend or foe is thought by many to be the source of this practice. Others believe that it stems from the gesture of showing an empty palm, indicating that the individual was unarmed and intended no harm— thus implying respectful or friendly intentions. In the navies of past centuries, a Sailor paid respect to a senior officer by taking off his hat, touching its brim, or making the motion of grasping the forelock of one's hair when uncovered.

Navy Regulations prescribe the hand salute to be rendered with the right hand, although it makes allowances for it to be given with the left. When your right arm is injured, for example, or if you were piping the boatswain's call with your right hand, it is permissible to salute with your left hand. In the Navy and Marine Corps, you must be covered (i.e., wearing a military hat, cap, or helmet) to salute, unless not saluting could be interpreted as disrespectful. Saluting customs are different in the Army and Air Force, where individuals may salute without headgear but may not salute with the left hand. Be aware that these differences in custom among the services should be modified if the circumstances warrant. Consider, for example, if you are in an office with several soldiers and none of you are covered. An Army officer enters and the soldiers jump to their feet, come to attention, and salute. Your naval custom would not include the salute, since you are uncovered, but not to salute would seem disrespectful under the circumstances, so you should do as the soldiers do and salute.

How to Salute

Saluting properly is a measure of your military bearing. Deviating from the standards below is a quick way to make yourself less of a Sailor.

- Salute from the position of attention if you are not moving, from a march if you are moving. You do not have to stop walking to salute.
- Bring your right hand up so that your fingertip is touching the lower edge of your hat or cap above and slightly to the right of the right eye.
- Keep your fingers joined, thumb alongside your index finger (not tucked), palm flat and inclined slightly toward you, and wrist straight. Your palm should not be visible to the person you are saluting. From the elbow to the tip of your finger, your arm should be as straight as physically possible.
- Your upper arm should be parallel to the deck, your forearm forming a 45-degree angle.
- Look into the eyes of the person you are saluting. Face the person to salute if you are standing, turn your head to face them if you are walking.
- Accompany the salute with an appropriate greeting—"Good morning, sir," "Good afternoon, ma'am," "Good evening, Lieutenant."
- Begin your salute when the officer is about six paces away. Hold your salute until the officer has completed his or her return salute.
- To end your salute, bring your hand smartly to your side, returning to attention if standing, returning to a natural swing if marching. Never flick the hand forward when terminating a salute.

[**3.1**] A Sailor saluting

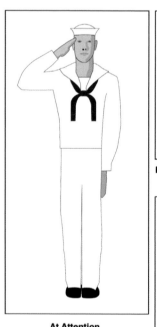

At Attention

Forearm Inclined at 45°

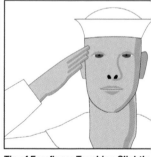

Tip of Forefinger Touching Slightly to Right of Right Eye

Upper Arm Parallel to Deck
Elbow Slightly Forward

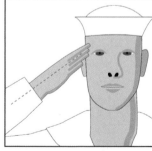

Hand and Wrist in a Straight Line
Palm Slightly Inward

[**3.2**] The proper way to execute a hand salute

Whom to Salute

Knowing whom to salute will save you from unnecessary embarrassment.

- Salute all commissioned and warrant officers of the seven uniformed services. This includes the five armed services (Army, Marine Corps, Navy, Air Force, and Coast Guard) as well as the National Oceanic and Atmospheric Administration (NOAA) and U.S. Public Health Service. (NOAA and PHS officers essentially wear Navy uniforms with slightly different insignia.)
- Salute someone you know to be an officer whether the individual is in uniform or civilian clothes. If not in uniform, the officer will say something to acknowledge your salute.
- Salute all foreign military officers. This can be tricky if you are not familiar with their uniforms, but if in doubt, salute.
- Salute high-ranking dignitaries (such as presidents, prime ministers, defense and service secretaries, etc.).
- Salute officers in a vehicle if you see the officer or see a sign that indicates that an officer is inside (such as admiral's or general's flags on the front fenders).
- Salute Medal of Honor recipients no matter what their rank and whether or not they are still in the service. This military custom is common among all the U.S. services.
- Salute all officers aboard ship on the first meeting of the day, but salute the commanding officer or flag officers on each meeting.
- Salute an individual executing an officer's duties no matter what their rank. Examples are a person standing Officer of the Deck (OOD) watch on the quarterdeck, or someone taking a division muster.
- WHEN IN DOUBT, SALUTE. It is better to err on the side of caution than to appear disrespectful to a superior.

When Not to Salute

There are circumstances when saluting is not called for. While it is still better to salute when inappropriate than to not salute when appropriate, knowing the proper time to render this important courtesy will serve you well. You should not salute when:

SALUTE OFFICERS WHEN MEETING, PASSING NEAR, ADDRESSING, OR BEING ADDRESSED

WHEN OVERTAKING A SENIOR THE SALUTE SHALL BE GIVEN WHEN ABREAST, WITH "BY YOUR LEAVE" SIR OR MA'AM

WHEN REPORTING (COVERED)

GUARDS SALUTE ALL OFFICERS PASSING CLOSE ABOARD

SENTRIES AT GANGWAYS SALUTE ALL OFFICERS GOING OR COMING OVER SIDE, PASSING CLOSE ABOARD

WHEN OFFICER MEETS DETAIL ASHORE OR AFLOAT, PERSON IN CHARGE SALUTES FOR DETAIL

UPON APPROACH OF OFFICER ONE CALLS ATTENTION, ALL SALUTE

ABOARD SHIP

ON FIRST DAILY MEETING SALUTE, ALL SALUTE

ABOARD SHIP

ON EVERY OCCASION, SALUTE THE CAPTAIN, OFFICERS SENIOR TO HIM OR HER, AND SENIOR OFFICERS FROM OTHER SHIPS

IN BOATS

ENLISTED PERSONNEL RISE AND SALUTE WHEN AN OFFICER ENTERS OR LEAVES (IF SAFETY PERMITS)

IN BOATS

WHEN OFFICER PASSES NEAR, OFFICER OR PETTY OFFICER IN CHARGE SALUTES; IF NONE PRESENT, ALL HANDS SALUTE

VEHICLES

RENDER SALUTES DUE THEM TO ALL OFFICERS IN VEHICLES (IF SAFETY PERMITS)

[**3.3**] When to salute

- At work or engaged in athletics or some other recreational activity.
- Injured and unable, such as when using crutches. Remember that if only your right arm is disabled, it is permissible to salute with the left.
- In combat or simulated combat conditions. Besides the obvious fact that there are more important things taking place, saluting can aid the enemy by identifying the person you are saluting as an officer, which could make him or her a target for enemy snipers.
- Carrying something with both hands and saluting would require you to put all or part of your load down. A verbal greeting is still appropriate in this case.
- In public places where saluting is inappropriate (such as on a bus or while standing in line at a theater). A verbal greeting is still appropriate, however.
- At mess. If you are addressed by an officer while eating, you should stop eating and sit at attention until the officer has departed. Courtesy dictates that the officer will keep the interruption brief.
- Guarding prisoners.
- In formation, salute only on command. Otherwise, the person in charge will salute for you.

Saluting While Armed

Some of the rules for saluting are the same and some are different when armed. If you are armed with a pistol in its holster or you are carrying a rifle at "sling arms," render the normal hand salute (except that at sling arms, you must reach across your body with your left hand to grasp the sling in order to keep it from swinging forward).

When carrying a rifle (other than at "sling arms"), there are three different ways in which to render a salute.

PRESENT ARMS

This is a formal rifle salute rendered to persons or colors when in formation or when posted as a sentry. As explained in **Chapter 2**, when ordered as a command, the preparatory command "Present" is pronounced with the emphasis on the second syllable, as in "pre-ZENT," followed by the command of execution "ARMS." Hold the rifle in front of you with the

WHEN IN RANKS, IF ADDRESSED COME TO ATTENTION

WHEN UNCOVERED AND IN INNER COURT OR OPEN PASSAGEWAY BETWEEN WINGS OF BUILDINGS

WHEN PART OF A DETAIL AT WORK

WHEN UNDER ACTUAL OR SIMULATED BATTLE CONDITIONS

AT MESS (IF ADDRESSED BY AN OFFICER, SIT AT ATTENTION)

WHEN CARRYING ARTICLES WITH BOTH HANDS

[**3.4**] When not to salute

barrel vertical, muzzle up, trigger guard to the front. Your left forearm should be parallel to the deck, your left hand grasping the rifle at the point of balance and your right hand holding the small of the stock.

RIFLE SALUTE AT ORDER ARMS

When not in formation or on sentry duty, execute the rifle salute at order arms. To salute from this position, move your left hand across your body, keeping your forearm, wrist, and hand flat as in a hand salute, and touch the rifle just below the muzzle.

RIFLE SALUTE AT RIGHT OR LEFT SHOULDER ARMS

When standing or marching at right or left shoulder arms, execute the rifle salute by moving your free arm across your body, parallel to the deck, palm down, keeping your forearm, wrist, and hand flat as in a hand salute, and touch the rifle at the rear of the receiver with the first joint of your index finger.

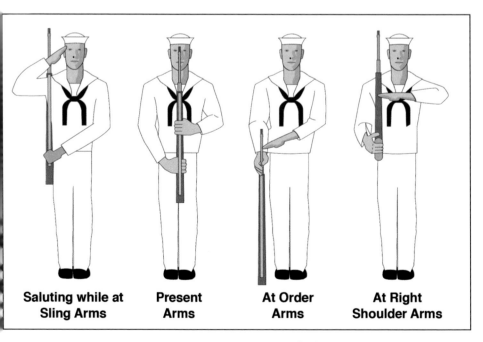

Saluting while at Sling Arms   **Present Arms**   **At Order Arms**   **At Right Shoulder Arms**

[3.5] Saluting while armed

HOW TO ADDRESS MILITARY PERSONNEL

There are really two different situations you must consider when it comes to addressing people in the Navy: introductions and conversation. Introducing people requires a degree of extra formality over merely addressing them in other conversation.

When you are introducing someone, you should use their entire title, but some—such as vice admiral or lieutenant commander—are too long and cumbersome to use in normal conversation, so you would shorten them by dropping the first part of their titles. You would introduce "Lieutenant Commander Jones" but you would then refer to her or him in conversation as "Commander Jones," or simply "Commander." However, if several people of the same rank are together, it is proper to use both title and name, such as "Admiral Taylor" or "Chief Smith," to avoid confusion.

In the military, rank establishes the order of introduction: introduce the junior to the senior, regardless of either one's age or gender. *Note:* See **Chapter 5 and** TAB 5-A for more information about addressing military personnel.

Officers

Officers are always addressed and referred to by their title or rank, such as admiral, captain, or commander. Some exceptions include:

- The Commanding Officer (CO). By tradition, the commanding officer of a ship or station, *no matter what his or her rank*, is addressed and referred to as "Captain."
- Doctors. An officer in the Medical Corps or Dental Corps may be addressed and referred to by rank *or* as "Doctor."
- Chaplains. A chaplain may be called "Chaplain" no matter what the rank.

SIR AND MA'AM

When conversing with an officer, you must use the appropriate amount of respect throughout the conversation. That includes the use of "sir" and "ma'am"—*every* time. *Never* allow your military bearing to slip and reply with "yeah" or "uh-huh," and never finish your thought without saying "sir" or "ma'am."

Use "sir" or "ma'am" only when directly addressing an officer, never when referring to them. In other words, you would say "the lieutenant told me to," never "Sir told me to."

It is also good practice to apply the same practices to chief petty officers, as in "Here is the report, Chief" or "I'll find out, Senior Chief."

Enlisted Personnel

A chief petty officer is addressed as "Chief Petty Officer Smith," or more informally as "Chief Smith" or "Chief," if you do not know his or her name. Master and senior chief petty officers are customarily addressed and referred to as "Master Chief Smith" and "Senior Chief Smith." If you do not know their names, just "Master Chief," or "Senior Chief" is appropriate. *Do not* shorten master chief or senior chief to just "chief."

Other petty officers are addressed and referred to by their specific ranks as well. For example, you would introduce PO2 Johnson as "Petty Officer Second Class Johnson" and address/refer to her as "Petty Officer Johnson."

Nonrated personnel—those in pay grades E-1 through E-3—are "Seamen" and should be introduced and addressed by that title and their names; for example, "Let me introduce Seaman Rachel Alexander" or "Seaman Alexander, you are needed topside."

Some Sailors with specialties have nicknames that are used informally. For example, medical technicians (usually only ones below chief) are addressed both in the Navy and Marine Corps as "Doc."

No, Yes, Aye, Aye, and Very Well

A negative response to a question is just the same as in civilian life, although it may be followed by "sir" or "ma'am" or "chief" (or "senior chief" and "master chief") as explained above. "No" is always no, but an affirmative answer can be answered with either "yes" or "aye, aye," depending on the circumstances.

The difference between saying "yes" and "aye, aye" is simple:

"Yes" means the opposite of "no":
    "Are you a seaman recruit?"
    "Yes, sir."
"Aye, aye" means "I understand and will obey":
    "See me after chow."
    "Aye, aye, ma'am."

When a senior wants to acknowledge that he or she has heard and understood a report from a junior, he or she may answer, "Very well." A junior *never* says "Very well" to a senior.

The use of "aye, aye" and "very well" may seem old fashioned, and they are—since both expressions come from centuries of naval usage—but these are a distinct part of the culture of life and work in the Navy and you mark yourself as a true Sailor by using these terms correctly.

FLAGS AND FLAG ETIQUETTE

Showing respect to the American flag is probably not new to you. In school, or perhaps in a scout troop, you may have recited the pledge of allegiance before starting the day's activities. You have probably been to a sporting event where the national anthem was played while people in the stadium stood as a mark of respect.

Although the American flag is, in truth, only a piece of colored cloth, what it *represents* causes us to want to show our respect. The American flag is a symbol of the democracy we value so highly, that men and women have died protecting, that is the essence of what the United States of America is truly about.

The American flag is a symbol of our nation and all of its people. Because of this, it is considered symbolically "alive" and is treated with dignity and respect. Since 1778, when the American flag was saluted for the first time by a ship of a foreign nation, the flag has played an important role in the history of our Navy.

As an American bluejacket, you will see the U.S. flag often, and you will participate in many ceremonies in which the flag plays a part and is honored. You may be called upon to fold an American flag, and you should know the proper way of doing it. (See TAB 3-A: Folding the Flag.)

Depending on how and where it is displayed, the flag of the United States may be called by several names.

- A flag carried on a staff is called the *national color*. When carried with the Navy flag or a battalion flag, they are referred to collectively as *the colors*.
- A U.S. flag carried by a vehicle is called the *national standard*.
- When flown from a ship, it is called the *national ensign*. The flag flown from a pole at naval shore stations may also be referred to as the ensign.

When a ship is in port, you will see another flag that is flown from a staff at the bow. Historically, Navy ships flew the blue portion of the ensign with the stars, which is called the *union jack*, but following the terrorist attacks on 9/11, that flag has been replaced with a flag considered to be the first Navy jack. This Revolutionary War flag is made of horizontal red and white stripes with a rattlesnake stretched diagonally across the stripes with the words "DONT TREAD ON ME" across the bottom. Note that the word "DONT" is spelled without the normal apostrophe (as in "don't") as it was done on the original flag.

[3.6] The current Navy Jack, here flown by an aircraft carrier on a special occasion. Normally the flag is flown from the jackstaff at the forward end of Navy ships when they are not under way.

The National Anthem

Many customs and ceremonies are associated with the national ensign. One that you will have some familiarity with is showing respect during the playing of the national anthem. Just as you would stand during the playing of "The Star-Spangled Banner" before a ballgame, all naval personnel show similar respect whenever the national anthem is played. You will do this differently depending on the circumstances.

IN UNIFORM AND COVERED

➡ Stand at attention, face the flag (or face the music if you cannot see the flag).

➡ Salute at the first note of the music. Hold the salute until the last note.

Note: On ships and naval stations, the playing of the national anthem is often preceded and followed by special bugle signals that tell you when to begin and end your salute. If those signals are being used, be sure to hold your salute until the second signal is sounded, rather than ending at the last note of the anthem. The second signal will always follow the anthem within a few seconds.

IN CIVILIAN CLOTHES

➡ Stand at attention, face the flag (or face the music if you cannot see the flag).

➡ Since 2008 servicemembers (including veterans and retirees) may render the hand salute (whether covered or uncovered) or may choose the traditional way for civilians to show their respect by placing the right hand over the heart—just as for the pledge of allegiance in school— at the first note of the music and hold it there until the last note. Men wearing hats remove them and hold them over their left shoulders so that their right hands are centered over their hearts. Women do not remove their hats. While either option is acceptable, saluting is a nice way to declare your service and is gender neutral.

IN FORMATION

➡ You will either be ordered to salute as a group by the formation commander or brought to attention while he or she renders a salute for the formation, depending upon the circumstances.

IN A BOAT

➡ You will either sit or stand at attention as safety dictates. The boat officer or coxswain will salute for all aboard.

DRIVING A MOTOR VEHICLE

➡ Pull over and stop if traffic safety permits. Sit at attention but do not salute.

DURING THE PLAYING OF A FOREIGN NATIONAL ANTHEM

➡ The same marks of respect prescribed during the playing of the U.S. national anthem are shown during the playing of another nation's anthem.

Passing of the Colors

Whenever the national color passes by you, as in a parade for example, stand and render a salute until the ensign has passed.

When you are passing the national color that is carried on a staff by a color guard, salute as you pass it.

Morning and Evening Colors

The ceremonies of hoisting the national ensign (raising the flag) at 0800 in the morning and lowering it at sunset are called *morning colors* and *evening colors*, respectively. These ceremonies take place every day on every Navy shore station in the world. Ships at sea do not observe either of these formal ceremonies, but ships in port—whether moored to a pier or anchored offshore—do observe both morning and evening colors. Aboard ships, the ceremonies have an added factor in that the jack (explained earlier) is hoisted and taken down from the jackstaff (at the bow) at the same time that the national ensign is hoisted or lowered from the flagstaff (at the stern) of the ship.

If there is more than one Navy ship in port at the same time, the one having the most senior officer (called SOPA, or "senior officer present afloat") holds colors and all the other ships follow the lead of SOPA. This ensures that all ships hold colors simultaneously, which makes for a much more impressive ceremony than if each ship acted independently.

The national ensign is always hoisted briskly and smartly, and lowered ceremoniously. The only exception to this practice is when the national ensign is hauled down briskly and smartly from the gaff as a ship shifts colors to the flagstaff when anchoring or mooring between the hours of 0800 and sunset.

MORNING COLORS

"First call" is sounded by a bugler, a loudspeaker, or on the ship's announcing (1MC) system precisely at 0755. Aboard ship, an alternative is for the officer of the deck to pass the word "first call to colors" over the 1MC. This serves to alert everyone that the morning colors ceremony will take place in five minutes. At the same time, a special yellow and green pennant called the PREP (for "preparative") pennant (see TAB 20-E: Signal Flags and Pennants) is hoisted to the yardarm on ships.

At 0800, the bugle sounds "Attention" (or the word is passed over the 1MC) and the national ensign and jack are hoisted. At that moment, the PREP pennant will be hauled to the dip (lowered to the halfway point) and remain there until the ceremony is completed. While the colors are being briskly hoisted, one of several things will happen:

- The band plays the national anthem (if the ship or shore station has a band).
- The bugler plays "To the Color" (if the ship or station has a bugler assigned).
- A recording of the national anthem is played over the 1MC.
- A recording of "To the Color" is played over the 1MC.
- Silence is observed while the colors are being hoisted (if none of the choices above are available).

During colors, everyone within sight or hearing renders honors. If you are outside, stop working (or whatever else you were doing when attention was sounded), face the colors, and salute. Remain saluting while the colors are being raised and the music (band or bugle) is playing. Drop your salute after the last note of the music but remain at attention until you hear the bugle call "Carry on." If you are aboard ship and cannot see the national ensign, face aft (toward the stern) because you know the colors are being hoisted there. If you are on a shore station and cannot see the national ensign, face in the direction you hear the music or whistles coming from. If you are in ranks, follow the orders of the person in charge of the formation.

If neither a band nor a bugle is available, a police-type whistle will be blown instead as follows: a single blast indicates "Attention," and those not in ranks render the hand salute. At the conclusion of the ceremony, three short blasts indicate "Carry on."

Once "Carry on" has been signaled either by bugle, by whistle, or verbally over the announcing system, you should resume what you were doing before the colors ceremony.

EVENING COLORS

Sunset is the time for evening colors in the Navy. The exact time of sunset changes depending on your latitude and the time of year but will be published each day in your ship's or station's POD (Plan of the Day). Five minutes before sunset, "First call to colors" is sounded just as in the morning and, if on board ship, the PREP pennant is raised to the yardarm. At sunset, the colors ceremony begins when "Attention" is sounded on a bugle or when a whistle is blown. PREP is hauled to the dip just as in the morning, and the procedures for standing at attention and saluting are the same as in the morning. While the national ensign is being lowered, the band will play the national anthem or the bugler (or a recording) will play "Retreat."

A significant difference in the two ceremonies is that at morning colors the national ensign is hauled up smartly (quickly), while at evening colors it is hauled down slowly and ceremoniously.

"Carry on" will signal the end of the ceremony just as it does in the morning.

REFLECTION

During the colors ceremony, you may of course think about whatever you like, but those who have grown to be proud of their service and to appreciate this nation through their years of experience will tell you that it is an excellent time to reflect upon what this Navy and this nation are all about, to think about what it is that makes the United States the greatest nation on Earth. If you are unmoved by the sight of your nation's flag bursting forth on a morning breeze in all its colorful glory, it is probably because you have not yet traveled the world and witnessed how other people live, have not yet experienced the pride of being a part of a crew that works hard and gives what it takes to make the U.S. Navy the best the world has ever seen. As you stand saluting in the evening twilight, watching your nation's colors slowly descend the mast to the haunting notes of the bugle playing "Retreat," do not be surprised if you feel a special bond with your nation and an appreciation for the sacrifices that have been made by people just like you in its defense. It is one of those moments that civilians never exactly share and which you will remember for the rest of your life whether you leave the Navy after one enlistment or remain in service for thirty years.

Shifting Colors

A custom unique to the sea services is shifting colors. As already discussed, the national ensign is flown from the flagstaff at the stern (and the jack is flown from the jackstaff at the bow) when a Navy ship is in port or at anchor. But when a ship gets under way—no longer moored to a pier or anchored—the national ensign is moved to the *gaff* (a short angled pole extending from the main mast that is higher up and toward the middle of the ship). When the last mooring line is brought on board, or the anchor is lifted clear of the bottom of the harbor (aweigh), a long whistle blast is blown over the ship's general announcing (1MC) system and the national ensign is hoisted to the gaff while, simultaneously, the national ensign and jack are taken down from the flagstaff and jackstaff, respectively. This is all done smartly (quickly); the jack and ensign should virtually disappear from the bow and stern while a different ensign leaps to the gaff. A ship that does not shift colors smartly will soon have a reputation it does not want!

When a ship anchors or moors to a pier the exact opposite procedure takes place. The ensign is taken down from the gaff and raised along with the jack at the bow when the first mooring line is passed to the pier or when the anchor touches bottom. All of this is done smartly, of course, to preserve the ship's reputation as "a taut ship" (efficient and proud).

Flying the Ensign While Under Way

Ships at sea do not observe morning or evening colors, but they do fly an ensign at the gaff from sunrise to sunset (except as noted below). The jack is not flown at sea.

When far out at sea and very few other vessels are around, the ensign is often taken down. This is done because a flag flying in the wind suffers a great deal of wear and tear, making it necessary to replace it frequently, and flying the national ensign at times when there is no one around to see it is wasteful. The ensign *is* flown at sea at the following times:

- Getting under way and returning to port
- When joining up with other ships
- When cruising near land or in areas of high traffic
- During battle

Dipping the Ensign

A very old custom of the sea is that merchant ships "salute" naval vessels by dipping their ensigns as they pass by. When a merchant ship of any nation that is formally recognized by the United States salutes a ship of the U.S. Navy, she lowers her national colors to half-mast. The Navy ship returns the salute by lowering her ensign to half-mast for a few seconds, then closing it back up. The merchant vessel then raises her ensign back up.

If a naval ship is at anchor or moored to a pier and a passing merchant ship dips her ensign, the salute should be returned by lowering the national ensign halfway down the flagstaff, pausing for a moment, then returning it to the peak. The flag flown at the bow is *not* dipped as well but remains two-blocked on the jackstaff.

If a naval vessel is under way and not flying the ensign (as discussed above) and a passing merchant ship dips her ensign in salute, the Navy ship will hoist her colors, dip for the salute, close them up again, and then haul them down again after a suitable interval.

Naval vessels dip the ensign only to answer a salute; they *never* salute first.

Half-Masting the National Ensign

When an official dies, it is often the practice to lower the ensign halfway down the mast or flag pole as a means of honoring the deceased official. The flag in this position is referred to as being at half-mast (outside the Navy, it is sometimes called half-staff). A list of officials so honored is contained in *United States Navy Regulations*.

More recently, the practice has been extended to occasions other than the loss of an official, such as in the aftermath of a terrorist attack.

The procedures for half-masting are as follows:

When the ensign is already flying. If the ensign is flying when word is received that the ensign is to be half-masted, it should be immediately lowered halfway.

When hoisting. If the ensign is not already flying, morning colors will be held as normal with the ensign being hoisted smartly all the way to the peak (top of the mast or flagstaff) and remaining there through the national anthem or "To the Color." Only then is it lowered ceremoniously to the half-mast position.

Memorial Day. The national ensign is brought to the peak through the end of the music and then half-masted using the procedures explained above. At 1200 (noon), a special gun salute is sounded called *minute guns*: one gun is fired every minute until twenty-one shots have been fired to honor those who have given their lives in the defense of our nation. At the conclusion of the firing, the national ensign is hoisted to the peak and flown that way for the remainder of the day. If a twenty-one-gun salute cannot be fired, the ensign is raised to the peak at precisely 1220.

During burial at sea. The ensign is at half-mast from the beginning of the funeral service until the body is committed to the deep.

Aboard ship in port, any time the national ensign is lowered to half-mast, so is the jack.

The exact half-mast position of the flag varies with the type of pole-mast being used:

Polemast (stationary flagpole). Half-mast position is three-fourths of the way to the peak.

Polemast with crosstree (yard). When at half-mast, the bottom of the union portion (blue field) shall be even with the crosstree.

Polemast with gaff. Half-mast position is halfway between the top and the bottom of the gaff.

Other Flags

Many other flags besides the national ensign are used in the Navy. There are flags that represent numbers and the letters of the alphabet and some with special meanings that are used by ships to communicate (see **Chapter 20 and** TAB 20-E), and there are other special flags used for a variety of purposes.

UNION JACK

Although this replica of the blue, star-studded field of the national ensign has been replaced by the first Navy jack as explained earlier in this chapter, the union jack is still carried in the flag inventory and has another purpose. It is hoisted at a yardarm (crossbar on a mast) when a general court-martial or a court of inquiry is in session.

[**3.7**] The union jack

COMMISSION PENNANT

The commission pennant is long and narrow, with seven white stars on a blue field and the rest of the pennant divided lengthwise, red on top and white below.

[**3.8**] A Sailor raises the commission pennant on a newly commissioned attack submarine.

The commission pennant flies, day and night, from the time a ship is commissioned until she is decommissioned (in other words, while she is in service as a U.S. Navy ship), except when a personal flag or command pennant is flying instead (as explained below). One other exception is that a Navy hospital ship flies a Red Cross flag instead of a commission pennant.

The commission pennant is hoisted at the after truck (top of the mast closest to the rear of the vessel) or, on board a mastless ship, at the highest and most conspicuous point available.

The commission pennant is also flown from the bow of a boat if the commanding officer is embarked (in the boat) to make an official visit.

The commission pennant is not a personal flag per se, but under certain circumstances it is used as the personal symbol of the commanding officer. Along with the national ensign and the jack, it is half-masted on the death of the ship's commanding officer. At the funeral of a ship's CO ashore, it is carried by a color bearer from a flagstaff and is draped in mourning by a black streamer. When a commanding officer transfers or the ship is decommissioned, it is the custom to present him or her with the commission pennant.

PERSONAL FLAGS

You will frequently hear the terms "flag officer" or "flag rank." These refer to admirals (or generals in other services) and have come about because officers in pay grades O-7 through O-10 in the Navy have special flags that are flown aboard ships or stations at which they are the senior rank.

For Navy admirals who are eligible for command at sea, the flags are blue with a number of white stars corresponding to their rank: one star for a rear admiral (lower half), two stars for a rear admiral (upper half), three stars for a vice admiral, and four stars for an admiral. For admirals not eligible for command at sea, including restricted line officers and officers in staff corps like supply, medical, judge advocate general, civil engineer, etc., the flags are white with blue stars. These flags may be mounted on a flagstaff in their offices, flown from their base headquarters flagpole, flown on the fenders of their official cars, and flown from the main truck (top of the tallest mast) on board ships in which they are embarked.

When an admiral takes a ship to be his or her headquarters, it is called the "flagship." The admiral's flag is folded and held in place by thread and hoisted to the peak of the main truck so that when the admiral boards, the

[3.9] During a change-of-command ceremony, the departing commanding officer of a guided-missile cruiser receives the commission pennant that flew on his ship during his time in command.

[3.10] The personal flag of a four-star admiral is flown on this submarine while she or he is embarked.

flag can be "broken" (opened up by yanking on the thread line) to signify the admiral's presence. This is why in traditional biographies of flag officers, the admiral's boarding of a new flagship is written as, "He broke his flag in USS *Neversail*."

The ship's commission pennant and the personal flag of an admiral are not flown at the same time, so if a vice admiral boards your ship, the commission pennant is hauled down from the after truck and the admiral's three-star flag is broken at the main truck. The admiral's personal flag remains flying for as long as the admiral is officially embarked, even if he or she leaves the ship for a period of less than seventy-two hours.

Some very high-ranking officials, such as the President, Secretary of Defense, Secretary of the Navy, and the Chief of Naval Operations, have their own specially designed personal flags, which are flown in the same manner as the starred flags of admirals.

[**3.11**] The Secretary of the Navy's flag flies aboard a ship while he or she is embarked.

COMMAND PENNANTS

Officers who are not admirals but have command of more than one ship or a number of aircraft rate a command pennant. These pennants are flown in the same manner as an admiral's personal flag. When commanding a force, flotilla, squadron, cruiser-destroyer group, or aircraft wing, the officer rates a "broad command pennant," which is white with blue stripes along the top and bottom. An officer in command of any other unit, such as an aircraft squadron, flies a "burgee command pennant," which is white with *red* stripes top and bottom.

ABSENCE INDICATORS

When a commanding officer or flag officer is temporarily absent, an absentee pennant is flown. The "substitute pennants" are used for this purpose (see TAB 20-E: Signal Flags and Pennants). When specific officers or officials depart the ship for a period less than seventy-two hours, their absence is indicated by hoisting the following pennants:

- **Admiral or unit commander.** First Substitute pennant flown from the starboard yardarm
- **Admiral's chief of staff.** Second Substitute flown from the port yardarm
- **Ship's commanding officer.** Third Substitute flown from the port yardarm
- **Civil or military official.** Fourth Substitute flown from the starboard yardarm
- (Secretary of Defense, Secretary of the Navy, etc.)

CHURCH PENNANT

While church services are conducted by a chaplain, the appropriate church pennant is placed on the hoist above the ensign. It is the only flag or pennant ever flown above the national ensign in this manner.

SPECIAL FLAGS AND PENNANTS

Both in port and at sea, it is the custom for ships to fly other flags or pennants with special meanings. Some of these will be discussed in the chapter on communications.

The senior officer present afloat (SOPA) will fly a special green and white flag (which is also the "starboard" pennant used in flag communications) so that all ships in sight will know where SOPA is embarked.

Ships who have earned them fly special pennants representing awards to the command—the Presidential Unit Citation (PUC), Navy Unit Commendation (NUC), and the Meritorious Unit Commendation (MUC)—from sunrise to sunset. These awards can be given to shore commands as well.

HONORS

Specific practices have come down to us through Navy history to acknowledge people of high ranks and to celebrate special events.

Manning the Rail

In the days of sail, a custom evolved in which the crew would "man the yards" by standing evenly spaced on all the ship's yards (crossbars on masts from which sails were suspended) and giving three cheers to honor a distinguished person. Today, the custom has become manning the *rail* since modern ships have few or no yards. To accomplish this, the crew is stationed at regular intervals along the rails and superstructure of a ship (along the edge of the flight deck on an aircraft carrier). This is done as a means of rendering honors to a president, the head of a foreign state, or the member of a reigning royal family. Sailors so stationed do not salute.

Although Navy Regulations call for ship's crews to be paraded at quarters when a ship enters or leaves port, it has also become the custom for ships to man the rail.

Dressing and Full-Dressing the Ship

Commissioned ships are "dressed" on national holidays and "full-dressed" on Presidents' Day and Independence Day. When a ship is dressed, the national ensign is flown from the flagstaff and usually from each masthead. When a ship is full-dressed, in addition to the ensigns a "rainbow" of signal flags is displayed from bow to stern over the mastheads, or as nearly so as the construction of the ship permits. Ships are only dressed and full-dressed in port, never under way, and only from 0800 to sunset.

[3.12] Naval Support Activity Bahrain receives the Navy Unit Commendation from the Chief of Naval Operations.

[3.13] Sailors man the rail on an aircraft carrier.

[3.14] A full-dressed guided-missile destroyer in honor of Presidents' Day while moored in Split, Croatia

Passing Honors

When naval vessels pass close aboard (600 yards for ships, 400 yards for boats) other naval vessels with officers more senior to them in command or embarked, it is the custom for the junior ship to initiate passing honors. Such honors are exchanged between ships of the U.S. Navy, between ships of the Navy and the Coast Guard, and between U.S. and most foreign navy ships.

Frequently, you will find that the entire process is accomplished using whistle signals or "blasts" blown with a police-type whistle. It is important that you know what the procedure is and what the whistles mean so that you are not embarrassed when the occasion arises to participate in a passing honors situation.

➡ The junior vessel announces "Attention to starboard" (or sounds one blast) or "Attention to port" (two blasts), depending upon which side of the vessel the senior ship is on.

➡ All members of the crew who are outside on the weather decks and not in ranks will stop what they are doing (unless their work is safety-related and it would be dangerous for them to stop) and face the direction indicated while standing at attention.

➡ The vessel being honored will likewise call its crew to attention facing the junior ship. Next, the word "Hand salute" is passed in the junior vessel (one blast) and the hand salute is rendered by all persons on deck.

➡ This also is returned by the senior vessel. "Two" (the command for ending the salute) is then passed by the senior vessel, followed by the junior (two blasts).

➡ Once the vessels are clear, "Carry on" is sounded (three blasts) and everything returns to normal routine.

Piping the Side

Piping the side is a customary part of the quarterdeck ceremony when a senior officer or a high-ranking civilian official comes aboard or leaves a ship. To carry out this honorary ceremony, the boatswain's mate of the watch pipes a special call—"Over the Side"—on the boatswain's pipe while Sailors form a cordon of two lines on either side of the gangway (entrance/exit to the ship). These Sailors are known as side boys and are paraded in pairs of different numbers based on the rank of the officer or official arriving—two, four, six, or eight.

➡ First, bells or tones are sounded over the 1MC corresponding to the number of side boys to which the arriving person is entitled. The bells themselves are *not* an honor—merely a message indicating to the crew how high in rank the visiting person is. They are sounded in pairs followed by a short pause; for six side boys, it would be "ding-ding . . . ding-ding . . . ding-ding."

➡ Immediately after the bells, the person being piped is announced by an abbreviated title, followed by the word "arriving" (or "departing"). This would include "United States" for the President or Vice President; "Navy" for the Secretary of the Navy; "Naval Operations" for the CNO; "DESRON TWO TWO" for the commander of Destroyer Squadron 22; or the name of the ship for a ship's commanding officer (i.e., "Michael Murphy" for USS *Michael Murphy*).

- The side boys salute on the first note of the pipe, holding their salute as the person being honored walks through the human passageway, and drop the salute together on the last note of the boatswain's pipe.
- Once the pipe is terminated, a final, single bell is sounded. This is customarily referred to as the "stinger."

Side boys must be particularly smart in appearance and well groomed, with immaculate uniforms.

Another tradition has evolved that is sometimes called "rainbow side boys." In this case, the dignitary is arriving on a flight deck and the side boys are formed up wearing an array of the different-colored jerseys that indicate what their jobs are on the flight deck.

[3.15] Rainbow side boys on an aircraft carrier

Gun Salutes

In the old days it took as long as twenty minutes to load and fire a gun, so that when a ship fired her guns in salute, thereby rendering herself temporarily powerless, it was considered a friendly gesture. That practice has come down through the years to be a form of honoring an individual or a nation.

The gun salutes prescribed by Navy Regulations are fired only by ships and stations designated by the Secretary of the Navy. Salutes are fired at intervals of five seconds, and always in odd numbers. A salute of twenty-one guns is fired on Washington's Birthday, Memorial Day, and Independence Day, and to honor the President of the United States and heads of foreign states. Other high-ranking government officials are honored by a lesser number of guns; for example, the vice president of the United States is honored by nineteen guns and the under secretary of the Navy receives a seventeen-gun salute. Senior naval officers are also honored by gun salutes, and the number of shots fired depends upon their rank. Some of the salutes for civil and military dignitaries are as follows:

21 guns—president or foreign king, queen, or royal family member
19 guns—vice president, foreign prime ministers, governors, chief justice of the United States, Joint Chiefs chairman, CNO, service chiefs, secretaries of state and defense, and the service secretaries.
17 guns—admiral
15 guns—vice admiral
13 guns—rear admiral (upper half)
11 guns—rear admiral (lower half)

Officers below the rank of rear admiral (lower half) do not rate a gun salute.

OTHER SHIPBOARD CUSTOMS

Ships have been plying the waters of the world for many centuries, and this long history has resulted in many unique customs. By observing these special customs, you will be forming a special link with Sailors from the past and keeping alive traditions that, in some cases, are thousands of years old.

The Bridge

When a ship is under way, the area known as the bridge serves as the control point for the vessel. A team of people will always be on watch serving the ship's special needs. The Officer of the Deck (OOD) heads that team and, serving as the captain's direct representative, is responsible for the safe navigation of the vessel and for carrying out the ship's routine. The OOD is assisted by a team of watchstanders, who carry out a number of functions such as steering the ship and making announcements on the general announcing (1MC) system to assist in maintaining the ship's routine.

There is a formality associated with the bridge, and many ships require all non-watch personnel to request permission from the OOD to come on the bridge, accompanying their request with a salute. This is more than a mere tradition because it allows the OOD to control access to the bridge, ensuring that the watch team is not inhibited in carrying out its important duties by having too many people in the way. Another custom that serves a useful purpose is that of calling out "Captain is on the bridge" by the first person to see the commanding officer enter the bridge area. This alerts the OOD and the other watchstanders to the captain's presence, which is important because it is the OOD's responsibility to report significant happenings to the captain and because the captain's authority supersedes that of the OOD when she or he is on the bridge.

The Quarterdeck

The quarterdeck in many ways replaces the bridge as the control point of the ship when the ship is not under way. It has both functional and ceremonial purposes and, just like the bridge, is manned by a watch team. The OOD shifts his or her watch from the bridge to the quarterdeck once the ship enters port, and until the ship gets under way again, the ship's routine is run from there. The location of the quarterdeck will vary according to the type of ship, and because the quarterdeck also normally serves as the point of entry and exit for the ship, it may actually move to different locations on board the same ship, depending upon which side is facing the pier or whether or not the ship is anchored and using boats.

Frequently the quarterdeck is marked off by appropriate lines, deck markings, decorative cartridge cases, or fancy work (nautical decorations made from pieces of line). The quarterdeck is always kept particularly clean and shipshape.

Watchstanders on the quarterdeck wear the uniform of the day and present a smart and military appearance at all times. Personnel not on watch should avoid the quarterdeck unless their work requires them to be in that area.

Larger vessels, such as aircraft carriers, may have two or more entry and exit points for the ship. Only one is designated as the quarterdeck, however.

Boarding and Departing the Ship

The officer of the deck in port, or the OOD's assistant—known as the junior officer of the deck (JOOD)—will meet all persons leaving or boarding the ship. There are specific procedures to be followed by Navy personnel when boarding or departing and, to avoid serious embarrassment, you must learn them.

Because of security considerations, you will nearly always be expected to show your ID card to the OOD (or her or his representative) whenever you board a naval vessel, whether you are a member of the crew or not.

BOARDING

If the ship is alongside a pier, you will use a "brow" (a walkway that bridges the gap between the pier and the ship) to come aboard. If the ship is anchored out in the water, you will, of course, ride in a boat to get to the ship, and to get from the water up to the ship's main deck you will use an "accommodation ladder" (a kind of stairwell that has been rigged over the side of the ship, leading up from the water to the main deck). The opening in the ship's rail, where you actually board the ship (whether you are using a brow or an accommodation ladder), is called the "gangway." Navy ships adhere to formal procedures during boarding.

→ At the gangway, you should turn and face aft (where the national ensign is flying from the flagstaff), come to attention, and smartly salute if the ensign is flying. On some larger ships, you will not be able to actually see the national ensign but you should salute facing aft anyway. You will know whether the national ensign is flying or not by the time of day. If it is after 0800 and before sunset, you will know that the ensign is flying. The OOD will return your salute to the national ensign.

➡ Next, turn to face the OOD (or her or his representative), salute, and say, "I request permission to come aboard, ma'am" (or "sir").

➡ The OOD will return your salute and say, "Permission granted" or "Very well," and you should proceed. (Note: These salutes take place no matter what the ranks of the individuals involved. If the OOD is a chief petty officer and the boarding individual is a commander, the latter will still salute the CPO, who, as OOD, represents the captain.)

➡ If you are not in uniform, you would not render the hand salute to the ensign, but instead face aft at attention and put your right hand over your heart. *United States Navy Regulations* states that "if covered, men shall remove their headdress with the right hand and hold it at the left shoulder, the hand being over the heart." Then return to attention, face the OOD, and request permission to come aboard.

➡ If you are not a member of the crew of the ship you are boarding, you should state the reason for your visit when requesting permission to come aboard.

DEPARTING

The procedure for leaving a ship is much the same as boarding, except that the steps are reversed. Step up to the vicinity of the gangway, salute the OOD, and say, "I request permission to go ashore, sir" (or "ma'am"). When the OOD says, "Permission granted" or "Very well" and returns your salute, drop your salute and step to the gangway. If the ensign is flying, face aft, salute smartly, and leave. If in civilian clothes, salute the ensign (but not the OOD) by placing your right hand over your heart.

CROSSING NESTS

Ships sometimes tie up in nests (clusters) alongside a tender or pier, and you may have to cross one or more ships to get to your own. The usual quarterdeck procedure described for boarding and leaving is modified somewhat in this case. When you board the inboard ship (the one closest to the pier), salute the colors and the quarterdeck and address the OOD by saying, "I request permission to cross, ma'am" (or "sir"). When the OOD says "Very well" or "Permission granted" and returns your salute, drop your salute and head across the ship to the brow that leads to the next ship in the nest.

It is not necessary to salute the colors on leaving, but be sure to do so when boarding the next ship in the nest. Repeat this procedure on each ship until you reach your own.

Officers' and CPO Country

The area on board ship where officers eat (the wardroom) and sleep (staterooms), as well as the passageways surrounding these areas, is known as "officers' country." Correspondingly, the area where chief petty officers eat and sleep is known as "CPO country" (colloquially, as the "goat locker," as a good-natured reference to chiefs as "old goats").

You should avoid these areas unless you are on official business. If your duties require you to enter any of these spaces, you should knock before entering and remove your cover. Watchstanders wearing a duty belt or a sidearm remain covered.

Enlisted Mess Deck

The eating area for enlisted personnel is called the mess deck and is treated with the same courtesy as the wardroom. Always uncover when on or crossing mess decks, except when you are on watch and wearing a duty belt or are under arms.

Divine Services

When religious services are held on board, the church pennant is flown, and word is passed that services are being held in a certain space of the ship and to maintain quiet about the decks. A person entering the area where services are held uncovers unless the services are for a religion that requires the head to be covered during worship.

Boat Etiquette

A ship is judged, among other things, by her boats and their crews. Whether in a working uniform or Service Dress Blue, crews should observe the courtesies and procedures that build and maintain their ship's reputation. Boats can play an important part in naval ceremonies, and each crewmember ought to know what is expected of the boat and of him or her.

Some boats will have only an enlisted person called a "coxswain" (pronounced "cock-sun") in charge, while others will have a "boat officer" specifically assigned to be responsible for boat and passenger safety.

BOARDING AND DEPARTING BOATS

The basic rule in Navy manners, as in civilian life, is to make way for a senior quickly, quietly, and without confusion. The procedure for entering boats and vehicles is *seniors in last and out first.*

If the boat is clearly divided into two sections (forward and aft), enlisted Sailors should sit in the forward section and officers in the aft section. In any case, the rule is that seniors take the seats farthest aft.

The boat coxswain salutes all officers boarding and leaving the boat. Enlisted personnel seated well forward in a large boat do not rise and salute when officers enter or leave. Enlisted personnel in the after section of a boat do rise and salute when a commissioned officer enters or leaves.

PASSING SALUTES

Boats exchange salutes when passing, as enlisted personnel and officers do when passing on shore. It is not the size or type of boat that determines seniority, but who is embarked; a small whaleboat carrying a commander is senior to a large boat with an ensign aboard. The coxswain or boat officer will usually be able to tell which boat is senior by the uniform of the passenger officer or the flag flown, but if they are in doubt, they will initiate a salute.

When one boat passes another, the coxswain and the boat officer (if there is one embarked) render a hand salute. Others in the boat stand or sit at attention. If standing, they face the boat being saluted; if seated, they sit at attention but do not turn toward the passing boat. The senior officer in the boat also salutes, while remaining seated, if he or she is visible from the other boat.

If a boat is carrying an officer or official for whom a salute is being fired by a saluting battery, the coxswain will slow the engine and disengage the clutch (if sea conditions permit) after the first gun is fired; the person being honored rises, if safety permits.

OTHER COURTESIES

There are some additional habits and practices that will not win or lose wars but are part of our heritage, so all Sailors should be aware of them. Commit these to memory to avoid embarrassment.

Calling Attention

Whenever the captain, officers senior to him or her, or important visitors approach an area or enter a room or ship's compartment where personnel are not at attention, the first person to see them coming should loudly call "Attention on deck!" ("Deck" is used whether or not you are on board a ship.) Everyone should immediately come to attention and remain that way until the senior person present gives the command to carry on or be seated. This courtesy applies both on and off ships.

"Gangway"

If an officer approaches a passage that is blocked, the first person to notice this should alert others to clear a path by calling "Gangway!" Everyone there should move out of the officer's way.

If enlisted personnel need to get through in a similar situation, they should clear a passage for themselves or others by saying "Coming through." "Make a hole" is not the correct term, although you will sometimes hear it being used.

"By Your Leave"

When it is necessary to overtake an officer while walking, approach on the officer's left side, salute when you are abreast, and ask, "By your leave, sir (or "ma'am")?" When the officer returns the salute and replies, "Very well," drop your salute and continue past.

Accompanying a Senior

Always walk to the left of someone senior to you. If the senior member is required either to render or return a salute, do likewise—saluting and dropping the salute when the senior does.

CEREMONIES

Special occasions call for special ceremonies in the Navy. You are likely to take part in a number of these during your time as a Sailor.

Official Visits

For official visits of high-ranking military officers and civil officials, Navy Regulations call for specific honors and ceremonies upon the arrival and departure of the dignitary. Several tables in the regulations describe the honors for personnel holding specific offices. These include:

Piping the side. Side boys are posted at the quarterdeck in pairs forming a cordon of two facing ranks through which the honoree will proceed. The total number differs for different civil and military ranks. The boatswain's mate pipes "Over the Side" from the time the dignitary's head becomes level with the deck until he or she has passed through the side boys, who salute through the duration of the pipe.

"Ruffles and Flourishes." Up to four "ruffles and flourishes" are played for honorees. If you have seen a formal ceremony for the president on TV, you will have heard four "ruffles and flourishes" prior to the playing of "Hail to the Chief."

Honors Music. Different songs are played for different honorees based on *United States Navy Regulations*. Admirals and Marine Corps generals receive the "Flag Officer's March." Army and Air Force generals receive the "General's March." Several high civilian officials receive the "Honors March" ("Stars and Stripes Forever"), while the vice president receives "Hail Columbia." The president, as mentioned, is honored with "Hail to the Chief."

Inspecting the Guard. The dignitary may inspect the guard of the day or honor guard.

Change of Command

When one commanding officer relieves another, a formal ceremony is held to honor the outgoing CO and to demonstrate the peaceful and lawful transfer of command. At its core, the ceremony has each officer reading his or her orders, formally acknowledging that the new CO has relieved the old, and then reporting that the change in command has been effected according to orders. The participants and often the whole crew will be in the seasonal full dress uniform to recognize the significance of this event.

Navy Birthday

Each 13 October, the Navy remembers all of its challenges and accomplishments since 1775. A cornerstone of the anniversary celebration is a birthday cake, usually cut ceremoniously with the first piece of cake shared by the oldest and the youngest Sailor present. Often, this observance is held as part of a formal dinner or a ball. Similar ceremonies might also be held for the anniversaries of different communities or corps within the Navy.

Special Ship Ceremonies

Formal ceremonies are conducted at significant moments of the life of a Navy ship, including the laying of the keel, launching, commissioning, and decommissioning. Each of these features specific rituals and acts that have come down through the centuries.

Keel-Laying Ceremony. A simple ceremony that marks the laying of the keel is the first major event in a ship's history.

Launching/Christening Ceremony. The newly completed ship is dedicated, given its name, and launched to the sea. This ceremony is known to many for the practice of having the sponsor break a bottle of champagne against the bow of the ship as it is launched into the water.

Commissioning Ceremony. This ceremony brings a ship into active service in the Navy, adding the title United States Ship (USS) to its name. The ship now flies the commission pennant.

Decommissioning Ceremony. The equivalent of a person's retirement, a solemn ceremony marks the end of a ship's active service and transfer to the reserve fleet for further disposition.

Personal Ceremonies

The Navy recognizes the importance of individuals and their service by recognizing certain milestone events.

Promotion and Frocking. Navy personnel are given higher levels of position in two ways. In one, enlisted personnel are *advanced* and officers are *promoted*. In the other, the individual is granted the authority to wear and use the new rank—but without the pay and allowances—before the actual date of the new rank. This is called *frocking*, after the practice of giving the frock coat of a new rank to Navy personnel in the age of sail. It is usually less formal than other ceremonies.

[3.16] Launching ceremonies are an old seafaring tradition. Here the ballistic-missile submarine USS *George Washington* slides down the ways amid much celebration in 1959.

Reenlistment. In this ceremony, a Sailor raises his or her right hand and again swears an oath to support and defend the Constitution of the United States. Reenlistment ceremonies often include families as close witnesses to this milestone in a Sailor's career. Many Sailors choose to reenlist at sites of historic significance or other places that hold special meaning.

Awards. Superior performance, whether through long-term dedication and achievement, selection as Sailor of the quarter, or courage in combat, is recognized in the Navy through the presentation of various awards. The award of personal decorations is usually performed by the commanding officer or a senior officer—the president in the case of a living recipient of the Medal of Honor. These ceremonies may be part of a routine command formation or a special event convened specifically to confer the award.

[3.17] A master chief and his family are piped ashore after twenty-five years of his service.

Retirement. The dedication of a Sailor over twenty or even thirty years of service is marked by a formal ceremony in which the command and the Navy pay tribute to the individual. Various awards, gifts, and/or letters of recognition are presented to the retiree and to the spouse or family as well. In a final gesture of respect, the retiree is "piped ashore" by passing through a dual line of shipmates while a boatswain's pipe sounds a farewell.

Funerals

Another kind of personal ceremony is the funeral. There is perhaps no more moving Navy ceremony. An escort, ranging in size from a squad for junior Sailors to a battalion for admirals, accompanies the deceased to the gravesite. Gun salutes are fired for admirals as minute guns (i.e., one a minute) in the number prescribed. For all others, three specific honors are rendered:

Three Volleys. A firing detail of at least five will fire three times in unison, a custom in military funerals that dates to the earliest use of firearms in warfare. (Note: while most firing parties use seven personnel firing rifles, the fact that they fire three times *does not* mean that this is a "twenty-one-gun salute." Gun salutes are performed by guns—i.e., cannon—not rifles, and are only performed for heads of state such as kings and presidents.)

"**Taps.**" During the Civil War, U.S. Army general Daniel Butterfield and his chief bugler, Oliver Norton, took a part of the lengthy bugle call for "lights out" and rearranged it into the notes that are now recognized as "Taps." The term originated from the Dutch word *taptoe*, which meant the shutting-off of the taps at the bar (and also gave us the word for the bugle call "Tattoo") as well as from the drum signal of "taps" that was played at the end of the day. As a signal of the time to rest, this was appropriated to military funerals to observe the deceased reaching the peace of eternal rest.

Flag Folding and Presentation. The national ensign is draped over the casket of a deceased Sailor, serving as the secular equivalent of the religious cloth that covers the casket, called the pall. After firing the volleys and the playing of "Taps," the casket bearers fold the flag for presentation to the deceased's next of kin.

BURIAL AT SEA

A special kind of funeral occurs when a Sailor is committed to the deep. Done out of necessity during war time, burial at sea can also be done at the request of a Sailor or his family.

Word is passed over the 1MC, "All hands bury the dead." The ship is stopped and colors are displayed at half-mast. The casket is placed on a board and covered with the ensign. When the indicated word of the committal is read, the body bearers tilt the board until the casket slides along it, under the national ensign, overboard into the sea. As it goes, the body bearers retain the board and the national ensign on board and stand fast. After the benediction, three volleys are fired and "Taps" is played.

MEMORIAL SERVICES

Although not recognizing specific individuals, the anniversaries of significant battles or events are sometimes commemorated by special ceremonies. These often involve the presentation of a floral wreath and the playing of "Taps."

Every year, the Battle of Midway (4–7 June 1941) is commemorated in various ways throughout the Navy.

Navy customs, courtesies, and ceremonies will not by themselves win wars, but they contribute to the special identification and unit cohesion that are important elements of being a Sailor. They make us both different and the same, while serving as a kind of glue that binds us to our nation, to our service, and to our shipmates, as well as to our unique heritage.

FOUR

PERSONAL CONDUCT

G ood order and discipline are important in any organization. But because mission accomplishment and human lives may be at stake in the military, and because American military organizations bring men and women together from all parts of the nation, often with different ethnic, religious, or cultural backgrounds, special standards of personal conduct are needed. These requirements take on additional importance because military service often entails performing your duties under difficult conditions, creating special challenges not always encountered in civilian walks of life.

First exposure to those standards of conduct begins at Boot Camp, and maintaining them continues throughout your military service. Salutes, special ceremonies, and the carrying out of orders, for example, are part of the military culture and are done without further explanation or instruction. These basics are aided by a number of additional written standards, some of which are unique to the Navy—such as "The Sailor's Creed" (see TAB 1-A: The Sailor's Creed), with its core values of honor, courage, and commitment—while others, like the Code of Conduct and the Uniform Code of Military Justice, apply to all the armed forces of the United States. Additional directives provide still more guidance to ensure that personal relations are maintained at levels compatible with military service. For your well-being and that of others, it is vital that you know what is expected of you in terms of personal conduct and that you not fail to meet those standards.

THE LAW OF ARMED CONFLICT

The United States follows public international law regulating conduct during armed hostilities known as "The Law of Armed Conflict," which is based on the concept that all people are entitled to basic human rights during times of war. These principles strike a balance between humanity and military necessity and are not a matter of choice. As a member of the U.S. armed forces, you must adhere to these principles at all times.

To ensure that hostilities are directed at enemy combatants and that unnecessary human misery and physical destruction is avoided, American military personnel must:

- fight only enemy combatants and safeguard noncombatants whenever possible
- destroy no more than the mission requires
- treat civilians humanely and respect their property as much as possible
- care for the sick and wounded, whether they are friendlies, neutrals, or enemies
- allow hostiles to surrender if they are attempting to do so
- treat prisoners of war and detainees fairly
- protect and respect chaplains as noncombatants
- protect and respect medical personnel and facilities
- prevent violations of these rules whenever possible
- report violations of these rules

CODE OF CONDUCT

Navy Regulations require you to be thoroughly familiar with the Code of Conduct for Members of the Armed Forces of the United States, more commonly referred to as simply the "Code of Conduct." The Code of Conduct will always be posted in an accessible place in every command, so you should have no problem reviewing it from time to time. The six articles of this code make it clear what is expected of you if you are in a combat situation and if you are unfortunate enough to become a prisoner of war (POW).

The articles of the code can be found in TAB 4-A: Code of Conduct for Members of the Armed Forces of the United States, and each is explained here. Read the Code carefully and think about what it says. Its importance cannot be overestimated.

ARTICLE I I am an American, fighting in the forces which guard my country and our way of life. I am prepared to give my life in their defense. ✦

As a member of the armed forces it is always your duty to oppose the enemies of the United States. This applies whether you are in active combat or confined as a prisoner of war.

Your responsibility is to guard "our way of life" and to be prepared to sacrifice your life if that is what it takes to accomplish this mission. You need only watch the evening news to know that there are problems in America, that this is not a perfect nation. But anyone who has traveled the world, as you may well do before your time in the Navy is over, will surely tell you that the United States of America is the greatest of all nations. And anyone who pays close attention to the evening news will also note that despite the many problems, there is a never-ending struggle to find solutions. This nation was born and continues to survive because Americans have always jealously guarded their freedom and have been willing to sacrifice themselves rather than yield their hard-won rights. You must do no less.

ARTICLE II I will never surrender of my own free will. If in command, I will never surrender the members of my command while they still have the means to resist. ✦

You must not surrender unless you have no other choice except senseless death. As long as you have the ability to resist being captured, either by engaging the enemy in combat or by evading, you must do so. If your continued resistance would result in your death and it would serve some useful purpose to the mission (such as delaying the enemy from taking an important position or providing additional time for others to escape), then you should not surrender. But if your continued resistance would result in your death and have no effect on the outcome of the mission, then surrender is acceptable.

This responsibility extends to anyone in command as well. The commander must not surrender the people in her or his command unless they can no longer fight or avoid capture and the only other choice is for them to die for no useful purpose.

> ARTICLE III If I am captured I will continue to resist, by all means available. I will make every effort to escape and aid others to escape. I will accept neither parole nor special favors from the enemy. ✦

The duty of a member of the armed forces to continue resistance by all means available is not lessened by the misfortune of capture. You should escape by any means possible and help others to escape. However, experience has proven that there may be times when escape is virtually impossible and that attempting to escape will only bring certain death to the escapee and possibly to his or her fellow POWs. In these circumstances, you should not attempt escape. For example, in Vietnam after several Americans tried unsuccessfully to escape from their prison in downtown Hanoi, it became apparent that the escapees were much too conspicuous in a city of hostile citizens and that escapees would have too far to go with no hope of local support in order to get to friendly forces. It was determined that escape was not a reasonable risk.

Parole agreements are promises given the captor by a POW to fulfill stated conditions (such as not to bear arms or not to escape) in consideration of special privileges (such as release from captivity or better living conditions). You must never sign or enter into any parole agreement without the consent of someone senior to you.

> ARTICLE IV If I become a prisoner of war, I will keep faith with my fellow prisoners. I will give no information or take part in any actions which might be harmful to my comrades. If I am senior, I will take command. If not, I will obey the lawful orders of those appointed over me and will back them up in every way. ✦

Providing information to the enemy, or any other action that harms a fellow prisoner, is shameful. Prisoners of war must not help the enemy identify fellow prisoners who may have knowledge of value to the enemy and who may therefore be interrogated and/or tortured.

Strong leadership is essential to discipline, and being in a POW situation does not lessen this. Without discipline, camp organization, resistance, and even survival may be impossible. Personal hygiene, camp sanitation, and care of the sick and wounded are imperative, and it is up to the leaders to ensure these things are accomplished to the best of everyone's ability.

Officers and petty officers (known as noncommissioned officers in the Army, Air Force, and Marine Corps) will continue to carry out their responsibilities and exercise their authority after capture. The senior line officer, petty officer, or noncommissioned officer within the POW camp or group will assume command according to rank or precedence, without regard to branch of service. Responsibility and accountability may not be evaded. If the senior officer or noncommissioned officer is incapacitated or unable to act for any reason, the next senior takes over.

> ARTICLE V When questioned, should I become a prisoner of war, I am required to give name, rank, service number, and date of birth. I will evade answering further questions to the utmost of my ability. I will make no oral or written statements disloyal to my country and its allies or harmful to their cause. ✦

United States Navy Regulations explains that the United States has agreed to abide by an international agreement entitled the Geneva Convention Relative to the Treatment of Prisoners of War, known more commonly as simply the "Geneva Convention," and as a member of the U.S. armed forces, you are subject to the requirements and protections of this agreement.

In accordance with the Geneva Convention, a POW is required to reveal her or his name, rank, service (social security) number, and date of birth. A POW may tell the enemy about his or her individual health or welfare and, when appropriate, about routine matters of camp administration, but the following are forbidden:

- Oral or written confessions, whether true or false
- Filling out questionnaires
- Providing personal-history statements

- Making propaganda recordings and broadcasts
- Signing peace or surrender appeals, criticisms, or any other oral or written communication on behalf of the enemy, or that is critical or harmful to the United States, its allies, its armed forces, or other prisoners

It is a violation of the Geneva Convention for captors to subject a POW to physical or mental torture or any other form of coercion to secure information of any kind. If, however, a prisoner is subjected to such treatment, he or she must strive to avoid by every means the disclosure of any information, or the making of any statement or the performance of any action, harmful to the interests of the United States or its allies, or that will provide aid or comfort to the enemy.

ARTICLE VI   I will never forget that I am an American, fighting for freedom, responsible for my actions, and dedicated to the principles which made my country free. I will trust in my God and in the United States of America. ✦

Should you become a prisoner, never give up hope and always resist enemy indoctrination. This will, of course, serve the best interests of the nation, but it will serve your best interests as well. The life of a POW is hard. If all nations lived up to the terms of the Geneva Convention as it is intended, a POW experience would be difficult enough, but Americans who have been captured by the enemy have, more often than not, been subjected to terrible living conditions and have often been tortured. Experience has proven that POWs who stand firm and united against the enemy help one another survive this ordeal.

After POWs are released, their conduct may be examined and evaluated. For this reason alone, you should strive to uphold the Code of Conduct while a POW. But, even more important, you will have to live with yourself after your release, and experience has proven that those POWs who upheld the Code of Conduct to the best of their ability are much better prepared to lead a normal life after their POW ordeal is over. Those who failed to uphold the Code to the best of their ability must live with the shame and dishonor of knowing that they failed their nation and their fellow POWs.

Hope that you never become a prisoner of war. Do everything in your power, consistent with honor, to avoid becoming a POW. But if you are captured, remember the Code of Conduct and uphold it. Your chances of survival will be enhanced, and your personal sense of honor will be undamaged.

UNIFORM CODE OF MILITARY JUSTICE (UCMJ)

As a civilian, you were subject to the criminal laws of local, state, and federal governments. To a large extent you still are. But by enlisting you have submitted yourself to the jurisdiction of the Uniform Code of Military Justice as well. The basic criminal laws of the Navy are stated in the UCMJ. It is a "uniform" code of law because Congress made it apply equally to the Army, Navy, Air Force, Marine Corps, and Coast Guard, no matter what a person's pay grade is. It is under this code that the various services bring criminal charges against personnel who violate military law. You have the right to see a copy of the UCMJ at any time, and it is always posted in an accessible place on every ship and station in the armed forces.

Absence Offenses

Many of the offenses that are covered in the UCMJ require no special explanation. Theft is theft and arson is arson, no matter what system of justice you answer to. But several articles deal with absence offenses, and they require some additional explanation and emphasis. Articles 85, 86, and 87 of the UCMJ deal with desertion, unauthorized absence (often referred to as simply "UA" or AWOL for absent without leave), and missing movement, respectively.

In civilian life, your presence at your job is very important, and in the case of some occupations such as doctor or fireman it can mean the difference between life and death. In the military, since defending the nation is your foremost reason for being, the potential for a life-or-death situation is always there. Whether you are the loader on a gun, the person who inspects parachutes, or the cook who prepares meals for the crew, you are an important part of a team that depends upon every member to function properly. Any mission, whether it is one involving combat, rescue, or routine operations, will be adversely affected if one or more of the team is not there to do his or her job. Because of this, unauthorized absence is considered a very serious breach of discipline and is subject to severe penalties.

Because of the punishment you may receive and because of your responsibility to the Navy and to your shipmates who are counting on you, you must make every effort to avoid being absent without proper authorization. This requires sensible planning on your part. Always leave extra time in your travel plans, whether you are facing a twenty-minute drive or a fourteen-hour flight. If, for reasons beyond your control, you are going to be late in returning, notify your duty station immediately. If you cannot get in touch with your duty station (for example, if you are attached to a ship and she got under way without you), contact the nearest naval activity or the American Red Cross. Don't use the mail, use the telephone. Furnish enough information so that your commanding officer can understand the situation and provide appropriate instructions. You can always reach the duty officer of any station or a shore patrol headquarters on any Navy base. In most cities, naval activities are listed in the telephone directory under "U.S. Government"; otherwise the information operator can give you the number. Also, even if you are in a region where there are no naval bases or installations, keep in mind that the Navy has recruiting offices in nearly every major U.S. city. The officer or petty officer on duty there can advise you of the best course to follow. If you are sick or in jail, a family member, a friend, the hospital, or the shore patrol can send a message for you. The bottom line is that there may be a valid excuse for your being late—such as sickness, accident, or other emergency—but there is never an excuse for not notifying your commanding officer, the nearest naval activity, or the American Red Cross.

Trials and Punishments

You have probably heard of the military term "court-martial," and you would be correct if you understood it to be roughly equivalent to a trial in civilian life. But be aware that some of the terminology and many of the procedures are different. There is also "nonjudicial punishment" that is unique to the military and is used for less serious offenses.

NONJUDICIAL PUNISHMENT (NJP)

This is basically a hearing in which the commanding officer (CO) handles a relatively minor offense rather than sending it to a court. While it is not a "trial" in the civil justice sense, it is held with formality and is not a pleasant experience for anyone involved. There is no right to an attorney at

NJP; rather, the offender appears without representation and the CO relies on inputs from the offender's division chief and division officer. Because these proceedings are nonjudicial, the offender may be punished but will not have a criminal record. In the Navy, NJP is usually referred to as "captain's mast."

On hearing the evidence, both for and against, the CO determines whether the accused is guilty or not and then, if necessary, assigns an appropriate punishment. Some of the punishments that a CO may award are restriction to the ship, extra duties, reduction in pay grade, correctional custody, and forfeiture of a portion of your pay.

The accused has certain rights during a captain's mast:

- To be present before the officer conducting the mast
- To be advised of the charges
- Not to be compelled to make any statement—the right to remain silent
- To be present during testimony of witnesses or the receipt of written statements
- To question witnesses or to have questions posed to witnesses
- To have available for inspection all physical and documentary evidence
- To present evidence on one's own behalf
- To be accompanied by a personal representative who may or may not be a lawyer and whose presence is arranged for by the accused
- To appeal the imposition of punishment to higher authority
- If assigned to a shore activity, to refuse captain's mast and demand trial by court-martial instead

OTHER "MASTS"

To avoid confusion, you should also be aware that there are other forms of "mast" in the Navy that have nothing to do with the UCMJ. Besides the captain's mast, you might find yourself involved in a "meritorious mast," which is used to present awards or commendations for achievement, or if you asked to see the CO for an important reason, this would be called a "request mast."

COURTS-MARTIAL

If an alleged offense is too severe to dispose of by captain's mast, or if the accused exercises his or her right to refuse NJP, the case will go to court-martial. There are three types of courts-martial: summary, special, and general.

Summary Court-Martial. If the offense is minor, and if nonjudicial action has been ruled out, the CO may refer the charges to trial by summary court-martial. This involves a summary or shortened procedure where actions are judicial in nature. One officer serves as the judge, jury, prosecution, and defense counsel. The officer takes evidence on the charges and makes judgment according to judicial standards. The accused has the right to consult with an attorney but does not have the right to be represented by an attorney during the proceedings. The accused may also refuse trial by summary court-martial and receive a special court-martial instead.

If an accused is convicted by summary court-martial, the court may impose punishments similar to, but generally tougher than, those imposed at NJP. A guilty finding at summary court-martial does not result in a federal criminal conviction but will be included in the member's service record.

Special Court-Martial. If a commanding officer feels that an alleged offense against a service person is moderate to severe, or if the accused has refused trial by summary court-martial, the CO may refer the charges to trial by special court-martial. A legally trained military judge oversees the trial and a minimum of a three-member jury decides guilt.

If you are brought before a special court-martial, you may waive the right to trial before the court-martial jury and face the military judge alone. If you decide to go with the jury, you may also request that there be one-third enlisted representation on the jury. You may have a military attorney assigned to you, you may request a specific military counsel, or you may hire your own civilian attorney at your own expense. Possible punishments include the possibility of a bad-conduct discharge and up to twelve months' imprisonment.

General Court-Martial. The general court-martial is reserved for more serious charges, such as common-law felonies (murder, rape, robbery, and arson) and more serious military charges, such as lengthy unauthorized absence and desertion. The court is composed of a military judge, five or more members who serve as the jury, and military defense and prosecution attorneys. The accused in a general court-martial may request trial before a military judge alone, but if he or she is enlisted and elects to be tried by the full court-martial, at least one-third of the court members must be enlisted persons.

This is by far the most serious of all military courts. Its sentencing power extends to the death penalty and life imprisonment. The *Manual for Courts-Martial* lists the maximum sentence that may be imposed for each offense by a court-martial under the UCMJ.

JOINT JURISDICTION

Although there are certain reservations, service personnel are also subject to civilian trial and punishment. Service personnel are not answerable to civil authorities for violations of a strictly military nature, such as unauthorized absence, desertion, or misbehavior before the enemy. These offenses are subject to trial by military authorities only. Service personnel, however, may be subjected to joint jurisdiction (both civil and military) for offenses such as murder, robbery, rape, or driving under the influence of drugs or alcohol. Under these circumstances, you could be tried twice for the same offense. This applies only in the case of state or local jurisdictions because they are considered separate from the federal government. A court-martial is included under federal jurisdiction, which means that the legal principle of "double jeopardy" prevents you from being tried by the federal government and a court-martial for the same offense.

RIGHT TO COUNSEL

Military law is a complex subject covered by thousands of books. The finer points of military law are not understood by most nonlegal personnel. But Navy lawyers are at your disposal, should the need arise, and will advise you at no cost on matters of military justice.

ENFORCEMENT

Although it is hoped that your personal conduct will be above reproach, there are enforcement mechanisms that can be employed when necessary. Besides those in your chain of command who are tasked with enforcing discipline, there are also specialized personnel who have disciplinary authority and responsibilities. Just as you would obey police officers in your neighborhood back home, so you should obey these naval personnel who have been charged with maintaining good order and discipline.

Shore Patrol and Other Armed Forces Police

The shore patrol (SP) is the military police force of the Navy. Personnel assigned shore-patrol duties can be officers and/or petty officers, and it is their duty to function much as any police force in civilian life does, providing assistance and maintaining order among naval personnel off ship or station. They are identified by brassards (armbands) with the letters SP.

The other services have police as well, called military police (MPs) in the Army and Marine Corps and air police (APs) in the Air Force. In some areas, a combined or unified armed-forces police detachment (AFPD) is organized, with military police from all the services under one command. You must obey all of these police, no matter what service they represent and no matter what their rank.

Military police from the various services assist military personnel and investigate accidents and offenses involving military personnel. They have the authority to stop, question, apprehend, or take into custody any member of the armed forces. You are required to show them your ID card, leave papers, or other orders, and to obey any directions they give you.

MAAs and Police Petty Officers

While SPs, MPs, and APs function as police off base, on board your ship or duty station certain personnel are assigned similar duties as masters-at-arms (MAA). They are appointed by the executive officer (second in command) and function as her or his assistants. Large ships or stations will have a chief master-at-arms (CMAA) with an appropriate number of assistants. Personnel are usually assigned to the MAA force for several months or longer. While acting as MAAs, they are relieved of most of their normal watches and duties.

Police petty officers usually remain with their divisions for work and watches, but they have additional duties that contribute to good order and discipline, such as making reveille (morning wakeup) and taps (shutting things down for the night), directing traffic during times of heavy personnel movement, and turning lights on and off at the appropriate times.

PERSONAL RELATIONS

Getting along in the Navy means more than just learning new duties, obeying regulations, standing watches, and carrying out assigned tasks. It also means working and living with all kinds of people. While this is part of the American ethic, it takes on particular significance when you find yourself in the crowded and challenging working conditions that are often a part of Navy life. Going to sea means a lot of people living and working in a relatively small area. It may mean not only putting up with crowded living conditions but also with extreme operating conditions and long working hours, in intense heat or bitter cold, sometimes for weeks or months at a time. The combination of these challenges coupled with the high standards of conduct demanded by the Navy means that you will have to place a great deal of emphasis on your personal behavior and on your relations with others.

Getting along with others is always in your own best interests. But even if it were not, you need to be aware that one of the quickest ways to end a successful career, and to face other harsh penalties as well, is to take part in such practices as ethnic discrimination and sexual harassment. The Navy is committed to fair and equitable treatment of all hands, by all hands, at all times, and simply will not tolerate anything less.

Ethnic Discrimination

Because Americans join the Navy from all walks of life and come from all parts of the country, you will be living and working with people of different races, people with different social and educational backgrounds, people of different religious faiths, people whose family background and customs are different from yours. All of these variations are defined as "ethnic" differences, and while they are very real and may be very evident, they must also be irrelevant in your relations with one another. Despite all these potential differences, the people you share the Navy with are guaranteed to have two things in common with you. They are people, and they are in the Navy. These are strong bonds when you think about it.

This is not to say that you must like everyone in the Navy. Human nature being what it is, it is almost guaranteed that you will meet, and even work closely with, some people you will not like. But your evaluation of individuals should be based upon their words and actions, not on their ethnic differences.

Men and women who have been in combat will tell you that they never gave a thought to the religion of the medic who stopped the bleeding of their wounds. They never once wondered if the pilot who was providing covering fire for them was black or white. They never asked about a fellow Sailor's family background before letting him help put out a fire on an aircraft loaded with live bombs.

The Navy has taken a great many steps to eliminate ethnic prejudice and discrimination. There are programs, educational campaigns, and regulations enacted to this end. All of these are important steps that need to be taken, but what is going to be the most effective means is how you deal with these matters. The following principles should guide you in your everyday activities:

- Treat each person as an individual and evaluate him or her on words and actions, not on ethnic makeup.
- Never tolerate ethnic discrimination in others. If a subordinate is practicing discrimination or exhibiting ethnic prejudice, correct it. If a superior is doing so, report it.
- If you are the victim of such activities, report it.

If you follow these guidelines at all times, you will be taking a large step toward the prevention of ethnic discrimination in the Navy, and you will be protecting yourself from the very serious consequences that are the result of such practices.

Sexual Harassment

It should come as no surprise to you that sexual harassment is prohibited in the Navy. Sexual harassment is defined, in simple terms, as making unwelcome advances toward another person. But human interaction is rarely simple. There can be a fine line between acceptable and unacceptable behavior when it comes to sexual interactions among individuals. Sexual harassment can be sexually oriented communications, comments, gestures, or physical contact. It can also be offers or threats to influence or alter, directly or indirectly, an individual's career or other conditions of service in order to secure sexual favors.

Despite the terminology used, sexual harassment is really about power, not about sex. Both men and women are capable of harassment and either men or women can be victims of it. An important point to keep in mind is that unwelcome behavior is determined by the *person being subjected to the behavior*, not the person doing it. Not everyone considers the same things welcome or unwelcome, so it only makes sense that it is the one on the receiving end who determines what is unwelcome. Some basic principles that will help guide you in your day-to-day activities:

- Any time sexually oriented behavior of any kind is introduced into the work environment or among coworkers, the behavior may constitute sexual harassment.
- If in doubt, don't do it.
- Never tolerate sexual harassment in others. If a subordinate is sexually harassing someone, correct it. If a superior is doing so, report it.
- If you are the victim of such activities, report it.

Men and women in the Navy have an obligation to each other and to their service to respect each other's dignity. That is the basis of civil rights and is required conduct for all service people.

Fraternization

Hundreds of years of Navy experience have demonstrated that seniors must maintain thoroughly professional relationships with juniors at all times. "Fraternization" is the term traditionally used to identify personal relationships that violate the customary bounds of acceptable senior-subordinate relationships.

While it is impossible to define every situation that might be considered fraternization, common sense dictates that activities that can affect a senior's ability to be objective are not appropriate. For example, dating, sharing living accommodations, intimate or sexual relations, commercial solicitations, private business partnerships, gambling, and lending or borrowing money are all activities that can impact senior-subordinate relationships.

Personal relationships that include any of these characteristics are forbidden under the following circumstances:

- between officers and enlisted personnel
- between chief petty officers (E-7 through E-9) and juniors (E-1 through E-6) who are assigned to the same command

- between instructors and students within Navy training commands
- between recruiters and recruits (or potential recruits)

Violations of these rules may result in disciplinary action under the Uniform Code of Military Justice (UCMJ).

One last caution: Fraternization rules are "service specific," which means they are not identical in each of the armed services. What is allowed or forbidden in another service, such as the Army, may or may not be allowed in the Navy, so do not make assumptions. If in doubt, ask for assistance from a senior in your chain of command to determine what is appropriate behavior and what might be considered fraternization.

Hazing

Good-natured fun, such as mild teasing, can enhance relationships among shipmates, but when it goes too far, it is no longer fun and is illegal. Your Navy has no tolerance for behaviors that are demeaning, humiliating, abusive, oppressive, or cruel to others. Neither must you.

Games or playing tricks on others that include such actions as shaving, taping, greasing, painting, tattooing, striking, threatening, forcing the consumption of food, alcohol, drugs, or any other substance are forbidden. Such practices as "tacking on," "pinning," and "blood wings" are a quick way to find yourself the subject of a court-martial. Following two simple rules will keep you from making a mistake that may do significant physical or psychological harm to others and bring serious consequences to you:

- Do not do anything to someone else that you would not want done to you.
- If you have any doubt, don't do it.

PUBLIC RELATIONS

Because you represent the U.S. Navy whenever you put on your uniform, you are in effect performing public relations duty every time you come into contact with someone outside the Navy. What people think about the Navy is influenced by what they see its members doing. This is true whether you are a seaman recruit or an admiral. When you put on the Navy uniform, you represent the U.S. Navy. It should be apparent that it is in your best interests as well as the Navy's that you never forget your importance as a representative of the service and always conduct yourself in a manner that will bring credit to you, your Navy, and the nation you serve.

Overseas Diplomacy

When you are visiting or working in other countries—and, as a Sailor in the U.S. Navy, the odds are that you will find yourself in one or more foreign nations at some point in your career—you represent not only the Navy but the United States of America as well. You will be on public relations duty, and you will, in effect, be an American ambassador as well. Fair or not, people in the other nations you visit will often judge all Americans by what you do.

24/7

From the time you join the service until you are discharged or retire, your duty and commitment to the Navy is a twenty-four-hours-a-day, seven-days-a-week obligation. This means that you must comply with the codes, standards, regulations, and policies described in this chapter and elsewhere in this book at all times, in all places. Unacceptable conduct is not excused because you are "not at work."

Finally, three simple rules will guide you well in your conduct as a Sailor in the United States Navy:

- Always be aware that you are a representative of the Navy and your nation.
- Always assume that someone is watching.
- Never do anything you would not want to read about online or in the newspaper or that you would not want to have to explain to your commanding officer or the people who raised you.

FIVE

NAVY TITLES

Among the things most alien to newcomers to the Navy are the many titles that people have. These titles fall into a number of categories, and understanding the distinctions among them can go a long way toward understanding the Navy (and the other services for that matter). Most people understand the concept of military "rank." One encounters this term in movies or television for example, where *generals* or *admirals* advise the president on how best to deal with a crisis, or *sergeants* and *lieutenants* share a quiet moment in a foxhole to talk of home just before the big battle begins.

While the military services share the terms and the usage of ranks, they do not all use the same titles for each. For example, a *major* in the Army, Air Force, and Marine Corps is a *lieutenant commander* in the Navy and Coast Guard. And, even more confusing, all the services use the title of *captain* but in some very different ways.

Generally less understood are the terms "billet" and "pay grade," as well as a number of other related ones, such as "rate," "rating," and "warfare specialty."

This chapter will help you understand the many titles that Navy people have and how to recognize them in the various alphanumeric designations that are often used to identify them. You will learn the rank structures, what the differences are in the various terms and, more practically, how to properly address Navy people, both in person and in writing.

SAILOR

Arleigh Burke, one of the Navy's most famous and revered admirals, sent a powerful message to his Navy when, despite his *many* titles and qualifications, he had "Sailor" prominently placed after his name on his granite tombstone in the U.S. Naval Academy cemetery.

As explained in **Chapter 1**, everyone in uniform in the U.S. Navy is a Sailor, no matter what his or her rank, gender, or occupational or warfare specialty.

Although you may see the term in lower case outside the Navy (and sometimes, mistakenly, within), Sailor is properly capitalized within the Navy. This is a result of decree (by the Secretary of the Navy) and by practice, and is meant to distinguish this term from more common uses in other contexts. A person enjoying an outing on a sailboat is a "sailor;" a man or woman serving in the U.S. Navy is a "Sailor."

BILLETS

To begin with, it is important to distinguish between a "billet" and a rank. A billet in the Navy is a current assignment and is much like a job title elsewhere in the world. Some examples of billet titles (among thousands) in the Navy are "Work Center Supervisor," "Combat Systems Officer," "Leading Seaman," "Executive Officer," "Deck Division Chief," "Ship's Secretary," and "G Division Officer."

One thing that distinguishes the military services from corporate America is that military people also have ranks in addition to their billets. Those who have worked in the federal government as civilians will find the idea of ranks a little less alien because of the "GS" (General Schedule) system that gives a government employee a GS rating, establishing what that person will be paid and placing him or her within a hierarchy of relative authority and responsibility. Ranks in the military are similar but with some notable differences. For one thing, people in the government have to *ask* to learn of another's GS rating, whereas military personnel wear their ranks on their sleeves, collars, and/or shoulders. But like GS ratings, ranks denote a person's qualification to take on responsibility and authority, and they also determine pay grades (as explained below).

All of this is to say that a newcomer to the Navy should be aware that billets and ranks are related. A person might need the *rank* of lieutenant in order to be eligible to fill a specific *billet*, such as being the weapons officer on a particular kind of ship, but the two are also separate in their own ways.

There are thousands and thousands of billets in the Navy just as there are many job titles in any large company. But there are a much smaller number of ranks, and you will go a long way toward understanding what the Navy is all about by learning about the Navy's (and the other services') ranks.

Before moving on to rank titles, one word of clarification about billets in the Navy: The heads of many units (such as ships, aircraft squadrons, etc.) are known by the generic billet title of "commanding officer." This is true of all the armed services. But, with a nod to tradition, the Navy *also* uses the term "captain" for many of these billets (as in, "He is the captain of that destroyer," or, "As captain of that cruiser, she has a great deal of responsibility."). But you will soon see that "captain" is also the name of a rank in the Navy (and in the other armed services as well—though at a different level). This means that the commanding officer of a destroyer might hold the rank of commander but still be called the "captain" of that ship. And the captain of an aircraft carrier usually holds the *rank* of captain as well!

DEFINITIONS

The terms *rank*, *rate*, *rating*, and *pay grade* are all related but are different in important ways. Officers in the Navy have ranks like lieutenant and captain. But Navy enlisted personnel have another system that includes the somewhat confusing terms of *rate* and *rating*.

It is helpful to understand that "pay grades," "ranks," and "rates" all refer to a person's relative position within the Navy—part of a hierarchy— while the term "rating" refers only to an occupational specialty.

Everyone in the Navy is either nonrated, rated, or a commissioned officer. Men and women who enlist in the Navy begin as nonrated personnel. Their knowledge is general in nature, the bulk of which is gained in Boot Camp. A combination of experience and specialized training will allow them to become specialists in a particular occupational field and eventually move up into a rated category and to advance (get promoted) through a number of levels. That occupational specialty is called a "rating" and when combined with a promotion becomes their "rate." Rated personnel are all called "petty officers." Nonrated and rated personnel together are referred to as "enlisted personnel." Commissioned officers are appointed using special criteria that usually include a college education and a special selection process (see **Chapter 1**).

PAY GRADES

Everyone wearing a Navy uniform has a pay grade. For that matter, everyone in the armed forces (Army, Navy, Air Force, Marine Corps, and Coast Guard) has a pay grade. A pay grade defines a person's relative standing in the Navy as well as determining how much money he or she will be paid. There are officer pay grades and enlisted (rated and nonrated) pay grades. Rated personnel whose technical skills and professional performance are outstanding may eventually earn a commission as a warrant officer, a special category that falls in between the other officer and the enlisted pay grades.

A new recruit enters the Navy as an E-1, which is the first enlisted pay grade. Pay grades E-1 through E-3 are the nonrated pay grades, meaning that they are not tied to a specific occupation. However, based upon screening and testing, recruits are placed within a broad occupational category—known as a general apprenticeship (such as seaman or airman)—for advancement through the nonrated pay grades. Specific advanced occupational training leads to advancement into the rated pay grades (E-4 through E-9). Officer pay grades are designated O-1 through O-10 and warrant officers have their own pay grades (W-1 through W-5).

See TAB 5-A: Pay Grades, Ranks, Rates, and Forms of Address in the Armed Forces for more information. There you will see that each pay grade has a specific name and that the names change as one moves up (gets promoted). Note that each of the armed forces has its own names for each pay grade and that some are the same for different services but others are different. You will also see that some confusion can arise as in the case of the term "captain," which is used for pay grade O-6 in the Navy and Coast Guard but is used for O-3 in the other services. As explained above, the term "petty officer" is used for pay grades E-4 through E-9 in the Navy and Coast Guard, but in the other services the equivalent term used is "noncommissioned officer."

RATINGS

As explained above, a rating is an occupational specialty in the Navy. You might call it a "job" or an "occupation" in the civilian world. In the

Navy, these "jobs" have traditional names like "boatswain's mate" or "quartermaster."

Remember not to confuse rating with the similar sounding "rate" (explained earlier), which is more like a rank and is tied to pay grade.

Before you can qualify for a rating, you must first work your way through the general apprenticeship levels (E-1 to E-3), which will help prepare you for your rating. Once you are promoted to E-4, you will have a rating, and, except in special circumstances, you will likely keep that rating for the rest of your career.

Ratings Categories

In order to advance beyond the E-3 pay grade, you must have a rating. This, of course, requires a significant amount of training and experience. Each of the Navy's ratings is identified by a two- or three-letter abbreviation such as ET (for electronics technician) or GSM (for gas turbine systems technician—mechanical). Each rating is further identified by a unique symbol, called a specialty mark, which becomes a part of your rating badge worn on the left sleeve of your dress uniforms. There are two categories of ratings: general and service. (See TAB 5-B: Navy Ratings for a complete listing of the current ratings with a short description and the symbol used with each.)

GENERAL RATINGS

Occupations for pay grades E-4 through E-9 are called general ratings. Each general rating has a distinctive badge. Examples of general ratings are operations specialist, gunner's mate, and logistics specialist. General ratings are sometimes combined at the E-9 level, when the work is similar. For example, the work done by a senior chief utilitiesman and by a senior chief construction electrician is very similar, so when these individuals are promoted to master chief, both would become master chief utilitiesmen. These are sometimes referred to as "compression ratings" and are identified in the description for those ratings where this applies (See TAB 5-B: Navy Ratings).

SERVICE RATINGS

Some general ratings are further subdivided into service ratings, which indicate some additional specialization. For example, the general rating of gas turbine systems technician (GS) is subdivided into two service ratings: GSE (electrical) and GSM (mechanical). There can be service ratings at any petty officer (PO) level; however, they are most common with E-4s through E-6s. In the higher pay grades (E-8 and E-9), service ratings often merge into a general rating. For example, those gas turbine systems technicians who specialized in electrical and mechanical systems (GSE and GSM) would become simply GSs once they are promoted to senior chief petty officer (E-8), because a senior chief gas turbine systems technician needs to know about both the electrical and mechanical systems. These are identified in TAB 5-B: Navy Ratings in the description for those ratings where this applies.

Current Ratings

In the days before the Civil War, the Navy had an urgent need for sail-makers but did not have any call for missile technicians. The number and types of ratings change as the needs of the Navy change. There are many occupational specialties in the Navy, and the skills required for each vary a great deal. Whether you enjoy working indoors or out, using hand tools or computers, are better in technical subjects or clerical, there are ratings that will suit your desires and abilities.

For a complete listing of current ratings and their specialty marks see TAB 5-B: Navy Ratings.

Specialty marks were added to enlisted uniforms beginning in 1866 and were designed to represent an instrument originally used to perform a particular task. For example, the mark for a quartermaster (QM), who works mainly in navigation, is a ship's helm, while the boatswain's mate (BM) mark is two crossed anchors. The custom of representing the type of work with a specialty mark for each rating continues, but many of the designs have been stylized or serve as a traditional representation of the skills needed and the tasks performed in that rating. For instance, the yeoman (YN), who performs administrative work in the Navy, is represented by crossed quills even though quills are no longer used as writing instruments.

General Apprenticeships

There are four general apprenticeship fields: seaman, fireman, airman, and constructionman. All naval personnel who are in pay grades E-1, E-2, or E-3 belong to one of these groups, and their particular status, reflecting both apprenticeship field and pay grade, is called their "general rate." Assignments to these general apprenticeships are based upon the individual's desires and aptitudes and the needs of the Navy. Each general apprenticeship field leads to one or more ratings. For example, a person hoping to be a boatswain's mate would first be a seaman; one wanting to be an engineman would first be a fireman; and a would-be aviation ordnanceman would first be an airman.

Some of the duties and skills of each general apprenticeship are described below:

- **Seaman (SN):** Keeps ships' compartments, lines, rigging, decks, and deck machinery shipshape. Acts as a lookout, member of a gun crew, helmsman, and security and fire sentry.
- **Fireman (FN):** Cares for and operates ships' engineering equipment (such as turbines, boilers, pumps, motors). Records readings of gauges, and maintains and cleans engineering machinery and compartments. Stands security and fireroom watches.
- **Airman (AN):** Performs various duties for naval air activities ashore and afloat. Assists in moving aircraft. Loads and stows equipment and supplies. Maintains compartments and buildings. Acts as a member of plane-handling crews.
- **Constructionman (CN):** Operates, services, and checks construction equipment (such as bulldozers and cranes). Performs semiskilled duties in construction battalions. Stands guard watches.

E-1s, E-2s, and E-3s are considered "general rates" and are identified by a two-letter combination that identifies their general apprenticeship and their pay grade. For example, someone who has gone into the construction general apprenticeship would start at the E-1 level as a CR (constructionman recruit); a promotion to E-2 would make that individual a CA (constructionman apprentice); and an E-3 would be a CN (constructionman). See TAB 5-C: General Rates for additional information.

Strikers

If you are seeking to be advanced to a specific rating, you are said to be "striking" for it. Personnel who are E-1s, E-2s, or E-3s and have achieved a significant level of experience or training toward a particular rating may be formally designated as a "striker." This is an official recognition of your progress and is an important step toward achieving that all-important promotion to petty officer. If you become a designated striker, it means that you have achieved the minimum skills required (through on-the-job experience and/or formal training) for a particular rating. A rating abbreviation will be formally added to your general rate abbreviation to indicate your achievement. For example, a seaman (SN) who demonstrates significant skills in the electronics technician (ET) rating would be designated as a striker by the new rating abbreviation ETSN.

RANKS AND RATES

Traditionally, in the Navy the term "rank" was applied only to the officer pay grades, and the term "rate" was used to describe the enlisted pay grades. In more recent times, this distinction has become less clear-cut, and enlisted pay grades are sometimes also referred to as ranks, but technically rate is the correct term to use.

The term "rate" really has two meanings. Like "rank," it is roughly equivalent to pay grade, and is often used that way. For example, "Seaman Apprentice" or "Petty Officer Third Class" are rates. But rate is more often considered a combination of pay grade and rating. Remember that rating refers to an occupation and only applies to petty officers (E-4s and above). If someone referred to you as a "quartermaster," he would be identifying you by your rating. But if she called you a "quartermaster second class," she would be referring to your rate (your occupation and your pay grade combined). This is somewhat confusing, but you can stay out of trouble if you remember that rating always refers to occupation and rate involves pay grade.

Rated Personnel

Petty officers (E-4 through E-9) are identified by a combination of letters and/or numbers that together represent the individual's pay grade and rating. The first two or three letters represent the general or service rating; the number or letter(s) following indicate the pay grade. TAB 5-D: Examples of Enlisted Career Advancement shows the progression of several Sailors who have had very successful careers in various ratings.

If your rate is "BM2," you are a petty officer second class (E-5) and your rating is boatswain's mate. A "CEC" is a construction electrician who has achieved the pay grade of a chief petty officer (E-7). A "BMCM" is a master chief boatswain's mate, and an "ABF3" is a third-class aviation boatswain's mate whose service rating specialty is fuels. As you can see, those few letters and/or numbers reveal a lot about the individual who has earned them.

Outstanding chief petty officers who are appointed to special positions in the Navy drop their rating designation and use the following identifiers with their names:

- Master Chief Petty Officer of the Navy—MCPON
- Fleet Master Chief—FLTCM
- Force Master Chief—FORCM
- Command Master Chief—CMDCM
- Chief of the Boat (on submarines only)—COB

NAVAL ENLISTED CLASSIFICATION (NEC) CODES

NEC is a special code used to identify an additional skill, knowledge, aptitude, or qualification not included in your general or service rating training. For example, if you are a boatswain's mate (BM), you would have many of the same skills and qualifications that other boatswain's mates have. But not all BMs are qualified tugmasters. If you became qualified as a tugmaster, the Navy would assign you an NEC code of BM-0161. That would tell the detailers—the administrative people at the Navy Personnel Command (NPC) in Millington, Tennessee, who match individuals to specific assignments in the Navy—that you have the knowledge and skills necessary to handle a tug. With that NEC code in your record, a detailer could then consider you for a billet (assignment) in a shipyard where a tugmaster is needed.

With a few exceptions, NECs are assigned to personnel by a special division at NPC (NPC PERS-4). Changes in your NECs are made only when a training command reports that you have completed a course (earning you a specialty code), when a command shows that your specialty code should be canceled, or when a command reports that you have earned a code through on-the-job training (OJT).

Because NECs identify billets and the personnel qualified to fill them, you should make sure your NECs actually reflect your qualifications. Not keeping your codes up to date may keep you from getting the duty you want. There is no limit to the number of NECs you may have, but the two most important ones will appear as your primary and secondary codes. All of them are kept in your permanent record at NPC and are available to the detailers there when you become eligible for reassignment.

There are seven types of NEC codes: entry series, rating series, special series, alphanumeric, numerical, tracking, and planning. These are explained in the *Manual of Navy Enlisted Manpower and Personnel Classifications and Occupational Standards—Volume II* (available online).

NAVAL AND OCCUPATIONAL STANDARDS

The Navy has established minimum capabilities for individuals in each rate and rating and has divided them into two categories: Naval Standards (NAVSTDs) and Occupational Standards (OCCSTDs).

NAVSTDs apply to all personnel at specific pay grades. For example, all E-6 personnel must know how to write enlisted performance evaluations.

OCCSTDS apply to specific rates, meaning that they apply to a Sailor's rating as well as his or her pay grade. For example, if you are a boatswain's mate third class, you must be able to operate an anchor windlass.

Both NAVSTDs and OCCSTDs are spelled out in Volume I of *Navy Enlisted Manpower and Personnel Classifications and Occupational Standards*, available at the Navy Personnel Command website (see **Appendix B: Online Resources**).

ADDRESSING SAILORS

There are rules for addressing Sailors in the Navy. The tables provided in TAB 5-A: Pay Grades, Ranks, Rates, and Forms of Address in the Armed Forces match ranks/rates/pay grades with the abbreviations and forms of address that you should use when referring to or communicating with other members of the armed forces.

The "Abbreviations" column lists the proper abbreviations of the ranks/rates *as they are used by the Navy and the other armed services.* Be aware that you will see other abbreviations used elsewhere; for example, civilian book publishers do not like to use all capital letters because they feel it is distracting on a printed page, and though the Navy's abbreviations have a certain military logic to them, they are not always clear to people not familiar with the Navy. As a result, you will often see such things as "Lt. Cmdr." (instead of LCDR), or "Vice Adm." (instead of VADM), or

"Smn" (instead of SN). But when dealing with or within the military, you will have more credibility if you use the military versions of abbreviations as shown in TAB 5-A.

The "Dear ———" column of the tables in TAB 5-A tells you how to properly address someone in correspondence. If, for example, you were going to send a letter to Seaman Apprentice Rebecca Smith, you would write her name on the outside of the envelope as "SA Rebecca Smith, USN." Inside the letter, you should again use the Navy abbreviation in the address part of the letter, but in the salutation, you should use the spelled-out form provided in TAB 5-A's column labeled "Dear ———." See the example below:

30 August 2017

SA Rebecca Smith, USN
USS *Ronald Reagan* (CVN 76)
FPO AP 96616-2876

Dear Seaman Smith:

Your copy of *The Bluejacket's Manual* was found in this office and is enclosed.

Sincerely,

J. Q. Adams

John Q. Adams

The last column in TAB 5-A ("Direct Address") tells you how you should address a Sailor in polite conversation, as in, "Good morning, Captain Halsey," or "Chief Williams, would you please explain why you have all those stripes on your lower left sleeve?"

When introducing a Sailor to someone else, you should use his or her full title the first time but then use the "direct address" form from then on. For example: "Doctor Thomas Dooley, this is Lieutenant Commander Stephen Decatur. Commander Decatur is headed for the Mediterranean next month."

Note that these addresses are mostly logical and simple, but there are a few quirks. In most cases, brevity rules. "Lieutenant Commander" becomes simply "Commander," "Seaman Apprentice" becomes "Seaman," and so on. Note, however, that you should not address a "Senior Chief Petty Officer" as "Chief," and that "Master Chief Petty Officer" does not become "Master." Keep in mind that chief petty officers are always referred to in that order, never "Petty Officer Chief." But you may (particularly when in less formal circumstances) drop the "petty officer" part. For example, the following is correct: "This is Chief Petty Officer Jane Jones. Chief Jones and Senior Chief Smith were shipmates together in USS *Independence* back before they were promoted to chief."

There are a few other "quirks" you should be aware of. There is only one Master Chief Petty Officer of the Navy, and he or she is the most senior enlisted Sailor in the Navy. He or she is referred to as "the MCPON" and is often addressed as "MCPON." As indicated in the table, this is pronounced "mick-pon" ("pon" rhyming with "John," not "loan"). The other armed services have similar positions as indicated in the tables.

Note that there are also multiple forms of E-9 and that their addresses require a little extra attention. This is a case where billets and ranks overlap a bit. A master chief petty officer who is assigned as the principal enlisted adviser to the commanding officer of a ship or some other unit would take on the title of "Command Master Chief Petty Officer"—more frequently referred to as simply "the Command Master Chief." A master chief who has been assigned as the principal enlisted adviser to a fleet commander would be a "Fleet Master Chief."

Note that a newly promoted admiral becomes a "Rear Admiral (Lower Half)" and if later promoted again would become a "Rear Admiral (Upper Half)." These odd titles are compromises reached after years of trying different titles. An O-7 was a "Commodore" during World War II; at one time, O-7s and O-8s both had the title of "Rear Admiral" with no distinctions in title; and for a while an O-7 was called a "Commodore Admiral." The titles shown in TAB 5-A are the correct ones at this time. A good-natured rear admiral (lower half) who had just received word that he had been promoted to rear admiral (upper half) quipped, "That's great news. Now I can wear my shoulder boards on my shoulders instead of my hips!"

One last clarification: As noted above, "Commodore" was a rank in the Navy for a time. Though that has changed, you may still encounter the term; but if you do, be aware that it is associated with a billet rather than a rank. This comes about when an officer who is not an admiral is given command of a group of ships, such as a destroyer squadron. Each ship has its own commanding officer (also known as "Captain" as explained earlier), so to avoid confusion (and to grant a degree of honor), the officer in charge of the group of ships is called the "Commodore." She or he may hold the rank of "Captain" but is referred to as "Commodore" by virtue of commanding more than one ship.

Titles are important in many walks of life, and the Navy is no exception. Although the material in this chapter is bewildering at first, it is nonetheless important and can be a source of embarrassment if you do not use these titles properly. Over time, they will become second-nature to you, but the sooner you learn them the better.

SIX

UNIFORMS

The uniforms you wear as a Sailor embody the history of the Navy and are a visible symbol of your dedication to the nation. Wearing the uniform sharply and according to rules and regulations reflects your professionalism and sense of pride in the service.

Your best source of information regarding uniforms is *U.S. Navy Uniform Regulations*, NAVPERS 15665 (often informally called "Uniform Regs"), which is issued by the Chief of Naval Personnel (CNP) at the direction of the CNO and carries the force of a lawful order. As with all references, be sure that you are using the current version of Uniform Regs—as of this writing, the current version is I (India). *It is strongly recommended that you check these regulations periodically and be alert to announced uniform changes.* As of this writing, there are a number of changes being contemplated. The Navy constantly evaluates uniforms and develops new components to improve fit, comfort, and military appearance of personnel in uniform. It is your responsibility to know current Uniform Regulations and to teach subordinates the correct way to wear Navy uniforms. The bottom line is that it can be highly embarrassing—and even dangerous in some circumstances—to be wearing the wrong uniform, so careful attention is warranted.

As stated earlier, www.usni.org/BlueAndGoldProfessionalBooks/The BluejacketsManual is a good place to check for updates to this book, including uniform changes as they become official.

Because of the wide variety of jobs performed in the Navy, there are multiple categories of uniforms, each with several variations. What uniform you wear with what variations is decided by the *prescribing authority*— defined in Uniform Regs as the area or regional commander. Your command will make it clear what uniforms have been prescribed, and this is often referred to as the *uniform of the day*.

UNIFORM TERMINOLOGY

Like most things in the Navy, there is a special vocabulary that is used when referring to uniforms. Some of it is official and some is traditional. You may hear the term *jumper*, for example, which refers to the special top that has a flap on the back collar. A *neckerchief* is a special "necktie" that is tied with a square knot and worn with the jumper. The term *trousers* (for pants) is not often used in the civilian world but still is in the Navy.

[**6.1**] Sailors in Service Dress Blue uniforms, showing the differences among officers, chiefs, and other enlisted personnel

Prescribed vs. Optional

As you will see below, there are a number of different uniforms that are worn by Sailors in the Navy. There are basic components that are the minimum required articles for each uniform, but there are also some variations that may be either *prescribed* or *optional*. Prescribable items are additional components to a uniform that are directed to be worn by the prescribing authority. Optional items are articles that you may choose to wear. It is important for you to know the difference between prescribed (you *must* wear) and optional (you *may* wear). Uniform Regs state: "Any procedures or components, regarding uniforms or grooming, not discussed in these regulations are prohibited." In other words, wearing unapproved components or insignia is forbidden. If something's not specifically authorized, then it is specifically *unauthorized*.

Nicknames

Unofficial nicknames are often used to describe Navy uniforms. The traditional uniform consisting of a jumper, neckerchief, and bell-bottomed trousers that many people associate with Sailors is sometimes called "Crackerjacks" because of its appearance on boxes or bags of the snack by that name. The cover worn with that uniform is sometimes referred to as a "Dixie cup."

Sailors will often refer to a uniform in a plural form, such as "blues," "whites," and "NWUs," but be aware that use of these informal terms can lead to confusion and embarrassment, so use them carefully. For example, "dress blues" doesn't really mean anything specific, as there are four different uniforms with the words "dress blue" in their title: Dinner Dress Blue, Dinner Dress Blue Jacket, Full Dress Blue, and Service Dress Blue. Use of the proper name of the uniform will ensure everyone understands what is to be worn.

Headgear

The Navy term describing hats or caps is *headgear*, although you will often hear the word *cover* used as well. Thus, "being covered" means wearing headgear.

Headgear is generally required to be worn outside and removed inside, but there are exceptions to this rule. Headgear is worn indoors during ceremonies or when armed (such as security personnel) and it is often not worn at sea—again, with exceptions.

[6.2] A Sailor wearing the traditional headgear sometimes informally called a "Dixie cup."

UNIFORM CATEGORIES

Uniform Regulations group the various combinations of clothing into categories: service, working, service dress, ceremonial, and dinner dress. The most common uniforms you will wear for everyday routine are the service and working uniforms. Others are prescribed for more formal occasions.

Service Uniforms

When prescribed as the uniform of the day these service uniforms are worn for office work, watch-standing, liberty, or business ashore. For E-6 and below, it consists of a short sleeve khaki shirt, blue trousers or slacks, and blue garrison cap. Various optional components include the blue V-neck sweater and all-weather coat. For E-7 and above, as well as officers, there are two service uniforms, "Service Khaki" (consisting of khaki trousers as well as shirts) and "Summer White" (all components—shirt, trousers, shoes, and cover—are white).

[6.3] A petty officer wearing the service uniform with khaki shirt and Navy blue trousers. The admiral (seated) is wearing a uniform windbreaker.

Working Uniforms

There are several versions of working uniforms—the Navy Working Uniform (NWU), Coveralls, and the Physical Training Uniform (PTU). Which to wear will depend on the type of work being performed, the location (whether you are at sea or ashore), and command policy.

NAVY WORKING UNIFORMS (NWUs)

As of this writing, the blue version (officially "NWU Type I") of the Navy Working Uniform is still authorized for wear but is being phased out (with 30 September 2019 as the current end date).

NWU Type III is being phased in as the replacement for the Type I. Black boots are the standard boots worn with NWU Type IIIs, but commanding officers may authorize the optional wear of the Navy-certified desert tan or coyote brown rough-side-out leather non-safety boots when wear of safety boots is not required. Sailors must buy these optional brown boots if they are not issued to them by their commands as organizational clothing.

A "Reverse U.S. Flag" patch (Fig. 6.6) may be authorized for wear on the right shoulder and a "Tactical DTOM" (Dont Tread on Me) patch (Fig. 6.7) may be authorized for wear on the left shoulder.

NWUs are designed for wear in circumstances that might damage or stain service or other uniforms. They are allowed for wear to and from work (with stops for such things as gas, groceries, banks, child day care, etc.). They are not liberty uniforms.

Various regions may have their own restrictions on wearing NWUs, so check local regulations. For example, in the National Capital Region (Washington, D.C., area), NWU is not authorized at places such as the Pentagon, the White House, Capitol Hill, and the National Mall.

Type II NWUs are similar but are a desert version, replacing the green components with tans and browns. They are typically worn only by Navy SEALs.

[6.4] Sailors in the blue Type I Navy Working Uniform (NWU)

[**6.6**] The "Reverse U.S. Flag" patch may be authorized for wear on the right shoulder of the NWU Type III.

[**6.5**] The Navy Working Uniform (NWU) Type III

[**6.7**] The "Tactical Dont Tread on Me" patch may be authorized for wear on the left shoulder of the NWU Type III.

COVERALLS

Your command may provide you coveralls for work that may permanently soil or damage your uniform. Normally, they may be worn only as an underway uniform or when authorized by commanding officers for environments ashore that warrant their use.

As of this writing, the Navy is testing new versions of coveralls that may be adopted for official use in the future.

Courtesy of
RGB Imaging

[**6.8**] Two Sailors wearing the Navy
Physical Training Uniform (PTU)

PHYSICAL TRAINING UNIFORM (PTU)

The PTU is designed primarily for group/unit physical training activities. It can, however, be worn both on and off base for fitness and leisure activities (such as picnics) unless determined otherwise by regional coordinators or commanding officers.

Basic components include the Navy PT shirt and shorts, athletic socks, and shoes. Optional items include a long-sleeve version of the PT shirt, sweat pants/shirt, watch cap, and command ball cap. Shirts other than the Navy PT shirt are not authorized. When worn in-port or for group PT, the shirt is tucked.

The PTU is not a substitute for the uniform of the day, and is not worn for business, for medical or legal appointments, or in the galley.

Service Dress Uniforms

There are two versions of the service dress uniforms: Service Dress Blue and Service Dress White. These uniforms are the equivalent of a civilian business suit. They are worn for occasions when dinner dress or full dress uniforms would be too formal. While the blue and white versions are generally worn by season, Service Dress Blue may be prescribed for wear year-round. If you are reporting to a new duty station and are unsure what the uniform of the day is, you will not go wrong to wear Service Dress Blue.

[6.9] Three Sailors on deck. The master chief in the center is wearing coveralls and the petty officer and officer are in Service Dress Blue.

[**6.10**] Three enlisted Sailors wearing their Service Dress Blue uniforms near the Pentagon

Ceremonial Uniforms

There are two versions of the ceremonial uniforms: Full Dress Blue and Full Dress White. On these uniforms, the Service Dress White or Blue uniform is modified by wearing large medals on the left, and ribbons that have no corresponding large medal on the right. White gloves may be issued for wear. These uniforms are worn on formal daytime occasions, such as change-of-command or retirement ceremonies, visits by foreign officials, presidential inaugurations, and state funerals.

Dinner Dress Uniforms

There are two versions of dinner dress uniforms: Dinner Dress Blue and Dinner Dress White. These are formal evening uniforms. Essentially, they are the blue and white service dress uniforms worn with miniature medals instead of ribbons. These uniforms are worn to official functions when civilians normally wear black tie. These are prescribable uniforms.

Optional versions of dinner dress uniforms that you may wear when Dinner Dress Blue or Dinner Dress White are prescribed are called Dinner Dress Blue Jacket and Dinner Dress White Jacket. These are formal evening uniforms consisting of a short jacket (blue for winter, white for summer), cummerbund, evening shirt with studs and cuff links, a bow tie, and high-waisted trousers for men and slacks for women. Women may wear either the knee-length or long formal skirt in lieu of slacks.

SPECIAL UNIFORM SITUATIONS

The diversity of activities and locations in the Navy sometimes requires special uniforms.

Organizational Clothing

For certain assignments, tasks, communities, or geographic locations, there may be a need for clothing outside of standard issue uniforms. For these situations, "organizational clothing" is issued by the command. It remains the property of the Navy and is returned to the command when the individual is transferred.

Organizational clothing that is worn with working uniforms includes such items as foul-weather jackets, flight jackets, flight suits, coveralls, firefighting proximity suits, etc. This clothing is worn only while performing duties for which the garments are designed.

Special Ceremonial Uniforms

The prescribing authority may authorize certain specific additions to standard uniforms for certain ceremonies. Members of color guards, honor guards, and ceremonial units such as parade marching elements that are under arms may be prescribed white leggings, standard white guard belts, and white gloves. No other accoutrements—including ascots, aiguillettes, and helmets—are authorized without specific authorization from the CNO, as is the case with the U.S. Navy Ceremonial Guard in Washington, D.C., and special drill units.

RANKS AND RATES ON UNIFORMS

Unlike most civilian occupations, members of the armed services wear specific uniforms, and on those uniforms there are also indications of rank or rate (See Chapter 5 for an explanation of these two terms). Depending on

[**6.11**] Members of a ship's crash and salvage crew wear fire-resistant proximity suits—a form of "organizational clothing."

the service and the uniform, ranks and rates can be displayed on collars, sleeves, headgear, shoulders, and/or centered on the chest.

Enlisted

In the Navy, enlisted personnel display their ranks in different ways depending upon which uniform they are wearing. For dress uniforms, ranks are worn on the upper left arm and sewn on. For service and working uniforms, ranks are worn on both collar points, either in metal or a sewn-on version.

TAB 6-A: Navy Enlisted Sleeve Markings shows the current system of rates as they are displayed on dress versions of uniforms (including ceremonial and evening dress). These are worn on the upper left sleeve. For E-2 and E-3 personnel, the rate is indicated by either two or three diagonal stripes. For petty officers, the basic structure is an eagle (traditionally called a "crow") with one, two, or three chevrons below and a rating symbol in between. (See TAB 5-B: Navy Ratings.) Figure 6.12 shows the rating badge for a gunner's mate second class. The two chevrons identify him as a petty officer second class, and the crossed-anchors rating symbol shows that he is a boatswain's mate. If his rating were gunner's mate instead of boatswain's mate, he would have crossed cannons instead of crossed anchors.

For service and working uniforms, a modified version is worn in the form of a metal collar or cap device that does not include a rating symbol. For petty officers first, second, and third class this consists of just the "crow" and appropriate number of chevrons, leaving out the rating symbol, as indicated in Figure 6.13.

[6.12] A typical sleeve marking for a petty officer second class

[6.14] A petty officer first class wearing the metal cap and collar devices of her rank

[6.13] Collar device for a petty officer second class

Chief petty officers wear a different form of collar and cap device that is a gold anchor with the letters "USN" in silver centered on the shank of the anchor. One silver star is added above the anchor for senior chiefs (E-8) and two stars for master chiefs (E-9). As the senior enlisted person in the Navy, the Master Chief Petty Officer of the Navy (MCPON) is the only person in the Navy who wears three stars above his or her anchor.

OTHER SERVICES

The Coast Guard, Marine Corps, Army, and Air Force have their own unique indications of rank. The Coast Guard is very similar to the Navy, except that Coast Guard devices include a federal shield that distinguishes them from the Navy devices. Marine Corps, Army, and Air Force enlisted personnel wear their sleeve markings on both sleeves, while the Navy and Coast Guard wear them only on the left arm. You may also see versions of these ranks worn as shoulder tabs, collar devices, etc.

[**6.15**] A master chief petty officer (center) poses with the Secretary of the Navy and the Master Chief Petty Officer of the Navy (MCPON). Note the two stars above the anchor on the master chief's cover and the three stars above the MCPON's anchor.

Since today's armed forces often work together, it is a good idea to refer to TAB 6-B: Enlisted Rank Devices of the Other Armed Services to know what the other services wear to indicate their ranks.

Officers

The collar and cap rank devices worn by officers are virtually the same for all the services, based on pay grade. An O-4 in any of the services is indicated by a gold oak leaf, even though the wearer would be a "lieutenant commander" in the Navy and Coast Guard and a "major" in the other services. See TAB 6-C: Officer Collar, Cap, and Shoulder Rank Devices in the Armed Services.

These same devices are also worn (in a larger size) on the shoulders in some cases, although Navy officers also have other shoulder devices—known as "shoulder boards"—that are similar in design to the markings worn on the lower sleeves (near the cuffs) of some uniforms, as shown in TAB 6-D: Navy Officer Shoulder Boards and Sleeve Markings.

Coast Guard officers wear shoulder boards and sleeve markings that are similar to those of Navy officers as shown in TAB 6-E: Coast Guard Officer Shoulder Boards and Sleeve Markings.

Warrant Officers in the Navy, Coast Guard, Marine Corps, and Army have their own rank devices as shown in TAB 6-F: Warrant Officer Rank Devices. There are no warrant officers in the Air Force.

LINE VS. STAFF

Most officers in the Navy are *line officers*, meaning that they are eligible for command at sea—that is, ships, submarines, and aviation units. Those officers all wear their rank collar devices on both collar points and a star above the stripes on their shoulder boards and sleeve markings (as shown in TAB 6-D).

Other officers, who are specialists—like doctors, lawyers, chaplains, civil engineers—are *staff officers*. They are not eligible for command at sea but can command shore facilities like Navy hospitals and construction battalions. These officers wear the same rank device on their right collar point that line officers do, but on the left they wear a distinctive device that indicates their specialty, like a cross for a Christian chaplain. See TAB 6-G: Line and Staff Corps Devices. This same distinctive device also replaces the star worn by line officers on their shoulder boards and sleeve markings.

NONUNIFORMITY IN UNIFORMS

Even though one of the purposes of uniforms is the uniformity that contributes to team-building, there are exceptions. One obvious exception is that officers, chiefs, and other enlisted personnel wear different uniforms, and another is the differences that occur according to rank. Other situations call for differences in uniforms as well.

Forbidden Items

U.S. Navy Uniform Regulations states, "No articles shall protrude from or be visible on the uniform." This applies to pens, key chain fobs, pins, jewelry, combs, cigarettes, and large wallets that are visible outside the pocket.

Permitted Items

Some additional items may be worn with your uniform, but in the interest of preserving uniformity and professional appearance, some restrictions apply.

COMMUNICATION DEVICES

Cell phones may be worn but only with working and service uniforms. These devices must be conservative in appearance and must not distract from the appearance of the uniform. Only one device can be worn, and it must be worn on the belt aft of the elbow so that it is not visible from the front and does not interfere with the proper wear of the uniform or with rendering military courtesies.

Earpieces and headsets or hands-free devices while in uniform are prohibited unless specifically authorized for the execution of official duties. In a vehicle, their wear is allowed only when permitted by local, state, and federal law.

EYEWEAR

Prescription glasses are of course authorized, but they may not be eccentric or faddish. This may be determined by your command if you are not sure.

Conservative sunglasses may be worn but not in military formations. Retainer straps are authorized for safety only, and must be plain, black, and worn snugly against the back of the head.

Tinted contact lenses may be worn but must be a natural color (blue, green, brown, etc.).

BACKPACKS, BRIEFCASES, ETC.

When wearing dress or ceremonial uniforms, bags will be hand-carried only. When wearing service or working uniforms, black or Navy blue backpacks may be worn over either the left shoulder or both shoulders, and computer bags may be worn across the left shoulder, the strap fore and aft. They may not be worn across the body diagonally, with the strap and bag on the opposite sides of the body. They must be either solid black or navy blue with no personal ornamentation and must conceal the bag's contents.

A full seabag may be worn over both shoulders or carried in hand.

Service Stripes

Service stripes, informally known as "hashmarks," indicate how long a Sailor has been in the service. Each stripe signifies the completion of four full years of active or reserve duty (or any combination thereof). These long diagonal stripes are worn on the left sleeve below the rating badge (on the forearm) by all enlisted personnel who have earned them. Service stripes are red when worn on your blue uniforms and Navy blue when worn on your white uniforms. Aviation personnel wearing the green uniforms (E-7s and above) also have dark-blue service stripes.

Enlisted personnel with a total of twelve years of active duty or drilling reserve service in the Navy or the Marine Corps who have fulfilled the requirements for successive awards of the Navy Good Conduct Medal, Reserve Meritorious Service Award, or Marine Corps Good Conduct Medal (see section on "Awards and Decorations," below) change the color of their rating badge and service stripes to gold on their Service Dress Blue, Service Dress White, Dinner Dress Blue, and Dinner Dress White jackets. Since each stripe represents four years of service, and it takes twelve years to qualify for the gold stripes and rating badge, you will have to have a minimum of three hashmarks before you can switch from red to gold.

Religious Apparel

Certain religious apparel may be worn with the uniform in specifically authorized manners and times. Certain items may be worn during organized worship services, while other components may be worn during normal duty hours.

As an example of religious articles and apparel that may be worn, headgear may be worn while in uniform if it is black or hair colored, without writing or symbols; can be completely covered by standard military headgear; and does not interfere with the proper wear or functioning of protective clothing or equipment. It cannot be worn in place of military headgear when military headgear is required.

It is important that you verify specifics with Uniform Regulations before wearing religious items.

AWARDS AND DECORATIONS

In the armed services, special awards are given to personnel who have done something beyond the normal expectations of duty. These awards are either medals or ribbons. Medals are metal pendants hung from pieces of colored cloth. Ribbons are rectangular pieces of colored cloth 1½ inches long and ⅜-inch high. Medals always come with a ribbon, but some awards consist of only a ribbon and do not have a corresponding medal.

The term "award" is used to describe any medal, ribbon, or attachment. "Decoration" is usually used to describe an award given to an individual for a specific act of personal gallantry or meritorious service.

Extraordinary bravery is what most people think of when they see these awards, and that is the reason behind some of the awards, but many others are given for other reasons. We have already mentioned the Good Conduct Medal (and ribbon), which is given to individuals in recognition of consistent achievement and conduct over a period of four years. The Purple Heart (medal and ribbon) is awarded to individuals who have been wounded in combat. The Meritorious Unit Commendation (ribbon only) is given to all members of a unit (an entire ship's crew, for example) when that unit has been singled out for some notable achievement. Some awards are issued for a particular war or campaign (such as the Global War on Terrorism Service Medal), and all who actively participate in those campaigns are given those awards. There are awards recognizing proficiency with rifles and pistols, a Humanitarian Service Medal (awarded to those involved in a rescue mission or similar operation), and a ribbon that represents service overseas. Some awards (such as the Silver Star and the Joint Service Commendation Medal) are the same for all the armed services, and others are unique to one service (such as the Combat Action Ribbon and the Sea Service Deployment Ribbon).

Awards are a source of pride, but some of that can be negated if you do not wear them properly on your uniform. See TAB 6-H: Wearing of Awards and TAB 6-I: Precedence of Awards for detailed information on when and how awards are to be displayed on your uniforms.

WARFARE AND OTHER QUALIFICATION INSIGNIA

Navy men and women may earn additional qualifications as their careers progress, and some of these are reflected in special insignia for their uniforms. For example, pilots wear gold wings, scuba divers wear a silver pin showing a diver's face-mask and regulator, and enlisted women or men who have qualified in surface warfare wear a silver pin consisting of a ship, crossed sabers, and ocean waves. (See TAB 6-J: Warfare and Qualification Insignia.) These qualifications may be in major warfare areas such as aviation or submarine warfare, or they may signify special occupations such as explosive ordnance disposal or parachuting. These insignia are usually metal pins attached to the uniform but may be embroidered or stenciled in some cases. Most of these special insignia are worn on the left breast above the ribbons and medals, but there are some exceptions. (For example, command insignia are worn on the right breast when the individual is actually in command and are moved to the left breast, below the ribbons/medals, once the individual is no longer in command.) If you earn more than one of these special insignia, you may wear a maximum of two, one above your ribbons and one below. (See *U.S. Navy Uniform Regulations*, NAVPERS 15665, for more information.)

MISCELLANEOUS UNIFORM ITEMS
Aiguillettes

These colored cords are worn by naval personnel who are serving as naval attachés, aides to high-ranking officials (such as admirals or the President of the United States), recruit division commanders, members of the U.S. Navy Ceremonial Guard, and personnel with various other specialized duties. There are service and dress versions, and they vary in color and the number of loops depending upon the duty assigned. Aides to the president, vice president, and foreign heads of state, as well as various other White House aides, all wear their aiguillettes on the right shoulder. All others are worn on the left shoulder.

Brassards

Brassards are bands of cloth, suitably marked with symbols, letters, or words, indicating a temporary duty to which the wearer is assigned, such as officer of the day (OOD), junior officer of the day (JOOD), master-at-arms (MAA), or shore patrol (SP). They are worn on the right arm, midway between shoulder and elbow, on outermost garments where they can be seen.

When authorized, mourning badges made of black crepe are worn by officers on the left sleeve of the outer garment, halfway between the shoulder and the elbow. Enlisted personnel wear it in the same position, but on the right sleeve.

Flight Deck Colored Jerseys

Sailors working on flight decks and airfields wear color-coded jerseys to identify their jobs as follows:

Purple Aviation fuel handlers

Blue Plane handlers, aircraft elevator operators, tractor drivers, messengers, and phone talkers

Green Catapult operators, arresting gear crewmen, maintenance personnel, cargo handlers, hook runners, photographers, quality control personnel, and helicopter landing signal enlisted personnel (LSEs)

Yellow Plane directors, aircraft handling officers, catapult officers, and arresting gear officers

Red Ordnancemen (weapons handlers), crash and salvage crews, and explosive ordnance disposal (EOD) personnel

Brown Plane captains and air wing line leading petty officers

White Squadron plane inspectors, landing signals officers, liquid oxygen (LOX) crews, safety observers, and medical personnel

Name Tags

You may be required to wear a personalized name tag for easy identification during conferences, VIP cruises, open houses, or similar occasions, or in the performance of duties where some easy method of identification by name is desirable or beneficial. Name tags are rectangular, not exceeding dimensions of 1 inch by 3½ inches, and may be any color as long as the same color is used throughout the command. Name tags are worn on the right breast, but are not worn when medals are prescribed.

Officer of the Day (Deck)   Junior Officer of the Day (Deck)   Shore Patrol

Geneva Cross   Master-at-Arms

[**6.16**] Brassards are worn on the right arm, midway between the shoulder and elbow.

[**6.17**] Flight deck personnel in their color-coded jerseys

GROOMING AND PERSONAL APPEARANCE

Your grooming is an instant indication of your professionalism as a Sailor and is an important component of your uniform appearance. Keeping yourself up to grooming and personal appearance standards is the Navy's expectation as spelled out in Uniform Regulations. The basic standard is that your hair, grooming, and personal appearance while in uniform shall present a neat, professional appearance. Defining additional terms such as "conservative" and "eccentric" is the responsibility of your command, not you. It is your job to know what is permitted in Uniform Regulations, to know what additional guidance your command has provided, and, if in doubt, to ask your leaders for guidance.

Men's Hair

Hair must be kept neat, clean, and well groomed. It must not be longer than four inches and may not touch the ears and collar, extend below eyebrows when headgear is removed, show under front edge of headgear, or interfere with properly wearing military headgear.

Hair above the ears and around the neck shall be tapered from the lower natural hairline upwards at least three-quarters of an inch and outward not greater than three-quarters of an inch to blend with hairstyle. Hair on the back of the neck must not touch the collar. "Blocking" or cutting a line to mark the edge of the hairline is not permitted. The only exception to this is for someone whose hair is curled or waved so much that the three-quarter-inch taper at the back of the neck is difficult to attain. Only then may the taper be combined with a line at the back of the neck. This applies to a very small percentage of male Sailors.

The "bulk" of the hair—defined as the distance that the mass of hair protrudes from the scalp—must not exceed two inches.

Hair coloring must look natural and complement the individual. Faddish colors and multicolored hair are not authorized.

Parting of the hair is limited to one part (cut, clipped, or shaved) that is natural, narrow, and runs fore and aft on the head.

Varying hairstyles, such as afros, are permitted if these styles meet the criteria of maximum length and bulk and tapered neck and sides and do not interfere with properly wearing military headgear.

Plaited or braided hair shall not be worn while in uniform or in a duty status.

Sideburns are permitted but must not extend below a point level with the middle of the ear, must be of even width (not flared), and must end with a clean-shaven horizontal line.

Men's Shaving and Facial Hair

The face must be clean shaven; no beards are permitted. Mustaches are authorized but shall be kept neatly and closely trimmed. No portion of the mustache shall extend below the lip line of the upper lip. It shall not go beyond a horizontal line extending across the corners of the mouth and no more than one-quarter inch beyond a vertical line drawn from the corner of the mouth. The length of an individual mustache hair fully extended shall not exceed one-half inch. Handlebar mustaches or other eccentricities are not permitted.

Personnel who are in various kinds of disciplinary status as a result of a court-martial or NJP, such as those in the brig, those serving restriction, or those awaiting separation by reason of misconduct, are not authorized to wear any facial hair except for valid medical reasons.

When shaved close to the skin, some men's facial hair grows at such a tight curl that the cut end pushes its way back into the nearby skin, creating a condition known as *pseudofolliculitis barbae* (PFB), or what is commonly called "shaving bumps." Those individuals will be referred to Medical for various stages of treatment. Depending on the severity of the condition, individuals may be granted permanent permission not to shave. Individuals in a temporary or permanent "no shave" status must still keep facial hair in good appearance and trimmed to a length of no more than one-quarter inch.

Women's Hair

Women's hair styles and cuts shall present a professional and balanced appearance while in uniform and when wearing civilian clothes in the performance of duty.

A hairstyle's appropriateness is evaluated by its appearance when headgear is worn. All headgear shall fit snugly and comfortably around the largest part of the head without distortion or excessive gaps. Hairstyles will not interfere with the proper wearing of headgear, protective masks or equipment. Hair (including a bun) is not to protrude from the opening in the back of the ball cap.

Hair length, when in uniform, may touch but not fall below a horizontal line level with the lower edge of the back of the collar. With jumper uniforms, hair may extend a maximum of one-and-a-half inches below the top of the jumper collar. Long hair, including braids, shall be neatly fastened, pinned, or secured to the head. Hair length shall be sufficient to prevent the scalp from being readily visible (except for documented medical conditions).

When bangs are worn, they shall not extend below the eyebrows. When headgear is worn, hair shall not show from under the headgear front.

Hair bulk (minus a bun) as measured from the scalp will not exceed two inches. The bulk of the bun shall not exceed three inches when measured from the scalp and the diameter of the bun will not exceed four inches. Loose ends must be tucked in and secured.

Lopsided and extremely asymmetrical hairstyles are not authorized. Angled hairstyles will have no more than a one-and-a-half inch difference between the front and the back length of hair. Layered hairstyles are authorized provided layers present a smooth and graduated appearance.

Hair, wigs, or hair extensions/pieces must be of a natural hair color (i.e., blonde, brunette, brown, red, gray, or black). Hair extensions/pieces must match the current color of hair. Wigs, hairpieces, and extensions shall be of such quality and fit as to present a natural appearance and conform to the grooming guidelines listed herein. Tints and highlights shall result in natural hair colors and be similar to the current base color of the hair.

HAIRSTYLES

Hairstyles must not detract from a professional appearance in uniform. Styles with shaved portions of the scalp (other than the neckline), those with designs cut, braided, or parted into the hair, as well as hair dyed using unnatural colors are not authorized. The unique quality and texture of curled, waved, and straight hair are recognized. All hairstyles must minimize scalp exposure.

While this list shall not be considered all inclusive, the following hairstyles are not authorized: ponytails; pigtails; braids that are widely spaced or protrude from the head; and locks. Locks, also called dreads, are strands of hair fused or coiled such that they cannot easily be combed out.

The intent is for pinned-up hair to be styled in a manner that prevents loose ends from extending upward or outward from the head. For example, when hair is in a bun, all loose ends must be tucked in and secured.

Braids are authorized but must be conservative and conform to the approved guidelines. When a hairstyle of multiple braids is worn, each braid shall be of uniform dimension, small in diameter (no more than one-quarter inch), and tightly interwoven to present a neat, professional, well-groomed appearance. Beads, decorative items, or other foreign material may not be braided into the hair. Multiple braids may be worn loose, or may be pulled straight back into a bun, within the guidelines herein.

When one braid is worn on each side of the head, both braids must be uniform in dimension and no more than one inch in diameter. Each braid must extend from the front to the back of the head near the lower portion of the hair line (i.e., braids are closer to the top of the ear than the top of the head to prevent interference with wearing of headgear).

A single French braid may be worn starting near the top of the head and be braided to the end of the hair. The end of the braid must be secured to the head and braid placement shall be down the middle of the back of the head.

Corn rows must be in symmetrical fore and aft rows and must be close to the head, leaving no hair unbraided. They must be no larger than one-quarter inch in diameter and show no more than approximately one-eighth inch of scalp between rows. Corn row ends shall not protrude from the head. Rows must end at the nape of the neck and shall be secured with rubber bands that match the color of the hair. Corn rows may end in a bun conforming to the guidelines listed herein, if hair length permits.

Two individual rolls, one on each side of the head, must be near the lower portion of the hair line (i.e., rolls are closer to the top of the ear than the top of the head and will not interfere with wearing of headgear). Rolls must be of uniform dimension and no more than one inch in diameter.

HAIR ACCESSORIES

The intent for accessories is to aid in controlling or styling the hair; the accessory itself should not be the reason for use. Therefore, they must be consistent with the hair color and be as unobtrusive as possible.

A maximum of two small barrettes, similar to hair color, may be used to secure the hair to the head. Additional hairpins, bobby pins, small rubber bands, or small thin fabric elastic bands may also be used to hold hair in place. Accessories used to form a bun are authorized if completely concealed.

Hair accessories shall not present a safety hazard. Headbands, scrunchies, combs, claws, and butterfly clips are examples of accessories that are not authorized. Hair nets shall not be worn unless authorized for a specific type of duty.

PT STANDARDS

During group command/unit physical training, commanding officers may relax female hair grooming standards with regard to having hair secured to the head. Hair restraining devices such as headbands may be worn, but must be consistent with the current hair color.

Hairpieces

Wigs or hairpieces shall be of good quality and fit, present a natural appearance, and conform to the grooming standards set forth in these regulations. They shall not interfere with the proper performance of duty nor present a safety hazard.

Men may wear wigs or hairpieces while in uniform or in a duty status only for cosmetic reasons to cover natural baldness or physical disfigurement.

Women may wear wigs or hairpieces while in uniform or in a duty status provided they meet women's normal grooming standards.

Cosmetics (Women)

Cosmetics may be applied in good taste so that colors blend with natural skin tone and enhance natural features. Exaggerated or faddish cosmetic styles are not authorized. Care should be taken to avoid an artificial appearance. Lipstick colors shall be conservative and complement the individual. Long false eyelashes shall not be worn when in uniform.

Cosmetic Permanent Makeup is authorized for eyebrows, eyeliner, lipstick, and lip liner only, but you must submit a Special Request Authorization Form (NAVPERS 1336/3) to your commanding officer expressing your desire to obtain permanent makeup. If a permanent makeup condition is deemed noncompliant by your commanding officer and removal or alteration is not feasible, you may be processed for involuntary separation.

Fingernails

Men's fingernails shall not extend past fingertips and must be kept clean. Women's fingernails shall not exceed one-quarter inch measured from the fingertip and must be kept clean. Nail polish may be worn, but colors must be conservative and complement the skin tone.

Jewelry

Conservative jewelry is authorized for all personnel and shall be in good taste while in uniform. Eccentricities or faddishness are not permitted. Jewelry shall not present a safety hazard.

While in uniform, only one ring per hand is authorized, plus a wedding/engagement ring set. Rings are not authorized for wear on thumbs.

Earrings are not authorized for men while in uniform or in civilian attire in a duty status. Men must also not wear earrings while in/aboard any ship, craft, aircraft, or in any military vehicle, on any base or in any other place under military jurisdiction, or while participating in any organized military recreational activities. Be aware that earrings may be prohibited while in some foreign countries.

Earrings are authorized for women, but in uniform they must be limited to one earring per ear, centered on the earlobes. They must be 4 mm to 6 mm (approximately one-eighth to one-quarter inch) in diameter ball and plain with shiny or brushed matte finish. They may be screw-on or with posts. Earrings are gold for female officers and CPOs and silver for enlisted personnel. Small single pearl earrings are authorized for wear with dinner and formal dress uniforms.

While in uniform, only one necklace may be worn, and it shall not be visible. Only one wristwatch and one bracelet may be worn. Ankle bracelets are not authorized while in uniform.

Body Piercing

No articles, other than earrings for women specified above, shall be attached to or through the ear, nose, or any other body part. The same restrictions that apply to earrings for men mentioned above apply to body piercing for both men and women.

Tattoos, Body Art, and Branding

Four criteria are used to determine whether tattoos, body art, or brands are permitted for Navy personnel: content, location, size, and cosmetic.

Tattoos/body art/brands located anywhere on the body that are prejudicial to good order, discipline, and morale or are of a nature to bring discredit upon the naval service are prohibited. For example, tattoos/body art/ brands that are obscene, are sexually explicit, or advocate discrimination based on sex, race, religion, or ethnic or national origin are prohibited. In addition, tattoos/body art/brands that symbolize affiliation with gangs, or supremacist or extremist groups or advocate illegal drug use are prohibited.

No tattoos/body art/brands are permitted on the head, face, or scalp. One tattoo on the neck is authorized if it does not exceed one inch in any direction. The neck area for purposes of this regulation is any portion visible when wearing a crewneck T-shirt or open-collar uniform shirt. In addition, otherwise permissible tattoos/body art/brands on the torso area of the body shall not be visible through white uniform clothing.

Individual tattoos/body art/brands below the elbow or knee have no size restrictions.

Cosmetic tattooing—medical or surgical procedures conducted by licensed, qualified medical personnel—to correct medical conditions requiring such treatment is permitted.

Mutilation

Intentional mutilation of any part of the body is prohibited. Mutilation is defined as the intentional radical alteration of the body, head, face, or skin for the purpose of and resulting in an abnormal appearance. Examples of mutilation include, but are not limited to:

- A split or forked tongue
- Foreign objects inserted under the skin to create a design or pattern
- Enlarged or stretched out holes in ears (other than a normal piercing)
- Intentional scarring on neck, face, or scalp
- Intentional burns creating a design or pattern

Dental Ornamentation

The use of gold, platinum, or other veneers or caps for purposes of dental ornamentation is prohibited. For purposes of this regulation, ornamentation is defined as decorative veneers or caps. Teeth, whether natural, capped, or veneered, will not be ornamented with designs, jewels, initials, etc.

[**6.18**] The uniform is a visible representation of the Navy's heritage and its special missions.

PRIDE AND PROFESSIONALISM

The rules and guidance provided in Uniform Regulations are intended to provide specifics when needed. This is helpful because our Navy brings together people of different genders, traditions, and cultural backgrounds. Such things as "it is inappropriate and detracts from military smartness for personnel to have their hands in their pockets" may not have occurred to a young person coming from a civilian background but are a real part of the military culture.

The Navy uniform, in its many variations, is a visible representation of the Navy's heritage and its special missions. Always wear your uniform with dignity and respect for what it stands for—and allow yourself a bit of self-indulgent pride for having earned the right to wear it!

SEVEN

NAVY MISSIONS
AND HERITAGE

In this chapter you will get a small taste of the Navy's heritage while learning about the Navy's missions. From the Revolutionary War on, the Navy you are now a part of has a long, proud history of successfully carrying out the missions assigned, when Sailors like you have been called upon to contribute to the defense and well-being of our nation. The time will come when you will be called upon to do the same.

MISSIONS

The United States, fourth largest nation in the world in terms of land area, has always been a maritime nation. Throughout the nation's history, interaction with the sea has played an important role in America's economy, defense, and foreign policy.

During the colonial period and in the early days of the Republic, it was much easier to travel from colony to colony or state to state by ship or boat than by horse or on foot. Fishing, whaling, and overseas trade were among the fledgling nation's most important businesses.

The War of 1812, fought just a few decades after the Revolution, was in no small part affected by a series of stellar U.S. naval victories over ships of the British Royal Navy, then the world's foremost sea power. A naval blockade and riverine warfare were essential elements in the Civil War, and the war against Spain at the end of the nineteenth century began with the sinking of the battleship *Maine* and was decided by American naval victories in Manila Bay and the waters off Cuba.

[**7.1**] The U.S. Navy has come a long way since its beginnings more than two centuries ago. Here, we see John Paul Jones leading a raid on Whitehaven off the southwestern coast of Scotland during the Revolutionary War.

[**7.2**] Named for the father of the U.S. Navy, the destroyer USS *John Paul Jones* fires a powerful guided missile from its vertical launching tubes.

American commerce would never have thrived without open sea lanes. Two world wars could not have been won without the lifelines maintained across the world's oceans, and American control of the sea was an essential element in the triumph over the Soviet Union in the Cold War. Today, the United States of America continues to look to the sea for these same things and relies upon its Navy to preserve and further the nation's maritime interests.

Being a maritime nation means having a comfortable relationship with the sea, using it to national advantage, and seeing it as a highway rather than as an obstacle. World War II provides an excellent example. By 1941 German dictator Adolf Hitler had conquered much of the land of Europe, but because Germany was not a maritime power, Hitler saw the English Channel (a mere twenty miles across at one point) as a barrier, and England remained outside his grasp. Yet the Americans and British were later able to strike across this same channel into Europe to eventually bring Nazi Germany to its knees. And in that same war, the United States attacked Hitler's forces in North Africa with ships, Sailors, and embarked soldiers, sailing clear across the Atlantic Ocean—a distance of more than three thousand nautical miles.

The navy of a maritime nation must be able to carry out a variety of strategic missions. Currently, the U.S. Navy has six important missions, all of which have been carried out effectively at various times in the nation's history and continue to be as important as ever in today's challenging world:

- All domain access
- Sea control
- Deterrence
- Forward presence and partnership
- Power projection
- Maritime security

All Domain Access

When the U.S. Navy first began defending the nation, the water's surface was the only naval domain. Armed ships capable of moving about on the waters of the world to defend the nation's interests carried out the Navy's missions. But as technology advanced, new domains opened up, requiring

[**7.3**] To a maritime nation, the sea is a highway rather than a barrier. Here, in 1944 the Navy projects its power across the English Channel to free Nazi-occupied Europe in what has become popularly known as "D-Day."

Sailors to go beyond the realm of the sea's surface into equally challenging new environments under the sea and above it. Today's Navy must maintain access to all of these domains in order to be able to carry out its vital missions.

As early as the American Revolution, Sailors were experimenting with vessels that could go under the water to take advantage of being unseen by the enemy. As time went on, this capability was more and more developed, and by World War I at the beginning of the twentieth century submarines were a major part of the war at sea. By the end of that same century, submarines had become formidable weapons, powered by nuclear energy and able to remain hidden and deliver devastating nuclear-tipped missiles to virtually anywhere on earth.

In that same twentieth century, the Navy took to the air, mastering the ability to fly airplanes off of ships as well as from naval air stations around the world. Propeller-driven, fixed-wing aircraft pioneered the way into the skies and were eventually joined by incredibly fast jets and by helicopters that have the ability to hover in one place and land on relatively small ships. No longer limited to the range of shipboard weapons, Navy ships could now project power across vast expanses of ocean and far inland.

Jet aircraft technology was accompanied by the development of guided missiles. These in turn led to greater and greater heights and eventually into outer space, where today satellites give the Navy vastly improved navigation, reconnaissance, and communications capabilities as well as greatly improving our ability to effectively control weapons and other vital systems.

As Sailors—aided by civilian scientists and engineers—ventured into the domains of sea, undersea, air, and space, these explorations and achievements led to further developments in other, less tangible, realms: the electromagnetic spectrum and cyberspace, impressive terms associated with more familiar things like radios, radars, and computers.

In little more than two hundred years the Navy has gone from sailing ships with limited capabilities to vastly more powerful ships, submarines, aircraft, missiles, satellites, electronic systems, and computers that carry out our nation's vital missions around the world.

Sea Control

Because navies are expensive, the newly created United States tried to do without one in the years immediately following the American Revolution. Within a year after the termination of hostilities with England, Congress ordered all major naval vessels sold or destroyed. The men who had fought for independence as Sailors in the Continental Navy during the Revolution were left high and dry by the new government's decision. Even John Paul Jones, our most famous naval hero during the American Revolution— recognized by many as the "father of the U.S. Navy"—left America and served as an admiral in the Russian navy. No money was allocated to the building of naval vessels in the first ten years following the Revolution, and George Washington, who had shown a keen understanding of the importance of naval power during the war, relied as president upon his secretary of war to oversee both the Army and the limited Navy we had retained. Thomas Jefferson viewed a navy as not only expensive but provocative and, when he became the nation's third president, relied on an inexpensive fleet of defensive gunboats to guard the nation's shores.

But these frugal measures did not last long. World events and human nature conspired to prove that a maritime nation cannot long endure without a navy. Almost immediately, the so-called Barbary pirates—the North African states of Morocco, Algiers, Tunis, and Tripoli, ruled by petty despots whose main source of income was derived from the seizure of ships or the extortion of protection money—began preying on defenseless American merchant shipping in the Mediterranean Sea. Additionally, the ongoing struggle between France and England made American ships and their crews tempting targets, and both nations began taking advantage of the helplessness of the Americans by seizing merchant ships and sailors on flimsy pretexts. Under these provocations, the cost of not having a navy soon outweighed the cost of having one. Spurred to reluctant action by these costly and insulting blows to U.S. sovereignty, Congress approved the reestablishment of a navy and the building of several ships.

In a series of engagements on the high seas in the next two decades, the fledgling U.S. Navy successfully defended the nation's right to use the world's oceans. During the Quasi-War with France (1798–1800), the frigate *Constellation* defeated two French frigates in separate engagements, and other American ships, including the feisty little schooner *Enterprise*, managed to capture more than eighty French vessels of various sizes and descriptions. In the War with Tripoli (1801–5), a band of American Sailors and Marines led a daring raid into the enemy's home harbor that earned them respect throughout much of the world. At the beginning of the War of 1812, the U.S. Navy had only seventeen ships while the British had more than six hundred, yet the Americans won a number of ship-to-ship battles. Considering the relative inexperience and small size of this new navy, American Sailors fought far outside their weight class. Naval leaders such as William Bainbridge, Oliver Hazard Perry, and Stephen Decatur, and warships such as *Constitution*, *Essex*, and *Niagara*, achieved enduring fame, and the motto "Dont Give Up the Ship" was etched into history. The new nation secured its rights and proved its ability to use the oceans of the world. Never again would the United States be powerless to defend itself at sea.

Ever since those early days, the U.S. Navy has been on station, ensuring America's right to use the sea for trade, for security, and for its growing role as a world power. As the nation grew stronger, the Navy also grew in size and capability. The early frigates that performed so well in battle with

[7.4] The frigate USS *Constitution*—nicknamed "Old Ironsides"—played a key role in the War of 1812 and is still in service today as a reminder of the Navy's proud heritage.

the French and British Navies during the Quasi War and the War of 1812 gave way to the ironclad monitors of the Civil War, and these were superseded by the big-gun, armored battleships and high-speed cruisers that won the Spanish American War in 1898.

In time, the United States emerged as a world power and the Navy's mission of preserving freedom of the seas became more vital than ever. New technology led to the development of new kinds of ships, such as destroyers and submarines, and the invention of the airplane and the aircraft carrier brought about the rise of naval aviation as a whole new component of the Navy. In the first half of the twentieth century the U.S. Navy was called upon to fight the greatest sea war in history when Germany and Japan challenged America's freedom of the seas. Maintaining that freedom was a major factor in the victory over the Soviet Union in the Cold War. Today the Navy continues its role of preserving our free use of the global oceans, and *that is where you come in.*

Deterrence

The most obvious reason for a maritime nation to have a navy is to ensure that no other nation attacks it by sea. Even when President Jefferson was trying to avoid having a navy in order to save money, he recognized this elemental need and tried to use his gunboat fleet as a deterrent to attack. One of the reasons for the United States building the Panama Canal in the early part of the twentieth century was to permit U.S. warships to move rapidly from coast to coast and thereby bring greater sea power and deter many a potential enemy from attacking our shores.

Improvements in technology—such as the development of high-speed aircraft, powerful missiles, and long-range submarines—gradually increased our vulnerability to attack, and the Navy continued to play a vital role in protecting the nation by deterring our enemies, both real and potential. In 1962 the Soviet Union placed offensive nuclear missiles in Cuba. President John F. Kennedy, a former Sailor, imposed a naval "quarantine" around the island and threatened nuclear retaliation as deterrent measures to keep the Soviets from using these missiles against the United States and other nations in the western hemisphere. This ultimately forced the Soviets to take the missiles out of Cuba.

Throughout the Cold War, the U.S. Navy's fleet of ballistic-missile submarines patrolled the oceans of the world, armed with nuclear weapons ready to be launched on very short notice against an aggressor nation. This massive firepower, coupled with the striking power of U.S. aircraft carriers, land-based missiles, and the U.S. Air Force's long-range aircraft, effectively deterred the Soviet Union. Without this deterrence, the United States would have been very vulnerable to attack and would have struggled to stand up to the extremely powerful Soviet Union in moments of crisis.

[7.5] Throughout the Cold War, the U.S. Navy's fleet of ballistic-missile submarines patrolled the oceans of the world, armed with nuclear weapons ready to be launched on very short notice against an aggressor nation.

An example of America's ability to deal with Soviet intimidation occurred during the Middle East War of 1973. Although neither the Soviet Union nor the United States was directly involved in that war between Israel and most of the Arab nations, the United States supported Israel while the USSR backed the Arab nations. When the Soviets began resupplying their clients by sending in massive quantities of weapons by airlift, the United States did the same for Israel. The U.S. Sixth Fleet took up station in the Mediterranean to provide protection for its aircraft flying into the war zone. When the war began going badly for the Arabs, the Soviets threatened to intervene. The United States responded by putting its forces on increased alert worldwide and by moving naval units into striking position. Faced with this deterrent, the Soviets thought better of their intervention and the war was ultimately ended and settled on equitable terms.

Several times the People's Republic of China has threatened to attack the Nationalist Chinese on the island of Taiwan, and each time the U.S. Navy has moved into position to successfully deter the Communists from attacking. Today, China is behaving more and more aggressively in the South China Sea, threatening to take control of islands and adjacent waters that are claimed by several of its Asian neighbors, such as Japan and the Philippines.

There are many such examples when the Navy has been called upon to deter others from taking actions that were seen as dangerous to the United States or were not in the nation's best interests. Just as an effective police patrol can deter criminals from committing crimes in a neighborhood, so the Navy preserves the peace and keeps our nation safe and prosperous by its mere existence and by its capabilities, forward presence, and its ability to patrol the waters of the world.

Forward Presence and Partnership

Another of the important missions of the Navy is based upon its ability to go virtually anywhere in the world. This capability allows the United States to be in a position to reassure our allies in a time of crisis, to intimidate potential enemies (a form of deterrence), to deliver humanitarian aid when disaster strikes, to rescue Americans or our allies from dangerous situations, or to be able to carry out offensive military action in a timely manner. This is called "forward presence" and explains why you may well find yourself serving on a deployment to a far corner of the world.

Sometimes the presence of a single destroyer visiting a foreign port is all that is needed to carry out this vital mission. On other occasions, a carrier strike group or an entire fleet moving into a region is used to send a stronger message of warning or support. If hostilities become necessary, having units already at or near enemy territory can be a major advantage.

In 1854 Commodore Matthew Perry used forward presence as a means to open diplomatic relations and, ultimately, trade with Japan, a nation that, until Perry's visit, had shunned contact with the outside world. During the latter part of the nineteenth century, American naval ships patrolled the waters of the Far East to provide protection for our economic interests and the many American missionaries in that part of the world. When war broke out with Spain in 1898, the U.S. fleet already present in the Far East was able to strike a quick and decisive blow against the Spanish fleet in the Philippines. Throughout the Cold War, the U.S. Navy kept the Sixth Fleet in the Mediterranean Sea and the Seventh Fleet in the Far East to reassure our allies in those regions that we were nearby and ready to respond in the event of a crisis. Today the Fifth Fleet makes our presence known in the Middle East and nearby regions.

Our modern American military forces also have great striking power through powerful armies and long-range aircraft, and some of those forces are maintained for quick response in Europe, the Middle East, and Asia. But that kind of forward presence can only exist at the invitation of other nations who are willing to give us bases on their territory. The Navy allows us to have a presence wherever there is water—almost everywhere. In times of increased tension, naval units can be moved to appropriate positions where American presence is needed, without having to negotiate any complicated diplomatic arrangements and without requiring much time.

Today, you often hear the term "globalization," which describes the increased interactivity of the world's nations. Used most often as an economic term, it explains how trade and financial activities are conducted among various countries, where raw materials might be grown or mined in one part of the world, converted into usable goods in another region, and purchased in still another, all relying on transportation systems (primarily ships) and world banking institutions to tie it all together.

This interconnectivity and dependence upon interwoven economic systems has led to a degree of globalization among the world's navies as well. Partnerships among nations with similar needs and interests are a natural offshoot of this global interconnectivity. The U.S. Navy maintains numerous partnerships with the navies of other nations through combined exercises, shared responsibilities, and special basing arrangements. These partnerships increase the effectiveness of the cooperating navies and contribute to the security of each nation.

Power Projection

Forward presence allows the Navy to be on station the world over, but just being there is not always enough. Sometimes, despite a nation's efforts to remain at peace, the use of force becomes necessary. When that occurs, the U.S. Navy has always been particularly effective in projecting American power where it is needed.

As early as the American Revolution, an American naval squadron sailed to the British-owned Bahamas to capture needed weapons, and John Paul Jones furthered the American cause by conducting a series of daring raids against the British Isles themselves.

In 1847, during the war with Mexico, the Navy transported a force of 12,000 Army troops to Vera Cruz and played a crucial role in the successful capture of that port city, ultimately leading to an American victory in that war.

Union ships not only carried out an effective blockade of Confederate ports during the Civil War, they also attacked key Southern ports and opened up the Mississippi River to Union use, effectively driving a wedge right into the heart of the Confederacy.

By escorting convoys, U.S. destroyers projected American power across the Atlantic to aid in an Allied victory during World War I. In World War II, American aircraft carriers, battleships, cruisers, destroyers, submarines, amphibious vessels, troop transports, oilers, ammunition ships, minesweepers, PT boats, and a wide variety of other ships carried the fight to the far corners of the world, slugging it out with powerful Japanese fleets in the Pacific, dueling with German submarines in the Atlantic, safely transporting incredible amounts of supplies to the many theaters of war, and landing troops on distant islands and on the African, Asian, and European coasts.

During the Korean, Vietnam, and Gulf Wars, naval power guaranteed our ability to project our power ashore, and naval aircraft, guns, and missiles inflicted significant harm on our enemies.

[**7.6**] A U.S. Navy ironclad gunboat during the Civil War

[**7.7**] A U.S. Navy swift boat on patrol in the South China Sea during the Vietnam War

When American embassies in Africa were bombed by terrorists in 1998, American cruisers, destroyers, and submarines retaliated, launching a Tomahawk-missile barrage at terrorist targets in Afghanistan and Sudan. In the following year, naval electronic warfare and strike aircraft were vital components of the air war in Kosovo, and in the opening years of the twenty-first century the Navy has already played key roles in the wars in Afghanistan and Iraq. Not only did the Navy launch some of the earliest strikes against the Taliban and al-Qaeda in Afghanistan, but tens of thousands of Navy personnel augmented Army and Marine Corps ground units who were stretched thin over two operational theaters.

When power needs to be projected, American naval forces have always been ready, willing, and able to accomplish the mission. As an American Sailor, you will sometimes hear yourself being described as the "tip of the spear" with good reason.

Maritime Security

Threats other than those posed by hostile nations can emerge, such as piracy, terrorism, weapons proliferation, and drug trafficking. Countering these irregular threats and enforcing domestic and international law at sea protects our homeland, enhances global stability, and secures freedom of navigation for the benefit of all nations.

In 1819 Congress declared the infamous slave trade to be piracy, and in response the Navy established an African Slave Trade Patrol to search for these dealers in human misery. In the decades leading up to the Civil War, the frigates *Constitution* and *Constellation* and many other Navy ships relentlessly plied the waters off West Africa, South America, and the Cuban coast, capturing more than one hundred suspected slavers.

In more modern times, the "War Eagles" of Patrol Squadron 16, flying out of Jacksonville, Florida, played a vital role in the capture of forty-one tons of cocaine, and USS *Crommelin*, working with USS *Ticonderoga*, intercepted a drug shipment of seventy-two bales of cocaine with an estimated street value of $36 million.

These operations are not what first comes to mind when one thinks about a navy, but they are becoming more and more typical as economic globalization and asymmetric threats emerge from adversaries often known as "non-state actors" in the twenty-first century.

Other Missions and Feats

Evacuating U.S. citizens from dangerous areas or situations has been a long-standing mission of the Navy, and helping people survive the ravages of natural disasters, such as earthquakes and hurricanes, is an unpredictable but vital task the Navy is often called upon to carry out.

Because of a potato blight in Ireland and western Scotland between 1846 and 1849, two million people either died or emigrated. In 1847 two Navy ships carried food that had been donated by Americans to the relief of thousands. To show their gratitude for having been saved from starvation, some of the residents named their children after the two ships, *Jamestown* and *Macedonian*.

In 2005 Navy ships arrived off America's southern coast to assist Gulf Coast residents in the aftermath of a devastating hurricane named Katrina. USS *Bataan* and USS *Iwo Jima*, ships designed and trained to conduct amphibious assault operations, instead used their Sea Stallion and Sea Hawk helicopters to conduct search-and-rescue missions, while Navy hovercraft evacuated victims and Seabees (Navy construction battalions) cleared debris and helped in many rebuilding efforts.

While combat operations are a well-known aspect of the Navy's history, there have been and will continue to be many occasions when the Navy is sent to save lives and help large numbers of people in distress. The Navy's expeditionary character and its great mobility make it uniquely positioned to provide assistance.

The U.S. Navy has also played an important role in other realms, such as exploration and scientific discovery. For example, a Navy exploration team led by LT Charles Wilkes took a squadron of ships around the world, exploring Antarctica and vast areas of the Pacific Ocean in the years 1838–42. His charts of the Pacific not only served mariners for many decades to come but were used in the invasion of Tarawa in the early part of World War II. Navy men Robert E. Peary and Richard E. Byrd were pioneers in polar exploration: Peary was the first man to reach the North Pole in 1909, and Byrd flew over the South Pole in 1929. When CAPT Edward L. "Ned" Beach Jr. and his crew took their nuclear submarine USS *Triton* around the world in eighty-three days in 1960, it was not the first time anyone had circumnavigated the earth, but it was the first time anyone had done it submerged for the entire voyage of 41,500 miles. In that same year, LT Don Walsh went deeper than any human being has ever been when he and

[**7.8**] The Navy and Coast Guard teamed up to provide assistance to New Orleans in the aftermath of Hurricane Katrina.

Jacques Picard took the bathyscaphe *Trieste* to the bottom of the Marianas Trench, 35,800 feet down (more than six and a half miles beneath the surface). Astronaut Alan Shepard was in the Navy when he became the first American in space, and astronaut Neil Armstrong had been in the Navy before he became the first man to walk on the moon.

The Navy has often led the way or played a crucial role in many realms of scientific and technological development, such as electricity, radio communications, radar technology, computer science, and nuclear engineering. Among her many achievements in computer science, RADM Grace Hopper invented COBOL, one of the important computer languages that led the way in computer development. Today, a ship bears her name. The world of nuclear engineering has been forever affected by the work of ADM Hyman Rickover, and VADM Charles Momsen, a Navy man known to his shipmates as "Swede," changed the deep-sea diving world by his inventions and his pioneering work.

[**7.9**] In 1960 CAPT Ned Beach and his crew sailed around the world submerged for the entire eighty-three-day trip. Their submarine, USS *Triton*, was equipped with two nuclear reactors.

Another Navy diver, Carl Brashear, worked his way up from cook to master diver, salvaging a nuclear weapon from the depths of the Atlantic and losing a leg in the process. His inspiring story was the basis for a major motion picture.

Another modern, multi-million-dollar movie included a reenactment of the feats of another Sailor who won the Navy Cross at Pearl Harbor. Dorie Miller was different from you only in circumstance, but how he responded to the Japanese attack on his ship USS *West Virginia*, manning guns and saving lives, later earned him the honor of having a ship named after him.

Boatswain's Mate James Elliott Williams left his southern rural home to join the Navy. In 1966 he was a petty officer first class in charge of a pair of patrol boats on narrow jungle waterways in Vietnam, when he found himself facing an entire enemy regiment trying to cross a canal. Without hesitation, Williams pressed the attack. Three hours later, more than a thousand enemy soldiers had been killed or captured and sixty-five enemy

[7.10] Messman Third Class Doris "Dorie" Miller receives the Navy Cross from ADM Chester Nimitz for his actions during the Japanese attack on Pearl Harbor on 7 December 1941.

vessels had been destroyed. Williams was awarded the Medal of Honor and later retired from the Navy as its most decorated enlisted member, having earned the Navy Cross, two Silver Stars, the Navy and Marine Corps Medal, three Bronze Stars, the Navy and Marine Corps Commendation Medal, the Vietnamese Cross of Gallantry, and three Purple Hearts. In a second career, he won the continued respect of his fellow South Carolinians by serving as a federal marshal.

For more than two centuries, Sailors of the United States Navy have been recording an impressive history of courage, resourcefulness, sacrifice, innovation, humanitarianism, combat skill, and dedication to duty. Now it is your turn to follow in their wakes and, circumstances permitting, leave your mark on the pages of this impressive record.

HERITAGE

As one who has chosen to take part in this ongoing story and to do your part in carrying out the important missions described above, you would do well to read and think about the history of the United States Navy. Even in the best fiction, you will not likely find a better story than the one that makes up the true story of the U.S. Navy in action. It is full of excitement, adventure, and heroism. It is also a story of harrowing moments and great challenges, and there are times when those who served before you made mistakes or were not up to the challenges placed before them, providing important lessons to be learned.

By learning about yesterday's Navy, you will be better prepared to serve today's Navy. You will better understand why the Navy is so important to national security, you will be inspired by the heroic actions of other Sailors who served before you, you will learn from the mistakes of the past, and you will share the pride of a heritage that became yours when you took the oath of enlistment. All of this will help you to do a better job and to feel good about why you are doing it.

While there are many good books, some magazines, and a few movies that will help you better understand the legacy you have been entrusted with, there are other ways that you can learn about and grow to appreciate the proud heritage you are now a part of. When you report to a ship, find out why she has the name she does. You may learn that the name once belonged to someone much like you, a Sailor carrying out the missions of the Navy to the best of his or her ability. You may also be surprised to learn that there may well have been other ships that have had the same name and have passed it on to this latest bearer of the name. When ships are lost in battle or die of old age, their name is often given to a newly built ship to carry on the legacy of the name. This is similar to the ongoing process you are now participating in. As older Sailors move on to retirement, they pass the legacy on to younger Sailors who then are entrusted to carry out the Navy's vital missions. This is obviously no small responsibility, but it is also a privilege that only a select group of Americans have had.

When you go ashore and notice a monument on the base, take a moment to read the accompanying plaque. It was placed there to honor some aspect of the Navy's—and *your*—heritage. You may find yourself walking just a little taller as you move on.

History can be the most boring thing in the world if it is merely a list of names and dates, but heritage is written in a special ink that is a blend of the blood of sacrifice, the sweat of hard work, and the tears of pride that will likely be yours when you realize the importance of what you are doing. Learn your heritage, be proud of it, and work hard to carry it on. This is your Navy!

EIGHT

NAVY ORGANIZATION

The Navy's organization is large, unique, and complicated, making it a challenge to understand. And because the Navy works so closely with the other services, it is not enough to merely understand how the Navy is organized; you must also have some idea of how it fits into the Department of Defense. This chapter will unravel some of the complexity and give you a better understanding of how the Navy is able to carry out its many assigned tasks.

AN ORGANIZATION WITH MANY DIFFERENT PARTS

One might think that setting up a navy organization would be a relatively simple thing; that ships would be organized into fleets to operate in certain waters of the world and that admirals would command those fleets; that a chain of command could be simply drawn from the commanding officers of ships to the commanders of fleets and ultimately to the senior-most admiral in charge of the whole navy. But this simplistic vision ignores the reality that there are actually a number of chains of command that must be understood if you are going to understand how the U.S. Navy is organized.

To begin with, the Navy consists of more than ships. There are also aircraft and submarines, SEALs, Seabees, Marines, and more that make up what we can collectively describe as the operating forces of the Navy. Sometimes you will hear the operating forces referred to as simply "The Fleet."

Further, these operating forces cannot function independently. There must be a supply system to ensure that the operating forces have fuel, ammunition, and the like. Some means of repairing the ships, aircraft, and other parts of the fleet must be in place, and medical facilities must be available to care for battle casualties and the sick. These and other considerations mean that there must be facilities ashore to support those ships and aircraft. These facilities are often referred to collectively as "The Shore Establishment."

And, as mentioned above, another complication stems from the realization that navies rarely operate alone, that modern warfare and readiness for war require all of the armed forces to operate together—or *jointly*—in various ways.

To add another complication, we sometimes operate with the armed forces of other nations. Although similar to "joint operations" with our own forces, we use the term "combined operations" to refer to operations involving other nations' forces.

And one more complicating factor comes from the fact that our nation is a democracy, and one of our governing principles is civilian control of the military, which means that there will be civilians in your chain of command, such as the President of the United States (who is commander in chief of the armed forces) and the Secretary of the Navy.

Some Things to Keep in Mind

In the military, the term "chain of command" is roughly synonymous with "organization." The former is a path of actual legal authority, while the latter is a little less formal, but for most purposes the two terms can be considered the same.

The factors mentioned above—the operating forces needing support from ashore, the need for joint operations among the services or combined operations among nations, and the necessity for civilian control of the armed forces—all combine to make for a more complicated organization than we might wish for, but understanding that organization can be helped by keeping certain things in mind.

TWO CHAINS OF COMMAND

To begin with, your unit (ship, squadron, etc.) is likely to be part of two separate (but sometimes overlapping) chains of command at the same time: an *administrative* chain of command and an *operational* chain of command.

[8.1] Modern warfare often requires Navy ships and aircraft to operate jointly with elements of the other services. Here, an Air Force stealth bomber can be seen at the top of the photograph.

[8.2] A U.S. Navy cruiser at the rear of a formation led by a German oiler and two Croatian missile boats in the Adriatic Sea

The administrative chain of command is what keeps the Navy functioning on a day-to-day basis so that the ships, aircraft, and other elements of the fleet are able to carry out operational tasks when assigned. This is the chain of command that takes care of the less colorful but essential elements of preparedness, such as training, repair, supply, personnel assignment, intelligence support, communications facilities, weather prediction, and medical treatment.

The operational chain of command controls forces (ships, aircraft, etc.) that are assigned to combat operations, operational readiness exercises, humanitarian relief missions, evacuations, etc., or are on station carrying out missions like sea control and deterrence.

The operating forces are more or less permanently organized in an administrative chain of command, while they are frequently reassigned to different operational chains of command as needs arise. For example, your ship or squadron may be involved in a scheduled fleet exercise (with its own specific operational chain of command) and suddenly be ordered to conduct a search-and-rescue operation in the aftermath of a typhoon, which will require a whole different chain of command.

DEPARTMENT OF THE NAVY VS. NAVY DEPARTMENT

To clarify one more possible area of confusion, *United States Navy Regulations* (NAVREGS) actually defines *three* principal elements within the Department of the Navy. Besides the operating forces and the shore establishment, NAVREGS also specifies "the Navy Department," which it defines as consisting of "the central executive offices of the Department of the Navy located at the seat of government . . . comprised of the Office of the Secretary of the Navy, the Office of the Chief of Naval Operations, and Headquarters, Marine Corps." This means that the terms "Department of the Navy" and "Navy Department" are defined as two different things: the former refers to the entire Navy organization—all operating forces (including the Marine Corps), the entire shore establishment, and all reserve forces—and the latter refers to the executive offices, most of which are located in Washington, D.C. As indicated early in this chapter, *complicated!*

DON AND DOD

The Department of the Navy (DON) is an integral part of the Department of Defense (DOD), which also includes the Army and the Air Force, and DON and DOD are intertwined to a significant degree.

There is a civilian head of the Navy, known as the Secretary of the Navy (SECNAV), and a military head, the Chief of Naval Operations (CNO). The CNO is subordinate to SECNAV.

The U.S. Marine Corps is part of the Department of the Navy, but is in many ways a separate service, having its own senior military commander (the Commandant of the Marine Corps) who serves on the Joint Chiefs of Staff but answers to the same civilian official (the Secretary of the Navy).

"TWO HATS"

Some individuals in this organizational structure may "wear two hats," an expression that means one person can actually have more than one job, and often those two (or more) jobs might be in different parts of the organizations described above. For example, the commander of the Navy's Fifth Fleet might also hold the position of "Commander of U.S. Naval Forces, Central Command" (a joint command position within the Department of Defense chain of command).

The Chief of Naval Operations "wears a number of hats" in that he or she is responsible for ensuring the readiness of the Navy's operating forces but is also the head of the shore establishment. And while this admiral is the senior military officer in the Navy, he or she also works directly for the civilian Secretary of the Navy and serves as a member of the Joint Chiefs of Staff in matters that involve working with the other armed services.

ALLIED CHAINS OF COMMAND

There are also allied chains of command that sometimes must be considered. For example, because the United States is a key member of the North Atlantic Treaty Organization (NATO), a U.S. Navy admiral can be the NATO Supreme Allied Commander Europe and be responsible for forces belonging to member nations as well as those of the United States.

HELPFUL HINTS

When dealing with the Navy's organization, keep in mind that you probably will not need to know every detail of that organization. The information provided is for an encompassing overview. Try to grasp the essentials—particularly those that apply directly to your job—but do not worry if you cannot remember exactly how it all fits together. Few people can.

Something else to keep in mind is that this organization frequently changes. Commands are renamed, offices shift responsibilities. Some confusion may be avoided if you do not assume that what you remember will always be the same. Also be wary of the Internet; while it is a wonderful information tool, it must be used with caution. Websites are not always kept up to date, and older (out-of-date) items sometimes show up when using a general search engine.

DEPARTMENT OF DEFENSE

As discussed above, the Department of the Navy (DON) is part of the Department of Defense (DOD), and some of the Navy's organization is directly intertwined with the DOD joint command structure. In its simplest breakdown, there are four principal components to DOD:

- The Secretary of Defense and his or her supporting staff in the Office of the Secretary of Defense (SECDEF/OSD)
- The Joint Chiefs of Staff and their supporting staff (JCS)
- The individual military departments (services): Army, Air Force, and Navy
- The Unified Combatant Commands (COCOMs)

Most people who watch even a little news are aware that there is a Secretary of Defense (SECDEF) heading up DOD and that he or she is assisted by a senior military officer known as the Chairman of the Joint Chiefs of Staff (CJCS), who can come from any of the services and whose principal duties include advising the President, the National Security Council, and the Secretary of Defense. Those people who are more informed may also know that the senior military officers of each service (the Chief of Naval Operations; the Commandant of the Marine Corps; the Chief of Staff of the Army; and the Chief of Staff of the Air Force) serve collectively as the Joint Chiefs of Staff (JCS) under the Chairman and the Vice Chairman. Probably less known is that there is another member of the JCS: the Chief of the National Guard Bureau.

Note that while the Marine Corps is a service within the Department of the Navy, the Commandant is a member of the Joint Chiefs of Staff.

The Coast Guard is another unique entity. It is, by law, the fifth military branch of the U.S. armed services, but it is assigned to the Department of Homeland Security, rather than DOD. And while the Coast Guard frequently operates in support of the Navy and DOD when it is called upon to perform national defense missions, the Commandant of the Coast Guard is not a formal member of the Joint Chiefs. During wartime or national emergency, the President can have the Coast Guard assigned to the Department of the Navy, but the last time this transfer occurred was just before and during World War II, and it is unlikely that it will ever happen again.

Both the Secretary of Defense and the Chairman of the Joint Chiefs of Staff have fairly large organizations working for them. Supporting SEC-DEF is a staff structure known collectively as the Office of the Secretary of Defense (OSD), which includes a deputy secretary of defense, a number of under secretaries, assistant secretaries, and other officials in charge of specific aspects of running DOD.

Likewise, the Chairman of the Joint Chiefs of Staff (CJCS) also has a support organization called "the Joint Staff."

For operational matters—such as contingency planning, responding to an international crisis, going to war, or participating in a major joint operational exercise—the chain of command is a bit different. This operational chain of command is sometimes referred to as the "U.S. National Defense Command Structure" and begins with the President of the United States in his constitutional role as commander in chief of the Armed Forces. It then goes through the Secretary of Defense (with the Chairman of the JCS and the service chiefs serving as principal advisers) to those generals and admirals known as "unified combatant commanders" (explained below).

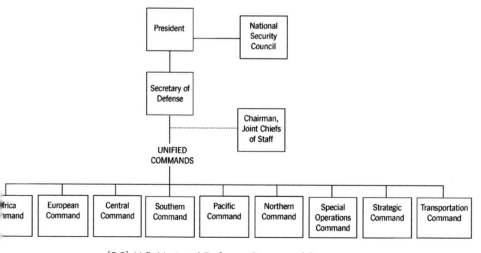

[8.3] U.S. National Defense Command Structure

It is important that you understand the role of the Chairman of the Joint Chiefs of Staff in the operational chain of command. The Chairman (with the assistance of the other Joint Chiefs) technically serves only as a principal *adviser* to the Secretary of Defense, but at SECDEF's direction he or she often issues directives to the unified combatant commanders, which can create the illusion that CJCS is in the chain of command between SEC-DEF and the unified commanders; however, these directives are always issued with the understanding that they originate with SECDEF, not CJCS.

Unified Combatant Commands

As described above there are a number of "Unified Combatant Commanders" who answer directly to the Secretary of Defense. These generals and admirals from the various services are sometimes referred to as just "unified commanders" or "combatant commanders" or "CCDRs." You may also see the abbreviation "COCOM" sometimes used, but CCDR is the correct abbreviation when referring to the commanders of these combatant commands.

Each CCDR is responsible for a specific geographic region of the world (sometimes referred to as an Area of Responsibility or AOR, such as Africa or Europe) *or* has a worldwide functional area of responsibility (such as all special operations or military transportation). It is through these CCDRs that the DOD and Navy operational organizations come together.

Currently, six of the nine CCDRs are responsible for specific geographic regions of the world:

Africa Command (AFRICOM) covers all of Africa except Egypt, with headquarters at Kelley Barracks in Stuttgart, Germany.

Central Command (CENTCOM) includes countries in the Middle East, North Africa, and Central Asia (most notably Afghanistan), with headquarters at MacDill Air Force Base in Florida.

European Command (EUCOM) covers more than fifty countries and territories, including Europe, Russia, Greenland, and Israel. Its headquarters is in Stuttgart, Germany. The commander of EUCOM simultaneously serves as the Supreme Allied Commander, Europe within the North Atlantic Treaty Organization (NATO), with its headquarters at Mons, Belgium.

Northern Command (NORTHCOM) is tasked with providing military support for civil authorities in the United States and protecting the territory and national interests of the United States including Alaska (but not Hawaii), Puerto Rico, Canada, Mexico, and the air, land, and sea approaches to these areas. NORTHCOM would be the primary defender against a mainland invasion of the United States. Its headquarters is at Peterson Air Force Base in Colorado.

Pacific Command (PACOM) is responsible for the gigantic Pacific Ocean area, to include parts of the Indian Ocean, and has its headquarters in Camp H. M. Smith, Hawaii.

Southern Command (SOUTHCOM) provides contingency planning and operations in Central and South America, the Caribbean, and the Panama Canal. SOUTHCOM's headquarters is in Doral, Florida.

The other three COCOMs have worldwide responsibilities that are functionally, rather than geographically, oriented.

Special Operations Command (SOCOM) oversees the various Special Operations Component Commands of the Army, Air Force, Navy, and Marine Corps and is headquartered at MacDill Air Force Base.

Strategic Command (STRATCOM) is charged with space operations (such as military satellites), information operations (such as information warfare), missile defense, global command and control, intelligence, surveillance, and reconnaissance, global strike and strategic deterrence (the United States nuclear arsenal), and combating weapons of mass destruction. STRATCOM is headquartered at Offutt Air Force Base in Omaha, Nebraska.

Transportation Command (TRANSCOM) provides air, land, and sea transportation for the Department of Defense, both in times of peace and times of war, and is headquartered at Scott Air Force Base in Illinois.

Each of these commands is more formally addressed with "United States" preceding (as in "United States Africa Command") and is sometimes abbreviated similarly (as in "USAFRICOM").

Remember that the CCDRs answer directly to the commander in chief (the President of the United States) through the Secretary of Defense, with the JCS serving as advisers and the CJCS sometimes passing orders from the President/SECDEF on to the CCDRs.

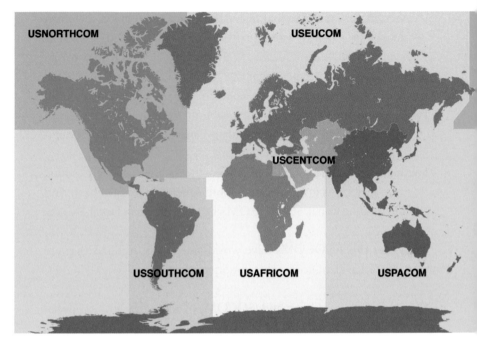

[**8.4**] Geographic Areas of Responsibility for Unified Commands

Service Component Commanders

Working directly for the CCDRs are the service component commanders. These are commanders who control personnel, aircraft, ships, and other elements—from their individual services—that can be made available to the unified commander for operations when needed. For example, the joint CENTCOM commander has the following service component commands assigned to carry out those operations that fall within CENTCOM's area of responsibility:

> United States Army Central Command (ARCENT)
> United States Central Command Air Forces (CENTAF)
> United States Naval Forces Central Command (NAVCENT)
> United States Marine Forces Central Command (MARCENT)

Sub-unified Commands

Some combatant commands have sub-unified commands assigned that are joint in nature, rather than service specific. For example, U.S. Cyber Command at Fort Meade is part of STRATCOM, but because it has personnel from the different services assigned, it is designated a "sub-unified command" rather than a service component command.

THE NAVY

As described above, the Navy is organized in two different (but related) ways at the same time: the operational chain of command and the administrative chain of command. Depending upon where you are assigned, you may be part of one or both of these organizations.

Both of these chains of command have the President of the United States at the top as commander in chief. Below the President is the Secretary of Defense, with the Chairman and the Joint Chiefs of Staff as his or her principal advisers. Below SECDEF, the chains are different. For operational matters, the SECDEF issues tasking orders directly to the unified combatant commanders (CCDRs), and for administrative matters, SECDEF relies upon the Secretary of the Navy to keep the Navy (and Marine Corps) manned, trained, and ready to carry out assigned missions.

The Operational Chain of Command

In centuries past, naval warfare could be effectively waged more or less independently, but in the modern age the importance of joint warfare cannot be overemphasized. In the vast majority of modern operations, whether they are combat, humanitarian, readiness, deterrent, or specialized, several or all of the U.S. armed forces must cooperate, coordinate, and combine their forces and plans to maximize their effectiveness and ensure mission accomplishment.

The Navy's operational chain of command is headed by the appropriate unified combatant commanders (CCDRs) described above. As previously mentioned, the officers commanding these combatant commands may be from any of the armed services (except the Coast Guard). The chain becomes purely naval below the CCDR with "naval component commanders" exercising operational control over one or more of the "numbered fleet commanders."

NAVAL COMPONENT COMMANDERS

CCDRs have component commanders assigned to them. Once a unified combatant commander has determined what assets (such as troops, ships, and aircraft) he or she will need to carry out a specific mission, that commander will rely upon the component commanders to provide those forces and coordinate their actions.

As already stated, this is the first level of command in the joint forces structure that is purely naval. There are a number of these naval component commands to meet the needs of the various unified combatant commands.

United States Pacific Fleet (USPACFLT or simply PACFLT). This naval component commander primarily serves the naval needs of the PACOM unified commander, and the primary AOR is the same as that of PACOM (Pacific and Indian Oceans), but PACFLT also provides assets to CENTCOM, SOUTHCOM, EUCOM, AFRICOM, and STRATCOM when required. PACFLT is headquartered at Pearl Harbor, Hawaii, and exercises control of both the Third and Seventh Fleets.

United States Naval Forces Europe (USNAVEUR or simply NAVEUR). From headquarters in Naples, Italy, COMUSNAVEUR plans, conducts, and supports naval operations in the European AOR during peacetime, crises, or war, answering directly to the EUCOM unified commander. He or she is supported by the Commander of the Sixth Fleet and by the Commander, Navy Region Europe (both are also headquartered in Naples, Italy).

United States Naval Forces Central Command (USNAVCENT or simply NAVCENT). Serving as naval component commander for the U.S. Central Command, NAVCENT, headquartered in Bahrain, is responsible for naval activities in the Arabian Sea, Persian Gulf, Red Sea, and part of the Indian Ocean. The vice admiral in command of this component also wears a second hat as Commander of the Fifth Fleet.

United States Fleet Forces Command (USFLTFORCOM or simply FLTFORCOM). Headquartered in Norfolk, Virginia, FLTFORCOM supports both STRATCOM and NORTHCOM as well as providing some naval support to EUCOM and CENTCOM. This component commander also serves as primary advocate for fleet personnel, training, maintenance, and operational issues, reporting administratively to the CNO.

United States Naval Forces Southern Command (USNAVSO or simply NAVSO). Headquartered at Naval Station Mayport, Florida, NAVSO's areas of operation are in South America, Central America, the Caribbean, and surrounding waters.

United States Naval Special Warfare Command (NAVSPECWARCOM or simply NAVSOC). Headquartered at the Naval Amphibious Base Coronado in San Diego, California, this is the naval component of the United States Special Operations Command.

United States Fleet Cyber Command/U.S. Tenth Fleet (FCC-C10F). Headquartered at Fort Meade, Maryland, this naval component command is an operational component of the U.S. Navy Information Dominance Corps and serves as the central operational authority for networks, cryptologic/signals intelligence, information operations, electronic warfare, and space capabilities in support of forces afloat and ashore.

NUMBERED FLEET COMMANDERS

Commanding the ships, submarines, and aircraft that operate in direct support of the naval component commanders are vice admirals in charge of the numbered fleets. Like the component commanders, these commanders have support staffs and facilities ashore, but the numbered fleet commanders also have a flagship from which to conduct operations at sea as missions require. Individual ships, submarines, and aircraft squadrons are assigned to different fleets at different times during their operational schedules. For example, a destroyer assigned to Third Fleet while operating out of its homeport of Pearl Harbor might later deploy to the Seventh Fleet in the western Pacific for several months. There are currently six numbered fleets in the U.S. Navy.

Fleet	Primary Operational Area
Third	Eastern Pacific Ocean
Fourth	Central and South American Waters
Fifth	Middle Eastern and South Asian Waters
Sixth	Mediterranean Sea
Seventh	Western Pacific Ocean/Indian Ocean
Tenth	Worldwide Cyber Domain

The apparent gaps (no First Fleet or Second Fleet, for example) is because of historical evolution rather than oversight. Numbered fleets come and go according to the current needs. For example, in World War II there were Eighth, Tenth, and Twelfth fleets to meet specific needs of that global conflict that were later deactivated.

Third Fleet. With shore headquarters in San Diego, California, Third Fleet operates primarily in the Eastern Pacific and supplies units on a rotational basis to Seventh Fleet in the Western Pacific and Indian Oceans and to Fifth Fleet in the Middle East.

Fourth Fleet. With shore headquarters in Mayport, Florida, Fourth Fleet has operational control of those units operating in the SOUTHCOM AOR.

Fifth Fleet. With shore headquarters in Bahrain on the Persian Gulf, Fifth Fleet has operational control of those units operating in the CENTCOM AOR.

Sixth Fleet. Operating in the Mediterranean Sea with shore headquarters in Gaeta, Italy, Sixth Fleet has both U.S. and NATO responsibilities (the latter as components of the NATO Strike and Support Forces, Southern Europe).

Seventh Fleet. With shore headquarters in Yokosuka, Japan, Seventh Fleet is responsible for the Western Pacific and Indian Oceans. The majority of units come from Third Fleet on a rotational basis, but there are some permanently assigned assets in the Seventh Fleet that are homeported in Japan.

Tenth Fleet. Headquartered at Fort Meade, Maryland, the Tenth Fleet operates worldwide in cyber space. It works with the Fleet Cyber Command to achieve the integration and innovation necessary for warfighting superiority across the full spectrum of military operations in the maritime, cyberspace, and information domains.

TASK ORGANIZATION

An entire fleet is too large to be used for most specific operations, but a particular task may require more than one ship. To better organize ships or

[8.5] The Tenth Fleet was reestablished in 2009. Tenth Fleet was first established in 1941 as the lead for antisubmarine warfare during World War II and successfully fulfilled that mission until it was disestablished in 1945.

other units into useful groups, the Navy developed an organizational system that has been in use since World War II. Using this system, a fleet can be divided into task *forces*, and they can be further subdivided into task *groups*. If these task groups still need to be further divided, task *units* can be created, and they can be further subdivided into task *elements*.

A numbering system is used to make it clear what each of these divisions is. The Seventh Fleet, for example, might be divided into two task forces numbered TF 71 and TF 72. If TF 72 needed to be divided into three separate divisions, they would be task groups numbered TG 72.1, TG 72.2, and TG 72.3. If TG 72.3 needed to be subdivided, it could be broken into task units numbered TU 72.3.1 and TU 72.3.2 (this "decimal" system might not sit well with your high school math teacher, but it works for the Navy). Further divisions of TU 72.3.1 would be elements numbered TE 72.3.1.1 and TE 72.3.1.2. This system can be used to create virtually any number of task forces, groups, units, and elements, limited only by the number of ships available.

Using the operational chain of command shown in Figure 8.6 we can imagine an example of how this system might work from one ship up through a CCDR.

Keep in mind that this shows only one path up the chain—there would also be other ships assigned to the various task elements and units, and there might be other task components (such as a Task Element 76.1.1.2 and Task Groups 76.2 and 76.3, etc.).

In this example, dock landing ship USS *Fort McHenry* (LSD 43) has been tasked with delivering Marines to one of several key locations in the Pacific as part of a larger operation that is responding to a crisis. Task Force 76 shown in the figure is responsible for carrying out amphibious operations in the Pacific operating area, and the commander (CTF 76) has divided her task force into two task groups, one to cover the eastern part of her area of responsibility (TG 76.1) and the other (TG 76.2) to cover the western part. CTG 76.1 has further divided his assigned forces into two task units (TU 76.1.1 and TU 76.1.2), the first tasked with transporting Marines to a troubled area and the other made up of destroyers to protect the transport unit. There are two LSDs assigned to TU 76.1.1, and the task unit commander has designated each of them as task elements, with each given a specific landing beach. The commanding officer of USS *Fort McHenry* has been designated CTE 76.1.1.1 to coordinate landing the Marines in her ship onto the northern beach, and the CO of the other LSD will do the same for the southern beach.

The Administrative Chain of Command

As mentioned above, there is a chain of command within the Navy that is parallel to the operational chain; this one involves many (but not all) of the same people who "wear more than one hat" in order to carry out functions within each chain. The administrative chain is concerned with readiness more than execution, focusing on such vital matters as manning, training, and supply, so that the operating forces are prepared to carry out those missions assigned by the operational chain of command.

SECRETARY OF THE NAVY (SECNAV)

SECNAV has an Under Secretary of the Navy as his or her direct assistant, and as can be seen in Figure 8.7, there are several Assistant Secretaries of the Navy (ASN) to handle specific administrative areas of the Navy.

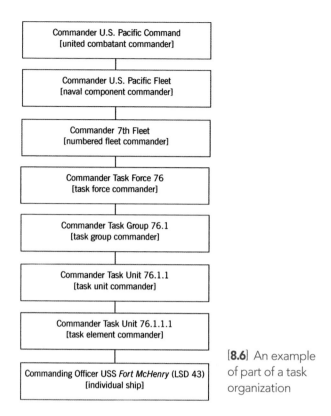

[**8.6**] An example of part of a task organization

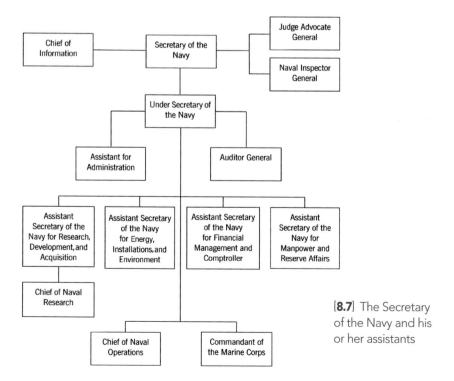

[**8.7**] The Secretary of the Navy and his or her assistants

In addition to these civilian assistants, SECNAV also has a number of military assistants, such as the Navy's Judge Advocate General, the Naval Inspector General, and the Chief of Information. Other military officers answer directly to SECNAV's civilian assistants, such as the Chief of Naval Research who reports to the Assistant Secretary of the Navy for Research, Development, and Acquisition, and the Auditor General who reports to the Under Secretary of the Navy.

CHIEF OF NAVAL OPERATIONS

Reporting directly to the Secretary of the Navy is the Chief of Naval Operations. The CNO is the senior military officer in the Navy and as such, he or she is a member of the Joint Chiefs of Staff (discussed above) and is also the principal adviser to the President and to the Secretary of Defense for naval matters. The CNO is always a four-star admiral and is responsible to the Secretary of the Navy for the manning, training, maintaining, and equipping of the Navy, as well as its operating efficiency. Despite the title "CNO," he or she is not in the operational chain of command.

Besides a Vice Chief of Naval Operations (VCNO), the CNO has a number of admirals working for him or her who oversee specific functions within the Navy, as indicated in Figure 8.8. Most of them are identified by the title "Deputy Chief of Naval Operations (DCNO)," the exception being the "Director of Naval Intelligence."

OPNAV Staff. Collectively, the CNO's staff is commonly referred to as "the Navy Staff" or "OPNAV" (derived from "operations of the Navy" but is better thought of as simply the "Office of the Chief of Naval Operations"). OPNAV also assists SECNAV, the under secretary, and the assistant secretaries of the Navy.

These admirals have staffs and subordinate commanders working for them, with many of these officers identified by subordinate "N-codes" as well. For example, the vice admiral who is assigned as DCNO for Integration of Capabilities and Resources has a number of rear admirals working for him or her as N85 (Expeditionary Warfare), N86 (Surface Warfare), N87 (Submarine Warfare), N88 (Air Warfare), and so on.

There are numerous other assistants to the CNO on the OPNAV staff, such as the Chief of Legislative Affairs (N09L), the Director of Naval Education and Training (N00T), the Surgeon General of the Navy (N093),

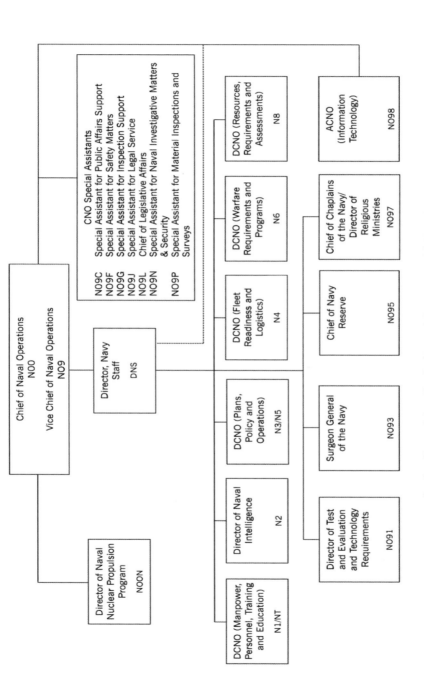

[8.8] Office of the Chief of Naval Operations (OPNAV)

who oversees all medical activities within the Department of the Navy, the Chief of Chaplains (N097), and the Director of Navy Reserve (N095).

The Director, Navy Staff directs OPNAV staff principal officials in support of CNO executive decision-making, delivers management support to the OPNAV staff, and serves as sponsor for thirty of the Navy's most important naval commands.

Shore Establishment. In addition to the OPNAV staff, there are a number of shore commands directly under the CNO that support the fleet, including the Office of Naval Intelligence, the Naval Security Group Command, the Naval Safety Center, the Naval Meteorology and Oceanography Command, the Naval Strike and Air Warfare Center, the Naval Legal Service Command, the Bureau of Naval Personnel, the Naval Education and Training Command, and the Bureau of Medicine and Surgery. A number of these commands are dual-hatted: for example, the head of the Bureau of Naval Personnel (BUPERS), known officially as the "Chief of Naval Personnel," is also the Deputy CNO for Manpower and Personnel (N1), and the Commander, Naval Education and Training Command serves as a member of the OPNAV staff, advising the CNO as the Director of Naval Education and Training (N00T).

Systems Commands. There are also five systems commands that oversee many of the technical requirements of the Navy and report to the CNO and SECNAV.

Naval Sea Systems Command (NAVSEA) is the largest and serves as the central activity for the building of ships, their maintenance and repair, and the procurement of those systems and equipment necessary to keep them operational. Among its many functions and responsibilities, NAVSEA also oversees explosive ordnance safety as well as salvage and diving operations within the Navy.

Naval Air Systems Command (NAVAIR) researches, acquires, develops, and supports technical systems and components for the aviation requirements of the Navy, Marine Corps, and Coast Guard.

Space and Naval Warfare Systems Command (SPAWAR) is responsible for the Navy's command, control, communications, computer, intelligence, and surveillance systems. These systems are used in combat operations, weather and oceanographic forecasting, navigation, and space operations.

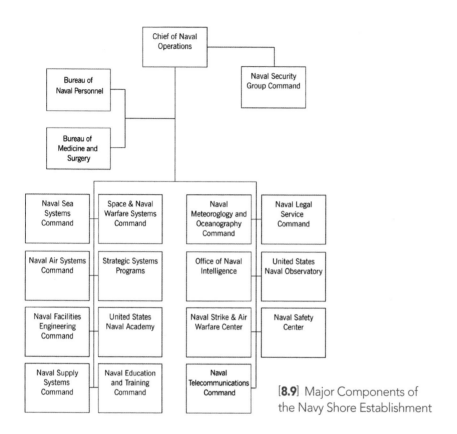

[8.9] Major Components of the Navy Shore Establishment

Naval Supply Systems Command (NAVSUP) provides logistic support to the Navy, ensuring that adequate supplies, such as ammunition, fuel, food, and repair parts, are acquired and distributed worldwide to naval forces.

Naval Facilities Engineering Command (NAVFAC) is responsible for the planning, design, and construction of public works, family and bachelor housing, and public utilities for the Navy around the world. NAVFAC manages the Navy's real estate and oversees environmental projects while keeping its bases running efficiently.

Type Commands. For administrative purposes, such as personnel manning, training, and scheduled repairs, the Pacific and Atlantic fleets have ships and aircraft classified and organized into commands related directly to their type. These groupings are called "type commands," and there are six.

Naval Surface Force, U.S. Atlantic Fleet (SURFLANT) administers to the needs and ensures the readiness of all surface ships (cruisers and destroyers, as well as amphibious, service, and mine warfare ships) assigned to the Commander of the U.S Fleet Forces Command (COMFLTFORCOM). The commander is known as COMNAVSURFLANT, and his or her headquarters are in Norfolk, Virginia.

Naval Surface Force, U.S. Pacific Fleet (SURFPAC) administers to the needs and ensures the readiness of all surface ships assigned to the Commander of the U.S. Pacific Fleet. The commander is known as COMNAVSURFPAC, and his or her headquarters are in San Diego, California.

Naval Submarine Force, U.S. Atlantic Fleet (SUBLANT) administers to the needs and ensures the readiness of all submarines assigned to the Atlantic Fleet. This commander is known as COMNAVSUBLANT, and his or her headquarters are in Norfolk, Virginia.

Naval Submarine Force, U.S. Pacific Fleet (SUBPAC) administers to the needs and ensures the readiness of all submarines assigned to the Commander of the U.S. Pacific Fleet. This commander is known as COMNAVSUBPAC, and his or her headquarters are in Pearl Harbor, Hawaii.

Naval Air Force, U.S. Atlantic Fleet (AIRLANT) administers to the needs and ensures the readiness of all aircraft assigned to the Atlantic Fleet. This commander is known as COMNAVAIRLANT, and his or her headquarters are at Norfolk, Virginia.

Naval Air Force, U.S. Pacific Fleet (AIRPAC) administers to the needs and ensures the readiness of all aircraft assigned to the Commander of the U.S. Pacific Fleet. This commander is known as COMNAVAIRPAC, and his or her headquarters is at North Island, California.

Even though there are separate type commanders on the different coasts, for coordination purposes, one is senior to the other and ensures compatibility of resources and procedures. For example, COMNAVSURFLANT is a three-star admiral and COMNAVSURFPAC is a two-star, the latter in charge of surface activities in the Pacific, yet deferring to her or his counterpart on the Atlantic to ensure coordinated action. This was not always the case, so that Sailors moving from one coast to the other often encountered very different rules and procedures.

Other Components in the Administrative Chain of Command. Below the type commanders are group commanders and below them are ship squadron commanders or air wing commanders. For example, below COMNAV-SURFLANT is Commander Naval Surface Group 2 with Destroyer Squadrons (DESRON) 6 and 14. Do not look for any regular pattern in these numbering systems, except that components on the East Coast are generally even-numbered and components on the West Coast are odd-numbered. The key point: just because Surface Group 2 has DESRONs 6 and 14 does not mean it will also have those numbers in between.

COMPLICATED BUT FUNCTIONAL

As you can see from the above, the Navy's organization is indeed complicated. But considering all that must be done to keep the world's most powerful Navy ready and able to carry out a very wide variety of missions, that organization is capable of meeting the many needs of the fleet as it serves the much larger defense establishment that guards the nation's vital interests and keeps Americans safe.

N-codes and task unit designations with multiple decimal points may seem intimidating at first, but those who operate within them are soon comfortable with it all. Once you are assigned to a specific command, you will quickly learn those parts of the chains of command that are important to you, and you will soon be using the Navy's alphabet soup of terminology with the best of them.

While it is good to be aware of these things early in your time in the Navy, you are likely to be more concerned about your immediate chain of command. The majority of Sailors will spend their early years on board a ship or a submarine, or in an aircraft squadron. The following sections explain those organizations in some detail.

SHIP AND SQUADRON ORGANIZATION

Because the missions and number of people assigned differ for each type of ship or aircraft squadron, each one is organized differently. An aircraft carrier, for example, has more departments and divisions than a destroyer, which is much smaller and has fewer people assigned. An aircraft carrier has need of an air department, but a submarine does not.

Despite these differences, all ships and squadrons have certain things in common. All commissioned ships and aircraft squadrons have a commanding officer who has overall responsibility and an executive officer who is second in command. All are divided into departments, and these are in turn subdivided into divisions.

[**8.10**] Different types of ships will be organized somewhat differently, but there are commonalities to all.

Ships

Every Navy ship operates under the authority of an officer assigned by BUPERS as that ship's commanding officer. The CO, as she or he is sometimes known, may be a lieutenant if the vessel is small, or a captain if the ship is very large. But no matter what the rank, the commanding officer is always called "Captain."

In case of absence or death, the CO's duties are assumed by the line officer next in command, whose official title is executive officer. The XO, as he or she is often called, is responsible for all matters relating to personnel, ship routine, and discipline. All orders issued by the XO have the same force and effect as though they were issued by the CO.

EXECUTIVE ASSISTANTS

Depending on the size of the ship, certain officers and enlisted personnel are detailed as executive assistants. All answer to the XO, but some, such as the ship's secretary, will work directly for the captain in some matters. These jobs may be full-time assignments or may be assigned to individuals as collateral (secondary) duties, depending upon the size of the ship's crew. Some are always filled by officers, others always filled by enlisted, but many can be either. Even those with "officer" in the title are sometimes filled by qualified enlisted personnel. A lot depends upon the size of the command and the relative qualifications of the individuals concerned.

The executive assistants are listed below in alphabetical order for convenience. Those listed are the most common; there may be others on board your ship as well.

Administrative Assistant. This individual can be an officer or a senior petty officer, and his or her duties are to relieve the XO of as many administrative details as possible. This individual will, under the XO's guidance, manage much of the ship's incoming and outgoing correspondence, take care of routine paperwork, and assist the XO with various other administrative functions.

Chaplain. Normally assigned only to larger ships, this specially qualified staff corps officer's duties are primarily religious in nature, but she or he is also involved in matters pertaining to the mental, moral, and physical welfare of the ship's company.

Chief Master-at-Arms. The chief master-at-arms (CMAA) is responsible for the maintenance of good order and discipline. The CMAA enforces regulations and sees that the ship's routine is carried out. This duty is normally carried out by a chief petty officer.

Career Counselor. The career counselor runs the ship's career-counseling program and makes sure that current programs and opportunities are known and available to crewmembers. His or her job is to stay informed about all of the Navy's current programs affecting the actual or potential careers of the men and women in the ship's crew.

Drug/Alcohol Program Adviser. Every Navy command is required to have at least one drug and alcohol program adviser (DAPA) on board. In larger commands, there should be one DAPA for every three hundred personnel assigned. DAPAs advise the CO and XO on the administration of the drug and alcohol abuse program aboard ship and on the approaches necessary to cope effectively with any problems that may exist in this area. The adviser must stay informed on all Navy policies and procedures on drug and alcohol education, rehabilitation, identification, and enforcement.

Educational Services Officer. The educational services officer (ESO) assists the XO in administering and coordinating shipboard educational programs for crewmembers.

Lay Leaders. When a chaplain is not available to meet the individual needs of crewmembers, a lay leader is appointed. For instance, if a unit has a Protestant chaplain, but no priest or rabbi, the command may appoint Roman Catholic and Jewish lay leaders. Those appointed must be volunteers, either officer or enlisted, and will receive appropriate training.

Legal Officer. The legal officer is an adviser and staff assistant to the CO and XO on the interpretation and application of the Uniform Code of Military Justice (UCMJ), the *Manual for Courts-Martial* (MCM), and other laws and regulations concerning discipline and the administration of justice within the command.

Personnel Officer. Assisting the XO in personnel matters, the personnel officer is responsible for the placement of enlisted personnel and for the administration and custody of enlisted personnel records. She or he will supervise the personnel office (if there is one) and oversee the processing of all enlisted performance evaluations, leave papers, identification cards, and transfer orders.

Postal Officer. The postal officer looks after the administration of mail services to the command. He or she must learn and stay current on all applicable postal regulations and supervise those personnel who handle the ship's mail.

Public Affairs Officer. The public affairs officer prepares briefing material and information pamphlets, assists with press interviews, generates newsworthy material about the unit's operation, and publishes the command's newspaper.

Safety Officer. On ships that do not have safety departments, the safety officer will advise the CO and XO on matters pertaining to safety aboard ship. She or he will be accorded department-head status for safety matters and will coordinate the ship's safety program.

Command Master Chief. The command master chief (CMDMC) assists the CO in matters of morale and crew welfare. See **Chapter 5** for more detail.

Senior Watch Officer. The senior watch officer is responsible for assigning and supervising all deck watchstanders, under way and in port. He or she coordinates the ship's watch bill, ensuring that trained personnel are equitably assigned to all necessary stations under all conditions. The senior watch officer is usually the most senior person among those who are standing watches.

Ship's Secretary. Administering and accounting for correspondence and directives, and maintaining officers' personnel records, are among the responsibilities of the ship's secretary. He or she also supervises the preparation of the captain's official correspondence.

Training Officer. The training officer coordinates the ship-wide training program. He or she will obtain and administer school quotas, provide indoctrination training to newly arrived personnel, coordinate with the operations officer in scheduling training exercises, and supervise the ship's personnel qualifications system (PQS).

Security Manager. The security manager is responsible for information systems and personnel security, the protection of classified material, and security education.

3-M Coordinator. The various aspects of the ship's maintenance and material management (3-M) program are supervised by the 3-M coordinator.

DEPARTMENTS AND DIVISIONS

Different ships have different departments, depending upon their size and mission. Some examples of commonly seen departments are engineering, operations, and supply. Ships whose primary mission is combat may have a weapons department, or it may be called combat systems on more sophisticated ships. Ships whose primary mission is logistical—involving replenishment of fuel, ammunition, or other supplies at sea—will often have a deck department.

Departments are subdivided into divisions, and divisions are often further subdivided into work centers, watches, and sections, with petty officers in charge of each.

Each ship's department has a department head, an officer who is responsible for its organization, training, and performance. The larger the ship, the more senior the department head will be. In a destroyer the department head is often a senior lieutenant, while in aircraft carriers department heads are usually commanders or lieutenant commanders.

Departments are often divided into divisions and have a division officer responsible for them. The division is the basic working unit of the Navy. It may consist of twenty specialists on small ships or as many as several hundred persons in an aircraft carrier. The division officer is the boss; he or she reports to the department head and is frequently a junior officer but can be a chief petty officer or a more senior petty officer if the situation calls for it. The division officer is the one officer with whom division personnel come into contact every day. The division chief and the leading petty officer are the division officer's principal assistants. Larger divisions may have more than one chief assigned and may even have other junior officers assigned as assistants.

In the first chapter of this book, you read about the chain of command, learning that it changes from assignment to assignment. When you report to your first ship, you will have a new chain of command that might begin with your section leader or work center supervisor, who reports to the division chief, who in turn reports to your division officer, who answers to the department head, whose boss is the executive officer, who reports directly to the captain, and so on.

Departments aboard ship belong to one of three different categories: command, support, or special.

COMMAND DEPARTMENTS

Depending upon the type of ship, some of the command departments frequently found on board are air, aircraft intermediate maintenance, combat systems, communications, deck, engineering, executive, navigation, operations, reactor, and/or weapons.

Air. The Air Department is headed by the air officer (informally referred to as the "air boss"), who supervises and directs launchings, landings, and the handling of aircraft and aviation fuels.

On a ship with only a limited number of aircraft, the department consists of a V division with the V division officer in charge. On ships with large air departments, additional divisions are assigned: V-1 (plane handling on the flight deck), V-2 (catapults and arresting gear), V-3 (plane handling on the hangar deck), V-4 (aviation fuels), and V-5 (administration). The division officers responsible for the first four divisions are known as the flight deck officer for V-1, the catapult and arresting gear officer for V-2, the hangar deck officer for V-3, and the aviation fuels officer for V-4.

Aircraft Intermediate Maintenance. The head of this department (usually referred to simply as "AIMD") is the aircraft intermediate maintenance officer, who supervises and directs intermediate maintenance for the aircraft on board the ship. The AIMD also keeps up ground-support equipment. When there is only one division in the department, it is called the IM division. Ships having more than one division include the IM-1 division (responsible for administration, quality assurance, production and maintenance/material control, and aviation 3-M analysis), the IM-2 division (for general aircraft and organizational maintenance of the ship's assigned aircraft), the IM-3 division (for maintenance of armament systems, precision measuring equipment, and aviation electronic equipment, known as "avionics"), and the IM-4 division (for maintenance of other aviation support equipment).

Combat Systems. Because of their complexity and sophistication, submarines and certain classes of cruisers, destroyers, and frigates have a combat systems department instead of a weapons department. Some of the functions covered by the operations department on those ships with a weapons department are included in combat systems on these vessels. Some of the divisions found in these departments are CA (antisubmarine warfare), CB (ballistic missile), CD (tactical data systems), CE (electronics repair), CF (fire control), CG (gunnery and ordnance), CI (combat information), and CM (missile systems).

Communications. In ships large enough to have a communications department, the head of the department is the communications officer, who is responsible for visual and electronic exterior communications. Her or his assistants may include a radio officer, a signal officer, a communications security material system (CMS) custodian, and a cryptosecurity officer. The department may be divided into CR (for radio) and CS (for signals) divisions. In smaller ships, the communications officer is a division officer reporting to the operations officer. In this case, the division is usually called OC division.

Deck. Some ships, such as aircraft carriers, have both a deck department and a weapons department; other ships have only one or the other, depending upon their mission. On ships with a deck department, the first lieutenant is the head of that department. which consists of divisions called 1st Division, 2nd Division, and so on. On ships that do not have a deck department, there is a division in the weapons department, usually called 1st Division, and the first lieutenant in this case is a division officer rather than a department head. Aboard those ships having only a deck department and not a weapons department, ordnance equipment, small arms, and other weapons are the responsibility of a division headed by a gunnery officer. Personnel assigned to the deck department (or division) carry out all seamanship operations, such as mooring, anchoring, and transferring cargo from ship to ship while under way.

Engineering. This department, headed by the engineering officer (also called the chief engineer), is responsible for the operation and maintenance of the ship's machinery, the provision of electrical power and freshwater, damage control, hull and machinery repairs, and the maintenance of underwater fittings. Ships large enough to have more than one division in the engineering department might have an M or MP division for main propulsion, A for auxiliaries, E for electrical, IC for interior communications, and R division for repair.

Executive. Some ships have an executive department made up of one or more divisions. (Aircraft carriers have an administrative department, which is similar in nature and function to the executive department in other ships.) This department is headed by the XO and may have an X division, which includes personnel assigned to work in the CO's office, XO's office, chaplain's office, print shop, security office, training office, legal office, and sick bay (when no medical officer is assigned). It may also include an I division used for the indoctrination of newly reporting personnel.

Navigation. This department, headed by the navigator, is responsible for the ship's safe navigation and piloting and for the care and maintenance of navigational equipment.

Operations. This department, often called "Ops," is headed by the operations officer, who is responsible for collecting, evaluating, and disseminating tactical and operational information. For ships with more than one division, the department might include OA, OC, OD, OE, OI, OP, OS, and OZ divisions. OA includes intelligence, photography, drafting, printing and reproduction, and meteorology. OC handles communications, but on ships having a large air contingent, such as aircraft carriers and amphibious assault ships, OC is the carrier air-traffic-control-center division. OD division covers the data-processing functions. OE is the operations electronics/material division. OI includes the combat information center (CIC) and sometimes the lookouts. OP is the photographic intelligence division. OS division handles communications intelligence. OZ is the intelligence and cryptologic operations division.

The following officers, when assigned, will usually report to the Ops officer: air intelligence, CIC officer, communications (COMM) officer, electronics material officer (EMO), electronic warfare (EW) officer, intelligence officer, meteorological officer, photographic officer, strike operations officer, and computer programmer (or computer-maintenance officer).

Reactor. Because they are nuclear powered, CVNs have this department in addition to the engineering department. The reactor officer, who heads this department, is responsible for the operation and maintenance of reactor plants and their associated auxiliaries. Divisions found in the reactor department include RA (auxiliaries), RC (reactor control), RE (electrical), RL (chemistry), RM (machinery), and RP (propulsion). Because of the special responsibilities of running a reactor plant and its obvious close ties with the engineering functions of the ship, the reactor and engineering officers must closely coordinate their activities.

Weapons. The weapons officer supervises and directs the use and maintenance of ordnance and (in ships without a deck department) seamanship equipment. On ships with antisubmarine warfare (ASW) arms and a weapons department, the ASW officer is an assistant to the weapons officer. Other assistants, depending upon the ship and its weapons capabilities, are the missile officer, gunnery officer, fire-control officer, and nuclear weapons officer. On some ships, the CO of the Marine detachment may also answer to the weapons officer.

Some of the divisions that may be included in the weapons department are F division (fire control), F-1 (missile fire control), F-2 (ASW), F-3 (gun fire control), G (ordnance handling), GM (guided missiles), V (aviation, for ships without an air department but with an aviation detachment embarked), and W (nuclear weapons assembly and maintenance).

SUPPORT DEPARTMENTS

Because of its obvious importance, most Navy ships will have a supply department. Smaller ships will have one or more hospital corpsmen assigned to handle the medical and health needs of the crew, but larger ships will have a medical department and a dental department with one or more doctors, dentists, nurses, and medical service corps officers assigned. Ships with one or more judge advocate general (lawyer) officers on board will have a legal department.

Supply. Headed by the supply officer, this department handles the procurement, stowage, and issue of all the command's stores and equipment. The supply officer pays the bills and the crew and is responsible for supervising and operating the general and wardroom messes, the laundry, and the ship's store. Ships large enough to have multiple divisions may have an S-1 division (general supply support), S-2 division (general mess), S-3 division (ship's stores and services), S-4 division (disbursing), S-5 division (officers' messes), S-6 division (aviation stores), and S-7 division (data processing).

Medical. The medical officer is responsible for maintaining the health of personnel, making medical inspections, and advising the CO on hygiene and sanitation conditions. Assistant medical officers may be assigned. H division is normally the only medical division.

Dental. The dental officer is responsible for preventing and controlling dental disease and supervising dental hygiene. Assistant dental officers are sometimes assigned to larger ships. D division is normally the only dental division.

Legal. The legal officer is responsible for handling all legal matters, particularly those pertaining to the UCMJ.

SPECIAL DEPARTMENTS
Certain ships have unusual missions and therefore require special departments. Included among these are aviation, boat group, deep submergence, repair, safety, transportation, and weapons repair.

Aviation. On a nonaviation ship with a helicopter detachment embarked, an aviation department is organized and headed by the aviation officer. The aviation officer is responsible for the specific missions of the embarked aircraft. His principal assistant may be a helicopter control officer, but often one officer performs both functions.

Boat Group. Amphibious ships often have a boat-group department whose responsibilities include the operation and maintenance of the embarked boats.

Deep Submergence. This specialized department, which is found on only a few naval vessels, launches, recovers, and services deep-submergence vehicles (DSVs) or deep-submergence rescue vehicles (DSRVs).

Repair. On ships with a large repair function, there will be a full department with a department head called the repair officer. On multiple-division ships, there may be an R-1 division (hull repair), R-2 division (machinery repair), R-3 division (electrical repair), R-4 division (electronic repair), and R-5 division (ordnance repair).

Safety. Larger ships, particularly those that conduct potentially hazardous operations on a routine basis, will have a safety department assigned.

Transportation. Only Military Sealift Command (MSC) transports have this department, headed by the transportation officer. The department is responsible for loading and unloading, berthing and messing, and general direction of passengers. On ships without a combat cargo officer, the transportation officer is also the liaison with loading activities ashore. Larger ships may have a T-1 division, which has the physical transportation responsibilities, and a T-2 division, which handles the administrative end of transportation.

Weapons Repair. This department, found only on tenders, usually has a single division, designated SR. A large department may be subdivided into the SR-1 division (repair and service) and the SR-2 division (maintenance of repair machinery).

AIRCRAFT SQUADRONS

Operating squadrons, like ships, have a CO, an XO, department heads, and division officers.

Commanding Officer

The CO, also known as the squadron commander, has the usual duties and responsibilities of any captain insofar as they are applicable to an aircraft squadron. These include looking after morale, discipline, readiness, and efficiency and issuing operational orders to the entire squadron.

Executive Officer

The XO, the second senior naval aviator in the squadron, is the direct representative of the CO. The XO sees that the squadron is administered properly and that the CO's orders are carried out. The executive officer, as second in command, will take over command of the squadron whenever the CO is not present.

Squadron Departments

Operational squadrons are organized into several departments, each with its own department head who is responsible for organization, training, personnel assignments, departmental planning and operations, security, safety, cleanliness of assigned areas, and maintenance of records and reports. Just as in ships, the number and functions of departments vary somewhat according to the squadron's mission. Most squadrons have at least four departments: operations, administration, maintenance, and safety. Many have a training department as well.

OPERATIONS

This department is responsible for aircraft schedules, communications, intelligence, navigation, and (in squadrons without a separate training department) squadron training. Working for the operations officer are a number of assistants with special duties, including the communications officer, classified material security officer, intelligence officer, navigation officer, tactics officer, landing signal officer, and (in squadrons without a separate training department) several training assistants.

ADMINISTRATIVE
The administrative department is responsible for official squadron correspondence, records maintenance, legal matters, and public affairs. An officer designated as first lieutenant ensures that squadron spaces and equipment are maintained and clean. Other assistants to the admin officer are the personnel officer, educational services officer, public affairs officer, legal officer, and command security manager. The personnel division takes care of personnel records, human resources management, and equal opportunity programs.

MAINTENANCE
This department is typically the largest in the squadron and oversees the planning, coordination, and execution of all maintenance work on aircraft. It also is responsible for the inspection, adjustment, and replacement of aircraft engines and related equipment including survival gear, as well as the keeping of maintenance logs, records, and reports.

SAFETY
The safety department head ensures squadron compliance with all safety orders and directives and is a member of the accident (investigation) board. The quality assurance division within the safety department is responsible for the prevention of defects by ensuring command compliance in programs and policies applicable to each aircraft platform.

TRAINING
Some squadrons have separate training departments to handle the training requirements of the squadron. Squadrons designated as fleet replacement squadrons (once known as readiness air groups or RAGs) exist to train new or returning squadron personnel in preparation for assignment to operational squadrons. Pilots and naval flight officers train in these squadrons after their initial basic flight training and before returning to an operational squadron after an extended assignment to other duties. Enlisted maintenance personnel are also trained in these squadrons in a special program known as FRAMP (Fleet Readiness Aviation Maintenance Personnel). Sometimes there is a separate FRAMP department.

The Navy's organization is complex and often confusing. While it is important for you to know your immediate organization and perhaps several levels above and below, you will not need to know all aspects. When you report to a new duty station, one of your early priorities should be to learn the organization of your new command and where it fits into the larger Navy. Rank and experience will determine how much else you will need to know.

NINE

SECURITY

The word security, as it is used in the Navy, can mean many things. Physical security involving the protection of ships and stations and all the people and equipment associated with them is a primary consideration. As you can probably imagine, information security is also an important consideration in the military—keeping a real or potential enemy from knowing your plans in peacetime, crisis, and war is another obvious example.

Naval personnel must always be security-minded and alert to external and internal threats. A few examples include saboteurs, terrorist attacks, civil disorders, riots, and spies.

EXTERNAL SECURITY

Twice in our nation's history, we have suffered the devastation and embarrassment of surprise attacks. On 7 December 1941, the U.S. Fleet and Army Air Corps units at Pearl Harbor, Hawaii, were surprised by an air attack from a Japanese fleet that caused severe damage and resulted in more than 2,500 deaths. On 11 September 2001, terrorists from several Middle Eastern countries, using hijacked American passenger aircraft, destroyed the World Trade Center in New York, severely damaged the Pentagon, and would likely have done further devastating damage were it not for the bravery and sacrifice of the passengers of United Airlines Flight 93, which crashed in Pennsylvania.

Those attacks and just plain common sense make it clear that we must expect attacks and take every precaution to prevent them or to minimize their effects should they occur. Threats to security may take many forms, and without resorting to outright paranoia, we must be alert to unexpected danger and implement preventative measures.

Force Protection Conditions (FPCONs)

Navy warfare publication NWP 3–07.2, *Navy Doctrine for Antiterrorism/ Force Protection*, states:

> The terrorist threat is not likely to diminish soon. On the contrary, events worldwide have shown the need for increased vigilance and preparation by U.S. Navy forces whether deployed or at home. Acts of terrorism are increasingly becoming the tactic of choice among those who wish to challenge the United States but do not have the capability or desire to directly confront U.S. forces using traditional military means.

To meet this need for "increased vigilance and preparation," the Navy has adopted the system of force protection measures created by the Department of Defense known as "Force Protection Conditions" (FPCONs), which provide a means of alerting commands of the degree of probability of a terrorist attack and of triggering a series of measures designed to increase the level of a unit's defense.

There are five levels of FPCONs beginning at "NORMAL" and progressing from "ALPHA" through "DELTA"—DELTA being the highest level of threat. Experience and logic make it clear that the threat of terrorism is always possible, therefore even "NORMAL" acknowledges this possibility and includes a number of defensive measures just in case. [Note: Because FPCONs are "joint" (pertaining to all services, not just the Navy), "ALPHA" is spelled this way, rather than the Navy way ("ALFA").]

FPCON NORMAL. *No known enemy threat exists.*
FPCON ALPHA. *There is an increased possible general threat of terrorist activity.*
FPCON BRAVO. *Increased and more predictable threat of terrorism.*
FPCON CHARLIE. *Imminent threat of terrorism.*
FPCON DELTA. *A localized, specific terrorist threat or an actual attack.*

See TAB 9-A: Force Protection Conditions (FPCONs) for more details, including specific actions to be taken.

As the FPCON increases, your command will have certain specific actions to take that will heighten security. As the degree of threat elevates, so will the degree of caution. Specific measures taken will depend upon the location and circumstances.

During times of heightened danger, extra watches may be assigned for added protection of the ship. For example, when the threat condition is high, strangers approaching the ship will be regarded with suspicion, even though they might appear to be ordinary visitors, salespersons, newspaper carriers, or delivery people. All individuals coming aboard will not only be identified by the OOD or his or her representative, but all items such as packages, parcels, briefcases, and toolboxes might be inspected. Persons standing gangway or quarterdeck watches assist the OOD in identifying approaching boats, screening visitors, and checking packages.

Sentries and guards posted for security purposes are always guided by written instructions and will be armed when the situation demands. Armed guards will be well trained in the use of their weapons and when to employ those weapons.

When ships are moored to a pier, attackers may mingle with a returning liberty party, pose as visitors, or sneak aboard. Moored or anchored ships are vulnerable to sneak attacks and sabotage, particularly at night. Ships can be approached by swimmers, small boats, or submarines. Sentries must know how to challenge approaching boats in order to identify occupants before they come alongside.

Security Reaction Forces

Sometimes called "Shipboard Reaction Forces" (SRF) or "Base Reaction Forces" (BRF), these are teams that have been specially trained and equipped to respond when a security emergency arises, such as intruders on your ship. Sailors (and sometimes Marines) assigned to these teams are ready to respond on a moment's notice much like volunteer firefighters in a community. In other words, they go about their normal duties and routines until called upon to respond to a security emergency.

You may be assigned to an SRF or BRF after you have been properly trained in weapons handling and other relevant topics. If you are not part of one of these teams, be sure to do what they tell you and do not impede

[**9.1**] As an armed sentry you will be well trained in the use of your weapons and when to employ them.

them in any way. If, for example, they come into your compartment and tell you to lie face down on the deck, do so immediately. Kissing steel is better than being wounded in an attack!

Bomb Threats

A bomb threat may happen anytime or anywhere. Many bomb threats are not real, but you should not assume that this is the case. If you receive a bomb threat by telephone, keep your head and take the following actions if at all possible:

- Keep the caller on the line and obtain as much information as you can.
- Write down the exact words of the caller (or as close to the exact words as possible) as quickly as you can.
- Try to determine the sex, approximate age, and attitude of the caller.

- Ask the caller when and where the bomb is to go off, what kind of bomb it is, what it looks like, and where the caller is calling from.
- Listen for background sounds that might give an indication of the caller's location.
- Note any accent or peculiarity of speech that may help identify the caller.

Each telephone at your command should have a copy of a "Telephonic Threat Complaint" form readily available to guide you if you receive a bomb threat.

There are certain other defensive actions you can take to reduce the chance of a real bomb attack:

- Strictly comply with and enforce procedures for personnel identification and access control by always carrying your own identification card and, if you are on watch, carefully examine the ID cards of personnel boarding your ship or visiting your command, particularly if you do not recognize them.
- Be suspicious of packages if you do not know where they came from.
- Be suspicious of any item that is obviously out of place.
- Maintain tight control of locks and keys.
- Lock spaces that are not in use.
- Report suspicious personnel and their actions.

Shipyard Security

Ships sent into shipyards for major repairs will have many civilians coming aboard to do their work. This increased traffic can make a ship more vulnerable to problems of theft, damage, and even sabotage, because it becomes more difficult to keep track of so many people on board. All workers coming aboard a ship must be identified. The shipyard itself will assist in this process by providing proper identification cards to its workers. Compartments containing classified matter must be secured, either by locks or with sentries. Shipboard personnel may be assigned as "fire watches" to each welder and burner who comes on board because of the increased potential for fire. Also, special precautions must be taken after each shift to inspect spaces for fire hazards.

WARTIME SECURITY

In times of war or when the potential for hostile action is very high, extra precautions must be taken to provide additional security to ships and stations. These precautions may be very elaborate and involve highly trained personnel, or they may be relatively simple and affect all hands.

Because modern technology enables an enemy to detect almost any electronic emission, a condition known as EMCON (emission control) may be set. When EMCON is imposed aboard ship, powerful equipment such as radio transmitters and radars will be shut down or tightly controlled. Even your personal radio and other electronic devices may be prohibited if they have signal-emitting characteristics, which many do.

In peacetime, ships display navigational lights for safety, but if military considerations take precedence (e.g., moving through waters where enemy ships or submarines may be present), navigational lights will be turned off. It is essential that you and your shipmates do not endanger the ship during such times. Smoking, for example, is now restricted to certain locations and prohibited during certain conditions; the glow of a cigarette can be seen for miles on a dark night. The light from an improperly shielded doorway will let a submarine make a successful periscope attack.

Sound travels better in water than in air. Unnecessary noises can aid an enemy in detecting a ship or submarine. When "quiet ship" is set, all banging and hammering will be prohibited, and everyone on board will be expected to avoid making any noises.

SECURITY OF INFORMATION

Some information—if obtained by an enemy, or a potential one—can be harmful to our nation. Obvious examples would be war plans, or the location of our forces during combat operations, or the codes that we use to keep things secret. Such information is labeled as "classified." That rather general term can be further specified into certain categories of national security classifications, such as Confidential, Secret, or Top Secret. Because the safety of the United States and the success of naval operations depend greatly on the protection of classified information, it is important that you understand what classified information is, who may have access to it, and what the important rules and guidance for safeguarding it are.

Security Classification

Information is classified when national security is at stake. It is assigned a classification, which tells you how much protection it requires. There are three main classifications, each of which indicates the anticipated degree of damage to national security that could result from unauthorized disclosure:

- Top secret—Exceptionally grave damage
- Secret—Serious damage
- Confidential—Damage

All classified material—such as messages, publications, electronic communications, software, equipment, or videos—must be plainly labeled with the appropriate classification. Following the classification, some material may have additional markings that signal extra precautions in handling. For example, "restricted data" means that the material pertains to nuclear weapons or nuclear power, and NOFORN indicates that the information cannot be disclosed to foreign nationals.

There is another category of government information, "for official use only" (FOUO). This is not considered classified information because it does not involve national security, but it is information that could be damaging in other ways and cannot, therefore, be divulged to everyone. Information such as the results of investigations, examination questions, and bids on contracts are "privileged information" and are kept from general knowledge under the designation FOUO.

Unauthorized disclosure, or "compromise," means that classified information has been exposed to a person not authorized to see it.

Security Clearance

Before you can be allowed to have access to classified information, you must have a security clearance. You will be assigned a security clearance based upon how much classified material you will need to work with in order to do your job. If you have a need to work with top-secret material, you must first receive a top-secret clearance. If all you will need to work with is confidential information, you will be assigned a confidential clearance.

The standards for clearances and information security are listed in the *Information Security Program Manual* (SECNAV M-5510.36). In general you must be trustworthy, of reliable character, and able to show discretion and good judgment. A person may be loyal to his or her country but unable to meet the standards for a position of trust and confidence. Conduct such as drug abuse, excessive drinking, and financial irresponsibility can lead to denial of clearance. This could cost a promotion, cause a rate conversion, or lead to separation from military service. A clearance may be denied or revoked because of a mental or emotional condition, general disciplinary causes, UA (unauthorized absence) or AWOL (absent without leave), falsification of official documents, or disregard for public laws or Navy regulations.

INVESTIGATIONS

Before you can be granted a security clearance, an investigation is conducted into your background to make certain that you can be trusted with classified information. Investigators will look into your past records and may question people who know you. This process can take a while, so you may be given an "interim" clearance based upon some preliminary investigating before your "final" clearance comes through. The word "final" in this case means that the investigation is over and that you have been granted the clearance you need. It is not "final" in the sense that it cannot be taken away. Should you involve yourself in any of the disqualifying activities mentioned above, such as drug use or financial irresponsibility, your clearance may be revoked.

Access and Need to Know

Security clearances are granted only when access to classified material is necessary to perform official duties and only at the appropriate level. If your job requires you to see confidential material but not secret or top secret, you will only receive a confidential clearance. This is no reflection on you or the level of trust the government places in you. If you are ever denied the access you need, *that* is a cause for concern, but as long as you receive the level of clearance required for the performance of your assigned duties, you should be satisfied.

It is very important to understand the concept of "need to know." Just because you have a secret clearance, that does not give you access to all secret material. Your secret clearance allows you to see all the secret material you *need to know* in order to do your job, but it does not entitle you to see information classified at that level in other locations or departments not related to your job. If circumstances change and your duties no longer require access, or require a lower level of access, your security clearance will be administratively withdrawn or lowered without prejudicing your future eligibility. Commanding officers may reinstate or adjust your security clearance as the need arises.

Safeguarding Classified Information

Classified information or material is discussed, used, or stored only where adequate security measures are in effect. When removed from storage for use, it must be kept under the continuous observation of a cleared person. It is never left unattended.

You are responsible for protecting any classified information you know or control. Before giving another person access to that information, it is your responsibility to determine that the person has the proper clearance and a need to know. If you are uncertain whether someone has the proper clearance and a need to know, find out before you allow him or her access. Never tell someone something classified just because he is curious, even if he has the proper clearance. Remember, there are two requirements for someone to have access to classified material: she must have the proper clearance and she must have an official need to know the information.

VOICE COMMUNICATIONS

Some radio circuits and telephones in the Navy are what we call "secure." This means they are protected by special equipment that encrypts (scrambles) your voice so that an enemy or someone not authorized cannot listen in and understand what you are saying. *But most are not secure.* Never discuss classified information over a telephone or a radio circuit unless you know that it is secure.

CENSORSHIP

In war or during certain peacetime emergency conditions, censorship of personal mail may be imposed. The intent of censorship is to avoid security violations that might occur through carelessness or lack of judgment in writing letters or sending electronic messages. Under such emergency conditions, all such communications written aboard a ship, or in a forward area, must be passed by a censor. When censorship is imposed, instructions will be issued explaining what can and cannot be discussed in letters. You should avoid subjects such as ships' movements, combat actions, or details of weapons in your communications under these circumstances.

Photographs may be censored as well. Cameras may be barred and all pictures taken aboard ship may require clearance for release.

Bear in mind that limitations may also be imposed upon all forms of communication, including telephone calls, texting, e-mails, and social media postings.

STOWAGE AND TRANSPORT

Classified material may not be removed from the command without permission. Authorized protective measures must be used when classified material is sent or carried from one place to another and it must be stowed (stored) properly. Do not, for example, take a classified manual home to study at night. It is admirable that you want to improve your knowledge so that you can do your job better, but you probably do not have the means to transport the material safely. You almost definitely do not have the means to stow it safely in your home. Do not take classified material home.

DISCOVERY OF CLASSIFIED INFORMATION

If you accidentally come across some classified material that has been left unguarded, misplaced, or not secured, do not read or examine it or try to decide what to do with it. Report the discovery immediately and stand by to keep unauthorized personnel away until an officer or senior petty officer arrives to take charge.

SECURITY AREAS

Spaces where classified materials are used or stowed or that serve as buffers are known as security areas. Some areas are more sensitive than others. A system has been developed to identify security areas properly. The government has established three types of security areas and identified them by levels. All three of these areas are clearly marked by signs with the words "Restricted Area." The level of the area is not identified on the signs, however.

Level I. No classified material is actually used or kept in a level I space. This space is used as a buffer or control point to prevent access to a higher-level security area. A security clearance is not required for access to a level I area, but an identification system is usually in place to control access to the area.

Level II. Classified material is stowed or used in these areas. Uncontrolled access to a level II area could potentially result in the compromise of classified information. Therefore, it is mandatory that anyone not holding the proper clearance be escorted while visiting a level II area.

Level III. Classified material is used in a level III area. Mere entry into the area risks compromise. An example would be a command and control center where large decision-making displays have classified information posted on them. Only people with the proper clearance and the need to know are permitted access to a level III area. All entrances must be guarded or properly secured.

Information Security Threats

Foreign nations and adversaries may be interested in a wide variety of classified information, to include new developments, weapons, techniques, and materials, as well as movements and the operating capabilities of ships and aircraft.

Those who try to collect such information cannot be stereotyped or categorized, which is why they succeed in their work. A person who has access to classified material should never talk to any stranger about any classified subjects. A foreign intelligence agent collects many odd little bits of information, some of which might not even make sense to the agent, but when they are all put together in the agent's own country they may tell experts much more than the Navy wants them to know.

Espionage agents prey upon the vulnerabilities of their intended targets. For example, service people with relatives in foreign countries can sometimes be intimidated into cooperation by threats to their relatives. People with financial problems or drug habits can be coerced into doing favors for the enemy. Some people may feel a need for attention. If a stranger offers to solve a problem you are having, you could be placed in the awkward position of accepting, without even knowing that your new friend is indeed from an unfriendly foreign nation. All this may sound like a scene from a spy movie but, unfortunately, it happens in real life. Enemy agents also like to infiltrate social gatherings where U.S. service personnel dance, drink, talk, text, and photograph. These agents may gather important pieces of information merely by listening to the conversation around them or by actively engaging in talk with service personnel. Then they pass on whatever is heard. Some agents even move into communities with service people so they can collect information from their neighbors.

Listed below are some ways to prevent being exploited by a foreign agent:

- Don't talk about a sensitive job to people who don't need to know—not even to your family or friends.
- Be especially careful about what you post online. Even seemingly routine information about yourself or your activities can help real or potential enemies piece together more important conclusions.
- Be careful what you say in social situations. Even seemingly trivial information can be valuable in the wrong hands.
- Be aware that telephone communications, text messaging, and e-mailing are all vulnerable to eavesdropping or hacking.
- Know how to handle classified material properly.

If you have personal problems you feel might be exploited, use the chain of command to solve them. No one in the Navy is going to hit you over the head because you have a problem that might be solved by a senior petty officer or officer. If one of them cannot help, go to a chaplain. Chaplains are in the service for more than religion; they are there to help, whatever your problem is.

REPORTING THREATS

Report any suspicious contact. If someone seems more curious about your job than seems normal and presses you for information in any way, report it to your superiors. If the person is innocent, no harm will come of it. If the person is guilty, you will have done a great service to your country by calling attention to the incident.

If you are contacted by someone who you are certain is attempting espionage, do not try to be a hero by taking action yourself. Report it!

Report any contact with someone you know who is from a nation that is hostile or potentially hostile to the United States, even if the contact seems innocent. Remember that spies rarely start out trying to get classified information from their targets. If you are unsure whether the nation is considered a potential threat, report it. In matters of security, it is always better to be overly cautious than not cautious enough.

If you feel that your superior in the chain of command cannot be trusted with the information you have to report, request permission to see the next higher-up. And the next, if necessary. If you feel you cannot approach the people in your chain of command, go to the Naval Criminal Investigative Service (NCIS) office. If you cannot find one, visit their website at www.ncis.navy.mil.

If you are going to make a report, make a note of the date, time, place, and nature of the encounter. Describe how you were approached and mention who else in the Navy was also approached. Provide names if you know them. State your own name, grade, social security number, and anything else you feel is pertinent.

CYBERSECURITY

Cyber threats come from a variety of sources including nation states, profit-motivated criminals, ideologically motivated hackers, extremists, and terrorists. When you log on to a Navy network or system, you're in the cyber battlespace.

If there are weaknesses in the Navy's defenses, they may be networks and computers that can be compromised by intruders with relatively limited resources. Cyber enemies only have to be successful once to do significant damage; we cannot afford to make any mistakes. Always practice good cyber discipline as described below.

> **Don't Take the Bait.** Always verify the source of e-mails and the links you may find in them. If you are directed to a site for an online deal that looks too good to be true, it probably is fraudulent. Phishing is a form of e-mail spoofing. By clicking on a link in what appears to be a legitimate e-mail, you may be directed to a fraudulent website that installs bad software on your computer or captures data you enter on the website. Opening an infected e-mail attachment can also install bad software on your computer.

"Phishing" is a scam used to dupe an e-mail user into revealing personal or confidential information, such as passwords, social security numbers, or credit card information, that a scammer can use to harm you or the Navy. "Spear-phishing" is a form of phishing that targets a specific organization. Spear-phishing e-mails appear to be from an individual or business you know. Spear-phishing attempts are not typically initiated by "random hackers" but are more likely to be conducted by those seeking financial gain, trade secrets, or military information. Signs that an e-mail may be a spear-phishing attempt include:

- Sender's name, organization, or company does not match the e-mail address or digital signature
- Words such as official, mandatory, urgent, etc.
- Link text may not match associated URL
- Unsolicited requests for personal information
- Poor grammar and multiple misspellings

When in Doubt, Throw It Out. Do not open suspicious links in e-mails, tweets, posts, messages, or attachments, even if you know the source.

Don't Connect Unauthorized Devices to Navy Networks. Connecting unauthorized devices, such as thumb drives and cell phones, to your computer is inviting trouble. Unauthorized devices may contain software that can allow an intruder inside the Navy's network. Do not allow convenience to take precedence over national and cybersecurity.

Remove Your Common Access Card (CAC). Remove your CAC when you are not using it. Don't make it easy for someone to access data on your computer when you're away.

Use a Better Password. Don't use easily guessed or weak passwords, and safeguard them so they can't be stolen. Password best practices include:

- Use different passwords for every account.
- Make passwords a minimum of eight characters long and include at least one number, one capital letter, one lowercase letter, and one special character.
- Select the first letter of each word in an easily remembered phrase for the letters in your password. For example, "stand Navy down the field, sails set to the sky" becomes "sNdtfsstts."
- Don't use names or words that can be found in any dictionary (including foreign languages).

- Don't use keyboard patterns.
- Routinely change passwords on all accounts.
- Do not change passwords in a serial fashion (e.g., password 2016 replaced with password2017).
- If you save your passwords to a file, password protect and encrypt the file.
- Don't write down your passwords or keep them in your wallet/purse.
- Don't allow your browser to store your passwords.

Safeguard Your Personally Identifiable Information (PII). Cyber adversaries can use information they have obtained about you to appear legitimate so they can trick you into surrendering data they need to breach our networks and systems. To protect your PII, be smart about providing information online and use good security practices when using social media sites.

Choose security questions that have answers not discoverable on the Internet—for example, do not choose the street you grew up on, your mother's maiden name, etc.—and don't conduct work-related business on your personal account.

Facebook, Twitter, LinkedIn, and other social media platforms are invaluable tools, but they can introduce security hazards. Personal profile information on these sites may be used by hackers for social engineering or phishing purposes. Also, be extra vigilant about friending bogus Facebook accounts, which can allow hackers to harvest sensitive user photos, phone numbers, and e-mail addresses for social engineering attacks.

Don't Use Peer-to-Peer (P2P) Programs. Don't use peer-to-peer (P2P) file sharing programs. These programs can spread bad software inside the Navy's network defenses.

Stay on Known, Good Websites. Use websites that are business related or known to not pose a hazard.

Don't Use Systems in Unauthorized Ways. The Navy has established policies to protect itself from compromise. Don't put others at risk by using systems in ways that are not authorized.

Complacency about cybersecurity makes the Navy vulnerable to compromises that could significantly affect operations. Your commitment to these cybersecurity best practices will protect the Navy's operational capabilities and contribute to our cyber fight. Think cybersecurity before you act.

From seamen recruits to admirals, security is the responsibility of everyone in the Navy. Just as you are alert to dangers of all types in your own home, so should you be always vigilant and protective of your Navy. Your life and those of your shipmates may very well depend on it.

TEN

SHIPS

Ships are the core element of the Navy. There are other important components—aircraft, construction battalions (known as Seabees), commando teams (known as SEALs), and shore installations, to name just a few—but ships have been the centerpiece of navies since ancient times. Because ships have been around in one form or another for thousands of years, they are steeped in tradition, yet modern ships are also prime examples of modern technology. The result is that Sailors must be able to use a very specialized vocabulary that ranges from ancient terms like "forecastle" and "bulkhead" to modern acronyms like "AMRAAM" and "LCAC."

Navy ships are highly complicated machines with their own propulsion plants, weapons, repair shops, supply spaces, and facilities for living, sleeping, and eating. Although there are great differences in the types and missions of ships, all ships have certain essential characteristics.

TERMINOLOGY

Armament is the combat "punch" of a ship. In some ships, that punch is primarily offensive, such as heavy-caliber guns or long-range missiles. Other ships, whose mission may be supportive, such as oilers or ammunition replenishment ships, carry armament that is primarily defensive in nature. A ship's armament may consist of guns, missiles, torpedoes, depth charges, rockets, mines, or aircraft. Most ships are armed with more than one type of weapon. An aircraft carrier, for example, uses her airplanes as the primary means of attack and defense, but she also may carry a close-in missile defense system to handle any attackers that may have penetrated her outer defenses.

[**10.1**] An *Arleigh Burke*–class destroyer under way on a distant sea

Survivability refers to those features that help a ship survive the effects of combat. Aside from weapons, a ship's sturdy construction is her best protection. Compartmentation, double bottoms, and other structural components all make a ship less vulnerable to attack or damage by other means. A ship's firefighting and flooding-control systems are also important components of her survivability.

Seaworthiness relates to hull design and other features that enable a ship to operate in high winds and heavy seas. A ship's stability, or the way she recovers from a roll, is an essential part of her seaworthiness. You will sometimes hear a ship referred to by her "sea-keeping abilities," which refers to how well she is able to perform her mission when the sea and weather conditions are bad.

Maneuverability is the way a ship handles in turning, backing down (going in reverse), moving alongside another ship, or evading enemy attacks. Many factors contribute to a ship's maneuverability, such as hull design, the size of her rudder, the power of her engines and how quickly they respond to changes, her draft (how much of the ship is under the water), or her sail area (how much of the ship is above the water where the wind can affect her).

Speed determines how quickly a ship can get to a scene of action, overtake an enemy, or avoid being overtaken, and plays a role in a ship's maneuverability and vulnerability. Key factors are the power of her engines in relation to her size and the shape of her underwater hull.

Endurance is the maximum time a ship can steam at a given speed. Most oil-powered ships can steam for days or even weeks without refueling. The Navy's nuclear-powered ships can cruise for years, limited only by their need to replenish food and other consumables.

No matter how specialized your professional training, you must still be thoroughly familiar with basic nautical terminology referring to ship construction. You will find that this terminology is used throughout the Navy whether you are on a naval air station, in a Navy school, or aboard ship. So you will need to learn this new vocabulary in order to communicate in your new profession. After a time, such language will become second nature to you, and you will find yourself using these terms naturally.

In some respects a ship is like a building. She has outer walls (forming the *hull* and *superstructure*), floors (*decks*), inner walls (*partitions* and *bulkheads*), corridors (*passageways*), ceilings (*overheads*), and stairs (*ladders*). But unlike a building, a ship moves, so you will also have to learn new terms for directions and getting around. For example, when you cross from a pier to a ship you are using the *brow* to go aboard, and what might be an entrance hall or foyer in a building is the *quarterdeck* on a ship. The front (*forward*) part of a ship is the *bow*; to go toward the bow is to go *forward*. The back (*after*) part of the ship is the *stern*; to go toward the stern is to go *aft*. Something located farther aft than another object is said to be *abaft* the other. The uppermost deck that runs the entire length of the ship from bow to stern is the *main deck*. (An exception to this rule is the aircraft carrier, whose main deck is the hangar deck, not the flight deck, which would seem to fit the normal definition of main deck. This came about because early aircraft carriers were created by starting with an existing ship and adding a flight deck above the main deck.) Above the main deck is the *superstructure*. "Floors" below the main deck are called *lower decks*. Those above the main deck are called *levels*. In a building you would go upstairs or downstairs, in a ship you go *topside* or *below*. The forward part of the main deck is the *forecastle* (pronounced "fohk-sul") and the after part is the *fantail*. As you face forward on a ship, the right side is *starboard*, and the left side is *port*. An imaginary line running full-length down the middle of the ship is the *centerline*. The direction from the centerline toward either side is *outboard*, and from either side toward the centerline is *inboard*. A line from one side of the ship to the other runs *athwartship*.

Although an explanation of the term *displacement* is technically more complicated, for most practical purposes this term refers to the weight of a vessel.

BASIC SHIP STRUCTURE

While you are not expected to be a naval architect, you will need to know some of the basics of ship construction in order to understand how ships work and where things are in relation to each other. This knowledge will not only keep you from getting lost on a ship, it may help you some day to save your ship or yourself should a disaster strike.

Submarines

Submarines are technically ships, but because they are designed to operate under water, they have very few topside features and practically no superstructure. About all that projects above the hull is the "sail," a streamlined tower that houses the periscopes and certain control stations, and where a few watchstanders can stand when the submarine operates on the surface.

Submarines have long, tub-like hulls with nearly circular cross sections and are built to withstand tremendous pressure. The hull consists of the bow compartment, containing living accommodations; the operations compartment, containing the control room, sonar, and radar rooms, the torpedo room, and some state rooms; the reactor compartment; the missile rooms (on fleet ballistic-missile submarines); and the engineroom. Submarines have special ballast tanks that can be quickly flooded when it is time to submerge, or pumped out when the sub is to surface.

The controls by which a submarine is maneuvered are more like those of an aircraft than those of a surface ship (which merely steers left or right), because a sub also moves up and down. In fact, when operating submerged, she banks in her turns and climbs and dives somewhat like an aircraft. Aside from these basic differences, a submarine is still a ship (although submariners traditionally refer to it as a "boat") and therefore contains many of the same systems and features found in a surface vessel.

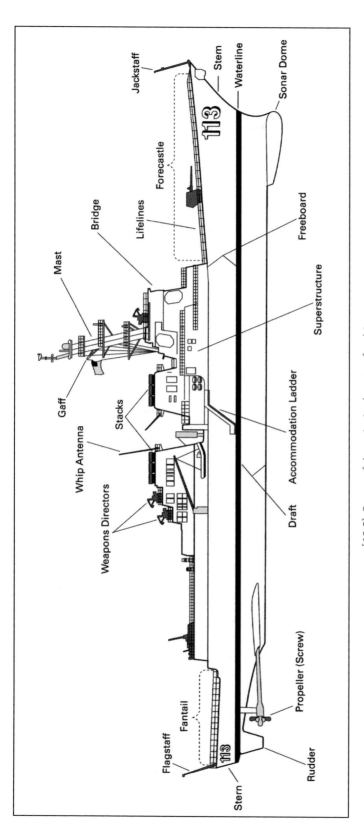

[10.2] Some of the principal parts of a ship

The Hull

The hull is the main body of the ship. Metal *shell plating* forms the sides and bottom, and the *weather deck* or *main deck* forms the top. Where the sides join the main deck is called the *gunwale* (rhymes with "funnel"). The outermost layer of plating and decking is called the *skin of the ship*.

The shape and construction of the hull depend on the type of ship. Ships designed for high-speed operations—destroyers and cruisers, for example—have long, narrow hulls with fine lines. Aircraft carriers and auxiliary ships have hulls with square center sections, vertical sides, and flat bottoms for greater carrying capacity. Submarines, designed to operate under water, have hulls that are rounded, like an egg, because that shape withstands great pressure.

The *keel* is the backbone of the ship. The keel usually looks like an I-beam running the full length of the ship along the bottom at dead center. The forward end of the keel, extended upward, is the *stem*; the after end, extended upward, is the *sternpost*. *Frames* are beamlike structures fastened at right angles to the keel, like ribs, and support the watertight skin or shell plating. Most ships built for the Navy also have *longitudinal frames* running fore and aft. The longitudinal and athwartships frames form an egg-crate structure in the bottom of the ship, which, when inner-bottom plating is welded to it, creates what is called a *double bottom*.

What would be interior walls in a building are called *bulkheads* if they are weight-supporting and watertight, and *partitions* if they are not. Solid (except for openings such as doors and ventilation ducts) "walls" inside the hull, extending from one side of the ship to the other, are called *transverse bulkheads*. Deck beams, transverse bulkheads, and *stanchions* (posts) support the decks and help strengthen the sides against water pressure.

When weight is added to a ship's inner bottom to balance her topside weight, making her more stable, it is called *ballast*. Some ships carry permanent concrete ballast; others pump saltwater into tanks to serve as temporary ballast, pumping it out when it is no longer needed.

Where the hull meets the surface of the water on a ship is called the *waterline*. Any part of the ship that is under water is below the waterline; any part of the ship that is in air is above the waterline.

Vertical extensions of the shell plating above the deck edge, which serve as a kind of solid fence, are called *bulwarks*. They shield deck areas from the direct effect of waves and keep personnel and equipment from going overboard. *Lifelines*, which are wire ropes mounted on short stanchions and stretched tight by turnbuckles, also form a kind of safety fence around the edges of the ship's weather decks (where there are no bulwarks).

The vertical distance from the waterline to the keel determines a ship's *draft*. Measured in feet and inches, *draft markings* are six-inch-high numbers marked on the hull near the stem and stern post. Because these numbers are six inches high and are six inches apart, the bottom of each number indicates foot marks and the top indicates half-foot marks.

That part of the ship's hull that extends from the waterline to the first weather deck is called *freeboard*.

To protect the ship's propellers (also called *screws*) from damage when coming alongside a pier or mooring next to another ship, steel braces are mounted at the stern directly above the propellers. These are appropriately called *propeller guards* (sometimes also called *screw guards*).

When a ship is properly balanced fore and aft (that is, the bow and stern are at the levels they were designed to be), the ship is said to be *in trim* or *trimmed*. If the bow is lower than the stern, the ship is said to be *down by the head* or *down by the bow*. When her stern is lower, she is said to be *down by the stern*.

A ship with one side higher out of the water than the other has a starboard or port *list*. This term is used as both a noun ("the ship has a two-degree list") and a verb ("she is listing two degrees"). List is a temporary condition caused by uneven loading of the ship. If, for example, fuel is added to the port-side tanks more rapidly than to the starboard-side tanks, the ship will list to port until the weight is balanced. List is measured in degrees by a device called an *inclinometer*, which is either a liquid-level or pendulum-like device mounted exactly at the ship's centerline. When the ship is perfectly level, the inclinometer reads "zero"; when she has a list, the inclinometer will tell you by how much.

Superstructure

All structures above the main deck are collectively referred to as the superstructure. Different kinds of ships have different types of superstructure. Often, the superstructure is topped off by one or more masts. At its simplest, a *mast* is a single pole fitted with a crossbar, called a *yardarm*, which extends above the ship and carries flag *halyards* (lines used to hoist the flags), navigational and signal lights, and various electronic devices. If the ship has two masts, the forward one is called the *foremast*, the after one the *mainmast*. Modern ships do not normally have three masts, but in the days of sail, when masts also played a role in the propulsion of the ship by supporting her sails, some ships had a third mast, called the *mizzen*, which was mounted after the mainmast. On single-masted ships, the mast, whether forward or amidships, is usually part of the superstructure and is simply called *the mast*.

The top of a mast is called the *truck*. The top of the foremast is the *foretruck*, while the top of the mainmast is the *main truck*. The *pigstick* is a slender vertical extension above the mast from which the ship's commission pennant or an admiral's personal flag flies. A pole called a *gaff* usually extends abaft the mainmast and is used to fly the national ensign when the ship is under way. The vertical *spar* (short pole) at the bow and the slightly *raked* (leaning backward) one at the stern are called the *jackstaff* and *flagstaff*, respectively. As discussed in **Chapter 3: Courtesies, Customs, and Ceremonies**, when a Navy ship is at anchor or moored to a pier it flies the "Dont Tread on Me" flag from the jackstaff and the national ensign on the flagstaff from 0800 to sunset. [Note: The jackstaff is so called because for much of the Navy's history, the union jack (star field portion of the national ensign) was flown at the forward end of the ship while in port; the Secretary of the Navy replaced the jack with the "Dont Tread on Me" flag after the war on terrorism was declared.]

The *stack* of a ship serves the same purpose as the smokestack on a power plant or the chimney on a house ashore: It carries off gases from the ship's engines and generators. (Nuclear-powered ships do not need stacks since their reactors produce no smoke or gas.) Some diesel-powered ships release their exhaust from the sides of the ship's hull rather than through a stack. On some ships, the masts and stacks have been combined to form large towers called *macks*.

Decks and Levels

Decks divide a ship into tiers or layers of compartments the way floors of a building divide it into stories. The deck normally consists of metal plates strengthened by transverse (athwartships) deck beams and longitudinal (fore and aft) girders. Decks above the waterline are usually *cambered* (arched) to provide greater strength and drain off water.

Decks are named according to their position and function in the ship. For purposes of compartment identification, decks are also numbered. The main deck is usually the uppermost of the decks that run continuously from bow to stern. The *second, third,* and *fourth decks,* continuous decks below the main deck, are numbered in sequence from topside down. A partial deck (that does not run continuously from bow to stern) is called a *platform.*

A partial deck above the main deck is numbered with a zero in front and called a *level* to distinguish it from the full decks. So the first partial deck above the main deck would be the 01 level, the next one up would be the 02 level, and so on. The term *weather deck* means just what it sounds like—a deck that is exposed to weather. *Flats* are removable plates or gratings installed as working or walking surfaces.

The *quarterdeck* is not a true deck or a structural part of the ship, but rather a *location* designated by the commanding officer as a place for ceremonies. Likewise, the word *mess deck* refers to a specific place where the crew eats and is not actually a deck in the strict sense of the word. A *flight deck* is the area used by airplanes and helicopters to land and take off.

Compartmentation and Watertight Integrity

Compartments are the rooms of a ship. Some compartments are actually called rooms, such as *wardroom, stateroom,* and *engineroom,* but generally speaking "room" is not used. Don't refer to the area where you sleep as the "bedroom" or the place where you eat as the "dining room." They are called *berthing compartment* and *mess deck,* respectively.

You will also hear the term *space* used often to describe a compartment or any enclosed area of a ship; for example, "supplies are kept in stowage spaces."

Each compartment on a ship has a unique identifier as explained in TAB 11-A: Shipboard Compartment Identification.

If a ship were built like a rowboat, one hole below the waterline could sink her. To prevent this from happening, naval ships are built with bulkheads that divide the hull into a series of watertight compartments. The term *watertight* means that when these compartments are sealed up, water cannot enter or escape. *Watertight integrity* is the overall quality of being watertight. A ship with good watertight integrity is far more survivable than one with poor watertight integrity. If a ship experiences flooding, the affected spaces can be sealed off and the other watertight spaces will keep the ship afloat. There are limits to this concept, of course. If enough compartments on a ship become flooded, the remaining watertight compartments may not have enough *buoyancy* (floatability) to keep the ship afloat. The more compartmentation a ship has, the more chance her crew has of confining the flooding to permit the ship to stay afloat (remain buoyant). The tradeoff is, of course, that too much compartmentation would interfere with the arrangement of mechanical equipment and with her operation.

An important bonus is that just as flooding can be isolated through this compartmentation system, so can fire.

Watertight doors allow access through bulkheads when opened but can prevent flooding and the spread of fire when closed. *Watertight hatches* serve the same purpose by providing sealable access through decks. Be sure to note the difference here. People—even some Sailors—often confuse doors and hatches on a ship. Ships have doors just as buildings ashore do. The difference between shipboard doors and those ashore is that those found on ships can be watertight or nonwatertight. Watertight doors contribute to the compartmentation and overall watertight integrity of the vessel, while nonwatertight doors serve the same kinds of purposes as those ashore—privacy and noise suppression. Watertight doors—set in framework above the deck with latches that can be locked closed—pass through bulkheads and nonwatertight doors pass through partitions. *Hatches*, on the other hand, are always horizontal—never vertical like a door—and allow passage through decks, not bulkheads or partitions. Technically the "door" used to close the hole in the deck made by a hatch should be called a "hatch cover," but in actual practice you will hear people referring to the hatch cover as just a hatch. This is acceptable, but you will also hear people refer to doors as hatches, and that is not acceptable.

All watertight fittings (both doors and hatches) are specially marked to tell you when it is all right to open them and when it is not. These markings will be explained in **Chapter 15: Damage Control**.

Obviously, holes must also be placed in watertight bulkheads and decks to allow ventilation ducts, fluid piping, and electrical and electronic cabling to pass through. These holes are specially constructed to prevent leaking and thereby preserve the watertight integrity of the ship.

Large ships have outer and inner *double bottoms*. These are divided athwartships and longitudinally into *tanks*, which are used to stow fuel oil or freshwater. (Note: The nautical term for "store," when it is used as a verb, is *stow*. When used as a noun, the correct term remains store. For example: "A load of stores was delivered to the ship and stowed below." The nautical term for "storage" is *stowage*.) These tanks can also be used to bring in seawater for ballast (to help keep the ship level).

Tanks at the extreme bow and stern, called the *forward peak* (or *fore-peak*) *tank* and the *after peak* (or *aftpeak*) tank, are used for trimming (leveling) the ship. Sometimes these tanks are used to carry potable (drinking) water. A strong watertight bulkhead on the after side of the forepeak tank is called the *collision bulkhead*. If one ship rams another head-on, the bow structure of the latter collapses at a point somewhere forward of the collision bulkhead, thus absorbing some of the shock of the collision and, it is hoped, preventing the flooding of compartments aft of it.

All tanks are connected to a pumping and drainage system so that fuel, water, and ballast can be transferred from one part of the ship to another or pumped overboard.

Ladders, Booms, and Brows

When a ship is not alongside a pier, her *freeboard* (distance from the water up to her main deck) causes a problem for boarding or leaving the ship. Boats coming alongside a ship will be too low for personnel to get out of the boat and up to the main deck. A special stairway leading from the deck down close to the water is suspended over the side to take care of this problem and is called an *accommodation ladder*. It has a platform at the bottom that serves as a landing for boats, and a suspended line, called a *sea painter* (often called merely *the painter*), to which boats secure themselves when coming alongside.

Some ships have *boat booms*, which are special spars swung out from the ship's side when the ship is moored or anchored. These special booms have lines suspended to the water for boats to tie up to, and they also have a *Jacob's ladder* (basically a rope ladder, although it can be made of metal or have wood components) that allows boat crews to climb into their boats or to leave their boats and come aboard the mother ship.

Boat booms require some athletic ability and are provided primarily for boat-crew use. Accommodation ladders are used by other ship's personnel and visitors.

When a ship is alongside a pier (or alongside another ship), boarding and departing are less difficult and can be accomplished by placing a simple crossway, called a *brow* (*not* a "gangplank"), to bridge the gap between the ship and pier (or between the two ships).

SHIPS' VITAL SYSTEMS

A number of systems are essential to every Navy ship. Without these important systems, ships could not carry out their missions. Because they carry out vital functions for the ship similar to functions for the human body, these systems are analogous to our nervous, circulatory, respiratory, and excretion systems.

Propulsion System

A ship is of little use unless it has mobility, and the source of that mobility is the ship's propulsion plant. In previous centuries, the source of propulsion was oars or sails, but in modern times more sophisticated forms are used.

OIL-FIRED STEAM PLANTS

For the better part of a century, steam has been the primary method of marine propulsion for sizable ships and is still used in many U.S. Navy vessels. Steam plants consist of boilers that transform freshwater into steam and turbines that convert that pressurized steam into usable power that turns the ship's propellers. Condensers convert the spent steam back into freshwater, which returns to the boilers to be reheated into energy-filled steam again. This "steam cycle," as it is called, is repeated over and over to provide the energy to propel a ship through the water. Even though this is a closed cycle—meaning that the water and steam are theoretically contained in the system and not allowed to escape—a certain amount of the freshwater is used up, so that a continuous supply of feed water is required for sustained operations. This is generated by distilling plants, which convert sea (salt) water into fresh water. A steam plant also needs a supply of fuel to provide the heat in the boilers, and this must be carried in fuel tanks on board—much as an automobile has a gas tank—and periodically replenished (either in port or from oilers at sea).

NUCLEAR POWER

Nuclear power is a very specialized form of steam propulsion. Instead of using oil-fired boilers, nuclear-powered ships have a reactor that produces the heat to convert freshwater to steam. Nuclear power plants give a ship the advantage of great endurance at high speed. Instead of refueling every few thousand miles like an oil-burning ship, a nuclear-powered ship can operate for years on one reactor core. Because there is no need to replenish oil, nuclear-powered ships can steam almost indefinitely, limited only by their need to replenish food and spare parts, and ammunition in wartime.

Another favorable feature of nuclear power is that, unlike conventional oil-fired systems, the generation of nuclear power does not require oxygen. This makes it particularly useful as a means of submarine propulsion, allowing the vessel to operate completely submerged for extended periods of time.

GAS TURBINES

Gas turbines are very similar to aircraft jet engines, but have been adapted for use on ships. The burning fuel spins turbines in the engines that convert the energy created by the burning fuel into usable power that turns the ship's propellers.

Although some of the principles are the same, some of the primary differences between these propulsion plants and those that use steam are that the gas turbines combine the functions of the boiler and the turbines into one element and gas turbines have no need of feedwater. This means that they are smaller, more efficient, and easier to maintain. They are also much more quickly "brought on the line" (turned on). A steam-powered vessel requires hours to prepare to get under way, while gas-turbine-powered ships can be ready in minutes.

The obvious advantages of gas-turbine technology have caused the U.S. Navy to build more and more of these ships. Whereas steam was once the main means of naval propulsion, today there are more gas-turbine ships in the Navy than ships with any other kind of propulsion.

DIESEL ENGINES

For relatively small ships that need no more than 5,000 to 6,000 horsepower, diesel engines are frequently used. Diesels take up less space and are more efficient than steam turbines. The diesel can be coupled directly to the shaft through reduction gears and perhaps a clutch, or it can drive a generator that produces current for the main drive.

Diesel engines are preferred over gasoline engines because highly volatile gasoline fumes are heavier than air and tend to collect in low places in a ship, making them very dangerous. Diesel fuel, which does not vaporize as readily, is much safer.

[**10.3**] A gas turbine systems technician
working on one of the ship's gas turbines

PROPELLERS

A vital component of a ship's propulsion system is the propeller(s). Some
ships have only one, others have two or more (an aircraft carrier has four
giant propellers). Another term you will hear when referring to ships' propellers is "screw."

Propeller shafts carry the power generated by the propulsion plant
to the propellers. In many ships, shafts run from a set of reduction gears
(which change the high-speed spin of the turbines into a more suitable
speed for the propellers) through long watertight spaces, called shaft alleys,
in the bottom of the ship. These shafts go out through the hull using special
watertight sleeves and are often supported outside the hull by struts. More
recent technology eliminates the use of reduction gears by using the energy
generated by gas turbines to drive electric motors that turn the propellers.

Propellers on some ships are fixed while others are of the controllable-
pitch type. Fixed propellers are solid in their construction and change
speed by speeding up or slowing down the spin of the whole propeller.

[**10.4**] A rare look at a destroyer's propellers

Controllable-pitch propellers, on the other hand, pivot their individual blades in such a way as to change the amount of thrust they create and thereby control the speed. For a fixed-type propeller to back down (go in reverse), it must be slowed down, stopped, and then spun in the opposite direction. A controllable-pitch propeller need only change the pitch sufficiently to reverse the thrust. For this reason, the latter type of propeller is much more common in modern naval ships.

BOW AND STERN THRUSTERS

Although technically not a part of the ship's propulsion system, some modern vessels have small thrusters mounted at appropriate points on the hull to assist in docking the ship. Usually mounted at or near the bow, these small propulsion units can be turned on to exert an additional force, usually sideways, on the ship's hull to move the bow in a desired direction. This can be very useful when trying to move a ship alongside a pier when coming into port or to move away from a pier when getting under way. These thrusters can be used for *very slow* propulsion in an emergency situation. Some vessels also have stern thrusters that essentially do the same for the after part of the ship.

The Steering System

The basic component of nearly every ship's or boat's steering system is the *rudder*. The simplest rudder design is a flat board or blade that extends into the water beneath the vessel's stern. When it is turned one way or the other while the vessel is moving, flowing water builds up on the front side and pushes the stern of the vessel in the opposite direction. Because the rudder acts by the force of water pushing against one side of it, there is no rudder action when the ship is motionless. And the greater the speed of the vessel through the water, the greater the effect the rudders have. For this reason, the rudder is usually mounted just astern of the screws, where the wash created by the moving propeller pushes directly against it and increases the turning effect.

The rudder is controlled by a *tiller* in an open boat (such as a motor whaleboat or motor launch) or by a wheel in the cockpit of a larger boat or on the bridge of a ship. This wheel is often called a *helm* on a ship. In a boat, the motion of the wheel is transmitted to the rudder by a cable or shaft. In a ship, the rudder is turned by an electric or steam engine in the steering-engine room. This electrical or hydraulic engine is controlled by the helm on the bridge. When the helm is turned on the bridge, it transmits a signal to the steering engine, which then moves the rudder.

Ships can have more than one rudder, but in the case of multiple rudders they do not act independently but are controlled together.

To prevent loss of control in case of damage to the bridge, there is usually a second steering wheel mounted elsewhere in the ship. This backup control station is called *secondary conn*. If that wheel is also disabled, the ship can be hand-steered by several Sailors using special gear in the steering-engine room. There is also a duplicate set of steering engines and connecting cables on naval vessels to serve as backup in the event of damage.

Ships or boats with two screws can be steered fairly well without a rudder by using the engines. If one screw turns faster than the other, the bow will swing toward the slower screw. If one screw goes ahead while the other goes astern, the bow of the ship will swing toward the backing screw. Boats, and even very large ships, can turn within the diameter of their own lengths using this method, which is appropriately called "twisting."

Mooring Systems

When ships are not under way, they must be secured in some way to keep them in place. A ship is *moored* when she is held in position by an anchor on the ocean bottom or is made fast either to a mooring buoy or a pier. To moor to a pier, a ship uses her *mooring lines*. To anchor or to moor to a special mooring buoy, the ship uses her *ground tackle* (such as anchors, anchor chains, or windlasses). Ground tackle is normally located on the forecastle, but some ships, particularly amphibious craft that run up onto beaches, may also carry a stern anchor, used to help pull them back off the beach when it is time to return to sea.

Electrical System

For ages, ships functioned without electricity, and for many years electrical power provided only a few important services, such as lights and a few motor-driven appliances. But today's modern ship uses an incredible amount of electrical power to carry out a wide array of functions. A modern ship depends upon its electrical power system to do many things, including powering complex weapon and communications systems, computing the solutions to a vast spectrum of tactical problems, powering ammunition hoists and aircraft elevators, detecting incoming enemy missiles and aircraft, providing lighting and temperature control, and running in-house television systems for entertainment. These and hundreds of other functions make electricity as vital to a modern warship as ropes were to a sailing vessel.

Ships generate their own electricity and all have backup systems to provide power when the primary system fails. Vital electrical circuits are also frequently duplicated so that power can continue to flow after battle damage occurs.

Ventilation System

This system supplies fresh air where it is needed and carries off unwanted exhaust. This system is made up of many subsystems that operate independently of each other.

Supply ventilation brings fresh, external air into the ship and, in the event of cold weather, heats the air by means of a preheater installed in the ducting. Exhaust ventilation carries away the air that has served its purpose and needs to be replaced. In those spaces containing equipment that generates heat or humidity (such as main engineering spaces, galley, or head facilities), the exhaust system is particularly vital. *"Recirc" ventilation* is provided to spaces containing electronic equipment (which requires a cool environment for proper operation), as well as to berthing, messing, and office spaces. As its name implies, this system recirculates internal air to prevent stagnation and, when necessary, draws the air through a cooling system to maintain the proper temperature.

In the event of fire, flooding, or some other danger requiring the isolation of a space or spaces, ventilation systems can be secured by de-energizing the fan motor and can be segregated by closing valvelike devices in the ducting (often found where the ducting penetrates decks, overheads, and bulkheads).

Potable Water System

Water for drinking, showering, and cooking is provided by the potable water system. Potable water is made in the ship's distilling units (evaporators) from saltwater taken from the sea and stowed in tanks specifically designated for potable water only. Piping systems carry the water from the tanks to the heads, galleys, and drinking fountains (scuttlebutts) for use.

Because the evaporators can only make so much water at a time, care must be exercised not to waste freshwater while a ship is under way or at anchor. You should never take what is popularly called a "Hollywood shower" while at sea. (This is the kind of shower you probably take at home, where you let the water run for as long as you are in the shower without giving any thought to water conservation.) While at sea, it is important to get in the habit of wetting down (quickly), turning the water off and leaving it off while you soap and scrub, and then turning the water on again just long enough to rinse off.

When moored to a pier where the appropriate connections are available, the ship's potable water system can be hooked up to receive freshwater. At these times, abundant freshwater is available so that the strict water conservation practices you use at sea are not necessary. The ship's potable water tanks will all be topped off (filled to capacity) before the ship gets under way.

Saltwater System

Saltwater is drawn out of the sea through underwater intakes and pumped throughout the ship using a different piping system from the one used for potable water. This water is available for firefighting when needed and is used on a routine basis as flushing water for the heads. It also is used as cooling water for certain items of machinery and electronic equipment and can be piped into tanks for ballast to stabilize the ship. Special sprinkler heads mounted all over the outside of the ship can be opened to allow a washdown of the ship to rid her of contaminants in the event of a chemical, biological, or radiological (CBR) attack.

Drainage System

The drainage system includes the piping, valves, and pumps that discharge water from the ship. Its functions include the removal of seawater that has entered the hull because of damage, collision, or heavy weather.

The main drainage system is composed of large piping located in the main engineering spaces and used for pumping their bilges (the lowest parts of the ship's hull where water collects). The secondary drainage system is composed of smaller piping located in other spaces, such as pump rooms and shaft alleys.

The main and secondary drainage systems are often coupled with the saltwater system to maintain the proper trim of the ship.

Since weather-deck drains collect natural rain and seawater, the drains connected to these areas are piped directly overboard. But internal drains (from sinks, showers, galleys, toilets, and urinals) are carefully controlled for environmental reasons. Drainage from these sources is collected in specially designed tanks for appropriate disposal.

Fuel System

This system includes fuel-stowage tanks, pumps, filling lines, transfer lines, and feed lines to the ship's boilers or engines. Like the other liquid systems aboard ship (potable water, saltwater, and drainage), the fuel system is also constantly monitored and fuel is moved about to help maintain proper trim.

Compressed Air System

Ships use compressed air for a number of purposes. Ejecting gases from guns after they have fired is one important use of this system. Compressed air is also used for charging torpedoes, operating pneumatic tools, running messages through dispatch tubes, powering automatic boiler controls, and various other uses. Compressors create the compressed air and special piping carries it where it is needed in the ship.

SPECIALIZED SPACES

Just as a building has specialized rooms or areas, such as the lobby, parking garage, heating plant, or boardroom, ships have special spaces with distinct purposes necessary to the operation or utility of the ship. Some ships have very special areas—such as Primary Air Control on an aircraft carrier—not found on all ships, but other special areas are found on most naval ships.

The Bridge

This is the primary control position for the ship when she is under way and the place where all orders and commands affecting the ship's movements and her routine originate. The captain will be on the bridge a lot of the time under way—especially during most special sea evolutions (such as refueling and rearming) and when the ship is entering and leaving port—but obviously cannot be there twenty-four hours a day. The *officer of the deck* (OOD)—a rotating watch position manned only by highly qualified personnel—is the captain's primary assistant in charge of safely running the ship, and is always on the bridge when the ship is under way.

There are various instruments and equipment on the bridge used to control the movements of the ship. The ship's helm and engine controls are located here, as well as radar repeaters, navigation light switches, wind indicators, radios, speed indicators, and compasses.

The bridge is sometimes referred to as the *pilot house.*

The Chart House

The chart house is normally just aft of the pilot house and on the same deck, but it can also be on another deck and some distance away. This is where the navigator and his or her team of quartermasters do much of their work. Using navigational equipment and instruments such as sextants, stadimeters, bearing circles, stopwatches, parallel rulers, dividers, protractors, position plotters, electronic devices, and navigational books and tables, the navigational team keeps a constant plot of the ship's position (location) at any given moment and a plan of where the ship is going.

Signal Bridge

This is an open platform located near (often just above) the navigational bridge and equipped with devices used to communicate visually, such as

[10.5] The bridge is the primary control position for a ship when she is under way.

signal searchlights and signal flags. The signal lights allow ships to communicate with one another by flashing the lights on and off in Morse code. The signal flags are kept in a specially designed stowage locker, known as a *flag bag*, which allows quick access to the flags. The lower ends of the halyards, on which signal flags are hoisted, are secured here so that the signalmen can quickly attach flags from the flag bag and hoist them into the air where other ships can see them.

Combat Information Center (CIC)

The combat information center is the nerve center of the ship. A lot of electronic equipment is installed in the CIC to process information received from a wide variety of sources, including radio, radar, sonar, electronic-warfare intercept receivers, IFF (identification friend or foe) transponders, visual communications, satellites, fathometers (depth gauges), and computers. All of this information is collected, processed, displayed, evaluated, and sent to other parts of the ship (or to other ships) for use in decision making and in properly employing the ship. CIC is the place where the ship's tactical operations are controlled. Such operations include the evaluation of targets, weapons firing, the control of friendly aircraft, surveillance operations, navigational assistance, submarine tracking, and many others.

Damage Control Central (DCC)

Damage Control Central serves as the central information site for matters affecting the safety of the ship. By monitoring conditions aboard ship and maintaining control of vital systems such as those used in firefighting and flooding control, and by maintaining careful records, damage-control charts, and liquid-loading diagrams, DCC sees that the ship is functioning efficiently and is prepared for any emergency conditions that may arise.

Storerooms

A ship cannot operate at sea for extended periods of time unless it has adequate stowage for consumable supplies and spare parts. These areas are known as storerooms. Some of these stowage areas are specially configured for a specific type of material.

Magazines

Magazines are used for the stowage of missiles, rockets, bombs, torpedoes, and gun ammunition. For obvious reasons, these important but potentially dangerous areas aboard ship are kept locked and under close control. They also are protected by various alarm and firefighting systems and are usually located in spaces well below the waterline so that, in case of fire, they can be quickly flooded.

Crew Accommodations

The living spaces aboard ship are essential to accommodate the needs of the crew. *Berthing* (sleeping) *compartments*, *heads* (bathrooms), *wardrooms* (living and dining areas for officers), officers' *cabins* (or *staterooms*), *galleys* (kitchens), *messes* (where enlisted personnel eat), laundries, barbershops, and *sick bay* (medical clinic) are all living areas necessary for the daily routine of the men and women who live aboard ship. Larger ships may have other spaces for the health and comfort of the crew, such as tailor shops, libraries, chapels, weight/aerobic rooms, and crew lounges. Virtually all ships have a *ship's store* where you can purchase toiletries, uniform items, *gedunk* (snacks), and—depending upon the size of the ship and its store—a variety of other items. An added benefit of using your ship's store is that the profits go to the ship's Morale, Welfare, and Recreation (MWR) fund.

Shops and Offices

Shops and offices can be found on virtually every Navy ship. The number of each depends upon the size and the purpose of the ship. An aircraft carrier will have hundreds. A patrol craft may have only one or two.

Most Navy ships will have at least an electrical shop and perhaps a machine shop as well. A tender, whose mission is maintenance and repair, will have many shops, including ones that do repairs and specialty work, such as instrument calibration, printing, photography, torpedo overhauls, and pump refurbishment. An aircraft carrier will have a large specialized repair facility called the aircraft intermediate maintenance department (AIMD), which performs a wide variety of maintenance functions to keep aircraft flying while the ship is at sea.

The captain and executive officer will probably have their own offices (or, on smaller ships, they will be combined into one, called the *ship's office*). On ships with adequate room, individual departments and divisions will have their own offices.

NAVAL SHIP AND SUBMARINE TYPES

The U.S. Navy operates hundreds of ships. Some of these are active ships, which means they are operational, ready to carry out missions, have a full complement of personnel and, unless they are temporarily undergoing heavy maintenance or repair, are fully capable of carrying out an assigned mission on short notice. The Navy also keeps a number of vessels in reserve status, which means that they are partially manned with active-duty personnel. The rest of the crew is made up of reserve personnel, who only man the ships periodically for training and when called upon in a national emergency.

The many different types of vessels in the Navy have specific functions. Some exist primarily to engage in combat with enemy forces (other vessels, aircraft, or land targets) and are generally referred to as *combatants*. These include aircraft carriers, cruisers, destroyers, frigates, littoral combat ships, amphibious ships, and patrol craft. Submarines are combatants but are often treated as a separate category from surface combatants because of their differences.

Considered part of the Navy's expeditionary forces, *amphibious ships* are often unofficially referred to as the "amphibs" or "gators." These ships work mainly where sea and land meet, and where assault landings are carried out by Navy–Marine Corps teams. Such operations call for a variety of types of ships. Many are *transports* of varied designs, used to sealift Marines and their equipment from bases to landing beaches. The differences lie in ship design and the way troops and their gear are moved from ship to shore, which can be done by means of landing craft, helicopters, tilt-wing aircraft, or tracked amphibious vehicles.

Other ships, called *auxiliaries*, exist to perform supporting functions, such as repairs, salvage operations, delivery of supplies (such as fuel, ammunition, food, and repair parts) needed to keep a ship operating, service as floating hospitals, and so on.

The Navy also operates a number of transport and auxiliary ships under what is called the Military Sealift Command (MSC). These ships usually have only a very small contingent of Navy personnel on board, and the majority of the crews are civilians. MSC ships have a support role and are not used as frontline combatants. They are considered to be "in service" rather than "in commission." Some ships, such as "roll-on, roll-off" vehicle cargo ships (T-AKRs) and transport oilers (T-AOTs) serve the Army and Air Force as well as the Navy.

Other MSC ships perform special-duty projects, such as laying and repairing of ocean-bottom cables used for detecting enemy submarines. Surveying ships (T-AGSs) and oceanographic research ships (T-AGORs) explore the oceans.

Of special interest is a group of various MSC ships of the Combat Logistics Force (CLF). As with other MSC ships, they have civilian officers and crews. They operate under Navy orders and have a military department of Navy personnel aboard, performing visual and radio communications and otherwise assisting the ship's civilian master and crew in operations with other naval units. These vessels include a variety of replenishment ships, fleet ocean tugs, and several specialized mission types that directly support the Navy by providing fuel, ammunition, stores, towing services, etc.

The various types of Navy ships currently in service are described in TAB 10-A: Ships and Craft.

Ship Identification

Most Navy ships have both a name and what we call a ship's *designation* to identify them. While the name is a convenient and traditional means of identification, there have been Navy ships bearing the same name throughout history, so the ship's designation—which is unique to that ship—is the only way to identify a specific ship. The ship's designation tells what type the ship is (such as destroyer, submarine, or cruiser) and assigns a unique *hull number* to the vessel.

Ships are also grouped into *classes* to identify those with identical, or nearly identical, characteristics.

NAME

The name is unique to a ship in that there can only be one Navy ship in commission at a time with a given name. But, as already mentioned, there may have been other ships with the same name in the past—in fact, it is fairly common practice in the Navy for ships to carry the name of an earlier ship that served with honor. For example, there have been eight U.S. Navy ships named "Enterprise." (*Note*: This count does not include the starship *Enterprise* of Star Trek fame, but the creator of the hit television and movie series, Gene Roddenberry, recognized the long tradition of passing on ship names and carried it on in his futuristic vision.)

The name of a Navy ship in commission (active or reserve) is preceded by the letters "USS," which stands for "United States Ship," for example, USS *Enterprise*. This practice began in 1907 when President (and former Assistant Secretary of the Navy) Theodore Roosevelt issued an executive order establishing this standard, so when you read about Navy ships before 1907 you may find them referred to differently.

MSC ships are considered to be "in service" rather than "in commission," and for this reason their names are preceded by the letters "USNS" (for United States Naval Ship) instead of "USS."

Sailors have traditionally (and unofficially) added nicknames to their seagoing homes. Some of these nicknames apply generally to the type, such as "flat tops" or "bird farms" for aircraft carriers and "tin cans" for destroyers. Specific ships also often have unofficial nicknames; among aircraft carriers, for instance, USS *Theodore Roosevelt* is known informally as the

"Big Stick" (referring to the president's famous quote "Speak softly but carry a big stick") and USS *Dwight D. Eisenhower* is "Ike" because that was the former president's nickname.

DESIGNATION

While a ship's name gives her some identity, the ship's designation—which consists of a combination of letters and numbers—tells you two additional things about a ship: her type and her place in the construction sequence. USS *Abraham Lincoln*, for instance, has the designation "CVN 72." CVN is her type classification, CV standing for aircraft carrier and N meaning nuclear propulsion; 72 indicates that she is the 72nd aircraft carrier authorized for construction. The term "hull number" actually refers only to the number part of the ship's designation, but you will commonly hear this term used instead of "ship's designation," as in "The ship's hull number is CVN 72." Ships' hull numbers are frequently painted on their bows and near the stern. Aircraft carriers have their hull numbers painted on the forward part of the flight deck and on the "island" (superstructure).

Since 1920 the Navy has used letter symbols to identify the types of ships and service craft, such as "DDG" for guided-missile destroyer and "CG" for guided-missile cruiser. This is called "type classification" and is used as part of the ship's designation. These may seem illogical at first (like "CV" for aircraft carrier) but as you become more familiar with these classifications, some patterns will emerge that will make some sense to you. See TAB 10-B: Ship Type Classifications for a list of some of the more common ones that you may encounter.

CLASS

Within a type classification of ships there are classes. Ships belonging to a particular class are built from the same plans and are very much alike; in many cases, they are identical except for the different hull number painted on their bows. The first ship built of a class determines the name of the class. For example, after World War II the United States redesigned its aircraft carriers to accommodate the newly invented jet aircraft then entering the fleet. The first of these new aircraft carriers to be built was commissioned as USS *Forrestal* (CV 59). She was the fifty-ninth aircraft carrier, but the first of this new class. Satisfied with these new ships, the Navy built three more—USS *Saratoga* (CV 60), USS *Ranger* (CV 61), and USS *Independence* (CV 62)—all of which are referred to as *Forrestal*-class carriers.

Later, some major improvements were deemed necessary, so the Navy redesigned its aircraft carriers significantly enough that they were considered a new class of carrier. The first of these new and different carriers was named USS *Kitty Hawk* (CV 63), so the next ship built after her, USS *Constellation* (CV 64), was considered a *Kitty Hawk*–class aircraft carrier. Some classes have only a few ships and others have hundreds.

As indicated in the beginning of this chapter, even though the Navy has evolved into a complex organization with various missions and many different kinds of equipment to accomplish them, ships are the core element of the Navy. Even imagined space travel and galactic conflict, such as in *Star Trek* and *Star Wars*, usually rely on space*ships* as the technological centerpiece. It should come as no surprise that this basic element is so embedded into Navy culture that even at shore installations floors are often referred to as decks, ceilings as overheads, etc. This is a source of pride that Sailors, Marines, and Coast Guardsmen emulate even though it often confuses and amuses civilians and those who serve in non-sea services.

ELEVEN

SHIPBOARD LIFE

As a Sailor in the U.S. Navy, you will more than likely serve aboard ship. In previous chapters, you have learned some things about shipboard organization and routine. You know, for example, that each day's events are listed in the Plan of the Day (POD). You have learned that there are certain rituals regarding the national ensign and that ships have a commanding officer we traditionally call "Captain," a second in command whose title is executive officer or XO. You know that each ship is organized into a variety of departments and divisions. In this chapter, you will learn more about the routine and the not-so-routine aspects of shipboard life.

STANDARD ORGANIZATION AND REGULATIONS OF THE U.S. NAVY (SORM)

If you had to learn a new set of regulations and an entirely different organization every time you moved from one division, department, or ship to another, you would waste a great deal of time and probably become very confused and not very efficient. The Navy has standardized everything—routine, regulations, and organization—as much as possible on all ships, so that transferring from one to another will require only minor adjustments on your part. The basis for this standardization is the current edition of the *Standard Organization and Regulations of the U.S. Navy* (OPNAVINST 3120.32), also known as the *Standard Organization and Regulations Manual*, and frequently referred to as "the SORM." Your daily and weekly routine aboard ship will be governed by this book, no matter which ship you might serve in. Your division and department will be organized in accordance with this manual, and the ship's governing regulations and instructions will have been drawn up using it as well, most likely giving it a ship's instruction number, such as "NEVERSINKINST 3120.32." Anytime you are assigned to a different ship, you should be sure to familiarize yourself with that ship's SORM.

Chapters in the SORM are as follows:

1. Unit Administration
2. Standard Unit Organization
3. Roles and Responsibilities
4. Watch Organization
5. General Guidance and Regulations
6. Unit Bills
7. Safety
8. Training
9. Ship Maintenance and Modernization
10. Unit Directives System
Appendix A. Acronyms

These chapters are discussed here and in other parts of *The Bluejacket's Manual*, but you would do well to periodically review the SORM itself to be sure you are properly informed and in compliance with this important publication. Copies will be available at your command and/or online.

General Guidance and Regulations

Chapter 5 of the SORM, entitled "General Guidance and Regulations," spells out those regulations that are common to all Navy ships, most of which will apply directly to you. For example, it contains rules concerning the proper operation of the ship's general announcing system (1MC), telling you that you must never use the 1MC without permission from the OOD. In chapter 5, you will also find that

- Alcohol must never be consumed aboard a Navy ship except when authorized for medicinal purposes.
- Wearing shoes while in a berth (bed) is forbidden.
- Gambling is illegal.

- Nothing is to be sold aboard ship except in the ship's store.
- Any electrical appliances brought on board must be approved by the ship's electrical officer.
- Freshwater must be conserved.
- Government property may not be removed from the ship without permission.
- Any communicable disease you have (or think you have) must be reported.
- Intoxication may lead to restraint.
- Red lights are the only lights authorized in certain areas at night (to preserve night vision for watchstanders).
- Cups, silverware, and other dining items must not be removed from the mess decks.
- Ship's parties and other social events or celebrations must not glorify or encourage the consumption of alcohol, include sexually suggestive activities, or show disrespect to religious beliefs.
- Frayed, torn, dirty, or otherwise mutilated clothing is prohibited.
- Paint and other flammable substances must be properly stowed.
- Pets are not allowed without permission of the commanding officer.
- Nothing should be thrown overboard without permission.
- Swimming over the side of the ship is not permitted without permission from the commanding officer.
- Personal mail may be subject to censorship for security reasons.
- Specific routes must be followed when going to general quarters stations. If you must go forward or up, do it on the starboard side of the ship; use the port side to go aft or down.

There are more regulations discussed in chapter 5. Because you will be held accountable for all applicable ones, you should make certain that you read and understand them.

Unit Bills

Chapter 6 of the SORM describes the various bills used to ensure that the required stations are manned for all important evolutions. Once these bills are set up on your ship, they tell you where you are supposed to be and what your duties will be for a given evolution. For example, the man overboard bill tells you where you are supposed to go and what you are supposed to do if anyone falls off the ship. If your ship is headed for some bad weather, the heavy weather bill explains who does what in order to prepare. Quite a few bills are listed and explained in chapter 6 to cover virtually every contingency, but not all of them apply to every type of ship. The unit bills covered in chapter 6 may be used as written or may be used as a guide in writing bills tailored for a specific ship.

The bills in chapter 6 are grouped according to the function they provide and are included as administrative, operational, emergency, or special.

ADMINISTRATIVE BILLS

Included in this group are the bills that take care of routine functions in the daily administration of the ship. Some of the bills found in this section are listed below.

Berthing and Locker Bill. This bill ensures that you and all your fellow crewmembers have a place to sleep and to stow your clothing and other personal effects.

Cleaning, Preservation, and Maintenance Bill. Procedures for cleaning and preservation (such as painting and lubricating) are provided so that department heads and division officers can make the appropriate personnel assignments.

Formation and Parade Bill. Identifies the areas of the ship to be used for various formations, such as morning quarters, personnel inspection, quarters for entering and leaving port, and ceremonial manning of the rail. Both fair- and foul-weather plans must be drawn up for many of these evolutions.

General Visiting Bill. Used to specify procedures for controlling visitors to the ship, ensuring adequate security for the ship and safety of the visitors.

Orientation Bill. Designed to provide an indoctrination program for newly reporting personnel, this bill calls for briefings and counseling on the ship's history, mission, organizations, regulations, routine, current operating schedule, and a variety of other topics.

Zone Inspection Bill. Under the guidance of this bill, the ship is divided into zones small enough to allow an experienced officer to conduct a thorough inspection in a reasonable amount of time. Zone inspections are conducted at least quarterly, and each zone has a senior officer (ideally a department head) assigned on a rotational basis to ensure a fresh look at the zone each time.

Other administrative bills include the official correspondence and classified material control bill, the personnel assignment bill, the personnel recall bill, and several types of security bills.

OPERATIONAL BILLS

These bills cover a wide variety of operations that a ship may conduct as part of its mission, such as operating the ship's boats, launching and recovering aircraft, fueling helicopters while they are hovering above your ship, collecting intelligence, defending the ship against attack while it is in port, preparing for heavy weather, operating in extreme cold, navigating under various circumstances, replenishing supplies while under way, rescuing individuals or other vessels in distress, putting divers in the water, performing salvage operations, and towing other vessels. Some of the other operational bills of special interest are discussed below.

Darken Ship Bill. When ships steam at night all unnecessary lights that can be seen outside the ship must be extinguished for navigational safety and to avoid enemy detection in war. When darken ship is set, the word will be passed over the 1MC to "set darken ship," and all topside doors and hatches must be closed and all ports blacked out. To perform efficiently during darken ship, you must be able to find your way around the ship's topside in complete darkness and know how to open and close doors, plug in telephones, locate switches, and handle all other equipment at your underway and general-quarters stations. During darken ship, only flashlights or hand lanterns with red lens covers can be used topside, and only when absolutely necessary.

Dry-Docking Bill. On occasion, ships need to come out of the water for major repairs to their hull, rudder, propellers, or other underwater fixtures. This is accomplished by putting the ship into a special dock that can be pumped dry, leaving the ship perched on special blocks so that workers can get to her underside. This is obviously a delicate operation that must be accomplished without error. The ship's dry-docking bill establishes the procedures and ensures that all personnel involved know what needs to be done.

EMCON Bill. Enemy forces with the right kind of equipment can locate your ship by picking up and homing in on the ship's emitters (equipment that puts electronic signals into the air, such as radar and radio). To counter this, the ship will have an emission control (EMCON) bill, which will ensure that the ship's emitters are turned off or very tightly controlled when the threat of enemy detection is a concern.

Equipment Tag-Out Bill. Common sense dictates that you must turn off the power before you work on a piece of electrical or electronic equipment, but aboard ship the power cutoff switch may be located some distance from the equipment it serves. The same is true for steam lines, fluid lines, and other potentially dangerous systems found aboard modern ships. Sometimes, for safety reasons, it is essential to turn off equipment you are not even working on; for example, if you are going up on the mast to change the bulb of the ship's masthead light, it is vital to turn off the radars and transmitting radio antennas to keep you from being harmed by them. The last thing you want to happen is for someone to turn on a piece of equipment accidentally or open a valve that presents a hazard to you. To prevent such accidents, ships employ equipment tag-out procedures, which involve labeling all secured components, making periodic announcements over the ship's general announcing (1MC) system, and ensuring interdepartmental coordination and cooperation.

Special Sea and Anchor Detail Bill. When ships get under way or return from sea, many more people must man stations and perform tasks not necessary during routine steaming. For example, the ship's anchors must be manned (either actually to anchor the ship or to be ready in case of an emergency) whenever the ship enters shallow water. This bill provides the organization necessary to ensure that the ship is properly manned and ready for safe navigation when entering or leaving port.

EMERGENCY BILLS

The nature of life at sea and the dangers encountered in wartime create the need for advance preparation for a wide variety of emergencies. The emergencies covered in this section of chapter 6 of OPNAVINST 3120.32 include aircraft crash and rescue, man overboard, nuclear-reactor casualties, nuclear-weapon accidents, and encounters with toxic gas.

Jettison Bill. Used when the ship's stability is threatened and can only be improved by throwing overboard (jettisoning) heavy items, particularly those located high in the ship. For example, a fire, collision, or some other disaster on an aircraft carrier may result in the ship taking on large quantities of water, which threatens stability. By throwing aircraft and flight-deck tractors off the flight deck the situation can be improved.

Emergency Steering Bill. Because steering is so vital to a ship, the crew must be able to improvise with emergency steering measures when the time comes. The emergency steering bill sets up the procedures for contending with this emergency.

SPECIAL BILLS
Several bills that do not fit into the other categories are listed as special bills.

Antisneak/Antiswimmer Attack Bill. When ships are in foreign ports, it is prudent to defend against sneak attacks. Because ships are particularly vulnerable to underwater attack by swimmers, extra measures of security must be employed to prevent such attacks.

Evacuating Civilians Bill. Crisis situations such as foreign wars or natural disasters sometimes require civilians to be evacuated. Because U.S. Navy ships are deployed to many parts of the world, they are often the most efficient means of carrying out evacuations. This bill provides the guidance for preparing for such a contingency.

Prisoners of War Bill. Should your ship be involved with the taking or transport of enemy prisoners of war, this bill establishes the procedures required in this situation.

Strip Ship Bill. During battle, many items found aboard ship during peacetime conditions can become very hazardous. Certain flammable materials in particular may be perfectly safe for shipboard use during normal conditions, but under combat conditions greatly enhance the ship's chances of sustaining lethal damage. The strip ship bill establishes procedures for removing these items in a methodical and logical manner.

Troop Lift Bill. Should your ship be required to transport troops from one place to another, this bill will help your ship properly organize for the task.

WATCH, QUARTER, AND STATION BILL

Most significant of all the bills found in your ship is the watch, quarter, and station (WQ&S) bill. This bill is prepared by your division officer and summarizes the personnel assignments within the division, based upon the other unit bills and the actual people assigned to the division. You should know where this bill is posted and be familiar with those parts that apply to you. Your name will actually appear on this bill, and it will list your responsibilities under various conditions.

Some ships are equipped with computer-generated systems that automate the WQ&S functions, while others continue to use the old WQ&S manual system, which uses a bulletin board–size chart to list all the required stations and the people who are assigned to them.

By referring to the WQ&S bill, you will see your bunk and locker number, your cleaning station, your in-port and at-sea watch assignments, your assignments during special situations covered by other unit bills (such as fire, collision, or rescue and assistance) and what you are supposed to do during various readiness conditions (explained below).

SHIPBOARD ROUTINE DUTIES

As you have probably gathered from the previous discussion, life aboard ship has many different aspects. Some days you may be taking part in evolutions such as entering and leaving port, refueling, receiving a helicopter, providing gunfire support, rescuing victims of some natural disaster, or any number of other activities that Navy ships take part in around the world. At other times, your day may include more routine (but important) functions, such as cleaning or performing upkeep maintenance or repairs.

Cleaning

The most basic form of preventive maintenance is cleaning. It is also among the least glamorous of the many duties you will perform while living aboard ship, but this function is just as vital as anything you will do. You may have heard the term "shipshape" used to describe something that is clean and well organized; this term did not come into the English language by accident. A dirty or improperly maintained ship will not function at peak efficiency and will create psychological as well as material problems that can mean the difference between victory and defeat when the time comes for the crew to perform under difficult circumstances.

Ships, by their very nature, cannot hire out to professional cleaning services, nor can they afford the luxury of having cleaning specialists in the crew whose only function is to do the cleaning. Therefore, the responsibility for cleanliness falls upon the crew, and these duties must be carried out in addition to other responsibilities that come with being a Sailor aboard ship.

As already discussed, the WQ&S bill will include your routine cleaning assignments so that you will know what your responsibilities are in this area. This does not mean that what is listed in the WQ&S will be your only cleaning assignments. You may be given additional assignments from time to time by crewmembers senior to you.

SWEEPERS

One of the routine evolutions you will likely encounter aboard ship is "sweepers." Shortly after reveille, at the end of the regular working day, and at other times as necessary, the word is passed on the ship's 1MC for sweepers. At these times, all men and women assigned as sweepers draw their gear, sweep and swab (mop) their assigned areas, and empty trash receptacles. If you are assigned as a sweeper or are placed in charge of a sweeper detail, make certain that trash and dirt are always picked up in a dustpan, never just swept over the side. Besides the potential environmental impact, sweeping dirt and trash over the side may result in the wind blowing it back on board, or it may stick to the side, giving the ship an unsightly appearance.

COMPARTMENT RESPONSIBILITY

Every compartment on a ship is assigned to a particular division for cleaning and maintenance responsibilities. While the members of the responsible division will be aware which spaces have been assigned to them, it is important to have some means to find out which division is responsible for a given space. On an aircraft carrier, for example, there are hundreds of compartments, and the executive officer may not be able to remember who is responsible for every space, but in his or her travels about the ship he or she may be disappointed in the condition of one of the passageways.

You may be going from one deck to another through a ladder well and notice that the nonskid surface is peeling up on one of the ladder rungs, creating a safety hazard. The carrier XO and you need an efficient system for finding the responsible division.

This basic but important need is met by compartment responsibility marking, commonly called a "Bullseye" as explained in TAB 11-A: Shipboard Compartment Identification. The last line on the Bullseye tells you which division is responsible for the space.

In addition to the Bullseye, each compartment has its own "Compartment Check-off List (CCOL)." This is a quick-reference checklist that lists the various damage control fittings such as watertight doors and firemain connections as well as ventilation ducts, fluid system components, and electrical components. This can be an invaluable source of information for routine maintenance as well as for emergency conditions.

If you are assigned duty as a berthing-compartment cleaner, you will be responsible for keeping the compartment scrupulously clean. This is extremely important, because the close living conditions aboard ship make cleanliness not only desirable but absolutely essential. Few things can affect the combat effectiveness of a unit more than the spread of communicable disease, and unpleasant living conditions can have serious effects upon morale.

Compartment decks are often covered with various substances for a variety of reasons. For example, nonskid materials are often applied to decks or ladder steps to prevent slipping, and decks near electronic equipment are frequently covered with special rubber matting to minimize the hazard of electrical shock.

You will frequently encounter tile on decks inside the skin of the ship. The tile used in the Navy is more resilient and presents fewer hazards than many forms you may have encountered in other walks of life (pun not intended). Tile-covered decks are maintained by sweeping loose dirt daily and wiping away spills as soon as possible. Frequent clamp-downs (cleaning with a wet swab) are important to prevent the buildup of unwanted substances. After a clamp-down, allowing the deck to dry and then buffing it with an electric buffing machine will improve the deck's appearance. For a more thorough cleaning when the deck is unusually dirty, apply a solution of warm water and detergent with a stiff bristle brush or circular scrubbing machine. Use water sparingly. Wet the deck with the cleaning solution, but do not flood it. Remove the soiled solution with a swab and rinse with clean water to remove residual detergent. Stubborn dirt and black marks left by shoes can be removed by rubbing lightly with a scouring pad or fine steel wool, or a rag moistened with mineral spirits.

Waxing will greatly improve the appearance of a tiled deck, but it should not be done to excess and should not be done when the ship is going out to sea or when heavy weather is anticipated. This is an added precaution against slipping, even though approved emulsion floor waxes are designed to be slip-resistant.

When rubber matting needs cleaning, it should be washed with a detergent solution, rinsed with a minimum amount of water, and dried.

Static conductive linoleum is ordinarily used as a deck covering in the medical operating room. This material should be cleaned in the same way as resilient deck covering, except that wax, oil, and polish should be avoided. These substances act as insulators and reduce the electrical conductivity of this type of deck covering. The deck's gloss may be increased by buffing lightly with fine steel wool and a floor-polishing machine.

Nonskid paint should be cleaned with a solution of one pint detergent cleanser and five tablespoons dishwashing compound or ten tablespoons of a substance called "metasilicate." This preparation is diluted with freshwater to make twenty gallons of solution. Apply with a hand scrubber and let it soak for five minutes then rinse with freshwater. Nonskid deck coverings should never be waxed or painted; otherwise, their nonskid properties will be reduced.

TOPSIDE SURFACES, DECKS, AND DECK COVERINGS

Topside surfaces, because of their constant exposure to weather and sea spray, must be kept clean in order to minimize the need to remove rust and other forms of corrosion. It is a lot easier and more economical to sweep and swab a deck than it is to remove rust and old paint and then repaint it.

There will be many inclement days at sea when weather and sea conditions prevent the crew from cleaning topside surfaces, but at the first opportunity these should be cleaned with freshwater and inspected for signs of rust and corrosion. If you see the beginnings of rust or signs of corrosion (aluminum surfaces, for example, will develop a white powdery residue in the early stages of corrosion), tend to the area immediately. A little work in the beginning will save a lot of work later.

FIELD DAY

Periodically, a field day is held. Field day is cleaning day, when all hands turn to and clean the ship inside and out, usually in preparation for an inspection by the captain or his representatives. Fixtures and areas sometimes neglected during regular sweepdown (such as overhead cables, piping, corners, spaces behind and under equipment) are thoroughly cleaned. Bulkheads, decks, ladders, and all other accessible areas are scrubbed; the "knife edges" around watertight doors and their gaskets are checked, and any paint, oil, or other substances are removed; brightwork is shined; and clean linen is placed on each bunk. Field days improve the ship's appearance and sanitary condition, preserve her by extending paint life, and reduce the dirt around equipment. Besides the obvious effects that dirt can have on health, appearance, and morale, accumulated dirt can cause sensitive electronic equipment to overheat and can cause serious abrasion problems for moving parts on machinery.

Maintenance

Just as a car must receive oil changes and other forms of periodic maintenance in order to keep functioning at peak efficiency, a ship and all of its many types of equipment must be maintained in order to meet all the challenges that may come along in both peace and war.

Broadly speaking, maintenance is either preventive or corrective. Preventive maintenance forestalls equipment or material failure. It includes such things as inspecting, cleaning, painting, lubricating, and testing. Corrective maintenance is another name for repair and becomes necessary when a piece of equipment fails or some part of the ship needs to be fixed. Such things as replacing worn-out parts in a piece of machinery, patching holes in the hull of one of the ship's boats, or rewiring an electronic component would be examples of corrective maintenance.

Because of the Navy's size and complexity, and the variety of equipment that must be maintained for ready use, a carefully planned program is required. The program must be the same for all equipment of the same type, regardless of the type of ship or location, so that a person transferred from one location to another can take on a new task easily. The Navy has such a program—the 3M (maintenance and material management) system.

THE MAINTENANCE AND MATERIAL MANAGEMENT (3M) SYSTEM

This system, explained in detail, establishes service-wide maintenance procedures so that you can maintain a piece of equipment using the same procedures no matter what ship you may be serving in. This system also standardizes the scheduling of maintenance so that it is the same everywhere you go. It also allows for the standardized collection of data, which is useful in analyzing the reliability of specific equipment and thereby leads to the improvement of maintenance scheduling and procedures. The two main features of the system with which you will be concerned are the planned maintenance system (PMS) and the maintenance data system (MDS).

Planned Maintenance System (PMS). PMS is designed to standardize and simplify maintenance procedures. It defines types of maintenance, sets up maintenance schedules, prescribes the tools and methods used for a particular type of maintenance, and helps you detect and prevent impending casualties. PMS also provides a good foundation for training in equipment operation and maintenance.

This portion of 3M also gives shipboard department heads the means to manage, schedule, and control the maintenance of their equipment. There are three major components of PMS: the PMS manual, maintenance schedules—cycle, quarterly, and weekly—and maintenance requirement cards (MRCs).

You will probably use MRCs almost daily. Your work center will have a complete set of them. When the weekly schedule names you for a job, use the appropriate MRC for step-by-step guidance while performing your task. The MRC has a periodicity code that tells when or how often a job is done (see TAB 11-B: 3M Periodicity Codes).

If the MRC indicates a "related maintenance," it means there are two jobs and that they should be done together. Safety precautions are listed for each job. Make sure you read, understand, and observe all precautions. The word "Caution" on an MRC means that a careless worker can damage the equipment; "Warning" means that the equipment could injure the worker. The section labeled "Tools, parts, materials, and test equipment" tells you exactly what to use. Don't substitute without authorization. If, for example, a particular grease is called for but not available, don't use just any grease. Check with your supervisor to see if there is an approved substitute.

Maintenance Data System (MDS). MDS is a management tool used by systems commands and fleet and type commanders to identify and correct maintenance and logistics support (supply) problems. This system has resulted in improvements in maintenance procedures, equipment design, the allocation of resources, and long-range cost accounting.

MDS is a means of recording planned and corrective maintenance actions. All maintenance actions, except daily and weekly preventive maintenance and routine preservation, are recorded in substantial detail using the MDS system. Recorded information concerns the number of man-hours required to make a repair, materials used, delays encountered, reasons for delay, and the technical specialty or activity involved. Once these data have been submitted using MDS forms and procedures, the information gathered is used to improve PMS and supply procedures, and can result in modifications to or replacement of equipment. The amount of time you spend recording information for the MDS system will be worthwhile because it is extremely valuable to those who must make important decisions on how to spend the Navy's money and how to improve equipment and procedures that will affect you and the others who must do the maintenance and operate the Navy's equipment.

PRESERVATION

One of the most effective means of preventive maintenance is what we call "preservation." Preservation may be accomplished in a number of ways, such as applying protective grease to machinery parts that are subject to corrosion or lubricating moving parts to reduce abrasion. Simple cleaning procedures are a basic form of preservation, and a common method of preserving the surface areas of ships is painting. Whether your stay in the Navy is one enlistment or a full thirty-year career, and no matter what your rating, chances are you will be expected to paint something at some time. The old saying, "If it moves, salute it; if it doesn't, paint it," is more humor than fact but it contains a kernel of truth. Paint is vital because it seals the pores of wood and steel, arrests decay, and helps prevent rust. It also promotes cleanliness and sanitation because of its antiseptic properties and because it provides a smooth, washable surface. Paint is also used to reflect, absorb, or redistribute light. And, properly applied, it can improve the appearance of things markedly.

Despite all of its advantages, paint that is improperly applied can cause many problems. Proper painting is a skill that must be learned. While experience is the best teacher, there are procedures and methods that you can learn to prepare yourself for the challenges of becoming a skilled painter. Before painting, you must be able to select suitable paints for the surfaces to be covered, and you must know how to effectively prepare those surfaces. Then you must learn the correct methods of actually applying the paint.

TYPES OF PAINT

Different surfaces require different kinds of paint. Different conditions (for example, whether the area will be exposed to water or air) will also dictate the kind of paint compounds that are to be used.

Primers are base coats of paint that adhere firmly to wood and metal, providing a smooth surface for finishing coats. They also seal the pores. Those applied on steel are rust inhibitors as well. At least two coats of primer should be used after the surface is cleaned to a bright shine. A third coat should be added to outside corners and edges. At least eight hours' drying time should be allowed between primer coats.

The ship's bottom (hull that is underwater all of the time, except when the ship is in dry dock) is painted with two special kinds of paint. Anticorrosive paint inhibits rusting and antifouling paint slows down the attachment and development of marine growth (popularly known as barnacles), which if allowed to grow can slow down a ship considerably. Remember that antifouling paint goes on after anticorrosive paint, because the former, if allowed to come into direct contact with the hull, will cause pitting.

The waterline area, which is sometimes underwater and sometimes exposed to air, is called the "boot topping" and is painted black with a special paint compound.

Vertical surfaces above the upper limit of the boot topping are given two coats of haze gray. Horizontal surfaces are painted with exterior deck gray, which is darker than haze gray. The underside of deck overhangs is painted white.

A nonskid deck paint is used on main walkways. It contains a small amount of pumice, which helps to give a better footing.

The top of stacks and top-hamper, subject to discoloration from smoke and stack gases, are painted black.

Depending on the use to which individual compartments are put, several color schemes are authorized or prescribed for interior bulkheads, decks, and overheads. Some spaces may be painted at the discretion of the individual ship, but many areas must be painted as prescribed by Naval Sea Systems Command (NAVSEASYSCOM). Deck colors, for example, are dark green in the wardroom and officers' quarters, dark red in machinery spaces, and light gray in enlisted living spaces. Common bulkhead colors are green for offices, radio rooms, the pilot house, and medical spaces; gray for the flag plot, combat information center, and sonar control; and white for storerooms and sanitary and commissary spaces. Overhead colors are either the same as bulkhead colors or white.

Many other types of paints are used for special purposes in the Navy. Aluminum surfaces require special primers and outer coats. Canvas preservatives, antisweat coating systems, varnishes, machinery paints, and many others are used aboard ship for different purposes. Never paint a surface without making certain that you have selected the correct paint. When in doubt, ask.

SURFACE PREPARATION

For paint to adhere to a surface, all salt, dirt, oil, grease, rust, and loose paint must be removed completely, and the surface must be thoroughly dry.

Salt and most dirt can be removed with soap or detergent and freshwater. Firmly embedded dirt may require scouring with powder or with sand and canvas. Do not use lye or other strong solutions because they might burn or soften the paint. When oil and grease fail to yield to scrubbing, they must be removed with diesel oil or paint thinner, and extreme caution is necessary. If you use diesel oil, scrub the surface afterward to remove the oil. After scrubbing or scouring, rinse the surface with freshwater.

To remove rust, scale, and loose paint, you need hand tools or power tools, paint and varnish removers, or blowtorches. Hand tools are usually used for cleaning small areas; power tools are for larger areas and for cleaning decks, bulkheads, and overheads covered with too many coats of paint. The most commonly used hand tools are sandpaper, steel wire brushes, and hand scrapers.

Sandpaper is used to clean corners and feather paint. Paint will adhere better to a clean surface that has been lightly sanded. A wire brush is useful for light work on rust or light coats of paint. It is also used for brushing weld spots and cleaning pitted surfaces.

Scrapers are made of tool steel, the most common type being L-shaped, with each end tapered to a cutting edge like a wood chisel. They are most useful for removing rust and paint from small areas and from plating less than one-quarter-inch thick, when it is impractical or impossible to use power tools.

Occasionally, it is necessary to use a chipping or scaling hammer, but care must be taken to exert only enough force to remove the paint. Too much force dents the metal, resulting in the formation of high and low areas. In subsequent painting, the paint is naturally thinner on the high areas. Consequently, thin paint wears off quickly, leaving spots where rust will form and eventually spread under the good paint.

The most useful power tool is the portable grinder. It is usually equipped with a grinding wheel that may be replaced by either a rotary wire brush or a rotary cup wire brush. Light-duty brushes, made of crimped wire, will remove light rust. Heavy-duty brushes, fashioned by twisting several wires into tufts, remove deeply embedded rust.

Scaling may be done with a chisel and pneumatic hammer. When using this tool, you must take care that the chisel strikes the surface at approximately a 45-degree angle.

The rotary scaling and chipping tool (commonly called a "deck crawler") is particularly helpful on large deck areas.

The electric disk sander is another handy tool for preparing surfaces. However, great care must be exercised in its use. If too much pressure is applied, or if the sander is allowed to rest in one place too long, it will quickly cut into the surface, particularly wood or aluminum.

Chemical paint and varnish removers are used mostly on wood surfaces but may be applied to metal surfaces that are too thin to be chipped or wire-brushed. Three types of removers are in general use: flammable, nonflammable, and water-base alkali. All three are hazardous, and safety precautions must be observed. These chemicals should be used only in well-ventilated spaces. Alkali remover is not to be used on aluminum or zinc because of its caustic properties.

Procedures for using these chemical removers are the same regardless of type. Wet the surface with a smooth coat of remover. Permit it to soak in until the paint or varnish is loosened, then lift the paint off with a hand scraper. After the surface is cleaned, wet it again with the remover and wipe

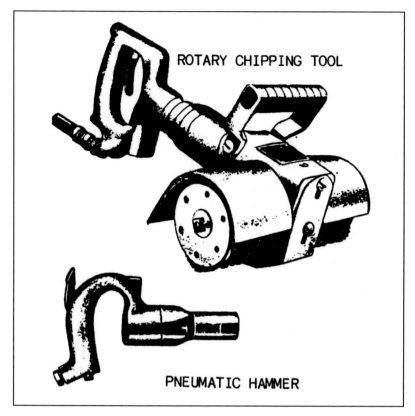

ROTARY CHIPPING TOOL

PNEUMATIC HAMMER

[**11.1**] The rotary chipping tool (more commonly called a "deck crawler") and the pneumatic hammer are useful tools for removing paint from decks and bulkheads.

[**11.2**] A Sailor using a disk sander aboard ship

it off with a rag. Finally, wash the surface thoroughly with paint thinner or soap and water. This final rinse gets rid of any wax left by the remover and any acids that may have been worked into the grain of the wood.

Holes, dents, and cracks in surfaces and open-grained woods should be filled before finishing.

Putty, wood fillers, and even sawdust mixed with glue can be applied to wood. Deep cracks in wooden booms, spars, and the like should first be caulked with oakum or cotton caulking and then covered with putty.

Epoxy cements are available for use on steel and aluminum surfaces. Methods of application vary with the type of cement, so carefully follow instructions.

All fillers should be allowed to dry and then sanded smooth before you apply the first finishing coat.

PAINTING USING BRUSHES AND ROLLERS

Smooth and even painting depends as much on good brushwork as on good paint. There is a brush for almost every purpose, so pick the proper brush and keep it in the best condition.

With a flat brush, a skillful painter can paint almost any shipboard surface. Flat brushes are wide and thick, hold a lot of paint, and give maximum brushing action. Sash brushes are handy for painting small items,

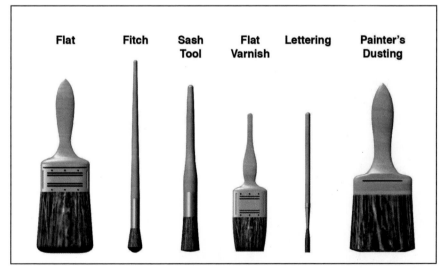

[11.3] Types of paint brushes used in the Navy

for cutting in at corners, and for less accessible spots. The fitch brush also is useful for small surfaces. The painter's dusting brush cleans surfaces.

Handling a paintbrush properly will pay dividends (meaning less work) in the long run. Grip paintbrushes firmly but lightly. Do not put your fingers on the bristles below the metal band. This grip permits easy wrist and arm motion; to hold the brush otherwise restricts your movement and causes fatigue.

When using a flat brush, don't paint with the narrow edge. This practice wears down the corners and spoils the shape and efficiency of the brush. When using an oval brush, don't let it turn in your hands. An oval brush, if revolved too much, soon wears to a pointed shape and becomes useless. Don't poke oversized brushes into corners and around moldings; this bends the bristles, eventually ruining a good brush. Use a smaller brush that fits into such odd spots.

Dip the brush into the paint halfway up the bristles. Remove excess paint by patting the brush on the inside of the pot. (If you oversoak the brush, paint will drip and run down the handle.) Hold the brush at right angles to the surface with the bristles just touching it. Lift the brush clear of the surface when starting the return stroke. If the brush is held obliquely and not lifted, the painted surface will have overlaps, spots, and a daubed appearance. A brush held at any angle other than a right angle will soon wear away at the sides.

For complete and even coverage, follow the Navy method and first lay on, then lay off. Laying on means applying the paint first in long strokes in one direction. Laying off means crossing your first strokes. This way the paint is distributed evenly over the surface, the surface is covered completely, and a minimum amount of paint is used.

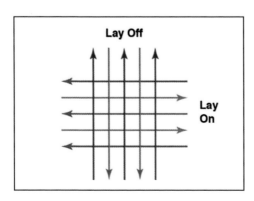

[11.4] The Navy method of painting

Always paint the overhead first, working from the corner that is farthest from compartment access. By painting the overhead first, you can wipe drippings off the bulkhead without smearing its paint. Coats on overhead panels should normally be applied in a fore-and-aft direction, those on the beams athwartships. But where panels contain many pipes running parallel with the beams, it is often difficult to lay off the panels fore and aft. In this case, lay off the panels parallel with the beams.

To avoid brush marks when finishing up a square, use strokes directed toward the last square finished, gradually lifting the brush near the end of the stroke while the brush is still in motion. Every time the brush touches the painted surface at the start of a stroke, it leaves a mark. For this reason, never finish a square by brushing toward the unpainted area; instead, brush back toward the area already painted.

When painting pipes, stanchions, narrow straps, beams, and angles, lay the paint on diagonally. Lay off along the long dimension.

Always carry a rag to wipe up dripped or smeared paint. Carefully remove loose bristles sticking to the painted surface.

Paint on interior surfaces must be applied in the lightest possible coat, only enough to cover the area. Heavy layers of paint are a fire hazard—the thicker they are, the faster they will burn; they are likely to entrap solvents and thinners that burn rapidly; they have a greater tendency to crack and peel; they are uneven, and may show marks and scratches more readily than thinner coats; and they do not penetrate as well as thinner coats or dry as well. Moreover, heavy layers of paint, which add noticeably to the weight of the ship, may cut her speed.

Using a paint roller is different from using a brush. The dip paint roller used in the Navy is equipped with a replaceable cylinder of knitted plush over a solvent-resistant paper core. It rotates on the shaft of a corrosion-resistant steel frame.

Large areas, such as decks and ship's sides (free of rivets, bolts, cables, pipes, and so on), can be covered with paint quickly by the roller method. Paint should be laid on and laid off the same way as with brushes. A moderate amount of pressure must be applied to the roller so that the paint is worked into the surface. If pressure is not exerted, the paint will not adhere and soon it will peel off. With the proper amount of pressure, a roller applies a more even coat and uses less paint than a brush.

CARE OF PAINTING SUPPLIES AND EQUIPMENT

Unfortunately, far too many good brushes and rollers are ruined simply because painters have little or no idea how to care for them. A perfectly good can of paint can be ruined after using only a little if the painter is careless. When painting, treat the paint, brushes, and rollers as though you paid for them yourself.

Do not let a brush stand on its bristles in a pot of paint for more than a few minutes. The weight of the brush bends the bristles, making it almost impossible to do a good paint job.

Never allow paint to dry on a brush. If you intend to leave a paint-filled brush for an hour or more, fold waxed paper or some other heavy paper around the bristles to keep air out. Twist the paper around the handle and secure it with rope yarn or sail twine. Cover your pot of paint, and place both it and the brush in a safe place. Before resuming your job, stir the paint thoroughly with a paddle—not with the brush.

At the end of the day, before turning in your paint and brush to the paint locker, clean as much paint from the brush as possible by wiping it across the edge of the paint pot or mixing paddle. Ordinarily, those working in the paint locker will clean and stow any brushes turned in. They may require your help, or you may be detailed to the job. If so, follow instructions carefully and thoroughly clean the brushes.

Paint lockers usually have containers with divided compartments for temporarily stowing brushes that have been used for different purposes, such as paint, varnish, or shellac. Most of these containers have tight covers and suspend brushes so that the bristles and the lower part of the ferrule (the brush's metal band) are covered by thinner or linseed oil. Brushes to be used the following day should be cleaned in the proper thinner and placed in the proper compartment of the container. Those not to be used again soon should be cleaned in thinner, washed in soap or detergent and water, rinsed thoroughly in freshwater, and hung to dry. After drying, they should be wrapped in waxed paper and stowed flat. Do not leave a brush soaking in water. Water causes the bristles to separate into bunches, flare, and become bushy.

Paint rollers are cleaned differently. The fabric cylinder should be stripped from the core, cleaned in the solvent recommended for a particular type of paint, washed in soap and water, rinsed thoroughly in freshwater, and replaced on the core to dry. Combing the fabric's pile while it is damp prevents matting.

Conservation

Every job in the Navy, whether it has to do with maintenance, cleanliness, or almost anything else, requires conservation. Conservation doesn't mean that you should set aside extra stores like a packrat because you think you might need them sometime. Nor does it mean that you should try to save a bit by using one coat of paint when two are required. Conservation means that you should make effective use of material and time to do the most work at the least possible cost. Although in many ways it is very different from your typical civilian corporation, the Navy is a business, and everything used—whether it is consumable supplies or your time—must be paid for. Just because all you do is sign a chit to draw something from supply does not mean it's free. Someone has to pay for it. And keep in mind that you, as an American taxpayer, help pay.

Inspections

Conducted to ensure the readiness of personnel and equipment and to maintain the high standards required of an impressive, combat-ready organization, inspections are a periodic part of shipboard life. Because inspections are similar in many ways to tests we have all encountered in school, it is only human nature to become somewhat apprehensive before an impending inspection. But besides their obvious necessity, inspections are a time for you to show what you can do, to demonstrate what you have learned, and to prove that you are the kind of person that will meet the unique challenges that life in the U.S. Navy sometimes brings. Whether it is a personnel inspection, a zone inspection, or some other type, it is an opportunity for you to excel. If you are properly prepared, it will be an enjoyable experience and will contribute to overall unit readiness. If you are not adequately prepared, an inspection can be a very uncomfortable experience.

If you are in charge of a compartment that is being inspected, present the space to the inspecting officer by saluting and greeting her or him in the following manner: "Good afternoon [morning], ma'am [sir]; Seaman Jones, compartment [name and number], ____ Division, standing by for inspection."

Life aboard ship is truly unique. In addition to the routines discussed in this chapter, you may find yourself standing watches (see **Chapter 13**), responding to an emergency or an emergency drill (see **Chapter 14**), or doing your part to carry out one or more of the Navy's many important missions (see **Chapter 7**).

TWELVE

SEAMANSHIP AND BOATS

As a Sailor, whether you eventually strike for boatswain's mate or logistics specialist, there are certain basic skills of seamanship you will need to know or at least be familiar with. Few Sailors can say they've never handled a line or tied a knot. All ships, whether they are patrol craft or aircraft carriers, use mooring lines to secure themselves to piers, anchors to hold them in place where there are no piers, and many other forms of equipment and skills that are unique but essential to ships and boats. As a Sailor, you will likely find yourself as part of boat crew, as a boat passenger, or using boats in some other fashion.

MARLINESPIKE SEAMANSHIP

The art of working with line or rope is called "marlinespike seamanship" or, sometimes, "marlinespiking." The name comes from a hand-held, spike-like tool used in working with wire rope, which is called a "marlinespike."

It is important to learn the special terminology associated with marlinespike seamanship, primarily because you want to avoid confusion. But there is a good secondary reason as well. There are certain measures of professionalism in the Navy that have no official status and have nothing to do with getting you promoted, but are used to size you up as a true Sailor rather than a landlubber. If you want to be recognized as a true Navy professional—to earn the respect of those more experienced than you—you should make an effort to think, act, and speak like a Sailor. This means you should use twenty-four-hour time, call a deck a deck (and not a floor), and know the difference between rope and line.

Lines, Ropes, and Wires

In the Navy, the term "rope" refers to both fiber and wire. Fiber ropes include those made of such natural materials as manila and hemp and those made of synthetic materials such as nylon. Here is the tricky part: Fiber rope is called "rope" only as long as it is still in its original coil. Once a piece has been cut to be used for some purpose (such as mooring or heaving), it is then called a "line." If you want to be considered a novice, call a line a rope. Rope made of wire (or a combination of wire and fiber) is usually called "wire rope" or simply "wire," even if it has been cut from its original coil and is being used for some specific purpose. There are some exceptions. The lifelines on ships, for example, are nearly always made of wire. You are probably safe if you forget about the word "rope" and use the words "line" and "wire."

What many would call a "loop" in a line is called a *bight* in the Navy. "Looping" a line around an object is called *taking a turn* or *taking a round turn*. A permanent loop on the end of a line is called an *eye*. Lines do not "break" in the Navy, they part. The free end of a length of line is called the *bitter end*.

Construction of a fiber line starts with small fibers, which are twisted until they form larger pieces called "yarns." Then the yarns are twisted in the opposite direction to form "strands," after which they are twisted in the original direction to become a line. The direction of this final twisting determines the "lay" of the line. Line can be either three- or four-strand, though three-strand is most common in the Navy. Nearly all three-strand line used in Navy ships is what we call "right-laid," meaning that the strands are twisted to the right. It is important to know this because you should always coil a line in the direction of its lay. For example, right-laid line should always be coiled in right-hand (clockwise) turns. This will prevent kinking and extend the life of the line.

Lines can also be formed by a different process called "braiding." Braided lines have certain advantages over twisted ones. They will not kink and will not flex open to admit dirt or abrasives. The construction of some, however, makes it impossible to inspect the inner yarns for damage. The more common braided lines are hollow braided, stuffer braided, solid braided, and double braided.

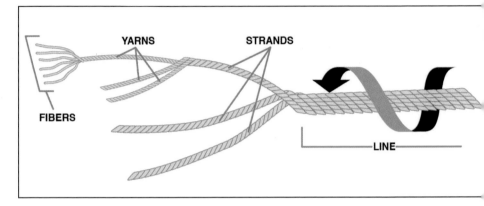

[**12.1**] The components of a line

FIBER LINES

Synthetic- and natural-fiber lines each have certain advantages and disadvantages. The common synthetic fibers—nylon, polyester (Dacron), polypropylene, and polyethylene (in descending order of strength)—ranging in size from one-eighth-inch to twelve inches in circumference, are generally stronger than natural fibers and not subject to rot. Nylon is more than twice as strong as manila, the most common natural fiber; it lasts five times as long and will stand seven times the shock load. Dacron gets stronger when wet, and polypropylene is so light it floats, both of which are obvious advantages in a marine environment. Most ships (smaller decks) use four-strand Aramid nylon line, due to its strength and no snap back.

The biggest disadvantages of synthetic line when compared to natural-fiber line is that synthetics stretch under heavy loads and it is more difficult to tell when they are going to part. Another disadvantage of synthetic line is that it does not hold knots as well as natural fibers. Some knots that are good for securing natural fibers, such as the square knot, are not adequate for synthetic materials. The *bowline* is one knot known to offer reasonable security when bending together or securing synthetic line.

Fiber lines are identified by their circumference and type; for example, "two-inch manila" or "three-inch nylon." Lines larger in circumference than five inches are called *hawsers*. Line that is less than one inch in circumference is usually called *small stuff*.

Synthetic-Fiber Lines. Before you use new three-strand synthetic, it should be *faked down*—or laid down in single turns—on deck and allowed to relax for twenty-four hours. The period can be shortened to about two hours by hosing down the line with freshwater.

When it is wet, synthetic line shrinks slightly but does not swell or stiffen. When tension is applied to the line, water squeezes out; under working loads, it appears as vapor.

Oil and grease do not cause synthetics to deteriorate, but they make them slippery. When this happens, the line should be scrubbed down. Spots may be removed by cleaning the line with light oils such as kerosene or diesel oil.

Sailors who work with natural-fiber line soon learn how to judge tension by the sound the line makes. Unfortunately, although synthetic line under heavy strain thins down considerably, it gives no audible indication of stress—even when it is about to part. For this reason, a *tattletale* line should be attached to synthetic line when it is subjected to loads that may exceed its safe working load. A tattletale line is a piece of smaller natural fiber line that is attached to a synthetic line at two carefully measured points so that it droops down. As the synthetic line stretches, the droop in the tattletale will get less and less. When the tattletale has become taut and is lying parallel to the synthetic line, you will know that the line is in danger of parting.

Natural-Fiber Lines. Because of their tendency to retain water and to rot, special care and handling are required when using natural-fiber lines.

Coils of line should always be stowed on shelves or platforms clear of the deck. They should never be covered in such a way that may prevent the evaporation of moisture.

Whenever possible, a wet line should be dried before stowing. If line must be stowed wet, it should be laid up on gratings in long fakes or suspended in some other way so that it will dry as quickly as possible. It should never be covered before it is dry.

To prevent cutting or breaking of the outer fibers, keep lines from rubbing against other objects whenever possible, particularly sharp or jagged ones. Avoid dragging line over ground where it can pick up dirt and other particles; these can work their way into the line and weaken the line by cutting the inner strands.

Under normal working conditions, the strength of line exposed to the elements deteriorates about 30 percent in two years. Lines should be inspected frequently for deterioration. Open the lay by twisting in the opposite direction and inspect the fibers. A white powdery residue indicates internal wear. After particularly heavy use, inspect the inside threads to see if all or a portion of the fibers are broken.

WIRE ROPE

The construction of wire rope is similar to that of fiber lines. Wire rope consists of individual wires made of steel or other metal, in various sizes, laid together to form strands. The number of wires in a strand varies according to the purpose for which the rope is intended. A number of strands are laid together to form the wire rope itself. Wire rope is designated by the number of strands per rope and the number of wires per strand. Thus, a 6 by 19 rope has 6 strands with a total of 19 wires per strand.

Wire rope made up of a large number of small wires is flexible, but small wires break so easily that the rope is damaged by external abrasion. Wire rope made up of a smaller number of larger wires is more resistant to abrasion, but less flexible.

Never pull a kink out of a wire rope by putting strain on either end. As soon as you notice a kink, uncross the ends by pushing them apart; this reverses the process that started the kink. Then turn the bent portion over, place it on your knee or some firm object, and push down until the kink starts to straighten out somewhat. Then lay it on a flat surface and pound it smooth with a wooden mallet.

Damage to a wire rope is indicated by the presence of what are called "fishhooks." These occur when individual wires break and bend back. If several occur near each other or along the rope's length, it is an indication that the wire rope is less reliable and may require replacement. Because of these "fishhooks," always wear gloves when handling wire.

You should inspect wire rope frequently, checking for fishhooks, kinks, and worn spots. Worn spots show up as shiny flattened surfaces. A wire rope with three broken wires in a strand is no longer useable.

Wire rope should never be stored in places where acid is or has been kept. Prior to storage, wire rope should be cleaned and lubricated.

Working with Line

Certain skills and practices, some of them simple and others more complicated, must be learned in order to work with line. The experts at working with line are the boatswain's mates, but every Sailor should be familiar with some of these skills.

STOWING LINE FOR READY USE

Once a line has been removed from the coil, it may be prepared for storage or ready use, either by winding on a reel or in one of the following ways:

- **Coiling down.** Lay the line down in circles, roughly one on top of the other. Right-laid line is always coiled down right-handed, or clockwise. When a line has been coiled down, the end that went down last on top is ready to run off. If you try to walk away with the bottom end, the line will foul up. If for some reason the bottom end must go out first, turn the entire coil upside down to free it for running.
- **Faking down.** The line is laid down as in coiling down, except that it is laid out in long, flat bights, one alongside the other, instead of in a round coil. A faked down line runs more easily than a coiled line.
- **Flemishing down.** Coil the line down first, then wind it tight from the bottom end, counterclockwise, bringing it tighter together so that it forms a close circular mat. This method of stowing a line not only keeps it ready for use, it looks good.

SECURING ENDS

Never leave the end of a line without what is called a *whipping*. This can be a piece of small stuff tied to the end of the line or a piece of tape wrapped around it to prevent the end of the line from unraveling. A good method to use for nylon line is to wrap a piece of tape around the end, leaving the tufted end of the strands exposed. You should then singe the exposed strands, causing them to melt together.

JOINING LINES TOGETHER WITH KNOTS, BENDS, AND HITCHES

The most obvious method of joining lines together is to tie them with a knot. But "bends" and "hitches" are also used for specific purposes because of the advantages they provide.

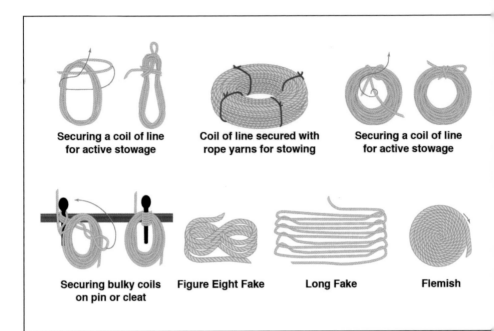

Securing a coil of line for active stowage

Coil of line secured with rope yarns for stowing

Securing a coil of line for active stowage

Securing bulky coils on pin or cleat

Figure Eight Fake

Long Fake

Flemish

[12.2] Different methods of stowing line

To a Sailor, a *knot* in a line usually means the line is tied to itself. When you tie two lines together, you have formed a *bend*. When you tie a piece of line to some other object, it is called a *hitch*. In many cases, these functions may overlap, so these terms are not absolute. One guiding principle is that knots are usually meant to be permanent and are therefore more difficult to untie than are bends and hitches.

There are big, thick books describing the many varieties of knots, bends, and hitches, but if you are comfortable with just a few, you will be able to take care of virtually any common situation. If you learn no others, be sure that you can at least tie a *square knot* (also called a reef knot) and a *bowline*. Others will prove useful in special situations, such as the *clove hitch* (used to fasten a line to an object—a good example would be a cowboy securing the reins of his horse to a hitching post), *figure eight* (used to put a temporary end to a line), *catspaw* (secures a cargo sling to a hook), *timber hitch* (good for lifting or securing logs, planks, and other long, rough-surfaced objects), and *carrick bend* (used to bend two hawsers together). The more knots, bends, and hitches you know, the better you will be able to use line to your advantage in a wide variety of situations.

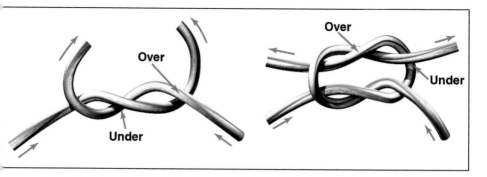

Over

Over

Under

Under

[**12.3**] Tying the square knot

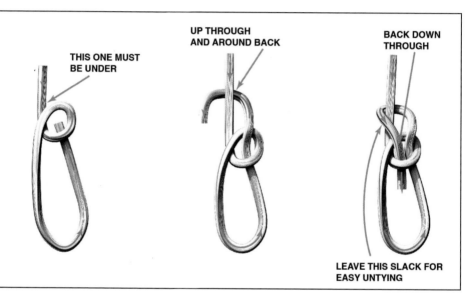

THIS ONE MUST
BE UNDER

UP THROUGH
AND AROUND BACK

BACK DOWN
THROUGH

LEAVE THIS SLACK FOR
EASY UNTYING

[**12.4**] Tying a bowline

Sometimes it is useful to secure two lines together side by side. This is accomplished by using a variety of what are called *seizings*.

When two lines are to be joined end to end in such a way as to merge them into one, they are *spliced*. A line can also be bent on itself and spliced to form a permanent loop on the end of the line or can be spliced back into itself (called a back splice) to secure an end to keep it from unraveling. If properly done, splicing does not weaken the line. A splice between two lines will run through, or over, another object more easily than a knot.

Ornamental knots are used to give your ship a smart nautical appearance and to promote safety and habitability. Just as with practical knots, bends, and hitches, there are virtual encyclopedias of ornamental work. Turk's heads, fox and geese, and sennits are just a few of the many forms of ornamental knots you may encounter during your time in the Navy.

Working with Wire Rope

The greater strength of wire rope as compared to fiber line is offset somewhat by its lesser flexibility and its tendency to rust if conditions are not right. Wire rope that is frequently exposed to weather or hard use requires some extra measures of protection to prolong its service life:

- **Worming.** The lay of the rope is followed between the strands with tarred small stuff. This keeps moisture from penetrating the interior of the rope and fills out the rope, giving it a smooth surface ready for parceling and serving.
- **Parceling.** This is accomplished by wrapping the rope spirally with long narrow strips of canvas, following the lay of the rope and overlapping turns to shed moisture.
- **Serving.** The final step in preserving wire rope is accomplished by wrapping small stuff snugly over the parceling, pulling each turn as taut as possible so that the whole forms a stiff protecting cover for the rope. A tool called a serving mallet is used for passing the turns in serving, and each turn is pulled taut by the leverage of the handle.

Remember this poetic rule:

Worm and parcel with the lay,
Turn and serve the other way.

MOORING

Mooring is defined as securing a ship to a pier, to another ship, to a mooring buoy, or by anchoring. In order to maximize pier space, Navy ships are also frequently moored to other ships, creating a nest of ships side by side alongside a pier or at an anchorage. When this is done alongside a pier, the ship closer to the pier is said to be "inboard" of the other(s), and ships farther from the pier are "outboard."

Mooring to a Pier

In order to properly moor a ship to a pier, certain standardized procedures make the operation efficient, and a knowledge of the appropriate terminology is essential. Standard commands, the deck fittings, and the lines themselves all are referred to in precise nautical terms that must be understood by Sailors in order to take part in the operation or to stand watches properly once a ship is moored.

In order to moor a ship properly, you will need to be able to identify certain items of equipment that are unique to ships. The lines used to secure the ship to the pier are called—no surprise—*mooring lines*. Each line is given its own unique name to make references to it clear and avoid confusion. Mooring line configurations and terms are explained in TAB 12-A: Mooring Line Configurations and Terms.

A mooring line will do no good without the necessary fittings on the ship and on the pier to which the mooring lines are secured. A *cleat* consists of a pair of projecting horns for belaying (securing) a line. *Bitts* are cylindrical shapes of cast iron or steel arranged in pairs on the ship's deck and on the pier, which are also used to belay lines. A *bollard* is a heavy cylindrical object with a bulbous top and a horn that is found on piers but not on ships. The eye or bight of a mooring line can be passed over it, and because of the bollard's design, the line will not slip off. A *chock* is different from the other fittings so far mentioned because lines are not secured to it but instead are passed through. Chocks come in three varieties—open, closed, and roller—and are used to feed lines in the direction you want, thereby increasing efficiency. A typical mooring configuration would have lines running from bitts aboard ship, through chocks, to a bollard (or a cleat or another set of bitts) on the pier.

To protect the sides of your ship from rubbing or banging against a pier (or against another ship if you are moored next to one), *fenders* and *camels* are used. Fenders are shock absorbers of various types (such as rubber shapes or clusters of line) suspended from the ship or pier to serve as cushions between them. Camels serve the same purpose, but instead of being suspended from the deck, they float in the water. Besides protecting the ship and pier from contacting each other, camels are used to keep aircraft carriers farther away from the pier because of their overhanging flight deck and elevators. If you moored an aircraft carrier to a pier without camels to hold it off, the elevators would, in many instances, lower right onto the pier or dangerously close to it.

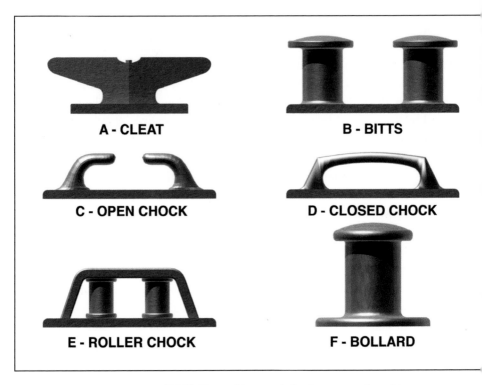

[**12.5**] Cleats, bitts, and chocks are used on ships to secure lines. Bollards are found on piers and on wharves.

To prevent rats from coming aboard your ship by using your mooring lines as convenient pathways, circular metal discs called *rat guards* are lashed to the mooring lines.

During the mooring process, a light line called a *messenger* is first sent over. Then, with the larger mooring line itself attached, it is hauled in. To help get the messenger across from the ship to the pier, a *heaving line*, *bolo*, or *line-throwing gun* is used, depending upon the distance of the ship from the pier. A heaving line is a light line with an orange rubber ball on the end; a bolo line is a nylon line with a padded lead weight or a monkey fist on it that is designed for throwing a greater distance by first twirling it in a circle to build up momentum before letting it go. A line-throwing gun is a modified rifle that can fire a special projectile with a line attached. It will reach farther than a heaving line or bolo but must be handled with a Sailor's knowledge and care. It is dangerous to use, particularly when people are standing on the pier.

LINE-HANDLING COMMANDS

During the process of mooring a vessel to a pier or to another ship, it is vital that the conning officer be able to communicate efficiently with the line handlers. To make sure there is no confusion, commands that are commonly used in mooring operations have been standardized. This system can only be efficient if both the conning officer and the line handlers know what the various commands are and what they mean. See TAB 12-B: Line-Handling Commands for some examples.

Anchoring

Mooring to a pier is nearly always the preferred method for a ship to spend its time when not under way. When alongside a pier, personnel can come and go and supplies are easily brought aboard. Because there are not always piers available, and because there are occasions when it is preferable not to be alongside a pier (such as when political unrest in a region makes defending the ship from terrorist attack a priority), ships have the ability to use anchors as a mooring alternative.

When anchored, boats must be used for transporting personnel and supplies to and from the ship. A careful watch on the sea and weather conditions must be kept and care exercised to ensure that the ship does not begin to move out of its anchorage by dragging its anchor.

The equipment associated with anchoring is called *ground tackle*. This includes the anchors themselves, the chains used to attach them to the ship, the windlasses used to *weigh anchor* (lifting the anchor back on board), and a variety of other components, such as shackles, chain stoppers, anchor bars, and detachable links.

ANCHORS

An anchor is a type of hook that embeds itself into the sea bottom to hold a ship in place. While the anchor itself is an important component of the process, the chain is also vital. The amount of chain used is very important because too much chain will allow the ship to move around too much within its anchorage, and too little may allow the ship to move out of its anchorage by dragging its anchor. The *shank* is the body of the anchor and the *flukes* are the "teeth" (or hook part) that actually bite into the bottom. Some anchors have a *stock*, which is a kind of crossbar that prevents the anchor from flipping over once it is lying on the bottom.

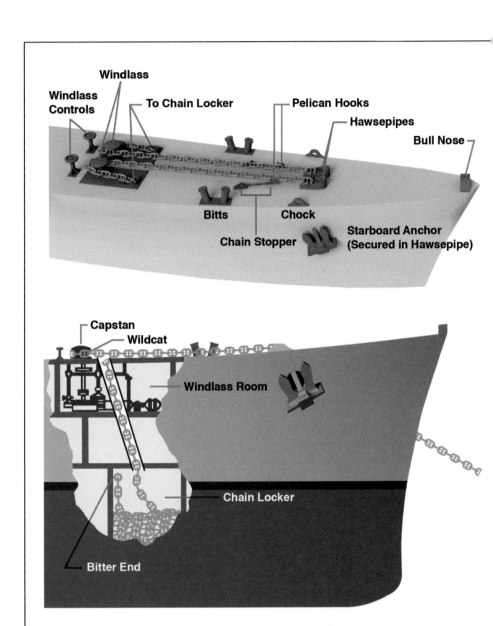

[**12.6**] A typical ground-tackle arrangement

Anchors are stored in a special tube in the ship's bow called a *hawse-pipe*. This tube also serves as a passage for the anchor chain, leading from the forecastle deck to the outer surface of the ship's hull closer to the water. When not in use, the anchor chain is stowed in a large compartment called the *chain locker*.

There are various types of anchors and different methods of anchoring. The most common method of anchoring is to drop one or two anchors in relatively shallow water and pay out enough chain to ensure that the ship will stay in place. In a *Mediterranean moor*, a ship usually has the stern moored to a pier and an anchor out on each bow. A *stream anchor*, now seldom used, is a small anchor dropped off the stern or quarter of a ship to prevent her from swinging to a current.

Stockless anchors, because they do not have the crossbar to get in the way, are easy to stow and were adopted by the Navy for this reason, despite the fact that they do not have the holding power of old-fashioned anchors.

Mushroom anchors have a bowl-shaped head at the end of the shank rather than hooks. Once used in older submarines, they are not used much anymore. They *are* very useful for keeping buoys in place because, once planted (particularly in groups of three), they are not easily dislodged and are therefore very reliable.

Lightweight (LWT) anchors are used on some Navy ships and craft. The commercially made Danforth anchor is also used aboard some Navy craft and small boats. LWT-type anchors have a great deal of holding power for their weights, relying on their ability to dig in rather than their dead weight (as is the case for the stockless types). For example, in a sand bottom, 10,000-pound LWT anchors are designed to have a holding power approximately equal to the 22,500-pound standard Navy stockless. Sizes below 150 pounds are used as boat anchors.

Two-fluke/balanced-fluke anchors are used by surface ships and the newest submarines. They are normally housed in the bottom of the ship rather than in a hawsepipe on the forecastle. They are sometimes used in place of bow anchors, which could strike the large, bulbous sonar dome that bulges out from the bow beneath the water.

Although no longer used for practical purposes, old-fashioned anchors are the traditional anchors you see represented on officers' and chief petty

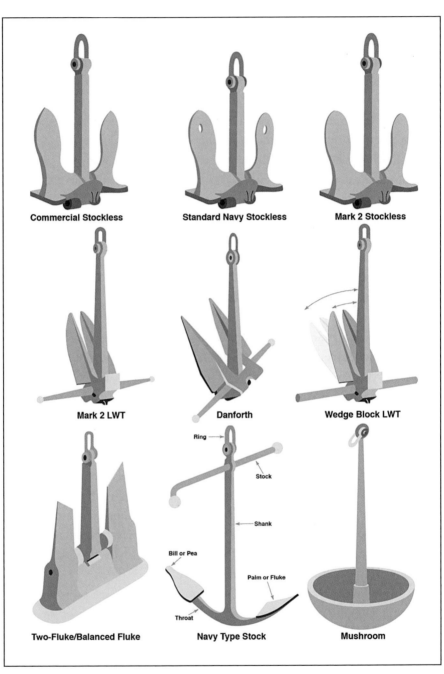

Commercial Stockless

Standard Navy Stockless

Mark 2 Stockless

Mark 2 LWT

Danforth

Wedge Block LWT

Two-Fluke/Balanced Fluke

Navy Type Stock

Ring

Stock

Shank

Bill or Pea

Palm or Fluke

Throat

Mushroom

[**12.7**] Types of anchors

officers' caps and on the rating badges, such as for boatswain's mates. Also known as "Navy-type stock anchors," they are commonly used as decorative items in front of Navy buildings and in various other locations.

CHAINS

Made of steel, Navy anchor chains vary in size according to the size of the ship and her anchors. Chain comes in 15-fathom lengths called *shots*. To understand this, you need to know that a *fathom* equals 6 feet. This means that a shot of anchor chain is 90 feet long. How many shots of chain a ship will carry depends upon the type of ship. Shots are connected to one another by *detachable links*. A special color-coding system is used to identify the various shots so that when the ship is anchored, you can tell, just by looking at visible chain on deck, how much chain has been payed out and is underwater. This system is explained in TAB 12-C: Anchor Chain Identification System.

OUTBOARD SWIVEL SHOTS

On most ships, standard outboard swivel shots, also called *bending shots*, attach the anchor chain to the anchor. They make it possible to stop off (secure) the anchor and break (unfasten) the chain between the windlass and the anchor so that the chain can then be attached to a mooring buoy (explained below). Outboard swivel shots consist of detachable links, regular chain links, a swivel, an end link, and a bending shackle (which actually attaches the anchor to the chain). Outboard swivel shots vary in length depending upon the size and type of ship but will not normally exceed 15 fathoms.

CHAIN STOPPERS

To hold the anchor securely in place when you are not actually in the process of letting it go or heaving it in, chain stoppers are attached to it. These consist of a shackle at one end (attaches the stopper to the deck of the ship) and a pelican hook (special hook that fits over a chain and can be securely closed—clamped on—or opened as needed) at the other. Several links of chain are included to give the stopper the desired length, and a turnbuckle is included that is used to adjust the stopper so that there is no slack in the chain once the stopper is attached. In other words, it makes the stopper taut. The stopper located closest to the hawsepipe is called the housing stopper. Other stoppers are called riding stoppers.

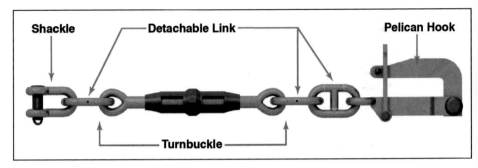

[**12.8**] A chain stopper

Stoppers are used for holding the anchor taut in the hawsepipe when not in use, for keeping the chain secure when the ship is riding to an anchor, and for holding an anchor in place when it is disconnected from the chain.

ANCHOR WINDLASS

The anchor windlass is used to hoist the bow anchor. Those ships with stern anchors have a similar device on the ship's fantail called the stern-anchor winch.

On combatant ships, the anchor windlass is a vertical type with controls, including a friction-brake handwheel that can be used to slow down and actually stop the anchor from running out any farther once it has been let go (dropped). Below deck is the drive motor with its electric and hydraulic components. Above deck is a smooth cylinder called a *capstan* that can use the motor power to heave around on mooring lines. Beneath the capstan is a wildcat that is fitted with ridges called *whelps*, which engage the links of the chain and prevent it from slipping while heaving it in. The wildcat may be disengaged from the shaft so that it turns freely when the anchor is dropped; as mentioned before, it is fitted with a brake to stop the chain at the desired length (called *scope*).

On some ships, the anchor windlass is a horizontal type above deck, with two wildcats, one for each anchor.

MOORING SHACKLES

As mentioned earlier, if mooring buoys are available the anchor chain may be detached from its anchor (leaving the anchor secured in its hawsepipe by the stoppers) and then attached to a mooring buoy. Mooring shackles

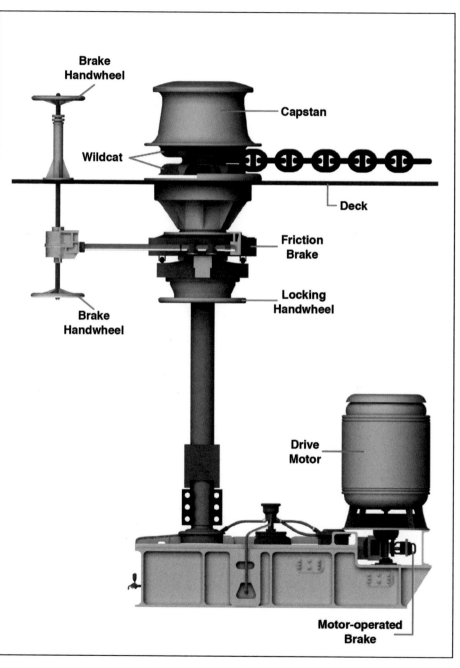

Brake Handwheel

Capstan

Wildcat

Deck

Friction Brake

Locking Handwheel

Brake Handwheel

Drive Motor

Motor-operated Brake

[**12.9**] Vertical-shaft anchor windlass

are used to make the attachment. Forged-steel mooring swivels with two links of regular chain at each end are inserted into the chain outboard of the hawsepipe to keep the chain from twisting as the ship swings.

THE ANCHOR DETAIL

The anchor detail is normally headed by the first lieutenant, who is assisted by one or more experienced boatswain's mates and a team of Sailors who perform the tasks associated with anchoring.

Whenever a ship is entering or leaving port, the anchor detail is set. This is true even if the ship has no intention of anchoring, because the ship's anchors can be used in an emergency situation to keep the ship from getting into serious danger—they serve as a kind of emergency brake. For example, a ship coming into or leaving a port often must travel through fairly restricted waters (such as a narrow channel) or into a small mooring basin. If the ship should suddenly lose its propulsion power, it might coast or drift into danger (such as running aground or colliding with other ships moored or anchored nearby). If the anchors are ready for letting go, they can be dropped and used to hold the ship in place temporarily until the problem can be fixed and propulsion restored.

DROPPING THE ANCHOR

With the anchor detail manned, the ship is carefully navigated into position by the officer of the deck (OOD) and his or her special sea (navigational) detail. When the ship is nearing the anchorage the bridge tells the forecastle to "stand by." Personnel on the forecastle will release all but one of the chain stoppers and the windlass brake so that the weight of the anchor is on the chain, which is being held by the one remaining stopper. When the ship is precisely in position, the bridge will tell the forecastle to let go the anchor. With everyone standing clear of the chain, a Sailor will knock the pelican hook on the stopper loose and, with a great roar, the anchor will plunge into the water and fall to the bottom. Allowing an anchor or its chain to run out using its own weight is called *veering*.

The Sailor controlling the windlass will set the brake soon after the anchor strikes bottom to prevent the chain from continuing to run and piling up. The OOD will normally back the ship to set the anchor (cause the flukes to dig into the bottom). Then the OOD will order the brake released on the windlass and will back the ship down some more to veer more chain until it is at the desired scope (length). Stoppers will then be set and the ship is anchored.

WEIGHING ANCHOR

When the ship is ready to get under way from its anchorage, the sea and anchor details are set and the forecastle detail will set the brake on the windlass and remove the stoppers. Upon command from the bridge, the windlass operator will begin heaving around to bring in the chain. Normally, she or he will heave around to short stay (all the chain is retrieved leading up to the anchor, but heaving is stopped just short of pulling the anchor out of the ground) and wait for orders to proceed.

When so ordered, heaving is continued, and the bridge is informed when the anchor is up and down (pulled out of the ground, but still resting on the bottom). Once the anchor is clear of the bottom (the weight of the anchor is on the chain), the report "anchor's aweigh" is sent to the bridge. At this point the ship is officially under way.

A *quick note for the novice Sailor*: Although it is incorrect, you will often see the Navy song referred to as "Anchor's Away." But "Anchor's Aweigh" is the grammatically correct title because it refers to the heaving in of the anchor. In practice (as on the Navy's official website), the title often leaves out the apostrophe, making the title "Anchors Aweigh."

A hose team will spray the chain as it emerges from the water to remove the mud and debris accumulated from the bottom. Once the anchor can be seen, the forecastle will report its condition to the bridge. Upon visual inspection of the anchor, the forecastle will report "anchor clear," or "anchor fouled" if it is tangled with a cable or some other object, or "anchor shod" if it has large amounts of mud on it. If it is ready to be housed (brought back into the hawsepipe), it will be heaved in and stoppers will be set to hold it in place.

STANDARD COMMANDS

Just as it is vital for clear, concise communications during line-handling operations, so is it important to have the same during anchoring operations. See TAB 12-D: Anchoring Commands.

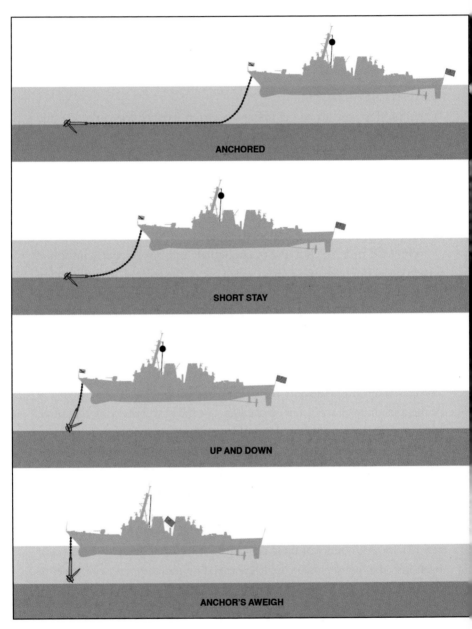

ANCHORED

SHORT STAY

UP AND DOWN

ANCHOR'S AWEIGH

[**12.10**] From anchored to under way

SCOPE OF CHAIN

The ship is held in place not only by the anchor itself but by the chain as well. *Scope* is the amount of chain the ship puts out to hold the ship in place. This amount varies with the depth of the water. The scope is normally five to seven times the depth of the water. For example, if your ship is anchoring in 10 fathoms (60 feet) of water, the OOD will use between 50 fathoms (300 feet) and 70 fathoms (420 feet) of chain to hold the ship in place.

Mooring to a Buoy

To avoid confusion, be aware that one does not moor to a navigational buoy. There are, in some locations in the world, special buoys that are securely attached to the bottom and are equipped for mooring a ship. Rather than use lines in this type of moor, a ship detaches its anchor chain from its anchor and then reattaches the chain to the buoy. This method has the advantage of allowing a ship to be securely moored in a specific location without having to use its own anchor or its mooring lines. The disadvantage is that, like anchoring, this method of mooring leaves the ship out in the middle of the water, necessitating the use of boats or helicopters to get personnel and supplies on and off the ship. This method of mooring is not as common as it once was but is still used in some ports.

TOWING

Most routine towing jobs in the Navy are handled by vessels that are specially equipped to handle these operations, such as harbor tugs, fleet tugs, salvage vessels, and submarine-rescue vessels. But other Navy ships must, in emergencies, be able to tow other vessels or be towed themselves.

The towing rig used varies among classes and types of ships, but includes certain common items. On the stern, most ships have a *towing-pad eye* that is used to attach the towing assembly, made up of a *chafing chain* with a large *pelican hook* made fast to a *towing hawser*. The hawser itself is usually a wire or synthetic hawser varying in length from 100 fathoms (600 feet) for a destroyer to 150 fathoms (900 feet) for a larger ship. It is normally attached to one of the towed ship's anchor chains, which has been disconnected from the anchor, run through the bull-nose, and veered to 20 to 45 fathoms.

The length of the towline—hawser and chain—is adjusted to hang in a deep underwater curve called a *catenary*, which helps to relieve surges on the line caused by movements of the two ships. Whether towing is done with two motor launches or two cruisers, the towline should be of such a scope (or length) that the two craft are in step, which means that they should both reach the crest of a wave at the same time. Otherwise, the towline will be whipped out of the water and may cause serious damage.

Once the towing hawser is rigged, the towing vessel gets under way very slowly. If the towing vessel moves too quickly, it may cause the line to part. Course changes must also be made slowly, never exceeding 15 degrees of rudder.

If you are involved in a towing operation, be aware that the towing line could part at any time and that, if it does, the potential for serious injury is very great. Never get any closer to a towing line than you have to.

DECK SEAMANSHIP

Despite all of their sophisticated electronics and modern engineering components, Navy ships must still rely on basic deck seamanship techniques to be able to move heavy loads about and to receive fuel, ammunition, and supplies on board. The principles—and, in fact, some of the actual equipment—used to accomplish these things are the same that Sailors have used for centuries. Mechanical winches may have replaced pure manpower in some cases, but the techniques and the rigs used are the same ones that Sailors used in the days of sail to get their work done. Because of this strong link to the past, many of the terms used in deck seamanship come down to us from centuries ago and will, therefore, take some getting used to.

Cargo Handling

Service and amphibious ships in the Navy, by the nature of their business, must be able to handle large amounts of cargo. But even combatants must be able to handle at least limited amounts. Therefore all ships have at least some cargo-handling equipment.

BASIC TERMINOLOGY

The most basic form of a cargo-handling rig is a boom attached to a kingpost that is operated by a combination of lines rigged for the purpose. A *kingpost* is a short, sturdy mast capable of supporting a large amount of weight. A *boom* is a sturdy pole that is attached to the kingpost by a swivel-type device called a *gooseneck*. The boom is lifted up and down by a *topping lift* and it is moved from side to side by *guys* (sometimes called *vangs*).

Rigging is a general term for wires, ropes, and chains used to support kingposts or other masts, or to operate cargo-handling equipment. *Standing rigging* describes lines that support but do not move. Examples of standing rigging are *stays*, which are rigged fore and aft to support masts, and *shrouds*, which are rigged athwartships to provide support. *Running rigging* includes movable lines such as topping lifts and guys.

One of the basic principles you must know if you are going to be able to work efficiently in handling cargo is that a device you probably would have called a pulley before becoming a Sailor is called a *block* and can be rigged to give you a significant mechanical advantage and thereby save you a great deal of work and energy. When blocks and lines are combined either to change the direction of an applied force or to gain a mechanical advantage, the combination is called a *tackle*. See TAB 12-E: Blocks and Tackles for a detailed explanation of these useful rigs.

BASIC RIGS

Perhaps the simplest cargo-handling rig is called a *single swinging boom*. If you have ever watched a crane at a construction site, this is comparable to a single swinging boom. The mechanical advantage of this rig can be increased by using one of the block-and-tackle combinations described in TAB 12-E: Blocks and Tackles.

Booms can be used singly or in pairs. One common use of a pair of booms is the *yard-and-stay rig*. One boom, called the *hatch boom*, is positioned over the ship's deck or over a cargo hatch and the other, called the *yard boom*, is swung out over the side to hang over the pier. The cargo hook is attached to a pair of whips run from the end of each boom. The one attached to the hatch boom is called the hatch whip and the one attached to the yard boom is called a yard whip. By alternately easing out and heaving around on the two whips, the cargo hook (with its cargo attached) can be moved from the pier to the ship or vice versa.

Underway Replenishment (UNREP)

Before the techniques of underway replenishment (UNREP) were developed, a ship that ran low on fuel, supplies, or ammunition had to return to port, or she had to stop and lie to while she was replenished by small boats.

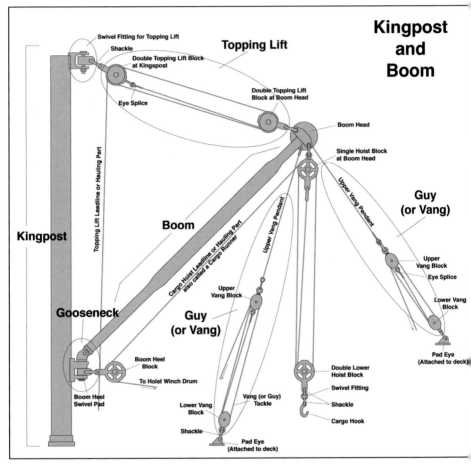

Kingpost and Boom

Swivel Fitting for Topping Lift

Shackle

Double Topping Lift Block at Kingpost

Eye Splice

Topping Lift

Double Topping Lift Block at Boom Head

Boom Head

Single Hoist Block at Boom Head

Topping Lift Leadline or Hauling Part

Kingpost

Boom

Cargo Hoist Leadline or Hauling Part also called a Cargo Runner

Upper Vang Pendant

Upper Vang Pendant

Guy (or Vang)

Upper Vang Block

Eye Splice

Lower Vang Block

Pad Eye (Attached to deck)

Gooseneck

Guy (or Vang)

Upper Vang Block

Boom Heel Block

To Hoist Winch Drum

Boom Heel Swivel Pad

Lower Vang Block

Shackle

Vang (or Guy) Tackle

Double Lower Hoist Block

Swivel Fitting

Shackle

Cargo Hook

Pad Eye (Attached to deck)

[12.11] A single swinging boom. The basic elements are the kingpost, boom, gooseneck, topping lift, and vangs (guys).

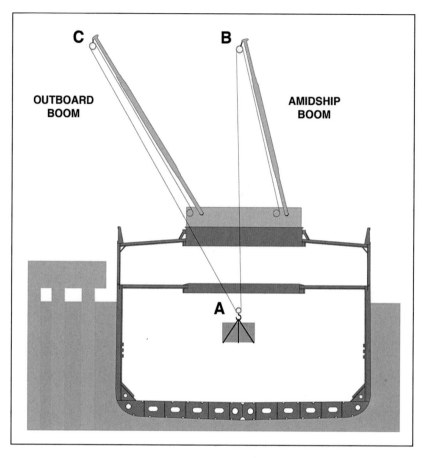

[**12.12**] A yard-and-stay rig

This was a serious handicap that severely limited the effectiveness of ships at sea. With modern techniques of UNREP, an entire fleet can be resupplied, rearmed, and refueled within hours, while it is proceeding on its mission.

There are two kinds of UNREP. One is called CONREP (for connected replenishment) and the other is called VERTREP (for vertical replenishment). CONREP is accomplished by ships coming alongside one another at a very close distance and exchanging fuel, ammunition, food, etc. VERTREP is accomplished using helicopters to lift items from one ship to another. The latter works well for things like food and ammunition but is not practical for fuel transfers. Frequently, you will hear the term UNREP used to mean CONREP.

[12.13] Underway replenishment (UNREP) allows ships to remain on station for long periods of time.

Some ships—such as replenishment tankers (AOR), oilers (AO), fast combat support ships (AOE), combat store ships (AFS), and ammunition ships (AE)—spend a great deal of their time conducting UNREPs. Other ships conduct UNREPs as necessary to keep themselves ready and on station. An aircraft carrier, for example, must UNREP with an ammunition ship to receive ordnance if it has been conducting strike operations, and might conduct periodic UNREPs with its accompanying destroyers to replenish their expended fuel.

TIDES, CURRENTS, AND WINDS

Despite all of the advances of modern technology, ships are still very much subject to the natural forces at sea and in coastal waters. Anyone who ventures onto the great waters of the world must do so with an understanding that tides, currents, and winds will have an effect on what he or she does. Whether you are piloting a small boat on a narrow waterway or are part of the team that turns an aircraft carrier into the wind to launch aircraft, the more you understand about how these forces work and what their effects will be, the better mariner you will be.

Tides

Tides are very important in naval operations. Amphibious landings are normally scheduled for high tide so that troops and equipment can land well up on a beach. In some harbors, deep-draft ships may be able to enter only

[**12.14**] Helicopters can provide vertical replenishment (VERTREP).

at high tide. Large ships are usually launched or dry-docked at high tide. Ships going alongside piers in channels subject to strong tides and currents normally wait for slack water, when the tide is neither ebbing nor flooding. Every Sailor whose responsibility is the handling of a vessel must understand the meaning and cause of various tidal conditions.

The term tide describes the regular rise and fall of the water level along a coast or in a port. The gravitational attraction of the moon is the primary cause of tides; it pulls water away from the earth. The earth's spinning motion also causes a bulge of water on the side of the earth opposite to the moon. Since the moon orbits the earth every twenty-four hours and fifty minutes, the result of these forces causes two low tides and two high tides at any given place during that period. The low and high tides are each twelve hours and twenty-five minutes apart. The sun also affects the tide, but it is so much farther away than is the moon that its pull is not nearly as great. It does, however, have an effect such that the rise and fall of tides are more complicated than they would otherwise be. Despite these variables, tides can be predicted with relative certainty and an experienced mariner will take advantage of this predictability whenever possible.

A tide rising—moving from low to high water—is said to be *flooding*. When the tide is falling, after high tide, it is said to be *ebbing*. The difference in depth between a high tide and the next low tide is considerable in many harbors; areas that are safe for a powerboat at high tide may be completely dry at low water. In some areas of the world, you might board a vessel from a pier in the morning by stepping directly across, using a level brow, and that same afternoon you would have to use a ladder to climb up to the main deck.

Currents

In most harbors and inlets, tides are the chief causes of currents; however, if the port is situated on a large river, its flow may also have a considerable effect on tidal currents. The flow of a large river will prolong the duration of an ebbing current, and the velocity of that current will be considerably greater as well.

Where currents are chiefly caused by the rise and fall of the tide, their direction and speed are largely governed by the shape of the shoreline and the contour of the ocean bottom. In a straight section of a confined waterway, the current tends to flow most rapidly in the center and much more slowly in the shallower water near either shore. If a boat goes with the current, the coxswain generally wants to stay near the center of the waterway. If a boat goes against the current, the coxswain stays as close to shore as the prevailing water depth will allow.

In many wide inlets, near the time of slack water the current may actually reverse itself in part of the inlet; while the ebb is still moving out of the main channel, a gentle flood may start near one shore. This condition, where it exists and is understood, can be helpful to a small-boat operator.

Where there is a bend in the channel, the current flows most strongly on the outside of the bend. This effect is very marked, particularly with a strong current. In some areas, a strong current can create rough water called tide rips. These are usually shown on charts and should be avoided. Every vessel, regardless of size, must make some allowance for the current's *set and drift* (direction and speed), which affects the course to be steered.

One more thing to bear in mind about currents: only on the coast does the turn of the current occur at the time of high water. In many ports, owing to the effect of the land's shape on water flow, there may be a very considerable difference between the time of high or low water and the time that the current starts to ebb or flood.

Winds

Modern naval vessels are not dependent on the wind for power, as sailing ships were, but at times the wind's effect on a ship can be considerable. Although sails are no longer used on naval vessels, the area of the ship's hull and superstructure exposed to the wind is still called *sail area*. The more sail area a ship has, the more effect wind has on it. For example, an aircraft carrier, with all of its massive sail area, will have a more difficult time moving toward a pier that has an offsetting (from the pier to the water) wind blowing than will a submarine, which is low to the water and has much less area exposed to the effects of the wind.

The natural wind that is blowing at any given time (the breeze you feel on your face, for example, when you are standing on a beach looking out to sea) is called *true wind*. You know that on a perfectly still day, when there is no wind blowing, you can easily have your cap blown off while riding in a convertible with the top down. This air flow, caused by the vehicle moving through the air, is called *relative wind* (its velocity is directly relative to the speed you are traveling). When the effects of these two are combined, the result is called *apparent wind*. For example, there will seem to be a lot more wind blowing if you drive down a road at high speed into the wind.

To illustrate these various winds, think about traveling in a small boat at a speed of 20 knots. If, when you start out, there is no (true) wind blowing, the relative wind (caused by your motion) will be 20 knots. An hour later, the wind has begun blowing out of the north at a speed of 10 knots. If you head north, the apparent wind will be 30 knots (20 relative + 10 true). If you head south, the apparent wind will be 10 knots (20 relative − 10 true).

If you head in any other direction the apparent wind will be something in between 10 and 20 knots depending upon the course chosen.

The effect of wind on ship operations can be beneficial or detrimental. During flight operations, an aircraft carrier most often heads into the wind, because the increased speed of the apparent wind helps aircraft take off and land by providing them more lift. A strong wind can make mooring a ship more difficult by keeping it off the pier or causing it to blow down on the pier too quickly.

At sea, the direction of the true wind is indicated by streaks of foam down the back sides of waves, while the direction of the apparent wind is shown by the way the ship's flags are blowing. True winds are described by the direction from which they are blowing. A north wind is blowing from the north toward the south, for example.

The side of the ship toward the wind is the *windward* side, and the side away from the wind is the *leeward* side. When the wind changes direction to the right, or clockwise, it *veers*; when it changes in the other direction (counterclockwise), it *backs*.

BOATS

The term "boat" refers to small craft limited in their use by size and usually not capable of making independent voyages of any length on the high seas. Do not make the mistake of calling a ship a "boat." It will mark you as a real landlubber. The exception to this is that submarines are more often than not called "boats."

The Navy uses thousands of boats, ranging from 9-foot dinghies to 135-foot landing craft. They are powered by diesels, outboard gasoline motors, or waterjets. Most boats are built of aluminum, fiberglass, or steel. Newer Navy boats are designed and built using the International System of units (also known as SI or metric), but older craft were designed using the English units system (feet and inches).

Types of Boats

The variety of boats is very large. Different types provide transportation, deliver supplies, assist in work and security, and participate in combat operations. A *standard boat* is a small craft carried aboard a ship to perform various tasks and evolutions, such as transporting personnel, moving supplies, and providing security. Other types have specialized capabilities. For example, *landing craft* are carried by various amphibious ships and are designed to carry troops, vehicles, or cargo from ship to shore under combat conditions, to unload, to retract from the beach, and to return to the ship. They are especially rugged, with powerful engines, and they are often armed. Landing craft are usually referred to by their designations (such as LCM or LCU) rather than by full names.

A very sophisticated landing craft used in today's fleet is the LCAC (landing craft, air cushion). As you can tell by the name, this unusual craft floats on a cushion of air that allows it to travel over water and right up onto land to deliver troops, equipment, and supplies. LCACs can clear an obstacle up to 4 feet high. They are 81 feet long and can carry a variety of vehicles or a load of more than 70 tons. Powered by 4 gas turbine engines, they are capable of speeds as high as 50 knots.

Workboats (WB) are found in shipyards and often carried on board salvage ships to assist in salvage operations, diving operations, underwater exploration, coastal survey, repair of other craft, and cargo transport between ships and shore.

[**12.15**] The LCAC uses a cushion of air to travel over both water and land to deliver troops, vehicles, and supplies ashore.

Rigid Hull Inflatable Boats (RHIB) are versatile boats designed for service as a standard ship's boat. The hull form is a combination of a rigid planing hull with an inflatable tube.

Personnel Boats (PE or PERS) are designed to transport personnel from ship to shore or from ship to ship. Those designed for officers are painted haze gray with white cabins. Those assigned for use by commanding officers, chief of staff, and squadron, patrol, or division commanders are called gigs and have a red stripe added just above the waterline. Personnel boats assigned to flag officers (admirals) are called barges. They have black hulls and a white stripe just above the waterline.

Utility Boats (UB), varying in length from 18 feet to 50 feet, are mainly cargo and personnel carriers or heavy-duty work boats. Many have been modified for survey work, tending divers, and minesweeping operations. In ideal weather, a 15-meter (50-foot) UB will carry 146 people, plus crew.

[**12.16**] A rigid hull inflatable boat (RHIB)

Utility boats are open boats, though many of the larger ones are provided with canvas canopies. The smaller utility boats are powered by outboard engines. The larger boats have diesel engines.

Punts are open square-enders, 14 feet long. They are either rowed or sculled, and are generally used in port by side cleaners.

SPECIAL BOATS

Some boats, used by shore stations and for special missions, are not normally carried on board ships. These include line-handling boats, buoy boats, aircraft rescue boats, torpedo retrievers, explosive ordnance disposal craft, utility boats, dive boats, targets, and various patrol boats. Many standard boats have been modified for special service.

[**12.17**] Personnel boats may become "gigs" when assigned to commanding officers or "barges" when assigned to flag officers.

[**12.18**] This 15-meter utility boat can carry 146 people.

Boat Crews

Most boats have permanently assigned crews. Crew size varies depending on the type of boat, but typically consists of the coxswain, an engineer, a bowhook, and sometimes a sternhook and a boat officer. All must be qualified swimmers.

Boat crews represent their parent vessel and should take pride in their appearance and that of their boat. The efficiency and smartness of a ship's boats and boat crews reflect the standards of the ship. Clean white uniforms can be hard to maintain on some ships, but custom dictates that every day the ship's laundry wash and press a uniform for each member of the duty boat's crew. Ship regulations frequently require crewmembers to wear sneakers. This is a safety factor, but it also avoids scuff marks and keeps the boats themselves looking good.

COXSWAIN

The coxswain is in charge of all personnel and equipment in the boat. Subject to the orders of the OOD and the senior line officer embarked, a coxswain otherwise has full authority and is responsible for the boat's appearance, safety, and efficient operation. The crew and passengers (including embarked troops) are required to cooperate fully with the coxswain. In fulfilling his or her responsibilities, the coxswain must be familiar with all details relating to the boat's care and handling. Equally important, the coxswain must be able to instruct the crew in all aspects of the general service and drills. The coxswain is also responsible for the appearance and behavior of the crew.

ENGINEER

The engineer ensures that the engine is in good condition and ready to run. Only the engineer should work on the engine. The engineer may also perform the duties of the sternhook.

BOWHOOK

The bowhook (pronounced to rhyme with "now") handles lines forward when the boat is coming alongside a pier or ship. The bowhook also tends fenders and forward weather cloths (canvases spread for protection against the wind). In an open boat, the bowhook usually sits on the forward thwart (cross-seat) on the starboard side, outboard. In bad weather, she or he may move to the lee side. The bowhook faces the bow and serves as a lookout.

When the boat approaches the landing, the bowhook should be ready to spring ashore with the *painter* (a length of line secured to the bow of the boat for towing or making fast) and take a turn on the nearest cleat. When the boat approaches a ship's side, the bowhook should be in the bow with the boathook, ready to snag the boat line and make it fast. The bowhook should always have a fender ready to drop over the side if a bump is unavoidable.

STERNHOOK
The sternhook, likewise, should be ready at once to jump ashore with the stern line. In an open boat, the sternhook normally sits on the starboard side, outboard on the after thwart, facing aft.

BOAT OFFICER
During heavy weather, and other times as deemed necessary, an officer (sometimes a chief petty officer) is assigned to each duty boat. A boat officer has authority over the coxswain. The boat officer does not assume the coxswain's responsibilities, or relieve the coxswain of his or her normal duties, but is there to oversee the boat operations and to ensure that safety is maintained at all times. The situation is somewhat like the relationship between the OOD and the commanding officer on the bridge. The coxswain and boat officer are responsible for the boat and for the safety and welfare of the crew and passengers.

Care of Boats
Maintenance greatly increases a boat's service life and ensures its operational readiness. The boat crew takes great care to prevent corrosion of metal-hulled boats by maintaining the paint and specified preservation coatings in good condition and ensuring that the proper number of zincs are used to prevent electrolytic corrosion.

Maintenance and repair of fiberglass hulls involve the same materials and techniques used on sports cars. Do not use laminates, resin, or hardeners without fully reading the instructions.

Repair minor damage, tighten loose bolts, and fix or replace leaking gaskets as soon as possible to prevent more repairs later. Secure all loose gear to avoid damage when the water gets rough. Keep the boat and its equipment free of dirt, corrosion, and accumulated grease.

Proper preventive maintenance is essential. Engine oil changes, battery servicing, and other maintenance should be performed in accordance with the planned maintenance system (PMS) for the boat. Gear housings, steering mechanisms, and other moving parts must be well lubricated. All rubber exhaust couplings should be checked for tightness and condition. When a boat is hoisted out of the water, the struts, propeller, sea suctions, and shaft bearings should be checked. Dog-eared propellers or worn shaft bearings cause heavy vibration, which may result in severe damage to the hull or engine.

Oil-soaked bilges are a fire hazard. When draining or filling fuel tanks or engine crankcases, avoid spilling diesel fuel or engine oil.

Fenders should be placed between boats when they are tied up.

Boat Customs and Etiquette

Just as Navy ships adhere to certain customs and traditions, so do Navy boats. See TAB 12-F: Boat Customs and Etiquette for additional information.

Boat Equipment

Every Navy boat in active service must have a complete outfit of equipment for meeting any ordinary situation. It is necessary to requisition part of the outfit. When a boat is turned in, its outfit also must be turned in, unless the boat is to be replaced by another of the same type. In that event, the outfit is retained. If a boat is to be replaced by one of a different type, the only items retained are those allowed for the new boat.

Hoisting and Lowering Boats

The process of hoisting and lowering boats is potentially dangerous and should be approached with the utmost attention to safety. While larger ships may use a crane to hoist and lower boats, *davits* are more commonly used. Davits are crane-like devices at the side edge of a ship's deck that are specially designed to hoist and stow boats aboard ship. Hoisting boats with double-arm davits is somewhat more complicated than lifting them with a crane. The boat is attached to the sea painter in the same manner as with a crane—particularly if the ship has headway and must therefore take the same precautions against broaching to when the boat is lifted.

There are a number of different kinds of davits in use in the Navy.

[**12.19**] Hoisting and launching boats are important seamanship skills.

Gravity davits are found on newer ships. Power is not required to lower boats. The boat lowers by gravity as it is suspended from the falls, and the descent speed is controlled with the boat's davit-winch manual brake. Several types of gravity davits are used. Depending on the design, a pair of modified davits may handle one to four boats; they are designated as single-, double-, or quadruple-davits. These are used mainly with amphibious craft.

An *overhead suspended davit* is a special gravity davit used beneath a sponson or other overhang found on aircraft carriers and helicopter landing ships.

A *slewing arm davit* (SLAD) is a mechanical davit with a single arm. The davit arm is mounted on a pedestal and rotates about a vertical axis when moving the boat outboard and inboard in a slewing type motion.

A *trackway davit* is a gravity davit consisting of an arm or arms mounted on rollers that run on an inclined trackway or trackways that are mounted on the deck. The incline on the trackway(s) is sufficient for gravity to cause the boat and arm(s) to move down the trackway(s) from the inboard position to the outboard position so that the boat may be lowered into the water.

LAUNCHING

Before swinging out a boat to be lowered, first make sure that the hull drain plugs are in. Each person in the boat wears a life jacket and hard hat and has a lifeline (monkey line) in hand. Run your sea painter outboard of everything on the ship, to the ship side of the bow, and belay with a toggle, so you can let it go without difficulty.

The boat's engine is started while the boat is in the air, but the clutch is never engaged until the falls are unhooked and hauled clear. In releasing the boat, the after fall is always unhooked first. Before starting ahead, take care that there are no trailing lines astern that might foul the screw. When the boat runs ahead and the painter slackens, the painter is thrown off by pulling out the toggle. The sea painter is hauled back to the ship by the light line attached to it.

HOISTING

When a boat comes alongside an underway ship to be hoisted in, the crew first secures the end of the sea painter. The shipboard end of the line is bent securely to a cleat or a set of bitts. The boat end of the painter is lowered by a light line and made fast to a forward inboard cleat. The sea painter is never bent to the boat's stern or to the side of the bow away from the ship. If it is, the boat, when riding to the painter, will dive against the ship's side and perhaps capsize. It is also important that the boat be driven ahead and allowed to drop back on the sea painter to position itself exactly under the crane before lifting. Otherwise, it may broach to (turn crossways to the flow of water) and capsize as it starts to leave the water.

Once the boat rides to the painter, its engine is secured and the slings are attached. Steadying lines are secured to the cleats on the outboard side of the boat and brought back on deck to hold it steady as it rises. The bowhooks and sternhooks must fend the boat off the side of the ship to prevent damage to either.

Ready Lifeboat

Regulations require that a ship at sea have at least one boat rigged and ready to be lowered for use as a lifeboat. The ship's boat bill states the exact specifications a lifeboat must meet and the equipment it must have.

At the start of each watch, the lifeboat coxswain musters the crew, checks the boat and gear, has the engine tested, and reports to the OOD. Depending upon current operations, the crew may be required to remain near the boat.

The ready lifeboat, usually a RHIB, is secured for sea in the davits, ready for lowering. The lifeboat has its sea painter already rigged, and the lifelines are cleared for running. The boat should have a full tank of fuel, and the lubricating oil reservoir should be full. Keep an extra can of oil on board. The bilge should be clean and dry and the boat plug in place. Life jackets are to be ready nearby or in the boat so the crew may don them quickly before lowering away.

Even though today's Navy is technologically advanced to an astonishing degree, many aspects of basic seamanship have changed little since the days of sail. Ships still use mooring lines and anchors much as the tall ships of yesteryear did, and boats are still an important part of the Navy's inventory. As a Sailor, you are tied to the sea—directly or indirectly—and you should know the basics of seamanship no matter what your rate. Besides being a point of pride, understanding the ways of the sea and how to cope with them may someday mean the difference between success and failure or even life and death.

THIRTEEN

WATCHSTANDING

Y ou may sometimes hear the term "24/7," meaning that something is occurring twenty-four hours a day, seven days a week—or more simply put, *all the time*. In the Navy this is more than an expression; it is a way of life, and it comes from the nature of what we do. Defending the nation is an around-the-clock job, requiring various people to continuously perform certain tasks, or to be ready to execute orders on a moment's notice. Just as police must remain on patrol and ready to respond quickly when needed, the nation's guardians must likewise be on the job without pause.

Since no individual can be on the job twenty-four hours a day, certain responsibilities must be carried out by different people taking turns for a specified number of hours at a time. This is similar to working shifts in factories or offices that operate around the clock. In the Navy, we call these shifts *watches*. They can involve a wide range of activities, from simply manning a radio or a telephone, to standing guard duty, to steering a ship, to operating a piece of machinery or electronic equipment, to monitoring intelligence indications and warnings, to . . . The possibilities are many. Another matter of terminology is that we refer to *standing* our watches, whether we are indeed on our feet or not.

During your time in the Navy it is likely that you will be required to stand watches—probably a number of different kinds. It is vitally important that you take watchstanding seriously, no matter what the task at hand. It is a mark of pride and a means of efficiency and, sometimes, a matter of survival that we stand our watches vigilantly at all times.

To cover all the watchstanding duties in the Navy would require a book much bigger than this one, but we will discuss a few of the more common types you might encounter.

SENTRY DUTY

We often associate guard duty with soldiers, yet people and equipment must be safeguarded in the Navy as well. You may find yourself standing sentry duty on a pier in a foreign country or walking the rounds on your ship as part of a security patrol or as a rover.

Requirements for standing sentry duty are the same as those for nearly all watches: keep alert, attend to duty, report all violations, preserve order, and remain on watch until properly relieved. Your immediate superior may be called the "petty officer of the guard," the "petty officer of the watch," the "officer of the deck," the "command duty officer," or some other title. For the purposes of this discussion, we will refer to your immediate superior as the petty officer of the watch. Whatever your superior is called, you must take your orders from that person. When you are detailed to a sentry watch, you will conduct yourself according to both special and general orders.

Special orders apply to a particular watch and will be rather specific. These orders will be passed on and explained to you before you assume the watch. You may receive these orders directly from the petty officer of the watch, or you may receive them from the sentry you are relieving.

The eleven general orders are the same throughout the Navy (and very similar in the other armed forces for that matter). You will—on any watch or duty, now and in the future—be responsible for carrying them out, even if no one has explained them to you or reminded you of them. For that reason, you must memorize these eleven general orders and be prepared to recite all or any of them whenever called upon to do so. Each of the general orders is listed and briefly explained below. For quick reference the orders (without accompanying explanations) are also included as TAB 13-A: The General Orders of a Sentry.

The General Orders of a Sentry

1. **Take charge of this post and all government property in view.**
   When you are a sentry, you are "in charge." This means that no one—no matter what his or her rank or position—may overrule your authority in carrying out your orders. The only way that you may be exempted

from carrying out your orders is if your orders are changed by your superior. For example, if your orders are to allow no one to enter a fenced-in compound, you must prevent everyone from entering, even if an admiral tells you it is all right for him or her to enter. The petty officer of the watch, or whoever is your immediate superior, may modify your orders to allow the admiral to enter, but without that authorization you must keep the admiral out. Situations such as this will not often—if ever—occur, but it is important that you understand the principles involved.

It is also your responsibility to know the limits of your post. This information will be conveyed to you among your special orders. You must also treat all government property that you can see as though it were your own, even if it is not technically part of your assigned post.

2. **Walk my post in a military manner, keeping always on the alert and observing everything that takes place within sight or hearing.**
Maintain a military posture, meaning do not slouch or scuffle; you are on duty in an important position and you should look like it as a means of conveying your authority and responsibility. "Keep your eyes peeled," as the expression goes. Be vigilant by looking around at all times. Do not hide from the rain or cold in poor weather. If you see or hear anything unusual, investigate it and, if needed, report it, depending upon the circumstances and your special orders.

3. **Report all violations of orders I am instructed to enforce.**
If, for example, someone is climbing a fence near your post, you must report it, even if the offender stops climbing and runs away after your challenge. In this case, even though it appears that the threat to security is over, there is no way for you to know whether this violator is the only one involved. And even though the climber may have just been seeking a shortcut back to her or his ship, you cannot be certain that there is not something more sinister involved. Let your superiors make the judgment calls; your job is to report what happens on or near your post.

4. **Repeat all calls from any post more distant from the guardhouse (quarterdeck) than my own.**
In these days of modern communications, sentries will probably have telephones or radios at their disposal with which to make their reports.

But if they do not, or if there is a power failure or some other reason that the modern equipment fails, the age-old practice of relaying the word is very important.

The term "guardhouse" in this general order refers to the command post or point of control for the watches. It might be the quarter-deck on board ship or a tent in the field.

5. **Quit my post only when properly relieved.**
You should not leave your post until your relief has come to take your place or until the petty officer of the guard has told you that the watch is no longer necessary. If the person relieving you is late, report it to the petty officer of the watch but do not quit your post. If you become ill and can no longer stand your watch, notify the petty officer of the watch and he or she will provide you a proper relief.

6. **Receive, obey, and pass on to the sentry who relieves me all orders from the commanding officer, command duty officer, officer of the deck, and officers and petty officers of the watch only.**
It is essential that you receive and obey all of the special orders that apply to your watch. It is also essential that you pass these orders on to your relief only.

7. **Talk to no one except in the line of duty.**
Having conversations about matters not pertaining to your duty is distracting and must be avoided. If someone tries to engage you in casual conversation while you are standing your watch, it is your responsibility to inform them that you are on duty and cannot talk with them until relieved of duty.

8. **Give the alarm in case of fire or disorder.**
While this is rather straightforward, keep in mind that a fire or disorder of some kind might be a deliberate distraction to keep you from observing some other disorderly or subversive activity. If you are certain that a fire is not meant to be a distraction, you should fight the fire if you have the means to do so. Remember, however, that your first responsibility is to report whatever is wrong.

9. **Call the OOD in any case not covered by instructions.**

   The rule here is "When in doubt, ask." If you are not sure what you are supposed to do in a particular situation, it is better to ask for clarification than to make an assumption or to guess.

10. **Salute all officers, and all colors and standards not cased.**

    Even though you are in charge of your post and everyone, including officers, must obey your instructions insofar as they pertain to your duties, you must still extend the appropriate military courtesies.

    Both terms, "colors" and "standards," refer to the national ensign. The national ensign may be referred to as "the colors" when it is fixed to a staff, mast, or pike (e.g., when flown from a flagstaff or carried in a parade). When it is fixed to a vehicle, it is called "the national standard." A flag is considered "cased" when it is furled and placed in a protective covering.

    If your duties allow, you should take part in morning or evening colors ceremonies, but do not sacrifice your vigilance in doing so. For example, if your assignment requires that you watch a certain area and the national ensign is being hoisted in a different direction, you should stand at attention and salute but do not face the colors; keep looking in the direction you are supposed to be watching.

11. **Be especially watchful at night, and during the time for challenging, to challenge all persons on or near my post, and to allow no one to pass without proper authority.**

    Challenging persons while you are on sentry duty is accomplished by a mix of custom and common sense. When a person or party approaches your post, you should challenge them at a distance that is sufficient for you to react if they turn out to have hostile intentions. You should say in a firm voice, loud enough to be easily heard, "Halt! Who goes there?" or "Who is there?" Once the person answers, you should then say, "Advance to be recognized." If you are challenging a group of people, you should say, "Advance one to be recognized." If you have identified the person or persons approaching, permit them to pass. If you are not satisfied with that person's identification, you must detain the person and call the petty officer of the watch.

When two or more individuals approach from different directions at the same time, challenge each in turn and require each to halt until told to proceed.

Armed Sentries

Standing sentry duty will usually mean that you are armed. In addition to sentry watches, other duties may require you to be armed, such as when carrying official mail, guarding prisoners, and, sometimes, being part of a shore patrol party.

No one is to be assigned to any duty requiring the use of a weapon until he or she has been properly trained in its use, including all safety precautions. Whenever you are armed, always treat your weapon with the utmost respect. See TAB 17-D: Proper Use of Small Arms for additional guidance.

SHIPBOARD WATCHSTANDING

When the ship is under way, a number of watch stations must be manned to keep the ship running safely. But even in port, many functions must be performed aboard ship around the clock to ensure that the ship is secure, providing certain "hotel" services for those who are living aboard and being ready for emergencies—including war. Shipboard watch organization is covered in chapter 4 of the current version of OPNAVINST 3120.32.

Conditions of Readiness (Cruising Conditions)

The appropriate watch organization is determined by the ship's condition of readiness. These are described below and also included as TAB 13-B: Conditions of Readiness, and it should be apparent that, generally speaking, the lower the number of the readiness condition, the more people will be required to be on watch. *Material* conditions of readiness (discussed in the chapter on "Damage Control") are set accordingly as well:

Condition I. Known as "general quarters." All hands are at battle stations, and the ship is in its maximum state of readiness. This condition is set on board ship if the ship is expecting combat or if some other emergency situation (such as a bad fire) occurs. Everyone on board has an assigned station that he or she must go to whenever Condition I is set.

Condition II. This condition is set only on large ships and is used when the ship is expecting to be in a heightened state of readiness for an extended period of time but the operations at hand are such that some relaxation of readiness is permissible.

Condition III. Wartime cruising with approximately one-third of the crew on watch. Weapon stations are manned in accordance with the threat, and other stations are manned or partially manned to fit the particular circumstances.

Condition IV. Normal peacetime cruising. Only necessary persons are on watch, while the rest of the crew engages in work, training, recreation, or rest as appropriate. This condition ensures an adequate number of qualified personnel are on watch for the safe and effective operation of the ship, yet allows for the most economical use of personnel in watch assignments.

Condition V. Peacetime watch in port. Enough of the crew is on board to get the ship under way if necessary or to handle emergencies.

Condition VI. Peacetime watch in port where only minimum personnel are required to keep an eye on the ship in order to maintain minimum security and to watch for fire or flooding. The ship will not be able to get under way without bringing more personnel on board and will require outside assistance to fight anything more than a minor fire.

There are also several variations of Condition I designed to meet special circumstances:

Condition IA. Personnel on station to conduct amphibious operations and a limited defense of the ship during landing operations.

Condition IAA. Personnel on station to counter an air threat.

Condition IAS. Personnel on station to counter a submarine threat.

Condition IE. Temporary relaxation from full readiness of Condition I for brief periods of rest and distribution of food at battle stations. This condition is set for brief periods during a lull in operations.

Condition IM. Personnel on station to take mine countermeasures.

Traditional Watch Structure

Literally hundreds of different kinds of watches are stood throughout the Navy to perform different functions. Watches can differ in length and when

they begin and end depending upon circumstances and command preferences. But there is a basic, traditional model that is either used in actuality
or is departed from as necessary (see TAB 13-C: Traditional Navy Watch
Structure). This model is based upon normal shipboard conditions and
has been traditional for centuries. It is based upon four-hour watches that
run around the clock. Four hours is the standard, because that was widely
accepted as the optimum time for a person to carry out the duties associated with operating a ship without suffering the dangerous effects of
fatigue. There is some disagreement about that standard, and studies have
been conducted to test other models. Consequently, you may encounter different ways of structuring watches at your command.

Ship's Bells

What began as a necessity has continued as a tradition. At various commands, you will hear bells ringing on the half hour that are very confusing
to the uninitiated.

For many centuries, Sailors did not have the luxury of a personal time-
piece. If watchstanders were to be relieved on time, some means of telling
the time had to be devised. A system that used a half-hour sandglass and
the ship's bell was created and has been used for hundreds of years. See
TAB 13-D: Ship's Bells for a description of this system that is still in use,
more out of tradition than function.

At the beginning of a watch, the sandglass was turned over to start it
running. As soon as it ran out, the watchstanders knew the first half hour
had passed, so they rang the ship's bell once and immediately turned the
sandglass over to start the second half hour. All on board the ship could
hear the bell so they could keep track of the time. When the sand ran out
the second time, the watchstanders again reversed the sandglass and rang
the ship's bell twice. They continued this until eight bells had been rung
(representing the passage of four hours or one complete watch). The watch
was then relieved, and the new watch team started the whole cycle over by
ringing one bell once the first half hour had passed, and so on.

This bell-ringing tradition (without the sandglass) continues on board
many Navy ships and at some other commands even though clocks and
watches are now used. Today, because bells are rung more out of tradition
than for real function, they are not normally rung between taps and reveille
(normal sleeping hours for Sailors not on watch), nor are they rung during divine services. A tradition, still observed in many Navy ships, is the

[**13.1**] Ship's bells—once an important part of shipboard watch-standing—are still a part of a proud heritage. Here, the bell of the attack cargo ship *Yancey* has been moved ashore for ceremonial purposes at Naval Air Station Meridian, Mississippi.

custom of the youngest member of the crew striking eight bells at midnight on New Year's Eve to ring in the New Year.

Watch Sections

On board ships and operational commands, you will more than likely be assigned to a watch section. When the word is passed that a specific section has the watch, everyone in that section immediately reports to her or his watch station. Different commands will have different numbers of watch sections, depending upon their size and the condition of readiness in effect.

Watch Stations

As already stated, there are hundreds of different watches in the Navy—too many to discuss all of them here, but several of the key shipboard stations are worth mentioning.

BRIDGE WATCHES

While a ship is under way, the bridge watch team ensures the safe navigation of the ship, supervises the daily routine, monitors communications, conducts drills, and generally oversees the safety and smooth operation of the ship. The *Officer of the Deck* (OOD) is in charge of this team and is the captain's direct representative for these duties.

Before an individual can stand OOD watches, the nature of the responsibilities involved requires that he or she must earn the trust of the captain. This is accomplished through an intensive training program that includes on-the-job training and relevant testing. Because no two ships are exactly alike—either in their physical layout or in their procedures—qualification as OOD on one ship does not automatically qualify the individual to stand OOD watches on other ships. OODs must requalify each time they join another ship.

Depending upon the ship, the OOD may be assisted by a *Junior Officer of the Deck* (JOOD) and, on larger ships, there may be a *Junior Officer of the Watch* (JOOW) as well.

With some exceptions, OODs, JOODs, and JOOWs are officers. Assisting them are a number of enlisted watchstanders.

The *Boatswain's Mate of the Watch* (BMOW) supervises and trains the enlisted members of the watch team, passes the word over the ship's general announcing (1MC) system, and assists the OOD and JOOD as directed. It is his or her responsibility that all deck watch stations are manned and that all hands in previous watch sections are relieved. Although it is the duty of the section leader and the division petty officer to instruct the people they send on watch, the BMOW must verify that every person on his watch team has been properly instructed and trained. A BMOW must also be a qualified helmsman, lee helmsman, and lookout.

The *Quartermaster of the Watch* (QMOW) is usually assigned from the navigation department. The QMOW maintains the ship's log and assists the OOD in navigational matters, including monitoring changes of weather and dealing with shipping. This watchstander is also a qualified helmsman.

The *Helmsman* steers the ship using the helm (steering wheel) as directed by the conning officer, and the *Lee Helmsman* controls the engines as directed by the conning officer.

Phone Talkers man sound-powered telephone circuits (explained in Chapter 20) to maintain communication with other key watch stations (such as the lookouts and engineering watchstanders), and the *Messenger* delivers messages to other parts of the ship, answers telephones, wakes up watch reliefs, and carries out other duties assigned by the OOD.

When the ship is under way, the OOD (or the JOOD or JOOW) will be in control (known as "having the conn") of the ship and will issue orders directly to the helm and lee helm to control the ship's movements. The captain can take the conn at any time if he or she so chooses.

LOOKOUTS

Another part of the ship's watch team are the ship's lookouts. Even though modern ships are equipped with modern electronic sensors, such as radar and sonar, they may not detect such things as smoke, small navigational markers, objects close to the ship, flares, or people in the water. The lookouts serve as the eyes of the ship to ensure safety and to provide amplifying information as needed.

You may very well stand lookout watches at some time during your stay in the Navy. As a lookout, you must do much more than keep your eyes open. You must know how to search in a way that will effectively cover your area of responsibility, and you must be able to report the location of an object to the OOD in a way that will give her or him the information she or he needs. You must watch for ships, planes, land, rocks, shoals, periscopes, discolored water, buoys, beacons, lighthouses, distress signals, floating objects of all kinds, and anything else unusual. You must not only be the eyes but the ears of the ship as well, and report sounds, such as fog horns, ships' bells, whistle buoys, airplanes, surf, and anything unusual. The golden rule of being a good lookout is, "If in doubt, report it." It is better to give the OOD too much information than to miss the one critical piece of information that can put the ship in jeopardy.

How many lookouts a ship will have at any given time depends upon the size and type of the ship and the conditions in which she is operating. Small ships will usually have only three lookouts: two in the vicinity of the bridge, port and starboard, and one after lookout somewhere astern. Larger ships may have more lookouts assigned to provide additional coverage. Each is stationed where he or she can best cover the surface and sky within his or her assigned zone. If lookouts are stationed any distance away from the OOD, they will wear sound-powered phones so that they may expeditiously send reports. It is good practice for a lookout to only use one of the earphones on the sound-powered set—placing the other on the side of his or her head—so that the free ear can be used to listen for relevant sounds as described above.

Low-visibility Lookouts. In fog or bad weather, additional lookouts are stationed immediately in the "eyes of the ship" as far forward as practical and on the bridge wings. Sound carries much farther in fog than on clear days, so a lookout must listen closely—especially if he or she is located in the bow—for whistles, bells, buoys, and even the wash of water against rocks or a nearby ship or boat. For this reason, fog lookouts do not wear sound-powered phones. An additional Sailor is assigned to man the phones at each fog lookout station to make reports to the OOD.

Binoculars. Contrary to widespread belief, it is not always better to search with binoculars. Several factors govern when and how they should be used. In fog, for instance, they should not be used at all. At night, however, they will enhance your vision and should be used often.

Keep in mind that while they significantly magnify, binoculars' field of view is usually only about 7 degrees, which is pretty narrow. This means you can see objects at considerably greater distances than with the naked eye, but you are able to view only a very small portion of your assigned sector while looking through them. To counter this limitation, you should use a special scanning technique when using binoculars to search for targets. This is a step-by-step method of looking. To understand this technique, try moving your eyes around a room or across the horizon rapidly and note that as long as your eyes are in motion, you see almost nothing. You may have noticed this if you ever saw a video shot by someone who was moving the camera too rapidly—everything is a blur. Now allow your eyes to move in short steps from object to object. You will be able to see what is there. When searching a seemingly empty stretch of sea, make yourself search your sector in short steps (approximately 5 degrees at a time), pausing between steps for approximately five seconds to see what, if anything, is in the field of view. At the end of your sector, lower the glasses and rest your eyes for a few seconds, then search the sector in the reverse direction with the naked eye.

As a sky lookout you should search from the horizon to the zenith (straight overhead), using binoculars only to identify a contact after you have spotted something with the naked eye. Move your eyes in quick steps—also about 5 degrees—across your sector just above the horizon, shift your gaze up about 10 degrees, and search back to the starting point. Repeat this process until the zenith is reached and you are looking straight up, then rest your eyes for a few seconds before starting over.

[**13.2**] Step-by-step scanning as a lookout

Lookout Reports. Every object sighted (called a "contact" in naval terminology) should be immediately reported to the OOD, no matter how insignificant it may seem to you. The report consists of several parts as applicable:

1. WHAT YOU SEE: Describe the contact quickly and briefly. Name the type or class of ship or aircraft if you recognize it; otherwise, simply report "ship," "plane," and so forth. If all you see is an object or a light but cannot make out any details, report it as simply a "contact."
2. BEARING: Always report contacts in relative bearings. These are given as three digits, spoken digit by digit.
3. RANGE: Estimate the contact's distance from your ship and report that in yards/miles. This is spoken digit by digit, except that multiples of hundreds and thousands are spoken as such.
4. TARGET ANGLE: Report target angle on all ships, given in three digits, spoken digit by digit.
5. POSITION ANGLE: Report position angle on all aircraft, given in one or two digits, spoken as a whole, not digit by digit.
6. MOVEMENT: Report whether the contact is moving from right to left, left to right, opening, closing, paralleling, high speed, slow speed, dead in the water, and so forth.

Because they do not always have access to a compass at their watch station, lookouts report objects in degrees of *relative bearing*. Navigational directions are described by true bearings where 000° represents true north,

090° is east, 180° is south, 270° is west, and other directions are in between as appropriate. Relative bearings are similar to true bearings except that they are oriented on the ship's bow instead of true north. Therefore, 000° represents the ship's bow when using relative bearings. Just as true bearings progress in a clockwise direction, so do relative bearings. If you want to report a periscope that is broad on the ship's starboard side, its relative bearing is 090°. A fishing boat dead astern would be reported as 180°R, and a buoy approximately halfway between would be 135°R.

Bearings are always reported in three digits and spoken digit by digit. For example, you would report a merchant ship broad on your port side as "two-seven-zero degrees relative."

Target angle is the relative bearing of your ship from another ship. This can be a little confusing at first, but to visualize what this is more clearly, imagine that you are on the other ship (the one you are reporting) and think about what would be the relative bearing of your actual ship as seen from there.

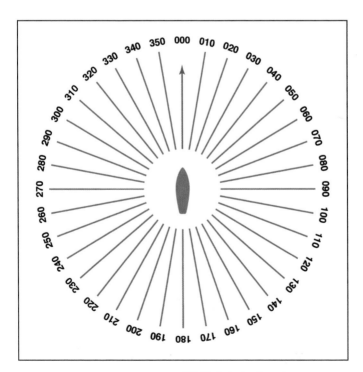

[**13.3**] Relative bearings are measured clockwise from the ship's bow to locate an object in relation to the ship.

An object in the sky is located by its relative bearing and position angle. The position angle of an aircraft is its height in degrees above the horizon, as seen from the ship. The horizon is considered to be zero degrees and directly overhead is 90 degrees. Position angles can never be more than 90 degrees, and they are given in one or two digits and spoken as a whole number, not digit by digit. To avoid confusion with relative bearings, the words "position angle" are always spoken before the numerals. Thus, if you spot an aircraft flying just a little above the horizon halfway between the bow and the starboard side of your ship, you would report it as "zero-four-five degrees relative, position angle ten." A helicopter hovering dead astern of your ship, about two-thirds of the way between the horizon and straight up, would be reported as "one-eight-zero degrees relative, position angle sixty."

Some examples of typical lookout reports are as follows:

BRIDGE—PORT LOOKOUT—SURFACE CONTACT BEARING TWO EIGHT ZERO—TWO THOUSAND YARDS—TARGET ANGLE ZERO NINER ZERO—MOVING FROM LEFT TO RIGHT SLOWLY.

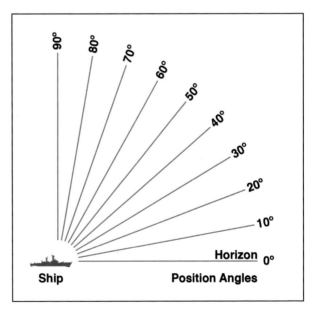

[**13.4**] Position angles locate objects in the sky.

BRIDGE—STARBOARD LOOKOUT—DESTROYER BEARING ONE ZERO ZERO—SIX MILES—TARGET ANGLE ZERO ONE ZERO—CLOSING RAPIDLY.

BRIDGE—STARBOARD LOOKOUT—F-14 JET FIGHTER BEARING ZERO FOUR ZERO—POSITION ANGLE THIRTY THREE—MOVING FROM RIGHT TO LEFT VERY RAPIDLY.

In the chapter on communications, you will find some additional guidance on proper reporting.

QUARTERDECK WATCHES

In port the OOD shifts the watch from the bridge to the quarterdeck. Although the ship is not under way, the OOD must still be vigilant about the safety of the ship, checking mooring lines or anchor chains as appropriate, monitoring weather conditions for any significant changes, and controlling access to the ship. The OOD and her or his watch team supervise and carry out the ship's routine, conduct honors and ceremonies as appropriate, control the ship's 1MC system, conduct drills, and carry out any additional orders from the captain, the executive officer, or the command duty officer—an officer placed in charge of the ship in the captain's absence.

Just as at sea, the OOD is assisted by a watch team in port. The OOD's principal assistant is the petty officer of the watch—sometimes called the BMOW just as when under way. There will nearly always be one or more messengers of the watch assigned and, depending upon circumstances, extra lookouts may be required. An anchor watch may be added to keep an eye on the anchor chain and report any excess strain or other problems to the OOD.

ENGINEERING WATCHES

The engineering watch team is headed by the *engineering officer of the watch* (EOOW). He or she is responsible for the safe and proper performance of all engineering watches and ensures that all engine orders from the OOD are promptly and properly executed. The EOOW is assisted by a number of *watchstanders* that vary depending upon the type of engineering plant.

DAMAGE-CONTROL WATCHES

The *damage-control watch team* is responsible for maintaining the proper material condition of readiness and for checking, repairing, and keeping in full operation the various hull systems affecting watertight integrity, stability, and other conditions that affect the safety of the ship.

COMBAT INFORMATION CENTER (CIC) WATCHES

The number and types of watches in CIC will vary considerably according to the condition of readiness and the types of operations being conducted. Under routine underway operations, there will be a *CIC watch officer* (CICWO) who will be assisted by one or more radar and radio operators. This team detects, reports, tracks, and evaluates air, surface, and submarine contacts during the watch.

When the potential for hostile action is increased, a *tactical action officer* (TAO) may be assigned by the commanding officer to take timely and decisive action in matters concerning the tactical employment and defense of the unit. The TAO is responsible for the safe and effective operation of combat systems.

DEPARTMENTAL DUTY WATCHES

Because members of the crew go ashore in port, it is important to have qualified personnel assigned to carry out normal or emergency departmental functions. Each department will assign a duty department head and additional personnel as necessary to be responsible for departmental functions. The supply department, for example, may assign a duty supply officer, a duty storekeeper, and duty cooks as necessary.

Logs

Many watch stations require a log, which is a permanent, written record of occurrences during a watch. Besides assisting watchstanders in keeping track of what has happened, logs can have legal status in a court of law and can be entered as evidence. For these reasons, log entries should be complete, accurate, and in standard naval language. Names and figures must be carefully recorded. The ship's deck log and the engineering log are examples of logs that are considered to be official records of a ship. Because of their legal status, no erasures may be made in any of these logs. When a correction is necessary, a line must be drawn through the original entry so it remains legible and the correct entry inserted. Corrections, additions, or changes in any log are made only by the person required to sign it, and initialed by that person in the margin of the page.

SHIP'S DECK LOG

This is the official chronological record of events occurring during a bridge or quarterdeck watch, which may concern the crew, operation, and safety of the ship, or may be of historical value. The OOD supervises the keeping of the log, and the QMOW, or other designated watchstander, actually writes the log. Each event is recorded in accordance with standing instructions. All log entries are made with a ballpoint pen, using black ink. Sample deck-log entries are contained in the *Watch Officer's Guide*.

The navigator examines the log daily, and the commanding officer approves it at the end of each month. The original ship's deck log goes to the chief of naval operations every month. A duplicate copy is kept on board for six months, after which it may be destroyed.

ENGINEERING LOG

This log is the official record of important information about the operation of the propulsion plant and auxiliary equipment. It contains entries such as the total miles steamed for the day, the ship's draft and displacement, engineering casualties experienced, and other pertinent information as described in OPNAVINST 3120.32.

Relieving the Watch

When relieving the watch, you should always report at least fifteen minutes before your watch is scheduled to begin so you can receive information and instructions from the off-going watch. Most ships muster oncoming watch sections to make sure each watchstander is ready ahead of time, but even if there is not a formal muster, you should always arrive early (at least fifteen minutes—longer if there is a lot going on). This is to allow you enough time to be sure that you fully understand all that is going on and all that is expected of you before you assume responsibility for the watch. Relieving the watch is a controlled and precise function and should always be treated as very serious business. Formality is the rule and casual behavior is clearly out of place.

The following steps are the minimum requirements for a good watch turnover if you are reporting to assume a watch:

1. State to the person you are relieving, "I am ready to relieve you." Use these exact words so there is no possibility of confusion. "What'cha got?" or "I'm ready" is not sufficient.

2. Once the off-going watch has explained everything that is going on or is likely to happen and you have asked all the questions you need to ask, you and the person you are relieving should report your readiness to assume the watch to the next senior person in the watch organization by saying, "Request permission to relieve the watch."

3. The senior watchstander will respond by saying, "Permission granted."

4. The off-going watch will render a salute to the senior watch-stander and state, "[The name of the watch station] properly relieved by [state your rate and name]."

5. You should then signify to all present that you have formally accepted the duties of the watch by saluting the senior watch-stander and stating, "I assume the duties of [watch station]." You should precede the latter by identifying yourself, particularly if it is dark as on the bridge at night. For example, you would say, "This is Seaman Garrett. I assume the duties of helmsman."

This procedure unequivocally transfers the responsibility for the watch from the previous watchstander to you. Thereafter, you assume complete authority and responsibility for the watch until someone follows the same procedure to relieve you of the watch.

NIGHT VISION

Night watches entail some extra preparations. If, for example, you were coming directly from a lighted compartment to a night watch as a lookout, you would be almost blind for a while. As your eyes become accustomed to the weak light, your vision gradually improves. After ten minutes you can see fairly well, and after thirty minutes you have your best night vision. This improvement is called *dark adaptation*.

Obviously, it is unsatisfactory to have someone standing a night watch who does not have 100 percent vision. To prevent this lost time while your eyes are adjusting to the dark, you must be sure that your eyes are not exposed to any white light, such as everyday light bulbs and fluorescent tubes, before going on watch. Fortunately, the human eye's ability to see in the dark is not affected by red light. That is why you will see only red lights on after dark in berthing compartments and at the various watch stations. Even with these precautions, there are places in the ship where you might encounter white light, such as on the mess decks where you might want to go get a sandwich or a cup of coffee before going on watch. To protect your eyes from any unwanted exposure to white light, you must put on specially designed red goggles before going on night lookout duty, at least a half hour before you must report for your watch. Be sure to leave them on for the full thirty minutes. These goggles prepare your eyes for darkness without affecting your ability to go about normal prewatch activities such as writing letters, getting dressed and ready for your watch, or even watching television. Even with this precaution, you should still give yourself at least an additional five minutes of adjusting to the outside conditions before actually assuming the watch. As you'll learn, it will probably take longer than that to get a full report from the person you are preparing to relieve.

Once you have assumed a watch at night, you must learn to use your "night eyes" effectively. Because of the way your eyes are made—the light receptors for white (daytime) light are in the center of your eye, while your night-vision receptors are located around the daylight ones, off center—you normally look directly at an object to see it best in the daylight, but in the dark you should look slightly to one side of an object to see it best. This will take some practice, but once you get used to it, you will be amazed at how well it works.

At night, it is easier to locate a moving object than a stationary one. But most objects in or on the water move relatively slowly. To counter this, move your eyes instead. This technique will significantly enhance your ability to pick up targets in the night. Slowly scan the area in broad sweeps instead of stopping to search a section at a time. If you think you see something while scanning, avoid the natural tendency to look right at it. Use the off-center technique to confirm the sighting and then report it.

Night-Vision Goggles (NVG). These special goggles may be available to you for enhanced night vision capability. They use ambient light to illuminate the darkness. Ambient light at sea at night comes mostly from the moon and stars. The more ambient light there is, the brighter and clearer the picture is for the user. All light, including color light, will stand out with the use of NVGs. The light is magnified to make it appear brighter than it really is. For example, a lit cigarette will look like a torch or bright flash light. Although colored light is picked up by NVGs very easily, you will not be able to distinguish what color you are seeing. The NVG display is monochromatic, which means it shows all lights, colored or white, in shades of green. Red light will be somewhat weaker to pick up. The brighter the actual light, the brighter it appears through NVGs, sometimes blinding the user of the goggles and making it nearly impossible to determine the source of the light.

[13.5] Night-vision goggles amplify the existing light. Here we see a guided-missile destroyer firing Tomahawk missiles.

WATCHES UNDER ARMS

Some watches—ashore and at sea—require the watchstander to be armed. In these cases, it is essential—both for safety and for efficiency—that you adhere to specific practices.

For relevant information regarding proper procedures in these special circumstances, see TAB 17-D: Proper Use of Small Arms.

As indicated at the beginning of this chapter, watchstanding is an essential part of the Navy. Watch stations exist to ensure readiness, safety, and efficiency, and good Sailors make it a habit to always stand their assigned watches seriously and efficiently, no matter what the assigned task. Your very life and that of your shipmates may well be at stake.

FOURTEEN

SAFETY AND EMERGENCIES

For the most part, U.S. Navy ships are very safe places to live and work. More than two hundred years of experience, a high state of training and readiness, and many technological developments have minimized the dangers that must necessarily exist in a vessel that ventures onto the sometimes unpredictable waters of the world carrying ammunition, fuel, and other potentially hazardous materials. But the safety enjoyed aboard an American naval vessel is only as effective as the safety practices of its individual crewmembers. You must not go around in constant fear while serving in a ship, but you must always be aware that there are dangers that must be protected against. Safety precautions are an essential element of shipboard life, and you owe it to yourself and to your shipmates to make safety precautions a part of your everyday routine. This chapter will introduce you to some of the more important safety precautions that must be continually practiced in the Navy.

Because accidents occasionally happen despite all attempts to prevent them, and because all of the safety precautions in the world cannot prevent hurricanes, enemy attacks, and other extraordinary situations, this chapter will also discuss emergencies you may face aboard ship and what to do when they occur.

SAFETY

As already stated, safety is a job for all hands at all times. Nearly every operation aboard a naval vessel poses potential danger. Going to sea often involves working with powerful machinery, high-speed equipment, volatile and exotic fuels and propellants, heavy lifts, high explosives, stepped-up electrical voltages, and the unpredictable forces of weather. It is the responsibility of all aboard ship to observe all safety precautions, both for themselves and for their shipmates.

Safety precautions for each piece of equipment used in the Navy are readily available and should be read and understood. The *Naval Ships' Technical Manual* (more often referred to as the NSTM), the *Standard Organization and Regulations of the U.S. Navy* (SORM), and other bureau and systems manuals contain written safety regulations.

Another important part of safety is the regular maintenance of equipment and systems. Maintenance involves much more than just cleaning and painting. For safety and efficiency, every item aboard ship—from the simplest valve to the most complicated electronic gear—must be clean and operable.

The following general instructions, listed alphabetically for easier reference, serve as an introduction to the most important principles regarding shipboard safety.

Aircraft Operations

During aircraft operations, only those personnel actually involved are allowed in the flight-deck area. All other personnel must remain clear or below decks. Personnel involved in flight operations must wear appropriate safety equipment (helmet, goggles, etc.). Passengers must be led to and from a helicopter or aircraft by a member of the transfer crew, handling crew, or flight crew.

Before aircraft operations can actually begin, the flight deck must be checked for loose materials that might cause damage if sucked into an aircraft engine. Loose gear must not be permitted in the flight deck area and must be stowed elsewhere or secured to the deck. Additionally, prior to the commencement of air operations, a procedure called a "FOD walk down" must be conducted. FOD stands for foreign object damage, and the procedure involves personnel forming a line across the flight deck and walking slowly along, carefully watching for any loose debris or objects that might cause damage. A single small screw or a chip of paint can spell disaster if sucked into an engine's turbines and must therefore be removed.

Be particularly careful around propellers and helicopter rotors. When turning, they are nearly invisible but are extremely dangerous. Rotor tips cover a wide area and often dip close to the deck when a helo lands or the ship moves with the waves. An aircraft making a turn while taxiing can put you in harm's way very quickly. The engine noise of the plane you are watching may drown out the noise of planes you are not watching. Don't move without looking in all directions, and don't direct all your attention to a single aircraft for very long.

Also beware of jet blast. Any place within 100 feet of a jet engine is dangerous. A jet blast can burn you, knock you down, or even blow you over the side.

Ammunition Handling

Everyone who handles ammunition must be instructed in safety regulations, methods of handling, and the stowage and uses of ammunition and explosives. Only careful, reliable, mentally sound, and physically fit Sailors are permitted to work with explosives or ammunition.

Anyone who knows of defective ammunition or other explosive ordnance, defective containers or handling devices, the rough or improper handling of ordnance, or the willful or accidental violation of safety regulations must report the facts to his or her immediate superior.

[14.1] Shipboard aircraft operations require special procedures and precautions.

Anyone supervising the inspection, care, preparation, handling, use, or disposal of ammunition or explosives must see that all regulations and instructions are observed, remain vigilant throughout the operation, and remind subordinates of the need for care and vigilance. Supervisors must also ensure that subordinates are familiar with the characteristics of explosive materials, the equipment used to handle them, all safety precautions, and the catastrophes that safety regulations are designed to prevent.

Matches, lighters, and any other spark- or flame-producing devices are not permitted in the vicinity of ammunition except under specific circumstances when necessary and when approved by the commanding officer.

Crews working with explosives or ammunition are limited to the minimum number of people required to perform the operation properly. Unauthorized personnel are not permitted in magazines or in the immediate vicinity of loading operations. All authorized visitors must be escorted.

The productivity of persons or units handling explosive ordnance must never be evaluated on a competitive basis that might lead to unsafe practices.

Live ammo, rockets, or missiles are loaded into guns or on launchers only for firing, except where approved by the Naval Sea Systems Command.

Nothing but inert (nonexplosive) ammo is used for drill purposes, except under certain special circumstances.

Supervisors must require good housekeeping in explosive spaces. Nothing is to be stored in magazines and other ammunition-handling spaces except explosives, their containers, and authorized handling equipment.

No warhead detonator should be assembled in or near a magazine containing explosives. Fuzing is performed only at a designated fuzing area.

Anyone supervising the inspection, care, preparation, handling, use, or disposal of ammunition or explosives must see that all regulations and instructions are observed, remain vigilant throughout the operation, and remind subordinates of the need for care and vigilance.

Boats

In motor launches, only the coxswain and the boat officer or senior line officer may ride on the coxswain's flat. No boat may be loaded beyond the capacities established by the commanding officer (published in the boat bill) except with his or her specific permission during emergencies.

[14.2] Anyone supervising the inspection, care, preparation, handling, use, or disposal of ammunition or explosives must see that all regulations and instructions are observed, remain vigilant throughout the operation, and remind subordinates of the need for care and vigilance.

To provide adequate traction, all members of a boat's crew wear rubber-soled shoes in the boat. Boat crews must demonstrate a practical knowledge of seamanship, rules of the nautical road, and safety regulations. Qualification for serving as a member of a boat crew is controlled by the ship's first lieutenant. The chief engineer is responsible for all boat engines and their electrical systems and will ensure that qualified personnel are available to operate and maintain them. Only personnel designated by the chief engineer will fuel the ship's boats, operate boat engines, or work with any component of the boat's electrical system, including the battery.

No one should ever board a boat from a boat boom unless someone else is standing by on deck or in a boat at the same boom (to render assistance in case of a fall or other difficulty).

All boats leaving the ship must have waterproof local chartlets with courses to and from their destinations plotted on them. They must have an adjusted and lighted compass installed and enough life preservers to accommodate each person embarked. These should be readily available for those times when rough seas, reduced visibility, or other hazards arise.

Chemicals

Adequate precautions must be taken when stowing, handling, and disposing of hazardous chemicals and materials. All chemicals, particularly unfamiliar ones, should be treated with respect. Unless you know otherwise for certain, always assume a chemical substance is hazardous and treat it accordingly.

A review of all potential hazards is not possible here, but substantial chemical-safety information is available in a number of references. Safety Data Sheets (SDS) are provided by the manufacturers of hazardous materials (HAZMAT) stored on board ship. SDS include information on immediate actions to be taken in case of emergencies (such as when chemicals are spilled or when personnel come into unprotected contact with these dangerous materials).

The *Naval Ships' Technical Manual* (NSTM) *670* has requirements and safety guidelines on a wide variety of hazardous chemicals, including cleaning agents, solvents, paints and associated chemicals, chlorinated hydrocarbons, mercury, oxidizing materials, corrosive liquids, and materials in aerosol containers.

Safety Precautions for Shore Activities (OPNAV Instruction 5100.23 series) includes information on the hazards of and precautions to be taken in using laboratory, photographic, and painting chemicals, as well as alkalis, acids, solvents, cleaning agents, cyanides, organic phosphates, toxic metals/dusts, and halogenated hydrocarbons.

Hazardous Material Information System (DOD Instruction 6050.5) lists hazardous items in federal stock, classifies material according to the type of hazard, and recommends proper stowage.

Afloat Supply Procedures (NAVSUP P-485) contains information on the receipt, custody, and proper stowage of hazardous materials.

Navy Hazardous Material Control Program (NAVSUP Instruction 5100.27) provides guidelines for procedures to follow when seeking information on the nature, hazards, and precautions of unknown chemicals and materials.

Electrical and Electronic Equipment

Electrical equipment includes generators, electrically powered machinery and mechanisms, power cables, controllers, transformers, and associated equipment. Electronic equipment includes radars, sonars, power amplifiers, antennas, electronic-warfare equipment, computers, and associated controls. The most important precautions with all such equipment are to treat them all with respect and never work on them alone.

As a basic rule, no one is to operate, repair, or adjust any electrical or electronic equipment unless he or she has been assigned that duty, except in definite emergencies. However, common sense must prevail here: electric lights and bulkhead-mounted electric-fan switches are exempted, for example. If you have any doubt about whether or not you should be operating a piece of electrical or electronic equipment, *don't*. An old Navy training film about electrical safety was titled "The Deadly Shipmate," and that is an apt description of electricity. It is truly a shipmate that can be relied upon to provide comfort, convenience, and combat readiness, but it is unquestionably deadly when improperly used.

You should never remove, paint over, destroy, or mutilate any name plates, cable tags, or other identification marks on electrical or electronic equipment. Never hang anything on, or secure a line to, any power cable, antenna, wave guide, or other piece of electrical or electronic equipment.

Only authorized portable electric equipment that has been tested and certified by the electric shop may be used. This includes personal electronic equipment (such as laptops, tablets, and cell phones).

Electric equipment should always be de-energized and checked with a voltage tester or voltmeter before being serviced or repaired. Circuit breakers and the switches of de-energized circuits must be locked or placed in the off position while work is in progress, and a suitable warning tag should be attached to them.

Work on live circuits or equipment is carried out only when specific permission has been received from the commanding officer. The person performing the work must be insulated from the ground and must follow all safety measures. Rubber gloves are worn and another person stands by to cut the circuit and render first aid if necessary. Medical personnel are alerted before such work begins.

Only authorized light fixtures with protective screens or shields are installed in machinery spaces.

Going aloft is defined as going onto upper areas of the superstructure or onto the ship's masts where there are radio, radar, or electronic-warfare antennas mounted. This can be very dangerous for a number of reasons. Electrical shock is an obvious hazard, but you can also be seriously injured by electronic emissions, struck by a rotating antenna, or injured in a fall. The emissions from such equipment can also charge the ship's rigging with enough electricity to do you serious harm. You should never go aloft unless adequate safety precautions have been employed, which will normally include securing all potentially hazardous pieces of equipment in the vicinity and making certain that equipment tag-out procedures are in effect to prevent the accidental energizing of secured equipment. These procedures are formalized and controlled by what is called a "man-aloft chit." This checklist requires all pertinent departments to be notified that someone is going aloft, so that they can take the appropriate safety precautions (turn off their antennas, etc.). As a precaution, duty department heads must sign the chit, acknowledging that a person is going aloft.

Because you do not have to be in actual contact with many of these pieces of equipment for them to do you serious harm—just being in the vicinity of a transmitting radar can do serious internal organ damage, for example—it is important to remember that an adjacent ship (one moored near you in port) can also be hazardous to you if you go aloft on your ship. In these situations, all necessary precautions must be taken on both ships before anyone may go aloft on either.

Electrical and electronic safety precautions must be conspicuously posted. Personnel are to be instructed and drilled in their observance, and anyone who routinely works on electrical and electronic equipment must be qualified to administer first aid for shock. He or she should also be capable of performing emergency resuscitation procedures and able to use airway breathing tubes. Instructions for these procedures are posted in spaces containing electronic equipment.

Rubber matting or vinyl sheeting is installed in areas where the potential for electrical shock exists.

Fire and Explosion Prevention

Reducing fire and explosion hazards is every Sailor's responsibility. Whenever possible, hazards should be eliminated, including anything that will burn. Replace these combustible materials with less flammable ones if you can. Limit the number of combustibles whenever possible. Those combustibles that are essential should be properly stowed and protected to reduce the chances of fire.

Whenever possible, you should prevent the accumulation of oil and other flammables in bilges and inaccessible areas. Stow oily rags in airtight metal containers and paint, brushes, rags, thinners, and solvents in authorized locations only. Do not use compressed air to accelerate the flow of liquid from containers of any type.

Forklifts

Forklifts should be operated only by those who have received training and hold a current forklift license. Before operating one, check its condition. Keep feet and hands inside the running line. No one other than the operator should ride a forklift, unless it has a second permanent seat.

On wet or slippery decks and when turning corners, always slow the forklift down. Never stand under loads being hoisted or lowered, and never permit anyone else to do so.

All cargo should be transported with the load-lifting rails tipped back. When you are moving, keep forks four to six inches above the deck, whether loaded or not. Do not exceed the specified load capacity. Lower and rest forks on deck when they are not in use.

Never bump or push stacks of cargo to straighten them. Forks should be worked all the way under their loads. Inspect each load before lifting. An unstable load should be rearranged or banded before being lifted.

Always come to a full stop before reversing the direction of travel.

When you complete your work, park the forklift in a fore-and-aft position near the centerline of the ship if possible, put on the parking brake, and secure it with chains or cables.

Hand Tools

You probably have worked with various tools before joining the Navy. Hammers, pliers, and screwdrivers are all common tools at home as well. If you have used these tools, you have learned that certain precautions must be taken in order to keep from injuring yourself. In most cases, injuries from these tools are minor—a bruised thumb or a pinched finger. But serious injury can also occur when a hand tool is not used in a safe manner and when certain precautions are not taken. Striking tools—hammers and chisels, for example—are particularly dangerous because they are used with sufficient force to cause serious injury if care is not exercised. Because of the importance and vulnerability of your eyes, safety goggles should be worn any time you use a striking tool. Also be sure that anyone else in the vicinity is wearing safety goggles as well, or have them leave the area before you begin your work. Flying chips can travel a good distance and do serious harm if everyone in the area is not protected.

Select the right hammer for the job. The head should be wedged securely and squarely on the handle, and neither the head nor handle should be chipped, cracked, or broken. Keep the hammer clean and free of oil or grease; otherwise it might slip from your hands, or the face of the hammer might glance off the object being struck. Grasp the handle firmly near the end, and keep your eye on the part to be struck. Strike so the hammer face hits the object squarely.

Chisels should be free of cracks or burrs and should be properly sharpened and tempered. Chisels should be held between the thumb and the other four fingers. On horizontal cuts, the palm should be up. Cup the chisel handle in the palm of your hand and exert pressure away from the body. Be sure no one is close enough to be hurt if the chisel slips.

Hydraulic Machinery

Hydraulically operated equipment can be extremely powerful. The lift in your hometown garage, which suspends entire automobiles six or more feet off the ground, is an example of a hydraulic system. Such equipment must never be used until all personnel are clear of moving parts. Imagine what would happen to you if you were under that garage lift when the mechanic decided to bring it down. While this is not a pleasant picture, it should serve to warn you of the danger associated with hydraulic machinery. Such things as elevators, periscopes, rudders, diving planes, gun mounts, and missile launchers are all moved using hydraulic machinery that makes that garage lift seem puny by comparison. Always treat hydraulic systems with respect and stand well clear when they are operating. Hydraulic machinery should always be secured and all equipment thoroughly checked if a hydraulic leak is detected or suspected.

Life Jackets

Anytime you go topside in heavy weather you must wear a life jacket. Being washed overboard is a very real danger when seas get rough, and being washed overboard without a life jacket greatly reduces your chances of ever seeing your ship, home, or family again. In addition to providing a layer of warmth and additional buoyance, modern life jackets are fitted with a signaling whistle, a sea-water activated strobe light, and an electronic Man Overboard Indicating (MOBI) device that directs ships in the area to a Sailor in the water.

Life jackets are also worn at times when the nature of your work increases the chances of your falling or being knocked overboard. Working on replenishment stations where booms or swinging cargo may push you over the side is one example of a time you will need to put on a life jacket. Life jackets are also worn when working over the side in port and at sea, whether you are suspended over the side on a stage or in a "boatswain's chair," or using a small boat. You are required to wear a life jacket when traveling in a small boat regardless of weather conditions.

Lifelines and Safety Nets

The lifelines (railings) on a ship are there to prevent people from falling overboard. You should never lean, sit, stand, or climb on any lifeline whether the ship is under way or in port. People working over the side in port may climb over lifelines when necessary, but only if they are wearing life jackets and safety lines that are tended by other people.

No lifeline should be dismantled or removed without specific permission from the first lieutenant, and then only if temporary lifelines are promptly rigged.

No weights should be hung or secured to any lifeline unless authorized by the commanding officer.

Safety nets are also rigged around flight decks to catch anyone who may be blown over the side by an aircraft's propeller wash or jet blast. You should never enter a flight-deck safety net except as authorized.

Line Handling

Lines are used for many purposes aboard ships. Experienced Sailors know that while lines are very useful, they can also be very dangerous. A mooring line (one that is used to secure a ship to a pier) that parts under strain is quite capable of instantaneously severing limbs. Always treat lines with respect. Do not, under any circumstances, stand in the bight (loop) of a line. If that line suddenly goes taut it can seriously injure you or drag you into danger. Never step on a line that is taut. It is foolish to try to check a line that is running out rapidly by stepping on it.

Synthetic lines (such as nylon) are widely used for mooring and rigging because of their durability and strength. These lines are characterized by high elasticity and low friction, so extra turns will be required when the line is secured to bitts, cleats, capstans, and other holding devices. Nylon line stretches one and a half times its original length and then snaps back with tremendous force if the line parts. Do not stand in its direct line of pull when heavy loads are applied.

Lines constructed from modern materials, such as Spectra, Aramid, and Kevlar, have a tremendously high breaking strength. When they do fail, they are designed to do so without any snapback. However, just as you would treat any gun as if it were loaded, you should approach any line with the idea that it can be very dangerous if it parts.

Materials Handling

You will probably—more than once—find yourself part of a working party that is bringing stores aboard or moving materials from one part of the ship to another. Particularly on reduced-manning ships, loading stores

[**14.3**] Experienced Sailors know that while lines are very useful, they can also be very dangerous.

can be an "all-hands evolution." Safety shoes (with toe protection) must be worn when handling heavy stores or equipment. Always wear gloves when carrying, lifting, or moving objects that have sharp edges or projecting points. Remove rings when wearing gloves.

Material should not be thrown from platforms or trucks to the floor or ground; use suitable lowering equipment if available.

Don't overload hand trucks. When working on a ramp or incline, keep the load below you—pull it up and push it down.

To lift a load by hand, stand close to it with your feet solidly placed and slightly apart. Bend your knees, grasp the object firmly, and lift by straightening your legs, keeping your back as straight as possible.

Paint-Removing Tools

Paint-removing tools, whether they are simple hand tools, such as a chipping hammer, or electrical and pneumatic tools, such as chippers, grinders, and scalers, are useful but potentially hazardous tools if not used with care. Because flying paint chips are an obvious hazard to your eyes, you must always wear protective goggles or face shields when using tools of this type. The high noise levels associated with these tools also require hearing protection equipment. Depending on where the work is being done and the airflow, a properly fitted respirator may be required as well.

Always check the rated speed of a grinding wheel before using; it should not be less than that of the machine or tool on which it is mounted. Grinders must have wheel guards to prevent injury.

To prevent a power tool from causing injury if it gets away from the user, the "deadman switch" automatically turns it off when not actually being held properly by the user. Always test this feature before operating a tool.

Personal Protective Equipment

You only have one body. And while you may have two eyes, ten fingers, and two hands, you really cannot spare any of them. Protective clothing and equipment (such as hard hats, gloves, earplugs and earmuffs, respirators, glasses and goggles, coveralls, and steel-toed shoes) were designed to help you keep your body intact and to ensure that all of your body parts continue to operate at peak efficiency. Use them!

Keep the body well covered (including gloves and rolled-down sleeves) to reduce the danger of burns when working near hot equipment.

Welding goggles and a protective welding jacket must be worn when brazing, welding, or cutting. Personnel assigned as fire watches during welding operations must also wear protective goggles.

Protective goggles should also be worn whenever working with corrosive substances such as acid, alkali, and vinyl paint.

Plastic face shields must be worn when handling primary coolant under pressure, and suitable eye protection—a shield, goggles, or safety glasses—must be used when buffing, grinding, or performing other tasks potentially hazardous to the eyes.

Do not wear clothing with loose ends or loops when working on or near rotating machinery.

Remember, you are guarding against both likely and unlikely injury that may occur. Use proper safety procedures and equipment, and challenge others to as well!

Radiation Hazard

As already discussed in the section about electrical and electronic safety, the high-powered radio-frequency energy emitted by electronic transmitting equipment (such as radios or radars) can cause serious injury if you get too close to it. Areas where this hazard exists will have warning signs posted to help you remain clear.

If you must work on equipment of this type, be sure to follow all safety precautions. For example, you should never inspect a radar's wave guide (a kind of rectangular pipe that carries the radar's signal between the antenna and the other components) for damage while it is activated because a leak can mean serious exposure to damaging radio-frequency energy.

Respect all posted hazard signs. Never assume a piece of equipment is secured unless you are absolutely certain and precautions have been taken to ensure that it is not accidentally re-energized.

Be aware that radio-frequency energy can also accidentally detonate or damage certain weapons. When these weapons are on deck or in other exposed areas for loading or maintenance, radiation hazard (RADHAZ) procedures will be put into effect. Follow all RADHAZ instructions and procedures, and if in doubt as to what you should or should not be doing, *ask*.

Radioactive Materials

Radioactive material is present in nuclear reactors and warheads, in the sources used for calibration of radiation-monitoring equipment, and in certain electronic tubes. Treat these objects with respect. Obey radiation warning signs and remain clear of radiation barriers unless your job requires you to do otherwise.

Radiation sources must be installed in the radiation-detection equipment or stowed in their shipping containers in a locked storage area. Spare radioactive electronic tubes and fission chambers are stored in clearly marked containers and locked stowage.

Replenishment at Sea

Ships often come alongside one another to transfer fuel, ammunition, or stores; this is called underway replenishment (UNREP). You may also hear the term CONREP (connected replenishment). Sometimes these transfers are accomplished by helicopters; this is vertical replenishment (VERTREP).

Safety regulations should always be reviewed immediately before each replenishment operation. Only essential personnel are allowed near any transfer station.

For UNREPs, topside personnel engaged in handling stores and lines must wear safety helmets and orange-colored, buoyant life-preserver vests. If the helmets are not equipped with a quick-acting breakaway device, you should fasten the chin strap behind your head or wear it unbuckled.

For VERTREPs, personnel may wear flight-deck vests and cranial impact helmets instead of the types used during UNREP.

Cargo handlers must wear safety shoes. Those handling wire-bound or banded cases wear work gloves.

If involved in a replenishment operation, be sure to keep clear of bights (loops) in the lines being used and keep at least six feet between you and any block or chock through which the lines pass. Keep clear of suspended loads and rig attachment points until loads have been landed on deck. Do not get between a suspended load and the rail or ship's superstructure. Be alert to the possibility of shifting cargo.

When line-throwing guns or bolos are used to throw lines between ships, the word will be passed just before the line is passed. If you are on the receiving ship, take cover while the line is being fired or thrown across.

Deck space near transfer stations should be covered with something slip-resistant.

During replenishments, a Sailor will be stationed well aft on the engaged side of the ship to act as a "lifebuoy watch." He or she will toss a life ring to anyone who falls or is knocked overboard and will immediately pass the word. Often another ship waiting her turn to replenish will follow behind those involved in replenishment operations to act as a lifeguard ship to retrieve anyone lost overboard. If no lifeguard ship is available, a boat or rescue helicopter should be kept ready for immediate use in rescuing anyone who falls overboard.

Measures must be taken to avoid hazards associated with radio-frequency hazards. This is important when handling ammunition and petroleum products. Dangerous materials, such as acids and compressed gases, are transferred separately from one another and from other cargo.

When transferring personnel by highline, only double-braid polyester line (hand-tended by at least twenty-five people) is used. Persons being transferred wear orange-colored life preservers (except patients in litters equipped with flotation gear). When the water temperature is 59° Fahrenheit or below, or when the combined outside air/water temperature is a total of 120° or below, immersion suits should be worn by personnel being transferred.

When fuels are received or transferred, no naked light (meaning all forms of lit candles, matches, cigars, cigarettes, cigarette lighters, and flame or arc welding and cutting apparatus) or electrical or mechanical apparatus likely to spark is permitted within 50 feet of an oil hose, an open fuel tank, the vent terminal from a fuel tank, or an area where fuel-oil vapors may be present. Portable electric lights used during fueling must have explosion-proof protected globes and must be inspected for proper insulation and tested prior to use. Portholes in the ship's structure on the engaged side are closed during fueling operations to prevent the accumulation of dangerous vapors inside the ship.

Safety Devices

Mechanical, electrical, and electronic safety devices must be inspected at intervals required by the planned maintenance system (PMS), by type-commander instructions, or as circumstances or conditions warrant. When practical and safe, these inspections are conducted when the equipment or unit is in operation. Machinery or equipment should never be operated unless safety devices are working.

No one should tamper with or render ineffective any safety device, interlock, ground strap, or similar device without the commanding officer's approval.

Safety Tags

DANGER, CAUTION, OUT OF COMMISSION, and OUT OF CALIBRATION tags and labels must be posted for the safety of personnel and to prevent misuse of equipment. Safety tags must never be removed without proper authorization.

Shore Power

When ships are moored to piers they will usually hook up to shore power instead of continuing to generate their own electricity as they must do at sea. This involves running heavy electric cables from the ship to terminal boxes on shore. As with all electrical equipment, shore-power cables and connections must be treated with great respect.

All onboard shore-power equipment must be checked for safety. Shore-power cables should be thoroughly inspected before using. Spliced portable cables are dangerous and should not be used except in an emergency. Cables should be long enough to allow for the rise and fall of the tide, but not so long as to allow the cable to dip in the water or become wedged between the ship and the pier. Cables should not rest on sharp or ragged edges such as ship gunwales. Personnel should not step or walk on shore-power cables.

Tanks and Voids

No one is permitted to enter any closed compartment, tank, void, or poorly ventilated space aboard a Navy ship until the space has been ventilated and determined to be gas-free by a qualified gas-free engineer. In an emergency, if a space must be entered without gas freeing, a breathing apparatus such as a self-contained breathing apparatus (SCBA) must be worn. In all cases, at least two persons must be present when such a space is occupied. One remains outside the space and acts as line tender and safety observer.

The space entered should be continuously ventilated, and a reliable person must be stationed at the entrance to keep count of the number of persons inside as well as to maintain communications. Suitable fire-extinguishing equipment must be on hand, nonsparking tools are to be used, and persons entering should not carry matches or lighters or wear articles of clothing that could cause a spark.

Toxic Materials

Solvents, refrigerants, paint thinner, fumigants, insecticides, paint removers, dry-cleaning fluids, antifreeze, and propellants for pressurized containers are all examples of toxic materials that may be hazardous if inhaled, absorbed through the skin, or swallowed. Even small amounts of some of these and similar substances can cause permanent blindness or death. The use of all hazardous materials is controlled by the medical officer or some other designated person. These substances should be used only in well-ventilated spaces, and contact with the skin should be avoided.

Welding

Welding is performed only with the permission of the commanding officer or officer of the deck. The area where "hot work" is done must be cleared of flammable matter.

Various synthetic materials yield toxic gases when burned or heated. Use caution when burning or welding resin-coated vinyl surfaces. Vinyl coating must be chipped or scraped clear in the work area whenever possible; welders, those standing fire watch, and others required to be in the immediate area must be equipped with respirators. Exhaust ventilation in the work area has a minimum capacity of 200 cubic feet per minute for each 3-inch suction hose.

Although ship's personnel do not normally do welding work on the hull, if such work is required proper precautions must be taken and the hull must be x-rayed at the first opportunity to determine if any structural damage has taken place.

Personnel are always assigned to function as a "fire watch" for the purpose of detecting and immediately extinguishing fires caused by welding operations. The watch usually consists of at least two persons—one with the operator, the other in the space behind, below, or above the site of cutting, grinding, or welding. Remember, heat generated by welding or burning passes through bulkheads and decks and can ignite material on the other side. If you are assigned as a fire watch, you must remain alert at all times, even though the assignment may grow boring. Make sure that the equipment you are issued is in working condition, and if you don't know how to operate it or have even minor questions, do not hesitate to ask for assistance. Inspect the work site with the welder. Make sure you know where all fire-fighting equipment is in the work space and adjoining spaces and know how to use it. Also make sure you know where and how to sound the fire alarm and know the assigned escape routes from the space.

When the hot-work operation is complete, fire watchstanders should inspect both sides of the work area and remain on station for at least thirty minutes to be sure that there are no more smoldering fires or sparks and that the hot metal has cooled to the touch.

Working Over the Side

At times it is necessary for work to be done over the side of a ship (such as for rust removal or painting). No work is done over the side without the permission of the OOD. Crews working over the side on stages, boatswains' chairs, and work floats or boats wear buoyant life preservers and are equipped with safety harnesses with lines tended from the deck above. When another ship comes alongside, all personnel working over the side should be cleared.

All tools, buckets, paint pots, and brushes used over the side must be secured by lanyards (pieces of line) to prevent loss overboard and injury to personnel below. Because working over the side in a dry dock is more hazardous than working over the side when the ship is in the water, you should use the same precautions that would be required when working aloft.

No person may work over the side while the ship is under way without permission of the OOD and the commanding officer.

EMERGENCIES

Despite all the safety precautions that are taken in the Navy, emergency situations will occasionally happen. The consequences of an emergency situation may depend to some degree upon luck and circumstances, but the preparedness and performance of the crew will be major determining factors.

Because of this, shipboard drills are frequently conducted so that you and the other members of the crew may prepare for those emergencies before they happen. Take advantage of these opportunities; they just may save your life or prevent serious injury someday.

General Quarters

During a major emergency—such as a serious fire or a gunboat attack—you will hear the continuous sounding of the general quarters alarm plus the words passed over the 1MC: "General quarters! General quarters! All hands man your battle stations!" If you hear this, don't try to find out what has happened. Just move! You will find out soon enough what is happening. Proceed as quickly as you can (being careful not to run into others or forget to duck when passing through low doors) to your assigned general quarters station. To ensure a smooth flow to stations, everyone adheres to the rule of "FUSDAP"—forward, up, starboard; down, aft, port. This means that if you need to go forward or up to get to your general quarters station, you should move to the starboard side of the ship. Conversely, if you need to move aft or down to a lower level, you must go to the port side of the ship. This will keep people from running into each other as they hurry to their stations. When everyone on board is at his or her battle (general quarters) station, the ship is most prepared for any emergency that may occur.

Man Overboard

When someone goes overboard, prompt action is essential. If you see someone go overboard, immediately sound the alarm, "Man overboard, port [starboard] side," and throw a life ring or life jacket. If a smoke float and a dye marker are available, drop them in, too. If possible, keep the person in sight. Everyone who sees the individual in the water should point at him or her. This will help the conning officer to bring the ship around to make a speedy recovery.

Every underway watch is organized to handle this situation. The conning officer maneuvers the ship to a recovery position. At the same time, the word is passed twice over the ship's 1MC system, and six or more short blasts are sounded on the ship's whistle. The lifeboat crew stands by to lower away when directed. If available, a helicopter may be launched. If the identity of the person is not known, a muster of the crew will be held to find out who is missing.

If you are the person who falls overboard, make every effort to keep your head. Hold your breath when you hit the water; the buoyancy of your lungs will bring you to the surface. There is a common misunderstanding that says the ship's screws will suck you under if you are too close to the ship. Because this isn't true, you should not waste your valuable energy by swimming frantically away from the ship. Use your energy to stay afloat and try to stay in one place. The ship will likely maneuver right back down her track toward you. Even if no one saw you go over, keep afloat and conserve your energy. Fight the impulse to panic. When a shipmate is missed, ships and aircraft begin an intensive search.

If a person goes overboard in port, the alarm is sounded as usual and the OOD follows the best available rescue procedure. Boats in the water assist in the emergency.

CBR Attack

In modern warfare, it is possible that an enemy may resort to what are commonly referred to as unconventional weapons. In the Navy, these are called CBR weapons, which stands for chemical, biological, and radiological. While these weapons are very different in some ways, many of the defensive measures employed against them are the same. In the event of a CBR attack, the crew can do a great deal to minimize casualties and damage.

[**14.4**] Rescue swimmers conducting a man overboard drill in the Arabian Sea

For those ships located at or near "ground zero" (the point of detonation) in a nuclear attack, or in an area of high concentration of biological or chemical agents, casualties and damage will, of course, be great. However, tests have shown that ships not receiving the direct effects of such attacks have a good chance of survival with relatively few casualties, and with weapons systems intact. If a formation of ships is widely dispersed as a defensive measure, it is probable that nearly all fleet units will escape the direct effects of a CBR attack.

PROTECTING THE SHIP

When a CBR attack is expected, the ship will go to general quarters and all topside areas will be washed down using the built-in countermeasure washdown system. The entire outer surface of the ship is kept wet so that CBR contaminants will wash overboard and not adhere to the external surfaces of the ship.

All nonvital openings of the ship are closed to maintain an envelope as gas-tight as possible. Some areas of the ship (such as engineering spaces) must continue to receive air from the outside; personnel who are manning stations in those spaces will have gas masks readily available.

PROTECTING PERSONNEL

The extreme effectiveness of some bacteriological agents, the toxicity of chemical agents, and the danger of radioactive fallout mean that specially designed protective clothing must be worn to increase the chances of survival. It is essential that this clothing be worn properly, so it is mandatory that all personnel be periodically retrained in the use of protective clothing and masks.

DETECTION OF CBR CONTAMINANTS

The detection of CBR agents—which generally are invisible, odorless, and tasteless and give no hint to the senses of their presence—requires special equipment and training.

Radioactive particles betray their presence by giving off several kinds of radiation, which can be detected by instruments known as radiacs (radiation, detection, indication, and computation). These instruments can be personal dosimeters, which measure the amount of radiation an individual has been exposed to, or they can be survey instruments used to detect the accumulated radiation in various parts of the ship.

In biological-warfare detection, samples must be taken, cultured, and subjected to thorough laboratory testing before the agent can be identified. This is slow, exacting work; if viruses are involved, they can greatly increase the difficulty of identification.

Chemical agents are somewhat easier to detect, but no one procedure can detect all known chemical agents. Some of these are lethal in extremely small concentrations and hence could be deployed upwind over a great area with devastating results.

The monitoring and surveying of ships and stations is a vital part of CBR defense. Locating a hazard, isolating contaminated areas, recording the results of a survey, and reporting findings up the chain of command are the functions of every military unit encountering contamination.

DECONTAMINATION

With early detection of CBR contamination, many lives can be saved by prompt and efficient decontamination. One of the most effective methods is flushing the contaminated surfaces with large amounts of water. The countermeasure wash-down system can be used for external surfaces, along with a more thorough subsequent scrubbing by personnel wearing protective clothing. For internal contamination, fire hoses and manual scrubbing are employed.

Emergency Destruction

In the event that your ship or station is in serious danger of being overrun or captured by enemy forces, the commanding officer may order the destruction of classified documents and equipment to prevent their falling into enemy hands. There are specific procedures for this and special equipment has been created for this purpose. As with all potential emergency situations, periodic drills will be conducted so that all involved personnel will be ready to carry out their duties in an expeditious manner.

Abandon Ship

Despite all precautions to prevent such a catastrophe, ships can sometimes be so badly damaged by battle or fire or some other cause that it becomes necessary for the crew to leave the ship before it sinks. During an emergency of this sort, many senior officers and petty officers may be lost as battle casualties, so you may find yourself with less supervision and assistance than usual. It is, therefore, a good idea to make sure you have a clear picture in your mind what you should do in the event the decision is made to abandon ship. Know your abandon-ship station and duties. Know all escape routes to the ship's topside from berthing spaces or working spaces below decks. Know how to inflate a life jacket. Know how to lower a boat or let go of a life raft. Know how to handle survival gear. And know how to do all of this in the dark! Disaster can strike suddenly at sea. A ship can go down within minutes of a collision or explosion. If you don't know what to do before this happens, there won't be time to find out after it does.

Abandon-ship stations and duties are noted on the Watch, Quarter, and Station Bill (see Chapter 11: Shipboard Life). Careful planning is required to determine who goes in which boat or raft, what emergency equipment is to be supplied, and who supplies it.

Only the commanding officer can order abandon ship. She or he will do so only after all efforts to save the ship prove futile. If the commanding officer is killed or incapacitated, the executive officer or next senior surviving officer will take command and make this decision if necessary.

When the abandon-ship alarm sounds, act fast. Take note of important information, such as water temperature, bearings and distance to nearest land, and friendliness of the inhabitants there. If there is time, this information will be passed to everyone by bridge personnel.

GOING OVER THE SIDE
Make certain your life jacket is secured properly and is equipped with a whistle, dye marker, and a flashing light. Use a cargo net, boat falls, fire hose, or line to help you get down to the water if you can, but don't slide down and harm your hands. If you have to jump, look out for wreckage or swimmers in the water. Do not dive head-first into the water; jump feet-first, with legs crossed and arms crossed across your chest, firmly gripping your triceps. If you have a pneumatic life jacket, don't inflate it until you are in the water—otherwise you will pop right out of it and possibly injure yourself because of the extreme buoyancy and force an inflated jacket exerts on your neck and body.

If possible, go over the windward side (in other words, jump into the wind) and swim upwind. If you go over the leeward side (side opposite the wind), the wind may blow the ship or burning oil down on you. Swim underwater to avoid burning oil; when you come up for air, splash the oil away as you break the surface. To protect yourself from underwater explosions, swim away for at least 150 yards, then climb aboard a raft, boat, or piece of wreckage, if possible; if that's not possible float on your back. Try to remain calm.

IN THE WATER

Rafts, boats, nets, and floating wreckage should be tied together; this makes it easier for searchers to find you. Wounded personnel should be put in boats or rafts first. Those strong enough to do so should hang on the sides if overcrowding is a problem.

In cold water, everyone must get into a raft or boat as soon as possible. If you must remain in the water, stay as still as possible to prevent heat loss. Heat escapes most rapidly from the head, hands, and feet; use whatever clothing is available to protect these areas. Numbness occurs in waters below 35° Fahrenheit. Breathe slowly and remain still. If overcrowding is a problem in cold waters, you may have to follow a rotation plan to get uninjured persons in and out of life rafts. Frostbite and immersion foot can occur quickly in cold water. Don't rub, as this will damage frozen tissues. Warm affected parts against your own body or a shipmate's.

In a hot climate, keep your shirt, trousers, cap, and shoes on—you'll need them for protection against sun and salt water.

BOAT HANDLING

In a power boat, the slowest possible speed will give the best mileage. If the boat is fitted for sails, use them and save the motor for an emergency. Otherwise, jury-rig a mast and sails out of oars, boat hooks, clothing, and tarpaulins. If wind and sea are driving you away from the nearest land or rescue area, rig a sea anchor (something dragged along behind the boat or raft in the water) to slow the drift.

ORGANIZATION

The abandon-ship bill assigns an officer or senior enlisted person to each boat or raft, but serious casualties may make you the senior person in a boat. If so, take charge.

Make the wounded as comfortable as possible. Make a list of all survivors, and try to list all known casualties. Inventory all water and provisions and set up a ration system based on the expected number of days to land. No one should eat or drink for the first twenty-four hours.

Organize a watch. Lookouts must be alert and know how to use available signal gear. Get under way for the nearest known land or well-traveled shipping route. Time permitting, the nearest landfall and coordinates by compass will be passed over the 1MC. Each boat and raft will be equipped with a compass.

Secure all gear so nothing will be lost. If you have fishing gear aboard, use it; otherwise, make some if you can. Rig a tarp for protection against the sun and to catch rainwater.

Try to keep all hands alert and cheerful. Save energy; unnecessary exertion uses up food and water.

EQUIPMENT

The vest-type life preserver is the most important item of abandon-ship equipment. Learn how to use it. The vest preserver goes over other clothes. Adjust the chest strap and fasten the snap hook into the ring; tie collar tapes to keep them down under your chin; and pull straps between the legs from behind, as tightly as possible without becoming uncomfortable. Adjust the straps on an unconscious person before he or she is put overboard; the design of this preserver will keep the person's head upright and prevent drowning.

The inflatable life preserver (commonly called a "rubber ducky") is carried in a pouch at your back and fastens around your waist on a web belt. It can be inflated with a carbon-dioxide cartridge or by blowing into the attached hose. To inflate the preserver, pull the pouch around in front, remove the preserver from the pouch, slip it over your head, and jerk the lanyard down as far as possible to release the gas into the chamber. For more buoyancy, you can add air through the mouthpiece of the oral inflation tube. To reduce buoyancy, open the valve on the tube. Never attempt deflation with the tube in your mouth.

Most Navy ships are equipped with inflatable lifeboats that are compact, relatively light, easily stowed, and easily launched. They are constructed of separate tubes so that if one or more is punctured the boat will still retain some buoyancy. The upper, lower, and canopy support tubes are inflated by carbon-dioxide cylinders; the thwart tubes are inflated with hand pumps. A fabric bottom is attached to the lower tube to support manually inflatable decks, which are equipped with hand lines and are removable for emergency use.

Life preserver donned, jacket tied at upper chest and waist; waist tie pulled snug, snap hook being fastened into ring on chest strap.

Leg straps being removed from back of preserver; will be led between legs

Both straps pulled between legs, one fastened to D ring on left side, other being fastened on right side.

Tying the collar.

[**14.5**] Donning the vest-type life preserver

The boat has a carrying case with a release cable extending outside; pulling the cables will open and inflate the boat in about thirty seconds. Normally the boat should be inflated in the water. As soon as the boat is inflated, use the boarding net and grab ladders to board it. The first person to enter stays at the entrance to help others; the second aboard goes to open the opposite entrance and help others board at that end.

Secured inside the boat is a waterproof equipment container filled with survival gear, including the following items: food-ration packets, canned water, can openers, de-salter kits, water-storage bags, batteries, sea dye marker, mirror, sponges, pocketknife, whistle, measuring cup, motion-sickness tablets, two-quart bailer, first-aid kit, signaling kit, fishing kit, and flashlights.

The signaling equipment is extremely important because life rafts are difficult to spot from the air and from the surface in heavy weather. The signal mirror you will find among the supplies provided, if used properly, can be seen at a distance of ten miles or more. To be effective, you must hold the mirror so that it reflects sunlight onto a nearby object. Then looking through the hole in the center of the mirror, you will see a bright spot that shows the direction of the reflected beam of sunlight. Keep your eye on the dot and move the mirror slowly until the mirror is reflecting the light onto the target.

The signal kit also contains distress signals for day and night use, which can also be used to provide wind-drift information to helicopters that have come to rescue you. One end of the signal tube produces an orange smoke for day use; the other end produces a red flare for night use. If it is very dark, you can tell which end is the flare by feeling the series of small bead-like projections embossed around the edge. Each signal flare will burn for about eighteen seconds.

Dye markers have a powder that produces a brilliant yellowish-green fluorescence when sprinkled on the water. In good conditions, the dye will be best seen for about an hour, but it will retain some of its color for up to four hours. From an altitude of three thousand feet, the detection range of the dye marker may be as great as ten miles. The range decreases as the dye deteriorates. Unless the moonlight is very bright, the dye is not effective at night.

Because water is essential for life, and seawater is not fit for consumption, you should never discard any article that will hold water. When it rains, every container that can hold water will be very valuable. To assist you in filling the containers, a rain-catcher tube is attached to the lifeboat canopy. Some types of rafts, such as those carried in aircraft, have primitive but effective solar stills for converting seawater into freshwater. In polar areas, freshwater can be obtained from old sea ice, which is bluish, splinters easily, and is nearly free from salt. Freshwater may also be obtained from icebergs, but be careful. As the iceberg's underwater portion melts, it gets top-heavy and can capsize without warning.

Fire

When fire breaks out on board a ship, the ship's bell is rung rapidly to get everyone's attention. At the end of the ringing, the bell is struck once distinctly to indicate that the fire is in the forward third of the ship, twice if the fire is in the middle third of the ship, or three times to indicate that the fire is in the after third of the ship. The word is then passed twice over the 1MC system, giving the exact location of the fire by compartment number and name if known.

If you discover a fire, it is important for you to get the word to the bridge (if the ship is at sea) or the quarterdeck (if in port). Always report the fire first, then take action to fight it if you can. If anyone else is around, you may send them to report the fire while you fight it, but do not make the mistake of trying to put out the fire without first making sure that it is reported. Too often, a fire has gotten out of control because a person tried to put it out without calling for help.

If you have begun to fight the fire, do not leave the scene until the fire or repair party arrives, unless you are endangered and must leave the scene for your safety. (See **Chapter 15: Damage Control** for more details on fire-fighting.)

A typical Navy ship is made of tons of metals floating on a vast—sometimes hostile—ocean, propelled by combustible fuels, loaded with ammunition and other explosives, using toxic materials, powered by thousands of volts of electricity. . . . *What can go wrong?* Despite all of these very real factors, Navy Sailors have good reason to believe they will survive until they reach retirement age—*if they follow the safety precautions* that experience, education, and common sense dictate.

FIFTEEN

DAMAGE CONTROL

Damage control (DC) is every Sailor's job—no matter what his or her rate or pay grade. A ship's ability to do her job, and indeed her survivability, may someday depend on her crew's damage-control response. Because basic DC qualification is a requirement for everyone on board, one of the first things a newly reporting individual receives is his or her damage-control personal qualification standards (PQS) package. This training package will guide you in learning about your ship, learning how to fight fires and control flooding, and reviewing basic first aid and the proper use of the ship's damage-control equipment.

The two major elements of damage control aboard ship are fighting fires and controlling flooding. The latter is often described as "maintaining the ship's watertight integrity." To accomplish these vital tasks, you need to have an understanding of some basic principles of flooding, combustion, and the Navy's DC organization. You also need to know how to work with equipment that you most likely never heard of before joining the Navy. You may also have to find in yourself an extra measure of courage and cool-headedness under pressure. Doing what is needed in a damage-control situation—with thousands of gallons of water rushing into a compartment you are trying to save, or the roar and heat of flames just a few feet away as you try to put down a fuel fire—can be a frightening experience. But if you prepare yourself by making sure that you know what is expected of you in case a DC situation arises, you will be able to keep your head in these stressful situations. Knowledge—understanding what the dangers are and how to combat them—is the most important ingredient to courage.

[**15.1**] All Sailors must be firefighters.

DAMAGE-CONTROL ORGANIZATION

The damage-control assistant (DCA) usually answers directly to the chief engineer and is responsible for preventing and repairing damage, training the crew in damage control, and caring for equipment and piping systems assigned to the organization.

Damage Control Central (DCC) is a special control station on the ship that serves as a central point from which damage control activities are monitored. DCC is the battle station for the DCA.

The ship's DC organization consists of two elements: the damage-control administrative organization and the battle organization. The former exists primarily to prevent damage on a routine basis while the latter is called into action to control damage once a problem has occurred.

DC Administrative Organization

To prevent or minimize damage, the ship will have an administrative organization in place to ensure that all DC-related preventive maintenance is accomplished on a routine basis. Each division in the ship will designate its own damage-control petty officer (DCPO). Under the supervision of the DCA and his or her specially trained DC personnel, these DCPOs will:

- Inspect division spaces daily for fire hazards and cleanliness.
- Perform preventive maintenance on selected damage-control systems and equipment, portable firefighting equipment, and access closures (doors, hatches, scuttles) within their division spaces.
- Maintain compartment check-off lists and the setting of specified material conditions of readiness within their division spaces.
- Aid in teaching division Sailors damage control, firefighting, and chemical-biological-radiological (CBR) warfare defense procedures.

DC Battle Organization

The ship's damage-control battle organization is directed from Damage Control Central (DCC) and includes a number (depending upon the size and mission of the ship) of repair parties and battle dressing stations (BDSs) at various locations throughout the ship. To aid the DCA and his assistants in coordinating the damage-control activities of the ship, DCC is equipped with a variety of graphic displays that show the subdivisions of the ship and her systems. These displays include:

- A casualty board to visualize damage and any corrective action in progress (based on repair-party reports)
- A piping diagram and stability board showing the vessel's liquid loading status, the location of flooding boundaries, the effect of flooding and liquid transfer on the ship's list and trim, and the corrective action taken
- A corrective damage-control status board
- An electrical systems status board
- An electronic casualty status board
- Deck plans to show the location of battle dressing stations and decontamination stations, and safe routes to them, as well as areas contaminated by CBR agents.

REPAIR PARTIES

A key element in the damage-control battle organization is the repair party. Repair parties may be subdivided and spread out to cover a greater area more rapidly, and to prevent loss of the entire party from a single hit. The number and ratings of personnel assigned to a repair party, as specified in the battle bill, are determined by the location of the station, the size of the area assigned to that station, and the total number of personnel available for all stations.

Each repair party will usually have an officer or chief petty officer in charge (called the repair locker officer or repair-party leader), a scene leader to supervise all on-scene activities (who also functions as the assistant repair-party leader), a phone talker, a number of messengers, and several people trained and equipped to don the appropriate clothing and equipment used in entering flooded or smoke-filled compartments. The repair party is rounded out by additional petty officers and nonrated persons from various departments.

Typical repair parties and teams are often designated as follows:

Repair 1   *Main-deck repair.* Includes a number of boatswain's mates who are familiar with the winches, capstans, and other equipment found on the ship's main deck.

Repair 2   *Forward repair.* Covers the forward third (roughly) of the ship's interior spaces.

Repair 3   *After repair.* Covers the after third (roughly) of the ship's interior spaces.

Repair 4   *Amidship repair.* Covers the middle third (roughly) of the ship (excluding engineering spaces).

Repair 5   *Propulsion repair.* Covers the engineering spaces of the ship. Composed of an engineering officer or chief and a broad cross-section of engineering ratings. Personnel assigned to Repair 5 must be qualified in the various engineering watch stations, as well as highly proficient in damage-control skills.

Repair 6   *Ordnance repair.* Comprised primarily of gunner's mates, fire-control technicians, and electrician mates. Responsible for damage control and emergency repairs to the ship's weapons systems and magazines. This party is sometimes subdivided into forward and after groups.

Repair 7   *Gallery deck and island structure repair.* This unit is used primarily on aircraft carriers and other ship types where it is needed.

Repair 8   *Electronics repair.* Comprised primarily of personnel with ratings in the various electronic specialties.

Because of their special needs, aircraft carriers and ships equipped for helicopter operations also have aviation-fuel repair teams and crash and salvage teams.

Ships that carry exceptionally large amounts of ordnance (ammunition ships and aircraft carriers, for example) have an explosive ordnance disposal (EOD) team made up of specially qualified personnel. These highly trained individuals are capable of disarming fuzed bombs and taking care of other ordnance-related emergencies.

Within each repair party there are hose teams; dewatering, plugging, and patching teams; investigation teams; shoring, pipe repair, structural repair, casualty power, interior-communications (IC) repair, and electrical repair teams; chemical detection, biological sampling, radiological monitoring, and CBR decontamination teams; and stretcher bearers.

In general, repair parties must be capable of the following:

- Evaluating and reporting correctly on the extent of damage in an area
- Maintaining watertight integrity (preventing leaks and flooding)
- Maintaining the ship's structural integrity (shoring up weakened decks and bulkheads)
- Controlling and extinguishing all types of fires
- Giving first aid and transporting the injured to battle dressing stations
- Detecting, identifying, and measuring the amount of chemical, biological, or radiological contamination, as well as carrying out decontamination procedures

The equipment needed by repair parties is stowed in repair lockers. Included are such things as patches for ruptured water and steam lines, broken seams, and the hull; plugs made of soft wood for stopping the flow of liquids in a damaged hull or in broken pipes; assorted pieces of wood used for shoring; radiological defense equipment; an electrical repair kit for isolating damaged circuits and restoring power; and tools for forcible entry, such as axes, crowbars, wrecking bars, claw tools, hacksaws, bolt cutters, oxyacetylene cutting torches, and portable exothermic cutting units. The equipment stowed in a repair locker is reserved for damage control only and should never be used for any other purpose.

Communication is vital to the damage-control organization. Systems used by repair parties and the DCA to communicate include battle telephone (sound-powered) circuits, interstation two-way (MC) systems, ship's service telephones, the integrated voice communications system (IVCS), wire-free communication (WFCOM), and messengers.

BATTLE DRESSING AND DECONTAMINATION STATIONS

Most ships have at least two battle dressing stations (BDS) equipped to handle personnel casualties. They are manned by medical personnel and are located so that stretcher cases may be brought directly to them by the repair party. Emergency supplies of medical equipment are also placed in first-aid boxes throughout the ship. Signs are also posted throughout the ship directing you to the nearest BDS.

To handle CBR problems, at least two "decontamination stations" are provided in widely separated parts of the ship, preferably near BDS. Signs pointing the way to these stations are painted with photoluminescent markings so that they can be seen in low-light conditions. To prevent recontamination after personnel have been decontaminated, each station is divided into two areas: a contaminated or unclean section with a washing area and a clean section. These stations are manned by trained medical and repair-party personnel to ensure that proper decontamination procedures are followed.

WATERTIGHT INTEGRITY

A ship cannot survive without maintaining its watertight integrity. Uncontrolled leaking or flooding in a ship obviously leads to its sinking. For this reason, ships are designed so that damage resulting in leaks or flooding can be controlled and its effects minimized. Because of these design features, ships can experience an amazing amount of damage and still survive if proper precautions are taken in advance and the right corrective action is taken once damage is sustained.

Compartmentation

As explained in Chapter 10: Ships, a network of bulkheads and decks—designed to prevent the flow of water or other fluids from one space to another when they are properly secured—protects a ship from sinking. If one compartment experiences flooding, it can be sealed off from the others so that only a portion of the ship's overall buoyancy is affected, thus reducing the danger of sinking. If a ship did not have this protection, one leak would cause the eventual sinking of the ship.

A ship is divided into as many watertight compartments as practical. In general, the more watertight compartments a ship has, the greater her resistance to sinking. This system, which permits the isolation of individual compartments, is useful not only to control flooding but also to prevent the spread of fire and smoke and to reduce the effectiveness of CBR attacks.

Closures

For ideal buoyancy and protection against fire and other dangers, each compartment within a ship would be completely sealed up all of the time. This is obviously not practical, since it would mean that no one could ever enter or leave a space on a ship. In order for a ship to function, it must have openings to permit passage through bulkheads and decks.

Because an opening in a deck or bulkhead obviously compromises watertight integrity, these openings must have closures (also called fittings) that can be used to restore watertight integrity when it is needed.

In ships, these closures are called *watertight doors* (WTD) when they seal openings in bulkheads, and *hatches* when they seal openings in decks. (Note: Technically, the term "hatch" refers to the *opening* in the deck, and the door-like structure that closes it is accurately called a "hatch cover," but you will often hear "hatch" used to describe the cover as well as the opening. This is generally acceptable. But you will sometimes also hear "hatch" used *incorrectly* to describe a WTD. This is not acceptable to a true Sailor.)

DOORS

Watertight doors are designed to resist the same amount of pressure as the bulkheads they are a part of. In other words, when closed properly, a WTD is just as strong as the bulkhead it serves. WTDs are sealed shut by rubber gaskets, which are fixed to the door in such a way as to create a seal between the door and bulkhead where they come into contact. This point of contact is called the *knife edge*. The "latches" that press the door shut and hold it there are called *dogs*.

On a WTD, the dogs will be placed all around the door to ensure a proper seal. Some doors have dogs that must be individually closed and opened. Others, known as *quick-acting watertight doors*, have mechanisms

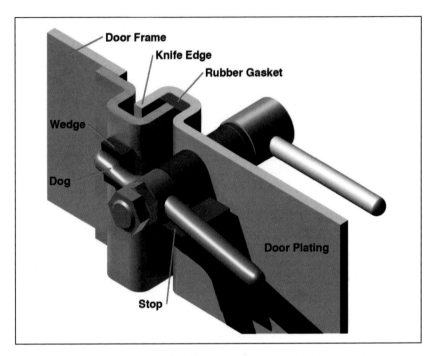

[**15.2**] "Dogs" are special latches used on watertight doors to ensure a watertight closure.

that operate all dogs simultaneously. Some doors, because of their location, do not need to be watertight. These are, not surprisingly, called *nonwatertight doors* (NWTD).

Some doors, though not watertight, are airtight (ATD) to retard the spread of flames or gases. Some doors have small tube-like openings in them that allow ammunition to be passed through without having to open the whole door. These are called *passing scuttles*. These too can be closed securely if flooding or contamination threatens.

Some openings, such as between offices, do not require watertight integrity and their doors look and function like normal doors you are used to seeing in buildings ashore. These are called *joiner doors*.

HATCH COVERS

Hatch covers (sometimes merely called "hatches" as explained above) can be thought of as horizontal doors that close the openings that allow access between decks. A hatch cover is either set with its top surface flush with the deck or set on top of a *coaming*, which raises the cover above the deck.

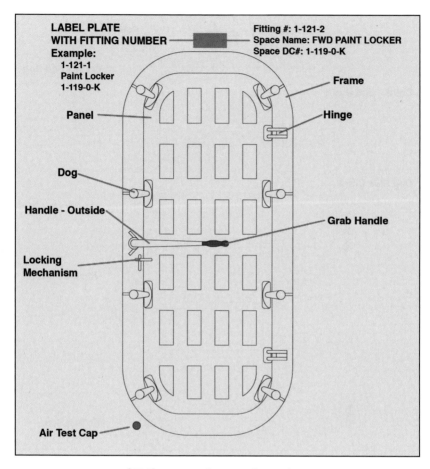

[**15.3**] An outside view of a quick-acting watertight door. Note the dogs all the way around for a tight seal.

Coamings are preferable in an area (such as on a weather deck) where water might wash over the deck. The coaming provides some protection that will prevent much of the water from pouring into the compartment below.

Some hatch covers, because they must cover relatively large openings in the deck, are heavy and difficult for one person to handle. To take care of this problem, larger hatch covers have an *escape scuttle*. This is a round opening with quick-acting closures that can be placed in the larger hatch cover to permit rapid escape from a compartment. Handwheels on both sides allow quick access or escape in an emergency. Escape scuttles are also sometimes placed directly through a deck or a bulkhead, without being part of a larger hatch cover.

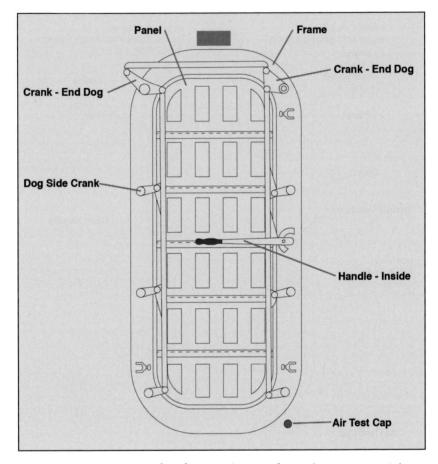

[**15.4**] An inside view of a quick-acting watertight door, showing how the dogs are linked together for simultaneous opening and closing.

Manholes provide access to spaces that must be entered only on rare occasions, such as voids and tanks used to store water and fuel. The covers to these openings are normally bolted in place. Manholes are also occasionally placed in bulkheads.

OTHER FITTINGS

Certain other fittings must be closed at times to prevent the unwanted flow of air or fluids. These would include certain valves and vents. For example, if an enemy aircraft sprays your ship with a toxic gas, it would be necessary to close the vents that bring air into the ship until the danger has passed.

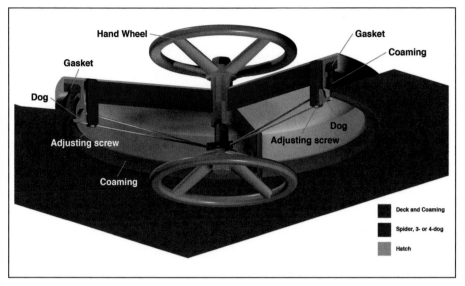

[**15.5**] A cutaway view of an escape scuttle showing the quick-acting handwheels above and below.

COMPARTMENT CHECK-OFF LISTS (CCOL)

In every compartment, posted where it can easily be seen, is a compartment check-off list. This list tells you every DC fitting (hatch, door, valve, vent, and so on) in that compartment. It also tells which division is responsible for that fitting, where it is located, and what it is used for. Other useful information, such as a list of all DC equipment (for example, fire extinguishers and hoses) is also included on this list. If you are familiar with the Navy's method of numbering compartments (see TAB 11-A: Shipboard Compartment Identification), you will find this check-off list very useful in locating important fittings and equipment. It is a good idea to take the time to study the compartment check-off list in those compartments in which you spend a lot of time (such as your berthing compartment or work spaces), so that you will know what types of damage-control fittings and equipment are in those compartments and where you can find them in an emergency.

There is also a computerized version of the CCOL that is a database kept by all Navy ships. It itemizes the location of all fittings and can be used by personnel responsible for the proper setting of material conditions of readiness.

USING AND MAINTAINING CLOSURES

Watertight doors and hatch covers will work longer and require less maintenance if they are closed and opened properly. When closing a door, first set one of the dogs opposite the hinges, with just enough pressure to keep the door shut. Then set a dog opposite the first one. Close the others, making sure you work with opposites as you go. This will maintain uniform pressure all around and cause less stress to the fitting.

When opening a door, start with the dogs nearest the hinges. This procedure will keep the door from springing and make it easier to operate the remaining dogs. Open the rest as you would when closing, shifting to opposite sides as you go.

Never paint the gaskets—the rubber must remain pliable for a proper seal—and never strike a knife edge, as dents or burrs will prevent a proper seal.

When closed, all watertight doors, hatches, scuttles, and manholes giving access to compartments must be securely "dogged" (closed down). Manhole covers should always be bolted except for inspection, cleaning, or painting. They must never be left open overnight or unattended when crews are not actually working in them.

When the ship sustains damage, watertight fittings should not be opened without permission from DCC. Extra caution is always necessary in opening compartments below the ship's waterline.

Material Conditions of Readiness

In order to determine when a ship's fittings should be opened for convenience and when they should be closed for safety, the Navy has devised a standardized system called the "material condition of readiness" system. This formal system permits the ship flexibility in adjusting to changing situations and thereby providing the right compromise between adequate safety and practical need. It should be fairly obvious, for example, that a ship at sea in a powerful storm is going to require a great deal more protection from flooding than is a ship moored to a pier in a safe harbor. To allow this flexibility, Navy ships have three basic material conditions of readiness that can be set to accommodate various situations, each representing a different degree of tightness and protection. These conditions are called *Xray*, *Yoke*, and *Zebra*. These conditions are explained in some detail in TAB 15-A: Material Conditions of Readiness.

DAMAGE REPAIRS

Timely and efficient repairs of damage to your ship may be necessary to keep her afloat. The difference between survival and sinking for your ship may depend upon how you and your shipmates are able to effect repairs. Damage-control drills will go a long way toward preparing you for this eventuality.

In an emergency repair situation, do your best with what you have. If you are calm, stay alert, and work quickly with the tools you have, you can do much to keep the ship afloat and make her ready for action again.

Any rupture, break, or hole in the ship's outer hull plating, particularly below the waterline, can let seawater in. If flooding is not controlled, the ship will sink. When the underwater hull is pierced, there are only two possible courses of action. The first, obviously, is to plug the holes. The second is to abandon the space or spaces where the penetration has taken place, then establish and maintain flood boundaries within the ship to prevent more extensive flooding.

There are two general methods of temporarily repairing a hole in the hull: put something *in it* or *over it*. In either case, the effect is to reduce the area through which water can enter the ship, or through which water can pass from one compartment to another. Holes may be effectively plugged by pounding in a wooden plug or stuffing it with something larger—such as a kapok life jacket or a mattress—depending upon the size of the hole. Prefabricated box patches may be placed over a hole with jagged or uneven edges, and a flexible sheet-metal patch may be appropriate for certain types of holes.

Cracks may be sealed using gaskets or some filler material such as caulking or oakum.

Shoring (perhaps best described as "bracing") is often used aboard ship to support ruptured decks, strengthen weakened bulkheads and decks, build up temporary decks and bulkheads against the sea, support hatches and doors, and provide support for equipment that has broken loose. Knowing the proper time to shore is a problem that cannot be solved by any one set of rules. Sometimes the need for shoring is obvious, as in the case of loose machinery or damaged hatches. But sometimes dangerously weakened supports under guns or machinery may not be noticeable. Although shoring is not always necessary, the best general rule is, "When in doubt, shore!"

The basic materials used in shoring are shores, wedges, sholes, and strongbacks. A *shore* is a portable beam. A *wedge* is a block, triangular on the sides and rectangular on the butt end. A *shole* is a flat block that may be placed under the end of a shore for the purpose of distributing pressure. A *strongback* is a bar or beam of wood or metal, often shorter than a shore, that is used to distribute pressure or to serve as an anchor for a patch. Many other pieces of equipment can also be used in connection with shoring.

FIRE PREVENTION AND FIGHTING

Fire is a constant threat aboard ship, and all measures must be taken to prevent it. Fires may start from spontaneous combustion, carelessness, hits by enemy shells, collision, or many other causes. If a fire is not controlled quickly, it could mean loss of the ship.

Whether you are a member of a repair party or not, it is essential that you learn all you can about fires—how they start, how to prevent them, and how to fight them.

Fire Basics

The old adage "Know thine enemy" is appropriate, for fire is the Sailor's deadly enemy, and if you understand the nature of fire, you will greatly improve your chances of keeping it from appearing and defeating it if it does.

THE FIRE TRIANGLE

The three essential elements for any fire to start and continue burning are *fuel*, *heat*, and *oxygen*. These three things make up what is called the "fire triangle." Remove any one of these three elements and you no longer have a triangle: the fire will be put out. Think about your backyard barbecue. To start the fire to cook the food, you need charcoal or gas (fuel), a match or lighter (heat), and good ventilation in the barbecue grill (oxygen). If the charcoal gets used up or the gas is turned off, the fuel is removed from the triangle and your cooking is over. If it rains, your fire will cool down (the heat is removed) and go out. If you place a tight cover over your grill and shut the ventilation openings, your fire will go out as soon as all of the oxygen inside is used up.

Aboard ship, the methods are the same as with your barbecue grill, although probably not as easy to accomplish. It is not always possible, for instance, or even practical, to eliminate fuel. If, however, a flammable liquid fire is being fed by a pipeline, the flow of fuel can be stopped by closing valves in the pipe.

Removing heat is the most common method of extinguishing a fire. The usual cooling method is to use lots of water.

Oxygen can be removed from a shipboard fire by using carbon dioxide (CO_2) to dilute the oxygen content of the air or by smothering the fire with a blanket of foam or sand.

CLASSES OF FIRE

Fires can be classified into four different types, identified by the first four letters of the alphabet. Once you know the class of fire you are dealing with, you will be able to fight the fire intelligently and in the most effective manner. Classes of fire and how to fight them are explained in TAB 15-B: Classes of Fire.

Fire Prevention

Any fire, however small, is bound to cause damage. For this reason, and because of the potential for disaster, a fire prevented is much preferred to a fire that must be fought.

The first step in fire prevention is to keep things squared away—clean, shipshape, and in their proper places. Keep flammable products (gasoline, oily rags, paint) away from fire-starting articles such as torches and sparking equipment. Don't take open flames near gasoline tanks, and don't bring flammable liquid near a welder's torch.

Make sure firefighting equipment is in the right place and in good condition. If a fire does start, you'll want to have the equipment on hand and ready to go. Even if you may not be able to prevent a fire from starting, you can prevent a little one from getting bigger.

The different classes of fire require different methods of prevention.

To prevent Class A fires, you should never throw lighted tobacco products or matches in trash cans and always be careful of where and how you stow rags and oily, paint-smeared cloth and paper. When welding or burning, maintain a proper fire watch, protect Class A materials from the open flame and hot droppings, and be sure to inspect the other side of a bulkhead where such "hot work" is taking place.

The danger of Class B fires requires some special methods of prevention. Be aware that in low places in the ship—such as bilges, tanks, and bottoms—there is the danger of the accumulation of flammable gasoline or oil vapors. Don't carry matches, lighters, or keys, and don't wear metal buttons or nylon clothing near gasoline or oil vapors. Use only non-sparking tools in areas where Class B substances have been or are stored. Don't turn on lamps, flashlights, or electrical equipment that are not certified as spark-proof in an area where gasoline or oil fumes can accumulate.

When working with electrical and electronic equipment, where the possibility exists of a Class C fire, do not paint or splash paint, oil, grease, or solvents on electrical insulation or wires. Report all frayed or worn wires and all sparking contacts, switches, and motors. Report any electrical equipment that is hot, smokes, or makes any unusual noise. In case of fire, secure all electrical equipment in the space. Don't use personal electrical and electronic equipment, such as hot plates, shavers, extension cords, stereos, or radios, unless they have been inspected and authorized by qualified engineering department personnel.

Protect Class D fuels from welding and burning operations. Do not store Class D fuels in areas that are susceptible to intense heat.

Fighting Fires

Despite the most careful precautions, fires can occur. If you discover a fire, report it immediately so that firefighting operations can begin. When reporting a fire, state the type of fire and its location (compartment name and designation), then do what you can to fight it. Always report the fire before taking any action. A delay of even half a minute might result in a minor fire becoming a major one.

After you have reported the fire, do what you can to fight or contain it. The efforts of one person may be enough to contain the fire until the fire party arrives. Use discretion, however. Do what you can *consistent with safety*. Your becoming a casualty will not help the fire party in its efforts.

To some extent, the procedures for fighting a fire depend on the conditions under which it occurs. Fires that break out during combat, normal steaming, or when a full crew is aboard are handled as battle casualties and the ship will likely go to GQ. These fires, which may occur in port or at sea, are normally fought by the firefighting party from the repair station in that section of the ship. Aboard larger ships, it may not always be feasible to go to GQ for every fire that occurs, so a nucleus fire party will handle those fires that can be kept isolated and under control. If control is lost, the ship will immediately go to GQ. When a fire occurs in port and only a partial crew is on board, the duty repair party handles it.

Fires that seem to be out may start again from a smoldering fragment or through vapor ignition. The final step in firefighting is the establishment of a *reflash watch* to keep an eye on the affected area for a sufficient amount of time, as determined by DCC.

Firefighting Equipment

All firefighting equipment is located in readily accessible locations and inspected frequently to ensure reliability and readiness. At any time, you may be called upon to serve on a repair/fire party, or you may be the only person present to combat a fire. If you don't know how to use the equipment, or what equipment to use, the result could be disastrous.

FIREMAIN

The firemain system is designed to deliver seawater to fireplugs, sprinkler systems, and AFFF (aqueous film-forming foam) stations throughout the ship. The firemain (also called simply "the main") has a secondary function of supplying flushing water and of providing coolant water for auxiliary machinery.

Firemain piping is configured as either a single line, horizontal loop, vertical loop, or composite system depending on the type of ship. On small combatant ships, a single-line system runs fore and aft near the centerline. On many larger combatant ships, horizontal-loop systems circle around the ship, providing versatility in case of damage. Some ships have vertical-loop systems winding through their superstructures. Composite systems (a combination of any of the other systems) are used on aircraft carriers because of their size and extensive compartmentation. There are many cross-connection points and cutout valves throughout the system to allow damaged sections of piping to be isolated or "jumped" by attaching hoses at bypass points. Risers (pipes that carry water vertically) and branch lines (horizontal pipes) lead from the main to fireplugs and AFFF systems throughout the ship.

Special attachments called "wye-gates" and "tri-gates" at the fireplugs allow two or three hoses to be attached simultaneously to one fireplug. Reducing fittings allows smaller hoses to be attached to larger fittings when necessary.

FIRE HOSES

The standard Navy fire hose has an interior lining of rubber, covered with two cotton or synthetic jackets. It comes in 50-foot lengths with a female coupling at one end and a male coupling at the other. The female coupling is connected to the fireplug. The male coupling is connected to another length of hose or to a nozzle. When rigging hoses, remember that the male end always points toward the fire and the female end of the hose is rigged in the direction of the fireplug.

Ships generally use 2½-inch hose on the weather decks and 1½-inch hose in the ship's interior. One or more racks at each fireplug are used to stow the fire hose. The hose must be faked on the rack so that it is free-running, with the ends hanging down and the couplings ready for instant use. On large ships, each weather-deck fire station has 100 feet of 2½-inch hose faked on a rack and connected to the plug. Below deck, 200 feet of 1½-inch hose are stowed by each plug, but only two lengths (100 feet) are connected to the plug. On smaller ships, 100 feet of 1½-inch hose are faked on the racks, with 50 feet connected to the plug. A spanner wrench for disassembling the connections is also stowed at each fire station. Spare lengths of hose are rolled and stowed in repair lockers.

SPRINKLER SYSTEMS

Sprinkler systems are installed in magazines, turrets, ammunition-handling rooms, spaces where flammable materials are stowed, and hangar bays. Water for these systems is piped from the firemain. Some systems are automatically triggered when a compartment reaches a certain temperature, but most are opened manually by control valves.

AQUEOUS FILM-FORMING FOAM (AFFF)

Aqueous film-forming foam (sometimes referred to as "light water"), a clear, slightly amber-colored liquid, is a concentrated mixture that was developed to combat Class B fires. In solution with water, it floats on the surface of fuels and creates a film (or blanket) that prevents the escape of vapors and thereby smothers the fire.

Permanently rigged AFFF stations are set up in high-risk and vital areas such as hangar bays on aircraft carriers. Usually called "HICAP" stations because of their high-capacity output, these systems do not need to be rigged before activating; they are ready for immediate use when needed.

Injection pumps and balance pressure proportioners are used on high-capacity AFFF systems. Individual HICAP stations are able to serve many different firefighting systems. When the station is activated, the pump injects AFFF concentrate into the piping downstream of the firemain control valve after it opens. The agitation of the water in the piping mixes the AFFF solution. The HICAP system can be activated from numerous local and remote stations, but it must be secured at the HICAP station itself. It is essential that the station be manned by qualified personnel once it is activated.

Portable AFFF systems require some rigging and servicing by the firefighting party. The male end of the hose line feeding seawater to an eductor is threaded into the female end of the portable eductor. A pickup tube (with a special ball-check valve that ensures one-way flow) must be inserted into a canister of AFFF. Seawater passing through the eductor causes a suction in the pickup tube that draws AFFF concentrate from the 5-gallon container. The eductor mixes the AFFF concentrate and seawater and delivers them to a 95-gallon-per-minute (gpm) variable-pattern AFFF nozzle, which is used to direct and distribute the solution.

To maintain the correct AFFF concentrate-to-water ratio, firemain pressure should be maintained. A pressure decrease due to friction in the hose could reduce pressure sufficiently to cause an improper AFFF concentrate and water mixture. Limiting the lengths of fire hose to 3 (for a total of 150 feet) and a rise of no more than one deck between the eductor discharge and the AFFF nozzle will maintain the needed pressure. Continuous use requires approximately 5 gallons per minute of AFFF concentrate. Fresh 5-gallon canisters of the concentrate must be provided as necessary to maintain the flow of AFFF.

PORTABLE EXTINGUISHERS

Two types of portable extinguishers used in the Navy are carbon dioxide (commonly called CO_2) and dry chemical (usually called PKP).

CO_2 extinguishers are used mainly for electrical (Class C) fires, but they are also effective on small Class A and B fires, such as an office trashcan or small amounts of oil, gasoline, and paint. Because CO_2 is heavier than air, it forms a smothering blanket over the fire. The extinguisher's effective range is four to six feet from the end of the horn.

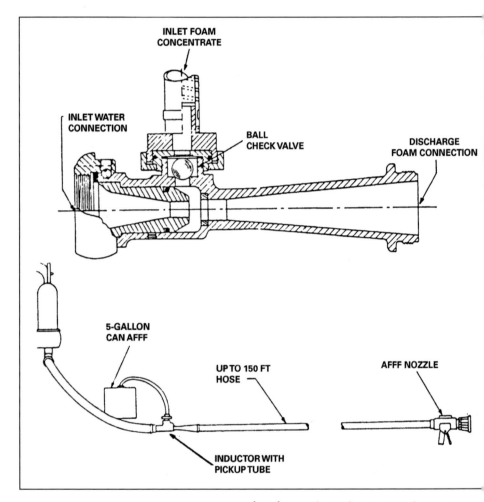

[**15.6**] An in-line eductor is used to mix AFFF concentrate and seawater.

To use the extinguisher, remove the locking pin from the valve, grasp the insulated handle of the horn with one hand, and squeeze the grip with the other. If you are in the open, approach the fire from the windward side (wind at your back). This extinguisher is quick to use, leaves no residue, and is not poisonous. But remember that CO_2 is capable not only of smothering fires but human beings as well. Use it sparingly in confined spaces. Also be aware that when released from the cylinder it expands rapidly to 450 times its stored volume, which causes the gas temperature to drop to minus 110° Fahrenheit. Contact with the skin can cause painful blisters.

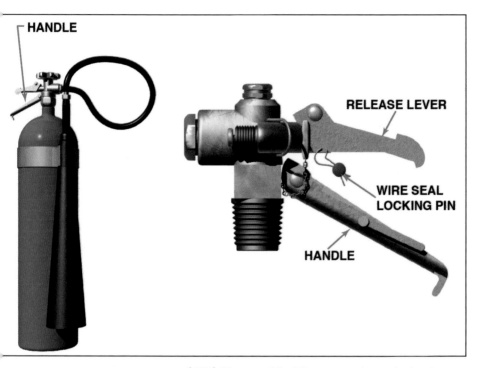

[**15.7**] The portable CO_2 extinguisher with detail of the handle, release lever, and locking pin.

Dry-chemical extinguishers are primarily used against Class B fires. The chemical used is purple potassium bicarbonate (similar to baking soda), also called "purple K powder" or "PKP."

PKP is nontoxic and four times as powerful as CO_2. It is also effective on Class C fires, but should not be used if CO_2 is available because it leaves a residue that may be harmful to the electronic components. PKP should not be used on internal fires in gas turbines or jet engines except in dire emergency for the same reason.

Handling the extinguisher is simple. Pull the locking pin from the seal-cutter assembly, tilting the bottle away from you and others for safety, and strike the puncture lever to cut the gas-cartridge seal. The extinguisher is then charged and ready for use. Discharge the chemical in short bursts by squeezing the grip on the nozzle and sweeping across the fire from side to side. Advance on the fire only if safe. When you are finished, invert the cylinder, squeeze the discharge lever, and tap the nozzle on the deck. This releases all pressure and clears the hose and nozzle of powder.

Dry chemical is an excellent firefighting agent, but its effects are temporary. It has no cooling effect and provides no protection against reflash. Therefore it may be backed up by AFFF. In confined spaces, PKP should be used sparingly. Prolonged discharge of the chemical reduces visibility and makes breathing difficult.

PUMPS

Pumps can be used to deliver water to fight fires or to dewater spaces, depending upon how they are rigged.

In firefighting, a significant amount of water may be discharged into the ship. For instance, a 2½-inch hose with a pressure of 100 pounds per square inch (psi) pumps nearly a ton of water per minute. Obviously, this water must be removed or the ship's stability will be greatly impaired.

Portable pumps may be powered by an internal combustion engine. When they are used below decks, the engine exhaust must be led outside the ship.

When a large height is unavoidable, it is possible to rig two pumps in tandem with a length of hose between them. The lower pump is activated first and primes the upper pump, which is then activated. Since the water being pumped is also cooling the pumps, the upper one must be carefully monitored to prevent overheating.

PROTECTIVE CLOTHING

Any clothing that covers your skin will protect it from flash burns and other short-duration flames. In situations where there is a likelihood of fire or explosion, keep covered as much as possible and protect your eyes with antiflash goggles.

If your clothes catch fire, don't run. This fans the flames. Lie down and roll up in a blanket, coat, or anything that will smother the flames. If nothing is available, roll over slowly, beating out the flames with your hands. If another person's clothes catch fire, throw the person down and cover him or her (except for the head) with a blanket or coat.

Aluminum-coated proximity suits are designed to protect the wearer from the radiant heat of fire. The suits offer only short-term protection. When worn by pilot-rescue personnel, the suits are continuously sprayed down to prevent overheating and should never make contact with actual flames. Proximity suits are used for open-air fires only and should never be used to combat fires inside the ship.

SELF-CONTAINED BREATHING APPARATUS (SCBA)

An invaluable piece of support equipment, the SCBA provides a supply of oxygen from a tank worn on the firefighter's back, giving the wearer the ability to go into compartments that have been robbed of adequate oxygen by a fire or that contain harmful gases, smoke, vapors, or dust.

AIR-LINE MASK

An alternative to the SCBA, which may be used for entering smoke-filled compartments to rescue crewmembers, is the air-line mask. Since it produces no oxygen of its own, it should never be used when actually fighting a fire. The mask is a demand-flow air-line respirator with a speaking diaphragm, monocular lens with adjustable head harness, breathing tube, and belt-mounted demand regulator. The mask comes with a 25-foot hose and quick-disconnect fittings. It is normally used with compressed air cylinders,

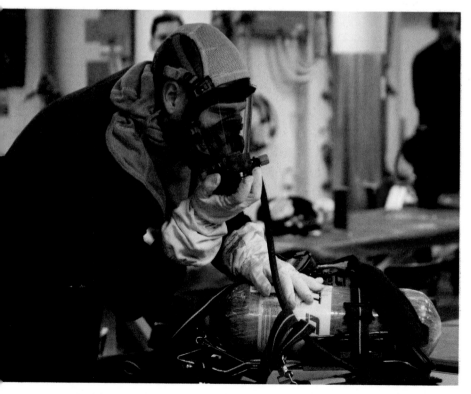

[15.8] A petty officer wearing a self-contained breathing apparatus (SCBA)

but when these are not available, low-pressure ship's-service air may be used as an alternative, provided it is reduced to the proper operating pressure.

Never use an oxygen cylinder with this equipment. Oil, grease, or oily water in the apparatus might combine with the oxygen and explode.

Before entering a space filled with toxic gases or smoke, check the mask to be sure it is working properly, then take a breath to determine whether there is sufficient airflow.

TENDING LINES

Tending lines are 50-foot lengths of nylon-covered steel wire with snap hooks at each end that allow a person to be found when smoke or darkness has reduced visibility. The tending line serves another useful function in that it can be used to communicate. In order to accomplish this, a standard set of signals is used throughout the Navy as follows:

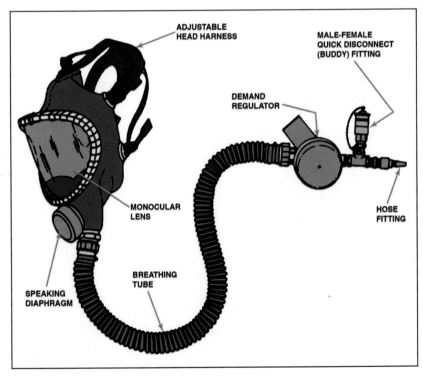

ADJUSTABLE
HEAD HARNESS

MALE-FEMALE
QUICK DISCONNECT
(BUDDY) FITTING

DEMAND
REGULATOR

MONOCULAR
LENS

HOSE
FITTING

SPEAKING
DIAPHRAGM

BREATHING
TUBE

[15.9] The air-line mask

	PULLS	MEANING
Tender to Wearer	1	Are you OK?
	2	Do you want to advance?
	3	Should I take up slack?
	4	Do you need help?
Wearer to Tender	1	I am OK.
	2	I am going to advance.
	3	I want you to take up slack.
	4	I need help.

One way to remember the line signal is to think of the acronym OATH: O (okay), A (advance), T (take up slack), H (help).

EMERGENCY-ESCAPE BREATHING DEVICE (EEBD)

The emergency-escape breathing device (EEBD), a fire-escape mask, consists of a head covering with a transparent face screen that can be donned quickly. Each EEBD provides the wearer with about fifteen minutes' breathing time, depending upon the physical exertion involved. This should enable the wearer to escape from any space. It is especially designed to protect against smoke inhalation.

SUPPLEMENTAL EMERGENCY EGRESS DEVICE (SEED)

Personnel working in engineering spaces wear SEEDs on their belts for easy access. Unlike the EEBD, the SEED does not provide protection for the eyes and nose, and it has a short operational time. It is meant only as a supplementary device, used temporarily to allow a watchstander to get to an EEBD.

ATMOSPHERE TESTING

All closed or poorly ventilated compartments (particularly those in which a fire has just occurred) are dangerous because the air in them may lack oxygen or contain toxic gases. Three steps should be taken as a matter of routine to test for combustible or toxic gases in confined spaces. The first step should be to test for oxygen content; the second for combustible vapors or gases; and the third for toxic substances. There are several types of atmosphere-testing indicators available for use by firefighting personnel.

Intended solely for the detection of oxygen deficiency in the atmosphere of a space, an *oxygen indicator* is designed to give a continuous reading of oxygen concentration from 0 to 25 percent. The oxygen indicator must be calibrated before each use. The sensing head of the indicator should be introduced into every part of the compartment, from top to bottom. If less than 20 percent oxygen is indicated, the compartment should be fully ventilated and retested. Before using the oxygen indicator, you should become very familiar with the instructions for its operation.

Combustible-gas indicators (explosimeters) are used to detect the level of explosivity of various flammable gases and vapors. Several different types of indicators are available, but all operate on the same principles. Operating instructions are attached to the inside of the case cover. This type of indicator can quickly, safely, and accurately detect all combustible gases or vapors associated with fuel oil, gasoline, alcohol, acetone vapors, illuminating gas, fuel gas, hydrogen, and acetylene in mixtures with air or oxygen. The indicator is sensitive to even small quantities of these substances. Although it does not actually identify specific combustibles, it indicates what their explosive level is. These instruments are equipped with flame arresters to prevent flashbacks.

The *Draeger toxic-gas detector* is a hand-operated, bellows-type aspirator pump into which the appropriate detector tube is inserted. The three gases commonly tested for are carbon monoxide, carbon dioxide (CO_2), and hydrogen sulfide.

DE-SMOKING

After a fire has been extinguished, it is usually necessary to remove the smoke from the affected compartment(s). This is done with natural or forced ventilation. In clearing the smoke out, several cautions should be noted:

- Be sure the fire is really out.
- Investigate the ventilation systems in the affected areas to make sure they are free of burning or smoldering materials.
- Have fire parties and equipment standing by the blower and controller of the ventilation systems.
- Obtain permission from DCC to open ventilation-system closures and start the blowers.

Portable ventilating equipment can be employed for de-smoking, although these devices are not as efficient or convenient as permanent ventilating systems. But when explosive vapors or fumes are present, it may be dangerous to use the ship's permanently installed ventilation systems. Under these circumstances, use only portable blowers.

Firefighting Parties

Every shipboard firefighting party consists of two hose teams known as the attack party. The no. 1 hose team is the *attacking unit*, and the no. 2 team is the *backup*.

The *scene leader* is in charge of the firefighting party. The scene leader's first duty is to get to the fire quickly, investigate the situation, determine the nature of the fire, decide what type of equipment should be used, and inform DCC. Later developments may require different or additional equipment, but the scene leader must decide what equipment is to be used first.

The *team leader* for each hose team directs the action of the nozzlemen and the other members of her or his team.

Nozzlemen man the nozzles of the hoses wearing complete battle dress plus gloves, flash hoods, a SCBA, and a miner's headlamp. Besides controlling the "business end" of the hose, nozzlemen help the scene leader investigate the fire when SCBAs are needed to enter a compartment.

Hosemen lead out the hose from the fireplug, remove kinks and sharp bends, and tend it while it is being used. When fighting the fire, they too wear SCBAs.

Investigators make continuous tours of inspection of those spaces adjoining the fire, looking for further damage, taking soundings (checking fluid levels in lower spaces), and leading personnel trapped in smoke-filled compartments to safety. In order to accomplish the latter, these team members also wear SCBAs.

Plugmen stand by to operate fireplug valves when ordered. They also rig and stand by jumper hoses (used to bypass damage) when necessary.

Accessmen clear routes to gain access to the fire by opening doors, hatches, scuttles, and other closures. They carry equipment to open jammed fittings and locked doors.

AFFF supplymen prepare foam-generating equipment and keep the system supplied with AFFF.

CO_2 *supplymen* carry CO_2 and PKP extinguishers.

The *closure detail* secures all doors, hatches, and openings around the area to isolate the fire. All ventilation closures and fans in the smoke and heat area are secured by this detail, which also establishes secondary fire boundaries by cooling down nearby areas.

The *electrician* de-energizes and re-energizes electrical circuits in the fire area and rigs power cables for portable lights, tools, and blowers.

The *hospital corpsman* provides on-scene first aid and is responsible for supervising the movement of seriously injured persons to sick bay for treatment.

The *phone talker* plugs into the nearest JZ sound-powered phone circuit to establish and maintain communication with DCC, either directly or through the local repair party. (See **Chapter 20: Communications** for an explanation of sound-powered phones.)

The *messenger* delivers messages between the scene leader and the repair-party leader.

Other personnel and equipment assigned to a firefighting party may include foam-equipment operators, additional hosemen, proximity suitmen (who wear special protective clothing that will allow them to get much closer to a fire than can someone with only normal protective clothing), a portable (oxyacetylene) cutting outfit (PCO) operator, the de-watering/de-smoking equipment team, and an atmospheric test equipment operator (who uses explosimeters, oxygen indicators, toxic-gas detectors, and other pieces of equipment to determine what dangers exist at the scene of the fire).

As Sailors, we all have a vested interest in keeping our ship afloat. Just as every Marine is famously a rifleman, so every Sailor must be a damage controlman. One of the deciding factors in the U.S. Navy's victory in World War II was our superiority over the Japanese in effective damage control. Our ships more often lived to fight another day when theirs did not.

SIXTEEN

NAVAL AIRCRAFT

Naval aircraft are an essential component of sea power. The U.S. Navy has thousands of aircraft in its inventory, organized into squadrons and air wings, that perform a wide variety of missions, many from the decks of ships and others from naval air stations. The many kinds of fixed-wing and rotary-wing (helicopter) aircraft flown by the Navy include fighter, attack, combined fighter-attack, antisubmarine, patrol, early warning, general utility, inflight refueling, transport, and trainer. Increasingly, unmanned aircraft (commonly referred to as "drones") are being used to accomplish various missions.

PRINCIPLES OF FLIGHT

Man has always wanted to fly. Legends from the very earliest times bear witness to this wish. Perhaps the most famous of these legends is the Greek myth about a father and son who flew with wings made of wax and feathers. It was not, however, until the successful flight by the Wright Brothers at Kitty Hawk, North Carolina, that the dream of flying became a reality. Since the flight at Kitty Hawk, aircraft designers have spent much time and effort in developing that first crude flying machine into the modern aircraft of today. To understand the principles of flight, you must first become familiar with the physical laws affecting aerodynamics.

Physical Laws Affecting Aerodynamics

Aerodynamics is the study of the forces that let an aircraft fly. Key to this study are Newton's Laws of Motion:

[**16.1**] Some of the many types of aircraft flown by the U.S. Navy

Newton's First Law of Motion

An object at rest will remain at rest, or an object in motion will continue in motion at the same speed and in the same direction, until an outside force acts on it. For an aircraft to taxi or fly, a force must be applied to it. It will remain at rest without an outside force. Once the aircraft is moving, another force must act on it to bring it to a stop. It will continue in motion without an outside force. This willingness of an object to remain at rest or to continue in motion is referred to as inertia.

Newton's Second Law of Motion

The second law of motion states that if an object moving with uniform speed is acted upon by an external force, the change of motion will be directly proportional to the amount of force and inversely proportional to the mass of the object being moved. Simply stated, this means that an object being pushed by 10 pounds of force will travel faster than it would if it were pushed by 5 pounds of force, and a heavier object will accelerate more slowly than a lighter object when an equal force is applied.

Newton's Third Law of Motion

The third law of motion states that for every action there is an equal and opposite reaction. This law can be demonstrated with a balloon. If you inflate a balloon with air and let it go without first tying the neck, the balloon will fly around as the air escapes from it. This is similar to what happens (only with more control) when a jet propels an aircraft through the air.

Airfoils

A fixed-wing aircraft depends on forward motion for lift. A rotary-wing aircraft depends on rotating airfoils for lift.

For a fixed-wing aircraft to fly, the wings are shaped in such a way that when the aircraft is propelled forward by the thrust of the engine(s), the air hitting the leading edge of the wing is split into two paths. The upper side of the wing has less air pressure acting on it than does the lower side. This difference in pressure causes air flowing along the underside of the wing to push the wing upward toward the lesser pressure on the upper side, thus creating lift. This special wing shape is called an *airfoil.*

Helicopters use the same principle, but their airfoils are the spinning rotors. The blades of these rotors are shaped like wings, and their spinning motion creates lift in the same manner as with the wings of a fixed-wing aircraft.

Forces Affecting Flight

An aircraft in flight is in the center of a continuous battle of forces. The conflict of these forces is the key to all maneuvers performed in the air. There is nothing mysterious about these forces—they are definite and known. The direction in which each force acts can be calculated. The aircraft is designed to take advantage of each force. These forces are *lift, weight, thrust,* and *drag.*

Lift is the force that acts in an upward direction to support the aircraft in the air. It counteracts the effects of weight. Lift must be greater than or equal to weight if flight is to be sustained.

Weight is the force of gravity acting downward on the aircraft and everything in the aircraft, such as crew, fuel, and cargo.

Thrust is the force developed by the aircraft's engine. It acts in the forward direction. Thrust must be greater than or equal to the effects of drag for flight to begin or to be sustained.

Drag is the force that tends to hold an aircraft back. Drag is caused by the disruption of the airflow about the wings, fuselage (body), and all protruding objects on the aircraft.

BASIC AIRCRAFT NOMENCLATURE

Because aircraft are such an important component of the Navy, you should be familiar with certain basic terms concerning the structure and capabilities of airplanes and helicopters.

The *fuselage* is the main body of the aircraft. The pilot controls the aircraft from the cockpit, which is located in the fuselage and positioned to provide needed visibility through a transparent canopy.

The *wings* are strong structural members attached to the fuselage; their airfoil shape provides the lift that supports the plane in flight. Wings are fitted with *flaps* that provide increased lift and can be used to reduce landing speed, which allows the aircraft to shorten the area needed for landing. The use of flaps during takeoff serves to reduce the length of runway needed.

The wings may carry fuel tanks, engines, and landing gear depending upon the aircraft's design. The wings may also be configured to carry guns, rockets, missiles and other weapons.

The tail assembly of a fixed-wing aircraft consists of *vertical and horizontal stabilizers, rudder(s),* and *elevators.* These components are key elements in the flight controls of the aircraft.

The *landing gear* usually means wheels, but in certain aircraft these may be replaced by skids, skis, or floats.

The *powerplant* develops the thrust or force that propels the aircraft forward, providing mobility and (in combination with the wings) the lift necessary to keep the aircraft aloft. In the case of helicopters, the powerplant provides the power to keep the rotors spinning, which keeps the aircraft aloft and allows it to hover as well as move through the air. The powerplant may consist of reciprocating (piston) engines that drive propellers, jet engines that develop thrust (turbojet and turbofan), or turbine engines and propellers or rotors in combination (turboprop or turboshaft).

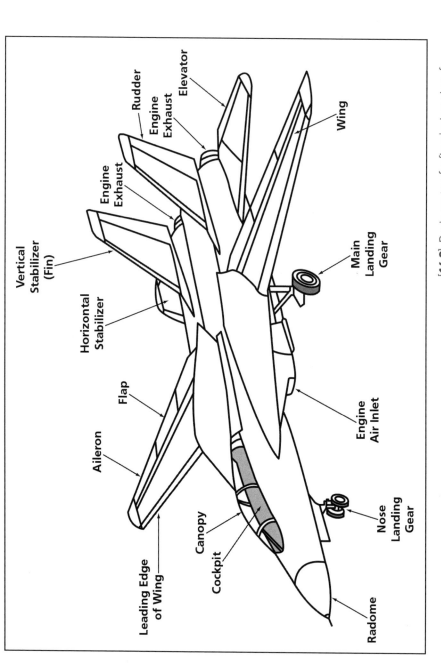

Vertical
Stabilizer
(Fin)

Rudder

Engine
Exhaust

Elevator

Engine
Exhaust

Wing

Horizontal
Stabilizer

Flap

Aileron

Main
Landing
Gear

Engine
Air Inlet

Leading Edge
of Wing

Canopy

Cockpit

Nose
Landing
Gear

Radome

[**16.2**] Basic parts of a fixed-wing aircraft

Helicopters (also called rotary-wing aircraft) are a special kind of aircraft. Instead of having wings as fixed-wing aircraft do, they have *rotors*, which are actually wings that rotate. The most common type have a single set of large rotors that provide the lift and a *tail rotor assembly* that counters the torque created by the main rotors. Some helicopters counteract the torque by having two sets of main rotors that spin in opposite directions. Helos (as they are often called) can lift vertically, hover in place, land in small areas, and fly backward as well as forward.

Another useful aircraft term is "Mach," which is commonly used to measure the speed capability of an aircraft or missile. Formally defined as the ratio of speed of an object to the speed of sound in the surrounding atmosphere, it is used as follows. An aircraft traveling at Mach 1 would be moving at the speed of sound. One going Mach 2 would be moving at twice the speed of sound, and Mach 1.5 would be moving at one-and-a-half times the speed of sound. Depending upon the altitude, temperature, and some other variables, the speed of sound varies, but a rough figure to use for approximation is 650 miles per hour. So an aircraft flying at Mach 2 would be moving at a speed of approximately thirteen hundred miles per hour. An aircraft that is able to fly faster than the speed of sound (Mach 1) is said to be "supersonic" and one that cannot is called "subsonic." A "hypersonic" aircraft flies at Mach 5 or greater.

Stealth technology has changed the appearance and actual structure of aircraft considerably. Stealth is accomplished by incorporating different materials and designing an aircraft's outer surface at various angles that will deflect a radar signal rather than return it to the transceiver from which it came, thereby making the aircraft virtually invisible to enemy radar.

TYPES OF NAVAL AIRCRAFT

There are many different types of aircraft in the U.S. Navy's inventory. Some of these were designed specifically for naval use, but many are used by the other armed forces as well. Some are fixed-wing aircraft while others are helicopters. See TAB 16-A: Types of Naval Aircraft for more information on the various types of aircraft currently in use by the Navy and the Marine Corps.

Fighters are used to destroy other aircraft and incoming missiles. They are the aircraft you would normally see involved in a "dogfight." Fighters are very fast and highly maneuverable. They patrol above friendly forces in what are called "combat air patrols" (CAP) and intercept and engage incoming enemy aircraft or missiles. They also penetrate enemy air space to engage the enemy's aircraft, and they escort other kinds of aircraft when they are carrying out their missions in hostile areas. All fighters are fixed-wing.

Attack aircraft are designed to destroy enemy targets, at sea and ashore, such as ships, vehicles, transportation systems, airfields, enemy troops, and so on. To accomplish these missions, attack aircraft are armed with various configurations of rockets, guided missiles, gun systems, torpedoes, mines, and bombs. Attack aircraft can be either fixed-wing aircraft or helicopters. The Navy used to have aircraft specifically designed as attack aircraft but currently relies on the F/A-18 Hornet to carry out both fighter and attack missions.

Patrol aircraft are tasked primarily with finding enemy forces. They are designed more for long range and time on station than for speed. Although they may be armed, sensors (such as radar, infrared, acoustic, and magnetic-detection devices) are their most important components.

Antisubmarine aircraft search out submarines visually, by radar and magnetic detection, or by signals sent from floating sonobuoys, and then destroy them with rockets, depth charges, or homing torpedoes. Both helicopters and fixed-wing aircraft are used for antisubmarine warfare.

Mine-warfare aircraft lay mines in enemy waters or sweep enemy mines from friendly waters or objective areas.

Command and control aircraft coordinate various operations within the battle space using sophisticated sensors, communications, and computer equipment.

Electronic warfare aircraft are designed and built specifically for tactical electronic warfare operations, such as jamming enemy radars for a significant tactical advantage.

Transport aircraft are used to carry cargo and personnel. As with any of the types of aircraft in the Navy's inventory, some are land based and others can be operated from aircraft carriers. Both helicopters and fixed-wing aircraft are used for transport missions.

Trainer aircraft are generally two-seat fixed-wing or rotary-wing aircraft that allow instructors and students to go aloft together to learn or perfect the techniques of flying.

IDENTIFYING AIRCRAFT

Many types, designs, and modifications of aircraft form the naval air arm of the Navy. Like ships, aircraft have names, usually chosen by the designers or developers and approved by the Navy. Unlike ships, these names do not apply to individual airplanes but to all of that same type, more like classes of ships. For example, one type of the Navy's combat aircraft is named "Hornet," and all the aircraft produced of that type are called Hornets. Individual aircraft are each identified with a unique serial number similar to the "Vehicle Identification Number" (VIN) on individual automobiles. This serial number is sometimes called a "tail number" because it is usually displayed on the tail of the aircraft.

The names are the most fun—there have been some great ones, like Phantom, Corsair, Hellcat, and Banshee—but they are the least revealing when it comes to type, mission, and so on. A more revealing system of letters and numbers is used to distinguish among the many types and variations of naval aircraft in service. This aircraft designation system—sometimes called the "Mission Design Series" (MDS)—is a combination of letters and numbers that tells you certain basic facts about the aircraft.

The bad news is that this system is a little intimidating at first—when you first encounter "F/A-18E/F," representing the Super Hornet, you can't help but think this is something only for cryptanalysts—but the good news is that it *is* mostly logical and definitely decipherable. Some more good news is that this system of identification is the same for all the armed forces. This system is explained in more detail in TAB 16-B: Identifying Military Aircraft.

Be careful that you do not confuse formal aircraft designations with other abbreviations that sometimes come into play. For example, a concept that has been in development for some time is the Joint Strike Fighter (JSF), a fighter aircraft designed from the beginning to meet the various needs of all the armed forces, rather than just one, as has often been the practice. This aircraft is often referred to as the JSF, but this is *not* an aircraft designation within the formal system.

One more thing to keep in mind (to avoid confusion) is that the current aircraft designation system has been in effect only since 1962, so if you are reading about aircraft in World War II, for example, the aircraft designations will not be the same.

AIRCRAFT ORGANIZATION

The basic organizational element for naval aircraft is the *squadron*. Some squadrons are carrier based, spending part of their time on board aircraft carriers; others are land based and, if their mission requires it, periodically deploy to other locations. Some squadrons are subdivided into detachments and are scattered to various ships or bases.

Though squadrons often have informal names that have more to do with morale than identification ("Black Knights," "Diamondbacks," etc.), they are officially identified by letter-number designations that, like ship hull numbers, tell something about their mission while giving them a unique identity. The first letter in a squadron designation is either a "V" or an "H." The V indicates fixed-wing aircraft and H is used for squadrons made up entirely of helicopters. If a squadron has *both* helicopters and fixed-wing aircraft, it is designated by a V. In the days when there was a third type of aircraft, the lighter-than-air (or dirigible) types, squadrons of those aircraft were designated by a Z.

The letter or letters following the V or H indicate the squadron's mission or missions. For example, a squadron whose primary purpose is training pilots to fly fixed-wing aircraft would be designated "VT." By adding a number, an individual squadron takes on a unique identity; for example, "VT-3." The numbers, in most cases, have some logic to them—such as even numbers indicating Atlantic Fleet squadrons and odd numbers designating Pacific Fleet—but movement and the periodic establishment and disestablishment of various squadrons has clouded some of the original intended logic.

Some of the squadron designations you might encounter are:

HM	helicopter mine countermeasures
HT	helicopter training
VA	attack
VAQ	tactical electronic warfare
VAW	carrier airborne early warning
VC	fleet composite
VF	fighter
VFA	strike fighter
VFC	fighter composite

VP	patrol
VQ	reconnaissance/strategic communications
VR	fleet logistics support
VRC	carrier logistics support
VS	sea control (antisubmarine warfare, etc.)
VT	training
VX	test and evaluation

Aircraft squadrons are typically grouped into larger organizational units called "air wings." A carrier air wing (CVW) is usually made up of about eight squadrons, each serving different but integrated purposes. With these various squadrons on board, an aircraft carrier can carry out a wide variety of missions.

While much of this book focuses on ships (primarily for space considerations), aircraft are a vitally important component of today's Navy. Powerful airwings are assigned to aircraft carriers, helicopter detachments operate off of destroyers and other ships, land-based patrol aircraft extend the Navy's reach, and logistical aircraft perform a vast array of vital missions. All of these functions and more make naval aviation an integral and essential part of the Navy's ability to carry out its many missions.

SEVENTEEN

NAVAL WEAPONS

The Navy's overall mission is to maintain sufficient military capability to effectively deter a would-be enemy from using military power against the United States and its allies, to defend against any attacks that might occur, and to take offensive action against the enemy once hostilities have begun. Weapons are the mainstay of the military. Without them, the Navy could not carry out its combat missions or defend its ships, planes, bases, and personnel.

TERMINOLOGY

To understand the weapons used by the Navy, one should first be familiar with the following terms.

Ordnance. This term applies to the various components associated with a ship's or aircraft's firepower: guns, gun mounts, turrets, ammunition, guided missiles, rockets, and units that control and support these weapons. (Note that the word is spelled "ordnance" and not "ordinance," which is something entirely different. This is a common error.)

Weapon system. When a number of ordnance components are integrated so as to find, track, and deliver fire onto a target, this is called a weapon system. For example, a gun would be called a weapon, but the gun plus the radars used to find and track the target and the ammunition-handling equipment used to load it would be called a weapon system.

[**17.1**] USS *Lake Erie* (CG 70) fires a standard missile from her vertical launcher.

Gun. In its most basic form, a gun is a tube (barrel), closed at one end, from which a projectile is propelled by the burning of gunpowder. A projectile (bullet) fired from a gun gets all of its traveling energy at the instant it is fired (unlike rockets and missiles whose burning fuels continue to propel them through the air).

Round. A unit of ammunition consisting of a projectile, a propellant, an igniting charge, and a primer. One shot.

Propellant. The explosive substance (such as gunpowder) that is ignited to produce the energy to move an object (such as a bullet) toward an intended target. Rockets and missiles also have propellants, but they continue to burn through part or all of the firing, whereas a projectile receives all of its energy at the moment of initial ignition.

Projectile. That component of ammunition that, when fired from a gun, carries out the tactical purpose of the weapon. In simplest terms, it is the "bullet." The parts of a typical gun projectile are the *body* (main part of the projectile; slightly smaller in diameter than the bourrelet), the *ogive* (curved forward portion of a projectile), the *bourrelet* (smooth machined area that serves as the bearing surface of the projectile during its travel through the bore of the gun), and the *rotating band* (circular ring made of copper or plastic that seals the forward end of the gun chamber to prevent the escape of propellant gases and engages the rifling in the bore to impart rotation to the projectile).

Rail gun. Under development and testing but not yet in use in the Navy, a rail gun uses magnetic "rails" instead of chemical propellants to launch projectiles at extreme ranges.

Laser Weapon System (LaWS). A directed energy weapon developed by the Navy for defensive purposes. It can be used to cripple a target's sensors or motors, detonate explosives, or destroy a small craft or drone.

Rocket. A weapon containing a propulsion section to propel the weapon through the air and an explosive section used to do damage to an enemy. A rocket is unable to change its direction of movement after it has been fired.

Missile. Originally called a "guided missile" this weapon is essentially a rocket (that is, it has a propulsion section and an explosive section), but also has a guidance section that allows its direction to be changed in mid-flight in order to better hit the target.

Ballistic missile. These are specialized missiles often associated with nuclear weapons. They are guided primarily during the relatively brief period when the missile is first launched and being powered to a very high

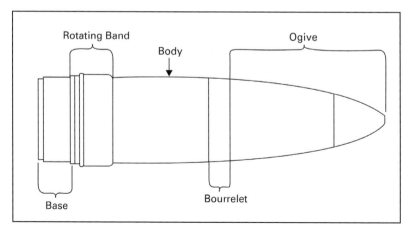

[**17.2**] The parts of a gun projectile

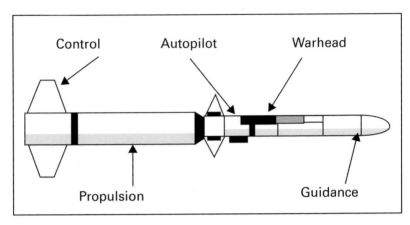

[**17.3**] The parts of a typical missile

(above the atmosphere) flight path. Using sophisticated calculations, they then rely on physical laws (gravitational effects, orbital mechanics, etc.) to carry them great distances until they then reenter the atmosphere and descend to the target.

Torpedo. A self-propelled underwater weapon used against surface and underwater targets. Some torpedoes function like underwater rockets in that they cannot be controlled once they have been launched, while other, more sophisticated versions can be guided, like an airborne missile, after they have been launched.

Mine. An underwater explosive weapon put into position by surface ships, submarines, or aircraft. A mine explodes only when a target comes near or into contact with it.

Depth charge. Antisubmarine weapons fired or dropped by a ship or aircraft, and set to explode either at a certain depth or in proximity to a submarine.

Bomb. Any weapon, other than a torpedo, mine, rocket, or missile, dropped from an aircraft. Bombs are free-fall (that is, they have no propulsion power to deliver them to the target) explosive weapons and may be either "dumb" (unguided) or "smart" (with a guidance system to steer them to their target).

Launcher. The device used to put a missile or rocket into the air. Older systems use an above-deck reloadable arm or box, but more modern systems use a vertical launch system (VLS), which uses tubes that are mounted in the ship's hull, expelling the missile through an open hatch

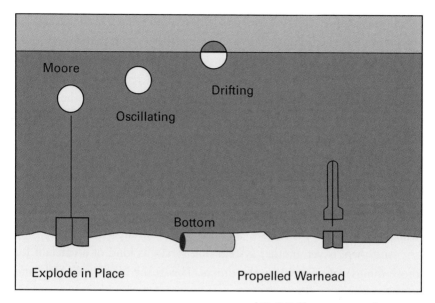

Moore

Oscillating

Drifting

Bottom

Explode in Place

Propelled Warhead

[**17.4**] Different types of mines

in the deck. (Also used to describe the device that puts a torpedo into the water.)

Warhead. That part of a missile, rocket, or torpedo that carries the explosive or some chemical package (for incendiaries, etc.).

Fire control. This is *not* the means for fighting fires (that is called "damage control" in the Navy), but it is the means used to control the firing of weapons. This can include the use of optics, radar, or laser beams and is the means for getting projectiles, missiles, and torpedoes onto a target.

WEAPONS DESIGNATIONS

You have probably noticed while reading other chapters in this book that the Navy is fond of designation systems (like the one for ship hull numbers that gives us such things as "CVN" and "DDG," and another for aircraft, the MDS system, which comes up with such things as "F/A-18E/F"). Though these systems can be bewildering at first, they really are useful for conveying a lot of information in a very compact way. Memorizing them is for the very brilliant or those with a lot of time on their hands. For the rest of us, being familiar with the basics—coupled with a willingness to refer to the various tables in this book—will go a long way toward making us smarter.

In this chapter you will encounter more of the same. In the section on missiles and rockets, you will encounter another system that makes sense out of such things as "AGM-88" and "RIM-2D." In the section on fire control, "Weapon Control Systems," you will find yet another similar (but different) system for identifying electronics equipment within the Department of Defense.

To make things just a bit more confusing, you will also encounter some weapons (particularly bomb guidance units, warheads, and some launchers) that are designated using a U.S. Air Force system that looks similar but is altogether different from the Navy system used to designate rockets and missiles. And you will find that the Navy uses some Army designations when referring to some of its weapons (small arms in particular).

And there is yet another system that serves as kind of a catchall for those things not covered by the others. This is the Navy's "MARK and MOD" system.

These various systems are explained in TAB 17-A: Weapons Designation Systems.

MISSILES AND ROCKETS

The chief advantage of rockets and missiles over gun and bomb systems is their extended range, and missiles are, of course, more effective than rockets because of their increased accuracy. The major disadvantage of these weapons is their added cost. Both missiles and rockets can be fired from either ships (including submarines) or aircraft.

Rocket and Missile Components

Rockets have three major components—the airframe, the powerplant, and the warhead. As already explained, missiles have a fourth component—the guidance system.

The *airframe* is the body of the rocket or missile, which determines its flight characteristics and contains the other components. It must be light, because the other parts are generally heavy. Airframes are made of aluminum alloys, magnesium, and high-tensile (high-stress) steel. These metals can withstand extreme heat and pressure.

The *powerplant* is similar in function to the engines of an aircraft except that the aircraft's engines are reusable while the missile's propulsion unit is expended in its one flight. The powerplant propels the rocket or missile, usually at very high speeds to minimize its chance of being shot down before reaching its intended target. Some must be able to operate at very high altitudes where there is little or no atmosphere and therefore are required to carry both the fuel and an oxidizer in order to sustain combustion. Other, less expensive powerplants are air-breathing plants that carry only the fuel, but they cannot operate above about 70,000 feet. Some rockets and missiles are equipped with additional boosters to extend the range.

The *warhead* is the part that does the damage. Its explosive may be conventional or nuclear or it may carry some chemical package to make smoke, fire, and so on.

Missile Guidance Systems

The guidance system in missiles constantly corrects the flight path until it intercepts the target. There are several different basic types of guidance systems: inertial, terrain following, homing, command, or beam riding. Many missiles use a combination of two of these systems—one guiding the missile through mid-course and the other used during the terminal stage. Components of these guidance systems will reside either in the missile itself or in the launch platform (ship, aircraft, etc.).

INERTIAL GUIDANCE

This type of guidance uses a predetermined path programmed into an on-board missile computer before launch. Missile speed and direction are checked constantly, and the computer makes corrections to keep it on course.

TERRAIN FOLLOWING GUIDANCE

Missiles using this sophisticated type of guidance are preprogrammed with known terrain characteristics along the intended flight path that the missile can "recognize" and use to maintain or adjust its course and altitude. Such information can be obtained from satellite imagery or other forms of intelligence.

HOMING GUIDANCE

In this type of guidance, the missile picks up and tracks a target by radar, optical devices, or heat-seeking methods.

In an *active* homing system, the missile itself emits a signal that is reflected off the target and picked up by a receiver in the missile.

In a *semiactive* homing system, the signal comes from the launching ship or plane rather than from the missile itself, is reflected off the target, and is then received by the missile, which uses the information received to correct its flight.

A *passive* homing system does not require either the missile or the firing ship or aircraft to emit a signal, but uses the target's emissions to home in on. For example, some passive homers use a target's own radar signals to home in on; a heat-seeking missile can home in on the heat put out by the target's engines.

COMMAND GUIDANCE

After the missile is launched on an intercept course, two separate radar systems track the target and the missile. A computer (on the launch platform—not the missile itself) evaluates how the missile is doing in relation to the target and transmits orders to the missile to change its track as necessary to ensure that it hits the target.

BEAM-RIDING GUIDANCE

This is an older system in which the missile follows a radar beam (transmitted by the launch platform) to the target. A computer in the missile keeps it centered within the radar beam. Several missiles may ride the same beam simultaneously. If the missile wanders outside the beam, it will automatically destroy itself.

Missile and Rocket Designations

Navy rockets and missiles are often identified by a three-letter designation, followed by a number. For example, the Sparrow missile is known as an AIM-7. The A tells you that the missile is launched from an airplane. If the first letter is an R, it means the missile is launched from a ship; U means that it is submarine-launched.

The second letter tells you the mission. I indicates air intercept (shoots down other aircraft), G means surface attack (ships or land targets), and U means the target is a submarine.

The third letter is either M (for missile) or R (for rocket).

The number(s) used differentiate between one similar system and another and represent the sequential development of the missile; for example, the first missile of a particular type that was developed was designated number 1 and the next was number 2, and so on. Just as with aircraft, major subsequent design modifications of the same weapon are identified by a follow-on letter, "A" for the first modification, "B" for the next, and so on. See TAB 17-A: Weapons Designation Systems for a more thorough explanation.

Missile Categories

Missiles can be launched from aircraft, ships, and submarines and, depending upon their intended target, may be categorized as air-to-air, air-to-surface, surface-to-air, and so on. Some missiles can be used against air and surface targets alike. See TAB 17-B: Types of Naval Weapons for more information on the Navy's missiles currently in use.

AIR-TO-AIR

The AIM-7 Sparrow, AIM-9 Sidewinder, and AIM-120 Advanced Medium-Range Air-to-Air Missile (AMRAAM) are carried by Navy fighter aircraft to shoot down enemy aircraft.

[**17.5**] Aviation ordnancemen preparing to load Sidewinder air-to-air missiles onto a Hornet fighter aircraft

AIR-TO-GROUND

Despite the name, these missiles can be used against ships at sea as well as inland targets.

SURFACE-TO-AIR

Mounted on ships, these missiles are designed to shoot down incoming enemy aircraft and missiles. These weapons can be used in concert with or instead of friendly interceptor aircraft.

CRUISE MISSILES

These missiles can be fired from surface ships to strike other surface ships and could therefore be called surface-to-surface missiles, but because they may also be fired from submarines or from aircraft to hit surface targets, they are more generically referred to as cruise missiles. More specifically defined as an unmanned, self-propelled guided vehicle that uses aero-dynamic lift (wings) to extend its range, a cruise missile is essentially an unmanned aircraft that is relatively inexpensive (compared to manned air-craft) to maintain and operate.

[**17.6**] The AGM-65 Maverick is an example of an air-to-ground missile.

[**17.7**] A Harpoon cruise missile is fired from a cruiser.

BALLISTIC MISSILES

By definition, ballistic missiles do not rely upon aerodynamic surfaces to produce lift and consequently follow a ballistic (free-fall) trajectory when thrust is terminated. A ballistic missile has a relatively short flight time, and defenses against it are difficult.

Some ballistic missiles are relatively simple weapons (such as the Scud missile used by Saddam Hussein during the Persian Gulf War), whereas others are highly sophisticated types (such as the Navy's Trident missile).

All extremely long-range missiles are ballistic. Intermediate-range ballistic missiles (IRBM) can reach targets up to fifteen hundred nautical miles away, whereas the intercontinental ballistic missile (ICBM) has a range of many thousands of miles. These weapons can be equipped with *multiple independently targetable reentry vehicles* (MIRV), which allow one missile to carry multiple warheads that can each be separately guided to a different target.

[17.8] A Trident ballistic missile fired from a submerged submarine

Missile Launching Systems

Earlier missile systems had "dedicated" launchers—separate magazine-loaded launchers for each type of missile. This took up valuable space on board ship and increased topside weight. Later launchers handled more than one type of missile, but still had to be individually loaded. The newest launcher is the Mark 41 VLS (vertical launch system). Missiles are carried in below-deck ready-to-launch tubes; any needed mix of missiles can be fired right from these tubes in quick succession without the delays that were involved in reloading topside launchers.

BOMBS

Although you will see the word "bomb" sometimes used in other contexts (such as "a suitcase bomb" or "a terrorist bombing"), for military purposes, bombs are normally considered to be ordnance dropped from aircraft that use gravity and the forces imparted by the aircraft's motion as the means of delivery (as opposed to rockets and missiles, which have their own means of propulsion).

There is an old joke that says, "Bombs are highly accurate and reliable weapons—they always hit the ground." Though this makes a good point about the nature of bombs as a weapon, its wisdom has been somewhat superseded by the advent of new technologies that include laser-guided bombs. These weapons—often called "smart bombs"—still use gravity and aircraft motion as the means of delivery, but these more sophisticated versions can be guided in flight and steered onto a target.

Bombs have four chief parts. The *case* is normally made of steel and contains the explosive. The *fuze* causes the bomb to explode when desired. The *fin* or *tail* assembly stabilizes the bomb during flight. An *arming-wire assembly* keeps the fuze from being armed until after the bomb is dropped.

Bombs are generally classed as explosive, chemical, or practice. General-purpose (GP) bombs, weighing anywhere from five hundred to two thousand pounds, are explosive-type bombs and are generally used against unarmored ships or ground targets that can be damaged by blast or fragmentation. Semi-armor-piercing (SAP) bombs are used against targets that

[**17.9**] Sailors loading a 2,000-pound bomb onto a Hornet attack aircraft

are sufficiently protected so as to require the bomb to have some penetration capability in order to be effective. Fragmentation bombs are usually smaller explosives dropped in clusters against troops and ground targets.

Chemical bombs contain specialized chemical agents that are used for a specific purpose. They can contain chemicals that are designed to disable or kill enemy personnel—such as mustard gas, phosgene, tear gas, or vomiting gas—or they can be smoke bombs containing white phosphorus that ignites during the explosion and spreads heavy smoke over the target area in order to conceal movements of ships or troops. Incendiary or napalm bombs, containing a mixture of gasoline or jet fuel and a thickening agent, are a form of chemical bomb that produces intense fire when ignited and are used against troops and ground targets.

Practice and drill bombs used in training may be loaded with sand or water and are inert (carry no explosive), so they will cause no damage other than simple impact. This makes them less dangerous than bombs fitted with explosives, but for training purposes and to develop safe practices they should be treated with the same respect as bombs carrying explosives.

See TAB 17-B: Types of Naval Weapons for more information on the Navy's bombs currently in use.

TORPEDOES

The torpedo is a self-propelled, explosive-carrying underwater weapon. Early torpedoes were basically of the "point-and-shoot" variety, but modern versions have a guidance system that markedly increases the accuracy of the weapon.

A torpedo consists of a tail, afterbody, midsection, and head. The *tail* section includes the screws, fins, and control surfaces. The propulsion system is contained in the *afterbody*. The *midsection* houses batteries, compressed air, or liquid fuel. The *head* contains the explosive charge, fuze, and any sensing (usually acoustic or magnetic) devices.

Torpedo guidance systems are either preset, wire-guided, or homing. *Preset* torpedoes follow a set course and depth after they are launched. *Wire-guided* torpedoes have a thin wire connecting the torpedo and the firing vessel, through which guidance signals can be transmitted to the torpedo to direct it to intercept the target. *Homing* torpedoes are either active, passive, or a combination of both (active/passive). The active versions depend on the sensing signals generated and returned to the torpedo through a

[**17.10**] A destroyer launches a torpedo.

sonar device inside the torpedo. Passive types pick up telltale signals (such as noise or magnetic disturbances) to home in on. In the active/passive mode, the torpedo searches passively until a target is acquired, then active terminal guiding finishes the target destruction.

Surface ships launch torpedoes from tubes mounted topside, or propel them to the target area with a rocket called an ASROC (antisubmarine rocket). Submarines launch torpedoes through specially designed tubes, and aircraft deploy their torpedoes by parachute so as to reduce the impact when the weapon strikes the water.

See TAB 17-B: Types of Naval Weapons for more information on the Navy's torpedoes currently in use.

MINES

Mines are passive weapons that are planted under the water to await the passage of enemy vessels to explode and do damage. Their advantage is that they operate independently (that is, no personnel are required to operate them once they have been planted). Their chief disadvantage is that they are indiscriminate (they can damage friendly or neutral vessels as well as enemy ones if precautions are not taken). You might be confused a bit if you read naval history and see the word "torpedo" used. In earlier times, what we now call a mine was called a torpedo. Today they are, of course, very different weapons.

Mines can be classified according to the method of actuation (firing), the method of planting, and their position in the water.

Mines may be actuated by contact or influence, or both. A contact mine fires when a ship strikes it. Influence mines may be actuated by the underwater sound generated in a passing ship's current, by the ship's magnetic field, or by the mine's sensitivity to reduced water pressure caused by a passing ship.

Mines may be planted by surface craft, submarines, and aircraft. Planting mines using surface craft is the most dangerous method because the ship doing the planting is vulnerable to attack. Submarines can plant mines more secretly and aircraft are able to plant mines quickly and with less risk.

Moored contact mines are anchored in place and float near the surface of the water where a ship might strike them. Bottom mines, which lie on the ocean floor, are used only in relatively shallow water. They are influence mines, set off by sound, magnetism, or pressure.

See TAB 17-B: Types of Naval Weapons for more information on the Navy's mines currently in use.

NAVAL GUNS

Guns have been a major component of naval armament for centuries. Early guns were highly inaccurate, often very dangerous devices that had to be loaded from the front end and aimed simply by pointing at a visible enemy. Today's guns are much more powerful and accurate, far safer, and aimed and controlled by sophisticated electronic and hydraulic systems.

Early cannon had smooth bores (inside the barrel) and usually fired round shot. Modern guns have rifling in their barrels, which is a network of ridges (called lands) and grooves shaped in a spiral that causes an elongated projectile to spin on its long axis (much as a well-thrown football). This increases the range and accuracy of the gun.

Guns are not nearly as important to naval ships as they once were. Sophisticated missile systems, with their greater range and superior accuracy, have taken the place of the gun as the mainstay of naval armament. There is, however, still a need for naval guns. Certain missions are better performed by guns, and missiles tend to be much more expensive.

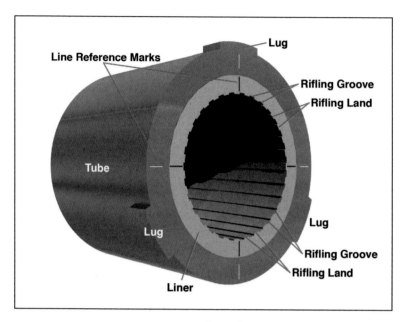

[**17.11**] Lands and grooves make up the rifling in a gun barrel.

[**17.12**] An MK 45 5-inch/62 gun firing from the forecastle of a destroyer; note that the projectile is visible.

U.S. Navy guns are classified by their inside barrel diameter and by their barrel length. These two figures are expressed in a rather cryptic manner that may seem confusing at first, but makes sense once you understand what it is telling you. The first figure in a Navy gun classification is the inside barrel diameter, expressed in inches or millimeters (mm). The second part follows a slash and, when it is multiplied by the first number, tells you the length of the gun's barrel. Thus, a 5-inch/54 gun would have an inside barrel diameter of 5 inches and a barrel length of 270 inches (5 x 54 = 270).

In years past, guns such as the 8-inch/55 and the 16-inch/50 were the main armament of large cruisers and battleships. Today, the most prevalent guns in the U.S. Navy are the 5-inch/54 (on cruisers and destroyers) and a specialized close-in weapons system (CIWS) known as the 20mm/76 Phalanx system, which is mounted on many ships as a protection against incoming missile attacks and localized surface attacks. Many Navy ships also carry saluting guns, which are used for ceremonial purposes and have no combat capability.

See TAB 17-B: Types of Naval Weapons for more information on the Navy's guns currently in use.

WEAPON CONTROL SYSTEMS

A weapon, however powerful, is only as good as its accuracy. The process by which a projectile, missile, bomb, or torpedo is guided to its target is called weapon control. A potential target is first detected by a sensor (radar, sonar, or lookout). It is then evaluated, either by human judgment, or by computer, or by a combination of the two. If the target is evaluated to be hostile, a decision is made, according to prescribed weapons doctrine, whether or not to engage. If the target is to be engaged, the appropriate weapon is selected. All available information is assimilated to produce a weapon-control solution that will guide the weapon to contact. The weapon is then fired.

Sensors

Before electronics arrived on the scene, enemies were detected and aimed at using the human senses, primarily the eyes. Modern weapons rely on electronic systems for detection of targets and to control weapons. Most common are radar and sonar. Both operate on the same principle but differ in the medium used.

In its most elemental form, radar (radio detection and ranging) uses a transceiver to send out (transmit) a radio-like electronic signal that reflects off a target and then returns the signal to a receiver where a very accurate timing system measures the amount of time that the signal took to travel to and from the target and, using the known speed of the signal, calculates the range to the target. A built-in direction-finding system also provides a bearing (direction) to the target.

Sonar works on the same principle, except that the signal used is sound rather than radio waves. Because radio signals work well in air and sound is more effective underwater, radar is used effectively in the detection of surface or air targets, but sonar is the sensor used in the detection of subsurface (underwater) targets.

Radar, sonar, and other Navy electronic equipments are identified by the Joint Electronics Type Designation System (JETDS). This system is explained in detail in TAB 17-C: Joint Electronics Type Designation System.

SMALL ARMS

The Navy also uses a variety of small arms (pistols, rifles, shotguns, grenade launchers, and machine guns) for various purposes, including sentry duty, riot control, and landing parties.

[**17.13**] The .50-caliber machine gun is the largest small arm used by the Navy.

Just as with larger Navy guns, small arms are differentiated by the inside diameter (bore) of the barrel. Like larger naval guns, this diameter may be expressed in either inches or millimeters, but unlike larger guns, small arms do not include a follow-on figure representing the length of the barrel. When the figure is in inches, it is referred to as "caliber" as in ".45-caliber pistol," but when it is expressed in millimeters, the term caliber is not used, as in "9mm pistol."

Shotguns are an exception. They are usually differentiated by "gauge," which still refers to the bore but is defined as the number of lead balls of that particular diameter required to make a pound. For example, it would take 12 lead balls of the diameter of the 12-gauge shotgun to equal one pound; 16 balls for the 16-gauge shotgun. This means that the 12-gauge shotgun has a larger bore than the 16-gauge, which seems backwards at first but makes sense when you think about it.

Any weapon with a bore diameter of 0.6 inches (.60-caliber) or less is called a small arm. The largest Navy small arm is the .50-caliber machine gun.

Small arms are considered to be "automatic" if holding down the trigger causes the weapon to continuously fire, and "semiautomatic" if the weapon reloads automatically when fired but requires another squeeze of the trigger to fire off another round.

[**17.14**] Sailors aboard a cruiser practicing with 9mm pistols

Some small arms you may encounter are identified by the Army system of terminology. An "M" preceding a number identifies a particular weapon, such as the "M14 rifle." Modifications are identified by a follow-on letter and number combination. For example, the M16 rifle has been modified twice as the M16A1 and M16A2 versions. Sometimes the Navy system of "Mark" (abbreviated "Mk") and "Modification" (abbreviated "Mod") is used, as in the "20mm Mk 16 Mod 5 machine gun." (See TAB 17-A: Weapons Designation Systems for an explanation of the "Mark and Mod system.")

Additional information about the use of small arms is provided in TAB 17-D: Proper Use of Small Arms.

The Navy uses many different kinds of weapons because it has many different missions to perform. As a Sailor, you may find yourself carrying a handgun, manning a machine gun, or squeezing the firing key of a missile launching system. The more you know about weapons, the better you will be prepared to use them safely and effectively.

EIGHTEEN

LEADERSHIP
AND DISCIPLINE

In the plotting room far below, Ensign Merdinger got a call to send up some men to fill in for the killed and wounded. Many of the men obviously wanted to go—it looked like a safer bet than suffocating in the plotting room. Others wanted to stay—they preferred to keep a few decks between themselves and the bombs. Merdinger picked them at random, and he could see in some faces an almost pleading look to be included in the other group, whichever it happened to be. But no one murmured a word, and his orders were instantly obeyed. Now he understood more clearly the reasons for the system of discipline, the drills, the little rituals . . . all the things that made the Navy essentially autocratic but at the same time made it work.

—*Walter Lord,* Day of Infamy

The scene described above actually took place aboard the battleship USS *Nevada* during the Japanese attack on Pearl Harbor at the beginning of World War II. Besides its dramatic appeal, this glimpse of history demonstrates an important fact of military life. The Sailors in *Nevada*'s plotting room did not carry out their orders because they wanted to, or because they were seeking a bonus in their paycheck. They did what Ensign Merdinger directed because their fears and sense of self-preservation were overcome by a combination of his leadership and their self-discipline. This is not easily achieved, yet in order for a military organization to function properly, particularly in life-threatening situations, leadership and discipline are absolutely vital.

LEADERSHIP

Leadership can be simply defined as the art of causing people to do what is required to accomplish a task or mission. But good leadership is not so easily defined. Good leaders are concerned with more than simply getting a job done. How the job gets done is also important. What good is a leader who gets a job done but loses the respect of his or her crew in the process? What good is a leader whose methods result in dissension, disorganization, ineffectiveness, poor morale, or bad results?

Leadership is characterized by responsibility and authority. As a leader, you are responsible for the tasks or missions assigned. You are also responsible for leading your subordinates in a manner that will not only get the job done but will preserve their dignity and minimize any negative effects that may be part of a difficult task. A leader's authority in the armed forces comes from the Uniform Code of Military Justice (UCMJ), which spells out the laws and the punishments that give the leader official power over her or his subordinates. Technically speaking, this authority is all a leader needs to make people do what he or she wants. But good leaders rely on much more than their authority to lead people. They recognize that subordinates are human beings just like themselves, not mere tools that can be used for a job and put back in a box. Good leaders find ways to cause individuals to carry out an assignment willingly rather than out of fear of reprisal.

Even though you start your Navy career as a follower, it will not be long before you will be called upon to exercise leadership. You might be selected as a recruit chief petty officer (RCPO) in boot camp, or become leading seaman in your division aboard ship, or be promoted to petty officer. So it is never too soon to begin thinking about how to be a good leader.

Principles

Because leadership is an art and not an exact science, there is no exact formula for success and it cannot be broken down into absolute rules. However, certain principles, if practiced on a consistent basis, will go a long way toward making you a good leader.

[**18.1**] Carrying the cutlass that symbolizes her role as leader, a recruit chief petty officer (RCPO) gets an early taste of leadership.

Reverse roles. This is a form of the so-called Golden Rule that appears in the culture of all civilized societies. Whenever you are dealing with subordinates, always treat them the way you would want to be treated if your roles were reversed. If you keep this principle in mind at all times, you will be well on your way to being a good leader.

Take responsibility. One of the fastest ways to lose the respect of your subordinates and undermine your leadership ability is to shirk responsibility. If you make an error, admit it. Do not try to hide your mistakes from your superiors or your subordinates. It will be very tempting to try to cover up your mistakes for fear that others will think less of you if they are revealed. This is magnified when you are in a leadership position. But very rarely does hiding a mistake work, and the damage done when you are discovered is always far greater than any damage that might occur from whatever mistake it was that you made in the first place.

Set the example. Always conduct yourself in a manner that will bring credit to yourself and will provide a model of behavior for your subordinates. Never say or imply that your subordinates should "do as I say, not as I do."

Praise in public; correct in private. When you have something good to say about your subordinates, do it so that all or many will hear. This will give added recognition to the individual(s) being praised, and it will inspire others to do well in hopes of being similarly recognized. When you have to correct a subordinate, do it in private. Embarrassing an individual adds nothing to the learning experience, and learning is the intended purpose of correcting someone who has done something wrong.

Be consistent but not inflexible. This is a difficult principle to uphold, because there are no clear guidelines. For the most part, consistency is extremely important and should be your goal. You should try to do things in a manner that your subordinates will come to know and expect so that they do not have to second-guess you. You should most especially be consistent in your praising and correcting and in your rewards and punishments. But you must also recognize that conditions and even people change. Because everything around you is not always the same, you must be flexible when that is what is needed. For example, you should be very consistent in expecting your subordinates to be on time for quarters every morning, but if an unexpected overnight snowfall has traffic slowed down one morning, you should not hesitate to excuse the latecomers.

Know your job. Few things are more uninspiring for subordinates than to recognize that their leader does not know her or his job. As a leader, you will earn the confidence and respect of those who work for you if you know everything you possibly can about your job. You should also strive to learn as much as you reasonably can about the jobs of your subordinates. Use this knowledge to improve your communications with subordinates, to instruct when necessary, and to monitor what they are doing. Do not use this knowledge to intrude on their work.

Do not micromanage. This ties in with the "know your job" principle. While it is important for you to assign, instruct, direct, and monitor, you should not overdo these things. Allow your subordinates to carry out their tasks in a manner that suits their abilities and preferences, as long as it is consistent with safety and efficiency. People appreciate clear instructions, concerns for their safety, and suggestions for efficiency, but they rarely like having someone looking over their shoulder during the entire job, telling them each and every step to take and exactly how to do it. When giving instructions and directions, try to sort out what is important for safety and efficiency from what is merely your personal preference. This will go a long way toward promoting a positive attitude when a subordinate is doing a job. He will feel "ownership" and a greater sense of accomplishment if allowed to put some of himself into a project.

Practice good followership. There are several advantages to being a good follower even when you have been made a leader. First, you will never become a leader if you have not been a good follower. No one is going to recommend you for a leadership position if you have been poor at responding to the leadership of others. Second, no leader is only a leader. Every leader is also a subordinate. The chain of command discussed in **Chapter 1** makes that clear. And even the president, who is commander in chief of the armed forces and at the top of the chain of command with no superior, must answer to the American people or he or she will not long remain their leader. To remain a leader, you must also be a good follower. The third, and most important, reason goes back to the second principle in this discussion. As a leader you must always set the example. If you do not, it will not take long for your subordinates to begin following your example, and it does not take a rocket scientist to figure out where that will leave you.

Don't be one of the gang. Nearly everyone wants to be liked, and being a good leader does not mean that you cannot also be liked. There is absolutely nothing wrong with a leader having a sense of humor and showing concern for each subordinate as an individual. But it is important to avoid the temptation of being too friendly, of putting your desire to be liked above your need to accomplish the mission. Whether it's as simple as an unpleasant clean-up job or as dramatic as having to tell people to place themselves in danger as Ensign Merdinger did at the beginning of this chapter, as a leader you are going to have to tell people to do things they do not want to do. You will not be able to do this if you have allowed yourself to be too friendly with your subordinates, to become "one of the gang."

Keep your subordinates informed. No one likes to be kept in the dark. Information and purpose tend to motivate. A person is usually better able to do a job if he or she understands why that job needs to be done and how it fits into the "big picture." For these reasons, you should keep your subordinates informed as much as possible. Sometimes, for security or other reasons, there will be things you cannot share with your subordinates. But unless these conditions exist, you should make it a common practice to give your subordinates as much information as you can about what they are doing and why they are doing it. This will improve morale and will often help them do a better job.

Keep in mind that different people may require different motivations. What works with one individual may or may not work with another. Some people respond best when given the freedom to do things their way within reasonable guidelines, while others prefer to be given specific directions. One seaman in your division might respond well to being told that the task at hand is for the good of the Navy, while another might need to be reminded of the consequences of his or her failure to do what is required. The point is that as a leader you must try to understand who the individuals are and what works best in motivating them to do what is required. Do not assume that "one size fits all" when it comes to leadership.

Every leader is a teacher. Leading is more than simply telling people what to do; it also requires telling them how to do it. Knowledge, patience, and thoroughness are some of the attributes of an effective teaching leader.

[**18.2**] A chief aviation boatswain's mate briefs Sailors before the start of flight operations on an aircraft carrier.

[**18.3**] Every leader must also be a teacher.

Leadership Styles

Leaders, like their followers, are individuals, and because of this you will quickly learn that different leaders have different leadership styles. Just because two different leaders seem very different in the way in which they lead does not necessarily mean that one is doing it wrong. Two athletes may have very different styles of playing, yet both can be quite good at what they do. Leaders, as well as athletes and anyone else who is striving to be successful, will do well to take advantage of their natural strengths and to compensate for their natural weaknesses. Some people are gifted with a natural sense of humor while others are inspirational speakers. Some people are naturally talkative while others are more sparing with their words. These characteristics are going to show themselves in each individual's leadership style, yet all can be effective leaders as long as they adhere to the basic principles discussed above.

Responsibility before Authority

It has probably occurred to you by now that much of leadership is merely common sense. Just by remembering and practicing the "reverse roles" principle, you will make few mistakes as a leader. But human nature is complex, and leadership is never easy. Whenever you are entrusted with a leadership role, whether you are leading one person or thousands, you must take it very seriously. Remember that with every leadership position comes added responsibility, as well as added authority. Always keep the responsibility foremost in your mind and the authority secondary, and you will be well on your way to being a good leader.

DISCIPLINE

The word "discipline" comes from a Latin word that means "to teach." What is being taught in a system of discipline is the controlling of an individual's actions, impulses, or emotions. Undisciplined children are those who have not been properly taught how and when to control their actions. Many times in our everyday lives we deliberately do things that are counter to our first impulse or what we may want to do, and this is usually a result of the discipline that was taught us by those who raised us. Self-discipline, for example, is what prevents us from getting into line ahead of others and what causes us to study for a test when we might be texting on our smart phone.

[**18.4**] Every promotion comes with added responsibility as well as authority.

Methods

Discipline is often confused with punishment, but the two words do not mean the same thing. Rewards and punishments are tools that are used to create and maintain discipline. As a child, you may have received an ice cream cone or a raise in your allowance for good behavior, and you more than likely were restricted from watching television or saw your allowance reduced because you did something you should not have done. If these things worked as they were meant to, someone probably referred to you at one time or another as a "well-disciplined child." This same system works when we are adults. Pay raises and parking tickets replace ice cream cones and allowance reductions, but the principles are the same. Parental guidance, religious beliefs, and other values contribute to discipline in individuals as well.

In the Navy, promotions and medals serve as rewards, while demotions and restricted liberty are sometimes imposed as punishments. Unit pride and patriotic devotion are some of the values relied upon to create a system of discipline that will ensure that Sailors will do what is expected of them even when it is different from what they may want to do. When discipline is working best within a unit, the individuals who make up the unit have a good attitude, do their work efficiently, and exhibit high morale. In a well-disciplined unit, the members often do the right thing because they *want* to, not because they have to. Such men and women perform with enthusiasm, individually or in groups, to carry out the mission of their organization, often with little guidance.

The Navy depends upon a blend of leadership and discipline to effectively accomplish its many missions. Discipline ensures obedience—even in dangerous or stressful situations—while good leadership promotes unit cohesion and maintains high morale, which in turn contributes to efficiency and effectiveness. As a Sailor, you will help yourself and your Navy by practicing good followership at all times and striving for good leadership when called upon to lead others.

NINETEEN

THE PAPER
NAVY

Although word processing, e-mail, and other electronic and digital advances have greatly benefited the Navy, there remain a number of special practices that originated in the days when paper was supreme and some means had to be developed to organize great volumes of it. Long before there were such things as search engines, the Standard Subject Identification Code (SSIC) system helped the Navy keep its paperwork organized. Without a scroll bar, organizing letters and directives into specific formats helped readers scan them quickly to find the parts they needed. Before firewalls and passwords, a system of protecting sensitive documents from prying eyes was developed.

Though these communications systems might be different if they were developed from scratch today, parts of them remain in effect and are still useful. Their existence alone makes understanding them essential if one is to function efficiently in this Navy world that is part nautical, part clerical, and part bureaucratic.

In this chapter, we will examine how the Navy communicates through correspondence and other means. We will explore the Navy Directives system, learn to decipher the SSIC system, and look at military classification of information. We will explain the logic of those numbers that appear on documents and learn how to make good use of the Navy's formats.

Although the Constitution, various treaties, and Congress supply the fundamental laws governing the Navy, they are really only broad outlines. The Navy has various publications and official directives setting forth specific procedures for the daily operation of the Navy Department and for the administration of personnel. Some of the more important documents that you are likely to encounter are listed in TAB 19-A: Important Navy Publications.

DECIPHERING THE NUMBERS

The Navy has long used numbers as a means of document identification. There are some numbering systems that do not do much more than uniquely identify a document, but more often than not, these numbers in themselves convey information in an abbreviated form that can be very useful. The Navy's SSIC system is the best example and is used in many ways Navy-wide. It is used as a means of identifying and filing correspondence, messages, official directives, and various other documents. Understanding how SSIC numbers work will take you a long way toward a better understanding of what is going on in the paper world of the Navy.

Standard Subject Identification Code (SSIC) System

To understand this system and how it is used, you must begin with a publication identified as the *SSIC Manual*. It is full of useful information that can help you navigate through the seas of paper you are likely to encounter at most Navy commands. It explains the SSIC system and includes a listing of the codes that the Navy uses to make documents identifiable for filing and research purposes. If you deal with Navy paper, you should keep a copy of it nearby.

The codes are four- or five-digit numbers that are linked to particular subjects. The general divisions of these codes and their subject matter are as follows:

1000–1999	Military Personnel
2000–2999	Information Technology and Communications
3000–3999	Operations and Readiness
4000–4999	Logistics
5000–5999	General Administration and Management
6000–6999	Medicine and Dentistry
7000–7999	Financial Management
8000–8999	Ordnance Material
9000–9999	Ships Design and Material

10000–10999	General Material
11000–11999	Facilities and Activities Ashore
12000–12999	Civilian Personnel
13000–13999	Aeronautical and Astronautical Material

Note: These are covered in more detail in TAB 19-B: Standard Subject Identification Codes. For the most detail, see the *SSIC Manual* itself.

These codes are assigned to various kinds of documents for identification and filing purposes. If you have a working knowledge of them, or if you keep a list of them handy, you can tell something about a document just by the assigned code. For example, if you received a document with the number 1414 on it, you would know that it had something to do with military personnel because of the 1000-series number assigned. Similarly, the number 4355 would have something to with logistics (because it falls between 4000 and 4999), and 7920 has something to do with financial management.

If you look in the *SSIC Manual*, you will see that the numbers are further broken down to assign more detailed subject matter to the numbers within each series. For example, within the 1000–1999 series (covering Military Personnel), you will see the following breakdowns:

1000–1099	General Military Personnel
1100–1199	Recruiting
1200–1299	Classification and Designation
1300–1399	Assignment and Distribution
1400–1499	Promotion and Advancement
1500–1599	Training and Education
1600–1699	Performance and Discipline
1700–1799	Morale and Personal Affairs
1800–1899	Retirement
1900–1999	Separation

From this list, you can see that the previously mentioned document with the number 1414 on it has something to do with "Promotion and Advancement" because it falls between 1400 and 1499. And because the SSIC further breaks down, as you see below, you would know that 1414 has something to do with enlisted qualifications.

1400	General
1401	Elections
1402	Selection Boards Record of Proceedings
1410	Requirements and Qualifications
1412	Officer Qualifications
1414	Enlisted Qualifications
1416	Officer Examinations
1418	Enlisted Examinations
Etc.	

You can see from the list above that there are some numbers that have no current assignment (1403 through 1409, for example). These numbers may be assigned specific subjects in the future if the need arises. These "missing" numbers can also be used *now* by a command to issue its own directives to cover a specific, related subject. For example, a command might decide to create a library of leadership books and articles providing advice on how to get promoted. The command might assign the number 1415 to the document establishing this special library, because the subject would seem to fall within this area but there is no number already covering it specifically.

You will encounter these SSIC numbers often. They are used on directives, naval messages, and letters for example. The more you know about them the better. No one can memorize them all, so you will have to rely on the *SSIC Manual* when you need a code to assign to something, or if you are trying to identify subject matter on an existing document, or you are trying to learn about a particular topic.

DIRECTIVES

You have probably heard of Navy Regulations, which you might expect to be a huge document that spells out the rules and procedures for running the Navy. In fact, you could read these regulations in an afternoon, and though they are important, only a small number of topics are covered, such as defining the positions of the SECNAV and the CNO, as well as the Commandant of the Marine Corps, establishing precedence among officers, defining standards of conduct, and the proper observance of ceremonies and customs.

So how does one know how to do the thousands of other things that are necessary for running such a large and complex organization? How does one know, for example, the proper means of keeping aviation ordnance records, or the rules for conducting proper psychological operations, or the procedures for conferring incentive awards, or the requirements for declassifying secret documents, or the means for effectively using the frequency spectrum, or the correct way of arranging ribbons on your uniform, or . . . The need for some means of detailing rules, procedures, policies, and the like is obvious. That is where the Navy Directives System comes in.

Before delving into this new world of complicated numbers and alien concepts, keep in mind what a gigantic task it is to try to organize so much information; keep in mind that it was conceived long before computer software was devised.

The Navy Directives System is intimidating at first. As you study it, you will be able to see a kind of logic in it and perhaps even appreciate the fact that it does manage to organize an incredible amount of information into a useful form.

Instructions and Notices

Two kinds of directives are issued by commands within the Navy Directives System. *Notices* are used to convey temporary (short-lived) information, and *instructions* are the means of establishing policies and procedures that are of a more permanent, long-term nature. For example, if the Bureau of Naval Personnel wanted to announce the procedures for a one-time shiphandling contest among junior officers, a notice would be used. But if the bureau wanted to establish the rules for an *annual* shiphandling competition that would occur year after year, an instruction would be issued.

Notices often contain a self-cancellation date, or their short-lived nature is evident within the text. For example, a notice inviting applicants for a one-time shiphandling competition might have a deadline for application included, so it would be obvious that the notice was no longer needed once that date had passed. Notices usually remain in effect for less than six months and never for more than a year. Instructions, however, remain in effect until superseded by a revised version of the instruction or until formally cancelled by a separate document.

Instructions and notices are issued at virtually all levels of command, from the Secretary of the Navy down to individual units. The good news is that you do not need to be familiar with those directives issued by commands outside your chain of command; the bad news is that you are responsible for being familiar with those directives issued by your command *and* for all those issued by commands that are above yours in the chain of command. So if you work in the CNO's office, you will be guided by a lot fewer instructions and notices than someone who is assigned to an aircraft carrier in the Atlantic Fleet—that individual must be familiar with the instructions and notices issued by the ship, by the group and fleet commanders, and on up to the CNO and SECNAV (see **Chapter 8: Navy Organization**).

IDENTIFICATION OF DIRECTIVES

Both instructions and notices are identified by the issuing authority's title, often abbreviated (as in "SECNAV" for Secretary of the Navy, or "OPNAV" for the CNO's office), followed by "INST" if it is an instruction, or "NOTE" if it is a notice. An identifying number follows that tells you something about the subject matter; this is one of the places where the SSIC system comes into play. The date of issuance is also an important identifying component for notices.

An appropriate example is the governing directive that explains all of this. It is issued by the CNO, has the title *Navy Directives Issuance System*, and is identified as:

OPNAVINST 5215.17

It is important to note that there is no other directive with that same identification. There might be a directive issued by another command with the same number, but then it would have a different originating command, such as SECNAVINST 5215.17 or COMPACFLT 5215.17. There might be a notice with the same number (less the decimal as explained below), such as OPNAVNOTE 5215. There might also be another directive with a very similar number, such as OPNAVINST 5215.18, but not another that is identical. That combination of command identifier, type of directive (INST or NOTE), and that exact number is unique to this one directive.

The Decimal Point. By now, you must be wondering why there is a decimal point and the number "17" appended to the SSIC code 5215 in the example above. If we checked the *SSIC Manual*, we would find the following:

5214	Reports Management
5215	Issuance Systems (Include Directives)
5216	Correspondence Management

We know that the "5215" in OPNAVINST 5215.17 deals with issuance systems, but the SSIC manual does not explain the decimal appendage. That part tells us that this particular directive is the seventeenth one issued by this command (OPNAV) on that particular subject. You could reasonably expect to find other documents identified as OPNAVINST 5215.16, OPNAVINST 5215.15, and so on, but do not be surprised if you do not; in this ever-changing Navy, directives with some or all of those previous numbers may have been cancelled.

Letter Appendages. You will often see a letter added to the end of the identifier. This tells us that the directive has been revised. If there is no letter appended, then you know the directive is the original and has not been revised. OPNAVINST 5215.17 has no letter following the number, so it is considered the original version. If the Chief of Naval Operations decides to change some things in this directive but keep it essentially the same, a new directive would be issued with the new identifier OPNAVINST 5215.17A. A subsequent revision would be identified as OPNAVINST 5215.17B and yet another would be OPNAVINST 5215.17C, and so on. If you encountered an instruction with the identifier 6224.1D, you would know that it was the fifth version of that particular instruction (original plus four lettered revisions: A, B, C, and D). Once a revised version is issued, the previous one is superseded and should be discarded.

IDENTIFYING NOTICES

Because they are temporary rather than long term, notices are identified differently from instructions. They still use an SSIC but you will not find a decimal or an appended letter attached. They are uniquely identified by a date instead. Despite the shared usage of SSICs, notices are easily discernible from instructions by the word "NOTE" following the issuing command's identification.

So if you encountered a directive with the identifier OPNAVNOTE 5215 of 30 August 2006, you would know by the word "NOTE" that it is a notice and not an instruction, and you would therefore know that it is of interest for a relatively short period of time after the date of issue (probably less than six months, as explained earlier). You would also know that it had something to do with the issuing of directives because of the SSIC 5215 (the same as the OPNAVINST 5215.17 discussed earlier).

A Few More Things to Know about Directives

Official directives are essential to the smooth running of the Navy. They deal with everything from the very important (such as establishing rules of engagement in a combat zone) to the rather trivial (such as how wide the margins must be when creating a directive).

Both instructions and notices are written using specific rules and formats that are spelled out in OPNAVINST 5215.17. Paragraphs will have identifying words at the beginning, like "Purpose" or "Background." This formality is useful in that you can get right to the meat of the directive by looking for those paragraphs identified with words like "Purpose," "Action," or "Responsibility" and avoiding those paragraphs beginning with words like "Background" and "Authority."

USMC Directives

In the event that you must deal with directives issued by the Marine Corps, it is helpful to know that what the Navy calls "Instructions" (long-term directives), the Marine Corps calls "Orders." And the Navy's short-term "Notices" are called "Bulletins" in the Marine Corps.

INTERNET EFFICIENCY

In the old days—not so very long ago—directives were typed up, reproduced, and distributed to all who needed them (often amounting to hundreds, even thousands, of pounds of paper). Today, most Navy directives are now maintained on websites, which makes them generally more accessible and more likely to be current.

For example, all of the SECNAV directives and those of the OPNAV can be found at **https://doni.documentservices.dla.mil/opnav.aspx**. You can find a directive by clicking on the tab labeled "Directives" and then selecting one of the dropdown choices, such as "All Instructions," "All Notices," and "SECNAV Instructions & Notices."

You will also see a link to "SECNAV Manuals." These are instructions that are large and comprehensive enough to qualify as manuals. Examples are the *SSIC Manual* and the *Department of the Navy Forms Management Manual*. Note that these instructions are kept separately at this link, rather than with all the other SECNAV instructions. *Note:* These instructions are exceptions to the usual format in that they are uniquely identified by dropping the "INST" and adding an "M" (for "manual") just before the SSIC, so that the *SSIC Manual* becomes SECNAV M-5210.2 and the *Department of the Navy Forms Management Manual* is SECNAV M-5213.1.

United States Navy Regulations has its own tab labeled "Regulations."

By clicking on the "Home" link in the upper right of the page, you will find some explanatory information and a section called "Subscribe to/Unsubscribe from Navy Issuances," which allows you to obtain e-mail notifications of updates as they occur.

NAVY CORRESPONDENCE

The Navy applies to its written correspondence the same precision it once applied to the setting of sails to maximize the propulsive power of the wind. These exacting procedures may stifle creativity, but they also ensure a degree of reliability that would not be guaranteed were such stringent procedures not prescribed.

The guiding directive is the *Department of the Navy Correspondence Manual* (SECNAVINST 5216.5). This manual is an important one with really useful information and guidance that should be on your desk or linked on your computer desktop if you write for the Navy. For a more user-friendly source that gives practical advice on naval writing, refer to *The Naval Institute Guide to Naval Writing* by Robert Shenk.

A detailed discussion of naval correspondence is beyond the scope of this book—the *Navy Correspondence Manual* is more than a hundred pages long—but some helpful summations can be found in TAB 19-C: Navy Letter Format.

NAVAL MESSAGES

Naval messages are used by virtually every Navy command to send important, official information quickly and reliably. Messages must be officially released by the commanding officer or his or her specifically designated representative(s) before they can be transmitted. Naval communications facilities, whether they are on a small ship or at a large communications station, ensure that officially released messages are accounted for to ensure that all intended recipients get the messages they are supposed to receive.

A naval message can be as simple as a one-line request from a ship asking a waterfront port facility for an extra tug or it can be a message released by the Secretary of the Navy or the Chief of Naval Operations that is intended for every person in the Navy. In fact, if you see a message marked "ALNAV" it is from the SECNAV, intended for "all of the Navy and the Marine Corps." If you see one marked "NAVADMIN," it is an administrative message from the CNO and is also intended for broad distribution. These messages are sequentially numbered so that all can be sure they do not miss one.

A naval message can be a daunting experience at first, but understanding the format and knowing where to look for specific pieces of information helps you to handle it.

Naval messages grew out of the days of Morse code radio transmissions and evolved into the era of radio teletype. When these came into being they were marvelous innovations that allowed the Navy to communicate in ways that were never possible before. A message could be sent to virtually the entire Navy in a very short period of time. A huge communications infrastructure grew out of this capability, involving a worldwide communications network of communications stations. As capacity grew, so did the amount of message traffic. Very exacting procedures were put into place to ensure that this increasingly large number of messages got to the intended recipients in a timely manner.

TAB 19-D: Navy Message Format provides some basic information about reading Navy messages.

While paper itself has been replaced in many ways by digital equivalents, *paperwork* still thrives. Record keeping, information dissemination, and other elements of data management and communication are important to the functioning of any large organization, and the Navy is no exception. Understanding the Navy's administrative systems will benefit you in many important ways.

TWENTY

COMMUNICATIONS

Communication is a vital part of the Navy. Ships must be able to communicate with each other when operating together, aircraft must be able to talk to one another and to the ships they are operating with, and fleet commanders must be able to report to and receive instructions from Washington, D.C. These are all forms of external communications and are extremely important. But just as important, the various stations within a ship must be able to communicate with one another—this is called internal communications. For example, the ship's damage-control parties must be able to communicate with Damage Control Central (DCC) and the bridge during an emergency, the bow lookouts must be able to report to the Officer of the Deck what they see and hear, and Primary Flight Control on an aircraft carrier must be able to communicate with Sailors moving aircraft about on the flight deck.

INTERNAL COMMUNICATIONS

The oldest form of internal communications in ships is the messenger. While messengers are still used, modern ships have other means available that are much faster than sending a runner. Simple buzzer and light signals are used to attract attention and to provide basic information about the current status of a system or component. Such things as rudder-angle indicators and engine-order telegraphs are more elaborate means of communicating equipment status. Computer links are used for sophisticated systems information, and synchro- and servo-systems are used with weapons systems to convey important information, such as where a gun is pointing. Larger ships have telephone systems similar to the ones you have used all your life. The ship's bell is also used to convey information to the crew, and even the "aboard/ashore board" used on the quarterdecks of many ships to indicate who is aboard at any given time is a means of internal communications.

The two most widely used forms of internal communications are the MC and J systems. MC systems include one-way loudspeaker systems and special box systems that allow various stations to talk back and forth to each other. J systems are the Navy's sound-powered phone systems that have the advantage of not requiring electrical power to function.

MC Systems

The chief advantage of these systems is that they electrically amplify the human voice so that it can be heard by many people at one time and in noisy conditions. Their major disadvantages are that they cannot be depended upon if electrical power is lost and they add noise to what may already be a noisy environment.

Some of the MC systems are what you might call public-address systems. The Navy calls them central-amplifier systems. They use a system of speakers (located where needed) to broadcast information, but the receiving stations cannot answer back.

Other MC systems are listed in TAB 20-A: MC Systems. These are made up of two-way boxes in different locations around the ship, which are wired to each other in such a way that the stations can talk to each other, either all at the same time or only one or a few at a time. These boxes are equipped with buttons that can be pressed so that only certain stations will hear what is being said. If you want to talk to all the stations on the circuit at the same time, push all of the buttons, but if only three of the stations on the circuit need the information you want to pass, you can press just the three buttons to those stations and not bother the others.

THE 1MC SYSTEM

In the old Navy, before the days of loudspeaker systems, the boatswain's mate passed any orders for the crew by word of mouth. The boatswain's mate of the watch (BMOW) sounded "Call mates" on his boatswain's pipe (a special whistle still in use today) to get the other boatswain's mates

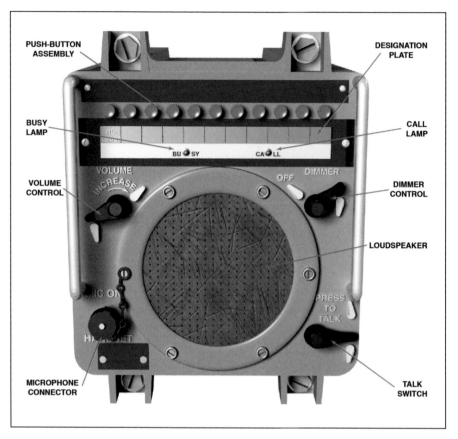

PUSH-BUTTON ASSEMBLY

DESIGNATION PLATE

BUSY LAMP

CALL LAMP

BUSY

CALL

VOLUME INCREASE

OFF DIMMER

VOLUME CONTROL

DIMMER CONTROL

LOUDSPEAKER

MIC ON

PRESS TO TALK

HEADSET

MICROPHONE CONNECTOR

TALK SWITCH

[**20.1**] A two-way MC unit

together, and they converged on the quarterdeck while answering repeatedly with the same call on their pipes. Upon hearing the information to be passed (called "the word" in the Navy), they dispersed throughout the ship to sing it out at every hatch.

While this procedure was colorful, it took a lot of time. Today a single boatswain's mate can quickly pass the word over the MC circuit to reach all or part of the ship at one time.

The ship's general announcing system, over which the word can be passed to every space in the ship, is designated the 1MC system. Transmitters are located on the bridge and quarterdeck so that the word can be passed by the OOD at sea and in port.

On some ships an announcement is preceded by a boatswain's call on her or his pipe to get the attention of the crew. A special call—"All

Hands"—is piped before any particularly important word, and a shorter call, called "Attention," is used before more routine announcements.

You will hear many different kinds of announcements over the 1MC. For most, the meanings will be obvious, but others will take some getting used to because they retain some of the Navy's traditional language. Listed below are some of the more common announcements heard over the 1MC, followed by a brief explanation. The words used here are typical but may differ somewhat from ship to ship.

"Air bedding." Mattresses and pillows are to be removed from your rack and taken topside where they should be draped over the ship's rail for a few hours to air out.

"Haul over all hatch hoods and gun covers." A rain squall is approaching. All open hatches must be closed and protective tarps must be rigged.

"Mail call." Incoming mail is available for pickup.

"Mess Gear. Clear the mess decks." All personnel not assigned as mess cooks or attendants should leave the mess decks' area so that preparations can be made for the next meal.

"The OOD is shifting his (her) watch from the bridge to the quarterdeck." This announcement alerts the crew that the OOD can now be found on the quarterdeck instead of the bridge. This occurs when the ship enters port. When the ship gets under way the opposite announcement would be made: "The OOD is shifting her (his) watch from the quarterdeck to the bridge."

"Reveille, reveille. All hands heave out and trice up." It's time to wake up and get out of your rack (bunk).

"Taps. Lights out. All hands turn in to your bunks and keep silence about the decks." It is time to go to bed. If you are not going to bed at this time, you must be as quiet as possible when in the vicinity of berthing compartments.

"Turn to. Commence ship's work." Passed in the morning to announce the beginning of the work day. After the noon meal, a slightly modified version is passed: "Turn to. Continue ship's work."

"Up all late bunks." All personnel who have been sleeping in (beyond reveille) because they had the midwatch the night before must now wake up.

The OOD is in charge of the 1MC. No call can be passed over it unless it is authorized by the OOD, the executive officer, or the captain.

Normally, the 1MC is equipped with switches that make it possible for certain spaces to be cut off from announcements of no concern to them. The captain, for instance, does not need to hear the call for late bunks, so his or her cabin can be cut out of the announcement.

Sound-Powered Telephones

In battle conditions or during other emergencies, a ship may lose some or all of its electrical power. Battery-powered communications systems are good only as long as the batteries hold out, and radio systems (such as walkie-talkies) are not always effective through steel bulkheads and decks (and they put radio signals into the air that might be detected by enemy forces in the vicinity). Because of these potential problems, ships must have some means of communicating internally that does not require an outside source of electrical power to function. For many decades, the Navy has relied upon a relatively simple but very reliable invention called the sound-powered telephone, which relies upon the energy generated by the user's voice to create enough current to power the circuit.

For many years, sound-powered circuits were a primary source of interior communications. In ships with the newer IVCS system (see below), sound-powered systems are now secondary.

You may stand a watch aboard ship that will require you to use a sound-powered telephone system. To do your job properly, you must have a basic understanding of the ship's sound-powered system and you must learn proper phone-talking procedures.

Sound-powered systems are recognizable as such by the letter J in their circuit designation. A detailed explanation of the sound-powered system is provided in TAB 20-B: Sound-Powered Communications System.

It is a good idea to familiarize yourself with the available jack boxes (outlets) in your work or watch station area. That way, if something happens to a circuit you are assigned to talk on, you will know what alternatives are available. For example, if you are assigned as a talker on the JA circuit during GQ and that circuit sustains battle damage, you will save valuable time if you know where any nearby XJA outlets are. Knowing other circuits in your area may prove useful as well.

Some sound-powered circuits, particularly the supplementary ones, have a handset similar to a normal telephone handset that is always attached. These handsets will have a button that must be held down while talking, and they are often accompanied by a buzzer system that will alert you that someone wants to talk to you on that circuit.

Far more common, however, is the sound-powered phone talker headset that is plugged into a sound-powered circuit outlet and worn by an individual who is specifically assigned as a talker on that circuit when needed.

USE OF THE SOUND-POWERED HEADSET

The typical headset used with the sound-powered phone has a headband that holds the receivers over the ears, a breastplate supported by a cloth neck strap, and a yoke that holds the mouthpiece transmitter in front of the mouth. The phone has a wire lead, which may be up to fifty feet long, with a jack on the end. The jack plugs into a box connected to the circuit.

To put the gear on, first unhook the right side of the neck strap from the breastplate, pass the strap around your neck and rehook it. Next, put on the earphones and adjust the headband so that the center of one or both earpieces is directly over your ear(s). In most cases, you will want to keep one ear uncovered so that you can hear what is going on around you. Keep the unused earpiece flat against the side of your head to keep unwanted noises from being picked up. Adjust the mouthpiece so that it is about an inch in front of your mouth. In making this adjustment, remember that the fine wire that goes to the transmitter can be broken if mistreated. Be sure that there are no sharp bends in it, and do not allow it to get caught between the transmitter and the yoke that supports it. Last, insert the plug into the jack box and screw the collar on firmly.

When you are wearing the headset, always keep some slack in the lead cord, and be sure it is flat on deck. If you have the cord stretched taut, someone may trip over it and damage the wires, injure him- or herself, or injure you. Do not allow objects to roll over or rest on the cord.

After plugging in the phones, test them with someone on the circuit. If they are not in working order, report that to the person in charge of your station and don a spare set; don't attempt to repair the set yourself.

Never secure the phones until you have permission to do so. When permission is given, do not just remove the phones and leave them. Unless someone is relieving you and takes the phones from you, always make up

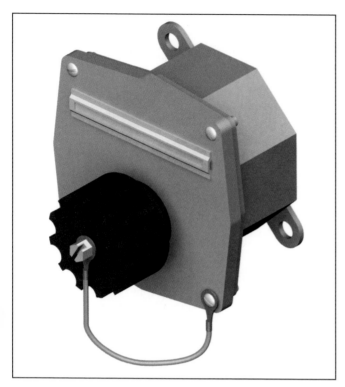

[**20.2**] A sound-powered telephone jack box

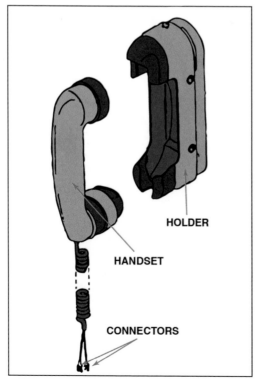

HOLDER

HANDSET

CONNECTORS

[**20.3**] A sound-powered handset

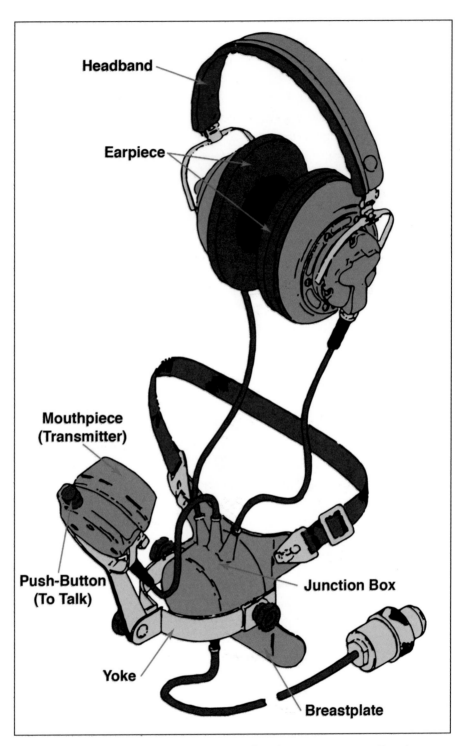

Headband

Earpiece

Mouthpiece
(Transmitter)

Push-Button
(To Talk)

Junction Box

Yoke

Breastplate

[**20.4**] A sound-powered headset

the phones for proper stowage. Remove the plug from the jack box by holding the plug in one hand and unscrewing the collar with the other. When the collar is detached, grasp the plug and pull it out, lay it carefully on the deck. Immediately screw the cover on the jack box; dust and dirt can cause a short circuit in a box that has been left uncovered. (If you see an uncovered jack box cover it, even though you are not responsible for the carelessness.) Remove the headpiece and hang it over the transmitter yoke. Coil the lead cord, starting from the end at the phone. Coil the lead in a clockwise direction, holding the loops in one hand. The loops should be eight to ten inches across, depending on the size of the space where the phones are stowed. When you are coiling the lead, be careful not to bang the plug against anything.

When the lead is coiled, remove the headpiece from the transmitter yoke and put the headband in the same hand with the coil. Use this same hand to hold the transmitter while you unhook one end of the neck strap from the breastplate. Fold the transmitter yoke flat, being careful not to put a sharp bend in the transmitter cord. Wrap the neck strap around both the coil of wire you created and the headband two or three times and snap the end back on the breastplate, then fold the mouthpiece back up against the junction box. You then have a neat, compact package to be stowed. Put the phones into their box, or hang them on the hook provided. Be careful not to crowd or jam the leads.

One of the advantages of a sound-powered phone set is that in an emergency the earpieces and mouthpieces are interchangeable—you can talk into an earpiece and listen using the mouthpiece if you need to. This advantage is also a disadvantage, because an uncovered earpiece allows unwanted sound into the circuit that can make it difficult for others on the circuit to hear. Headset phones should, therefore, always be unplugged when not in use. If they are left plugged in, the earpieces will pick up noise and carry it into the circuit.

Never place the phones on the deck. Not only may someone step on them, but decks are good conductors of noise, which the phones can pick up.

SOUND-POWERED PHONE-TALKING TECHNIQUE

The way you ordinarily talk is not the way you should talk on a sound-powered phone. The person on the other end of the line cannot see you, may not know you, and may be unfamiliar with the things you are talking about.

When you are functioning as a shipboard sound-powered phone talker, you must speak clearly, be specific, and act businesslike. Use a strong (not loud), calm voice and speak slowly, pronouncing each word carefully. Don't mumble, run things together, or talk with gum or other objects in your mouth.

Because sound-powered circuits are open to all stations simultaneously, circuit discipline is essential to prevent too much noise and confusion. Send only official messages. Do not engage in idle chit-chat. Each phone talker is a key link in the ship's interior communications chain. Unauthorized talking means that the chain is weakened. Don't engage in it, and don't permit others to, either.

Keep the button in the off position except when you are actually talking. Avoid allowing anger, impatience, or excitement to be noticeable in your voice. Be professional. Few things can be as helpful or as reassuring as a calm voice in the middle of a crisis. Always use standard terms and phraseology, avoiding slang.

When talking on a sound-powered telephone (or on a radio circuit and even a standard telephone), your voice does not have the same clarity that it does when speaking face to face with someone. That is one of the reasons why the Navy insists upon standardized terminology when communicating. You have already learned that course headings and bearings are always given as three digit numbers (zero-four-five) while position angles are spoken as "forty" or "seventy," for example. Numbers are often spoken individually rather than in the more conventional (but confusing) manner you were used to in civilian life. Because the numbers "five" and "nine" sound very much alike on a sound-powered circuit or on a radio, the number "nine" is always pronounced "niner" in the Navy. This will seem strange to you at first, but after a while it will become second nature. Standardization of speech helps the listener to know what is being said by providing additional clues that will help overcome the reduced sound quality in these communication instruments.

One of the most valuable tools in maintaining clarity and avoiding confusion in communications is the use of the phonetic alphabet (see TAB 20-C: The Phonetic Alphabet). The letters C, D, E, P, V, T, and Z all sound very much alike on a sound-powered phone, for example. By using their phonetic equivalents (Charlie, Delta, Echo, Papa, Victor, Tango, and Zulu) there is no chance of someone misunderstanding what letter you mean.

If you say, "We need part number six alfa" instead of "six a," there is no chance that someone will confuse that with part 6k (which would be "six kilo"). The phonetic alphabet can also be used to spell out words that someone is having difficulty understanding.

It is absolutely mandatory that you memorize the phonetic alphabet. You will be lost in the Navy without it.

SOUND-POWERED MESSAGE FORM

When using sound-powered telephones, most messages have three parts, given in the following order:

- the name of the station called
- the name of the station calling
- the information to be sent

This format must always be followed. Call the station the message is for, identify your station, then transmit the message. It may seem strange to keep repeating these things, but keep in mind that there will probably be a number of people plugged into the circuit at the same time and they cannot see each other, so it is important to identify who you are and who you are talking to. Remember the order: who to, who from, what about. If you are on the anchor detail stationed on the forecastle and want to call the bridge, you would say:

"Bridge [who to], Forecastle [who from];
anchor secured [what about]."

When receiving a message, first identify your station, then acknowledge for the message with the words "aye, aye" or, simply, "aye." This means that you heard the message and understood it. It does not mean "yes." For example, if your station is the forecastle and the bridge has just ordered the anchor to be let go: "Forecastle, Bridge; let go the anchor." Acknowledge that you understood what was said by answering with: "Forecastle, aye, aye" (or, "Forecastle, aye").

This does not mean that you (or anyone else) will let the anchor go. It means simply that you understood what was being said. When you pass this word on to the chief in charge of the anchor detail, she or he may tell you to tell the bridge that the anchor cannot yet be let go because the stopper is jammed. By saying "Aye, aye" you merely were saying "I heard and understood what you said."

You should note that in the above answer the forecastle did not say "Bridge, Forecastle, aye," but merely said "Forecastle, aye." This is because it is obvious who is being answered and to say "Bridge" would be unnecessary. It is acceptable (in fact, preferable) to abbreviate your conversation in this manner as long as it does not add to the confusion.

If you did not understand what was said, you should not answer "Aye, aye," but should say, "Bridge, Forecastle; repeat."

The following is a typical conversation you might have on the 1JV sound-powered circuit if you are on the forecastle as part of the anchor detail. For clarity, *your words will appear in italics.*

"Forecastle, Bridge; is the starboard anchor ready to let go?"
"Bridge, Forecastle; we are having trouble with the stopper."
"Forecastle, Bridge; report when the anchor is ready."
"Forecastle, aye."

[A minute goes by while the boatswain's
mates are trying to free the stopper.]

"Bridge, Forecastle; the First Lieutenant says the bale is bent."
"Forecastle, Bridge; repeat."
"Bridge, Forecastle; the First Lieutenant says the bale is bent."
"Forecastle, Bridge; the 'what' is bent?"
"Bridge, Forecastle; 'bale.' Bravo, alfa, lima, echo."
"Bridge, aye."
"Forecastle, Bridge; the Captain says he will back the ship down
    to keep us in our intended anchorage while you work on the
    stopper."
"Forecastle, aye."
"Bridge, Fantail; we have a small fishing boat astern of us."
"Bridge, aye."

In the last exchange, you can see that the talker at the fantail station, who is also on the circuit, warns the bridge that there is a fishing boat astern. This illustrates the importance of stations identifying themselves on the circuit when they speak. All of the prefacing with "Bridge, Forecastle" and "Forecastle, Bridge" in the above conversation seems unnecessary and awkward until you realize that there are other stations on the circuit, and it is important to know who is talking to whom in order to avoid confusion.

CIRCUIT TESTING

To find out if all of the stations on the circuit are manned and ready, the control-station talker would run a check of the circuit. For example, if the damage-control circuit is manning up and the control station (DCC) wanted to verify that all stations are on the line, the DCC talker would initiate the check by saying, "All Stations, Central; testing."

Each talker on the circuit then would acknowledge in the assigned order.

> "Repair One; aye, aye."
> "Repair Two; aye, aye."
> "Repair Three; aye."
> "Repair Four; aye, aye."

Normally each station answers in order, but does not wait more than a few seconds if the station ahead of it fails to acknowledge. If Repair Two fails to answer, Repair Three should, after giving Repair Two a few seconds to answer, go ahead and acknowledge for his or her station. If you were the talker in Repair Two and just came on the line while the check was going on, you should report in at the end, after all the other stations have made their reports in sequence. Do not try to jump in out of sequence—it may cause unnecessary confusion.

Integrated Voice Communications System (IVCS)

IVCS (spoken as "I-Vicks") combines the features of sound-powered phones, dial telephones, and intercom units into one sophisticated system with many advanced operating features. IVCS is capable of interfacing with other shipboard communications systems and consists of terminals (user access devices), computer-controlled interior communications switching centers (ICSCs), and a number of special accessories. In the event of a loss of electrical power, a battery backup system keeps IVCS operating. Using "NETS" voice circuits, some of the more common ones are:

NET 15—Command Net; used for Combat Information Center (CIC) coordination

NET 25—Combat Systems Equipment Control

NET 27—Electronic Control

NET 29—Underwater Systems Control

NET 66—AEGIS/Air Weapons Control

NET 74—Surface Weapons Systems Control

NET 80—Damage Control

NET 85—Electrical Service/Engineering Systems Control

Voice Tubes

A voice tube is exactly what it sounds like—a metal tube that allows stations to communicate with one another simply by talking into it. Large cones are fitted onto the ends of the tube to amplify the sound of your voice. Voice tubes require no electrical power, but their effectiveness decreases in direct proportion to the length of the tube, so they are used for short-distance communication only. A typical voice-tube installation would connect the bridge wings to the helm, enabling the conning officer to pass orders to the helmsman without having to come into the pilot house from the bridge wing.

EXTERNAL COMMUNICATIONS

External communication involves two or more ships, stations, or commands. A ship communicates externally by a wide variety of methods, including messenger delivery, mail, flaghoist, semaphore, flashing light, radio, facsimile (FAX), teletype, whistle signals, and foghorns. The most significant forms of communicating are visual and electronic.

Visual Signaling

Despite this age of high technology when satellites and radios transmit communications at incredible speed, the oldest form of communication can still play a vital role in the Navy. Visual communication has a distinct advantage over other forms. For all its advances, science has yet to produce a silent form of electronic communication, one that cannot be detected by advanced technological equipment. Visual communication fills the need for a reliable, silent, and relatively secure means of communication at ranges up to fifteen miles.

The three main types of visual signal are flashing light, flaghoist, and semaphore.

FLASHING LIGHT

Letters and numbers are broken down into short and long flashes of light known as Morse code. A transmitting signalman sends messages one letter at a time with a slight pause between each letter. The receiving signalman flashes a light for each word received until the message is complete.

Flashing-light signaling is accomplished by two methods, directional and nondirectional. With the directional method, the sender aims his light directly at the receiving ship or installation. The ship's standard signal-searchlight is most often used. The signal-searchlight is mounted to the ship's rail or to a special stand and is worked with levers attached to a blinking screen, which allows the light to be quickly shown and blocked (to form the short and long flashes required for Morse code). (See TAB 20-D: Morse Code.)

A blinker tube (or blinker gun) and a multipurpose lamp may also be used. These are portable, battery-operated lights with trigger switches to control flashes.

The nondirectional method is also called all-around signaling. Most of it is done by yardarm blinkers, lights mounted near the ends of the port and starboard yardarms on the mainmast and controlled by a signal key, similar to an old-fashioned telegraph, located on the signal bridge. This method is best for sending messages to several ships at once.

Lights used at night can be seen by an enemy, so an alternate system called "Nancy" uses invisible infrared light. Messages sent by this system can be seen only by those who have a special Nancy receiver, which gathers infrared rays and converts them to visible light. Nancy, with a range of from 10,000 to 15,000 yards, can be used only at night and is a more secure method of communication.

FLAGHOIST

This system uses special flags with individual meanings that can be hoisted on lines called *halyards* so that they can be seen by other ships in the vicinity. This is an effective system of visual signaling, but it can be used only in daytime. There is a signal flag for each letter of the alphabet, a set of flags for each numeral 0 through 9, a set of pennants for each numeral 0 through 9, and other flags and pennants with special meanings. A complete set of signal flags will have sixty-eight flags and pennants. (See TAB 20-E: Signal Flags and Pennants).

Because only a limited number of flags can be hoisted at a time, spelling out messages is not practical. Instead, short combinations of flags have been listed in special code books to have specific meanings. For example, instead of trying to spell out the words "Engage the enemy with swords and cutlasses," a code book could assign the letters/numbers "WX8" to have that meaning. As long as both ships have the appropriate code book, one could hoist those three flags to convey that longer message. The only limitation to a system like this is the size of the code book used.

Most ships carry only two or three complete sets of flags, but special substitute pennants may be employed to repeat flags that are already flying. The first substitute repeats the first flag or pennant in the same hoist, the second substitute repeats the second flag or pennant, and so on. With this system, there is virtually no limit to the combinations of flags and pennants that may be displayed (except for halyard space) and thousands of different signals can be sent.

Some signal flags have special meanings when used alone:

Bravo	Ship is handling explosives or fuel oil.
Five	Ship is broken down; cannot maneuver on its own.
Oscar	Man overboard.
Papa	Personnel recall. All hands return to ship.
Quebec	Boat recall. All boats return to ship.

SEMAPHORE

Semaphore requires little in the way of equipment and is relatively simple once the user becomes accustomed to it. Words are transmitted by holding the arms in a specific position to represent individual letters. When sender and receiver are close, as when their ships are alongside one another for UNREP, no special equipment is necessary. The semaphore characters are made simply by moving the hands to the proper positions. At greater distances, flags attached to short staffs held by the sender will make the signals much more visible. Standard semaphore flags are usually fifteen to

[**20.5**] Signal flags are hoisted on halyards to send coded messages.

eighteen square inches, and each staff is just long enough to grasp firmly. Most semaphore flags issued to the fleet today are fluorescent and made of sharkskin. For night semaphore, flashlights with special light-diffusing cones attached are held in the same manner as semaphore flags.

A good signalman can send or receive about twenty-five five-letter groups a minute. Only thirty positions need to be learned to be able to communicate by this method.

[**20.6**] Semaphore requires little in the way of equipment and is relatively simple once the user becomes accustomed to it.

Semaphore is much faster than flashing light for short-distance transmissions. It may be used to send messages to several ships at once if they are in suitable positions but works best when used one on one. Because of its speed, semaphore is better adapted than the other visual methods for longer messages.

Although semaphore's usefulness is limited somewhat by its short range, it is more secure than flashing light or radio because there is less chance of interception by an enemy or unauthorized persons. Speed and security, therefore, are the two factors favoring the use of semaphore. (See TAB 20-F: Semaphore Signaling System).

Electronic Communications

Electronic communications used in the Navy take many forms. In the earliest days of radio, signals were sent by something called "continuous wave," which relied on Morse code as the means for transmitting signals. Later, voice radio came into being and revolutionized naval tactical communications. Other advances followed, including teletype, satellite communications, facsimile (FAX), and e-mail.

VOICE RADIO

While you will certainly reap the benefits of modern electronic communications in the Navy, you will not be involved in using most forms unless you strike for radioman. One form, however, you may use on a frequent basis while standing watches or taking part in various operations. Voice radio or radiotelephone communications (RT) is often used as a fast, convenient, and efficient means of communicating. Ship to ship, ship to aircraft, aircraft to aircraft, ship to boat, and so on, voice radio is essential for many operations. Because of this, every Sailor should be able to communicate effectively using radio telephones, and because radios operate somewhat differently from the telephones you are used to, you will need to learn a few new things in order to be an effective radio communicator.

For example, you must begin by *unlearning* a particularly bad habit that has, for some reason, made its way into many movies and television programs. The oft-used expression "over and out" makes no sense whatsoever, yet you will hear it used time and again on the big and little screens. In radiotelephony, "over" is a shorthand way of saying, "I am finished talking and now it is your turn." "Out" means "I am finished talking and we have nothing more to talk about, so I am signing off." In short, "out" is roughly equivalent to "goodbye" on a telephone. So when actors say "over and out," they are, in essence, saying, "I am finished talking and now it is your turn, so good-bye." Needless to say, this makes no sense. Never, never, never say "over and out" on a Navy radio circuit unless you enjoy being the butt of jokes.

Other words and phrases, called "prowords," have special meanings when used in voice radio communications. See TAB 20-G: Radiotelephone Prowords for a list of the more common ones.

Voice radio transmissions take the following form: the station called followed by the words "this is" and the identification of the station doing the calling. For example, if the call sign of your station is "Tango Charlie" and you are trying to call station "Delta Whiskey," you would say, "Delta Whiskey, this is Tango Charlie." The following example illustrates a radio conversation between these two stations. (Note: Prowords are in UPPER CASE.)

"Delta Whiskey, THIS IS Tango Charlie, OVER."

"Tango Charlie, THIS IS Delta Whiskey, ROGER, OVER."

"Delta Whiskey, THIS IS Tango Charlie. When will your last boat be departing? OVER."

"Tango Charlie, THIS IS Delta Whiskey. The last boat will depart one hour before sunset. OVER."

"Delta Whiskey, THIS IS Tango Charlie. The Chief of Staff wants you to wait until General Scarloni arrives. OVER."

"Tango Charlie, THIS IS Delta Whiskey. Spell last name of general. OVER."

"Delta Whiskey, THIS IS Tango Charlie. I SPELL: sierra, charlie, alfa, romeo, lima, oscar, november, india. OVER."

"Tango Charlie, THIS IS Delta Whiskey. SAY AGAIN all after lima. OVER."

"Delta Whiskey, THIS IS Tango Charlie. I SAY AGAIN all after lima: oscar, november, india. OVER."

"Tango Charlie, this is Delta Whiskey. WILCO. OUT."

TRANSMITTING RULES AND TECHNIQUES

Because RT is used so widely in ships, aircraft, and motor vehicles, everyone should understand the basics of circuit discipline. Under most circumstances, the following practices are specifically forbidden:

- Violation of radio silence
- Unofficial conversation between operators
- Transmitting in a directed net without permission
- Excessive tuning and testing
- Unauthorized use of plain language (no encryption)
- Use of profane, indecent, or obscene language

Listen before transmitting—break-ins cause confusion. Speak clearly and distinctly; slurred syllables and clipped speech are difficult to understand. Speak slowly, so that the recorder has a chance to understand the entire message the first time. This way, you'll save time and avoid repetitions. Use standard pronunciation, not regional accents.

Keep the correct distance (about two inches) between your lips and the microphone. Speak in a moderately strong voice to override background noise. While transmitting, keep your head and body between sources of noise and the microphone.

Keep the volume of the headset earphone or speaker low. Pause momentarily, when possible, during your transmission by releasing the transmit button; pausing allows any other station with higher-precedence traffic to break in. Transact your business and get off the air. Preliminary calls are unnecessary when communications are good and the message is short. Do not hold the transmit button in the push-to-talk position until you're ready to transmit. Apply firm pressure to the transmit button to prevent an unintentional release.

SECURE VOICE COMMUNICATIONS

If a transmission is in plain language (unencrypted), anyone can intercept and read it. Important messages may be encrypted and sent in a code or cipher known only to the sender and receiver. Codes are word-for-word substitutions, and both sender and receiver must use the same code book. Ciphers are letter-for-letter substitutions, which may require a machine for encoding and decoding. Encrypted message may be copied by anyone, but without the code book or cipher machine it is difficult or impossible to read.

Modern communications equipment often includes automatic encryption devices that "scramble" voice radio transmissions so that they are unreadable by unwanted parties and "unscrambled" by the intended receiver who has matching encryption/decryption devices.

Communications—whether routine or tactical—are an essential element in the Navy's functioning and can mean the difference between success and failure. From the ancient art of semaphore to sophisticated satellite systems, the Navy takes advantage of many forms of communication, many of which will likely affect you as a Sailor.

TWENTY-ONE

THE BENEFITS OF SERVING

Serving in the U.S. Navy is something that will likely be a source of pride for you. But no one expects you to survive or thrive on pride alone. Just as in any profession, Sailors are paid for their work. And just as there are special demands and sacrifices that go with life in the Navy, there are also benefits that come with the job.

The Navy provides a growing number of apps—such as "New to the Navy"—that have some information on pay and benefits, but the best source of information about these benefits is your command career counselor. These counselors are trained specialists who have all the latest information on the benefits available to Sailors.

Another excellent source of information is the latest edition of *The Military Advantage: The Military.com Guide to Military and Veterans Benefits*, written by Terry Howell and published by the Naval Institute Press.

Following is a less-detailed but useful summary to give you a good general idea of some of what the Navy provides to its Sailors in pay and benefits.

PAY AND ALLOWANCES

Sailors receive two kinds of financial remuneration while they are in the Navy: *pay* and *allowances*. There are certain legal and economic distinctions between the two, but the most practical way to distinguish them is that pay is much like the salary a civilian would receive in her or his job and is, therefore, subject to federal income tax. Allowances are extra payments designed to help you meet certain expenses of Navy life. Some allowances are not subject to federal income tax while others are.

Because there are these two types of remuneration in the Navy (some taxable and some not), when comparing how much money Sailors make with how much their civilian counterparts make, a dollar-for-dollar comparison is not entirely accurate.

When discussing pay and allowances, I may provide examples just to give you an idea of approximately what we are talking about, but be aware that these amounts change often, so it is best to refer to the latest edition of *The Military Advantage* or to check online for the latest amounts.

Basic Pay

Basic pay depends on your pay grade and years of service. It is the same for every Sailor in that same pay grade with the same amount of time served. It is the largest single part of a Sailor's paycheck.

Those "paychecks" are paid twice a month, usually on the first and the fifteenth, through the direct-deposit system (DDS). Pay and entitlements are electronically transferred to the banking institution of your choice. With DDS, no matter where you are—aboard ship, on shore, at an overseas station, in a travel status, or on leave—when payday rolls around, you will have immediate access to your money because your pay will be in your accounts, on time.

Allowances

BASIC ALLOWANCE FOR SUBSISTENCE (BAS)

All Sailors receive Basic Allowance for Subsistence (BAS) to cover meals. When serving in a capacity where meals are provided, such as aboard ship, BAS will be deducted from your pay.

BASIC ALLOWANCE FOR HOUSING (BAH)

This allowance is nontaxable and is based on a variety of factors. The amount of BAH varies considerably, depending upon your pay grade, whether you have dependents (spouse and children), whether or not government quarters are available and used, and some other possible variables, depending upon your individual situation. Geographic location has a significant effect on the amount; living in Southern California is considerably more expensive than living in portions of the South, and the government takes that into consideration when determining the amount of BAH you are to be paid.

CLOTHING ALLOWANCES

You may receive clothing allowances at various times during your service, depending upon whether your specific duties require special kinds of clothing. These include *Initial Clothing Allowances, Cash Clothing Replacement Allowances, Extra Clothing Allowances,* and *Clothing Maintenance Allowances.*

FAMILY SEPARATION ALLOWANCE (FSA)

If you have dependents (are married with or without children), you may be entitled to some additional money when separated from them as a result of government assignment, such as an unaccompanied tour overseas or on a ship on overseas deployment. There are specific requirements and restrictions, depending upon marital status, length of separation, whether or not accompaniment is authorized, and some other considerations.

Other Forms of Pay and Allowances

There are ways that your paycheck may be increased. There are travel and transportation allowances, cost of living allowances (COLA), hostile fire/imminent danger pay, special duty assignment pay, hardship duty pay, reenlistment bonuses, and a number of others that you may or may not be eligible for.

Leave and Earnings Statement (LES)—A Key Document

You should review your monthly *Leave and Earnings Statements* (LES) to keep track of your pay and allowances. The Defense Finance and Accounting System provides the *myPay* system online (**mypay.dfas.mil**) where you may review your pay and other benefits as well as make discretionary changes (such as allotments) without having to resort to paper forms.

Allotments

Through allotments you may assign part of your pay regularly to a bank or an insurance company. Once the appropriate forms have been filled out, the specified monthly amount is automatically deducted from your paycheck and payments will automatically be made by the Navy.

ADVANCEMENT

Advancement in the Navy means better pay, more privileges, greater responsibility, and increased pride. Advancement to petty officer rates in the Navy are made through centralized competition. Because the requirements sometimes change, it is always best to consult with your personnel office or educational services office for the latest information. Additional information can be found in the *Advancement Manual for Enlisted Personnel—BUPERS 1430.1* (Series). While the Navy will assist you in many ways, meeting the requirements for advancement in rate is ultimately up to you. Think ahead and prepare, so that you are ready for advancement once you have met the time-in-rate (TIR) requirements.

Keep in mind that not all ratings have the same opportunities for advancement. Training, promotion, bonuses, and duty locations are rating specific. Contact your command career counselor for the latest information.

General Requirements

While there are a number of requirements for advancement (time in rate, awards earned, exam scores, etc.), the most heavily weighted aspect is your performance. Throughout your Navy career, you will receive performance evaluations describing how well you perform your duties. What those evaluations in your record say about you is the most important factor in determining whether you will be advanced. Advancement to E-3 depends entirely upon your performance and you having spent the required amount of time as an E-2. If you have a favorable recommendation for advancement on your most recent evaluation, you will be automatically advanced to E-3 when you have served the required time in rate (see below). One of the ways to advance to E-4 through E-7 is to compete in the semiannual or annual Navy-Wide Advancement Examinations (NWAE) for advancement in rate. Before you can take these exams you must meet certain eligibility requirements. You must be recommended for advancement by your commanding officer (CO) or officer in charge (OIC), meet physical readiness and body fat standards, and must complete the required leadership courses for E4 and above.

TIME IN RATE (TIR)

You must spend a minimum length of time in any given rate before you can even try to advance to the next higher one. This period is called "time in rate" and is designed to ensure that a Sailor spends some time at each level gaining experience before she or he is eligible for advancement to the next higher rate. The specific TIR requirements do change from time to time, but currently they are as follows:

E-1 to E-2	9 months as an E-1
E-2 to E-3	9 months as an E-2
E-3 to E-4	6 months as an E-3
E-4 to E-5	12 months as an E-4
E-5 to E-6	36 months as an E-5*
E-6 to E-7	36 months as an E-6*
E-7 to E-8	36 months as an E-7
E-8 to E-9	36 months as an E-8

* Time in Rate can be 24 months if your CO grants an "Early Promote Waiver."

Keep in mind that these are minimum times. Except for advancement to E-3, you should not expect to necessarily get advanced within these periods of time. Few people do.

NAVAL STANDARDS (NAVSTDS) AND OCCUPATIONAL STANDARDS (OCCSTDS)

Volume one of the *Manual of Navy Enlisted Manpower and Personnel Classifications and Occupations Standards* (NAVPERS 18068) lists the minimum things you should know or be able to do in order to be eligible for your next advancement. NAVSTDS are general military requirements that do not apply to a specific rating and that all Sailors at each pay grade should know. OCCSTDS are the job tasks you should know for the specific rating (such as quartermaster or logistics specialist) and pay grade you are trying to achieve. Keep in mind that there will be questions related to both on your exam. Also keep in mind that you are responsible for knowing not only those NAVSTDS and OCCSTDS for the rate you are trying to achieve but also all those of the lower rates. In other words, if you are preparing to be advanced to quartermaster second class, you should be studying and reviewing the NAVSTDS for E-2 through E-5 and the OCCSTDS for QM3 as well as QM2.

PREPARATION AIDS

For most advancements you must take a written advancement examination. The people who write these exams have also prepared guides to help you study. For each rate there is a Bibliography for Advancement-in-Rate Exam Study (known more commonly as a BIB).

The BIB for your rate gives you a list of all the publications that will help you prepare for advancement such as training courses, instructions, and technical manuals. BIBs can be obtained from your educational services officer (ESO) or from the Internet at the Navy Credentialing Opportunities Online (COOL). The reference material listed in the BIB is examination specific, so you should download a new one in advance of each advancement exam you take.

Training Manuals (TRAMANs) and Non-Resident Training Courses (NRTCs). To help you prepare for advancement, the Navy supplies TRAMANs that serve as textbooks and NRTCs (often called "correspondence courses"), which are courses based on the TRAMANs that you can take without having to go to a school. See your educational services officer or command career counselor for assistance in determining which courses to take and how to obtain them. Most are available on the Internet at the Naval Education and Training Command (NETC) website (**www.netc.navy.mil/**).

PERSONAL PREPARATIONS

Next to good performance, perhaps the most important requirement for your advancement is a good study plan. There is a lot of material to review no matter what rate you are trying to achieve, so you must make time on a regular basis to prepare yourself for the advancement exam. Try studying three days a week right after breakfast or every night before taps—whatever works best for you. Try to allot at least an hour, but settle for less on occasion rather than not study at all. Every little bit helps. Remember to ask your peers and leadership about Rating Stand Down Study Groups and Advancement Training Teams in your area. These can provide additional study materials and assist you in focusing your study efforts.

When it comes time to take the exam you have been preparing for, it is a good idea not to attempt any last-minute studying the night before. Relax. Go out for dinner if possible. Take a walk, spend some time with friends, or have a moderate workout at the gym. Most important of all, get a good night's sleep.

EXAM DAY

While taking the exam, pace yourself. Begin by reading all the questions and the answer choices. Then go through the exam again, this time answering all those questions you are certain you know. Go through again with the time remaining and work on those questions you are not certain about. Take an educated guess rather than leave a question blank. You will not be graded by the number of wrong answers, but on the number of correct responses.

CAREER DEVELOPMENT BOARD (CDB)

To ensure that your career is progressing and developing as it should, your command will conduct a CDB. These boards are conducted after you first report aboard (within thirty days), after you have been aboard for six months, again at twelve months, and then at least once a year thereafter until you transfer to your next command. In most cases, members of the CDB are the command master chief, command career counselor, personnel officer, educational services officer, mentors, and leaders from your division. These people will provide you with sound career information and advice so that you can make informed decisions about your career. For example, if you are having difficulty advancing in a timely manner, the CBD will find ways to help you. Or if you wanted to apply for an officer program, the CDB would assist you in determining your eligibility and help with the application requirements.

Advancements

Obviously the Navy cannot advance everyone who wants to be advanced. Because the Navy needs only a certain number of petty officers, it is not even always possible to advance everyone who passes the examination and meets all advancement requirements. The Navy has therefore devised an equitable system to select the most qualified Sailors for advancement.

FINAL MULTIPLE SCORE (FMS)

Once you have met all the requirements and have taken the competitive examination, your results will be computed as a "final multiple score." This is determined by combining a number of factors to determine who, of all those competing, will be advanced. The factors for E4–E6 include how you did on the written examination, your performance marks, how long you have served in your current pay grade, how many awards you have received, your level of education, and whether or not you have taken the exam before and how well you did. You will receive a certain amount of credit for each of these factors, depending upon what pay grade you are seeking, and the end computed result will be your FMS. Your FMS is then compared to the FMSs of everyone else competing for advancement in your rating and pay grade. The Navy determines how many people it needs to advance, and those with the highest FMSs are advanced. For example, if you are seeking advancement from seaman to QM3, and the Navy needs one hundred new QM3s, you will be advanced if your FMS was among the top one hundred of those who are competing. If one hundred or more people did better than you once the FMSs are calculated, you will not be advanced. But if only ninety-nine or fewer did better, you will be a new QM3. The factors to determine an E-7 FMS are the results of your examination and your performance marks.

PASSED BUT NOT ADVANCED (PNA)

For every written examination there is a minimum passing grade established. If you pass the exam but do not end up with a high enough FMS to be advanced, you are designated as PNA, which means "passed but not advanced." This is certainly frustrating, but it's not all bad news. PNA points are factored into your FMS, but points are only creditable from the most recent five advancement cycles in that pay grade. For each advancement cycle, 1.5 PNA points are awarded to candidates in the top 25 percent of standard scores as well as in the top 25 percent of PNAs who passed the NWAE but did not advance and were not invalidated. The maximum cumulative PNA point total that may be credited to candidates is 15. You can see that it is a good idea to take the exam each time it is offered even if you feel that you have little chance of being one of those who will get advanced.

SELECTION BOARDS (E7–E9)

Advancement to E7–E9 is completed via a selection board process. Each enlisted selection board consists of a captain who serves as president; a fleet, force, or senior command master chief who serves as the senior enlisted adviser to the president; a senior recorder; and officers and master chief petty officers serving as board members. The board members are divided up into various panels responsible for reviewing the records of candidates in one general occupation area (i.e., deck, engineering, medical, supply, etc.). Additionally, a sufficient number of assistant recorders (chief and senior chief petty officers) are employed to ensure the smooth handling and accounting of records. Advancement across the Navy is vacancy driven, therefore quotas are developed to determine the maximum number of candidates that may be selected for advancement. The quotas are to be filled by the "best qualified" candidates competing for advancement. While the quota may not be exceeded, should it be determined by a panel that there is an insufficient number of "qualified" candidates in a rating, the panel may recommend not using all the quotas.

The candidate's records are reviewed within the panel and recommendations are made to determine who will be advanced and who will not be advanced. Once the panel has made its recommendation, the panel briefs the president, who ensures the panel's recommendation is in accordance with Navy policy. The next step is to obtain a majority vote of "yes" from a group of other panels to agree that the list of selects and non-selects is in the best interest of the Navy. After all panels have completed the process for the eligible candidates, a final list is forwarded to the Chief of Naval Personnel for approval.

MERITORIOUS ADVANCEMENT PROGRAM

In addition to the traditional advancement exam process, Sailors can also advance to pay grades E4–E6 through the Meritorious Advancement Program (MAP). MAP authorizes commanding officers to recognize their best Sailors through on-the-spot advancement. The program is intended to give the command triad (commanding officer/executive officer/command master chief) more flexibility to reward Sailors who display outstanding performance by immediate advancement to the next level of responsibility. Very few MAP quotas are released each year, which means the competition is fierce. Any Sailor that strives to be selected to advance through the MAP program is expected to be the top performer in his or her command. If selected for MAP advancement, he or she will immediately assume the title and responsibility of the next pay grade and be entitled to wear the uniform and earn pay at the new rank.

BECOMING AN OFFICER

There are a number of ways to become an officer in the U.S. Navy. Minimum requirements are that you must be a U.S. citizen and must meet certain age, physical, and service requirements. In general, a college degree is also a requirement, but there are exceptions. If you are interested in any of the programs briefly described below, you should contact your educational services officer or command career counselor for additional information and assistance. Be aware that you will likely incur additional active-duty service obligations with these programs.

United States Naval Academy (USNA)

Most midshipmen are appointed from among high school or prep school graduates, but about 10 percent of every entering class consists of prior enlisted Sailors and Marines. To be a candidate for appointment, you must be a U.S. citizen, at least seventeen but not more than twenty-three years of age in the entering year, and unmarried with no children, and you must meet minimum scores on the math and verbal Scholastic Aptitude Test (SAT) or the American College Test (ACT). You must also meet certain physical requirements and be recommended by your commanding officer.

Midshipmen pay no tuition, room, and board and are paid while attending the Academy in Annapolis, Maryland, for four years. Upon graduation, they receive a bachelor of science degree and a commission in the Navy or Marine Corps.

Applicants who do not make the initial cut for the Naval Academy but could—in the opinion of the USNA Admissions Board—profit from an additional year of academic preparation may be offered the opportunity to attend the Naval Academy Preparatory School (NAPS) in Newport, Rhode Island. If you wish to be considered for NAPS, you must state your willingness on your USNA application.

Naval Reserve Officers Training Corps (NROTC)

You may also compete for NROTC scholarships. To be eligible, you must be a U.S. citizen, be a high school graduate or equivalent, be physically qualified, have a good performance record, and be under twenty-seven and a half years of age on 30 June of the year you become eligible for commissioned status. Tuition, fees, books, uniforms, and a monthly subsistence allowance are paid by the scholarship program. The program is available at more than fifty civilian colleges and universities. NROTC students may earn a bachelor's degree in various academic fields, although at least 80 percent of the program's participants must be majoring in engineering, mathematics, physics, or chemistry.

Active-duty Sailors who are selected as NROTC scholarship recipients are released to the Inactive Ready Reserve (IRR) while attending school and do not receive pay and allowances.

Officer Candidate School (OCS)

If you have a bachelor's degree (BA, BS) from an accredited academic institution, you may be eligible to attend OCS at Newport, Rhode Island. The program is about twelve weeks long and provides basic knowledge of the naval profession. You will also receive specialized follow-on training after OCS to further prepare you for your initial fleet assignment as an officer. If you are an E-4 or below, you will be designated as an officer candidate and advanced to E-5 for pay purposes upon reporting to OCS. If you are an E-6 or above, you will continue to be paid in your current grade. Besides having the required degree, you must meet age and physical requirements, and you must be a U.S. citizen.

Seaman to Admiral-21 (STA-21) Program

STA-21 is a commissioning program that provides an excellent opportunity for highly motivated active-duty enlisted personnel. Although the applicant's history of fleet performance will receive consideration during the selection process, emphasis will also be placed on the identification of those applicants who possess both the academic and leadership potential necessary to become outstanding naval officers. STA-21 has two components. The first is an eight-week course of intensive officer preparation and indoctrination at Officer Training Command in Newport, Rhode Island. The second part consists of full-time, year-round study for up to thirty-six months at an NROTC-affiliated university.

Warrant Officer Program

Chief petty officers (pay grades E-7 to E-9) may apply for the warrant officer program. There is no age requirement, but applicants must have completed at least twelve but not more than twenty-four years of naval service. Appointments are made to the grade of chief warrant officer (W-2). E-9s with two years in grade may apply for appointment to chief warrant officer (W-3).

Other specific requirements are that a candidate must be a U.S. citizen, have a high school diploma or equivalent, have a good performance record, be physically qualified, and be recommended by the commanding officer. Applications are considered by a board convened by the Secretary of the Navy annually. Applicants accepted into the warrant officer program must agree to remain on active duty for three years from the date they are promoted to chief warrant officer.

Limited Duty Officer (LDO) Program

The LDO program is open to warrant officers with one year's time in grade as of 1 September in the year application is made. The program is also open to enlisted applicants in pay grades E-6 through E-8. Enlisted applicants must have completed at least eight but not more than sixteen years of active naval service. E-6 personnel must compete in the E-7 examination and be designated LDO selection-board-eligible.

The LDO program has some of the same basic requirements as the warrant officer program. Warrant officers who are accepted into the LDO program are appointed to the grade of lieutenant (junior grade); enlisted applicants who are accepted are appointed as ensigns.

Because those appointed through this program are specialists in a particular field (having come from an enlisted rating), officers who receive their commissions as LDOs continue to receive assignments related to their specialties. For example, a gunner's mate who is commissioned through the LDO program is likely to be assigned to a ship as the weapons officer. Because these officers are "limited" to assignments related to their specialties, they are called "limited duty officers."

Other Commissioning Opportunities

Besides the programs listed above, there are a number of other ways for you to earn a commission. All commissioning programs are covered in a consolidated manual called the *Enlisted to Officer Commissioning Programs Application Manual* (OPNAVINST 1420.1). See your educational services officer for assistance.

ENLISTED SERVICE RECORD

All of this information about you—pay grade, rating, rate, NECs—has to be recorded somewhere so that you and the Navy can keep track of it. This is accomplished by your enlisted service record. It is the Navy's official file on you. Service records used to be kept on paper, but today your record of service is kept in an Electronic Service Record (ESR).

You can access your ESR through the Navy Standard Integrated Personnel System (NSIPS). This online service provides twenty-four-hour access to your training data and career counseling records as well as your Electronic Service Record (ESR). You should make sure your ESR is correct and up to date as much as possible, especially if you are nearing a major event such as going up for promotion or getting transferred to a new duty station. Promotion and selection boards use a Performance Summary Record (PSR), which is based on the information in your ESR, so it is important that your information is accurate.

Your record is important during your Navy career and after. While you are in the Navy, your service record will be used to help decide what assignments you will get and whether or not you will be promoted. When you leave the Navy, you may need information from your record for the collection of veterans' benefits, for federal or civilian employment, or for school credits.

Like most things in the military, there is a standardized way of keeping service records. You will not have to know the details of this standardization unless your chosen rating is in the administrative occupational field (personnel specialist or yeoman), but an understanding of the basic arrangement will help you find your way around your record when you review it for accuracy. In your record, you will find information divided into the following categories:

- Personal Information—Such information as your full name, address, dependency information (important data about your spouse and children if you have any), emergency contact information (whom to notify in the event of an emergency such as hospitalization), insurance information, religious accommodations, and other relevant information about you.
- Training, Education, and Qualifications—Courses and schools you have completed (both military and civilian, Personnel Qualification Standards (PQS) completed, warfare qualifications you have earned, information about your educational benefits, etc.
- Performance—A record of your duty assignments, performance evaluations, honors, awards, court memorandums, and other related materials.
- e-Leave—Used to keep track of your leave (vacation) time. Here you can submit leave requests, obtain approval, check in and out, etc.
- Professional History—Here you will find a record of your duty stations, copies of your orders, promotion history, etc.
- PCS Travel—When you receive Permanent Change of Station (PCS) orders transferring you from one duty station to another, this system will ensure your travel arrangements for both you and your

dependents are in order and will take care of related matters such as assigning you a sponsor at your new command.

- Service, Obligations, and Agreements—This is where you will find what service obligations you have (primarily how much time—via contract and extensions—you have agreed to serve in the Navy).
- Administrative Remarks—This is a chronological record of significant miscellaneous entries that are not included elsewhere in your record, or where more detailed information may be required to clarify entries on other pages of your record.
- NSIPS Summary of Changes—This section is used only by administrative personnel who are overseeing your record.

GENERAL BENEFITS AND SERVICES

There is no doubt that the pay in today's Navy is one of the real benefits. There are others, such as commissary (grocery store) and exchange (department store) privileges, medical and dental care for Sailors and their dependents, and an extensive educational program.

Family Housing

The family housing program includes public quarters (government rental units), mobile-home parks, government-insured privately owned projects, and leasing of privately owned units. The Navy tries to make sure adequate housing facilities are available for Sailors and their families at a reasonable cost and within reasonable commuting distance.

Because on-base housing is a popular benefit, being more convenient and less expensive than renting or buying a place to live off base, there is usually a waiting list. When you are preparing to transfer to a new duty station, you should contact the housing office at your new location as soon as possible to see what the housing situation is and to get on the list as soon as you are eligible.

Where Navy housing is not available, housing referral offices will provide assistance in locating private housing in the community.

Health Benefits

Under the Uniformed Services Health Benefit Program (USHBP), care is provided in Uniformed Services Medical Treatment Facilities (USMTFs) when possible. Other care is provided in civilian facilities at full or partial expense to the government when necessary.

[**21.1**] Family housing at Trumbo Point, an annex of Naval Air Station Key West

Active-duty members must be provided all necessary medical care. The primary source of care for all eligible beneficiaries is the USMTF. When care is not available from the USMTF for an active-duty member, it may be provided at government expense under the Non-Naval Medical Care Program and must be preauthorized. Each USMTF can provide acute medical and surgical care to varying degrees. Since not all USMTFs have the same medical capabilities, the health benefits adviser (HBA) should be contacted to determine what services are available.

Dependents and retired personnel are provided care at a USMTF if space, facilities, and proper medical staff are available.

Servicemembers Group Life Insurance (SGLI)

You are eligible for a special life insurance policy provided by the U.S. government. Currently you may elect to take up to $400,000 of life insurance coverage. The monthly cost to you is 7 cents per every $1,000 of coverage, with an additional mandatory $1.00 per month for "Traumatic Injury Protection." You may opt out or take less than the maximum amount of coverage, but you must choose to do so. If you do nothing, you will automatically be enrolled at the maximum amount. You must also specify who will receive the money if you opt in, and that will be a part of your official service record.

Death Benefits

If you should die while on active duty, your next of kin will receive a death gratuity (currently $100,000) tax free. If you have dependents, they would be eligible for certain benefits to help them financially, including housing and health care assistance, as well as additional Social Security benefits. Death benefits would also occur if you should die within 120 days after leaving the Navy, and if the death is determined to be service-related.

Leave

All personnel on active duty, from seaman to admiral, earn vacation time just as civilians do, but in the military it is called "leave." If Sailors want some time off to go back to their hometown to visit friends and relatives, they must submit a request, using the chain of command, specifying the exact days they want to be away. Because of the operational needs of the Navy, you cannot take leave whenever you feel like it. You will be an important member of the crew of a ship or station, so your absence will have to be carefully planned in order to keep things running smoothly while you are gone. You should not make airline reservations or other firm plans until your leave request has been approved.

Earned at the rate of two and a half days each month, this amounts to a total of thirty days of leave per year. The only exceptions are time spent in the brig or if you are absent without authorization for twenty-four hours or more. "Earned leave" is the amount credited to you on the books at any given date. Under certain circumstances, you may be permitted to take more leave than you are entitled to. This is called "advance leave" and will give you a negative balance. Advance leave is paid back as you earn it through continued service.

As leave accumulates, it is carried over from one fiscal year to the next. Except for special circumstances involving extended deployments or hostile conditions, no more than sixty days can be carried over on the books. This means that if you have sixty-seven days of leave on the books on 30 September (the end of the fiscal year), you will lose seven days of leave. For this reason, you should keep track of the leave balance on your LES and plan accordingly.

Persons discharged under honorable conditions with leave still on the books are paid a lump sum equal to the daily rate of basic pay they are earning at the time of discharge for each day. The most leave a Sailor can "sell back" in a military career is sixty days. Those discharged with a negative leave balance will pay back approximately a day's pay for each day's leave owed.

Your commanding officer has the authority to grant all earned leave on a yearly basis, plus up to forty-five days' advance leave. Personnel lacking enough earned leave during an emergency can be granted advance leave up to sixty days.

"Convalescent leave" is an authorized absence while you are under medical care and treatment. It must be authorized by your commanding officer on orders of a medical officer, or by the commanding officer of a military hospital. It is usually granted following a period of hospitalization and is not charged as leave.

Occasionally, a death in the family or some other serious consideration will require you to need leave in a hurry. This is called "emergency leave," and the procedures are, of course, different from those of routine leave requests. The best way for your family to get in touch with you in an emergency is to contact the American Red Cross by calling 1-877-272–7337; after verifying the situation, the Red Cross will immediately notify the Navy.

Overseas Schools for Family Members

The Department of Defense (DOD) operates many educational facilities for minor family members of all U.S. active-duty military and DOD civilian personnel stationed overseas. There are many DOD schools overseas with a portion of them Navy-sponsored. Army and Air Force schools in many countries are also open to Navy family members. From first grade through high school, family members can receive an education overseas at the government's expense.

Child Care

The Navy operates child-development centers at almost all naval installations. This program provides high-quality child care in conveniently located child-development centers at moderate cost to Sailors (fees are based on pay grade). Additionally, at naval installations having government housing, family child care is provided in government housing and is run by government-certified child-care providers. Commanding officers of installations that have child-care centers may establish priority of access in child-development centers (for example, single parents and dual military couples).

Counseling Assistance

The Navy has human relations experts ready to advise and help Sailors with difficult personal and family affairs. Navy chaplains, like ministers or priests at home, can offer counseling as well as perform religious ceremonies like baptisms, marriages, and funerals.

Personal help is available through Fleet and Family Support Centers (FFSC), where program specialists and clinical counselors assist with adaptation to Navy life and provide services and skills for self-sufficiency and personal success. These specialists offer a wide variety of programs and services, including counseling for problems relating to alcoholism and drug abuse, the effects of discriminatory practices in and out of the Navy, and family and personal affairs, including the successful management of the challenges of deployment. They can help Sailors with debt management, estate planning, and other financial services.

A legal-assistance officer can help you draw up wills, powers of attorney, deeds, affidavits, contracts, and many other documents. She or he also can advise you on transfers of property, marriage and divorce, adoption of children, taxation, personal injury, and other legal problems. The advice is free, and may help you avoid a lot of trouble. All matters are treated confidentially.

The Navy's Sexual Assault Prevention and Response Program (SAPR) provides both prevention programs and victim assistance. Fleet-wide training programs aim at eradicating sexual assaults, while special reporting procedures and professional counseling services tend to the needs of those who have been victimized.

Caring for Families

The Family Advocacy Program provides help with problems of child and spouse abuse. Services include prevention classes and individual help for victims and offenders as well as working closely with military and civilian agencies in dealing with these issues.

The Exceptional Family Member (EFM) program ensures that the special needs of family members are met by ensuring the servicemember's assignments are compatible with those needs. Because special needs cannot be met at every duty station throughout the world, EFM enrollment is mandatory for active-duty sponsors who have family members with chronic illness or incapacity, mental illness, or learning disabilities.

Relocation assistance services help Sailors and families adjust to new duty stations. Typical services include destination area information, intercultural relations training, settling-in services, and help in finding a home.

Help is available for civilian spouses in locating and obtaining local employment. Workshops are offered on how to search for a job, plan a career, write a résumé, have a successful job interview, and network.

New parents may take advantage of programs of identification, screening, home visitation, information, and referral for new and expectant parents. Prevention education programs and referrals to community support services are also offered.

Military OneSource

This service is available twenty-four hours a day and serves as a "one-stop" place to go whenever service members or their family members need assistance of any kind. This program can be accessed by calling **1-800-342-9647** or by visiting the Military OneSource website, **www.militaryonesource.mil.**

Morale, Welfare, and Recreation (MWR)

Morale, welfare, and recreation (MWR) programs provide many different recreational, social, and community support activities for all Navy personnel and their dependents.

Sports and fitness programs are designed to provide the Navy community with facilities and programs that enhance the overall quality of life and contribute to physical and mental readiness. The base-level sports and fitness program consists of informal or recreational sports (where individuals participate for fun and fitness) and organized (intramural) sports (i.e., individual, dual, team, and meet events) where the element of competition is included for events within and between individual commands. Some MWR programs also offer "Captain's Cup Field Day" competitions that are designed to build morale and teamwork while providing a means to have a great deal of fun.

The higher level sports program (armed forces sports program) is for active-duty members who demonstrate exceptional athletic abilities. Competitive forums for the higher level sports program include Navy trial camps, which are used to evaluate and select athletes for Navy teams and the armed forces championships. These two competitive forums provide a pathway for athletes to represent the armed forces in competition at the international level.

Outdoor recreation facilities may include outdoor equipment rental centers, parks, picnic areas, archery ranges, recreational vehicle (RV) parks, skeet and trap ranges, campgrounds, stables, marinas, beaches, swimming pools, cabins, cottages, off-base recreational areas, outdoor obstacle/challenge courses, paintball competition courses, and climbing walls. Instructional classes, outdoor equipment rentals, specialty equipment sales, organized group activities, special events, self-directed activities, and seasonal/geographic activities are also provided in various areas.

An information, tickets, and tours (ITT) program is located on virtually every shore installation in the Navy. ITT serves the military community with local recreation information (on and off base), entertainment tickets, and local tour services. Additionally, a hotel reservation system is available to assist travelers in finding quality, low-cost accommodations while on vacation.

Auto Skills Centers at some bases provide automotive enthusiasts with a quality, value-based program for the repair and maintenance of their vehicles. These are not service stations, but are facilities where patrons can work on their vehicles and learn automotive skills.

The Navy golf program is offered at over forty bases, providing course play, snack bars, pro shops, driving ranges, and cart rentals, as well as classes and personalized lessons.

The Navy bowling program offers open and league bowling, and special youth programs at many shore facilities.

The Navy Club System provides food, beverage, entertainment, and recreation programs at most bases.

Service Organizations

Many organizations provide assistance and services to Sailors and their families. Three of the most important are the Navy–Marine Corps Relief Society, the USO, and the American Red Cross.

NAVY–MARINE CORPS RELIEF SOCIETY

Supported entirely by private funds, the Navy–Marine Corps Relief Society assists Sailors/Marines and their families in time of need. Though not an official part of the Navy, this society is the Navy's own organization for taking care of its people. It is staffed and supported largely by retired/formal naval personnel and provides financial aid to those in need in the form of an interest-free loan, a grant, or a combination of both.

[21.2] Young bowlers at a Navy bowling alley on the base in Yokosuka, Japan

UNITED SERVICES ORGANIZATION (USO)

The USO provides programs, entertainment, and services at more than 180 USO locations worldwide, including Afghanistan, Djibouti, Kuwait, the United Arab Emirates, Germany, Italy, Japan, Iraq, South Korea and the United States. Since 1941 the USO has attended to servicemembers' morale by bringing entertainment to forward deployed forces, often hosting comedians, musicians, and athletes who voluntarily support those who defend.

AMERICAN RED CROSS

The American Red Cross supplies financial aid to naval personnel, does medical and psychiatric casework, and provides recreational services for the hospitalized. It also performs services in connection with dependency discharge, humanitarian transfer, emergency leave, leave extensions, and family welfare reports.

Some Important Numbers

Websites are wonderful things, but sometimes we need to actually talk to someone to get the support we need. Here are some important numbers to keep in a safe place for those times that you may (hopefully *not*) need them:

American Red Cross	1–877–272–7337
Military Crisis Hotline	1–800–273–8255
Sexual Assault Crisis Support	1–877–995–5247
National Domestic Violence Hotline	1–800–799–7233
National Suicide Prevention Lifeline	1–800–273–8255

EDUCATIONAL BENEFITS

Your professional education begins with recruit training and continues throughout your naval career, whether it lasts for four years or thirty. You may attend one or more Navy vocational/technical schools, may be able to receive college credit for military training and experience, and may also qualify for specialized training (such as nuclear engineering or diving school).

But the Navy also places very high value on personal development, recognizing that additional education is not only a potential morale factor but also can make for a better Sailor for reasons that should be obvious.

Men and women who have the desire and the ability to expand their personal educational horizons will find a number of programs offering correspondence courses, tuition assistance, college opportunities, high school equivalency, and other ways to improve themselves. You will discover that there is never a shortage of educational opportunities in the Navy.

Educational Programs

THE "GI BILL"

One of the best educational opportunities for servicemembers is the so-called GI Bill. This first came into existence after World War II and has gone through several iterations since, the most recent one being the "Post-9/11 GI Bill." Providing significant financial benefits to servicemembers—including tuition costs, a monthly housing stipend, and additional money for books and other expenses—the amounts available vary according to your state of enrollment (full or part time), number of units taken, and the amount of active-duty service. Too complicated to explain in detail here, this outstanding benefit is explained online at a number of websites—including **www.benefits.va.gov/gibill/**.

One important benefit that has been added to the Post-9/11 GI Bill is that some benefits can be transferred to dependents. This transferability option allows eligible servicemembers to transfer all or some unused benefits to their spouse or dependent children. The Department of Defense (DOD) determines whether or not you can transfer benefits to your family. Once the DOD approves benefits for transfer, the new beneficiaries apply for them at the Veterans Administration (VA). More information is available at **www.benefits.va.gov/.**

DEFENSE ACTIVITY FOR NON-TRADITIONAL EDUCATION SUPPORT (DANTES)

Despite the rather labored acronym, this program helps servicemembers pursue their education goals and earn degrees or certifications while continuing to serve. DANTES maintains three online catalogs that list distance learning courses and programs:

- An "Independent Study Catalog" lists more than six thousand high school, undergraduate, graduate level, and examination preparation courses from regionally accredited institutions.
- An "External Degree Catalog" lists academic programs available from regionally accredited colleges and universities that have little or no residency requirements for degree completion.
- A "Catalog of Nationally Accredited Distance Learning Programs" lists courses and degree programs from various national accrediting bodies. Subjects range from "Appliance Repair" to "Zionism and Judaism in Israel."

NAVY COLLEGE PROGRAM (NCP)

This program helps Sailors earn college degrees by providing them academic credit for Navy training, work experience, and off-duty education. The NCP also enables Sailors to obtain a college degree while on active duty. While the NCP is primarily geared toward enlisted Sailors, officers have access to some NCP components.

NAVY COLLEGE AT SEA PROGRAM (NCPACE)

Part of the Navy College Program, NCPACE allows Navy and Marine Corps servicemembers to pursue education while on sea-duty assignments. In many cases an instructor will be assigned to a ship or unit to provide on-site instruction. Both undergraduate and graduate courses are available through NCPACE.

[21.3] A petty officer first class receives a master of science degree during Southern Illinois University and Navy College's thirty-sixth annual graduation ceremony at Naval Base Coronado. The mission of Navy College is to provide academic support for Sailors across the fleet seeking technical and college education.

THE SEAMAN TO ADMIRAL-21 PROGRAM

STA-21 is a commissioning program that provides selected active-duty Sailors a full scholarship to attend a top-notch university. Through this program enlisted Sailors move on to careers as naval officers.

SERVICEMEMBERS OPPORTUNITY COLLEGES (SOC)

The Navy version of this degree program is known as "SOCNAV" and consists of colleges that offer associate's and bachelor's degree programs on, or accessible to, Navy installations worldwide. Each college in the network accepts credits from all the others. SOCNAV guarantees that Sailors can continue toward completion of a degree even though the Navy may transfer them to various locations.

MILITARY PROFESSIONAL STUDIES AND POSTGRADUATE PROGRAMS

The Department of Defense operates several graduate schools for military officers seeking to earn their postgraduate degrees. These include the following schools:

- Naval Post Graduate School
- Naval War College
- Army War College
- Air War College
- Air Force Institute of Technology
- Judge Advocate General's School of the Army
- National Defense Intelligence College
- School of Advanced Air and Space Studies
- Uniformed Services University of Health Sciences

Financial Assistance Programs for Educational Purposes

THE NAVY TUITION ASSISTANCE PROGRAM

Helping to cover up to 100 percent of the cost of an active-duty Sailor's education, this benefit is available to Sailors who meet the following qualifications:

- Must have served one year on board in his or her *first* permanent duty station (this requirement may be waived by CO)
- Will serve on active duty through the last day of the academic course
- Has passed the most recent physical fitness assessment or received a waiver
- Has taken her or his most recent advancement exam, if applicable, and is recommended for advancement or promotion
- Has not received a nonjudicial punishment (NJP) within six months, or is not pending administrative separation
- Is not under instruction in initial skills training or in a duty under instruction training status

NAVY–MARINE CORPS RELIEF SOCIETY'S EDUCATION ASSISTANCE PROGRAM

Offering interest-free loans and grants for undergraduate/post-secondary education at an accredited two- or four-year education, technical, or vocational institution in the United States, this financial assistance is available for children of active-duty, retired, or deceased Sailors and Marines and for spouses of active-duty and retired Sailors and Marines. Loan and grant amounts range from $500 to $3,000 per academic year to cover tuition, books, fees, room, and board. The money is paid directly to the student's academic institution and repayment of these interest-free loans must be by military payroll allotment.

THE NAVY COLLEGE FUND
Also known as a GI Bill "kicker," this financial resource is available to those who sign up for the GI Bill. Qualified applicants can receive, upon enlistment, more than $15,000 in addition to their GI Bill education funding.

STUDENT LOAN REPAYMENT PROGRAM (LRP)
College students or graduates who qualify receive, upon enlistment, up to $65,000 toward student loans.

STAYING OR LEAVING
The Navy is not forever. Sailors may stay for only one enlistment or may choose to make a full career of the Navy, remaining until it is time to retire. Once you complete your enlistment, you may be eligible to reenlist—sometimes called "shipping over." Reenlistment is not a right; it is a privilege. To earn that privilege, Sailors must be recommended for reenlistment by their commanding officer, be physically qualified, and meet certain standards of performance. Another consideration will be the "needs of the service"—how much your particular specialty is needed. In cases where the need is significant enough, you may be offered a sizable reenlistment bonus.

Reenlistment
Sailors may ask to reenlist for anywhere from two to six years. In cases where a reenlistment bonus is available, the more years you ship over for, the more money you will receive.

In some cases, Sailors may ask to extend their current enlistment rather than reenlist. Extensions may be granted at any time during an enlistment for special circumstances, such as wishing to qualify for advancement, or to make an upcoming cruise or deployment, or to gain entry into a service school or a special program. Extensions are executed in increments of one or more months, not to exceed a total of forty-eight months on any single enlistment.

Reenlistment ceremonies can be done virtually anywhere that is safe. The Navy gladly accommodates unusual venues to enhance the memorable experience.

Navy Reserve

One other option—between active duty and separation—is service in the Navy Reserve. This is a way that you can leave active duty to pursue a civilian career but continue to serve and receive certain benefits. Although fewer or modified, there are many benefits that come with reserve service. But it is very important to realize that with those benefits come obligations, including the possibility of being called to active duty in times of need.

Discharges

When Sailors leave the Navy, whether voluntarily or involuntarily, they receive a formal discharge, and the type of discharge they receive can have a significant effect on their eligibility for continued benefits. Certain discharges eliminate some veterans' rights and benefits, and many employers will reject a former military person who cannot produce an honorable-discharge certificate.

[21.4] An unusual reenlistment ceremony taking place in the Gulf of Aqaba

An *honorable discharge* means what it sounds like: separation from the service with honor. It is given to Sailors who have performed well and are leaving the service voluntarily at the end of their obligated service or are being asked to leave for reasons of disability or for the convenience of the government (fewer Sailors authorized, for example). To receive an honorable discharge, the final average of a Sailor's performance marks must meet minimum specifications and he or she cannot have been convicted by a general court-martial, or convicted more than once by a special court-martial.

General discharges are given under honorable conditions for those whose conduct and performance, though technically satisfactory, has not been good enough to deserve an honorable discharge.

The discharges you especially do not want are (in order of increasing severity), the *undesirable discharge* (UD), *bad conduct discharge* (BCD), and *dishonorable discharge* (DD). The UD is given by administrative action for misconduct or breach of security, the BCD only by approved sentence of a general or special court-martial, and the DD only by approved sentence of a general court-martial.

Retirement

Although it is unusual for young people to think seriously about such things, the retirement benefits of military service are something you should consider before leaving the Navy. Too complicated to go into in detail here—and frequently up for review for possible changes—retirement from military service has always been worthwhile, occurring earlier than in most civilian occupations and generous enough to warrant serious consideration. No one should use this benefit as the sole reason for remaining in the Navy, but if you are considering the pros and cons of remaining in service or leaving the Navy, this should be one of the considerations. You should talk with your career counselor to get the latest information about this important benefit.

Thrift Savings Plan

Another thing to consider is the Thrift Savings Plan offered by the Navy. This is an added benefit that you can choose to supplement your retirement. The plan allows you to have some of your pay automatically deducted and invested. There are several options available, and a visit to the Command Financial Specialist (CFS) is the best way to find out the details.

[**21.5**] A chief petty officer and his family pass through side boys at his retirement ceremony.

Adjusting

Whether you leave the Navy after only one "hitch" or eventually retire from service, there will be a period of adjustment once you leave naval service. There is a certain amount of social and psychological shock that comes from leaving military society, where rules and paths are well defined. Even though you were a civilian before you joined the Navy, going back to the civilian world will take some adjustment. You always looked sharp in your uniforms and passed every inspection with flying colors, but you may find that dressing yourself for a new job is a real challenge. You will probably be surprised at how missing a little sleep is a much bigger deal to civilians than it is to military personnel. You may find that what is early morning to your civilian coworkers is midday to you. You will probably get some quizzical looks the first time you ask a coworker where the scuttlebutt is or explain that you are "going topside for a minute."

Don't expect this transition to happen overnight. It may take weeks, months, or even longer. The important thing to remember is that it is perfectly normal and that you are not the first who has had to make this adjustment.

It is important to bear in mind that your years of service in the Navy have strengthened you as a person, taught you a great many things, and prepared you to handle many of the challenges of life. You will likely have learned the importance of leadership and followership, and you will know the importance of self-discipline and a strong work ethic. You should not be cocky, but you should be confident. As a former Sailor, there isn't much you can't handle.

THE GREATEST BENEFIT

Perhaps the single greatest benefit that Sailors receive while serving in the U.S. Navy is the satisfaction of knowing that they are serving their nation. By being a part of the finest Navy the world has ever seen, whether in the throes of combat or carrying out the daily routine, you are helping to preserve freedom in the United States of America, and that is a special satisfaction not found in many walks of life.

Another benefit that most Sailors enjoy is the opportunity to travel, to do for free what other people pay significant sums of money to do. But there is another, more significant, aspect to travel as well. You will likely return from your travels with a much deeper appreciation of what you have here in this great nation. Seeing other parts of the world enlarges one's vision, offers unique insights into different cultures, and makes clear that we are privileged to be inhabitants of this wondrous planet. But it also allows us to compare and contrast, and with few exceptions, the end result is a great surge of gratitude that *we are Americans!*

We are incredibly fortunate to have vast resources at hand and a standard of living that is the envy of most of the world. We have a form of government that, although it cannot solve every problem and may not always make the best choices, is rooted in the soil of individual freedom and human rights, and has a long record of striving to do what is right. One does not have to go very far beyond our borders to realize how fortunate we are, to compare how others live and what many must endure, and serving in the U.S. Navy means you are likely to have that opportunity.

To enjoy such privileges is a pleasure; to *defend them is an honor.*

TABS

Tabs consist of reference information that you will find useful as you go about the business of being a Sailor:

- much like *appendices* in traditional books
- designed to be referred to for specific information rather than completely read
- identified by numbers corresponding to the associated chapter and letters for reference purposes
- also identified by a title that briefly describes what it contains

Introductory Tabs (identified by a number only) provide some additional material, including a listing of major topics related to the Tab and its associated chapter and lists of additional references for those who care to learn more about the topics covered.

TABS by Subject Matter

SUBJECT	TAB
3M Periodicity Codes	11-B
Addressing Military Personnel	5-A
Aircraft, Identifying Military	16-B
Anchor Chain Identification System	12-C

SUBJECT	TAB
Anchoring Commands	12-D
Awards, Precedence	6-I
Awards, Wearing	6-H
Bells, Ship's	13-D
Blocks and Tackles	12-E
Boat Customs and Etiquette	12-F
Classes of Fire	15-B
Classifications of Ships	10-B
Coast Guard Officer Shoulder Boards and Sleeve Markings	6-E
Code of Conduct	4-A
Conditions of Readiness (Cruising)	13-B
Conditions of Readiness (Material)	15-A
Core Values of the U.S. Navy	1-B
Correspondence (Letter Format)	19-C
Cruising Conditions	13-B
DOD Organization	8-A
Electronics Designation System	17-C
Enlisted Rank Devices of the Other Armed Services	6-B
Fire, Classes	15-B
Flag, Folding	3-A
Flags, Signal and Pennants	20-E
Folding the Flag	3-A
Force Protection Conditions	9-A
Forms of Address in the Armed Services	5-A
FPCONs	9-A
General Orders of a Sentry	13-A
General Rates	5-C
Identifying Military Aircraft	16-B

SUBJECT	TAB
Joint Electronics Type Designation System	17-C
Letter Format	19-C
Line and Staff Corps Devices	6-G
Line-Handling Commands	12-B
Material Conditions of Readiness	15-A
MC Systems	20-A
Message Format	19-D
Mooring Line Configurations and Terms	12-A
Morse Code	20-D
Naval Aircraft, Types	16-A
Naval Weapons, Types	17-B
Navy Enlisted Sleeve Markings	6-A
Navy Officer Shoulder Boards and Sleeve Markings	6-D
Navy Organization	8-A
Navy Publications	19-A
Navy Time	1-C
Officer Collar, Cap, and Shoulder Rank Devices	6-C
Organization, DOD	8-A
Organization, Navy	8-A
Pay Grades	5-A
Phonetic Alphabet	20-C
Precedence of Awards	6-I
Prowords, Radiotelephone	20-G
Publications	19-A
Radiotelephone Prowords	20-G
Ranks and Rates	5-A
Ratings	5-B
Sailor's Creed	1-A

TAB 1 Welcome Aboard

Because the Navy is both a military service and a sea service, to make the transition from civilian to Sailor you must learn the ways of both.

Major Topics Covered:

- ⚓ Chain of Command
- ⚓ Core Values
- ⚓ Navy Terminology
- ⚓ Dates and Time
- ⚓ Liberty and Leave

To Learn More:

- ⚓ www.usni.org/BlueAndGoldProfessionalBooks/TheBluejackets Manual
- ⚓ Recruit Training Command, www.bootcamp.navy.mil/
- ⚓ Navy Terms, www.navy.com/glossary.html
- ⚓ Navy Traditions, www.navy.mil/navydata/traditions/html/navy term.html
- ⚓ *Honor, Courage, Commitment: Navy Boot Camp* by J. F. Leahy (Naval Institute Press, 2013)
- ⚓ *Basic Training for Dummies* by Rod Powers (John Wiley & Sons, 2011)
- ⚓ *The Parent's Guide to the U.S. Navy* by Thomas J. Cutler (Naval Institute Press, 2016)
- ⚓ *Naval Ceremonies, Customs, and Traditions*, 6th ed., by Royal W. Connell and William P. Mack (Naval Institute Press, 2004)
- ⚓ Post-RTC Training, www.navy.com/about/locations/training -centers.html
- ⚓ *Time Conversion* (NAVEDTRA 14252)

Associated Tabs:

- ○ TAB 1-A: The Sailor's Creed
- ○ TAB 1-B: The Core Values of the United States Navy
- ○ TAB 1-C: Navy Time

1-A The Sailor's Creed

I am a United States Sailor.
I will support and defend the Constitution of the
United States of America and I will obey the orders
of those appointed over me.
I represent the fighting spirit of the Navy and those
who have gone before me to defend freedom and
democracy around the world.
I proudly serve my country's Navy combat team
with Honor, Courage, and Commitment.
I am committed to excellence and fair treatment of all.

1-B The Core Values of the U.S. Navy

Throughout its history, the Navy has successfully met all its challenges. America's naval service began during the American Revolution, when on 13 October 1775 the Continental Congress authorized a few small ships, creating the Continental Navy. Esek Hopkins was appointed commander in chief and twenty-two officers were commissioned, including John Paul Jones.

From those early days of naval service, certain bedrock principles or core values have carried on to today. They consist of three basic principles.

Honor: "I represent the fighting spirit of the Navy . . ." Accordingly, we will: conduct ourselves in the highest ethical manner in all relationships with peers, superiors, and subordinates; be honest and truthful in our dealings with each other, and with those outside the Navy; be willing to make honest recommendations and accept those of junior personnel; encourage new ideas and deliver the bad news, even when it is unpopular; abide by an uncompromising code of integrity, taking responsibility for our actions and keeping our word; fulfill or exceed our legal and ethical responsibilities in our public and personal lives twenty-four hours a day. Illegal or improper behavior or even the appearance of such behavior will not be tolerated. We are accountable for our professional and personal behavior. We will be mindful of the privilege to serve our fellow Americans.

Courage: "I will support and defend . . ." Accordingly, we will: have courage to meet the demands of our profession and the mission when it is hazardous, demanding, or otherwise difficult; make decisions in the best interest of the navy and the nation, without regard to personal consequences; meet these challenges while adhering to a higher standard of personal conduct and decency; be loyal to our nation, ensuring the resources entrusted to us are used in an honest, careful, and efficient way. Courage is the value that gives us the moral and mental strength to do what is right, even in the face of personal or professional adversity.

Commitment: "I will obey the orders . . ." Accordingly, we will: demand respect up and down the chain of command; care for the safety, professional, personal, and spiritual well-being of our people; show respect toward all people without regard to race, religion, or gender; treat each individual with human dignity; be committed to positive change and constant improvement; exhibit the highest degree of moral character, technical excellence, quality, and competence in what we have been trained to do. The day-to-day duty of every Navy man and woman is to work together as a team to improve the quality of our work, our people and ourselves.

These are the CORE VALUES of the United States Navy.

1-C Navy Time

Civilian time	(24-hour clock)	Spoken as
Midnight	0000 or 2400	
1:00 a.m.	0100	"Zero-one-hundred" or "Oh-one-hundred"
2:00 a.m.	0200	"Zero-two-hundred" or "Oh-two-hundred"
3:00 a.m.	0300	
3:30 a.m.	0330	"Zero-three-thirty" or "Oh-three-thirty"
4:00 a.m.	0400	

Civilian time	(24-hour clock)	Spoken as
5:00 a.m.	0500	
6:00 a.m.	0600	
6:15 a.m.	0615	"Zero-six-fifteen" or "Oh-six-fifteen"
7:00 a.m.	0700	
8:00 a.m.	0800	
9:00 a.m.	0900	
10:00 a.m.	1000	"Ten-hundred"
11:00 a.m.	1100	"Eleven-hundred"
11:47 a.m.	1147	"Eleven-forty-seven"
12 Noon	1200	
1:00 p.m.	1300	"Thirteen-hundred"
2:00 p.m.	1400	
3:00 p.m.	1500	
3:59 p.m.	1559	"Fifteen-fifty-nine"
4:00 p.m.	1600	
5:00 p.m.	1700	
6:00 p.m.	1800	
7:00 p.m.	1900	
8:00 p.m.	2000	"Twenty-hundred"
8:01 p.m.	2001	"Twenty-oh-one"
9:00 p.m.	2100	
10:00 p.m.	2200	
11:00 p.m.	2300	"Twenty-three-hundred"
12 Midnight	2400 or 0000	"Twenty-four-hundred" or "Zero-zero-zero-zero"
12:01 a.m.	0001	"Zero-zero-zero-one"

TAB 2 Military Drill

Close order drill is an efficient way to keep groups of people together in an orderly fashion, it is an effective method of promoting discipline, and it provides experience in giving and following commands.

Major Topics Covered:

- ⚓ Formations
- ⚓ Commands
- ⚓ Facing Movements
- ⚓ Marching

To Learn More:

- ⚓ **www.usni.org/BlueAndGoldProfessionalBooks/TheBluejackets Manual**
- ⚓ *Basic Military Requirements* (NAVEDTRA 14325)
- ⚓ *Marine Corps Drill and Ceremonies Manual* (MCO P5060.20), **www.usna.edu/Chapel/_files/documents/information/MCO%20 P5060%2020%20W%20CH%201_11.pdf**

TAB 3 Navy Customs, Courtesies, and Ceremonies

Because the Navy is both a military service and a sea service, to make the transition from civilian to Sailor you must learn the ways of both.

Major Topics Covered:

- ⚓ Saluting
- ⚓ Addressing Military Personnel
- ⚓ Flags and Flag Etiquette
- ⚓ Honors
- ⚓ Shipboard Customs
- ⚓ Courtesies
- ⚓ Ceremonies

To Learn More:

- ⚓ www.usni.org/BlueAndGoldProfessionalBooks/TheBluejackets Manual
- ⚓ *Basic Military Requirements* (NAVEDTRA 14325)
- ⚓ *Flags, Pennants, & Customs* (NTP 13)
- ⚓ *Military Requirements for Petty Officers Third and Second Class* (NAVEDTRA 14504)
- ⚓ *Naval Ceremonies, Customs, and Traditions*, 6th ed., by Royal W. Connell, USN, and William P. Mack (Naval Institute Press, 2004)
- ⚓ *United States Navy Regulations*, Chapter 12, "Flags, Pennants, Honors, Ceremonies, and Customs"
- ⚓ Flag Etiquette, www.military.com/flag-day/flag-ettiquette-dos -and-donts.html
- ⚓ *Social Usage and Protocol Handbook: A Guide for Personnel of the U.S. Navy* (OPNAVINST 1710.7A)
- ⚓ *Signalman 3 & 2* (NAVEDTRA 14244)

Associated Tabs:

- ○ TAB 3-A: Folding the Flag

3-A Folding the Flag

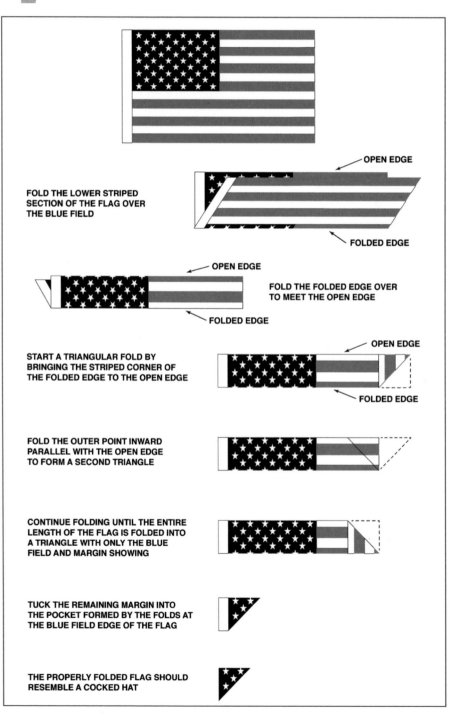

FOLD THE LOWER STRIPED SECTION OF THE FLAG OVER THE BLUE FIELD

OPEN EDGE

FOLDED EDGE

OPEN EDGE

FOLD THE FOLDED EDGE OVER TO MEET THE OPEN EDGE

FOLDED EDGE

START A TRIANGULAR FOLD BY BRINGING THE STRIPED CORNER OF THE FOLDED EDGE TO THE OPEN EDGE

OPEN EDGE

FOLDED EDGE

FOLD THE OUTER POINT INWARD PARALLEL WITH THE OPEN EDGE TO FORM A SECOND TRIANGLE

CONTINUE FOLDING UNTIL THE ENTIRE LENGTH OF THE FLAG IS FOLDED INTO A TRIANGLE WITH ONLY THE BLUE FIELD AND MARGIN SHOWING

TUCK THE REMAINING MARGIN INTO THE POCKET FORMED BY THE FOLDS AT THE BLUE FIELD EDGE OF THE FLAG

THE PROPERLY FOLDED FLAG SHOULD RESEMBLE A COCKED HAT

TAB 4 Personal Conduct

Good order and discipline are vital to military organizations because military service often entails performing your duties under difficult conditions, creating special challenges not always encountered in civilian walks of life. Three simple rules serve as primary guidance:

- Always be aware that you are a representative of the Navy and your nation.
- Always assume that someone is watching.
- Never do anything you would not want to read about online or in the newspaper or that you would not want to have to explain to your commanding officer or the people who raised you.

Major Topics Covered:

- ⚓ The Law of Armed Conflict
- ⚓ Code of Conduct for Members of the Armed Forces of the United States
- ⚓ Uniform Code of Military Justice
    - ~ Non-judicial punishment
    - ~ Courts-Martial
    - ~ Right to Counsel
- ⚓ Personal Relations
    - ~ Ethnic Discrimination
    - ~ Sexual Harassment
    - ~ Fraternization
    - ~ Hazing
- ⚓ Public Relations & Overseas Diplomacy

To Learn More:

- ⚓ www.usni.org/BlueAndGoldProfessionalBooks/TheBluejackets Manual
- ⚓ *Basic Military Requirements* (NAVEDTRA 14325)
- ⚓ *Legalman* (NAVEDTRA 14351)
- ⚓ Law of Armed Conflict, www.icrc.org/eng/assets/files/other/law1 _final.pdf

- ⚓ Law of Armed Conflict, archive.defense.gov/pubs/law-of-war -manual-june-2015.pdf
- ⚓ Law of Armed Conflict, www.loc.gov/rr/frd/Military_Law/pdf /LOAC-Deskbook-2012.pdf
- ⚓ Uniform Code of Military Justice, www.ucmj.us/
- ⚓ Navy Judge Advocate General (JAG), www.jag.navy.mil
- ⚓ Navy Judge Advocate General Manual (JAGMAN), www.jag.navy .mil/library/instructions/JAGMAN2012.pdf
- ⚓ Equal Opportunity, www.public.navy.mil/bupers-npc/support /21st_Century_Sailor/equal_opportunity/Pages/default.aspx
- ⚓ *Navy Equal Opportunity Policy* (OPNAV INST 5354.1F)
- ⚓ Navy Sexual Assault Prevention & Response, www.navy.mil/local /sapr

Associated Tabs:

- ○ TAB 4-A: Code of Conduct for Members of the Armed Forces of the United States

4-A Code of Conduct for Members of the Armed Forces of the United States

For an explanation of each of the articles in the Code, see Chapter 4.

ARTICLE I   I am an American, fighting in the forces which guard my country and our way of life. I am prepared to give my life in their defense. ✦

ARTICLE II   I will never surrender of my own free will. If in command, I will never surrender the members of my command while they still have the means to resist. ✦

ARTICLE III   If I am captured I will continue to resist, by all means available. I will make every effort to escape and aid others to escape. I will accept neither parole nor special favors from the enemy. ✦

ARTICLE IV If I become a prisoner of war, I will keep faith with my fellow prisoners. I will give no information or take part in any actions which might be harmful to my comrades. If I am senior, I will take command. If not, I will obey the lawful orders of those appointed over me and will back them up in every way. ✦

ARTICLE V When questioned, should I become a prisoner of war, I am required to give name, rank, service number, and date of birth. I will evade answering further questions to the utmost of my ability. I will make no oral or written statements disloyal to my country and its allies or harmful to their cause. ✦

ARTICLE VI I will never forget that I am an American, fighting for freedom, responsible for my actions, and dedicated to the principles which made my country free. I will trust in my God and in the United States of America. ✦

TAB 5 Navy Titles

There are many titles associated with service in the Navy. And to further complicate things, the different military services share some titles and use different ones for others. Understanding all of this can be challenging.

Major Topics Covered:

- Billets
- Pay Grades
- Ranks
- Naval Enlisted Classification (NEC) Codes
- Warfare Specialties
- Forms of Address
- Rates and Ratings

To Learn More:

- www.usni.org/BlueAndGoldProfessionalBooks/TheBluejackets Manual
- *Basic Military Requirements* (NAVEDTRA 14325)
- *Personnel Specialist: Basic Training Manual* (NAVEDTRA 15006A)
- Officers' Ranks, www.navy.mil/navydata/ranks/officers/o-rank.html
- Ratings, http://www.public.navy.mil/bupers-npc/organization/nav mac/workforceclassification/Documents/Enlisted%20Navy%20 Ratings%20List.pdf

Associated Tabs:

- TAB 5-A: Pay Grades, Ranks, Rates, and Forms of Address in the Armed Forces
- TAB 5-B: Navy Ratings
- TAB 5-C: General Rates
- TAB 5-D: Examples of Enlisted Career Advancement

5-A Pay Grades, Ranks, Rates, and Forms of Address in the Armed Forces

NAVY

PAY GRADE	RANKS/ RATES	ABBREVIATIONS[a]	DEAR—[b]	DIRECT ADDRESS[c]
O-11	Fleet Admiral	FADM	Not currently in use.	
O-10	Admiral	ADM	Admiral	Admiral
O-9	Vice Admiral	VADM	Admiral	Admiral
O-8	Rear Admiral (Upper Half)	RADM	Admiral	Admiral
O-7	Rear Admiral (Lower Half)	RDML	Admiral	Admiral
O-6	Captain	CAPT	Captain	Captain
O-5	Commander	CDR	Commander	Commander
O-4	Lieutenant Commander	LCDR	Commander	Commander
O-3	Lieutenant	LT	Lieutenant	Lieutenant
O-2	Lieutenant (Junior Grade)	LTJG	Lieutenant	Lieutenant
O-1	Ensign	ENS	Ensign	Ensign
W-5	Chief Warrant Officer	CWO5	Chief Warrant Officer	Warrants are usually addressed by their specialty; as in "Boatswain," "Gunner," etc.

PAY GRADE	RANKS/ RATES	ABBREVIATIONS[a]	DEAR—[b]	DIRECT ADDRESS[c]
W-4	Chief Warrant Officer	CWO4	Chief Warrant Officer	
W-3	Chief Warrant Officer	CWO3	Chief Warrant Officer	
W-2	Chief Warrant Officer	CWO2	Chief Warrant Officer	
W-1	Warrant Officer	Not currently in use.		
E-9	Master Chief Petty Officer of the Navy	MCPON	MCPON	MCPON (pronounced "mick-pon")
"	Fleet Master Chief Petty Officer	FLTCM	Fleet Master Chief	Fleet
"	Force Master Chief Petty Officer	FORCM	Force Master Chief	Force
"	Command Master Chief Petty Officer	CMDCM	Command Master Chief	Master Chief
"	Master Chief Petty Officer	MCPO	Master Chief	Master Chief
E-8	Senior Chief Petty Officer	SCPO	Senior Chief	Senior
E-7	Chief Petty Officer	CPO	Chief	Chief
E-6	Petty Officer First Class	PO1	Petty Officer	Petty Officer

PAY GRADE	RANKS/ RATES	ABBREVIATIONS[a]	DEAR—[b]	DIRECT ADDRESS[c]
E-5	Petty Officer Second Class	PO2	Petty Officer	Petty Officer
E-4	Petty Officer Third Class	PO3	Petty Officer	Petty Officer
E-3	Seaman	SN	Seaman[d]	Seaman[d]
E-2	Seaman Apprentice	SA	Seaman[d]	Seaman[d]
E-1	Seaman Recruit	SR	Seaman[d]	Seaman[d]

[a] Use the "Abbreviation" column for addressees on letters and envelopes (e.g., "LCDR Stephen Decatur USN").

[b] Use the "Dear" column (followed by person's surname) for salutations and introductions (e.g., "Dear Commander Decatur").

[c] Use the "Address" column when addressing someone directly (e.g., "Good morning, Commander," or, "Force, the admiral wants to see you on the flag bridge").

[d] Note that, depending upon occupational specialty, "Seaman" is replaced with "Fireman," "Airman," "Constructionman," or "Hospitalman."

MARINE CORPS

PAY GRADE	RANKS	ABBREVIATIONS	DIRECT ADDRESS[a]
O-10	General	Gen	General
O-9	Lieutenant General	LtGen	General
O-8	Major General	MajGen	General
O-7	Brigadier General	BGen	General
O-6	Colonel	Col	Colonel
O-5	Lieutenant Colonel	LtCol	Colonel
O-4	Major	Maj	Major

PAY GRADE	RANKS	ABBREVIATIONS	DIRECT ADDRESS[a]
O-3	Captain	Capt	Captain
O-2	First Lieutenant	1stLt	Lieutenant
O-1	Second Lieutenant	2ndLt	Lieutenant
W-5	Chief Warrant Officer	CWO5	Chief Warrant Officer (Gunner)
W-4	Chief Warrant Officer	CWO4	Chief Warrant Officer (Gunner)
W-3	Chief Warrant Officer	CWO3	Chief Warrant Officer (Gunner)
W-2	Chief Warrant Officer	CWO2	Chief Warrant Officer (Gunner)
W-1	Warrant Officer	WO	Warrant Officer (Gunner)
E-9	Sergeant Major of the Marine Corps	SgtMaj	Sergeant Major
E-9	Sergeant Major	SgtMaj	Sergeant Major
"	Master Gunnery Sergeant	MGySgt	Master Gunnery Sergeant (Master Guns)
E-8	Master Sergeant	MSgt	Master Sergeant (Top)
"	First Sergeant	1stSgt	First Sergeant
E-7	Gunnery Sergeant	GySgt	Gunnery Sergeant (Gunny)
E-6	Staff Sergeant	SSgt	Staff Sergeant
E-5	Sergeant	Sgt	Sergeant
E-4	Corporal	Cpl	Corporal

PAY GRADE	RANKS	ABBREVIATIONS	DIRECT ADDRESS[a]
E-3	Lance Corporal	LCpl	Lance Corporal
E-2	Private First Class	PFC	Private First Class (PFC)
E-1	Private	Pvt	Private

[a] Use the "Address" column when addressing someone directly (e.g., "Good morning, Gunny"). Addresses in parentheses are used informally.

COAST GUARD

PAY GRADE	RANKS (AND RATES)	ABBREVIATIONS	DIRECT ADDRESS[a]
O-10	Admiral	ADM	Admiral
O-9	Vice Admiral	VADM	Admiral
O-8	Rear Admiral (Upper Half)	RADM	Admiral
O-7	Rear Admiral (Lower Half)	RDML	Admiral
O-6	Captain	CAPT	Captain
O-5	Commander	CDR	Commander
O-4	Lieutenant Commander	LCDR	Commander
O-3	Lieutenant	LT	Lieutenant
O-2	Lieutenant (Junior Grade)	LTJG	Lieutenant
O-1	Ensign	ENS	Ensign
W-4	Chief Warrant Officer	CWO4	All warrants are addressed as "Mister" or "Ms."
W-3	Chief Warrant Officer	CWO3	
W-2	Chief Warrant Officer	CWO2	

PAY GRADE	RANKS (AND RATES)	ABBREVIATIONS	DIRECT ADDRESS[a]
W-1	Warrant Officer	Not currently in use	
E-9	Master Chief Petty Officer of the Coast Guard	MCPOCG	MCPOCG (pronounced "mick-pog")
"	Area Command Master Chief Petty Officer	CMC	Master Chief
"	Command Master Chief Petty Officer	CMC	Master Chief
"	Master Chief Petty Officer	MCPO[b]	Master Chief
E-8	Command Senior Chief Petty Officer	CSC	Senior Chief
"	Senior Chief Petty Officer	SCPO[b]	Senior
E-7	Command Chief Petty Officer	CCPO	Chief
"	Chief Petty Officer	CPO[b]	Chief
E-6	Petty Officer First Class	PO1[b]	Petty Officer
E-5	Petty Officer Second Class	PO2[b]	Petty Officer
E-4	Petty Officer Third Class	PO3[b]	Petty Officer
E-3	Seaman[c]	SN (AN or FN)	Seaman[c]

PAY GRADE	RANKS (AND RATES)	ABBREVIATIONS	DIRECT ADDRESS[a]
E-2	Seaman Apprentice[c]	SA (AA or FA)	Seaman[c]
E-1	Seaman Recruit[c]	SR	Seaman

[a] Use the "Direct Address" column when addressing someone directly (e.g., "Good morning, Commander," or "Master Chief, the admiral wants to see you on the flag bridge").

[b] Rating abbreviations (such as BMC or QM2, etc.) are used more often than the rate abbreviations CPO, PO2, and so on.

[c] Note that, depending upon occupational specialty, "Seaman" is replaced with "Airman" or "Fireman."

ARMY

PAY GRADE	RANKS	ABBREVIATIONS	DIRECT ADDRESS[a]
O-10	General	GEN	General
O-9	Lieutenant General	LTG	General
O-8	Major General	MG	General
O-7	Brigadier General	BG	General
O-6	Colonel	COL	Colonel
O-5	Lieutenant Colonel	LTC	Colonel
O-4	Major	MAJ	Major
O-3	Captain	CPT	Captain
O-2	First Lieutenant	1LT	Lieutenant
O-1	Second Lieutenant	2LT	Lieutenant
W-5	Chief Warrant Officer	CW5	Mister

PAY GRADE	RANKS	ABBREVIATIONS	DIRECT ADDRESS[a]
W-4	Chief Warrant Officer	CW4	Mister
W-3	Chief Warrant Officer	CW3	Mister
W-2	Chief Warrant Officer	CW2	Mister
W-1	Warrant Officer	WO1	Mister
E-9	Sergeant Major of the Army	SMA	Sergeant Major
"	Command Sergeant Major	CSM	Sergeant Major
"	Sergeant Major	SGM	Sergeant Major
E-8	Master Sergeant	MSG	Master Sergeant
"	First Sergeant	1SG	First Sergeant
E-7	Platoon Sergeant	PSG	Sergeant
"	Sergeant First Class	SFC	Sergeant
E-6	Staff Sergeant	SSG	Sergeant
E-5	Sergeant	SGT	Sergeant
E-4	Corporal	CPL	Corporal
E-4	Specialist	SP4	Specialist
E-3	Private First Class	PFC	Private
E-2	Private Second Class	PV2	Private
E-1	Private	PVT	Private

[a] Use the "Address" column when addressing someone directly (e.g., "Good morning, Sergeant").

AIR FORCE

PAY GRADE	RANKS	ABBREVIATIONS	DIRECT ADDRESS[a]
O-10	General	Gen	General
O-9	Lieutenant General	Lt Gen	General
O-8	Major General	Maj Gen	General
O-7	Brigadier General	Brig Gen	General
O-6	Colonel	Col	Colonel
O-5	Lieutenant Colonel	Lt Col	Colonel
O-4	Major	Maj	Major
O-3	Captain	Capt	Captain
O-2	First Lieutenant	1st Lt	Lieutenant
O-1	Second Lieutenant	2nd Lt	Lieutenant
W1–5[b]			
E-9	Chief Master Sergeant of the Air Force	CMSAF	Chief
"	Chief Master Sergeant	CMSgt	Chief
E-8	Senior Master Sergeant	SMSgt	Sergeant
E-7	Master Sergeant	MSgt	Sergeant
E-6	Technical Sergeant	TSgt	Sergeant
E-5	Staff Sergeant	SSgt	Sergeant
E-4	Senior Airman	SrA	Airman

PAY GRADE	RANKS	ABBREVIATIONS	DIRECT ADDRESS[a]
E-3	Airman First Class	A1C	Airman
E-2	Airman	Amn	Airman
E-1	Airman Basic	AB	Airman

[a] Use the "Address" column when addressing someone directly (e.g., "Good morning, General").

[b] There are no warrant officers in the Air Force.

 ### 5-B Navy Ratings

A rating is an occupational specialty in the Navy. You might call it a "job" or an "occupation" in the civilian world. Before Sailors can qualify for a rating, they must first work their way through the "general apprenticeship levels" (E-1 to E-3), which helps prepare them for a rating. In order to advance beyond the E-3 pay grade, Sailors must have a rating. Once promoted to E-4, they have a rating and, except in special circumstances, will likely keep that rating for the rest of their careers.

Each of the Navy's ratings is identified by a two- or three-letter abbreviation such as ET (for electronics technician) or GSM (for gas turbine systems technician—mechanical). Each rating is further identified by a unique symbol, called a specialty mark, that is included on a rating badge worn on the left sleeve of dress uniforms.

There are two categories of ratings: general and service. Occupations for pay grades E-4 through E-9 are called general ratings. Each general rating has a distinctive badge. Examples of general ratings are operations specialist, gunner's mate, and logistics specialist.

Some general ratings are further subdivided into service ratings, which indicate some additional specialization. For example, the general rating of gas turbine systems technician (GS) is subdivided into two service ratings: GSE (electrical) and GSM (mechanical). There can be service ratings at any petty officer level; however, they are most common with E-4s through E-6s. In the higher pay grades (E-8 and E-9), service ratings sometimes merge into a general rating. For example, those gas turbine systems technicians who specialize in electrical and mechanical systems (GSE and GSM) become simply GSs once they are promoted to senior chief petty officer (E-8), because a senior chief gas turbine systems technician needs to know about both the electrical and mechanical systems.

General ratings are sometimes combined at the E-9 level, when the work is similar. For example, the work done by a senior chief utilitiesman and that done by a senior chief construction electrician is very similar, so when these individuals are promoted to master chief, both become master chief utilitiesmen. These are referred to as compression ratings.

Specialty marks were added to enlisted uniforms beginning in 1866 and were often designed to represent an instrument originally used to perform a particular task. For example, the mark for a quartermaster (QM), who works mainly in navigation, was a ship's helm, while the boatswain's mate (BM) mark used two crossed anchors. The custom of representing the type of work with a specialty mark for each rating continues, often using traditional (sometimes obsolete) instruments, such as crossed quills for yeoman (YN), who performs administrative work in the Navy, even though quills are no longer used as writing instruments.

Each rating—with its specialty mark—is briefly described below. When a general rating also has service ratings, these are included in the description. Compression ratings are also included. Those ratings that merge into compression ratings are also noted.

AB

Cross anchors, winged

Aviation Boatswain's Mate

ABs operate, maintain, and repair aircraft catapults, arresting gear, and barricades. They operate and maintain fuel- and lube-oil transfer systems. ABs direct aircraft on the flight deck and in hangar bays before launch and after recovery. They use tow tractors to position planes and operate support equipment used to start aircraft. (**Service ratings:** ABE [launching and recovery equipment]; ABF [fuels]; ABH [aircraft handling])

AC

Microphone, winged

Air Traffic Controller

ACs assist in the essential safe, orderly, and speedy flow of air traffic by directing and controlling aircraft under visual (VFR) and instrument (IFR) flight rules. They operate field lighting systems, communicate with aircraft, and furnish pilots with information regarding traffic, navigation, and weather conditions. They operate and adjust GCA (ground-controlled approach) systems. They interpret targets on radar screens and plot aircraft positions.

AD

Two-bladed
propeller, winged

Aviation Machinist's Mate

ADs maintain jet aircraft engines and associated equipment or engage in any one of several types of aircraft maintenance activities. ADs maintain, service, adjust, and replace aircraft engines and accessories, as well as perform the duties of flight engineers. (**Compression rating:** AF [Aviation Maintenanceman])

AE

Globe, winged

Aviation Electrician's Mate

AEs maintain, adjust, and repair electrical-power generating, converting, and distributing systems, as well as lighting, control, and indicating systems in aircraft. They also install and maintain wiring and flight and engine instrument systems, which include automatic flight control, stabilization, aircraft compass, attitude reference, and inertial navigation systems. (**Compression rating:** AV [Avionics Technician])

AG

Circle on vertical
arrow, winged

Aerographer's Mate

The Navy has its own weather forecasters, AGs, who are trained in meteorology and the use of aerological instruments that monitor such weather characteristics as air pressure, temperature, humidity, wind speed, and wind direction. They prepare weather maps and forecasts, analyze atmospheric conditions to determine the best flight levels for aircraft, and measure wind and air density to increase the accuracy of anti-aircraft firing, shore bombardment, and delivery of weapons by aircraft.

AM

Crossed mauls,
winged

Aviation Structural Mechanic

The maintenance and repair of aircraft parts (wings, fuselage, tail, control surfaces, landing gear, and attending mechanisms) are performed by AMs working with metals, alloys, and plastics. AMs maintain and repair safety equipment and hydraulic systems. (**Service rating:** AME [safety equipment]) (**Compression rating:** AF [Aviation Maintenanceman])

AO

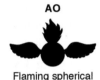

Flaming spherical
shell, winged

Aviation Ordnanceman

Navy planes carry guns, bombs, torpedoes, rockets, and missiles to attack the enemy on the sea, under the sea, in the air, and on land. AOs are responsible for maintaining, repairing, installing, operating, and handling aviation ordnance equipment; their duties also include the handling, stowing, issuing, and loading of munitions and small arms.

AS

Crossed maul and
spark, winged

Aviation Support Equipment Technician

ASs perform intermediate maintenance on "yellow" (aviation accessory) equipment at naval air stations and aboard carriers. They maintain gasoline and diesel engines, hydraulic and pneumatic systems, liquid and gaseous oxygen and nitrogen systems, gas-turbine compressor units, and electrical systems.

AT

Helium atom,
winged

Aviation Electronics Technician

ATs perform preventive and corrective maintenance on aviation electronic components supported by conventional and automatic test equipment. They repair the electronic components of equipment associated with weapons, communications, radar, navigation, antisubmarine warfare sensors, electronic warfare, data links, fire control, and tactical displays. (**Compression rating:** AV [Avionics Technician])

AW

Spark-pierced electron
orbits over wave, winged

Naval Air Crewman

AWs perform a wide variety of functions in many of the Navy's aircraft, such as operating electronic equipment (radars, radios, etc.), performing search-and-rescue techniques, etc. (**Service ratings:** AWF [mechanical]; AWO [operator]; AWR [tactical helicopter]; AWS [helicopter]; AWV [avionics])

AZ

Two-bladed propeller
on open book, winged

Aviation Maintenance Administrationman

AZs perform clerical, administrative, and managerial duties necessary to keep aircraft maintenance activities running smoothly. They plan, schedule, and coordinate maintenance, including inspections and modifications to aircraft and equipment.

BM

Crossed anchors

Boatswain's Mate

BMs train, direct, and supervise others in marlinespike, deck, and boat seamanship; ensure proper upkeep of the ship's external structure, rigging, deck equipment, and boats; lead working parties; perform seamanship tasks; are in charge of picketboats, self-propelled barges, tugs, and other yard and district craft; serve in or are in charge of gun crews and damage-control parties; and use and maintain equipment for loading and unloading cargo, ammunition, fuel, and general stores.

BU

Carpenter's square
on plumb bob

Builder

Navy BUs are similar to civilian construction workers. They may be skilled carpenters, plasterers, roofers, cement finishers, asphalt workers, masons, painters, bricklayers, sawmill operators, or cabinet-makers. BUs build and repair all types of structures, including piers, bridges, towers, underwater installations, schools, offices, houses, and other buildings. (**Compression rating:** CU [Constructionman])

CE

Spark on telephone pole

Construction Electrician

CEs are responsible for the power production and electrical work required to build and operate airfields, roads, barracks, hospitals, shops, and warehouses. The work of Navy CEs is like that of civilian construction electricians, powerhouse electricians, telephone and electrical repairmen, substation operators, linemen, and others. (**Compression rating:** UC [Utilities Constructionman])

CM

Double-headed wrench on nut

Construction Mechanic

CMs maintain heavy construction and automotive equipment (buses, dump trucks, bulldozers, rollers, cranes, backhoes, and pile drivers) as well as other construction equipment. They service vehicles and work on gasoline and diesel engines, ignition and fuel systems, transmissions, electrical systems, and hydraulic, pneumatic, and steering systems. (**Compression rating:** EQ [Equipmentman])

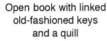

CS

Open book with linked old-fashioned keys and a quill

Culinary Specialist

CSs operate and manage Navy dining facilities and bachelor enlisted quarters. They are cooks and bakers in Navy dining facilities ashore and afloat, ordering, inspecting, and stowing food. They maintain food service and preparation spaces and equipment and keep records of transactions and budgets for the food service in living quarters ashore.

CT

Crossed quill and spark

Cryptologic Technician

Depending on their special career area, CTs control access to classified material, translate foreign-language transmissions, operate radio direction-finding equipment, employ electronic countermeasures, and install, service, and repair special electronic and electromechanical equipment. CTs require special security clearances. (**Service ratings:** CTI [interpretive]; CTM [maintenance]; CTN [network]; CTR [collection]; CTT [technical])

DC

Crossed fire axe and maul

Damage Controlman

DCs perform the work necessary for damage control, ship stability, firefighting, and chemical, biological, and radiological (CBR) warfare defense. They instruct personnel in damage control and CBR defense and repair damage-control equipment and systems.

EA

Measuring scale fronting level rod

Engineering Aide

EAs provide construction engineers with the information needed to develop final construction plans. EAs conduct surveys for roads, airfields, buildings, waterfront structures, pipelines, ditches, and drainage systems. They perform soil tests, prepare topographic and hydrographic maps, and survey for sewers, water lines, drainage systems, and underwater excavations. (**Compression rating:** CU [Constructionman])

EM

Globe with longitude, latitude lines

Electrician's Mate

The operation and repair of a ship's or station's electrical powerplant and electrical equipment are the responsibilities of EMs. They also maintain and repair power and lighting circuits, distribution switchboards, generators, motors, and other electrical equipment.

EN

Gear

Engineman

Internal-combustion engines, either diesel or gasoline, must be kept in good order; this is the responsibility of ENs. They are also responsible for the maintenance of refrigeration, air-conditioning, and distilling-plant motors and compressors.

EO

Bulldozer

Equipment Operator

EOs work with heavy machinery such as bulldozers, power shovels, pile drivers, rollers, and graders. EOs use this machinery to dig ditches and excavate for building foundations, to break up old concrete or asphalt paving and pour new paving, to loosen soil and grade it, to dig out tree trunks and rocks, to remove debris from construction sites, to raise girders, and to move and set in place other pieces of equipment or materials needed for a job. (**Compression rating:** EQ [Equipmentman])

EOD

Mine on crossed torpedo and aircraft bomb

Explosive Ordnance Disposal Technician

EODs render safe all types of ordnance, both conventional and unconventional, improvised, chemical, biological, and nuclear. They perform a wide variety of ordnance-related tasks, including underwater location, identification, render-safe, demolition, recovery, and disposal of foreign and domestic ordnance. They also support military and civilian law enforcement agencies.

ET

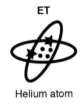

Helium atom

Electronics Technician

ETs are responsible for electronic equipment used to send and receive messages, detect enemy planes and ships, and determine target distance. They must maintain, repair, calibrate, tune, and adjust electronic equipment used for communications, detection and tracking, recognition and identification, navigation, and electronic countermeasures.

FC

Rangefinder with inward spark on each side

Fire Controlman

FCs maintain the control mechanism used in weapons systems on combat ships. Complex electronic, electrical, and hydraulic equipment is required to ensure the accuracy of guided-missile and surface gunfire-control systems. FCs are responsible for the operation, routine care, and repair of this equipment, which includes radars, computers, weapons-direction equipment, target-designation systems, gyroscopes, and rangefinders.

FT

Rangefinder

Fire Control Technician

FTs maintain advanced electronic equipment used in submarine weapons systems. Complex electronic, electrical, and mechanical equipment is required to ensure the accuracy of guided-missile systems and underwater weapons. FTs are responsible for the operation, routine care, and repair of this equipment.

GM

Crossed cannons

Gunner's Mate

Navy GMs operate, maintain, and repair all gunnery equipment, guided-missile launching systems, rocket launchers, guns, gun mounts, turrets, projectors, and associated equipment. They also make detailed casualty analyses and repairs of electrical, electronic, hydraulic, and mechanical systems. They test and inspect ammunition and missiles and their ordnance components and train and supervise personnel in the handling and stowage of ammunition, missiles, and assigned ordnance equipment.

GS

Turbine with ducting

Gas Turbine Systems Technician

GSs operate, repair, and maintain gas-turbine engines, main propulsion machinery (including gears, shafting, and controllable-pitch propellers), assigned auxiliary equipment, propulsion-control systems, electrical and electronic circuitry up to printed circuit modules, and alarm and warning circuitry. They perform administrative tasks related to gas-turbine propulsion-system operation and maintenance. (**Service ratings:** GSE [electrical]; GSM [mechanical])

HM

Caduceus

Hospital Corpsman

HMs assist medical professionals in providing health care to service people and their families. They act as pharmacists, medical technicians, food-service personnel, nurses' aides, physicians' or dentists' assistants, battlefield medics, X-ray technicians, and more. Their work falls into several categories: first aid and minor surgery, patient transportation, patient care, prescriptions and laboratory work, food-service inspections, and clerical duties.

HT

Crossed fire axe and maul
with carpenter's square

Hull Maintenance Technician

HTs are responsible for maintaining ships' hulls, fittings, piping systems, and machinery. They install and maintain shipboard and shore-based plumbing and piping systems. They also look after a vessel's safety and survival equipment and perform many tasks related to damage control.

IC

Telephone receiver
over globe

Interior Communications Electrician

ICs operate and repair electronic devices used in a ship's interior communications systems—SITE TV systems, public-address systems, electronic megaphones, and other announcing equipment—as well as gyrocompass systems.

IS

Magnifying glass
and quill

Intelligence Specialist

Military information, particularly classified information about enemies or potential enemies, is called "intelligence." Intelligence specialists analyze intelligence data. They break down information to determine its usefulness in military planning. From these intelligence data, they prepare materials that describe in detail the features of strategic and tactical areas all over the world.

IT

Four sparks

Information Systems Technician

ITs are responsible for the Navy's vital command, control, communications, computer and intelligence systems, and equipment. They use state-of-the-art multimedia technology such as fiber optics, digital microwave, and satellites on a global basis and work with telecommunications equipment, computers, and associated peripheral devices. (**Service rating**: ITS [submarines])

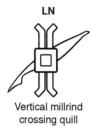

LN

Vertical millrind
crossing quill

Legalman

Navy LNs are aides trained in the field of law. They work in Navy legal offices performing administrative and clerical tasks necessary to process claims, to conduct court and administrative hearings, and to maintain records, documents, and legal-reference libraries. They give advice on tax returns, voter-registration regulations, procedures, and immigration and customs regulations governing Social Security and veterans' benefits and perform many duties related to courts-martial and nonjudicial hearings.

LS

Crossed keys

Logistics Specialists

LSs are the Navy's supply clerks. They see that needed supplies are available, including everything from clothing and machine parts to forms and food. They serve as civilian warehousemen, purchasing agents, stock clerks and supervisors, retail sales clerks, store managers, inventory clerks, buyers, parts clerks, bookkeepers, and even forklift operators. They also provide postal system services for the Navy to ensure an efficient interface between the U.S. Postal Service and the fleet.

MA

Star embossed in
circle within shield

Master-at-Arms

MAs help keep law and order aboard ship and at shore stations. They report to the executive officer, help maintain discipline, and assist in security matters. They enforce regulations, conduct investigations, take part in correctional and rehabilitative programs, and organize and train Sailors assigned to police duty. In civilian life, they would be detectives and policemen.

MC

Orbiting satellite with lightning bolts

Mass Communications Specialist

MCs are public affairs and visual information experts. They present the Navy story to audiences in the Navy and to the rest of the world through a variety of media. MCs write and produce print and broadcast journalism news and feature stories for military and civilian newspapers, magazines, television, and radio. They use photography, web design, graphic design, and other related skills in the performance of their duties.

MM

Three-bladed propeller

Machinist's Mate

Continuous operation of the many engines, compressors and gears, refrigeration, air-conditioning, gas-operated equipment, and other types of machinery afloat and ashore is the job of the MM. In particular, MMs are responsible for a ship's steam propulsion and auxiliary equipment and the outside (deck) machinery. MMs may also perform duties in the manufacture, storage, and transfer of some industrial gases. (**Service ratings**: MME (auxiliary); MMN [nuclear]; MMW [weapons])

MN

Floating mine

Mineman

MNs test, maintain, repair, and overhaul mines and their components. They are responsible for assembling, handling, issuing, and delivering mines to the planting agent and for maintaining mine-handling and mine-laying equipment.

MR

Micrometer and gear

Machinery Repairman

MRs are skilled machine-tool operators. They make replacement parts and repair or overhaul a ship engine's auxiliary equipment, such as evaporators, air compressors, and pumps. They repair deck equipment, including winches and hoists, condensers, and heat-exchange devices. Shipboard MRs frequently operate main propulsion machinery in addition to performing machine-shop and repair duties.

MT

Guided missile and
electronic wave

Missile Technician

MTs perform organizational and intermediate-level maintenance on ballistic-missile weapons systems; they also operate and maintain their fire-control systems, guidance subsystems, and associated test equipment, as well as missile and launcher/tuber groups and all ancillary equipment. They operate and maintain strategic weapons systems, associated ship/weapon subsystems, and test and handling equipment.

MU

Lyre

Musician

MUs play in official Navy bands and in special groups such as jazz bands, dance bands, and small ensembles. They give concerts and provide music for military ceremonies, religious services, parades, receptions, and dances. Official unit bands usually do not include stringed instruments, but each MU must be able to play at least one brass, woodwind, or percussion instrument. Persons are selected for this rating through auditions.

NC

Anchor crossed
with quill

Navy Counselor

NCs offer vocational guidance on an individual and group basis to Navy personnel aboard ships and at shore facilities and to civilian personnel considering enlistment in the Navy. They assess the interests, aptitudes, abilities, and personalities of individuals. An NCR (Navy Counselor Recruiter) focuses on bringing people into the Navy and helps new recruits make early career decisions. NCCs (Navy Career Counselors) primarily work with personnel further along in their careers, assisting them with such things as advancing their education, converting their ratings, and improving their chances for retention and promotion.

ND

U.S. Navy Mark-V diving helmet and breastplate

Navy Diver

NDs perform underwater construction, salvage, repair, maintenance, demolition, reconnaissance, and search-and-rescue tasks using a variety of diving equipment. They also support Special Warfare and Explosive Ordnance Disposal personnel (see SO and EOD ratings).

OS

Arrow through oscilloscope

Operations Specialist

OSs operate radar, navigation, and communications equipment in a ship's combat information center (CIC) or on the bridge. They detect and track ships, planes, and missiles. They operate and maintain IFF (identification friend or foe) systems, ECM (electronic countermeasures) equipment, and radiotelephones. OSs also work with search-and-rescue teams.

PR

Parachute, winged

Aircrew Survival Equipmentman

Parachutes are the lifesaving equipment of aviators when they have to bail out. In times of disaster, a parachute may also be the only means of delivering badly needed medicines, goods, and other supplies to isolated victims. PRs pack and care for parachutes as well as service, maintain, and repair flight clothing, rubber life rafts, life jackets, oxygen-breathing equipment, protective clothing, and air-sea rescue equipment. An Aircrew Survival Equipmentman was originally called a "Parachute Rigger," which explains the rating abbreviation "PR."

PS

Book with quill

Personnel Specialist

Those Sailors in the PS rating provide enlisted personnel with information and counseling related to Navy occupations, opportunities for general education and job training, requirements for promotion, and rights and benefits. PSs maintain and audit pay and personnel records and determine military pay and travel entitlements. They prepare financial and accounting reports related to individual pay and travel transactions and operate associated accounting systems.

QM

Ship's helm

Quartermaster

QMs are responsible for ship safety, skillful navigation, and reliable communications with other vessels and shore stations. In addition, they maintain charts, navigational aids, and records for the ship's log. They steer the ship, take radar bearings and ranges, make depth soundings and celestial observations, plot courses, command small craft, conduct honors and ceremonies with passing ships, maintain signaling equipment, and send and receive visual signals by flashing light, semaphore, and flaghoist. QMs stand watch and assist the navigator and officer of the deck (OOD).

RP

Globe on anchor within compass

Religious Program Specialist

RPs assist Navy chaplains with administrative and budgetary tasks. They serve as custodians of chapel funds, keep religious documents, and maintain contact with religious and community agencies. They also prepare devotional and religious educational materials, set up volunteer programs, operate shipboard libraries, supervise chaplains' offices, and perform administrative, clerical, and secretarial duties. They train personnel in religious programs and publicize religious activities.

SB

Cutlass and cocked flintlock pistol on an anchor

Special Warfare Boat Operator

SBs drive a variety of special warfare craft. They support SEALs and other Special Operations Command forces during their maritime and riverine missions and conduct unconventional small boat operations such as coastal/riverine patrols. They collect intelligence on enemy military installations in coastal areas, perform parachute/helicopter insertion operations, and support military and civilian law enforcement operations.

SH

Crossed key and quill

Ship's Serviceman

Both ashore and afloat, SHs manage barbershops, tailor shops, ships' uniform stores, laundries, dry-cleaning plants, and cobbler shops. They serve as clerks in exchanges, convenience stores, gas stations, warehouses, and commissary stores. Some SHs function as Navy club managers.

SO

Flintlock pistol on an anchor and trident

Special Warfare Operator

SOs are better known as SEALs—an acronym from one of their primary missions: conducting insertions/extractions from the sea, air, or land. SOs also conduct covert, special operations missions in virtually any environment throughout the world, capture high-value enemy personnel and terrorists, collect information and intelligence through special reconnaissance missions, carry out small-unit, direct-action missions against military targets, and conduct underwater reconnaissance and demolition of natural or man-made obstacles prior to amphibious landings.

ST

Earphones pierced by arrow

Sonar Technician

STs operate sonar and other oceanographic systems. They manipulate, control, evaluate, and interpret data for surface and submarine operations. STs coordinate submarine and auxiliary sonar and underwater fire-control interface, operate surface-ship underwater fire-control systems and associated equipment for the solution of antisubmarine warfare problems, and perform organizational and intermediate maintenance on their respective sonar and allied equipment. (**Service ratings**: STG [surface]; STS [submarine])

SW

I-beam suspended from hook

Steelworker

SWs rig and operate all special equipment used to move or hoist structural steel, structural shapes, and similar material. They erect or dismantle steel bridges, piers, buildings, tanks, towers, and other structures. They place, fit, weld, cut, bolt, and rivet steel shapes, plates, and built-up sections used in the construction of overseas facilities. (**Compression rating**: CU [Constructionman])

UT

Valve

Utilitiesman

UTs plan, supervise, and perform tasks involved in the installation, operation, maintenance, and repair of plumbing, heating, steam, compressed-air systems, fuel-storage and -distribution systems, water-treatment and -distribution systems, air-conditioning and refrigeration equipment, and sewage-collecting and disposal facilities. (**Compression rating**: UC [Utilities Constructionman])

YN

Crossed quills

Yeoman

YNs perform secretarial and clerical work. They greet visitors, answer telephone calls, and receive incoming mail. YNs organize files and operate duplicating equipment, and they order and distribute supplies. They write and type business and social letters, notices, directives, forms, and reports. They maintain files and service records.

5-C General Rates

Even though some Sailors in pay grades E-1 through E-3 may not yet have a rating, they still work within the general parameters of the occupational field (apprenticeship) that they seek. Sailors who are aspiring to ("striking for" in Navy parlance) a particular rating will have the appropriate "general rate" for that general field. As you can see below, a Sailor seeking a rating within the category of engineering would have the general rate of "Fireman" while a Sailor seeking a rating in aviation would be an "Airman."

General Apprenticeship	E-1	E-2	E-3
Seamanship, Operations, Administration, etc.	SR (Seaman Recruit)	SA (Seaman Apprentice)	SN (Seaman)
Engineering and Maintenance	FR (Fireman Recruit)	FA (Fireman Apprentice)	FN (Fireman)
Construction	CR (Constructionman Recruit)	CA (Constructionman Apprentice)	CN (Constructionman)
Aviation	AR (Airman Recruit)	AA (Airman Apprentice)	AN (Airman)

5-D Examples of Enlisted Career Advancement

The example below shows the advancement of a typical general rating (Boatswain's Mate).

Pay Grade	Rate	Title
E-9	BMCM	Master Chief Boatswain's Mate
E-8	BMCS	Senior Chief Boatswain's Mate
E-7	BMC	Chief Boatswain's Mate
E-6	BM1	Boatswain's Mate First Class
E-5	BM2	Boatswain's Mate Second Class
E-4	BM3	Boatswain's Mate Third Class
E-3	SN	Seaman
E-2	SA	Seaman Apprentice
E-1	SR	Seaman Recruit

This example shows the advancement of a typical service rating (Aircrew Survival Equipmentman). Note that this individual became a "designated striker" for her rating at the E-3 level.

Pay Grade	Rate	Title
E-9	PRCM	Master Chief Aircrew Survival Equipmentman
E-8	PRCS	Senior Chief Aircrew Survival Equipmentman
E-7	PRC	Chief Aircrew Survival Equipmentman
E-6	PR1	Aircrew Survival Equipmentman First Class
E-5	PR2	Aircrew Survival Equipmentman Second Class
E-4	PR3	Aircrew Survival Equipmentman Third Class
E-3	PRAN	Aircrew Survival Equipmentman Airman
E-2	AA	Airman Apprentice
E-1	AN	Airman Recruit

In this example, this Sailor began his career in the construction general apprenticeship, was then rated as a Construction Electrician and merged with the Utilitiesman rating at the E-9 level. This is an example of a compression rating.

Pay Grade	Rate	Title
E-9	UCCM	Master Chief Utilitiesman
E-8	CECS	Senior Chief Construction Electrician
E-7	CEC	Chief Construction Electrician
E-6	CE1	Construction Electrician First Class
E-5	CE2	Construction Electrician Second Class
E-4	CE3	Construction Electrician Third Class
E-3	CN	Constructionman
E-2	CA	Constructionman Apprentice
E-1	CR	Constructionman Recruit

In this example, this Sailor began her career in the aviation general apprenticeship and then was rated as an Aviation Boatswain's Mate, with a service rating in fuels. That service rating is indicated by the addition of a third rating letter—"F" in this case. Had her service rating been in aircraft handling, the F would be replaced by H, so that her rating would be ABH instead of ABF.

Pay Grade	Rate	Title
E-9	ABFCM	Master Chief Aviation Boatswain's Mate
E-8	ABFCS	Senior Chief Aviation Boatswain's Mate
E-7	ABFC	Chief Aviation Boatswain's Mate
E-6	ABF1	Aviation Boatswain's Mate First Class
E-5	ABF2	Aviation Boatswain's Mate Second Class
E-4	ABF3	Aviation Boatswain's Mate Third Class
E-3	AN	Airman
E-2	AA	Airman Apprentice
E-1	AR	Airman Recruit

TAB 6 Uniforms

Because of the wide variety of jobs performed in the Navy, there are multiple categories of uniforms, each with several variations. What uniform you wear with what variations is decided by the *prescribing authority*—defined in *U.S. Navy Uniform Regulations* as the area or regional commander. Your command will make it clear what uniforms have been prescribed, and this is often referred to as the *uniform of the day*.

The best source of information regarding uniforms is *U.S. Navy Uniform Regulations*, NAVPERS 15665 (often informally called "Uniform Regs"), which is issued by the Chief of Naval Personnel (CNP) at the direction of the CNO and carries the force of a lawful order. As with all references, be sure that you are using the current version of "Uniform Regs"—as of this writing, the current version is I (India).

Major Topics Covered:

- ⚓ Uniform Terminology
- ⚓ Categories of Uniforms
- ⚓ Ranks on Uniforms
- ⚓ Awards and Decorations
- ⚓ Warfare and Other Qualification Insignia
- ⚓ Grooming and Personal Appearance

To Learn More:

- ⚓ www.usni.org/BlueAndGoldProfessionalBooks/TheBluejackets Manual
- ⚓ *Basic Military Requirements* (NAVEDTRA 14325)
- ⚓ Uniforms and Insignia, **www.navy.com/about/uniforms.html #enlisted-rate**
- ⚓ Uniform Regulations, **www.public.navy.mil/bupers-npc /uniforms/uniformregulations/Pages/default.aspx**
- ⚓ *Navy and Marine Corps Awards Manual* (SECNAVINST 1650.1H)
- ⚓ Navy Awards, **awards.navy.mil/awards/webbas01.nsf/(vwWeb Page)/home.htm?OpenDocument**
- ⚓ Navy Awards Precedence, **www.public.navy.mil/bupers-npc /support/uniforms/uniformregulations/Pages/NavyAwards PrecedenceChart.aspx**

⚓ Women's Hair Standards, **www.navy.mil/ah_online/um/female hair.html**

⚓ Navy Uniform Support Center, **www.mynavyexchange.com/nex /uniforms**

Associated Tabs:

- TAB 6-A: Navy Enlisted Sleeve Markings
- TAB 6-B: Enlisted Rank Devices of the Other Armed Services
- TAB 6-C: Officer Collar, Cap, and Shoulder Rank Devices in the Armed Services
- TAB 6-D: Navy Officer Shoulder Boards and Sleeve Markings
- TAB 6-E: Coast Guard Officer Shoulder Boards and Sleeve Markings
- Tab 6-F: Warrant Officer Rank Devices
- Tab 6-G: Line and Staff Corps Devices
- TAB 6-H: Wearing of Awards
- TAB 6-I: Precedence of Awards
- TAB 6-J: Warfare and Qualification Insignia

6-A Navy Enlisted Sleeve Markings

In this example, the markings are for a Sailor who is a boatswain's mate and therefore includes crossed anchors—the symbol associated with that rating. The crossed anchors would be replaced by the appropriate rating symbol (see TAB 5-B: Navy Ratings) for other ratings.

These markings are for winter uniforms and would be different for summer uniforms with all features ("crow," rating symbol, and chevrons) in dark blue on white. Note that the chevrons for E-7 and above are gold instead of red; this indicates twelve or more years of good conduct service and can occur at any pay grade once this milestone has been reached.

6-B Enlisted Rank Devices of the Other Armed Services

The Coast Guard, Marine Corps, Army, and Air Force have their own unique indications of rank. Only the Navy and Coast Guard include their occupational specialties on their sleeve markings, while the other services do not. Another difference is that the Marine Corps, Army, and Air Force wear their sleeve markings on both sleeves, while the Navy and Coast Guard wear them only on the left arm.

Master Chief Petty Officer
of the Navy/Coast Guard
E-9

Master Chief Petty Officer,
Fleet/Force/Command
Master Chief Petty Officer
E-9

Senior Chief Petty Officer
E-8

Chief Petty Officer
E-7

Petty Officer First Class
E-6

Petty Officer Second Class
E-5

Petty Officer Third Class
E-4

Seaman
E-3

Seaman Apprentice
E-2

(none)

Seaman Recruit
E-1

[**6-A**] Navy enlisted sleeve markings

Sergeant Major
of the Marine Corps
E-9

Master Gunnery Sergeant
Sergeant Major
E-9

Master Sergeant
First Sergeant
E-8

Gunnery Sergeant
E-7

Staff Sergeant
E-6

Sergeant
E-5

Corporal
E-4

Lance Corporal
E-3

Private First Class
E-2

(none)

Private
E-1

[6-B-1] Marine Corps enlisted ranks

Sergeant Major
of the Army
E-9

Sergeant Major
Command Sergeant Major
E-9

Master Sergeant
First Sergeant
E-8

Sergeant First Class
E-7

Staff Sergeant
E-6

Sergeant
E-5

Corporal, Specialist
E-4

Private First Class
E-3

Private
E-2

(none)

Private
E-1

[6-B-2] Army enlisted ranks

Chief Master Sergeant
of the Air Force
E-9

Chief Master Sergeant
First Sergeant
Command Chief Master Sergeant
E-9

Senior Master Sergeant
First Sergeant
E-8

Master Sergeant
First Sergeant
E-7

Technical Sergeant
E-6

Staff Sergeant
E-5

Senior Airman
E-4

Airman First Class
E-3

Airman
E-2

(none)
Airman Basic
E-1

[6-B-3] Air Force enlisted ranks

6-C Officer Collar, Cap, and Shoulder Rank Devices in the Armed Service

These collar, cap, and shoulder devices are virtually the same for all the services, based on pay grade. An O-4 in any of the services is indicated by a gold oak leaf, even though the wearer would be a "lieutenant commander" in the Navy and Coast Guard and a "major" in the other services.

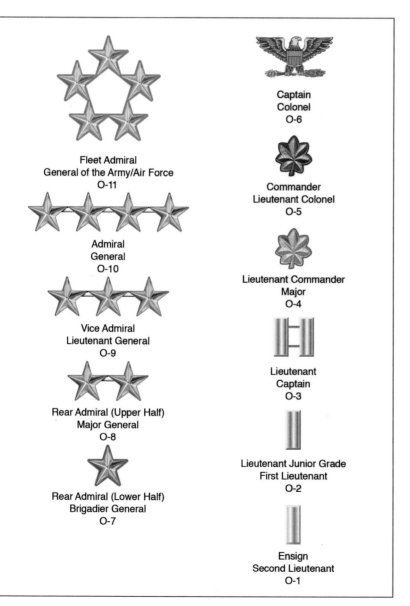

Fleet Admiral
General of the Army/Air Force
O-11

Admiral
General
O-10

Vice Admiral
Lieutenant General
O-9

Rear Admiral (Upper Half)
Major General
O-8

Rear Admiral (Lower Half)
Brigadier General
O-7

Captain
Colonel
O-6

Commander
Lieutenant Colonel
O-5

Lieutenant Commander
Major
O-4

Lieutenant
Captain
O-3

Lieutenant Junior Grade
First Lieutenant
O-2

Ensign
Second Lieutenant
O-1

6-D Navy Officer Shoulder Boards and Sleeve Markings

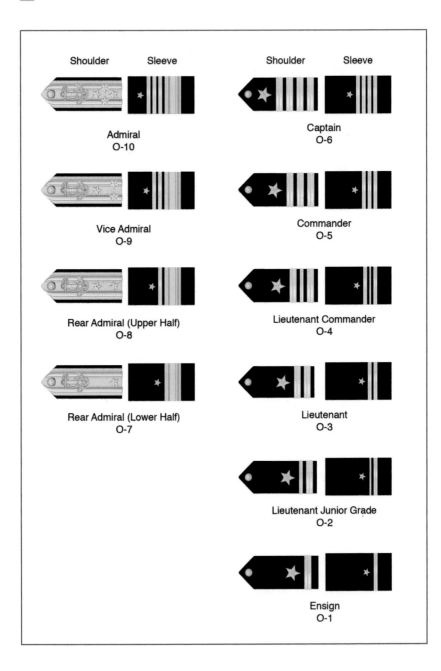

6-E Coast Guard Officer Shoulder Boards and Sleeve Markings

Coast Guard officers have similar shoulder boards and sleeve markings to those worn by Navy officers. The main difference is the use of the same federal shield worn by enlisted personnel in the Coast Guard.

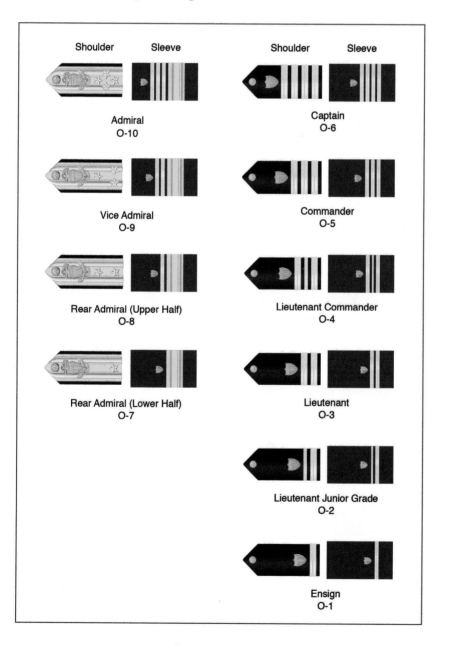

6-F Warrant Officer Rank Devices

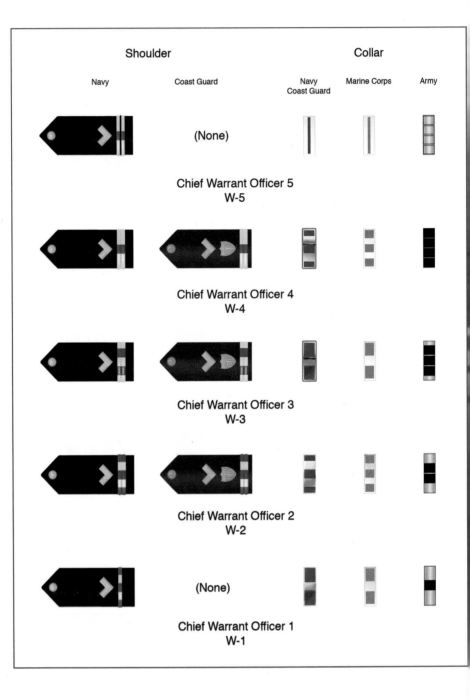

Shoulder		Collar		
Navy	Coast Guard	Navy Coast Guard	Marine Corps	Army

6-G Line and Staff Corps Devices

Navy Line Corps

Christian

Jewish

CHAPLAIN CORPS SYMBOLS

Muslim

Hindu

Buddhist

Medical Corps

Nurse Corps

Dental Corps

Medical Services Corps

Supply Corps

Judge Advocate General Corps

Legal Community

Civil Engineer Corps

6-H Wearing of Awards

Awards are either medals or ribbons. Medals are metal pendants hung from pieces of colored cloth. Ribbons are rectangular pieces of colored cloth 1½ inches long and ⅜-inch high. Medals always come with a ribbon, but some awards consist of only a ribbon and do not have a corresponding medal.

The term "award" is used to describe any medal, ribbon, or attachment. "Decoration" is usually used to describe an award given to an individual for a specific act of personal gallantry or meritorious service.

Only wear your medals on very formal occasions when the prescribed uniform is full dress. Miniature versions of the medals are worn with dinner-dress uniforms. Ribbons are worn on dress uniforms but not on working ones.

When you earn your first ribbon wear it centered a quarter of an inch above your left breast pocket. As you add ribbons, you will build them in rows of three. You may see members of other services wearing large numbers of ribbons in rows of four, but in the Navy the most you can wear in a row is three. If you have a number not divisible by three, the uppermost row contains the lesser number, with the extra one or two ribbons centered over the row beneath. On full-dress occasions, when you are wearing your medals, line them up in rows of three, side by side, or you may put five in a row if you overlap them. Any awards that only have a ribbon (no corresponding medal) must be worn on the right breast when full-size medals are worn. Do not wear any ribbons, however, when you are wearing miniature medals (dinner-dress occasions).

If you earn the same award more than once, you will not receive the medal or ribbon again, but will receive a special metal attachment that goes on the original medal or ribbon. Other attachments are also sometimes added to awards to represent something other than repeated awards (such as the number of missions flown or an "S" on a pistol or rifle ribbon to indicate qualification as a sharpshooter).

It is important that you wear your awards in the proper order. Whenever you earn a new award, you must determine where it goes in relation to the other awards you have already earned.

TAB 6-I: Precedence of Awards lists the medals and ribbons you might earn while in the Navy in their order of precedence, which determines how they are to be worn on your uniform. The awards with the higher precedence are worn closer to your heart (called "farthest inboard"). For example, if you have earned an Armed Forces Expeditionary Medal, a Navy Unit Commendation, a Combat Action Ribbon, a Navy and Marine Corps Achievement Medal, and a National Defense Service Medal, you would arrange them in two rows, with three ribbons on the lower row and two on the upper row. Since the Navy and Marine Corps Achievement Medal has the highest precedence (nearest the top of the list) it would go on the top row, closest to your heart (farthest inboard). Next to it would be the Combat Action Ribbon. The bottom row would have the Navy Unit Commendation farthest inboard, with the National Defense Service Medal next in line (in the middle), and the Armed Forces Expeditionary Medal last, on the bottom row, farthest from the heart (farthest outboard).

 6-1 Precedence of Awards

The precedence of decorations authorized for personnel of the Navy and Marine Corps is listed below. *U.S. Navy Uniform Regulations*, NAVPERS 15665, provides further information regarding the precedence and appropriate wear of all personnel, unit, and service awards.

In general, awards are worn in the following order:

- U.S. Military Personal Decorations
- U.S. Military Unit Awards
- U.S. Campaign and Service Awards
- Foreign Military Personal Decorations*
- Foreign Military Unit Awards
- Multilateral Military Service Awards (United Nations, NATO, etc.)
- Foreign Military Service Medals
- Marksmanship Awards

  * Foreign awards are worn in the order of receipt; if from the same-country, that country's precedence is used for those ribbons.

PRECEDENCE OF AWARDS

(1) Medal of Honor
(2) Navy Cross
(3) Defense Distinguished Service Medal
(4) Distinguished Service Medal
(5) Silver Star Medal

(6)   Defense Superior Service Medal

(7)   Legion of Merit

(8)   Distinguished Flying Cross

(9)   Navy and Marine Corps Medal

(10)   Bronze Star Medal

(11)   Purple Heart Medal

(12)   Defense Meritorious Service Medal

(13)   Meritorious Service Medal

(14)   Air Medal

(15)   Joint Service Commendation Medal

(16)   Navy and Marine Corps Commendation Medal

(17)   Joint Service Achievement Medal

(18)   Navy and Marine Corps Achievement Medal

(19)   Combat Action Ribbon

(20)   Presidential Unit Citation

(21)   Joint Meritorious Unit Award

(22)   Navy Unit Commendation

(23)   Meritorious Unit Commendation

(24)   Navy "E" Ribbon

(25)   Prisoner of War Medal

(26)   Good Conduct Medal

(27)   Navy Reserve Meritorious Service Medal

(28)   Navy Fleet Marine Force Ribbon

(29)   Navy Expeditionary Medal

(30)   National Defense Service Medal

(31)   Korean Service Medal

(32)   Antarctica Service Medal

(33)   Armed Forces Expeditionary Medal

(34)   Vietnam Service Medal

(35)   Southwest Asia Service Medal

(36)   Kosovo Campaign Medal

(37)   Afghanistan Campaign Medal

(38)   Iraq Campaign Medal

(39)   Global War on Terrorism Expeditionary Medal

(40)   Global War on Terrorism Service Medal

(41)   Korea Defense Service Medal

(42)   Armed Forces Service Medal

(43)   Humanitarian Service Medal

(44)   Military Outstanding Volunteer Service Medal
(45)   Sea Service Deployment Ribbon
(46)   Navy Arctic Service Ribbon
(47)   Navy Reserve Sea Service Ribbon
(48)   Navy and Marine Corps Overseas Service Ribbon
(49)   Navy Recruiting Service Ribbon
(50)   Navy Recruit Training Service Ribbon
(51)   Navy Ceremonial Guard Ribbon
(52)   Navy Basic Military Training Honor Graduate Ribbon
(53)   Armed Forces Reserve Medal
(54)   Navy Reserve Medal
(55)   Philippine Republic Presidential Unit Citation
(56)   Republic of Korea Presidential Unit Citation
(57)   Vietnam Presidential Unit Citation
(58)   Republic of Vietnam Gallantry Cross Unit Citation
(59)   Republic of Vietnam Meritorious Unit Civil Actions Citation
(60)   United Nations Service Medal
(61)   United Nations Medal
(62)   NATO Medal
(63)   Multinational Force and Observers Medal
(64)   Inter-American Defense Board Medal
(65)   Republic of Vietnam Campaign Medal
(66)   Kuwait Liberation Medal (Saudi Arabia)
(67)   Kuwait Liberation Medal (Kuwait)
(68)   Rifle Qualification Award
(69)   Pistol Qualification Award

6-J Warfare and Qualification Insignia

Navy men and women may earn additional qualifications as their careers progress, and some of these are reflected in special insignia for their uniforms. These qualifications may be in major warfare areas such as aviation or submarine warfare, or they may signify special occupations such as explosive ordnance disposal or parachuting. Most of these are worn on the left breast above the ribbons and medals, but there are some exceptions. If you earn more than one of these special insignia, you may wear a maximum of two, one above your ribbons and one below.

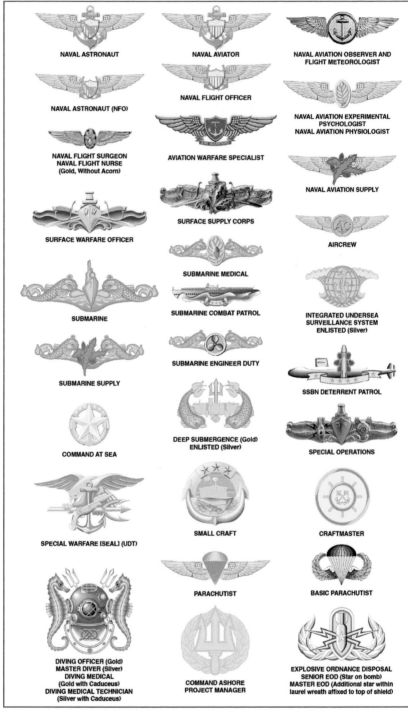

[6-J] Some examples of warfare and qualification insignia

7 Navy Missions and Heritage

"The mission of the Navy is to maintain, train and equip combat-ready naval forces capable of winning wars, deterring aggression and maintaining freedom of the seas."

—*Navy Mission Statement*

Throughout the nation's history, interaction with the sea has played an important role in America's economy, defense, and foreign policy through the performance of important missions. Currently, the U.S. Navy has six important missions, all of which have been carried out effectively at various times in the nation's history and continue to be as important as ever in today's challenging world.

Major Topics Covered:

- All domain access
- Sea control
- Deterrence
- Forward presence
- Power projection
- Maritime Security
- Heritage

To Learn More:

- **www.usni.org/BlueAndGoldProfessionalBooks/TheBluejackets Manual**
- *Basic Military Requirements* (NAVEDTRA 14325)
- *Military Requirements for Petty Officers Third and Second Class* (NAVEDTRA 14504)
- *Military Requirements for Petty Officers First Class* (NAVEDTRA 14145)
- Navy Missions, **www.navy.com/about/mission.html**
- *How We Fight: Handbook for the Naval Warfighter*, available from U.S. Government Printing Office and online at: **http://navy reading.dodlive.mil/files/2015/08/HWF-Book-Combined-Final - 27-Apr-15.pdf**

⚓ *A Cooperative Strategy for 21st Century Seapower*, **www.navy.mil /local/maritime/**

⚓ Naval History and Heritage Command, **www.navy.mil/local/nav hist/index.asp**

⚓ *A Sailor's History of the U.S. Navy* by Thomas J. Cutler (Naval Institute Press, 2005)

⚓ *The U.S. Navy: A Concise History* by Craig L. Symonds (Oxford University Press, 2015)

⚓ *The Naval Institute Historical Atlas of the U.S. Navy* by Craig L. Symonds & William J. Clipson (Naval Institute Press, 2001)

⚓ *United States Naval Aviation 1910–1995* by Roy A. Grossnick (Naval History & Heritage Command, 1997)

TAB 8 Organization

The Navy's organization is large, unique, and complicated, making it a challenge to understand. It is an organization with many different parts, and because the Navy works so closely with the other services, it is not enough to merely understand how the Navy is organized; you must also have some idea of how it fits into the Department of Defense.

Major Topics Covered:

- ⚓ Chains of Command
- ⚓ DOD Organization
- ⚓ Navy Organization
- ⚓ Combatant Commands (COCOMS)
- ⚓ Naval Component Commands
- ⚓ Fleets
- ⚓ Task Organization
- ⚓ Ship Organization
- ⚓ Aircraft Organization

To Learn More:

- ⚓ www.usni.org/BlueAndGoldProfessionalBooks/TheBluejackets Manual
- ⚓ *Basic Military Requirements* (NAVEDTRA 14325)
- ⚓ *Military Requirements for Petty Officers Third and Second Class* (NAVEDTRA 14504)
- ⚓ *Military Requirements for Petty Officers First Class* (NAVEDTRA 14145)
- ⚓ *Airman* (NAVEDTRA 14014A)
- ⚓ Organization of the Department of Defense (DOD), www.defense .gov/About-DoD/DoD-101
- ⚓ Navy Organization, www.navy.mil/navydata/organization/org -top.asp
- ⚓ *Standard Organization and Regulations of the U.S. Navy* (OPNAV INST 3120.32D)

Associated Tabs:

> ○ TAB 8-A: Notes on Navy and Department of Defense (DOD) Organization

8-A Notes on Navy and Department of Defense (DOD) Organization

The following notes provide a summary of the details in **Chapter 8: Navy Organization.**

There is more than one chain of command in the Armed Forces:

- The *operational* chain of command is used to carry out specific missions (like an airstrike or a humanitarian relief effort).
- The *administrative* chain of command takes care of support functions (like personnel manning, repairs, etc.).
- Navy forces may be part of a *joint* chain of command that includes elements from other services (Army, Air Force, etc.).
- U.S. forces are often part of *allied* chains of command as well. These are considered "combined" forces rather than joint.

The Department of Defense (DOD) consists of four principal components:

- The Secretary of Defense and his or her supporting staff
- The Joint Chiefs of Staff and their supporting staff
- The individual military departments (services): Army, Air Force, and Navy
- The Unified Combatant Commands

The Navy is one of the five armed services. The others are the Army, Air Force, Marine Corps, and Coast Guard. When working together, the services are said to be "joint." The heads ("service chiefs") of each service are:

- The Chief of Naval Operations
- The Chief of Staff of the Army
- The Chief of Staff of the Air Force
- The Commandant of the Marine Corps
- The Commandant of the Coast Guard

The Marine Corps is part of the Department of the Navy but is in many ways a separate service as well.

The Coast Guard is the fifth branch of the U.S. armed services and often works closely with elements of the Department of Defense, but it is currently organized as part of the Department of Homeland Security.

The National Guard and Air National Guard are reserve components of the U.S. armed forces and are under the dual control of their local state government and the federal government (Army and Air Force, respectively).

The Joint Chiefs of Staff serve as principal advisers to the President and Secretary of Defense but are not actually in the operational chain of command. Each of the service chiefs (except the Commandant of the Coast Guard) are members of the Joint Chiefs, as are the Chairman and Vice Chairman and the chief of the National Guard Bureau.

The Unified Combatant Commanders (also known as "Combatant Commanders" or "Unified Commanders") answer directly to the Secretary of Defense. There are currently nine *unified commands*:

- Africa Command (AFRICOM)
- Central Command (CENTCOM)
- European Command (EUCOM)
- Northern Command (NORTHCOM)
- Pacific Command (PACOM)
- Southern Command (SOUTHCOM)
- Special Operations Command (SOCOM)
- Strategic Command (STRATCOM)
- Transportation Command (TRANSCOM)

Note: Each of these commands is more formally addressed with "United States" preceding (as in "United States Africa Command") and is sometimes abbreviated similarly (as in "USAFRICOM).

The Department of the Navy (DON):

- is subordinate to the Department of Defense (which is headed by a civilian Secretary of Defense, who is assisted by a military Chairman of the Joint Chiefs of Staff).

- is administratively headed by a civilian Secretary of the Navy, who is assisted by a military head known as the Chief of Naval Operations (CNO).
- is not the same as the "Navy Department," which is formally defined as being part of the DON and consists of "the central executive offices of the Department of the Navy located at the seat of government . . . comprised of the Office of the Secretary of the Navy, the Office of the Chief of Naval Operations, and Headquarters, Marine Corps."

The Navy's operational forces (commonly called "The Fleet") consist of ships, aircraft, submarines, SEALs, and so on.

The Navy's operational chain of command is typically structured as follows (from top to bottom):

- President of the United States (constitutionally the "Commander in Chief of the Armed Forces")
- Secretary of Defense
- Unified Combatant Commanders (such as PACOM) depending upon the locale and the mission; these are "joint" commands so they may be commanded by an officer from one of the other services
- Naval Component Commander (such as PACFLT); purely naval (as opposed to joint) so there will be a Navy officer in command
- Numbered Fleet Commander (such as COMSEVENTHFLT)
- Task Organization (variable and can consist of all or some of the following (in descending order):
  - task force
  - task group
  - task unit
  - task element
  - individual unit (such as a ship, aircraft squadron, SEAL team, etc.)

The naval component commands are:

- United States Fleet Forces Command (USFLTFORCOM or FLTFORCOM)
- United States Pacific Fleet (USPACFLT or PACFLT)
- United States Naval Forces Europe (USNAVEUR or NAVEUR)

- United States Naval Forces Central Command (USNAVCENT or NAVCENT)
- United States Naval Forces Southern Command (USNAVSO or NAVSO)
- United States Fleet Cyber Command
- United States Naval Special Warfare Command (NAVSPECWAR-COM or NAVSOC or NSWC)

There are currently six numbered fleet commands in the Navy that operationally support the naval component commanders:

Fleet	Primary Operational Area
Third	Eastern Pacific Ocean
Fourth	Central and South American Waters
Fifth	Middle Eastern and South Asian Waters
Sixth	Mediterranean Sea/African Waters
Seventh	Western Pacific Ocean/Indian Ocean
Tenth	Worldwide Cyber Domain

Task Organization permits commanders to better organize ships or other units into useful groups based around specific tasks. Using this system, a fleet can be divided into task forces and they can be further subdivided into task groups. If these task groups still need to be further divided, task units can be created and they can be further subdivided into task elements. A numbering system for identifying the various parts of a task organization starts with the appropriate fleet and then subdivides according to tasks using something that looks like a decimal system on steroids:

- Seventh Fleet
- Task Force 76
- Task Group 76.1 (Task Group 76.2, etc., as needed)
- Task Unit 76.1.1 (Task Unit 76.1.2, etc.)
- Task Element 76.1.1.1 (and so on . . .)

The administrative chain of command keeps the Navy functioning on a day-to-day basis by taking care of the essential elements of preparedness like training, repair, supply, personnel assignment, medical treatment, and so on. Unlike the operational chain, it is purely naval, rather than joint. The administrative chain of command is structured as follows:

- The SECNAV, who is a civilian and has a second in command known as the Undersecretary, as well as several Assistant Secretaries who handle specific areas, such as Manpower and Reserve Affairs.
- Subordinate to SECNAV is the *Chief of Naval Operations* (CNO), who is a naval officer and has a second in command known as the Vice Chief of Naval Operations, as well as a number of deputies with specific areas of responsibility such as Naval Intelligence. The CNO and his staff are organized as the Office of the Chief of Naval Operations, better known as "OPNAV."
- Below SECNAV and OPNAV is the *shore establishment*, consisting of various activities that support the operating fleet by handling such things as Training, Medicine, and Intelligence. Some of the various components of the shore establishment are:
  - Bureau of Naval Personnel
  - Bureau of Medicine and Surgery
  - Naval Education and Training Command
  - Strategic Systems Programs
  - Naval Legal Service Command
  - Naval Meteorology and Oceanography Command
  - Office of Naval Intelligence
  - Naval Safety Center
  - Naval Strike and Air Warfare Center
  - Naval Systems Commands (see below)

Navy systems commands oversee many of the technical requirements of the Navy and report to the CNO:

- Naval Sea Systems Command (NAVSEA)
- Naval Air Systems Command (NAVAIR)
- Space and Naval Warfare Systems Command (SPAWAR)
- Naval Supply Systems Command (NAVSUP)
- Naval Facilities Engineering Command (NAVFAC)

For administrative purposes, ships and aircraft are organized into six **type commands** that reflect their commonality and their geographic location:

- Naval Surface Force, U.S. Atlantic Fleet (SURFLANT)
- Naval Surface Force, U.S. Pacific Fleet (SURFPAC)
- Naval Submarine Force, U.S. Atlantic Fleet (SUBLANT)
- Naval Submarine Force, U.S. Pacific Fleet (SUBPAC)
- Naval Air Force, U.S. Atlantic Fleet (AIRLANT)
- Naval Air Force, U.S. Pacific Fleet (AIRPAC)

Within the type commands, ships and aircraft are further organized into manageable **group commands** with component **ship squadrons** and **air wings,** consisting of individual ships and aircraft squadrons.

TAB 9 Security

From seamen recruits to admirals, security is the responsibility of everyone in the Navy. Just as you are alert to dangers of all types in your own home, so should you be always vigilant and protective of your Navy. Your life and those of your shipmates may very well depend on it.

Major Topics Covered:

- ⚙ External Security
- ⚙ Force Protection Conditions (FPCONs)
- ⚙ Wartime Security
- ⚙ Security of Information
  - ~ Security Classification
  - ~ Security Clearance
  - ~ Voice Communications
  - ~ Stowage and Transport of Classified Information
- ⚙ Cybersecurity

To Learn More:

- ⚓ **www.usni.org/BlueAndGoldProfessionalBooks/TheBluejackets Manual**
- ⚓ *Department of the Navy Personnel Security Program* (SECNAV M-5510.30)
- ⚓ *Navy Doctrine for Antiterrorism/Force Protection* (NWP 3–07.2)
- ⚓ *U.S. Navy Social Media Handbook*

Associated Tabs:

- ○ TAB 9-A: Force Protection Conditions (FPCONs)

 9-A Force Protection Conditions (FPCONs)

FPCON NORMAL—*NO KNOWN ENEMY THREAT EXISTS*
Applies when only a *general* threat of possible terrorist activity exists. Only routine security measures are required.

Actions to be taken:

- Remind all personnel to be suspicious and inquisitive of strangers.
- Be alert for abandoned parcels or suitcases and for suspicious unattended vehicles in the vicinity.
- Report unusual activities to the Officer of the Deck.
- Secure and periodically inspect spaces not in use.
- Review pier and shipboard access control procedures including land and water barriers.
- Ensure sentries, roving patrols, the quarterdeck watch, etc., have the ability to communicate with one another.
- Coordinate pier and fleet landing security requirements with other services, allies, local law enforcement, etc., in the area and identify or establish ways to communicate with them.

FPCON ALPHA—*THERE IS AN INCREASED POSSIBLE GENERAL THREAT OF TERRORIST ACTIVITY*

This condition is set when it is believed that the possibility of an attack has increased but nothing specific is known about that possibility. FPCON ALPHA can be sustained for very long periods of time.

Actions to be taken:

- Muster, arm, and brief security personnel on the threat and rules of engagement.
- Keep key personnel who may be needed to implement security measures on call.
- Randomly inspect vehicles entering pier.
- Randomly inspect hand-carried items and packages before they are brought aboard.
- Establish procedures for screening food, mail, water, and other supplies and equipment entering the ship.
- Regulate shipboard lighting as appropriate to the threat environment.
- Increase frequency of security drills.
- Establish internal and external communications, including connectivity checks with the local operational commander, agencies, and authorities that are expected to provide support, if required.

- When in a non–U.S. Navy controlled port:
    - ➤ deploy barriers to keep vehicles away from the ship if possible (100 feet in U.S. ports and 400 feet outside the United States as the minimum standoff distances)
    - ➤ rig hawse pipe covers and rat guards on lines, cables, and hoses
    - ➤ consider using an anchor collar
    - ➤ raise accommodation ladders and stern gates when not in use

FPCON BRAVO—*INCREASED AND MORE PREDICTABLE THREAT OF TERRORISM*

This will be set when specific information suggests probable violence, but specific targets have not been identified. Because the resulting increased security measures that will be implemented may affect the operational capabilities of units and may have an impact on relations with local authorities, this condition should be downgraded when possible (but not at the expense of security).

Actions to be taken:

- Set Material Condition Yoke (secure all watertight doors and hatches), main deck and below.
- Consistent with local rules and regulations:
    - ➤ post armed pier sentries as necessary
    - ➤ establish unloading zones
    - ➤ move all containers as far away from the ship as possible (100 feet in the United States, 400 feet outside the United States as the minimum standoff distances)
- Local threat, environment, and fields of fire should be considered when selecting weapons.
- Restrict vehicle access to the pier. Discontinue parking on the pier.
- Post signs in the local language to establish visiting and loitering restrictions.
- Before allowing visitors aboard, inspect all their hand-carried items and packages. Where available, use baggage scanners and walk-through or handheld metal detectors to screen visitors and their packages prior to boarding the ship.

- Implement measures to keep unauthorized craft away from the ship. Authorized craft should be carefully controlled.
- Raise accommodation ladders, etc., when not in use.
- Clear ship of all unnecessary stages, camels, barges, and lines.
- Review liberty policy in light of the threat and revise it as necessary to maintain safety and security of ship and crew.
- Conduct division quarters at foul weather parade.
- Avoid conducting activities that involve gathering a large number of crewmembers on the weatherdecks. Where possible, relocate such activities inside the skin of the ship.
- Ensure an up-to-date list of bilingual personnel for the area of operations is readily available.
- If they are not already armed, arm the quarterdeck and consider arming the sounding and security patrol.
- Review procedures for expedient issue of firearms and ammunition to the shipboard security reaction force and other members of the crew.
- Instruct watches to conduct frequent, random searches of the pier, including pilings and access points.
- Conduct visual inspections of the ship's hull and ship's boats at intermittent intervals and immediately before getting under way.
- Hoist ship's boats aboard when not in use.
- Terminate public visits. In U.S. government–controlled ports, host visits (family, friends, small groups sponsored by the ship) may continue at the commanding officer's/master's discretion.
- After working hours, reduce entry points to the ship's interior by securing infrequently used entrances. Safety requirements must be considered, however.
- Where applicable, obstruct possible helicopter landing areas.
- Where possible, monitor local communications (ship-to-ship, TV, radio, police scanners).
- As appropriate, inform local authorities of actions being taken.
- If the threat situation warrants, deploy picket boats to conduct patrols in the immediate vicinity of the ship. Brief boat crews and arm them with appropriate weapons considering the threat, the local environment, and fields of fire.

- When in a non-U.S. Government-controlled port:
    - ➤ identify and randomly inspect authorized watercraft, such as workboats, ferries, and commercially rented liberty launches, daily
    - ➤ direct liberty boats to make a security tour around the ship upon departing from and arriving at the ship, with particular focus on the waterline and under pilings when berthed at a pier
    - ➤ remove any excess brows/gangways
    - ➤ maintain the capability to get under way on short notice or as specified by standard operating procedures
    - ➤ consider the layout of fire hoses and brief designated crew personnel on procedures for repelling boarders, small boats, and ultra-light aircraft

FPCON CHARLIE—*IMMINENT THREAT OF TERRORISM*

Applies when an incident has occurred or some specific intelligence has been received indicating that some form of terrorist action or targeting against personnel or facilities is likely. Because prolonged implementation of Charlie measures may create hardship and affect the activities of the unit and its personnel, this condition should be maintained when necessary but not beyond.

Actions to be taken:

- Consider setting Material Condition Zebra (secure all access doors and hatches), main deck and below.
- Cancel liberty. Execute emergency recall.
- Prepare to get under way on short notice. If conditions warrant, request permission to sortie/get under way.
- Block unnecessary vehicle access to the pier.
- Coordinate with local port authorities to establish a small-boat exclusion zone around the ship.
- Add additional personnel to watch teams as appropriate.
- Energize radar and sonar.
- Rotate screws and cycle rudder(s) at frequent and irregular intervals to deter or thwart attacks.
- Consider staffing repair locker(s).

- If available and feasible, consider use of airborne assets (such as embarked helicopters) as an observation platform.
- Activate an antiswimmer watch.
- In non-U.S. government-controlled ports and if unable to get under way, consider requesting armed security augmentation from area Combatant Commander.

FPCON DELTA—*A LOCALIZED, SPECIFIC TERRORIST THREAT OR AN ACTUAL ATTACK*

This condition will normally be set only by units that have been attacked or are very likely to be attacked. Only on very rare occasions (such as 11 September 2001) would this condition be set over a larger area. FPCON Delta measures are not intended to be sustained for substantial periods.

Actions to be taken:

- Fully implement all measures of lower FPCON levels.
- Permit only necessary personnel topside.
- If possible, cancel port visit and get under way.
- Employ all necessary weapons to defend against attack.

TAB 10 Ships

Even though the Navy has evolved into a complex organization with various missions and many different kinds of equipment to accomplish them, ships are the core element of the Navy. Even imagined space travel and galactic conflict, such as in *Star Trek* and *Star Wars*, usually rely on space-*ships* as the technological centerpiece. It should come as no surprise that this basic element is so embedded into Navy culture that even at shore installations floors are often referred to as decks, ceilings as overheads, etc. This is a source of pride that Sailors, Marines, and Coast Guardsmen emulate even though it often confuses and amuses civilians and those who serve in non-sea services.

Major Topics Covered:

- ⚓ Ship characteristics
- ⚓ Ship construction
- ⚓ Ship systems
- ⚓ Ship types
- ⚓ Ship classifications

To Learn More:

- ⚓ www.usni.org/BlueAndGoldProfessionalBooks/TheBluejackets Manual
- ⚓ *Basic Military Requirements* (NAVEDTRA 14325)
- ⚓ Naval Vessel Register, www.nvr.navy.mil
- ⚓ *Navy Program Guide* (current year)
- ⚓ *The Naval Institute Guide to Ships and Aircraft of the U.S. Fleet,* 19th ed., by Norman Polmar (Naval Institute Press, 2013)
- ⚓ Ship information, http://www.navy.mil/navydata/our_ships.asp

Associated Tabs:

- O TAB 10-A: Ships and Craft
- O TAB 10-B: Ship Type Classifications

10-A Ships and Craft

For reference purposes, ships and craft are separated into two groups, combatants and auxiliaries. Combatants are listed alphabetically by their type ("cruiser" or "destroyer," for example) followed by their ship type classification ("CG" or "DDG," for example). See TAB 10-B for a complete list of classifications. Auxiliaries are grouped according to their general functions (underway replenishment, fleet support, and service craft).

COMBATANTS

Aircraft Carriers (CVN)

These enormous ships have been described as the "world's largest combatant ships and the world's smallest airfields." They are longer than 3 football fields laid end-to-end, can displace as much 100,000 tons and carry between 60 and 80 aircraft of various types. The number of personnel required to operate an aircraft carrier and its aircraft is nearly 5,000.

Aircraft carriers carry an assortment of aircraft capable of performing a wide variety of missions, including air support to troops ashore, bombardment missions, antisubmarine operations, rescue missions, reconnaissance, and antiair warfare. Because of their powerful engines and four screws, carriers are capable of high speed, and they are capable of staying at sea for long periods of time, making them a potent weapon in a wide variety of scenarios.

[**10-A-1**] Aircraft carrier (CVN)

Besides having a huge flight deck for loading, launching, and recovering many different types of aircraft, CVNs also have a large hangar deck beneath the flight deck where aircraft can be safely stowed and maintained. This area is so large that it can accommodate such things as boxing matches, concerts, and basketball games.

Equipped with catapults for launching and arresting gear for recovering, CVNs can handle specially designed fixed-wing aircraft as well as helicopters.

Amphibious Assault Ships (LHA/LHD)

Of all the Navy's ship types, only CVNs are larger than these. They resemble CVNs, but with both a flight deck and a well deck, they are capable of simultaneous air and landing-craft operations. Unlike CVNs, these ships do not have the catapults or arresting gear needed for normal fixed-wing aircraft and can only operate helicopters and vertical-landing-and-take-off fixed-wing aircraft. They can also function as sea-control ships, when necessary, by operating antisubmarine helicopters and AV-8B Harrier V/STOL (vertical/short takeoff and landing) airplanes.

Amphibious Command Ship (LCC)

Originally designed to function as command centers for amphibious operations, LCCs currently serve as fleet flagships, providing control and communication facilities for the fleet commander and her or his staff.

There are currently only two LCCs in the Navy: USS *Blue Ridge* (LCC 19) and USS *Mount Whitney* (LCC 20). Although these ships were commissioned in 1971, they have been modernized and are expected to remain in service until 2039.

Amphibious Transport Dock (LPD)

These ships are similar to the LSD (see below) in that they deliver troops and equipment in landing craft or vehicles carried in a well deck and floated out through a stern gate, but their helicopter capacity is more extensive, including hangar facilities where aircraft can be stowed and maintained. The modern *San Antonio*–class LPDs are 684 feet long and displace 25,000 tons. They have 20,000 square feet of space that can accommodate a large number of vehicles, have 34,000 cubic feet for cargo, and can accommodate as many as eight hundred troops. Their medical and dental facilities are larger and more capable than those on the LSDs. Other advanced

[**10-A-2**] Amphibious assault ship (LHA)

[**10-A-3**] Amphibious command ship (LCC)

features include an enclosed mast and sensor (radar, electronic warfare, etc.) array that makes them harder to detect and allows easier maintenance, state-of-the-art C4ISR (command, control, communications, computers, intelligence, surveillance, and reconnaissance) and self-defense systems, a shipboard wide-area network linking shipboard systems with embarked Marine Corps platforms, and significant quality of life improvements.

Coastal Riverine Force

This force extends the Navy's reach from traditional "blue water" (oceans and seas) areas into coastal (sometimes called "green water") and riverine ("brown water") areas. It uses a variety of small, combat-capable craft ranging from rubber combat raiding craft to 85-foot coastal patrol boats.

[**10-A-4**] Amphibious transport dock (LPD)

[**10-A-5**] Coastal Riverine Squadron 1 patrol boats

Cruisers (CG)

During World War II, there were heavy cruisers (CA) and light cruisers (CL), the difference being primarily in their gun armament. Today, the Navy's cruisers are all *Ticonderoga*-class guided-missile (designated CG) ships, which are powered by gas turbines and equipped with the very sophisticated Aegis combat system that can handle multiple engagements at the same time.

These ships displace about 10,000 tons and are particularly potent in antiair missions, but are capable of a number of other missions as well, including antisurface and antisubmarine. They are equipped with a variety of weapons, including missiles that can knock out incoming raids from enemy aircraft or missile attacks. With other specially designed missiles, they are able to deliver an offensive punch, hitting land or sea targets at substantial distances.

Destroyers (DDG)

In today's Navy, destroyers perform a wide range of duties. They can serve as part of a screen unit in a carrier task group, protecting it from various forms of attack. They can detect and engage enemy submarines, aircraft,

[**10-A-6**] Guided-missile cruiser (CG)

missiles, and surface ships. In an amphibious assault, a destroyer's weapons can help protect against enemy forces at sea and ashore. In short, destroyers have a well-deserved reputation of being the "workhorses" of the fleet.

Previous classes of destroyer were rather small—some displacing as little as 400 tons—but today's *Arleigh Burke*–class destroyers displace more than 8,000 tons and are over 500 feet long. Modern destroyers are powered by gas-turbine engines and can go from "cold iron" (meaning no engines on the line) to full speed in twelve minutes, in sharp contrast to their steam-powered predecessors, which took hours to power up. The weapons of today's destroyers include torpedoes, guns, antisubmarine rockets, and a variety of missiles. Before the inclusion of missiles, destroyers were designated DDs, but all of today's destroyers are equipped with sophisticated missile systems and are therefore designated as DDGs. Like the *Ticonderoga*-class cruisers, *Arleigh Burke*–class destroyers are equipped with the Aegis system, making it the most potent class of destroyer ever built.

[**10-A-7**] *Arleigh Burke*–class guided-missile destroyer (DDG)

Another, even more sophisticated destroyer is the *Zumwalt* class. These ships are in many ways very different from any other destroyers. Designed to operate alone or as part of a task force, their capabilities include enhanced survivability in the face of enemy aircraft, missiles, submarines, mines, and small boat attacks. Given the hull number 1000, the Navy currently plans on building three of these technological wonders.

Dock Landing Ship (LSD)

These ships have a well deck inside the vessel that can be flooded so that waterborne landing craft and vehicles can be floated out of the ship's stern gate. They also have a limited capacity (a flight deck but no hangar space) for handling troop-carrying helicopters or *Osprey* hybrid aircraft. LSDs are equipped with a vehicle turning area and tactical logistics communication spaces to facilitate and coordinate troop/vehicle movement and logistics. These ships have a doctor and dentist assigned as ship's company, two dental examination rooms, and one medical operating room.

[**10-A-8**] *Zumwalt*-class guided-missile destroyer (DDG)

[**10-A-9**] Dock landing ship (LSD)

Expeditionary Transfer Docks (T-ESD)/
Expeditionary Mobile Base Ships (T-ESB)

The Expeditionary Transfer Dock (T-ESD) is a large (785 feet long and displacing approximately 80,000 tons), highly flexible ship that provides logistics movement from sea to shore in order to support a broad range of military operations. These ships can operate within "Maritime Prepositioning Ship Squadrons" that are stationed at key points in the world to be mobile sea bases that are ready to support U.S. military operations during times of crisis. Designed to support the delivery of needed equipment, they have sophisticated vehicle delivery systems and 25,000 square feet of stowage space for vehicles and equipment, as well as 380,000 gallons of fuel storage capacity.

Later versions include a flight deck, berthing spaces to accommodate 250 troops, and repair spaces among other things, and are called "Expeditionary Mobile Base Ships" (T-ESB).

[**10-A-10**] An artist's rendering of the Military Sealift Command expeditionary transfer dock USNS *Montford Point* (T-ESD1).

Frigates (FF) and Littoral Combat Ships (LCS)

The frigate first appeared in the U.S. Navy during World War II as the destroyer escort (DE). In 1975 destroyer escorts were redesignated as frigates (FF). The inclusion of missiles further transformed them into FFGs.

Another class of ship began as a littoral combat ship (LCS), but because "L" has traditionally been used for amphibious ships (originally meaning "landing"), these ships are expected to transition to the more appropriate designation of FF.

These ships have been designed to allow them to be configured (or reconfigured) for different missions, depending upon "modules" that can be added or removed. The same ship can be configured for surface, anti-submarine, or mine countermeasures, depending upon what modules are used. If missile systems are added, they will likely be re-designated as FFGs.

Although their missions are the same, these ships are being built in two distinct variants: the *Freedom* variants have more traditional designs built primarily of steel and all have *odd* hull numbers, while the *Independence* variants have an all-aluminum "stabilized monohull" (that looks something like a catamaran when viewed from astern) and they all have *even* hull numbers.

[**10-A-11**] *Freedom-*class littoral combat ship (LCS)

[**10-A-12**] *Independence*-class
littoral combat ship (LCS)

Landing Craft, Air Cushion (LCAC)

This specialized landing craft is usually carried by larger amphibious ships (such as LPDs and LHDs). Because it rides on a cushion of air, it can operate on both land and water. LCACs are used to transport the weapons systems, equipment, cargo, and personnel of the assault elements of a Marine Air-Ground Task Force from ship to shore and across the beach. They can carry heavy payloads, such as an M-1 tank, at high speeds. Air cushion technology allows this vehicle to reach more than 70 percent of the world's coastline, while only about 15 percent of that coastline is accessible by conventional landing craft.

Landing Craft, Mechanized and Utility (LCM/LCU)

Landing craft are used by amphibious forces to transport equipment and troops to the shore. They are also used to support civilian humanitarian/ maritime operations. Capable of transporting cargo, tracked or wheeled vehicles, and troops from amphibious assault ships to beachheads or piers, LCMs are 74 feet long and have a bow ramp for onload/offload, while the larger LCUs are 135 feet long and have both bow and stern ramps for onload/offload. LCUs have the ability to operate at sea for up to ten days.

[**10-A-13**] Landing craft, air cushion (LCAC)

[**10-A-14**] A pair of LCMs headed for the beach

[**10-A-15**] An LCU carrying a pair of tanks

Littoral Combat Ships
See **Frigates (FF) and Littoral Combat Ships (LCS)** above.

Mine Countermeasures Ships (MCM)
These ships have fiberglass sheathed wooden hulls and use sonar and video systems, cable cutters, and a mine detonating device that can be released and detonated by remote control to remove or destroy enemy mines.

Patrol Coastal Ships (PC)
PCs are used for a variety of missions including special warfare and coastal interdiction operations. They include patrol craft of the *Cyclone* (PC 1) class. Measuring 170 feet long with a 35-knot speed and armed with two 25mm guns, Stinger missiles, and lighter weapons, PCs are considerably smaller than frigates but larger than coastal and riverine craft.

[10-A-16] Mine countermeasures ship (MCM)

[**10-A-17**] Patrol coastal ship (PC)

Submarines (SSN/SSBN/SSGN)

The Navy has three basic types of submarine: attack submarines designated SSN, fleet ballistic-missile submarines designated SSBN, and guided-missile submarines designated SSGN. All U.S. submarines currently are nuclear powered.

The primary mission of attack submarines is to attack other submarines and ships, but they are also assigned secondary missions, which may include surveillance and reconnaissance, direct task-force support, landing-force support, land attack, minelaying, and rescue. An SSN's principal weapons are high-speed, wire-guided torpedoes and cruise missiles for use against surface and land targets.

Fleet ballistic-missile submarines have a strategic mission, in that they are meant to deter or participate in a nuclear-missile exchange. Their highly sophisticated, very potent ballistic missiles are capable of hitting targets many thousands of miles away and causing tremendous destruction. These vessels must remain submerged for long periods of time, virtually out of contact with the rest of the world, waiting to carry out a mission that could be devastating to the whole world. This is a stressful environment for the crews, and to alleviate some of that stress, SSBNs are operated during alternate periods by two separate crews. One is called the blue crew and the other the gold crew. On return from an extended patrol, one crew relieves

[**10-A-18**] Attack submarine (SSN)

the other, and the ship returns to patrol following a brief period alongside her tender or in port. The relieved crew enters a month-long period of rest, recreation, and leave, followed by two months of training. This system allows each crew time ashore, while keeping the entire force of SSBNs cruising on deep patrol except for very brief periods.

The primary missions of the guided-missile submarine are to conduct land attacks and to insert and support Special Operations Forces (SOF). Secondary missions are similar to those of the SSNs and include intelligence, surveillance and reconnaissance (ISR), battle space preparation, and sea control. Armed with up to 154 Tomahawk or Tactical Tomahawk land attack missiles, they have the ability to carry and support a team of 66 SOF personnel for up to 90 days. Clandestine insertion and retrieval of these Special Operations Forces are enhanced by the ability to host dual dry deck shelters.

[**10-A-19**] Fleet ballistic-missile submarine (SSBN)

AUXILIARIES

Underway-Replenishment Ships

If they are going to be combat effective, warships must be able to remain at sea for weeks at a time with fuel, provisions, parts, and ammunition. The U.S. Navy is highly proficient at underway replenishment (UNREP) techniques that use special cargo-handling gear to make transfers from one ship to another while the two are steaming abreast or, in some cases, astern. Vertical replenishment (VERTREP) is a form of UNREP in which cargo-carrying helicopters are used to transfer goods from one ship to another. Much of the UNREP capability of the Navy today is carried out by Military Sealift Command (MSC) ships, such as oilers (T-AO), ammunition ships (T-AE), and fast combat support ships (T-AOEs).

[**10-A-20**] Fast combat support ship (T-AOE)

Fleet Support Ships

UNREP vessels are only one type of the auxiliaries that help carry out the Navy's many missions. A number of other ships play vital roles in keeping the fleet operating at peak efficiency. For example, salvage vessels provide rapid firefighting, dewatering, battle-damage repair, and towing assistance to save ships that have been in battle or victims of some other disaster from further loss or damage. Equipped with specialized equipment and manned by salvage divers, these ships can also perform rescue and salvage operations underwater.

Service Craft

Also among the Navy's waterborne resources is a large and varied group of service craft. Some are huge vessels like the large auxiliary floating dry docks that can take very large vessels aboard and raise them out of the water for repairs. Barracks craft accommodate crews when their ships are being overhauled or repaired. Lighters are barges used to store and transport materials and to house pier-side repair shops. Some gasoline barges, fuel-oil barges, and water barges are self-propelled; those that are not depend on tugs. Floating cranes and wrecking derricks are towed from place to place as needed. Diving tenders support diving operations, and ferryboats or launches, which carry people, automobiles, and equipment, are usually located at Navy bases, where facilities are spread out over large distances. Best known of the service craft are the harbor tugs, large and small, that aid ships in docking and undocking, provide firefighting services when needed, perform rescues, and haul lighters from place to place.

[**10-A-21**] A large harbor tug (YTB) showing off some of her firefighting capability

10-B Ship Type Classifications

Used as part of a ship's official designation, the Navy uses letter symbols to identify the types of ships and service craft. This is called "type classification." Some of the more common type classifications are listed below. Keep in mind that many of these type classifications are not in use currently, but they are listed because you may come across them historically or they may be reactivated at some later date.

ACS	Auxiliary crane ship
AD	Destroyer tender
AE	Ammunition ship
AFDL	Small auxiliary floating dry dock
AFDM	Medium auxiliary floating dry dock
AFS	Combat store ship
AFSB	Afloat forward staging base
AGF	Miscellaneous command ship
AGM	Missile range instrumentation ship
AGOR	Oceanographic research ship
AGOS	Surveillance ship
AGS	Surveying ship
AH	Hospital ship
AK	Cargo ship
AKR	Vehicle cargo ship
AO	Oiler
AOE	Fast combat-support ship
AOR	Replenishment oiler
AOT	Transport oiler
APL	Barracks craft (non-self-propelled)
ARC	Cable repair ship
ARDM	Medium auxiliary repair dry dock
ARS	Salvage ship
AS	Submarine tender
ASR	Submarine rescue ship
ATF	Fleet ocean tug
AVB	Aviation logistics support ship
BB	Battleship

CA	Heavy cruiser
CC	Command ship
CG	Guided-missile cruiser
CGN	Guided-missile cruiser (nuclear propulsion)
CL	Light cruiser
CLG	Guided-missile light cruiser
CSP	Causeway section, powered
CV	Multipurpose aircraft carrier
CVA	Attack aircraft carrier
CVHE	Escort helicopter aircraft carrier
CVN	Multipurpose aircraft carrier (nuclear propulsion)
CVS	Antisubmarine warfare aircraft carrier
DD	Destroyer
DDG	Guided-missile destroyer
DE	Destroyer escort
DER	Radar picket escort ship
DL	Destroyer leader
DLG	Guided-missile destroyer leader
DLGN	Guided-missile destroyer leader (nuclear propulsion)
DSRV	Deep-submergence rescue vehicle
EDD	Self-defense test ship
FF	Frigate
FFG	Guided-missile frigate
FFR	Radar picket frigate
FFT	Frigate (reserve training)
FSF	Fast sea frame
IX	Unclassified miscellaneous
JHSV	Joint high speed vessel
HST	High speed transport
HSV	High speed vessel
LCAC	Landing craft, air cushion
LCC	Amphibious command ship
LCM	Landing craft, mechanized
LCPL	Landing craft, personnel, large
LCS	Littoral combat ship
LCU	Landing craft, utility
LCVP	Landing craft, vehicle and personnel

LHA	Amphibious assault ship (general purpose)
LHD	Amphibious assault ship (multipurpose)
LPD	Amphibious transport dock
LPH	Amphibious assault ship (helicopter)
LSD	Dock landing ship
LSSC	Light SEAL support craft
LST	Tank landing ship
MCM	Mine countermeasures ship
MCS	Mine countermeasures support ship
MHC	Coastal minehunter
MLP	Mobile landing platform
MPFUB	Maritime prepositioning force utility boat
MSC	Coastal minesweeper
MSO	Ocean-going minesweeper
PB	Patrol Boat
PBR	River patrol boat
PC	Patrol coastal ship
PCE	Patrol escort
PCF	Fast patrol craft ("swift boat")
PCG	Guided-missile patrol craft
PCH	Patrol craft (hydrofoil)
PG	Patrol combatant
PGG	Guided-missile patrol combatant
PHM	Patrol combatant missile (hydrofoil)
PT	Patrol torpedo boat
PTF	Patrol torpedo boat, fast
RAB	Riverine assault boat
RCB	Riverine command boat
RPB	Riverine patrol boat
SBX	Mobile radar platform
SDV	SEAL delivery vehicle
SLWT	Side-loadable warping tug
SS	Submarine
SSAG	Auxiliary submarine
SSBN	Ballistic-missile submarine (nuclear propulsion)
SBX	Sea-based X-band radar ship
SSC	Ship to shore connector

SSG	Guided-missile submarine
SSGN	Missile (non-ballistic) submarine (nuclear propulsion)
SSN	Submarine (nuclear propulsion)
YC	Open lighter
YCV	Aircraft transportation lighter
YD	Floating crane (non-self-propelled)
YDT	Diving Tender
YFB	Ferry boat or launch
YFD	Yard floating dry dock
YFN	Covered lighter
YFNB	Large covered lighter
YFND	Dry dock companion craft (non-self-propelled)
YFNX	Lighter (special purpose)
YFP	Floating power barge (non-self-propelled)
YLC	Salvage lift craft, light (non-self-propelled)
YOGN	Gasoline barge
YON	Fuel oil barge
YOS	Oil storage barge
YP	Yard patrol (patrol craft, training)
YR	Floating workshop (non-self-propelled)
YRB	Repair and berthing barge (non-self-propelled)
YRBM	Repair, berthing, and messing barge (non-self-propelled)
YRDH	Floating dry dock workshop, hull (non-self-propelled)
YRDM	Floating dry dock workshop, machine (non-self-propelled)
YRR	Radiological repair barge (non-self-propelled)
YSD	Seaplane wrecking derrick
YTB	Large harbor tug
YTL	Small harbor tug
YTM	Medium harbor tug
YTT	Torpedo trials craft
YWN	Water barge
YWO	Waste oil barge

Ships of the Military Sealift Command (MSC) are distinguished from other Navy ships by having a "T" before their letter designations. Below are some examples of MSC ship types.

T-AE	Ammunition ships
T-AFS	Combat stores ship
T-AG	Offshore petroleum distribution system ship
T-AGOS	Ocean surveillance ship
T-AGS	Oceanographic survey
T-AH	Hospital ship
T-AK	Maritime prepositioning ship
T-AKE	Dry cargo ship
T-AKR	Vehicle cargo ship
T-AO	Oiler
T-AOE	Fast combat support ship
T-AOT	Transport oiler (tanker)
T-ARC	Cable repair
T-ARS	Rescue and salvage ship
T-ATF	Fleet ocean tug
T-MLP	Mobile landing platform

Notes: When these classifications are paired with a hull number (as in DDG 51, or CVN 76) there should not be a hyphen in between (as in DDG-51)—although, in truth you will frequently see this (incorrectly) done. When a "T" is used to designate a ship as an MSC asset, a hyphen *is* used to separate it from the rest of the classification (as in T-AO, or T-MLP).

TAB 11 Shipboard Life

As a Sailor in the U.S. Navy, you will more than likely serve aboard ship. Life aboard ship is truly unique, requiring a special organizational structure that is standard in some ways and tailored in others. Just finding your way around in a ship (especially an aircraft carrier!) can be a real challenge, but the good news is that the Navy has a system for "navigating" on board a ship that is both universal and logical, once you understand how it works. The importance of cleanliness in such a close environment cannot be overemphasized, and because ships are both complex and subject to significant environmental challenges, maintaining them requires a great deal of knowledge and attention to detail.

Major Topics Covered:

- ☸ Shipboard Organization
- ☸ Shipboard Routine
- ☸ Cleaning
- ☸ Maintenance & Preservation
- ☸ Inspections

To Learn More:

- ⚓ **www.usni.org/BlueAndGoldProfessionalBooks/TheBluejackets Manual**
- ⚓ *Basic Military Requirements* (NAVEDTRA 14325)
- ⚓ *Military Requirements for Petty Officers Third and Second Class* (NAVEDTRA 14504)
- ⚓ *Military Requirements for Petty Officers First Class* (NAVEDTRA 14145)
- ⚓ *Standard Organization and Regulations of the U.S. Navy* (OPNAVINST 3120.32D)

Associated Tabs:

- ○ Tab 11-A: Shipboard Compartment Identification
- ○ Tab 11-B: 3M Periodicity Codes

11-A **Shipboard Compartment Identification**

The Navy has a system of compartment identification that helps you find your way around any ship, provides information useful for proper cleaning and maintenance, and provides information needed for damage control.

FINDING YOUR WAY

Trying to find your way around a multideck ship that is several hundred feet long can be a difficult process. Just as a town or city has a system using street signs and addresses to help you find your way around, so does a Navy ship. Each compartment on a ship has an identifier that is roughly equivalent to a street address in a city. Once you understand this system, you will know where you are at any given place on a ship, and you will be able to find any space on a ship even if you haven't been there before.

Every space aboard ship is assigned an identifying number-letter symbol, which is marked on a label plate above the entrance(s) to the space and on a sign on the bulkhead inside the space (the latter is commonly called the "Bullseye"). Compartment identifiers contain the following information in the following format:

Deck number – Frame number – Number representing the space's relation to the centerline of the ship – Letter(s) explaining the function of the compartment

EXAMPLE: 4–95–3–M

The *deck number* is the first part of the compartment number. Since the main deck of a ship is always numbered "1," we know that our example compartment is three decks below the main deck. If our example had been numbered "04," we would know that it was four decks *above* the main deck. If a compartment extends through more than one deck (such as an engineering space that must be large enough to hold a boiler or turbines), the deck number of that compartment refers to the bottommost deck.

The second number refers to the *frame number*. As explained earlier in this chapter, frames are beamlike structures that are fastened to the keel and run athwartships. They are numbered sequentially, fore to aft, so that the frame nearest the stem of the ship would be numbered "1" and the next one aft would be numbered "2," and so on. When you are first assigned to a ship, it is a good idea to find out and memorize the number of frames she has, because then you will have a better idea what part of the ship you are in once you know the frame number of the compartment. In our example compartment, the frame number is 95. If we know that the ship has a total of 207 frames, we would then be able to figure out that we are located almost halfway between the bow and stern of the ship. The frame number always refers to the forwardmost bulkhead of a compartment.

The third part of the compartment identifier refers to the compartment's relation to the centerline. Compartments located directly on the centerline are numbered "0" (zero). Those on the starboard side of the centerline are numbered with odd numbers, and those on the port side are numbered evenly. The first compartment on the starboard side of the centerline would be numbered "1," the next one outboard would be numbered "3," the next one outboard of that one would be "5," and so on until we reach the skin of the ship. The first compartment on the port side of the centerline would be numbered "2," and the ones outboard of it would be "4," "6," and so on. Our example compartment is identified by the number "3," so we know that it is the second compartment off the centerline on the starboard side of the ship.

The fourth and last part of the compartment identifier is the letter that identifies the compartment's primary function. Spaces where goods are stowed for delivery to other ships or stations, rather than merely stowed for future use of the ship itself, are identified by a two-letter symbol, but all others are simply one letter. From the list of compartment letter identifiers below, it can be seen that our example compartment is used for the stowage or handling of ammunition.

A   Stowage spaces: store and issue rooms; refrigerated compartments

AA   Cargo holds: cargo holds and refrigerated compartments

C   Control centers for ship and fire-control operations (normally manned): the combat information center (CIC); internal communications (IC) rooms; plotting rooms; pilot house; electronic equipment-operating spaces

E   Engineering control centers (normally manned): main machinery spaces; evaporator rooms; steering-gear rooms; pump rooms; auxiliary machinery spaces; emergency generator rooms

F   Oil stowage compartments (for use by the ship itself, that is, not as cargo): fuel-, diesel-, and lubricating-oil compartments

FF   Oil stowage compartments (cargo): compartments carrying various types of oil as cargo

G   Gasoline stowage compartments (for use by the ship itself): gasoline tanks, cofferdams, trunks, and pump rooms

GG   Gasoline stowage compartments (cargo): spaces for carrying gasoline as cargo

J   JP-5 (aviation) fuel (ship or embarked aircraft use): jet-fuel stowage spaces

JJ   JP-5 fuel (cargo): spaces for carrying JP-5 fuel as cargo

K   Chemicals and dangerous materials (other than oil and gasoline)

L   Living spaces: berthing and messing spaces; staterooms; washrooms; heads; brig; sick bay; and passageways

M   Ammunition spaces: magazines; handling rooms; turrets; gun mounts; shell rooms; ready service rooms

Q   Miscellaneous spaces not covered by other letters: laundry; galley; pantries; wiring trunks; unmanned engineering; electrical and electronic spaces; shops; offices

T   Vertical access trunks: escape trunks

V   Voids: spaces that are normally empty

W   Water stowage spaces: drainage tanks; freshwater tanks; peak tanks; reserve feedwater tanks

THE "BULLSEYE"

As mentioned above, every compartment on a Navy ship has what is commonly known as a "Bullseye" that provides some essential information about that compartment in an abbreviated form. Located inside the compartment itself, the Bullseye consists of a twelve- by fifteen-inch rectangle that is photoluminescent (so that it can be found in low-light conditions) with two-inch black letters in its center. It is, whenever possible, located at eye level where it can easily be seen. The information in this rectangle is standard throughout the Navy. Below is an example of a Bullseye:

4–95–3–M

FR 95–99

GM

The first line tells you the compartment number as described above. The second line tells you the extent of the compartment in terms of how many frames it spans (in this example, five frames), and the last line tells you which division is responsible for the space (in this case "GM Division.")

DAMAGE-CONTROL FUNCTION

The subject of damage control is treated in some detail in **Chapter 15**, but it is important to note here that the Bullseye's compartment-responsibility marking system serves another important function besides telling you which division is responsible for a particular space. It also serves to identify the compartment quickly so that anyone can report it in the event of a fire or other emergency. If you discovered a fire in this space, you could report it without confusion, even if you had never been to this space before and were not familiar with it. By reading its number off the first line, you could tell the damage-control party exactly where they needed to go to fight the fire. This saves valuable time, which would be especially essential in the example used above since the space identified in this example is a magazine used for stowing ammunition!

 11-B 3M Periodicity Codes

See **Chapter 11** for an explanation of the 3M (Maintenance and Material Management) System.

D	Daily
2D	Each Second Day
3D	Each Third Day
W	Weekly
2W	Each Second Week
M	Monthly
2M	Each Second Month
Q	Quarterly
A	Annually
18M	Each 18 Months
24M	Each 24 Months
C	Cycle*
R	Situational**

   * Cycle means that the designated maintenance is to be done once between major overhauls (approximately every 3 years).

** Situational requirements include such things as "before getting under way" or "after firing the guns."

TAB 12 Seamanship and Boats

All Sailors must have at least a basic understanding of seamanship. No matter what part of the Navy you serve in, such knowledge will likely serve you well.

Major Topics Covered:

- ☸ Working with lines and ropes
- ☸ Mooring with lines and anchors
- ☸ Towing
- ☸ Underway replenishment
- ☸ Boats
    - ~ Types
    - ~ Crews
    - ~ Customs

To Learn More:

- ⚓ www.usni.org/BlueAndGoldProfessionalBooks/TheBluejackets Manual
- ⚓ *Basic Military Requirements* (NAVEDTRA 14325)
- ⚓ *Seaman* (NAVEDTRA 14067)
- ⚓ *Boatswain's Mate* (NAVEDTRA 14343A)
- ⚓ *Chapman Piloting & Seamanship*, 67th ed., by Jonathan Eaton (Hearst, 2013)
- ⚓ *Navy Towing Manual* (Naval Sea Systems Command)
- ⚓ *Boat Crew Seamanship Manual* (COMDTINST M16114.5C) by U.S. Coast Guard (2014)

Associated Tabs:

- ○ TAB 12-A: Mooring Line Configurations and Terms
- ○ TAB 12-B: Line-Handling Commands
- ○ TAB 12-C: Anchor Chain Identification System
- ○ TAB 12-D: Anchoring Commands
- ○ TAB 12-E: Blocks and Tackles
- ○ TAB 12-F: Boat Customs and Etiquette

12-A Mooring Line Configurations and Terms

Mooring lines are referred to by both numbers and by names. They are numbered starting with the forward-most one (number 1) and continuing aft in sequence. Mooring lines are named by a combination of their location, their use, and the direction in which they tend as they leave the ship.

Once a ship is moored to a pier or to another ship, it is important to prevent the ship from moving along (laterally) and to keep it from moving up and down (parallel to) the pier. Mooring lines are designed to prevent these two things. Lines that prevent ships from drifting away from the pier—in other words, that control lateral movement—are rigged perpendicular, or nearly so, to the pier and are called *breast line*s. Lines that prevent or minimize forward and aft movement—in other words, motion parallel to the pier—are rigged nearly parallel to the pier and are called *spring lines*.

The mooring configuration will differ depending upon the size of the vessel being moored and the surrounding conditions, such as tides, currents, and weather, but a standard six-line moor will illustrate most of what you need to know about mooring a ship to a pier. The first line farthest forward is called the *bow line* and runs through the *bull-nose* (chock on the very front of the ship) and then to the pier. The next line aft is numbered "2" and is called the *after bow spring*. This name is derived from the fact that it tends (goes) aft, is located in the forward half of the ship (hence the word "bow"), and is a spring line. In this case it prevents the forward motion of the ship. Moving aft along the ship's main deck, the next line you would encounter would be the number three line, and it is called the *forward bow spring*. This, too, is a spring line because it keeps the ship from moving backward along the pier. The other parts of its name tell you it is located on the forward part of the ship (bow) and that it tends forward. The next two lines aft would be numbers four and five and they would be called the *after quarter spring* and the *forward quarter spring*, respectively. These lines are also spring lines and function the same as their counterparts on the bow. Because they are located on the after half of the ship, they are identified by the word "quarter" instead of "bow." The final line in a standard six-line configuration is called the *stern line*. Like the bow line, this line is usually rigged as a breast line, meaning that it runs perpendicular (or nearly so) to the pier and is used to prevent lateral (in and out) movement of the ship in relation to the pier. Larger ships will, of course, rig more lines to secure the ship more effectively to the pier or another ship. Those rigged in the middle (amidships) of the ship are called *waist lines*. So an extra line rigged amidships to keep the ship snug to the pier, for example, would be called a "waist breast line." If more lines are rigged, they still follow the rule of numbering from forward, so that the last line aft on a ship moored with eleven lines would be numbered "11."

Once the ship is settled into her berth and all mooring lines have been rigged, they are usually doubled up. This is a somewhat misleading term because the way doubling up is accomplished results in three lines (actually parts of the same line) going from the ship to the pier instead of just one at each location.

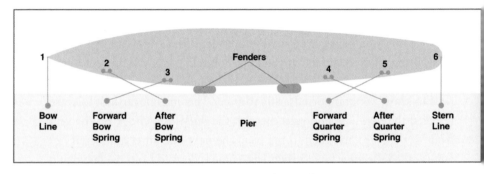

[**12-A-1**] A six-line moor. Note the fenders used to keep the ship from rubbing against the pier.

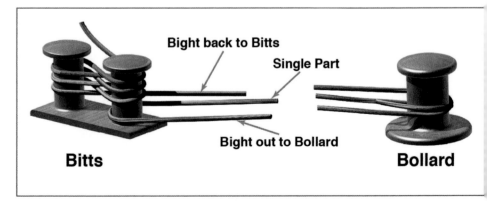

[**12-A-2**] Doubling up

12-B Line-Handling Commands

During the process of mooring a vessel to a pier or to another ship, it is vital that the conning officer be able to communicate efficiently with the line handlers. To make sure there is no confusion, commands that are commonly used in mooring operations have been standardized. This system can only be efficient if both the conning officer and the line handlers know what the various commands are and what they mean. Below are some examples of the standard commands used and what they mean.

COMMAND	MEANING
Stand by your lines.	Man the lines; be ready to cast off or take in.
Pass number one.	Pass the number one line to the pier and place the eye over the appropriate bollard or other fitting, but take no strain.
Take a strain on number two.	Put number two line under tension.
Slack number four.	Let all tension off the number four line.
Ease the bow line.	Let most of the tension off the bow line.
Hold number six.	Do not let the number six line pay out at all. Best accomplished by taking turns around a cleat or set of bitts so that the line can't slip.
Check the stern line.	Do not pay out the stern line but let it slip rather than part the line.
Heave around on number one.	Pull in the number one line using the capstan—the mechanical device that can be used to efficiently pull in a line.
Avast heaving.	Stop the capstan.
Take in number three.	Retrieve the number three line. Bring your line back aboard your ship.
Cast off number five.	Take the number five line off the bollard or the fitting and let it go. This command is used to tell line handlers on the pier or on an adjacent ship to return the number five line to the ship it belongs to.

12-C Anchor Chain Identification System

A special color-coding system is used to identify the various shots so that when the ship is anchored, you can tell, just by looking at visible chain on deck, how much chain is out and underwater.

SHOT NUMBER	COLOR OF DETACHABLE LINK	NUMBER OF ADJACENT LINKS PAINTED WHITE	TURNS OF WIRE ON LAST WHITE LINK
1 (15 fathoms)	Red	1	1
2 (20 fathoms)	White	2	2
3 (45 fathoms)	Blue	3	3
4 (60 fathoms)	Red	4	4
5 (75 fathoms)	White	5	5
6 (90 fathoms)	Blue	6	6

Each of the detachable links that marks the beginning of another shot of chain is painted either red, white, or blue. The links on either side are painted white (the number of links corresponding to the number of shots), and pieces of wire are also twisted onto the last white link to further aid in identification (the latter is useful in the dark when you cannot see the links clearly but can feel the turns of wire). Every link in the last shot of chain is painted red and every link in the next-to-last shot is painted yellow. This will give you warning that you are almost out of chain.

12-D Anchoring Commands

COMMAND	MEANING
Stand by.	Brake is released on the windlass so that the weight of the anchor is on the chain stopper.
Let go.	The pin is removed from the pelican hook and a Sailor with a maul knocks the bail loose on the pelican hook so that it will release the stopper and the chain can run freely.

Pass the stoppers.	With the brake set, the stoppers are fastened around the chain to hold it in place, then the brake is released.
Heave around to.	The windlass brings the chain in until the short stay anchor is just about to break ground.
Anchor's up and down.	The anchor is about to come free but is still on the bottom.
Anchor's aweigh.	The anchor is clear of the bottom and the ship is under way (no longer moored).
Anchor is in sight.	The anchor detail on the forecastle can see the anchor well enough to report its condition.
Anchor is clear.	There is little or no debris from the bottom clinging to the anchor.
Anchor is shod.	The anchor is caked with mud or other debris from the bottom.
Anchor is fouled.	The anchor has hooked onto a cable or some other underwater obstruction that will prevent it from being brought into the hawsepipe.

 12-E Blocks and Tackles

In the Navy, a *block* is essentially what civilians call "pulleys." When blocks are combined with lines, they can be used to change the direction of an applied force (such as allowing you to pull down in order to lift something up) or, even better, they can be used to provide a significant mechanical advantage (which translates to "less work"). These combinations of blocks and lines are called *tackles*.

The simplest tackle is called a *single whip* and is made by running one line that has been attached to something (such as the end of a boom) through one block. This tackle gives you no mechanical advantage and is used solely to cause a change of direction in the force applied; for example, it allows you to lift a load straight up while you are pulling downward.

For obvious reasons, most tackles are rigged to achieve a mechanical advantage. The simplest tackle that provides this advantage is called a *runner*. Like the single whip, it uses only one line and one block, but by attaching the load to the block itself and allowing the block to move instead of attaching it to something, you gain a 2:1 mechanical advantage. (Note: In all cases described here, there is a certain amount of work lost because of friction, but the mechanical advantages gained are close enough for us to approximate them for simplicity.) That means that you will be able to lift a 120-pound load by using only 60 pounds of actual force—your load will seem only half as heavy as it actually is.

If you think about it, you can see that a runner would not be a very easy tackle to use because it is difficult to control, so a more common way to gain the same 2:1 advantage is to use two blocks (one moving and the other fixed) in a rig we call a *gun tackle*.

You have probably noticed that some blocks have more than one *sheave* (the "wheels" inside the block). Using a block with one sheave, combined with a block that has only two, we came up with a new rig called a *luff tackle*. This rig gives you a 3:1 mechanical advantage, which means your 120-pound load can now be lifted with only 40 pounds of force (it seems to weigh only one-third as much now).

Taking it another step, two blocks with two sheaves each can be rigged into a tackle we call a *twofold*. As you might have guessed, this rig provides an advantage of 4:1, meaning that you need only apply 30 pounds of force to lift your 120-pound load.

You may have noticed a pattern here that will help you to determine the theoretical mechanical advantage of a rig without having to come back to this book to look it up. If you look at the number of lines that are going in and out of the moving (not the fixed) block, it will tell you the mechanical advantage. For example, look at both the runner and the gun tackle. The number of lines running in and out of the moving block is two. This means the mechanical advantage is 2:1. The number of lines running in and out of the moving block on the twofold is four, so the mechanical advantage is 4:1.

Still more sheaves can be used in a two-block rig to gain even more advantage, but the friction factor begins to become sizable as you add more sheaves and lines so that the mechanical advantage is significantly degraded.

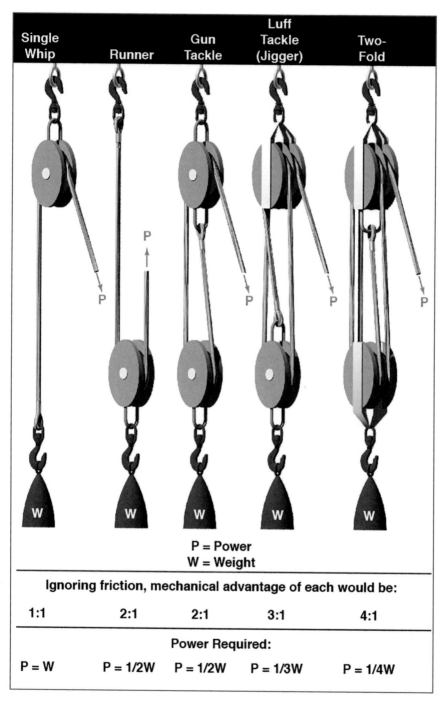

Single Whip	Runner	Gun Tackle	Luff Tackle (Jigger)	Two-Fold

P = Power
W = Weight

Ignoring friction, mechanical advantage of each would be:

1:1	2:1	2:1	3:1	4:1

Power Required:

P = W	P = 1/2W	P = 1/2W	P = 1/3W	P = 1/4W

[12-E] Blocks and tackles

12-F Boat Customs and Etiquette

Just as Navy ships adhere to certain customs and traditions, so do Navy boats.

Whenever Navy personnel board a boat, junior personnel embark first and seniors last. When the craft arrives at its destination, seniors will disembark first and juniors last. While embarked, seniors sit aft and juniors forward.

When under way, it is customary for boats to exchange salutes just as personnel and ships do. The coxswain (or boat officer, if embarked) will attend to all salutes, and the coxswain of the junior boat will initiate the salute and idle the boat's engine during the exchange. The rest of the boat crew will stand at attention. Passengers will remain seated but come to seated attention (sit erect, looking straight ahead, and not talking).

FLAGS AND PENNANTS

The national ensign is displayed from Navy boats when:

- they are under way during daylight in a foreign port
- ships are dressed or full dressed
- they are alongside a foreign vessel
- an officer or official is embarked on an official occasion
- a uniformed flag or general officer, unit commander, commanding officer, or chief of staff is embarked in a boat of his or her command or in one assigned for his or her personal use
- when prescribed by the senior officer present

Since small boats are a part of a ship, they follow the motions of the parent ship regarding the half-masting of colors.

When an officer in command is embarked in a Navy boat, the boat displays from the bow the officer's personal flag or command pennant—or, if not entitled to either, a commission pennant.

In a boat assigned to the personal use of a flag or general officer, unit commander, chief of staff, or commanding officer, or when a civil official is embarked, the following flagstaff insignia are fitted at the peak:

Spread eagle. For an official whose authorized salute is nineteen or more guns, such as Secretaries of the Navy, Army, Air Force, Chief of Naval Operations, and the Commandant of the Marine Corps.

Halberd. For a flag or general officer whose official salute is fewer than nineteen guns and for a civil official whose salute is eleven or more but fewer than nineteen guns (assistant secretaries of defense down to and including consuls general).

Ball. For an officer of the grade or relative grade of captain in the Navy and for a career minister, counselor, or first secretary of an embassy, legation, or consul.

Star. For an officer of the grade or relative grade of commander in the Navy.

Flat truck. For an officer below the grade or relative grade of commander in the Navy and for a civil official on an official visit for whom honors are not prescribed.

Note: The head of the spread eagle and the cutting edges of the halberd must face forward. The points of the star must face fore and aft.

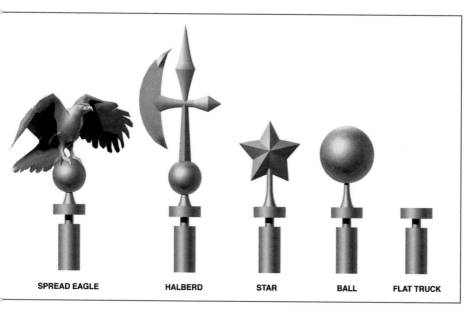

SPREAD EAGLE   HALBERD   STAR   BALL   FLAT TRUCK

[**12-F**] Flagstaff insignia

BOAT MARKINGS

Admirals' barges are marked with chrome stars on the bow, arranged as on the admiral's flag. The official abbreviated title of the flag officer's command appears on the stern in gold letters—CINCPACFLT (for Commander in Chief Pacific Fleet), for example.

On gigs assigned for the personal use of unit commanders not of flag rank, the insignia is a broad or burgee replica of the command pennant with squadron or division numbers superimposed. The official abbreviated title of the command, such as DESRON NINE, appears on the stern in gold letters.

The gig for a chief of staff not of flag rank is marked with the official abbreviated title of the command in chrome letters, with an arrow running through the letters. Other boats assigned for staff use have brass letters but no arrows.

Boats assigned to commanding officers of ships are called gigs and are marked on the bow with the ship type or name and with the ship's hull number in chrome letters and numerals. There is a chrome arrow running fore and aft through the markings. On boats for officers who are not in command or serving as chiefs of staff, the arrow is omitted and letters are brass. The ship's full name, abbreviated name, or initials may be used instead of the ship's type designation. An assigned boat number is sometimes used instead of the ship's hull number.

Other ship's boats are marked on the bow either with the ship's type and name or with her initials, followed by a dash and the boat number—for example, ENTERPRISE-1. These markings also appear on the stern of most boats. Letters and numbers are painted black. Numerals are painted as identifiers on miscellaneous small boats such as line-handling boats, punts, and wherries.

TAB 13 Watchstanding

Watchstanding is an essential part of the Navy. Watch stations exist to ensure readiness, safety, and efficiency, and good Sailors make it a habit to always stand their assigned watches seriously and efficiently, no matter what the assigned task. Your very life and that of your shipmates may well be at stake.

Major Topics Covered:

- ※ Sentry Duty
- ※ Shipboard Watches
- ※ Conditions of Readiness
- ※ Ship's Bells
- ※ Lookout Techniques
- ※ Logs

To Learn More:

- ⚓ **www.usni.org/BlueAndGoldProfessionalBooks/TheBluejackets Manual**
- ⚓ *Basic Military Requirements* (NAVEDTRA 14325)
- ⚓ *Seaman* (NAVEDTRA 14067)
- ⚓ *Standard Organization and Regulations of the U.S. Navy* (OPNA-VINST 3120.32D)
- ⚓ *Lookout Training Handbook* (NAVEDTRA 12968-D)
- ⚓ *Sound-Powered Telephone Talkers' Training Manual* (NAVEDTRA 14232)
- ⚓ *Quartermaster* (NAVEDTRA 14338A)

Associated Tabs:

- ○ TAB 13-A: The General Orders of a Sentry
- ○ TAB 13-B: Conditions of Readiness (Cruising Conditions)
- ○ TAB 13-C: Traditional Navy Watch Structure
- ○ TAB 13-D: Ship's Bells

13-A The General Orders of a Sentry

1. Take charge of this post and all government property in view.
2. Walk my post in a military manner, keeping always on the alert and observing everything that takes place within sight or hearing.
3. Report all violations of orders I am instructed to enforce.
4. Repeat all calls from posts more distant from the guardhouse (quarterdeck) than my own.
5. Quit my post only when properly relieved.
6. Receive, obey, and pass on to the sentry who relieves me all orders from the commanding officer, command duty officer, officer of the deck, and officers and petty officers of the watch only.
7. Talk to no one except in the line of duty.
8. Give the alarm in case of fire or disorder.
9. Call the OOD in any case not covered by instructions.
10. Salute all officers, and all colors and standards not cased.
11. Be especially watchful at night, and during the time for challenging, to challenge all persons on or near my post, and to allow no one to pass without proper authority.

13-B Conditions of Readiness (Cruising Conditions)

Condition I. Known as "general quarters." All hands are at battle stations, and the ship is in its maximum state of readiness. This condition is set on board ship if the ship is expecting combat or if some other emergency situation such as a bad fire occurs. Everyone on board has an assigned station that he or she must go to whenever Condition I is set.

Condition II. This condition is set only on large ships and is used when the ship is expected to be in a heightened state of readiness for an extended period of time but the operations at hand are such that some relaxation of readiness is permissible.

Condition III. Wartime cruising with approximately one-third of the crew on watch. Weapon stations are manned in accordance with the threat, and other stations are manned or partially manned to fit the particular circumstances.

Condition IV. Normal peacetime cruising. Only necessary persons are on watch, while the rest of the crew engages in work, training, recreation, or rest as appropriate. This condition ensures an adequate number of qualified personnel are on watch for the safe and effective operation of the ship, yet allows for the most economical use of personnel in watch assignments.

Condition V. Peacetime watch in port. Enough of the crew is on board to get the ship under way if necessary or to handle emergencies.

Condition VI. Peacetime watch in port where only minimum personnel are required to keep an eye on the ship in order to maintain minimum security and to watch for fire or flooding. The ship will not be able to get under way without bringing more personnel on board and will require outside assistance to fight anything more than a minor fire.

There are also several variations of Condition I designed to meet special circumstances:

Condition IA.   Personnel on station to conduct amphibious operations and a limited defense of the ship during landing operations.

Condition IAA.   Personnel on station to counter an air threat.

Condition IAS.   Personnel on station to counter a submarine threat.

Condition IE.   Temporary relaxation from full readiness of Condition I for brief periods of rest and distribution of food at battle stations. This condition is set for brief periods during a lull in operations.

Condition IM.   Personnel on station to take mine countermeasures.

13-C Traditional Navy Watch Structure

Period	Known as
0000–0400	Midwatch
0400–0800	Morning Watch
0800–1200	Forenoon Watch
1200–1600	Afternoon Watch

1600–1800   First Dog Watch*
1800–2000   Second Dog Watch*
2000–2400 (0000)   Evening Watch (Also called the "First Watch")

   * The First and Second Dog Watches straddle the time when the evening meal is traditionally served. Those with the First Dog Watch eat the evening meal after being relieved and those with the Second Dog Watch eat before relieving the watch.

 13-D Ship's Bells

BELLS	MID	MORNING	FORENOON	AFTERNOON	DOGS	EVENIN
1 Bell	0030	0430	0830	1230	1630	2030
2 Bells	0100	0500	0900	1300	1700	2100
3 Bells	0130	0530	0930	1330	1730	2130
4 Bells	0200	0600	1000	1400	1800	2200
5 Bells	0230	0630	1030	1430	1830	2230
6 Bells	0300	0700	1100	1500	1900	2300
7 Bells	0330	0730	1130	1530	1930	2300
8 Bells	0400	0800	1200	1600	2000	2400 (0000

Bells are rung at the times indicated. Note that each watch is divided into eight half-hour segments, with each one being signaled by an additional bell until the maximum of eight is reached; then the cycle is repeated for the next watch.

Bells are rung in pairs. For example:

- 3 bells would be rung as "ding-ding," one-second pause, then "ding."
- 4 bells would be rung as "ding-ding," one-second pause, then "ding-ding."
- 5 bells would be rung as "ding-ding, one second pause, then "ding-ding," another one-second pause, then "ding."

TAB 14 Safety and Emergencies

For the most part, U.S. Navy ships are very safe places to live and work. But the safety enjoyed aboard an American naval vessel is only as effective as the safety practices of its individual crewmembers. Safety precautions are an essential element of shipboard life, and you owe it to yourself and to your shipmates to make safety precautions a part of your everyday routine.

Major Topics Covered:

- ☸ Safety procedures while dealing with:
    - ➤ Aircraft operations
    - ➤ Ammunition
    - ➤ Boats
    - ➤ Chemicals and toxic materials
    - ➤ Electrical and electronic equipment
    - ➤ Tools and machinery
    - ➤ Mooring lines
    - ➤ Radioactive materials
    - ➤ Unreps
- ☸ Emergencies
    - ~ General quarters
    - ~ Man overboard
    - ~ CBR attack
    - ~ Abandon ship

To Learn More:

- ⚓ **www.usni.org/BlueAndGoldProfessionalBooks/TheBluejackets Manual**
- ⚓ *Basic Military Requirements* (NAVEDTRA 14325)
- ⚓ *Military Requirements for Petty Officers Third and Second Class* (NAVEDTRA 14504)
- ⚓ *Military Requirements for Petty Officers First Class* (NAVEDTRA 14145)
- ⚓ *Airman* (NAVEDTRA 14014A)
- ⚓ *Damage Controlman* (NAVEDTRA 14057)

15 Damage Control

Damage control is every Sailor's job—no matter what his or her rate or pay grade. The two major elements of damage control aboard ship are fighting fires and controlling flooding.

Major Topics Covered:

- ☸ Repair Parties
- ☸ Maintaining Watertight Integrity
    - ~ Compartmentation
    - ~ Closures
    - ~ Material Conditions of Readiness
- ☸ Damage Repairs
- ☸ Fire Prevention and Fighting
    - ~ The Fire Triangle
    - ~ Classes of Fire
    - ~ Firefighting Equipment

To Learn More:

- ⚓ **www.usni.org/BlueAndGoldProfessionalBooks/TheBluejackets Manual**
- ⚓ *Basic Military Requirements* (NAVEDTRA 14325)
- ⚓ *Damage Controlman* (NAVEDTRA 14057)
- ⚓ *Military Requirements for Petty Officers First Class* (NAVEDTRA 14145)
- ⚓ *Damage Control PQS* (NAVEDTRA 43119-J)

Associated Tabs:

- ○ TAB 15-A: Material Conditions of Readiness
- ○ TAB 15-B: Classes of Fire

15-A Material Conditions of Readiness

As explained in **Chapter 15**, several material conditions of readiness have been defined to prevent flooding or the spreading of fire and smoke or contamination resulting from a chemical, biological, radiological (CBR) attack. Various fittings (watertight doors, hatch covers, scuttles, and manhole covers) on a ship are in place to close off openings that might otherwise allow this dangerous free flow from one part of the ship to others. These fittings have special markings on them to identify which ones should be closed depending upon the material condition of readiness in effect.

> Condition Xray provides the least protection but the most convenience. It is set when the ship is in little or no danger, such as when she is at anchor in a well-protected harbor or secured at home base during regular working hours. During this condition, all closures (such as watertight doors and hatch covers) **marked with a black or circled X** are secured. They remain closed when the higher conditions of readiness Yoke and Zebra are set.

> Condition Yoke provides more protection than condition Xray and is set when a ship is involved in routine underway operations. In port, Yoke is set after regular working hours and is also maintained at all times during war. Yoke closures, **marked with a black or circled Y**, are secured during conditions Yoke and Zebra (but not Xray).

> Condition Zebra provides the maximum protection and is set before going to sea or when entering port during wartime. It is also set immediately, without further orders, whenever general quarters (GQ) stations are manned. Condition Zebra can also be set to localize and control fire and flooding when GQ stations are not manned. When condition Zebra is set, all closures (doors, hatches, porthole covers, and valves) **marked with a red Z, a circled red Z, or a red Z within a black D** are secured.

This basic system is modified to allow for special circumstances as follows:

> Circle Xray and Circle Yoke fittings may be opened without special permission when going to or from GQ stations, when transferring ammunition, or when operating vital systems during GQ. These fittings must be immediately closed once the need to have them open has passed.

> Circle Zebra fittings may be opened during prolonged periods of GQ, when the condition of readiness is modified by the commanding officer to enable personnel to prepare and distribute battle rations,

open limited sanitary facilities, and ventilate battle stations, and it provides access from ready rooms to the flight deck. When open, these fittings must be guarded for immediate closure if necessary.

Dog Zebra fittings are secured during condition Zebra, but are also secured separately during darken ship conditions. These are doors, hatches, or porthole covers that if left open would allow light from inside the ship to be seen outside. The reason for these fittings is obvious in wartime, because allowing lights to show outside at night might help the enemy to detect your ship. Dog Zebra fittings are also important in peacetime conditions, because stray lights coming from inside a ship can make it confusing for mariners to see your navigational lights properly, and because stray bright lights can temporarily blind watchstanders so that they cannot see in the darkness.

William fittings, marked with a black W, are specialized fittings that are normally kept open during all material conditions and are only closed under extraordinary conditions as determined by the damage control assistant, chief engineer, and commanding officer. An example of a William fitting is a sea-suction valve that supplies important engineering equipment and fire pumps.

Circle William fittings, marked with a circled black W, are normally kept open but must be secured against CBR attack. These are primarily ventilation-system closures that must be secured to prevent the spread of CBR contaminants (radiation, chemical gases, and germs or viruses).

Remember that it is the responsibility of all hands to maintain the material condition in effect. If it is necessary to break the condition, permission must be obtained (from the OOD or DCC). A closure log is maintained in DCC at all times to show where the existing condition has been broken; the number, type, and classification of fittings involved; the name, rate, and division of the man or woman requesting permission to open or close a fitting; and the date a fitting was opened or closed.

15-B Classes of Fire

There are four classes of fire, and each requires different methods of extinguishing. The various equipment referred to here is explained in **Chapter 15**.

Class Alfa. These fires involve solid substances—wood, cloth, paper—that usually leave an ash. Class Alfa fires are usually characterized by white smoke. Explosives are included in this category. The usual means of extinguishing Class A fires is with water. In a large fire, the flame is usually knocked down (cooled) with fog (spray), then a solid stream of water is applied to break up the material. Fog is then used for further cooling.

Class Bravo. Class B fires involve flammable liquids, such as oil, gasoline, or paint. These fires usually are characterized by heavy black smoke. For small fires CO_2 is effective. For large fires other agents, such as water and aqueous film-forming foam (AFFF), must be used. Never use a solid stream of water to fight Class B fires. It will only make the fire worse because the water penetrates the fuel's surface, flashes to steam, scatters the fuel, and spreads the fire. Spaces subject to major fuel- or lube-oil spills (firerooms, enginerooms, or fuel-transfer and manifold rooms) are equipped with HALON 1301 (fluorocarbon gas) dispensing systems that, when activated, will knock down a Class B fire.

Class Charlie. Fires in electrical or electronic equipment are classified as Class C. A fire of this type is usually characterized by smoke with a bluish tint along with arcs, sparks, and a distinctive smell you are not likely to forget once you have experienced it. The primary extinguishing method is to de-energize the equipment, which reduces the fire to Class A or B. The preferred extinguishing agent is CO_2, since it does not leave any residue that may harm or interfere with the efficient operation of the equipment. PKP (a special firefighting chemical powder, see below) may be used as a last resort, but its corrosiveness will further damage the equipment.

Class Delta. Fires involving combustible metals (for example, magnesium, sodium, or titanium) and any fires that require special handling fall into the category of Class D. Special metals are used for building certain parts of aircraft, missiles, electronic components, and other equipment. An example is the magnesium aircraft parachute flare, which can burn at a temperature above 4,000° Fahrenheit. Water used on this type of fire will break down into its natural elements of hydrogen and oxygen, which by themselves are unstable and liable to cause small explosions. You should use low-velocity fog at extreme range and remain upwind of this type of fire, and stay behind cover as much as possible. One important safety precaution: the intense light produced by this type of fire can easily cause permanent damage to the eyes, so never look directly at the fire and wear protective welder's goggles with very dark lenses if they are available.

COMBUSTIBLE	CLASS OF FIRE	EXTINGUISHING AGENT
Wood, paper, fabric	A	1. Fixed water sprinkling 2. Solid water stream or fog 3. Foam (AFFF) 4. Dry chemical (PKP) 5. CO_2
Explosives, propellants	A	1. Magazine sprinkling 2. Solid water stream or fog 3. Foam (AFFF)
Paints, spirits, flammable liquid stores	B	1. CO_2 (fixed system) 2. Foam (AFF) 3. Installed sprinkling system 4. High-velocity fog 5. Dry chemical (PKP) 6. CO_2
Gasoline	B	1. Foam (AFFF) 2. CO_2 (fixed system) 3. Water sprinkling system 4. Dry chemical (PKP)
Fuel oil, JP-5, diesel oil, kerosene	B	1. Foam (AFFF) 2. Dry chemical (PKP) 3. Water sprinkling or fog 4. CO_2 (fixed system)
Electrical and radio apparatus	C	1. CO_2 2. High-velocity fog 3. Fog foam or dry chemical (only if CO_2 not available)
Magnesium alloys	D	1. Jettison overboard 2. Wide-angle fog

TAB 16 Naval Aircraft

Naval aviation is a critical component of the Navy's ability to carry out full-spectrum operations—from delivering humanitarian assistance and disaster relief at home and overseas, to maritime security operations to ensure safe passage of commercial vessels, to high-intensity sea control and power projection in a major contingency. Helicopters and fixed-wing aircraft operating from nuclear aircraft carriers, large-deck amphibious ships and shore stations, and helicopters operating from amphibious ships, cruisers, and destroyers—complemented by advanced unmanned aerial vehicles—are key contributors to the capabilities of the U.S. Navy and Marine Corps.

Major Topics Covered:

- ⚓ Principles of Flight
- ⚓ Aircraft Nomenclature
- ⚓ Types of Naval Aircraft
- ⚓ Identifying Aircraft
- ⚓ Aircraft Organization

To Learn More:

- ⚓ www.usni.org/BlueAndGoldProfessionalBooks/TheBluejackets Manual
- ⚓ *Airman* (NAVEDTRA 14014A)
- ⚓ *Navy Program Guide* (current year)
- ⚓ *How We Fight: Handbook for the Naval Warfighter,* available from U.S. Government Printing Office and online at **http://navy reading.dodlive.mil/files/2015/08/HWF-Book-Combined-Final -27-Apr-15.pdf**

Associated Tabs:

- ○ TAB 16-A: Types of Naval Aircraft
- ○ TAB 16-B: Identifying Military Aircraft

16-A **Types of Naval Aircraft**

For cross-reference purposes, aircraft are presented alphabetically by names with their designations following. Types of aircraft are then discussed in more detail arranged alphabetically by their letter-number designations.

Aries II	EP-3E
Blackjack	RQ-21A
Clipper	C-40A
Fire Scout, Navy	MQ-8B
Goshawk	T-45A/C
Greyhound	C-2A
Growler	EA-18G
Harrier	AV-8B
Hawkeye	E-2C/D
Hercules	C-130T / KC-130J
Hornet	F/A-18 C/D
Huron	C-12
King Stallion	CH-53K
Lightning II	F-35A/B/C
Mercury	E-6B
Navy Fire Scout	MQ-8B
Orion	P-3C
Osprey	MV-22 B/C
Pegasus	T-44C
Poseidon	P-8A
Prowler	EA-6B
Sea Dragon	MH-53E
Sea Hawk	MH-60R/MH-60S/SH-60F
Sea Ranger	TH-57 B/C
Shadow	RQ-7B
Stingray	MQ-25A
Super Hornet	F/A-18E/F
Super Stallion	CH-53E
Texan II	T-6A/B
Tiger	F-5N/F
Turbomentor	T-34C
Venom	UH-1Y
Viper	AH-1Z

AH-1Z VIPER

This cutting-edge attack helicopter delivers state-of-the-art dynamics, weapons, and avionics to incorporate the latest in survivability. With anti-armor capability, it engages and defeats a broad array of threats at impressive standoff ranges. Whether it's providing cover for advancing ground forces or escorting assault support helicopters en route to a landing zone, the AH-1Z is called on when Marines need serious firepower from the air.

AV-8B HARRIER

A single-seat, light attack aircraft that supports Marine operations ashore by attacking surface targets and escorting friendly aircraft. It can operate day or night in all weather conditions and its vertical/short takeoff and landing (V/STOL) capability allow it to operate from a variety of amphibious ships, rapidly constructed expeditionary airfields, and damaged conventional airfields.

[16-A-1] AH-1Z Viper

[16-A-2] AV-8B Harrier

C-2A GREYHOUND

Provides critical logistics support to carrier strike groups. Its primary mission is the transport of high-priority cargo, mail, and passengers between carriers and shore bases, and it can deliver a combined payload of ten thousand pounds over a distance of more than one thousand nautical miles. The interior arrangement of the cabin can readily accommodate cargo, passengers, and litter patients. Priority cargo such as jet engines can be transported from shore to ship in a matter of hours. A cargo cage system or transport stand provides restraint for loads during launches and landings.

C-12 HURON

A military variant of the commercial King Air series aircraft that incorporates a cargo door with an integral air-stair door to permit easy entry and egress. The flight deck and cabin are pressurized for high altitude flight, and with an effective payload capacity of up to 4,215 pounds, the cabin can readily be configured to accommodate passengers, cargo, or both. The mission of the C-12 Huron is to provide rapid, high-priority movement of personnel and cargo; range clearance, courier flights, medical evacuation and humanitarian rescue; multi-engine pilot training; and testing assets.

[16-A-3] C-2A Greyhound

[16-A-4] C-12 Huron

C-20G

A military variant of the commercial Gulfstream IV aircraft with a cargo door that provides long-range, medium airlift logistics support for fleet battle groups.

C-26

A military variant of the commercial Model SA-227-DC (Metro 23) aircraft series manufactured by Fairchild Aircraft Corporation. The cabin can be configured to accommodate up to nineteen passengers, two and a half tons of cargo, or a combination of both. Two variants—the RC-26D and the EC-26D—are used to support operations at missile firing ranges.

C-37

Variations of this modified commercial Gulfstream aircraft provide executive transport to the Secretary of the Navy, the Chief of Naval Operations, and other executive-level personnel.

C-40A CLIPPER

Provides critical logistics support to the Navy. Ordered by the Navy to replace its fleet of C-9B Skytrains, the C-40A is the newest logistics aircraft to join the Navy.

[16-A-5] C-20G

[**16-A-6**] C-40A Clipper

C-130T HERCULES

The primary mission of the Hercules, often called "the workhorse of the fleet," is to satisfy Navy-specific fleet essential airlift requirements world-wide, to include a flexible response to the fleet and short-notice operational requirements for both training and deployed units. The C-130T operates from shore installations to provide intratheater logistics support for all aspects of naval power. A four-engine, turbo-prop aircraft capable of landing and taking off from short, rough dirt runways, it can transport up to ninety-two personnel, or 42,000 pounds of cargo, and can be configured to perform air medical evacuation missions carrying up to seventy litters.

CH-53E SUPER STALLION

This heavy-lift helicopter has been in service since the 1980s and is being replaced by the CH-53K King Stallion. (See MH-53E for another variant of this venerable fleet workhorse.)

[**16-A-7**] C-130T Hercules, here configured as the Blue Angels support aircraft known to many as "Fat Albert"

[**16-A-8**] CH-53E Super Stallion

CH-53K KING STALLION

This helicopter will eventually replace the aging Super Stallions to provide essential heavy-lift capabilities. The King Stallion has more powerful engines with greater lift and endurance capabilities. Among its many capabilities, this aircraft is capable of transporting thirty combat-loaded troops.

E-2C/D HAWKEYE

The E-2 Hawkeye is the Navy's all-weather, carrier-based, tactical battle management, airborne early warning, command-and-control aircraft. The Hawkeye provides all-weather airborne early warning, airborne battle management, and command and control functions for the carrier strike group and joint force commander. Additional missions include surface surveillance coordination, air interdiction, offensive and defensive counter air control, close air support coordination, time-critical strike coordination, search-and-rescue airborne coordination, and communications relay.

The E-2C is gradually being replaced by the more advanced E-2D, but E-2Cs will continue to serve until at least 2023.

[16-A-9] E-2C/D Hawkeye

E-6B MERCURY

Provides a survivable communications link between national decision-makers and the country's arsenal of strategic nuclear weapons. The E-6B enables the President of the United States and the Secretary of Defense to directly contact submarines, bombers, and missile silos protecting our national security through deterrence.

EA-6B PROWLER

A twin-engine aircraft designed for carrier and advanced base operations, the Prowler provides an umbrella of protection for strike aircraft, ground troops, and ships by jamming air defense systems and communications. Its primary mission is suppression of enemy air defenses in support of strike aircraft and ground troops by interrupting enemy electronic activity and obtaining tactical electronic intelligence within the combat area.

EA-18G GROWLER

A variant of the U.S. Navy F/A-18F two-crew strike fighter airframe, the EA-18G combines the combat-proven F/A-18F strike fighter platform with an advanced airborne electronic attack suite. Its mission is identical to the EA-6B and will eventually replace that airframe in the Navy.

[**16-A-10**] E-6B Mercury

[**16-A-11**] EA-6B Prowler

[**16-A-12**] EA-18G Growler

EP-3E ARIES II

The Navy's only land-based signals intelligence (SIGINT) reconnaissance aircraft. The EP-3E is based on the P-3 Orion airframe and provides fleet and theater commanders near-real-time tactical SIGINT worldwide. With sensitive receivers and high-gain dish antennas, the EP-3E exploits a wide range of electronic emissions from deep within targeted territory.

F-35A/B/C LIGHTNING II

Also known as the "Joint Strike Fighter," this highly sophisticated fighter aircraft combines advanced stealth capabilities with cutting-edge sensor components that make the aircraft difficult for enemies to detect and even more difficult to defeat. The F-35A version is a "conventional takeoff and landing" (CTOL) variant (i.e., uses runways) that is used primarily by the Air Force. The F-35B variant is a "short takeoff/vertical landing (STOVL) that is designed to operate from short-field bases or air-capable ships. The F-35C variant is designed to take off and land primarily from aircraft carriers using catapult and arresting-wire technology.

[16-A-13] EP-3E Aries II

F/A-18C/D HORNET

The F/A-18 is an all-weather attack aircraft that can also be used as a fighter. In its fighter mode, the F/A-18 is used primarily as an escort and for fleet air defense. In its attack mode, it is used to attack ashore and afloat targets for force projection and to support forces ashore.

F/A-18E/F SUPER HORNET

The F/A-18E/F is an all-weather fighter/attack aircraft that looks to the untrained eye much like the F/A-18C/D Hornet but is actually a larger, more capable aircraft. One way to tell which aircraft you are seeing is that the Hornet has rounded air intakes under the forward edge of the wings, while the Super Hornet's air intakes are angular (almost square). The "E" version is a single-seat aircraft, and the "F" version has a two-person crew.

[**16-A-14**] F-35B Lightning II

[**16-A-15**] F/A-18C Hornet

[**16-A-16**] F/A-18E Super Hornet

KC-130J HERCULES

A multi-mission tactical tanker and assault support aircraft that can conduct in-flight refuelings or be reconfigured to deliver precision firepower.

MH-53E SEA DRAGON

A mine-countermeasures derivative of the CH-53E Super Stallion, this version is heavier and has a greater fuel capacity than the Super Stallion. Capable of transporting up to fifty-five troops, the MH-53E can carry a 16-ton payload fifty nautical miles, or a 10-ton payload five hundred nautical miles. In its primary mission of airborne mine countermeasures, the MH-53E is capable of towing a variety of mine countermeasures systems.

MH-60R SEA HAWK

The MH-60R continues the legacy of the SH-60B mission by conducting ASW and ASUW from the decks of cruisers, destroyers, and frigates, and also deploys as a carrier-based squadron. The MH-60R adds a dipping sonar, multimode inverse synthetic aperture radar, enhanced electronic support measures, self-defense suite, digital torpedoes, and air-to-ground weapons. Additional missions include search and rescue, medical evacuation, vertical replenishment, naval surface fire support, and communications relay.

[16-A-17] KC-130J Hercules refueling two helicopters

[**16-A-18**] MH-53E Sea Dragon

[**16-A-19**] MH-60R Sea Hawk

MH-60S SEA HAWK

A twin-engine helicopter used for anti-surface warfare, naval special warfare support, special operations support, combat search and rescue, search and rescue, logistics, drug interdiction, anti-piracy operations, humanitarian relief operations, and airborne mine countermeasures. The MH-60S also has an upgraded weapons system that allows it to deploy as a gunship in support of the anti-surface warfare mission area.

MQ-8B FIRE SCOUT

An unmanned aerial vehicle, the Fire Scout has the ability to autonomously take off from and land on any aviation-capable warship that is equipped with the appropriate ship control station and also at unprepared landing zones close to the forward edge of the battle area. It can carry out surveillance, find tactical targets, track and designate targets, and provide accurate targeting data to strike platforms such as strike aircraft, helicopters, and ships. This unmanned aerial vehicle (UAV) is also able to carry out battle damage assessment.

[16-A-20] MH-60S Sea Hawk

[**16-A-21**] MQ-8B Fire Scout

MV-22 B/C OSPREY
This unusual aircraft is a hybrid of aircraft and helicopter technology that rotates the engines to either a vertical or horizontal configuration to allow it vertical takeoff capability or to fly like a conventional aircraft. Both the "B" and "C" (enhanced) versions are in service.

P-3C ORION
As the Navy's land-based, long-range, antisubmarine warfare patrol aircraft, the P-3C has advanced submarine detection sensors such as directional frequency and ranging sonobuoys and magnetic anomaly detection equipment, and can carry a mixed payload of weapons internally and on wing pylons. The P-3C's mission evolved in the late 1990s and early twenty-first century to include intelligence, surveillance, and reconnaissance of the battle space, both at sea and over land. It will eventually be replaced by the P-8 Poseidon.

P-8A POSEIDON
Derived from the globally deployed, commercially supported Boeing 737–800 airframe, the Poseidon maintains the latest capabilities of the P-3C and a state-of-the-art flight station and navigation/communication system. Additionally, the P-8A will incorporate in-flight refueling capabilities yielding extended ranges and time-on-station previously unavailable in the P-3C Fleet.

[**16-A-22**] MV-22B Osprey in "helicopter mode"

[**16-A-23**] MV-22B Osprey in "fixed-wing mode"

[**16-A-24**] P-3C Orion

[**16-A-25**] P-8A Poseidon

RQ-7B SHADOW

This UAV is employed by the Marine Corps to provide Marine Air Ground Task Force commanders with both planned and immediate air reconnaissance. The RQ-7B carries electro-optical and infrared sensors to provide day and night imagery as well as a laser spotter to support targeting. It serves in the air reconnaissance function to produce intelligence, target acquisition, and battle damage assessment. It also supports the command and control function by serving as a platform for airborne communications relay.

RQ-21A BLACKJACK

A small, tactical UAV designed to provide intelligence, surveillance, and reconnaissance capabilities to amphibious assault ships, Marine Corps units, and Navy special warfare operators.

T-6A/B TEXAN II

A tandem-seat, turbo-prop trainer whose mission is to train Navy, Marine Corps, and Coast Guard pilots and naval flight officers.

[16-A-26] RQ-7B Shadow

[**16-A-27**] RQ-21A Blackjack

[**16-A-28**] T-6B Texan

T-34C TURBOMENTOR
Used to provide primary flight training for student pilots, this aircraft is currently in the process of being replaced by the T-6 Texan II.

T-44C PEGASUS
A pressurized, twin-engine, fixed-wing aircraft used to train Navy, Marine Corps, and Coast Guard pilots to fly multi-engine aircraft such as the P-3, P-8, E-6, E-2/C-2, HC-144, and C-130.

[**16-A-29**] T-34C Turbomentor

[**16-A-30**] T-44C Pegasus

T-45A/C GOSHAWK

This Navy version of the British Aerospace Hawk aircraft is used for inter-mediate and advanced portions of the Navy/Marine Corps pilot training program for jet carrier aviation and tactical strike missions, and the Naval Flight Officer Training Program. There are two versions of T-45 aircraft in operational use at this time, the T-45A and T-45C derivatives. The T-45A, which became operational in 1991, contains an analog design cockpit, while the newer T-45C (delivery began in 1997) is built around a new dig-ital (glass cockpit) design. All T-45A cockpits will be digitized through the required avionics modernization program.

TH-57 B/C SEA RANGER

A derivative of the commercial Bell Jet Ranger 206, the Sea Ranger's pri-mary mission is to provide advanced helicopter training to Navy, Marine Corps, and Coast Guard pilots. The TH-57 has two variants—TH-57B and TH-57C models. The TH-57B is used for visual flight rules training and the TH-57C is used for instrument flight rules training.

[16-A-31] T-45C Goshawk

[**16-A-32**] TH-57C Sea Ranger

UH-1Y VENOM

Provides a blend of all six Marine Aviation functions, including offensive air support, assault support, command and control, and aerial reconnaissance. This utility helicopter is often also called the "Super Huey" (reflecting the fact that it is a modern variant of the famous UH-1 "Huey") and the "Yankee" (reflecting its variant designation).

X-47B

The Navy is developing an unmanned aircraft-carrier-based reconnaissance and strike capability to support air wing operations.

[**16-A-33**] UH-1Y Venom

[**16-A-34**] The X-47B unmanned carrier-based aircraft is under development.

16-B Identifying Military Aircraft

There are thousands of aircraft in the Navy, and identifying them can be a bit of a challenge. To accomplish this, they have names and official letter and number designations to distinguish one from the other. This designation system (sometimes called the "Mission Design Series") is explained in some detail below, followed by a simpler version for those who do not need or want quite so much precision. In fact, you can probably skip to that section ("The Simpler Way") if you do not deal with aircraft much and only need the basics, but I recommend you review the intervening sections first for a better understanding, even if you eventually rely on the shorter version.

Probably the simplest way to begin deciphering these designations is to remember this: *one thing common to all aircraft designations is the dash (hyphen).* Whether the aircraft is a C-2A, or an EA-18G, or an F/A-18 E/F, there is always a dash in the designation. If you use that as your starting point, you will have a consistent reference from which to begin cracking this code. Think of the dash in this system as being much like the decimal point in a number system. In mathematics, where numbers appear in relation to the decimal point indicates their value (tens, hundreds, positive, negative, etc.); in the aircraft designation system, where letters or numbers appear relative to the dash helps you understand their meaning.

In the forthcoming explanation, let's take a few examples from the real world by "decoding" the following aircraft designations: T-45A, SH-60F, EA-18G, NKC-135A, and F/A-18E/F.

LEFT OF THE DASH

Letters to the left of the dash can be a bit confusing, but once deciphered, they tell you a lot about a particular aircraft.

Type or Basic Mission

Let's begin with the first letter to the left of the dash. It tells you one of two things: either the *type* or the basic *mission* of the aircraft.

By "type," we mean whether it is a regular airplane (with fixed wings, engine(s), etc.) or some special kind of aircraft, like a helicopter. It's important to realize that *there is no letter for a regular fixed-wing aircraft type* (it is assumed by omission), but the following letters are used to tell you that the aircraft is a special type, as indicated:

G	glider
H	helicopter
Q	UAV (unmanned aerial vehicle)
S	spaceplane
V	V/STOL (vertical/short takeoff and landing)
Z	lighter than air (dirigible, etc.)

By "mission," we mean the primary purpose of the aircraft. The following letters describe aircraft missions as indicated:

A	attack
B	bomber
C	transport
E	special electronic installation
F	fighter
L	laser
O	observation
P	patrol
R	reconnaissance
S	antisubmarine
T	trainer
U	utility
X	research

Now comes the tricky part. If the aircraft is a special *type* (such as a glider or a helicopter), the first letter to the left of the dash will be one of those from the type list previously shown: G, H, Q, S, V, or Z. If it is *not* one of these special types (in other words, it's just a regular fixed-wing airplane), then there is *no letter* indicating type. It will be understood that no type letter indicates a regular fixed-wing airplane type. If that is the case, then the first letter to the left of the dash will be one from the *mission* list above: A, B, C, E, and so on.

Because the first letter to the left of the dash will indicate *either* the type or the mission of the aircraft, and the two lists do not overlap (except in one instance), for simplicity you can combine the two lists into one and translate them appropriately (keeping in mind that the letter used is indicating either a type or a mission). [Note: The one overlap could be confusing but is a minor problem because the overlap is the letter "S" for both type (spaceplane) and mission (antisubmarine). You are not likely to encounter this problem—spaceplanes are pretty rare, at least for now, and should be obvious in context—but it is worth mentioning just in case.]

In our examples from above, we know that the T-45A is a fixed-wing airplane with a primary mission of *training*; the SH-60F is a *helicopter*; the EA-18G is a regular airplane with a primary mission of *attack*; and the NKC-135A is a fixed-wing airplane with *transport* as its primary mission. The F/A-18E/F is a bit of a special case: the slash between the F and the A indicates that this is a regular airplane that has *two* primary missions: it is both a *fighter* and an *attack* aircraft. (Didn't want to make this *too* easy!)

Modified Mission

Now, let's look to another letter to the left of the dash. This letter (if there is one) is called the mission modifier. The following letters, when appearing in this position, have these meanings:

A	attack
C	transport
D	director
E	special electronics
F	fighter
H	search and rescue/MEDEVAC (medical evacuation)
K	tanker
L	cold weather
M	multi-mission
O	observation
P	patrol
Q	drone (unmanned)
R	reconnaissance
S	antisubmarine
T	trainer
U	utility
V	staff
W	weather

These letters can be combined with *either* a type or a mission indicator in the first position to the left of the dash to tell you more about what an aircraft is used for. In our examples, the T-45A has no mission modifier, so it remains simply a trainer aircraft; the "S" of the SH-60F helicopter tells us that it is used for antisubmarine warfare; the EA-18G's original attack mission was modified by adding an "E" for special electronics; and the NKC-135A is used as a tanker (for refueling other aircraft in the air). Because the two letters ("F" and "A") are separated by a slash in the F/A-18E/F, the F is not a mission modifier but is considered coequal with the A, so this is an aircraft that is capable of carrying out both fighter and attack missions with equal capability.

To better understand this process, consider that the H-60 helicopter has been modified into several different versions in today's Navy. The SH-60 version is used for antisubmarine warfare; the HH-60 is a helicopter of the same basic design, but this version is used for search-and-rescue purposes; and there are other versions as well.

Status Prefix

One more place to the left of the dash is sometimes (not very often) occupied by a letter called the status prefix. These letters are used for aircraft that are in a special status as follows:

G	grounded
J	special test (temporary)
N	special test (permanent)
X	experimental
V	prototype
Z	planning

The only one of our selected examples that has a letter in this position is the NKC-135A, and we can see from the list above that it is being used for a special test (permanently). You will not often see these letters used, but it is good to be aware of them should you encounter them.

Left-of-the-Dash Summary

Before moving to the right side of the dash, review the table below for a summary of all items that *may* appear to the left of the dash in an aircraft designation.

STATUS PREFIX	MODIFIED MISSION	BASIC MISSION	VEHICLE TYPE
G –Permanently Grounded	A - Attack	A- Attack	D - UAV Control Segment
J - Special Test (Temporary)	C - Transport	B - Bomber	G - Glider
N - Special Test (Permanent)	D - Director	C - Transport	H - Helicopter
X - Experimental	E - Special Electronics	E - Special Electronic Installation	Q - Unmanned Aerial Vehicle (UAV)
Y - Prototype	F - Fighter	F - Fighter	S - Spaceplane
Z - Planning	H - Search/Rescue/ MEDEVAC	L - Laser	V - VTOL/STOL
	K - Tanker	O - Observation	Z - Lighter-Than-Air Vehicle
	L - Cold Weather	P- Patrol	
	M - Multi-mission	R - Reconnaissance	
	O - Observation	S - Antisubmarine	
	P - Patrol	T - Trainer	
	Q - Drone	U - Utility	
	R - Reconnaissance	X - Research	
	S - Antisubmarine		
	T - Trainer		
	U - Utility		
	V - Staff		
	W - Weather		

RIGHT OF THE DASH

Now it is time to consider what is on the *right* side of the dash. This side is a bit easier because it does not require any memorization or any "crib notes" for translation.

Design

You will recall that earlier we established that aircraft designations are sometimes referred to as the MDS (Mission Design Series) system. The letters to the left of the dash make up the "mission" part of that, and the letters and numbers to the right comprise the "design" and "series" parts.

Immediately to the right of the dash is the design number. All this number means is that this aircraft is a specific design of the particular type or mission. The first design of a patrol aircraft was designated "P-1," and when a whole new design of an aircraft for patrolling was accepted by the Defense Department, it was designated "P-2," and so on.

In our chosen examples, the T-45A is the forty-fifth design of a trainer aircraft that has been accepted by DOD; the SH-60F is the sixtieth helicopter design; the EA-18G is the eighteenth attack aircraft design; and the NKC-135A is the 135th transport design. The F/A-18E/F is once again a bit of an aberration; it is *not* the eighteenth fighter/attack design, but *is* the eighteenth fighter design accepted by DOD. (Reason does not always prevail.)

Series

Many times the basic design of an aircraft is modified in some way, so that it is no longer the same aircraft as originally designed, but it has not been changed enough to warrant calling it a whole new design. To indicate this significant modification (version), a series letter is appended to the design number. The aircraft in its original design is considered to be "A" in the series. The first modification would be "B," the next would be "C," and so on. "I" and "O" are not used because they might be confused with one and zero.

So we now know that the T-45A and the NKC-135A are both original designs (as indicated by the "A" series indicator) and that the SH-60F has been modified five times and the EA-18G six times.

The F/A-18C/D is, once again, a special case. There are actually two different versions of the Hornet in service; one has only one seat and is designated the "C" version, whereas the "D" version has two seats. Because both are in service you will often see them listed as "C/D" when referring to them generically.

THE SIMPLER WAY

All the above information is provided for those who want to know precisely what the aircraft designation system is telling them. But below I have compiled all the codes covering type, mission, and status into one list. In truth, if you use this list to decipher the information to the left of the dash without concerning yourself where these particular letters fall, you will know the essentials about the aircraft and only rarely get confused.

Most of the time, the letters will be clear in context. For example, if you are given a picture of an aircraft that has the designation ZSH-7A and it has rotating blades on it, the chances are the "Z" indicates that it is in "planning" rather than being a "lighter-than-air" craft, and the "S" more than likely indicates "antisubmarine" rather than "spaceplane." So, use the letters below without worrying about where they fall to the left of the dash and you will, *in most cases*, know all you need to about an aircraft.

A	attack
B	bomber
C	transport
D	director
E	special electronic installation
F	fighter
G	glider *or* grounded
H	helicopter *or* search and rescue
J	special test (temporary)
K	tanker
L	laser *or* cold weather
M	multi-mission
N	special test (permanent)
O	observation
P	patrol
Q	drone (unmanned)
R	reconnaissance
S	antisubmarine *or* spaceplane
T	trainer
U	utility
V	V/STOL *or* staff *or* prototype
W	weather
X	research *or* experimental
Z	lighter than air *or* planning

TAB 17 Naval Weapons

Weapons are the mainstay of the military. Without them, the Navy could not carry out its combat missions or defend its ships, planes, bases, and personnel.

Major Topics Covered:

- ✸ Weapons Designations
- ✸ Missiles and Rockets
- ✸ Bombs
- ✸ Torpedoes
- ✸ Mines
- ✸ Guns
- ✸ Small arms

To Learn More:

- ⚓ **www.usni.org/BlueAndGoldProfessionalBooks/TheBluejackets Manual**
- ⚓ *Basic Military Requirements* (NAVEDTRA 14325)
- ⚓ *Seaman* (NAVEDTRA 14067)
- ⚓ *Gunner's Mate* (NAVEDTRA 14324A)
- ⚓ *Principles of Naval Weapon Systems*, 2nd ed., by Craig Payne (Naval Institute Press, 2010)
- ⚓ *Navy Program Guide* (current year)
- ⚓ *How We Fight: Handbook for the Naval Warfighter* – available from U.S. Government Printing Office and online at **http://navy reading.dodlive.mil/files/2015/08/HWF-Book-Combined-Final -27-Apr-15.pdf**

Associated Tabs:

- ○ TAB 17-A: Weapons Designation Systems
- ○ TAB 17-B: Types of Naval Weapons
- ○ TAB 17-C: Joint Electronics Type Designation System
- ○ TAB 17-D: Proper Use of Small Arms

17-A Weapons Designation Systems

MISSILE AND ROCKET DESIGNATIONS

Navy rockets and missiles are often identified by a specialized system of letters and numbers as shown in the table below.

STATUS (OPTIONAL)		LAUNCH PLATFORM		MISSION		TYPE	
J	special test, temporary	A	air	D	decoy	L	launch vehicle
N	special test, permanent	B	multiple	E	special electronics installation	M	guided missile
X	experimental	C	coffin	G	surface attack	N	probe
Y	prototype	F	individual	I	intercept aerial	R	rocket
Z	planning	G	runway	Q	drone		
		H	silo stored	T	training		
		L	silo launched	U	underwater attack		
		M	mobile	W	weather		
		P	soft pad				
		R	ship				
		S	underwater				

Note that the letters in the first column ("Status") are optional, which means that you will not always see them used—in fact, you will *rarely* see them used. Most often you will encounter three letters (representing the launch platform, the mission, and the type) followed by a number. For example, the Navy's Sparrow missile is identified as an "AIM-7."

- The first letter ("A") tells you that this weapon is launched from an aircraft.
- The second letter ("I") tell you that the weapon's mission is to shoot down other aircraft ("intercept aerial").
- The third letter ("M") tells you that this weapon is a guided missile.

The number following the letters and the dash is a unique identifier for that particular rocket or missile. In other words, if the Navy developed another air-to-air missile it would also be identified by the letter combination of "AIM" but would have a number other than 7 to distinguish it from the Sparrow.

Just as with aircraft designations, if there are subsequent major modifications (versions) to the basic design of a particular rocket or missile, they are indicated by a follow-on alphabetically sequential letter (A, B, C, and so on). For example, the third modification of the AIM-7 would be designated AIM-7C, the fourth would be AIM-7D, and so on.

MARK AND MOD SYSTEM

The Navy assigns MARK and MOD numbers to many types of equipment not covered by other designation systems. Bombs, torpedoes, guns, fire control systems (and the gun directors within them), rocket motors, missile launchers, warheads, and so on fall within this system, which has been around since World War II.

The system is less revealing in some ways than some of the other designation systems, but it is relatively simple. Beginning with a simple word description of the item (such as "torpedo" or "launcher"), it is then specified by a unique MARK number and followed by a MOD number. For example:

Torpedo, MARK 46 MOD 5

The MARK number is assigned sequentially and is the means of distinguishing one similar item from another. If the Navy accepts a modified version, that is indicated by the MOD number. The original version is designated MOD 0 and the first modified version is MOD 1.

According to MIL-STD-1661 (the governing instruction for this system—which you do not want to read unless you really have to), the *name* of the item is to *precede* the MARK number, and it is to be separated from the latter by a comma, as you see in the example above. (Talk about "military precision"!)

The governing instruction also calls for the words "MARK" and "MOD" to be written unabbreviated and in uppercase. However, the instruction allows some variations, and in actual practice, you may well see MARK as "MK" (or even "Mk") and you may also see "Mark" and "Mod" used. Therefore, the following variations are acceptable and you will see them used often:

Mark 46 Mod 4 Torpedo
MK 46 MOD 4 Torpedo
Mk 46 Mod 4 Torpedo

Although the MOD part of the system is important in some contexts, it is often expendable in normal usage. So you will often see, for example, the MARK 46 MOD 5 Torpedo referred to as simply the "MARK 46 Torpedo" (or "MK 46 Torpedo" or "Mk 46 Torpedo").

Dashes and other punctuations should not be used (and are not sanctioned by the governing instruction), but in truth you will see such things as these:

Mark-46 Mod 4 Torpedo
Mk.46 Mod 4 Torpedo

The instruction goes on to say that items with adjective descriptors, such as a "missile launcher," should be written in "reverse nomenclature" (with a separating comma) as in "launcher, missile." There is a reason for this standardization. When these items are listed in inventory documents and the like, they will be grouped more logically when alphabetized. In other words, all the torpedoes will be listed together:

Torpedo, MARK 14 MOD 5
Torpedo, MARK 46 MOD 5
Torpedo, MARK 48 MOD 1

And all fire control systems will be grouped together:

Fire Control System, Gun, MARK 75 MOD 2
Fire Control System, Gun, MARK 86 MOD 1
Fire Control System, Guided Missile, MARK 13 MOD 1

Experimental

The prefix "EX" is used instead of "MARK" for experimental items. If an EX item is adopted for operational use, it will use MARK from then on but will retain the originally assigned number. When an item is redesignated from EX to MARK, the MOD numbers are restarted from zero. For example, if an experimental item is designated EX 37, and the MOD numbers 0 through 3 were assigned during development, once the item is put into operational service, the new designation would be MARK 37 MOD 0. However, if more than one of the versions (modifications) is put into service, say EX 37 MOD 1 and EX 37 MOD 3, the new item designations would be MARK 37 MOD 0 and MARK 37 MOD 1. It *is* logical, if not pretty.

LASER-GUIDED BOMBS

A joint Navy–Air Force program, laser-guided bombs (LGB) are highly accurate munitions with a laser guidance unit fitted onto the nose that is used to guide the bomb onto the target. These guidance units are used with various bombs, such as the MK 83 1,000-pound bomb. The bomb-dropping aircraft (or some other source) illuminates the target with a laser beam and the bomb follows the reflection of that beam onto the target.

Like joint direct attack munitions (JDAM), these weapons are also designated using the Air Force system, so you will encounter such designations as GBU-10 (using the MK 84 bomb), GBU-12 (using the MK 82), and GBU-16 (using the MK 83).

 17-B Types of Naval Weapons

The Navy's weapons are listed below in alphabetical order by their more commonly used names or acronyms.

AARGM. *See* Advanced Anti-Radiation Guided Missile.

Advanced Anti-Radiation Guided Missile (AARGM). An air-to-ground missile used for destruction of enemy air defenses. Similar to the High-speed Anti-Radar Missile (HARM), it is a more sophisticated weapon that targets enemy radar systems by homing in on their electronic emissions while minimizing collateral damage.

Advanced Medium-Range Air-to-Air Missile (AMRAAM). An all-weather, all-environment, radar-guided missile developed as a follow-on to the Sparrow missile series. AMRAAM is smaller, faster, and lighter and has improved capabilities against very low-altitude and high-altitude targets in an electronic countermeasure environment. Its active radar, in conjunction with an inertial reference unit and microcomputer system, makes the missile less dependent on the aircraft fire control system, enabling the pilot to aim and fire several missiles at multiple targets. The AMRAAM is a result of a joint U.S. Navy and U.S. Air Force development effort and is in service with numerous NATO and allied countries.

Aegis. The Aegis Weapon System (AWS) is a centralized, automated weapons control system that was designed as a total weapon system, from detection to kill. The heart of the system is the AN/SPY-1, an advanced, automatic detect-and-track, multi-function phased-array radar. This high-powered (four megawatt) radar is able to perform search, track, and missile guidance functions simultaneously, with a tracking capacity of more than one hundred targets.

AMRAAM. *See* Advanced Medium-Range Air-to-Air Missile.

Anti-Submarine Rocket (ASROC). An anti-submarine rocket that carries a torpedo, allowing a ship to attack a submarine from a safer distance than would be required to simply launch the torpedo from a standard shipboard launcher. The vertical launch ASROC (VLA) is launched from vertical missile tubes in Aegis-equipped ships.

ASROC. *See* Anti-Submarine Rocket.

AWS. *See* Aegis.

Bombs, General Purpose. *See* MK 80 Series General-Purpose Bombs.

CIWS. *See* Phalanx.

Evolved Sea Sparrow. An improved version of the Sea Sparrow, this missile is faster and has an improved payload and range.

HARM. *See* High-Speed Anti-Radar Missile.

Harpoon. Because Harpoons can be fired from virtually every combatant in the Navy (surface ships, submarines, and aircraft) the Harpoon is designated as the RGM-84, the UGM-84, and the AGM-84. It has a range of more than seventy-five miles, and a version called SLAM-ER (for Stand-Off Land Attack Missile-Extended Range) is used to attack land or sea targets at greater distances.

High-Speed Anti-Radar Missile (HARM). Designated AGM-88, this missile is designed specifically to knock out enemy radars (by homing in on their electronic emission) at sea and ashore.

JDAM. *See* Joint Direct Attack Munition.

Joint Direct Attack Munition (JDAM). Jointly developed with the U.S. Air Force to provide increased accuracy for air-launched bombs, the JDAM kit converts a "dumb bomb" (one that is simply dropped from an aircraft without any additional guidance) into a "smart bomb" by adding a special assembly that includes an inertial navigational system and a global positioning system component for guidance control.

These can be attached to 500-, 1,000- and 2,000-pound bombs (see MK 80 Series General-Purpose Bombs).

Joint Stand-Off Weapon (JSOW). The JSOW is an air-launched weapon that can be dropped on a target from as far away as sixty nautical miles (known as a "stand-off range"). Currently, two variants of JSOW are in the fleet: AGM-154A, which uses electronic guidance to hit targets, and AGM-154C, which adds a terminal imaging infrared seeker and a special two-stage warhead.

JSOW. *See* Joint Stand-Off Weapon.

Laser Joint Direct Attack Munition (LJDAM). Basically a JDAM with a modular laser sensor to provide moving target kill capability. The laser sensor kit is field-installed (meaning attached on board ship or at an airfield, rather than at a factory) on the 500-pound version of JDAM.

LCDB (Low Collateral Damage Bomb). *See* MK 80 Series General-Purpose Bombs.

LJDAM. *See* Laser Joint Direct Attack Munition

Maverick. The AGM-65 is a short-range, air-to-surface missile designed for day or night sea warfare (antiship) and land interdiction missions. The AGM-65E/E2 is a laser-guided missile employed by F/A-18 Hornet and AV-8 Harrier aircraft. The AGM-65F is an infrared-guided missile employed by Navy patrol aircraft.

MK 38 25mm machine gun. This single-barrel, air-cooled, heavy machine gun is effective up to two thousand yards. Designed for ship self-defense from small craft attacks and other localized attacks.

MK 45 5-inch 54/62 caliber gun. This fully automatic naval gun provides surface combatants accurate naval gunfire against fast, highly maneuverable, surface targets, air threats, and shore batteries during amphibious operations.

MK 46 30mm Gun Weapon System (GWS). A remotely operated naval gun system that uses a 30mm high-velocity cannon, a forward looking infrared sensor, a low-light television camera, and a laser rangefinder for shipboard self-defense against small, high-speed surface targets. The gun can be operated locally at the gun turret or remotely from a remote operating console.

MK 48 Torpedo. This heavyweight torpedo is used solely by submarines and is employed as their primary antisubmarine and anti-surface ship weapon. Its latest version, MK 48 Mod 7 common broadband advanced sonar system torpedo, is optimized for both deep and littoral waters and has advanced counter-countermeasure capabilities.

MK 50 Torpedo. A highly capable undersea weapon for U.S. Navy aircraft and surface ships. It is an advanced lightweight digital torpedo designed for use against faster, deeper-diving and more sophisticated submarines.

MK 54 Torpedo. This lightweight torpedo integrates existing torpedo hardware and software from the older MK 46, MK 50, and MK 48 torpedoes with state-of-the-art digital signal processing technology. It incorporates an advanced guidance and control section and tactical software improvements to increase shallow water counter-countermeasure capability significantly at reduced lifecycle costs.

MK 67 Submarine-Launched Mobile Mine (SLMM). This submarine-deployed mine was developed from an older torpedo and is used for clandestine mining in hostile environments.

MK 80 Series General-Purpose Bombs. Originally created in the late 1940s, these bombs have been the standard air-launched bomb for Navy and Air Force services ever since. Designed to provide blast and fragmentation effects and used extensively in a number of configurations including laser-guided bombs, joint direct attack munitions (JDAM), and air-delivered mining applications. The unguided versions of the general-purpose bomb can also be delivered in free-fall or delayed modes depending upon mission requirements. The three basic versions of these bombs are:

> MK 82 500 pound (BLU 111)
> MK 83 1,000 pound (BLU 110)
> MK 84 2,000 pound (BLU 117)

The MK 80 system is being replaced by the newer "BLU" (for "Bomb-Live Unit) series as indicated above. The Navy's MK 80 series bombs remaining in inventory are filled with H-6 high explosive. The newer BLU series bombs incorporate a PBXN-109 explosive that provides less sensitive characteristics and is considered safer to handle and stow.

The Navy's newest member to the BLU series is the BLU-126 that is designed as a low-collateral warhead. It is identical to the BLU-111 with the exception of the amount of PBXN-109 explosive filler. The aft end of the BLU-126 bomb is packed with approximately twenty-seven pounds of explosive filler, with the remainder of the bomb being filled with inert material. It is sometimes referred to as the LCDB (for Low Collateral Damage Bomb).

Phalanx. The Phalanx Close-In Weapons System (CIWS) combines a 20mm Gatling gun with search and tracking radar to provide surface ships with terminal defense against anti-ship missiles. Phalanx automatically detects, tracks, and engages air warfare threats. A special "man-in-the-loop" system allows local control to counter small craft attacks or other localized threats.

Quickstrike Mines. A family of shallow-water, aircraft-laid mines. Versions include the MK 62, MK 63, and MK 65, which are converted general purpose bombs of the 500-pound, 1,000-pound, and 2,000-pound sizes, respectively.

Rolling Airframe Missile (RAM). Designated RIM-116 this surface-to-air missile was developed jointly with the Federal Republic of Germany and provides ships with a low-cost self-defense system against anti-ship missiles and asymmetric air and surface threats.

Sea Sparrow. A modified version of the Sparrow air-to-air missile, this missile is carried by ships having no Standard missile capabilities. This missile has a range of about ten nautical miles and is designed to provide close-in protection when other means of anti-air defense have been ineffective.

Shrike. Designated AGM-45, this missile is delivered by fighter aircraft and is designed to home in on enemy antiaircraft radars.

Sidewinder. The AIM-9 is an all-weather heat-seeking (infrared) missile with a range of five to ten nautical miles depending upon conditions. It has been through a number of modernizations, and the current fleet weapon is the AIM-9M.

SLAM-ER. *See* Harpoon.

SLMM. *See* MK 67 Submarine-Launched Mobile Mine.

Sparrow. Designated the AIM-7, this highly maneuverable radar-guided missile can attack enemy aircraft from any direction in virtually all weather conditions and has a range of more than thirty nautical miles.

Standard Missile. The U.S. Navy's primary surface-to-air air defense weapon is an integral part of the Aegis Weapon System (AWS) aboard *Ticonderoga*-class cruisers and *Arleigh Burke*–class destroyers and is launched from the MK 41 Vertical Launcher System (VLS). Its primary missions are fleet area air defense and ship self-defense. It has a range of about ninety nautical miles, but an extended-range version can reach as far as two hundred nautical miles.

TASM. *See* Tomahawk.

TLAM. *See* Tomahawk.

Tomahawk. An all-weather, ship- or submarine-launched cruise missile, the Tomahawk has proven to be a highly survivable weapon due to its low radar detectability and terrain/wave-skimming flight. Designated BGM-109, it can be used in several variations, including a TASM (Tomahawk anti-ship missile) and a TLAM (Tomahawk land-attack missile).

Trident II. The Navy's fleet ballistic missiles are submarine-launched ICBMs with MIRV capability and were designed for strategic deterrence and attack. The earliest version was the Polaris, followed by the Poseidon. Today, U.S. fleet ballistic-missile submarines carry the Trident missile. The most advanced version, the Trident II (UGM-133), has a range of more than six thousand miles and is capable of carrying up to eight independent thermonuclear warheads.

VLA (Vertical Launch ASROC). *See* Anti-Submarine Rocket.

 17-C **Joint Electronics Type Designation System**

Radar, sonar, and other Navy electronic equipments are identified by this system, sometimes referred to by its acronym "JETDS." First developed during World War II, it was originally called the "Army-Navy Nomenclature System." Even though it is now a joint system including the Air Force, Coast Guard, and Marine Corps, it still retains the prefix identifier "AN" (for "Army-Navy"), and you will sometimes hear it called the "AN System."

The rest of the designation consists of three letters plus a number (with an optional letter sometimes following). Each letter tells you something about the equipment, and the number is the model number that is unique to that design.

As with other designation systems, different versions (modifications) of the same basic equipment are indicated by a sequential alphabetical letter; the original version has no letter, the first modification would be "A," the second "B," and so on.

The table below provides the meanings of the three letters that are the main part of the system.

INSTALLATION		TYPE OF EQUIPMENT		PURPOSE	
A	piloted aircraft	A	invisible light, heat radiation (i.e., infrared)	A	auxiliary assembly
B	underwater, mobile (submarine)	B	COMSEC (secure communications)	B	bombing
D	pilotless carrier (missile, drone, UAV)	C	carrier (electronic wave or signal)	C	communications
F	fixed ground	D	RADIAC (radioactivity detection, identification, and computation)	D	direction finding, reconnaissance, and surveillance
G	general ground	E	laser	E	ejection or release
K	amphibious	F	fiber optics	G	fire control or searchlight directing
M	mobile ground	G	telegraph or teletype	H	recording or reproducing
P	portable (by man)	I	interphone and public address	K	computing
S	surface ship	J	electromechanical	M	maintenance or test
T	transportable (cannot be operated while in motion)	K	telemetering	N	navigation aid

INSTALLATION		TYPE OF EQUIPMENT		PURPOSE	
U	general utility	L	countermeasures	Q	special or combination
V	vehicle	M	meteorological	R	receiving or passive detecting
W	water (surface/ underwater combination)	N	sound in air	S	search and detecting (range and bearing)
Z	piloted/pilotless airborne combination	P	radar	T	transmitting
		Q	sonar and underwater sound	W	automatic flight or remote control
		R	radio	X	identification or recognition
		S	special or combination	Y	surveillance and control
		T	telephone (wire)	Z	secure
		V	visual/visible light		
		W	armament (only used if no other letter applies)		
		X	fax or television		
		Y	data processing		
		Z	communications		

For example, you might encounter the JETDS designator

AN/SPY-1D

The "AN" simply tells you that this is a designation within JETDS. Because that is the only function of these letters, you will often see them dropped, so you might simply see "SPY-1D" referring to this same equipment. When the "AN" *is* used, it is followed by a slash (/) to avoid confusion. The three letters following tell us the most about the equipment:

- The first letter ("S" in our example) indicates *where* this equipment is installed (the "platform" using it).
- The second letter ("P" in our example) tells us the *type* of equipment.
- The third letter ("Y" in our example) defines the *purpose* of the equipment.

So, we can determine that the AN/SPY-1D is a surveillance and control (Y) radar (P) that is installed on surface ships (S).

The number after the letters ("1" in our example) is the *model number*. Each new model of an equipment is normally assigned the next number in sequence, so if the Navy acquired a new surveillance and control radar for use on surface ships, it would be designated "SPY-2."

The appended letter at the end ("D" in our example) tells you that this is a modified version from the original design. The first (original) version would have no suffix. The first modification uses "A," the second would be "B," and so on. The letters "I," "O," "Q," "S," "T," "X," "Y," and "Z" are not used for modifications for reasons too complicated to go into here. Since our example uses the letter "D"—the fourth letter of the alphabet— we can assume that this radar system has been significantly modified four times since the original design first appeared.

With what we now know about electronic designations, we can determine that an

AN/PRC-66B

is a portable (P) radio (R) used for communications (C) purposes with a model number of "66," and this is the second modification (B) to the original design.

 17-D Proper Use of Small Arms

As part of your military duties, you may be required to carry and perhaps even use a firearm. You will, of course, receive practical training in the use of weapons before you will be expected to carry one, but certain universal fundamentals will help to prepare you.

WATCHSTANDING UNDER ARMS

Make certain that you know the special orders of your watch pertaining to weapons. In some situations, your orders will be to carry your weapon with a clip or magazine of ammunition inserted but no round (bullet) in the chamber; in others, you will be expected to carry your clips or magazines in a pouch on your belt and only insert them when imminent danger threatens.

When being relieved of the watch while carrying a loaded weapon, you should remove the clip or magazine from the weapon, point it in a safe direction, and check the chamber, making sure there are no rounds present. Release the slide, and with the weapon still pointed in a safe direction, let the hammer go home (return it to the uncocked position). Your relief should repeat this procedure after you have turned the weapon over to him or her.

WHEN TO FIRE

Armed personnel are authorized to fire their weapons only under the following conditions:

- To protect their own lives or the life of another person where no other means of defense will work
- To prevent the escape of a dangerous prisoner
- To prevent sabotage, arson, or other crimes against the government after all other means have failed

SAFETY PRECAUTIONS

The following general safety precautions apply whenever you are handling any type of firearm:

FOUR IMPORTANT RULES:

- TREAT EVERY WEAPON AS IF IT WERE LOADED (*even if you are sure it is not*).
- NEVER POINT A WEAPON AT ANYTHING YOU DO NOT INTEND TO SHOOT, AND POSITIVELY IDENTIFY YOUR INTENDED TARGET BEFORE FIRING.
- KEEP WEAPON ON "SAFE" UNTIL YOU INTEND TO FIRE.
- WHEN HOLDING A WEAPON, KEEP YOUR FINGER STRAIGHT AND OFF THE TRIGGER UNTIL YOU ARE READY TO ACTUALLY AIM AND FIRE.

Additionally:

- Know your weapon—its shooting characteristics, its safeties, and its loading and handling procedures.
- Be aware of the safety of innocent bystanders.
- Warning shots are prohibited.
- Always make sure the bore (inside of barrel) is clear and that all oil and grease have been removed from the outside of the weapon before firing.
- Use only the proper size of ammunition.
- Point the weapon in a safe direction when loading.
- Unload firearms before transporting them unless they may be needed during the transit.
- Unload unattended weapons. If you have weapons at home, stow them with trigger locks installed and keep ammunition out of the reach of children.
- Do not climb trees or fences with a loaded firearm if it can be avoided.
- Do not pull a firearm toward you by the muzzle.
- Be aware of the possibility of ricochet when firing. Keep in mind that a bullet may skip like a stone on water if fired at a shallow angle over a hard or liquid surface.
- It should be obvious that firearms and alcohol don't mix. Also, be aware that many prescription drugs also have side effects that can add to the danger of handling weapons.
- Never play around when carrying a weapon.

FIRING TECHNIQUES

When firing a small arm, whether on a target range or in an actual real-life combat situation, remembering some basic rules will help you to be more effective.

Proper sight alignment is essential to accuracy. Although it may seem illogical to you, the point at which you are aiming should be resting on top of the two aligned sights. When aiming, you want the front and rear sights to be perfectly aligned and the target appearing to rest directly on top of them.

1

PERFECT ALIGNMENT. TOP OF FRONT SIGHT LEVEL WITH TOP OF REAR. EQUAL LINE OF LIGHT ON EITHER SIDE OF FRONT SIGHT IN REAR SIGHT NOTCH. PERFECT SHOT.

2

FRONT SIGHT LOWER THAN TOP OF REAR, EQUAL LINE OF LIGHT ON EITHER SIDE OF FRONT SIGHT IN REAR SIGHT NOTCH. SHOT TOO LOW.

3

TOP OF FRONT SIGHT HIGHER THAN TOP OF REAR. EQUAL LINE OF LIGHT ON EITHER SIDE OF FRONT SIGHT IN REAR SIGHT NOTCH. SHOT TOO HIGH.

4

TOP OF FRONT SIGHT LEVEL WITH TOP OF REAR, TOO MUCH LIGHT ON RIGHT SIDE OF FRONT SIGHT IN REAR SIGHT NOTCH. SHOT TO LEFT, 9 O'CLOCK.

5

TOP OF FRONT SIGHT HIGHER THAN TOP OF REAR. TOO MUCH LIGHT ON LEFT SIDE OF FRONT SIGHT IN REAR SIGHT NOTCH. SHOT HIGH AND RIGHT.

6

TOP OF FRONT SIGHT LEVEL WITH TOP OF REAR, TOO MUCH LIGHT ON LEFT SIDE OF FRONT SIGHT IN REAR SIGHT NOTCH. REVOLVER "CANTED," SHOT LOW AND RIGHT.

7

TOP OF FRONT SIGHT LEVEL WITH TOP OF REAR, TOO MUCH LIGHT ON RIGHT SIDE OF FRONT SIGHT IN REAR SIGHT NOTCH. REVOLVER "CANTED." SHOT LOW AND LEFT.

[**17-D**] Effects of correct and incorrect small arms sight alignment

Blackening your sights will prevent glare. Use a smudge pot, carbide lamp, candle, cigarette lighter, or ordinary match to blacken your sights.

Take a normal breath before firing, exhale part of it, and hold the rest as you squeeze the trigger. Squeeze the trigger steadily—do not jerk it. If your sight alignment shifts while you are squeezing, do not release the pressure on the trigger; hold it while you realign the sights, then continue squeezing. You should be surprised when the weapon fires.

See OPNAVINST 3591.1 (series) *Small Arms Training and Qualification* for more detailed instructions and procedures.

TAB 18 Leadership and Discipline

Leadership is characterized by responsibility and authority. Leaders are responsible for the tasks or missions assigned and are also responsible for leading subordinates in a manner that will not only get the job done but will preserve their dignity and minimize any negative effects that may be part of a difficult task. Good leaders find ways to cause individuals to carry out an assignment willingly rather than out of fear of reprisal.

Major Topics Covered:

- ☸ Leadership Principles
- ☸ Leadership Styles
- ⚓ Discipline

To Learn More:

- ⚓ **www.usni.org/BlueAndGoldProfessionalBooks/TheBluejackets Manual**
- ⚓ *Basic Military Requirements* (NAVEDTRA 14325)
- ⚓ *Military Requirements for Petty Officers Third and Second Class* (NAVEDTRA 14504)
- ⚓ *Military Requirements for Petty Officers First Class* (NAVEDTRA 14145)
- ⚓ *Military Requirements for Chief Petty Officers* (NAVEDTRA 14144)
- ⚓ *Saltwater Leadership: A Primer on Leadership for the Junior Sea-Service Officer* by Robert O. Wray Jr. (Naval Institute Press, 2013)
- ⚓ *Navigating the Seven Seas: Leadership Lessons of the First African American Father and Son to Serve at the Top in the U.S. Navy* by Melvin G. Williams Sr. and Melvin G. Williams Jr. (Naval Institute Press, 2011)
- ⚓ *In the Shadow of Greatness: Voices of Leadership, Sacrifice, and Service from America's Longest War* by the U.S. Naval Academy Class of 2002 (Naval Institute Press, 2012)
- ⚓ *Leadership Embodied: The Secrets to Success of the Most Effective Navy and Marine Corps Leaders*, 2nd ed., edited by Lt. Col. Joseph J. Thomas, USMC (Naval Institute Press, 2013)

⚓ *The U.S. Naval Institute on Naval Leadership*, The U.S. Naval Institute Wheel Book Series, edited by Thomas J. Cutler (Naval Institute Press, 2015)

⚓ *The Noncommissioned Officer and Petty Officer: BACKBONE of the Armed Forces* (CreateSpace Independent Publishing Platform, 2015)

⚓ *Leading with the Heart: Coach K's Successful Strategies for Basketball, Business, and Life* by Mike Krzyzewski and Donald T. Phillips (Grand Central Publishing, 2001)

⚓ *The Trident: The Forging and Reforging of a Navy SEAL Leader* by Jason Redman and John Bruning (HarperCollins, 2013)

TAB 19 The Paper Navy

Despite the increasing reliance on computers, the Navy's administrative systems are based on paper forerunners, and it is important for you to understand these systems as they currently exist. Correspondence, directives, and many other paper-based systems are essential to the smooth operation of today's Navy.

Major Topics Covered:

- ⚓ The Standard Subject Identification Code (SSIC) System
- ⚓ Directives (Instructions and Notices)
- ⚓ The Internet as Admin Ally (Saving Trees)
- ⚓ Naval Messages

To Learn More:

- ⚓ **www.usni.org/BlueAndGoldProfessionalBooks/TheBluejackets Manual**
- ⚓ *Department of the Navy Records Management Program: Standard Subject Identification Code (SSIC) Manual* (SECNAV M-5210.2)
- ⚓ *Department of the Navy Correspondence Manual* (SECNAV M-5216.5)
- ⚓ *Personnel Specialist: Basic Training Manual* (NAVEDTRA 15006A)
- ⚓ *The Naval Institute Guide to Naval Writing*, 3rd ed., by Robert Shenk (Naval Institute Press, 2011)
- ⚓ *Time Conversion* (NAVEDTRA 14252)
- ⚓ *Navy Directives Management Program Manual* (OPNAV M-5215.1)

Associated Tabs:

- ⭕ TAB 19-A: Important Navy Publications
- ⭕ TAB 19-B: Standard Subject Identification Codes (SSIC)
- ⭕ TAB 19-C: Navy Letter Format
- ⭕ TAB 19-D: Navy Message Format
- ⭕ TAB 19-E: Time Zones of the World

19-A Important Navy Publications

The following list is by no means all-inclusive, but it is a good start toward understanding the foundation of the paper Navy. Note that some of these publications have combinations of letters and numbers following them in brackets (like OPNAVINST 3120.32 and JAGINST 5800.7); these are explained in **Chapter 19: The Paper Navy**. Some of these publications are "joint" ones that apply to all the armed services and others are Navy only. Joint publications are often supplemented by Navy publications that cover any differences or additions.

United States Navy Regulations (NAVREGS)
Often referred to as "Navy Regs," this publication outlines the organizational structure of the Department of the Navy (DON) and sets out the principles and policies by which the Navy is governed.

Standard Organization and Regulations of the U.S. Navy (OPNAVINST 3120.32)
Sets forth regulations and guidance governing the conduct of all members of the U.S. Navy and sets the standards for the organization of naval units. Though not technically correct, to understand its function you might think of this as a kind of addendum to *United States Navy Regulations*. This is a much bigger publication than NAVREGS with a lot more information.

Standard Subject Identification Code (SSIC) Manual (SECNAV M-5210.2)
This is described in more detail later in this chapter. It provides a numerical coding system that is useful in the filing and identification of documents.

Standard Navy Distribution List (SNDL) (OPNAVNOTE 5400)
The SNDL lays out the administrative chain of command and provides addresses for fleet units and shore activities.

Naval Military Personnel Manual (NAVPERS 15560)
Often called the MILPERSMAN, this is a very important publication that affects you in many ways—including applications for various educational programs, transfers, discharges, and separations.

Manual for Courts-Martial, United States
This publication describes the types of courts-martial established by the Uniform Code of Military Justice (UCMJ), defines their jurisdiction, and prescribes their procedures. It also covers such matters as nonjudicial punishment (NJP), reviews of court-martial proceedings, new trials, and limitations on punishment. This manual applies to all the armed services.

Manual of the Judge Advocate General (JAGINST 5800.7)
Often referred to as the "JAGMAN," this manual covers legal and judicial matters that apply only to the naval service. Included among these are instructions regarding boards of investigation and examining boards— their composition, authority, and procedures.

Joint Federal Travel Regulations
Issued in three volumes, only the first volume deals with actual travel. JFTR interprets for all services the laws and regulations concerning the manner in which transportation is furnished, travel for family members, the transportation of household goods, reimbursement for travel expenses, and similar information.

U.S. Navy Travel Instructions (NAVSO P-1459)
Amplifies the rules laid down in volume 1 of the JFTR specifically for the Navy.

Department of Defense Military Pay and Allowance Entitlements Manual
DODPM covers statutory provisions for entitlements, deductions, and collections on military pay and allowances.

Navy Pay and Personnel Procedures Manual (NAVSO P-3050)
The PAYPERSMAN contains detailed information about the procedures of the military pay system for members of the Navy.

Enlisted Transfer Manual (NAVPERS 15909)
The TRANSMAN is the official manual for the distribution and assignment of enlisted personnel; it supplements the MILPERSMAN.

Navy and Marine Corps Awards Manual (SECNAVINST 1650.1)
Usually referred to as "The Awards Manual," this is issued by the SECNAV for guidance in all matters pertaining to decorations, medals, and awards, including how they are worn.

Manual of Advancement (BUPERSINST 1430.16)
This addresses the administration of the Navy advancement (promotion) system. It explains the basic policies outlined in MILPERSMAN on eligibility requirements for advancement; the preparation of forms; the ordering, custody, and disposition of Navy-wide exams; the administration of examinations for advancement; changes in rate or rating; and the procedures for actual advancement.

Department of the Navy Correspondence Manual (SECNAV M-5216.5)
Spells out the proper procedures and formats for preparing various forms of Navy correspondence, such as letters, memoranda, e-mail, etc.

Department of the Navy Information Security Program (SECNAV M-5510.36)
Establishes policies and procedures for classifying, safeguarding, and declassifying national security information.

Small Arms Training and Qualification (OPNAVINST 3591.1)
Provides detailed instructions and requirements for small arms use and safety, including proper gun range procedures as well as real-world techniques.

 19-B Standard Subject Identification Codes (SSIC)

1000–1999: Military Personnel
Subjects relating solely to the administration of military personnel. Civilian personnel subjects are included in the 12000 series. General personnel subjects relating to both civilian and military personnel are included in the 5000 series.

2000–2999: Information Technology and Communications
Includes subjects relating to general information technology matters and to communications systems and equipment

3000–3999: Operations and Readiness
Subjects related to such matters as operational plans, fleet operations, operational training and readiness, warfare techniques, operational intelligence, research and development, and geophysical and hydrographic support

4000–4999: Logistics

Topics related to the logistical support of the Navy and Marine Corps, including procurement, supply control, property redistribution and disposal, travel and transportation, maintenance, construction and conversion, production and mobilization planning, and foreign military assistance

5000–5999: General Administration and Management

Includes subjects relating to the administration, organization, and management of the Department of the Navy, including general personnel matters concerning *both* civilian and military personnel, records management programs, security, external and internal relations, audiovisual management, law and legal matters, office services, office automation, and publication and printing matters

6000–6999: Medicine and Dentistry

Medical matters such as physical fitness, general medicine, special or preventive medicine, dentistry, and medical equipment and supplies

7000–7999: Financial Management

Financial administration of the Department of the Navy, including budgeting, disbursing, accounting, auditing, industrial and other special financing matters, and statistical reporting

8000–8999: Ordnance Material

All types of ordnance material and weapons, including ammunition and explosives, guided missiles of all types, nuclear weapons, fire control and optics, combat vehicles, underwater ordnance materials, and miscellaneous ordnance equipment

9000–9999: Ships Design and Material

Such matters as the design and characteristics of ships, and their material and equipment

10000–10999: General Material

Those general categories of materials not included in the specialized material groups, such as ordnance and ships. It includes personnel material, general machinery and tools, audiovisual equipment and accessories, and miscellaneous categories including metals, fuels, building materials, electrical and electronic categories, and diving and hyperbaric systems equipment.

11000–11999: Facilities and Activities Ashore

Ashore structures and facilities, fleet facilities, transportation facilities, heavy equipment, utilities and services, and other similar subjects

12000–12999: Civilian Personnel

Includes subjects relating solely to the administration of civilian personnel. Military personnel subjects are included in the 1000 series. General personnel subjects relating to both civilian and military personnel are included in the 5000 series.

13000–13999: Aeronautical and Astronautical Material

Aeronautical and astronautical material, including parts, accessories, and instruments; special devices; armament; aerological equipment; weapons systems, types of aircraft; and astronautic vehicles

19-C Navy Letter Format

If you are familiar with a basic business letter format, you will find that Navy letters have essentially the same kind of information. But there are some added features, and the format is noticeably different. Both kinds of letters have in common a letterhead, the date, the addressee, and the signature, but a standard Navy letter differs in a number of ways.

Below is a sample standard Navy letter. The format you see here is generally the same for all Navy letters although some may have additional features added, such as classification markings if the letter contains information that must be safeguarded from enemy eyes.

Note that in the upper right hand corner of our sample letter there is a four-digit number ("2310" in our sample). You may have correctly guessed that this is an SSIC that can be used to ensure that the letter is filed (and can later be retrieved) by both sender and receiver according to its subject matter.

The serial number below the SSIC is assigned to identify who within the command originated the letter and as an internal means of keeping track

2310
Ser N3/103
30 August 2007

From: Commanding Officer, Naval Test Wing Atlantic (VX-1)
To: Commander Naval Air Warfare Center Weapons Division, Point Mugu, CA
         (Code 327100E)

Subj: ORGANIZATIONAL MESSAGE RELEASE AUTHORITY VIA NAM-
         DRP DEFICIENCY REPORT (DR) WEBSITE

Ref: (a) NTP 3(J) Telecommunications Users Manual

Encl: (1) Sample NAMDRP Deficiency Report
         (2) Message Form

1. Per ref (a), the following personnel are authorized to release organizational messages for this command using the NAMDRP Deficiency Report (DR) form using
enclosures (1) and (2) as guidelines.

Name	Rank/Rate
David Jones	LT
Stephanie Decatur	AT1
W.T. Door	AE1
Corey Spondents	ATCS

2. At least one of the named individuals will be available for releasing messages at all
times.

    a. Personnel will be given specific rotational assignments.

    b. A monthly bill will be maintained by the senior watch officer.

3. This list supercedes all previous authorizations.

C. C. Garrett
Christopher C. Garrett

[**19-C**] A typical Navy letter

of outgoing correspondence. These numbers may vary considerably from command to command and are primarily of interest to clerical personnel.

The date should always be in military format—day-month-year—on a standard Navy letter.

There can be little doubt who is the originator of this letter because there is both a letterhead identifying the command and a "From" line. Standard Navy letters have both "From" and "To" lines ensuring that it is clear who is sending and who is meant to receive the communication.

Additional features of a standard Navy letter are as follows:

- "Via" ensures the appropriate levels of the chain of command are kept informed. *Optional*—used only if there are intermediate levels of command involved.
- "Subj" (subject) makes it clear what the letter is about at a quick glance (for those of us who do not have all SSICs committed to memory).
- "Ref" (reference[s]) lists (with alphabetic identifiers in parentheses) any other letters or documents that can or should be referred to in order to better understand the contents of this letter. *Optional*—used when necessary or helpful, but not required if this letter can be understood without additional references.
- "Encl" (enclosure[s]) lists (with numerical identifiers) any documents that are being included with this letter. *Optional*.

Note that the paragraphs in the text are all numbered and are *not* indented. Sub-paragraphs are indented and identified by lowercase letters (a, b, c, etc.). If there are sub-sub-paragraphs, these are further indented and numbered with parentheses around them. The *Correspondence Manual* prescribes further breakdowns of sub-paragraphs.

This standard format may seem a bit over-prescribed, but once you become comfortable with it, you will realize that it really does help you find what you are looking for quickly. Just reading the subject line can often tell you whether a letter is of interest to you. Seeing who the letter is from (and to whom it is addressed) can give you some idea of the letter's importance. The cited references can often be useful in further understanding what the letter is about.

If you have to compose a Navy letter, use one of the sources mentioned earlier (the *Department of the Navy Correspondence Manual* or *The Naval Institute Guide to Naval Writing*). Another method is to use actual letters as samples.

19-D Navy Message Format

Naval messages can be very short or very, very long, but they all have certain things in common. When reading a naval message, look for clues in finding the parts that are important to you. Below is a real naval message (edited for space considerations) that the Chief of Naval Operations sent out in the aftermath of Hurricane Katrina in the fall of 2005. *The numbers to the left of the message are there for our reference purposes and would not be there in a real naval message.*

Note that naval messages are all in uppercase letters; this stems from the days when teletype machines were the primary means of sending naval messages. As you read the message, keep in mind that some of it is there primarily for the communicators who must create, transmit, and account for the message. If you see a line preceded by a three-letter code, such as "ZNR" and "ZEN," the information on that line is for the communicators and you can ignore it (unless you are a communicator).

The main things to look for in a naval message as you scan from top to bottom are the following:

> DATE-TIME GROUP
> FM
> TO
> MESSAGE CLASSIFICATION
> SUBJ
> TEXT (Single sequential numbers marking text paragraphs)

DATE-TIME GROUP

Near the top of every message (line 3 in our sample message) is a "Date-Time Group" (DTG), which tells you the approximate time and date that the message was sent. It is important because it uniquely identifies the message and because you can tell when the message was sent.

```
1    RAAUZYUW RUEWMFU0966 2622350-UUUU—RUCRNAD.
2    ZNR UUUUU ZUI RUENAAA0966 2622350
3    R 192346Z SEP 05 PSN 675154K28
4    FM CNO WASHINGTON DC
5    TO NAVADMIN
6    ZEN/NAVADMIN @ AL NAVADMIN(UC)
7    INFO ZEN/CNO CNO
8    BT
9    UNCLAS
10   NAVADMIN 236/05
11   MSGID/GENADMIN/CNO WASHINGTON DC/DNS//SEP//
12   SUBJ/TAKING CARE OF OUR OWN//
13   REF/A/GENADMIN/CNO WASHINGTON DC/161133ZSEP2005//
14   AMPN/REF A IS TASK FORCE NAVY FAMILY PLANNING ORDER//
15   RMKS/1. HURRICANE KATRINA DIRECTLY IMPACTED AN ESTIMATED 18,000 NAVY
16   FAMILIES. IN FACT, MANY OF THE SAILORS PROVIDING RELIEF TO LOCAL
17   CITIZENS ARE IN NEED OF RELIEF THEMSELVES. MOST HAVE LOST
18   SOMETHING; SOME HAVE LOST EVERYTHING.
19   2. WE NEED LONG-TERM SOLUTIONS. THAT'S WHY I ORDERED THE ESTABLISHMENT OF TASK
20   FORCE NAVY FAMILY (TFNF). TFNF WILL CONDUCT FULL SPECTRUM COMMUNITY SERVICE
21   OPERATIONS TO PROVIDE A RAPID AND COORDINATED RETURN TO A STABLE ENVIRONMENT FOR
22   OUR AFFECTED NAVY FAMILY. THAT'S THE MISSION.
23   3. AND WHEN I SAY FULL SPECTRUM, I MEAN IT. AS STIPULATED IN REF
24   (A), FULL SPECTRUM COMMUNITY SERVICE OPERATIONS WILL INCLUDE BUT ARE
25   NOT LIMITED TO: 1) FULL ACCOUNTING OF AFFECTED NAVY FAMILY MEMBERS;
26   2) AVAILABILITY OF TEMPORARY HOUSING; 3) WAY AHEAD FOR PERMANENT
27   HOUSING WHERE AUTHORIZED; 4) FINANCIAL ASSISTANCE AND COUNSELING; 5)
28   RETURN TO SCHOOL FOR CHILDREN; 6) TRANSPORTATION OPTIONS FOR
29   RELOCATION, WORK AND SCHOOL; 7) ACCESS TO HEALTH CARE SERVICES; 8)
30   ACCESS TO PASTORAL AND FAMILY COUNSELING SERVICES; 9) ACCESS TO
31   CHILD CARE; 10) ACCESS TO LEGAL SERVICES, INCLUDING CLAIMS SUPPORT;
32   AND 11) EMPLOYMENT SUPPORT.
33   4. JUST TO BE CLEAR, THE NAVY FAMILY CONSISTS OF: NAVY SERVICE
34   MEMBERS (ACTIVE AND RESERVE, OTHER SERVICE MEMBERS ASSIGNED TO NAVY
35   COMMANDS OR TENANTS ON NAVY INSTALLATIONS PENDING CONCURRENCE OF
36   THEIR RESPECTIVE SERVICES) AND THEIR FAMILIES; NAVY RETIREES AND THEIR FAMILIES;
37   CIVILIAN EMPLOYEES OF DEPARTMENT OF THE NAVY AND THEIR FAMILIES; AND MAY INCLUDE
38   CERTAIN EXTENDED FAMILY MEMBERS (DEFINED AS PARENTS, PARENTS-IN-LAW, GUARDIANS,
39   BROTHERS, SISTERS, BROTHERS-IN-LAW, SISTERS-IN-LAW) OF DECEASED, INJURED,
40   OR MISSING NAVY SERVICE MEMBERS, NAVY RETIREES OR DON CIVILIANS WITHIN THE JOA;
41   FAMILY MEMBERS IN THE JOA OF NAVY SERVICE MEMBERS/CIVILIANS.
42   5. I WANT THE NET CAST WIDE, AND I WANT IT HAULED IN OFTEN. THERE
43   ARE PEOPLE HURTING OUT THERE — OUR PEOPLE AND THEIR LOVED ONES —
44   AND WE WILL DO ALL WE CAN TO ALLEVIATE THEIR PAIN. I LIKEN IT TO A
45   MAN OVERBOARD. YOU SHIFT THE RUDDER OVER, GO TO FLANK SPEED, AND
46   PLUCK THE SAILOR OUT OF THE WATER. IN MY VIEW, WE VE GOT NEARLY
47   45,000 PEOPLE IN THE WATER RIGHT NOW, AND WE RE GOING TO PICK THEM
48   UP.
49   6. HURRICANE KATRINA DEVASTATED CITIES AND TOWNS. IT TOOK LIVES.
50   BY DAMAGING OUR BASES IN THAT REGION, IT EVEN CHIPPED AWAY AT SOME
51   OF OUR COMBAT CAPABILITY. BUT IT DID NOT DESTROY THE HUMAN SPIRIT.
52   IT DID NOT DESTROY THE NAVY FAMILY. NO STORM CAN WIPE THAT OUT. WE
53   WILL STAND BY THE NAVY FAMILY AS THE NAVY FAMILY HAS STOOD BY US. I
54   KNOW I CAN RELY ON YOUR SUPPORT.
55   7. ADM MIKE MULLEN SENDS.//
56   BT
57   #0966
```

[19-D] A typical Navy message

The DTG always appears in the same format: six numbers followed by a "Z" and then a three-letter abbreviation for the month and a two-digit number for the year. In most cases all you will care about is the date that the message was sent; the month and year are obvious but the day is less so because it is represented by the first two digits of the six that appear before the "Z." It is always in two digits, so the seventh of the month would appear as "07." So, looking at the DTG on our example message, we know that it was sent on 19 September 2005.

The "Z" in the DTG makes sense when you know what it is. You are probably aware that the time in New York is different from that in Los Angeles (three hours earlier, to be exact). Because there are different time zones all around the earth, using local time in a date-time group could be confusing. To avoid confusion, naval messages all use the same time zone—that of Greenwich, England—no matter where the sender is located and no matter what the local time is. Each time zone is identified by a letter of the alphabet—see TAB 19-E Time Zones of the World—and the letter designating Greenwich is "Z."

One more thing to keep in mind about the DTG is that each message sent by a particular originator has a unique DTG, and this is used to reference that particular message. In other words, no other message originated by the CNO will have this same DTG, and if he or she or anyone else wants to refer to this message in another message, they will do so by that unique DTG.

FM

The line that begins with "FM" (line 4 in our example) is short for "from" and tells us who sent the message; in this case, the CNO.

TO

Likewise, the "TO" line (line 5 in our example) tells you whom the message is meant for. It might designate one or more individual addressees (like USS PREBLE or DESRON 15) or it might use a more efficient collective address as in this case ("NAVADMIN" means it is a special message from the CNO that is meant for the entire Navy). If there is more than one addressee, each is on a separate line, and sometimes the list can be quite long if the message is meant to go to a lot of different addressees.

MESSAGE CLASSIFICATION

Depending upon where you work and what you do, you may have access to classified material. In terms of naval messages, you can tell what the classification is (or is not) by looking between the addresses and the subject line. Line 9 in our sample message is the message classification; in this case, the message is unclassified; you can tell by the abbreviation "UNCLAS." If the message were classified it would have the words "CONFIDENTIAL," "SECRET," or "TOP SECRET" instead, and you would have to have the appropriate security clearance to read it.

SUBJ

Although the "SUBJ" line (line 12 in or sample) is not at the top of a naval message, it can be a real time-saver because it reveals the subject of the message. Train your eyes to look for that first, and many times you can tell right off whether the message is of interest to you. If you are an engineer working on submarine sonar systems and the "SUBJ" line reads "AVIA-TION FUEL INVENTORIES," chances are you can ignore it. Be careful, however. Subject lines are not always clear and may not accurately reflect the message content (or all of it); naval messages are drafted by human beings, after all. A line with a SUBJ of "PREPARING ADMIRAL BRIEFS" may not be about laundry!

TEXT

To read the important part of a naval message—to get to the meat of the matter—look for the text, which is easily identifiable because *the paragraphs are numbered* with a period following. You can see in our example that a little way in on line 15 is a "1." That is the first paragraph of the message. The second paragraph is identified by a "2" (line 19 in our sample), the third by a "3" (line 23), and the others at lines 33, 42, 49, and 55. Be careful not to confuse the numbers with a single parenthesis following (beginning at line 25) with paragraph numbers. These are numbered items on a list within paragraph 3.

19-E Time Zones of the World

In the international time zone system, the surface of the earth is divided into twenty-four zones, each extending through 15° of longitude, with the initial zone lying between longitudes 7½° east and 7½° west of the prime meridian. (*Longitude* is the name given to the imaginary lines that run lengthwise, north and south, between the North and South Poles. They have east and west designators.) The time system is named after Greenwich, England, because the zero meridian passes directly through that town. Each zone represents a different time in the 24-hour-day cycle, with a 1-hour variation between each time zone. To further aid in zone referencing, each time zone has a numerical, a literal (letter) and, to aid in the mathematical computation, a "+" or a "-" designator.

The zero meridian (*prime meridian*) is the imaginary line running down the center of the initial time zone; thus, this time zone is designated "0" (zero) in the numbering system.

The remaining zones are numbered consecutively, 1 through 12, both east and west of 7½° longitude, through 180° longitude. The longitudes of 180° east and 180° west are the same imaginary line. This meridian is the *International Date Line.*

Let's pause to consider what appears to be a contradiction. We stated that the earth is divided into twenty-four time zones; however, we have accounted for twenty-five zones (twelve east of zone 0, twelve west of zone 0, and zone 0 itself, a total of twenty-five zones). This contradiction will be resolved later in the discussion of the International Date Line and the requirement to have a point at which we shift from one day to another. For now, let's agree there are only twenty-four time zones.

In addition to all zones having an assigned number, each zone also has a letter designator.

The initial time zone, again because of its division by the zero merid-ian, is designated zone "Z" or ZULU. (Use the phonetic alphabet—see TAB 20-C: The Phonetic Alphabet—to pronounce the letters of the time zones.) With twenty-five designators, we use every letter of the English alphabet except "J."

Like the numbering system, the letters begin with the ZULU (0) time zone and progress to the east and west, consecutively. The zones to the east of ZULU are lettered "A" through "M" (ALFA through MIKE) and the zones to the west of ZULU are lettered "N" through "Y" (NOVEMBER through YANKEE). Remember, beginning at ZULU and reading from left to right, we have zones ALFA through MIKE (eastern hemisphere). Returning to ZULU and reading from right to left, we find zones NOVEMBER through YANKEE (western hemisphere). Don't forget to omit "J" in the eastern hemisphere.

Each zone has a designation of either "+" or "-" in addition to the numerical and literal designators. In time-conversion computations, you will see the reason for these designators. Learning the "+" and "-" designation system is easy. All zones of the western hemisphere have the designation "+." All zones of the eastern hemisphere have the designation "-".

With the exceptions of zones MIKE and YANKEE, which we will discuss later, each time zone spans 15° of longitude, with the twenty-four principal meridians bisecting (dividing in half) each zone. At the equator, each degree of longitude spans sixty nautical miles (NMs). Thus, a time zone spans nine hundred NMs (15 x 60 = 900).

Now we come to a very important point in our discussion. Since we are considering the MIKE and YANKEE zones to be a single zone, it follows that the time in MIKE is *always* the same as that in YANKEE. This is where the International Date Line comes into play, for whenever this line is crossed, whether from east to west or from west to east, the *day must change*. Since we have already established that there is a one-hour difference between each of the twenty-four time zones, it is clear that there is always a situation where it is a day earlier or later in one part of the world than it is in another.

RULE: IT IS ALWAYS THE SAME TIME IN ZONE MIKE AS IT IS IN ZONE YANKEE, BUT IT IS *NEVER* THE SAME DAY.

When you cross the International Date Line, apply the sign of the departed hemisphere. For example, to go from the MIKE zone into the YANKEE zone, subtract one day. MIKE is in the eastern (or the "-") hemisphere. To go from the YANKEE zone into the MIKE zone, add one day.

YANKEE is in the western (or the "+") hemisphere. From "-" to "+," subtract; from "+" to "-", add. Another method is simply to remember to add a day when crossing the line westbound and subtract a day when crossing eastbound.

Probably the best way to remember whether to add or to subtract the hour is to take the case of the four time zones spanned by the contiguous United States (ROMEO through UNIFORM). Most of us have, at some time or other, watched a sporting event being played on the West Coast while we were physically located on the East Coast. In cases where the contest was held in the late afternoon or early evening in California, it was frequently dark in New York. Obviously, it was earlier in the day in California than it was in New York. Therefore, we can say with confidence that whenever we are traveling from a westerly direction toward a point eastward, we must add an hour each time we pass from one time zone into another. The opposite is also certainly true. When traveling from an easterly direction toward a point westward, we must subtract an hour for each new zone entered. This rule will hold true regardless of your location in the world: west to east—add, east to west—subtract. Additionally, when the 0000 hour is reached, the day changes accordingly.

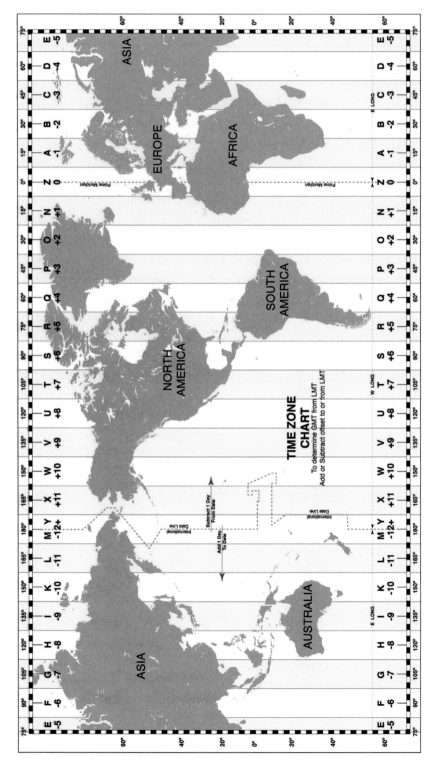

[19-E] Time zones of the world

20 Communications

Both internal and external communications are essential to the Navy. There are a variety of ways in which this is accomplished, from the very basic semaphore system to highly sophisticated satellite systems. Communications among Sailors, ships, aircraft, commanders in headquarters, etc., are vital to mission accomplishment.

Major Topics Covered:

- ⚙ MC Systems
- ⚙ Sound-Powered Telephone Systems
- ⚙ Visual Signaling
    - ~ Flashing Light
    - ~ Flaghoist
    - ~ Semaphore
- ⚙ Voice Radio

To Learn More:

- ⚓ **www.usni.org/BlueAndGoldProfessionalBooks/TheBluejackets Manual**
- ⚓ *Basic Military Requirements* (NAVEDTRA 14325)
- ⚓ *Electronics Technician Volume 3: Communications* (NAVEDTRA 14088)
- ⚓ *Sound-Powered Telephone Talkers' Training Manual* (NAVEDTRA 14232)
- ⚓ *Communication Instructions: Radiotelephone Procedures* (ACP) 125(F)
- ⚓ *Signalman 3 & 2* (NAVEDTRA 14244)
- ⚓ *U.S. Navy Social Media Handbook*

Associated Tabs:

- ○ TAB 20-A: MC Systems
- ○ TAB 20-B: Sound-Powered Communications System
- ○ TAB 20-C: The Phonetic Alphabet

20-A MC Systems

Many MC systems are available for shipboard use, but not all of them will be found on every ship. They are listed below. [*Note:* Those systems with an asterisk are central amplifier (one-way) systems; the others are all two-way networks.]

*1MC	General Announcing
*2MC	Propulsion plant
*3MC	Aviators
4MC	Damage control
*5MC	Flight deck
*6MC	Intership
7MC	Submarine control
8MC	Troop administration and control
*9MC	Underwater troop communication
18MC	Bridge
19MC	Aviation control
21MC	Captain's command
22MC	Electronic control
23MC	Electrical control
24MC	Flag command
26MC	Machinery control
27MC	Sonar and radar control
*29MC	Sonar control and information
30MC	Special weapons
31MC	Escape trunk
32MC	Weapons control
35MC	Launcher captains
39MC	Cargo handling
40MC	Flag administrative

42MC	CIC coordinating
44MC	Instrumentation space
45MC	Research operations
*46MC	Aviation ordnance and missile handling
47MC	Torpedo control
50MC	Integrated operational intelligence center
51MC	Aircraft maintenance and handling control
53MC	Ship administrative
54MC	Repair officer's control
55MC	Sonar service
58MC	Hangar-deck damage control
59MC	SAMID alert

20-B Sound-Powered Communications System

- **Sound-Powered Phones are identified by the letter "J" in their designation.**

- **An additional letter after the J represents the general purpose of the circuit.** For example, the letter S after the J in a circuit identifies that circuit as one used to gather sensor information (such as radar or sonar), the letter L would be used by lookouts to pass information to the bridge, CIC, and other stations that may need it, and so on.

- **Numbers may precede the J to differentiate different circuits of the same general type.** For example, on a ship that has only one primary weapons system, the circuit connecting key weapons stations would be simply designated the JC circuit. But on a ship with two major weapons systems, there would be two separate circuits, designated 1JC and 2JC. On most ships, the surface-search radar circuit is designated the 21JS while the air-search radar circuit is designated the 22JS.

- **Vital circuits are duplicated by what are called auxiliary circuits.** Even though these circuits connect the same stations as the primary circuit, the wires connecting them are deliberately run through different parts of the ship so that damage to one is less likely to result in simultaneous damage to the other.

- Supplementary circuits are short, direct lines used to connect key stations that need a source of quick, reliable communications. For example, a supplementary connects the captain's sea cabin and the bridge, so that the OOD can quickly notify the captain of matters of importance. Because supplementary circuits are not manned, most of these circuits contain a buzzer system so that one station can alert another that communications between the two are desired.
- The letter X precedes both auxiliary circuits and supplementary circuits, but you can tell the difference because the latter do not have an additional letter after the J. For example, the XJL and X22JS circuits are alternates of the JL and 22JS primary circuits, while the X1J and X8J would be supplementary circuits.
- Individual stations on a circuit are distinguished from each other by the addition of yet another number at the end of the sequence. For example, 22JS7 identifies outlet number 7 on the 22JS circuit. Other outlets on the same circuit would be assigned individual numbers like 22JS6 and 22JS8, and so on.

Some of the more common sound-powered circuits you may encounter aboard ship are listed below.

JA	Captain's battle circuit
JC	Weapons control
JL	Lookouts
JW	Navigation
JX	Communications
1JV	Maneuvering and docking
21JS	Surface-search radar
22JS	Air-search radar
61JS	Sonar information
2JZ	Damage control

These circuits, and others like them, are manned when necessary but will remain unused at other times. For example, the JL circuit will be manned at all times while at sea but is unused when the ship is moored to a pier.

20-C The Phonetic Alphabet

As you look over the phonetic alphabet, you will notice certain idiosyncrasies. For example, the letter "Alfa" is spelled with an f instead of ph. This is because some of our allies do not have a ph in their language. Also note that "Whiskey" ends in "key," not "ky," and "Juliett" ends in two ts.

Pay close attention to the pronunciation of each letter. Note that in the table provided, each word is accented on the syllable in capital letters. This is no time for individuality—it is essential that everyone say these words as much the same as is possible to avoid any confusion, which is the whole purpose. The letter p should be pronounced "pah-PAH," not "POP-ah" as most Americans are more likely to say. L is "LEE-mah," not "LYE-mah," and q is "kay-BECK," *not* "quee-BECK."

a	alfa	AL-fa
b	bravo	BRAH-voh
c	charlie	CHAR-lee
d	delta	DEL-tah
e	echo	ECK-oh
f	foxtrot	FOKS-trot
g	golf	GOLF
h	hotel	hoh-TELL
i	india	IN-dee-ah
j	juliett	JEW-lee-ett
k	kilo	KEY-loh
l	lima	LEE-mah
m	mike	MIKE
n	november	no-VEM-ber
o	oscar	OSS-cah
p	papa	pah-PAH
q	quebec	kay-BECK
r	romeo	ROW-me-oh
s	sierra	see-AIR-rah
t	tango	TANG-go
u	uniform	YOU-nee-form
v	victor	VIK-tah

w	whiskey	WISS-key
x	Xray	ECKS-ray
y	yankee	YANG-key
z	zulu	ZOO-loo

Note: The phonetic alphabet has been around for a long time, but has not always been the same. During World War II, the phonetic alphabet began with the letters "Able, Baker, Charlie," K was "King," and S was "Sugar," for example. After the war, when the NATO alliance was formed, the phonetic alphabet was changed to make it easier for the people who speak the different languages found in the alliance. That version has remained the same, and today the phonetic alphabet begins with "Alfa, Bravo, Charlie," K is now "Kilo," and S is "Sierra."

20-D Morse Code

International Morse code is standard for all naval communications transmitted by flashing light. The code is a system in which letters, numerals, and punctuation marks are signified by various combinations of dots (.) and dashes (–). A skilled signalman sends code in evenly timed dots and dashes, in which a dot is one unit long, a dash three units long. There is a one-unit interval between dots and dashes in a letter, a three-unit interval between letters of a word, and a seven-unit interval between words.

A	Alfa	. –
B	Bravo	– . . .
C	Charlie	– . – .
D	Delta	– . .
E	Echo	.
F	Foxtrot	. . – .
G	Golf	– – .
H	Hotel	. . . .
I	India	. .
J	Juliett	. – – –
K	Kilo	– . –
L	Lima	. – . .

M	Mike	– –
N	November	– .
O	Oscar	– – –
P	Papa	. – – .
Q	Quebec	– – . –
R	Romeo	. – .
S	Sierra	. . .
T	Tango	–
U	Uniform	. . –
V	Victor	. . . –
W	Whiskey	. – –
X	Xray	– . . –
Y	Yankee	– . – –
Z	Zulu	– – . .
1	One	. – – – –
2	Two	. . – – –
3	Three	. . . – –
4	Four	. . . . –
5	Five	. . . . .
6	Six	– . . . .
7	Seven	– – . . .
8	Eight	– – – . .
9	Nine	– – – – .
10	Ten	– – – – –
.	Period	. – . – . –
,	Comma	– – . . – –
?	Question Mark	. . – – . .
;	Semicolon	– . – . – .
:	Colon	– – – . . .
-	Hyphen	– . . . . –
'	Apostrophe	. – – – – .

20-E Signal Flags and Pennants

Flag	Name Written Spoken	Flag	Name Written Spoken	Flag	Name Written Spoken
	A **ALFA** AL-FA		**M** **MIKE** MIKE		**Y** **YANKEE** YANG-KEE
	B **BRAVO** BRAH-VOH		**N** **NOVEMBER** NO-**VEM**-BER		**Z** **ZULU** ZOO-LOO
	C **CHARLIE** CHAR-LEE		**O** **OSCAR** OSS-CAH		**ONE - 1** WUN
	D **DELTA** DEL-TAH		**P** **PAPA** PAH-**PAH**		**TWO - 2** TOO
	E **ECHO** ECK-OH		**Q** **QUEBEC** KAY-**BECK**		**THREE - 3** THUH-REE
	F **FOXTROT** FOKS-TROT		**R** **ROMEO** ROW-ME-OH		**FOUR - 4** FO-WER
	G **GOLF** GOLF		**S** **SIERRA** SEE-AIR-RAH		**FIVE - 5** FI-YIV
	H **HOTEL** HOH-**TELL**		**T** **TANGO** TANG-GO		**SIX - 6** SIX
	I **INDIA** IN-DEE-AH		**U** **UNIFORM** YOU-NEE-FORM		**SEVEN - 7** SEH-VEN
	J **JULIETTE** JEW-LEE-**ETT**		**V** **VICTOR** VIK-TAH		**EIGHT - 8** ATE
	K **KILO** KEY-LOH		**W** **WHISKEY** WISS-KEY		**NINE - 9** NINE-ER
	L **LIMA** LEE-MUH		**X** **XRAY** ECKS-RAY		**ZERO - 0** ZEE-ROH

Pennant and Name	Written and Spoken	Pennant	Written and Spoken	Pennant	Written and Spoken
1	**PENNANT ONE** WUN		**CODE OR ANSWER** CODE OR ANSWER		**PORT** PORT
2	**PENNANT TWO** TOO		**SCREEN** SCREEN		**SPEED** SPEED
3	**PENNANT THREE** THUH-REE		**CORPEN** CORPEN		**SQUAD** SQUAD
4	**PENNANT FOUR** FO-WER		**DESIG** DESIG		**STARBOARD** STBD
5	**PENNANT FIVE** FI-YIV		**DIV** DIV		**STATION** STATION
6	**PENNANT SIX** SIX		**EMERGENCY** EMERG		**SUBDIV** SUBDIV
7	**PENNANT SEVEN** SEH-VEN		**FLOT** FLOT		**TURN** TURN
8	**PENNANT EIGHT** ATE		**FORMATION** FORM		**FIRST SUB** 1st
9	**PENNANT NINE** NINE-ER		**INTERROGATIVE** INT		**SECOND SUB** 2nd
0	**PENNANT ZERO** ZEE-ROH		**NEGAT** NEGAT		**THIRD SUB** 3rd
			PREP PREP		**FOURTH SUB** 4th

20-F Semaphore Signaling System

20-G Radiotelephone Prowords

PROWORD	EXPLANATION
AUTHENTICATE	The station called is to reply to challenge that follows.
AUTHENTICATION IS . . .	The transmission authentication of this message is _____.
BREAK	I hereby indicate the separation of the text from other portions of the message.
CALL SIGN	The group that follows is a call sign (identification of a station).
CORRECTION	An error has been made in this transmission. Transmission will continue with the last word correctly transmitted.
FIGURES	Numerals or numbers follow.
I SAY AGAIN	I am repeating my transmission (or the portion indicated).
I SPELL	I will spell the next word phonetically.
OUT	This is the end of my transmission to you and no answer is required or expected. (Equivalent to "Goodbye" on a telephone.)
OVER	This is the end of my transmission to you and a response is necessary. Go ahead; transmit.
RELAY (TO)	Transmit this message to all addressees immediately following.
ROGER	I have received your last transmission satisfactorily.
SAY AGAIN	Repeat your last transmission.
SILENCE	[Repeated three or more times.] Cease transmissions on this net immediately. Silence will be maintained until lifted.
SILENCE LIFTED	The silence that was imposed on this net is now ended. You are free to transmit.

PROWORD	EXPLANATION
SPEAK SLOWER	Your transmission is too fast. Reduce your talking speed.
THIS IS	This transmission is from the station whose designator immediately follows.
WAIT	I must pause for a few seconds.
WAIT, OUT	I must pause for longer than a few seconds.
WILCO	I have received your signal, understand it, and will comply. [Since the meaning of "Roger" is included in that of "Wilco," the two prowords are never used together.]

TAB 21 The Benefits of Serving

Just as there are special demands and sacrifices that go with life in the Navy, there are also benefits that come with the job.

Major Topics Covered:

- ⚓ Pay and Allowances
- ⚓ Advancement
- ⚓ Service Record
- ⚓ Navy Housing
- ⚓ Health Benefits
- ⚓ Leave
- ⚓ Child Care
- ⚓ Counseling
- ⚓ Educational Benefits
- ⚓ Discharges
- ⚓ Retirement

To Learn More:

- ⚓ **www.usni.org/BlueAndGoldProfessionalBooks/TheBluejackets Manual**
- ⚓ *The Military Advantage: The Military.com Guide to Military and Veterans Benefits* by Terry Howell (Naval Institute Press, current edition)
- ⚓ Navy Pay Charts, **www.dfas.mil/militarymembers/payentitlements /military-pay-charts.html**
- ⚓ Navy Pay and Benefits, **www.public.navy.mil/bupers-npc/career/ payandbenefits/Pages/default2.aspx**
- ⚓ *Enlisted to Officer Commissioning Programs Application Administrative Manual* (OPNAVINST 1420.1B)

APPENDIX A
NAVY TERMS AND ABBREVIATIONS

A person entering a new trade must learn the vocabulary of that trade. As you have probably already surmised, the Navy has a language all its own. In the list below, you will find many commonly used naval terms and acronyms. Words that appear in the definitions and are defined elsewhere in the glossary are italicized.

Most of the terms you will have to learn pertain to shipboard life, but you should be aware that you will hear these terms used ashore in naval establishments as well. For example, Sailors will, more than likely, call a floor in a hallway at the Pentagon "a deck in the passageway."

1MC—ship's announcing system
abaft—farther aft, as in "abaft the beam"
abeam—abreast; on a relative bearing of 090 or 270 degrees
aboard—on or in a ship or naval station
accommodation ladder—a ladder resembling stairs that is suspended over the side of a ship to facilitate boarding from boats
adrift—loose from moorings and out of control (applied to anything lost, out of hand, or left lying about)
AFFF—aqueous film-forming foam
AFPD—armed-forces police detachment
aft—toward the stern (not as specific as abaft)
after—that which is farthest aft
afternoon watch—the 1200 to 1600 watch

aground—that part of a ship resting on the bottom (a ship "runs aground" or "goes aground")

ahoy—a hail or call for attention, as in "Boat ahoy"

AIMD—aircraft intermediate maintenance department

AIRLANT—Naval Air Force, U.S. Atlantic Fleet

alee—downwind

all hands—the entire ship's company

aloft—generally speaking, any area above the highest deck

alongside—by the side of the ship or pier

amidships—an indefinite area midway between the bow and the stern; "rudder amidships" means that the rudder is in line with the ship's centerline.

anchorage—an area designated to be used by ships for anchoring

anchor cable—the line, wire, or chain that attaches a vessel to her anchor

AOR—area of responsibility

AP—air police

ARG—amphibious ready group

armament—the weapons of a ship

ashore—on the beach or shore

ASN—assistant secretary of the Navy

ASROC—antisubmarine rocket

astern—behind a ship

ASUW—anti-surface warfare

ASVAB—Armed Services Vocational Aptitude Battery

ASW—antisubmarine warfare

ATD—airtight door

athwart—across; at right angles to

auxiliary—extra, or secondary, as in "auxiliary engine"; a vessel whose mission is to supply or support combatant forces

avast—stop, as in "avast heaving"

aweigh—an anchoring term used to describe the anchor clear of the bottom (the weight of the anchor is on the cable)

AWOL—absent without leave

Aye, aye—Reply to a command or order, meaning "I understand and will obey"

BAH—Basic Allowance for Housing

barge—a blunt-ended craft, usually non-self-propelled, used to haul supplies or garbage; a type of motorboat assigned for the personal use of a flag officer

barnacles—small shellfish attached to a vessel's undersides, pilings, and other submerged structures, the accumulation of which can slow a vessel down

BAS—Basic Allowance for Subsistence

batten down—the closing of any watertight fixture

battle lantern—a battery-powered lantern for emergency use

BCD—bad conduct discharge

BDS—battle dressing station

beam—the extreme width (breadth) of a vessel, as in "a CV has a greater beam [is wider] than a destroyer"

bear—to be located on a particular bearing, as in "the lighthouse bears 045 degrees"

bear a hand—provide assistance, as in "bear a hand with rigging the brow"; expedite

bearing—the direction of an object measured in degrees clockwise from a reference point (*true bearings* use true north as the reference, *relative bearings* use the ship's bow as the reference, and *magnetic bearings* use magnetic north)

belay—to secure a line to a fixed point; to disregard a previous order or to stop an action, as in "belay the last order" or "belay the small talk"

below—beneath, or beyond something, as in "lay below" (go downstairs); or "below the flight deck"

bend—two lines tied together (see "knot" and "hitch")

berth—bunk; duty assignment; mooring space assigned to a ship

BIBS—Bibliography for Advancement-in-Rate Exam Study

bight—a loop in a line

bilge—lowest area of the ship where spills and leaks gather; to fail an examination

billet—place or duty to which one is assigned

binnacle—a stand containing a magnetic compass

binnacle list—list of persons excused from duty because of illness

bitt—cylindrical upright fixture (usually found in pairs) to which mooring or towing lines are secured aboard ship or on a pier

bitter end—the free end of a line

block—roughly equivalent to a pulley

BLS—basic life support

BMOW—boatswain's mate of the watch

board—to go aboard a vessel; a group of persons meeting for a specific purpose, as in "investigation board" boat—a small craft capable of being carried aboard a ship

boat boom—a spar rigged out from the side of an anchored or moored ship to which boats are tied when not in use

boatswain's chair—a seat attached to a line for hoisting a person aloft or lowering over the side

boatswain's locker—a compartment, usually forward, where line and other equipment used by the deck force are stowed

bollard—a strong, cylindrical, upright fixture on a pier to which ships' mooring lines are secured

bolo line—a line with a padded lead weight or a monkey fist on it that is designed for greater distance when throwing a line (as from a ship to a pier)

boom—a spar, usually movable, used for hoisting loads

boot topping—black paint applied to a ship's sides along the waterline

bow—the forward end of a ship or boat

bowhook—member of a boat's crew whose station is forward

break out—to bring out supplies or equipment from a stowage space

breast line—mooring line that leads from ship to pier (or another ship, if moored alongside) at right angles to the ship and is used to keep the vessel from moving laterally away from the pier (another ship)

BRF—Base Reaction Force

bridge—area in the superstructure from which a ship is operated

brig—jail

brightwork—bare (unpainted) metal that is kept polished

broach to—to get crosswise to the direction of the waves (puts the vessel in danger of being rolled over by the waves)

broad on the bow or quarter—halfway between dead ahead and abeam, and halfway between abeam and astern, respectively

broadside—simultaneously and to one side (when firing main battery guns); sidewise, as in "the current carried the ship broadside [parallel] to the beach"

brow—a walkway used for crossing from one ship to another, and from a ship to a pier (*Note:* Although you sometimes hear it used to describe a brow, "gangplank" is not a naval term.)

bulkhead—a vertical partition in a ship (never called a wall)

buoy—an anchored float used as an aid to navigation or to mark the location of an object

BUMED—Bureau of Medicine and Surgery

BUPERS—Bureau of Naval Personnel

cabin—living compartment of a ship's commanding officer

CAC—Common Access Card

camel—floating buffer between a ship and a pier (or another ship) to prevent damage by rubbing or banging (similar to a fender except that a camel is in the water whereas a fender is suspended above the water)

can buoy—a cylindrical navigational buoy, painted green and odd-numbered, which in U.S. waters marks the port side of a channel from seaward

carry away—to break loose, as in "the rough seas carried away the lifelines"

carry on—an order to resume previous activity after an interruption

CASEVAC—casualty evacuation

CBR—chemical, biological, and radiological

CCDR—combatant commander (unified combatant commander)

CCOL—compartment check-off list

centerline—an imaginary line down the middle of a ship from bow to stern

CFL—command fitness leader

chafing gear—material used to protect lines from excessive wear

chain locker—space where anchor chain is stowed

chart—nautical counterpart of a road map, showing land configuration, water depths, and aids to navigation

chart house—the navigator's work compartment

chip—to remove paint or rust from metallic surfaces with sharp-pointed hammers before applying paint

chock—deck fitting through which mooring lines are led

chow—food

CIC—combat information center

CINCPACFLT—Commander in Chief Pacific Fleet

CIWS—close-in weapons systems

CJCS—Chairman of the Joint Chiefs of Staff

cleat—a permanent fixture mounted to a bulkhead, deck, or pier that has a pair of projecting horns for belaying (securing) a line

CMAA—chief master-at-arms

CMC—command master chief (general)

CMDCM—command master chief petty officer (rate abbreviation)

CNO—Chief of Naval Operations

CO—commanding officer

coaming—raised area around a hatch that prevents water from pouring down through the opening when the hatch cover is open

COB—chief of the boat

COCOM—combatant command

COD—carrier on-board delivery

Colors—the national ensign; the ceremony of raising and lowering the ensign

combatant ship—a ship whose primary mission is combat

commission pennant—a long, narrow, starred and striped pennant flown only on board a commissioned ship

COMNAVCRUITCOM—Commander, Navy Recruiting Command

companionway—deck opening giving access to a ladder (includes the ladder)

compartment—interior space of a ship (similar to a "room" ashore)

conn—the act of controlling a ship (similar to "driving" ashore); also the station, usually on the bridge, from which a ship is controlled

CONREP—connected replenishment

CONUS—continental United States

COSAL—coordinated shipboard allowance list

course—a ship's desired direction of travel, not to be confused with heading

cover—to protect; a shelter; headgear; to don headgear

coxswain—enlisted person in charge of a boat (pronounced "cock-sun")

CPO—chief petty officer

crow's nest—lookout station aloft

CTOL—conventional takeoff and landing

cumshaw—a gift; something procured without payment

CV—aircraft carrier

DANTES—Defense Activity for Non-Traditional Education Support

darken ship—to turn off all external lights and close all openings through which lights can be seen from outside the ship

davits—mechanical arms by means of which a boat is hoisted in or out

Davy Jones' locker—the bottom of the sea

DC—damage control

DCA—damage-control assistant

DCC—Damage Control Central

DCNO—Deputy Chief of Naval Operations

DCPO—damage-control petty officer

DD—dishonorable discharge; destroyer

dead ahead—directly ahead; a relative bearing of 000 degrees

dead astern—180 degrees relative

deck—horizontal planking or plating that divides a ship into layers (floors)

deck seamanship—the upkeep and operation of all deck equipment decontaminate—to free from harmful residue of nuclear or chemical attack

deep six—to throw something overboard (see also "jettison")

DEERS—Defense Enrollment Eligibility Reporting System

DELREP—delay in reporting

dinghy—a small boat, sometimes equipped with a sail, but more commonly propelled by outboard motor or oars

dip—to lower a flag partway down the staff as a salute to, or in reply to a salute from, another ship

distance line—a line stretched between two ships engaged in replenishment or transfer operations under way (the line is marked at twenty-foot intervals to aid the conning officer in maintaining the proper distance between ships)

division—a main subdivision of a ship's crew (1st, E, G, etc.); an organization composed of two or more ships of the same type

DJMS—Defense Joint Military Pay System

DLA—Dislocation Allowance

dock—the water-space alongside a pier

DOD—Department of Defense

dog—a lever, or bolt and screws, used for securing a watertight door; to divide a four-hour watch into two two-hour watches

dog down—to set the dogs on a watertight door

dog watch—the 1600–1800 or 1800–2000 watch

DON—Department of the Navy

double up—to double mooring lines for extra strength

draft—the vertical distance from the keel to the waterline

dress ship—to display flags in honor of a person or event

drift—the speed at which a ship is pushed off course by wind and current

drogue—sea anchor

dry dock—a dock, either floating or built into the shore, from which water may be removed for the purpose of inspecting or working on a ship's bottom; to be put in dry dock

EAOS—end of active obligated service

ebb—a falling tide

EEBD—emergency-escape breathing device

eight o'clock reports—reports received by the executive officer from department heads shortly before 2000

EMCON—emission control

ensign—the national flag; an O-1 pay grade officer

EOD—explosive ordnance disposal

escape scuttle—an opening with quick-acting closures that can be placed in the larger hatch cover to permit rapid escape from a compartment

ESO—educational services officer

ESR—Electronic Service Record

EW—electronic warfare

executive officer—second officer in command (also called "XO")

eyes—the forward most part of the forecastle

fake—the act of making a line, wire, or chain ready for running by laying it out in long, flat bights, each one alongside and partially overlapping the other

fantail—the after end of the main deck

fathom—unit of length or depth equal to six feet

fender—a cushioning device hung over the side of a ship to prevent contact between the ship and a pier or another ship

field day—a day devoted to general cleaning, usually in preparation for an inspection

firemain—shipboard piping system to which fire hydrants are connected

first lieutenant—the officer responsible, in general, for a ship's upkeep and cleanliness (except machinery and ordnance gear), boats, ground tackle, and deck seamanship

first watch—the 2000–2400 watch (also called evening watch)

five-star admiral—a rank above admiral; no longer used (also known as "fleet admiral")

flag officer—any officer of the rank of rear admiral (lower and upper half), vice admiral, or admiral

flagstaff—vertical staff at the stern to which the ensign is hoisted when moored or at anchor

fleet—an organization of ships, aircraft, marine forces, and shore-based fleet activities, all under one commander, for conducting major operations

fleet admiral—a rank above admiral; no longer used (also known as "five-star admiral")

flood—to fill a space with water; a rising tide

FLTCM—fleet master chief petty officer

FMS—final multiple score

FOD—foreign object damage

FORCM—force master chief petty officer

fore and aft—the entire length of a ship, as in "sweep down fore and aft"

forecastle—forward section of the main deck (pronounced "FOHK-sul") foremast—first mast aft from the bow

forenoon watch—the 0800–1200 watch

forward—toward the bow

foul—entangled, as in "the lines are foul of each other"; stormy

FOUO—for official use only

FPCON—Force Protection Condition

gaff—a light spar set at an angle from the upper part of a mast (the national ensign is usually flown from the gaff while under way)

galley—space where food is prepared (never called a kitchen)

gangway—the opening in a bulwark or lifeline that provides access to a brow or accommodation ladder; an order meaning to clear the way

general quarters—the condition of full readiness for battle

gig—boat assigned for the commanding officer's personal use

GMT—General Military Training; Greenwich Mean Time

GPO—Government Publishing Office (formerly Government Printing Office)

GPS—Global Positioning System

GQ—*general quarters*

ground tackle—equipment used in anchoring or mooring with anchors

GS—General Schedule

gunwale—where the sides join the main deck of a ship or boat (pronounced "GUN-nel")

halyard—a light line used to hoist a flag or pennant

handsomely—steadily and carefully, but not necessarily slowly

hard over—condition of a rudder that has been turned to the maximum possible rudder angle

hashmark—a red, blue, or gold diagonal stripe across the left sleeve of an enlisted person's jumper, indicating four years of service

hatch—an opening in a deck used for access

haul—to pull in or heave on a line by hand

hawser—any heavy line used for towing or mooring

HAZMAT—hazardous materials

head—the upper end of a lower mast boom; compartment containing toilet facilities; ship's bow

heading—the direction toward which the ship's bow is pointing at any instant

headway—motion or rate of motion as a vessel moves through the water in a forward direction

heave—to throw, as in "heave a line to the pier"

heave around—to haul in a line, usually by means of a capstan or winch

heaving line—a line with a weight at one end, heaved across an intervening space for passing over a heavier line

helm—steering wheel of a ship

helmsman—person who steers the ship by turning her helm (also called steersman)

helo—helicopter

highline—the line stretched between ships under way on which a trolley block travels back and forth to transfer material and personnel

hitch—to bend a line to or around an object (see "knot" and "bend"); an enlistment

holiday—space on a surface that the painter neglected to paint

hull—the shell, or plating, of a ship from keel to gunwale

hull down—a lookout term meaning that a ship is so far over the horizon that only her superstructure or top hamper is visible

IC—interior communications

ICBM—intercontinental ballistic missile

IFF—identification friend or foe

IFR—instrument flight rules

inboard—toward the centerline

island—superstructure of an aircraft carrier

ISR—intelligence, surveillance, and reconnaissance

IVCS—Integrated Voice Communications System

jack—starred blue flag (the American flag without the stripes); once flown at the jackstaff of a commissioned ship not under way (now replaced by the "Dont Tread on Me" flag).

jackstaff—vertical spar at the stem on which the "Dont Tread on Me" flag is hoisted

Jacob's ladder—a portable rope or wire ladder

JAG—judge advocate general

JCS—Joint Chiefs of Staff

JDAM—joint direct attack munition

JETDS—Joint Electronics Type Designation System

jettison—to throw overboard

jetty—a structure built out from shore to influence water currents or protect a harbor or pier

joiner door—a nonwatertight door (such as a door between offices)

JOOD—junior officer of the deck

JOOW—junior officer of the watch

jump ship—to desert a ship

jury rig—any makeshift device or apparatus; to fashion such a device

kingpost—a short, sturdy mast capable of supporting a large amount of weight; used in handling cargo

knock off—quit, cease, or stop, as in "knock off ship's work"

knot—one nautical mile per hour; also a line tied to itself (see "bend" and "hitch")

ladder—means of going from one deck to another (can be vertical like a traditional ladder; can also be a flight of steps)

landing craft—vessel especially designed for landing troops and equipment directly on a beach

landing ship—a large seagoing ship designed for landing personnel and heavy equipment directly on a beach

lanyard—any short line used as a handle or as a means for operating some piece of equipment; a line used to attach an article to the person, as a pistol lanyard

lash—to secure an object by turns of line, wire, or chain

launch—to float a vessel off the ways in a building yard; a type of powerboat, usually over thirty feet long

lay—movement of a person, as in "lay aloft"; the direction of twist in the strands of a line or wire

LCAC—landing craft, air cushion

LCM—landing craft, mechanized

LCPL—landing craft, personnel, large

LCU—landing craft, utility

LDGP—low drag, general purpose (bombs)

LDO—limited duty officer program

lee—an area sheltered from the wind; downwind

leeward—direction toward which the wind is blowing (pronounced "loo-ard")

LES—leave and earnings statement

LGB—laser-guided bombs

LHA—amphibious assault ship

LHD—amphibious assault ship

liberty—sanctioned absence from a ship or station for a short time for pleasure rather than business

life jacket—a buoyant jacket designed to support a person in the water

lifelines—in general, the lines erected around the edge of a weather deck to prevent personnel from falling or being washed overboard; more precisely (though not often used), the topmost line (from top to bottom, these lines are named lifeline, housing line, and foot-rope)

line—a length of rope that is being used for some purpose

list—transverse inclination of a vessel (when a ship leans to one side)

log—a ship's speedometer; book or ledger in which data or events that occurred during a watch are recorded; to make a certain speed, as in "the ship logged 20 knots"

look alive—admonishment meaning to be alert or move faster

lookout—person stationed topside on a formal watch who reports objects sighted and sounds heard to the officer of the deck

LOX—liquid oxygen

LPO—leading petty officer

LSD—dock landing ship

LSE—landing signal enlisted personnel

lucky bag—locker under the charge of the master-at-arms; used to collect and stow deserter's effects and gear found adrift

MAA—*master-at-arms*

magazine—compartment used for the stowage of ammunition

main deck—the uppermost complete deck (An exception is the aircraft carrier, where the main deck is defined as the hangar bay rather than the flight deck, which arguably fits the criterion of the definition.)

mainmast—second mast aft from the bow on a vessel with more than one mast; the tallest mast on a vessel (On a ship with only one mast, it is usually referred to simply as "the mast.")

main truck—the top of the tallest mast on a vessel

make fast—to secure (attach)

man—to assume a station, as in "to man a gun"

manhole—an opening that is normally closed but provides access to spaces that are entered only on rare occasions (like voids and tanks used to keep fuel or water)

man-o'-war—a ship designed for combat

MARCENT—U.S. Marine Forces Central Command

marlinespike—tapered steel tool used to open the strands of line or wire rope for splicing

marlinespike seamanship—the art of caring for and handling all types of line and wire

master-at-arms—a member of a ship's police force

mate—a shipmate; another Sailor

MCM—*Manual for Courts-Martial*

MCPO—master chief petty officer

MCPON—Master Chief Petty Officer of the Navy

MDS—Maintenance Data System

mess—meal; place where meals are eaten; a group that takes meals together, as in officers' mess

messenger—a line used to haul a heavier line across an intervening space; one who delivers messages

midwatch—the watch that begins at 0000 and ends at 0400

moor—to make fast to a pier, another ship, or a mooring buoy; also, to anchor

mooring buoy—a large anchored float to which a ship may moor

morning watch—the 0400–0800 watch

motor whaleboat—a double-ended powerboat

MP—military police

MRC—maintenance requirement card

MSC—Military Sealift Command

MSTS—Military Sea Transportation Service

MUC—Meritorious Unit Commendation

muster—a roll call; to assemble for a roll call

MWR—Morale, Welfare, and Recreation

NAS—Naval Air Station

NAVAIR—Naval Air Systems Command

NAVCOMP—Comptroller of the Navy

NAVEDTRA—Navy Education and Training

NAVFAC—Naval Facilities Engineering Command

NAVMILPERSCOM—Navy Military Personnel Command

NAVSEA—Naval Sea Systems Command

NAVSHIPSTECHMAN—*Naval Ships' Technical Manual*

NAVSO—Executive Offices of the Secretary of the Navy (Navy Staff Office)

NAVSTA—Naval Station

NAVSTDS—Naval Standards

NAVSUP—Naval Supply Systems Command

NCIS—Naval Criminal Investigative Service

NCP—Navy College Program

NEC—Navy Enlisted Classification

nest—two or more boats stowed one within the other; two or more ships moored alongside each other

NETC—Naval Education and Training Command

NEX—Navy Exchange

NJP—nonjudicial punishment

NKO—Navy Knowledge Online

NME—National Military Establishment

NMT—Navy Military Training

NOAA—National Oceanic and Atmospheric Administration

NOFORN—information that cannot be disclosed to foreign nationals

NOS—National Ocean Service

NPC—Navy Personnel Command

NRTC—Non-Resident Training Courses

NSIPS—Navy Standard Integrated Personnel System

NSTC—Naval Service Training Command

NUC—Navy Unit Commendation

nun buoy—a navigational buoy, conical in shape, painted red and even-numbered, which marks the starboard side of a channel from seaward

NWTD—nonwatertight door

NWU—Navy working uniform

OBA—oxygen-breathing apparatus

OCCSTDS—Occupational Standards

OCS—Officer Candidate School

OINC—officer in charge

OJT—on-the-job training

on the beach—ashore; a seaman assigned to shore duty, unemployed, retired, or otherwise detached from sea duty

OOD—officer of the deck

OPNAV—Office of the Chief of Naval Operations

OPSEC—operational security

OSD—Office of the Secretary of Defense

OTH—other than honorable

outboard—away from the centerline

overboard—over the side

overhaul—to repair or recondition; to overtake another vessel

overhead—the underside of a deck that forms the overhead of the compartment next below (never called a ceiling)

P2P—peer-to-peer (file sharing programs)

P-Days—processing days

PACFLT—United States Pacific Fleet

party—a group on temporary assignment or engaged in a common activity, as in "line-handling party," or a "liberty party"

passageway—a corridor used for interior horizontal movement aboard ship (similar to a hallway ashore)

pay out—to feed out or lengthen a line

PCS—permanent change of station

PSR—Performance Summary Record

PFA—physical fitness assessment

PFB—*pseudofolliculitis barbae* (shaving bumps)

PHA—physical health assessment

PHS—U.S. Public Health Service

pier—structure extending from land into water to provide a mooring for vessels

pigstick—small staff from which a commission pennant is flown

PII—personally identifiable information

pilot house—enclosure on the bridge housing the main steering controls

piloting—branch of navigation in which positions are determined by visible objects on the surface, or by soundings

pipe—to sound a particular call on a boatswain's pipe

pitch—vertical rise and fall of a ship's bow and stern caused by head or following seas (see "roll")

plane guard—destroyer or helicopter responsible for rescuing air crews during launch or recovery operations

plank owner—a person who was assigned to the ship's company when he or she was commissioned

Plan of the Day—schedule of a day's routine and events ordered by the executive officer and published daily aboard ship or at a shore activity (see *POD*)

PMS—planned maintenance system

PNA—passed but not advanced

PO—petty officer

POD—*Plan of the Day*

pollywog—a person who has never crossed the equator (pejorative)

port—to the left of the centerline when facing forward

POW—prisoner of war

PQS—Personnel Qualification Standards (System)

PRD—projected rotation date

PREP—preparative pennant

PRT—Physical Readiness Test

PSD—personnel support detachment

PTU—physical training uniform

PUC—Presidential Unit Citation

QMOW—quartermaster of the watch

quarterdeck—deck area designated by the commanding officer as the place to carry out official functions; station of the officer of the deck in port

quartermaster—an enlisted assistant to the navigator

quarters—stations for shipboard evolutions, as in "general quarters," "fire quarters"; living spaces

quay—a solid structure along a bank used for loading and offloading vessels (pronounced "key")

radar—a device that uses reflected radio waves for the detection of objects; derived from "radio direction and ranging"

RADHAZ—radiation hazard

range—the distance of an object from an observer; an aid to navigation consisting of two objects in line; a water area designated for a particular purpose, as in "gunnery range"

rat guard—a hinged metal disk secured to a mooring line to prevent rats from traveling along the line into the ship

RCPO—recruit chief petty officer

RDC—recruit division commander

reef—an underwater ledge rising abruptly from the ocean's floor

relief—a person assigned to take over the duties of another

replenishment—to resupply a ship or station

RHIB—rigid hull inflatable boat

ride—to be at anchor, as in "the ship is riding to her anchor"

riding lights—navigational lights shown at night by a moored vessel

rig—to set up a device or equipment, as in "to rig a stage over the side"

rigging—a general term for wires, ropes, and chains used to support kingposts or other masts, or to operate cargo-handling equipment. *Standing rigging* describes lines that support but do not move. Examples of standing rigging are *stays*, which are rigged fore and aft to support masts, and *shrouds*, which are rigged athwartships to provide support. *Running rigging* includes movable lines such as topping lifts and guys.

roll—side-to-side movement of a ship while under way (see "pitch")

rope—fiber or wire line (fiber rope is usually referred to as line, while wire rope is called rope, wire rope, or wire)

ropeyarn Sunday—a workday or part of a workday that has been granted as a holiday for taking care of personal business

RT—radiotelephone (voice radio)

RTC—Recruit Training Command

rudder—device attached to the stern that controls a ship's direction of travel

running lights—navigational lights shown at night by a vessel under way

running rigging—see "rigging"

SAMID—Ship's Anti-Missile Integrated Defense

SBP—Survivor Benefit Program

scope—length (of anchor chain)

SCPO—senior chief petty officer

scuttle—a small opening in a larger door or hatch cover that can be used to pass through without having to open the larger (heavier) door

scuttlebutt—a drinking fountain (originally, a ship's water barrel, called a "butt") that was tapped (scuttled) by the insertion of a spigot from which the crew drew drinking water; rumor (the scuttlebutt was once a place for personnel to exchange news when the crew gathered to draw water)

sea anchor—a device streamed from the bow of a vessel for holding it end-on to the sea

SEAL—Sea-Air-Land (Navy special forces personnel)

seamanship—the art of handling a vessel; skill in the use of deck equipment, in boat handling, and in the care and use of line and wire

sea painter—a length of line secured to the bow of a boat for towing or making fast (attaching)

sea state—condition of waves and the height of their swells

seaworthy—a vessel capable of withstanding normal heavy weather

SECDEF—Secretary of Defense

SECNAV—Secretary of the Navy

second deck—first complete deck below the main deck

secure—to make fast (firmly attach), as in "secure a line to a cleat"; to cease, as in "secure from fire drill"

SEED—supplemental emergency egress device

service force—organization providing logistic support to combatant forces

SGLI—Servicemembers Group Life Insurance

shake down—the training of a new crew in operating a ship

shellback—a person who has crossed the equator

shift colors—to change the arrangement of colors upon getting under way or coming to moorings ship—any large seagoing vessel capable of extended independent operation; to take on water unintentionally

ship over—to reenlist in the Navy

ship's company—all hands permanently attached to a ship or station; the crew

shipshape—neat, clean, taut

shoal—a structure similar to a reef, but more gradual in its rise from the floor of the ocean

shole—a flat piece of material (such as wood) that is placed under the end of a shore to distribute pressure

shore—land, usually that part adjacent to the water; a timber used in damage control to brace bulkheads and decks

shroud—see "rigging"

SI—International System of Units (metric system)

sick bay—shipboard space that serves as a hospital or medical clinic

side boy—one of a group of seamen who form two ranks at the gangway as part of the ceremonies conducted for visiting officials

side light—one of a series of running lights (the starboard side light is green and the port side light is red)

sight—to see for the first time, as to sight a ship on the horizon; a celestial observation

SIGINT—signals intelligence

SIQ—sick-in-quarters

skylark—to engage in irresponsible horseplay

slack—to allow a line to run out; undisciplined, as in a "slack ship"

SLAD—slewing arm davit

SLAM—standoff land attack missile

small craft—any less-than-ship-size vessel

smart—snappy, seamanlike, shipshape

SOC—Special Operations craft

SOF—Special Operations Forces

SOPA—senior officer present afloat

SORM—*Standard Organization and Regulations of the U.S. Navy*

sound—to determine the depth of water; to dive deep (of marine animals); a body of water between the mainland and a large coastal island

SP—shore patrol

spar—the nautical equivalent of a pole

special sea detail—crewmembers assigned special duties when leaving and entering port

splice—to join lines or wires together by intertwining strands; the joint so made

spring line—a line that is rigged from ship to pier to prevent or minimize forward and aft movement—in other words, motion parallel to the pier

square away—to put in proper order; to make things shipshape

square knot—simple knot used for bending two lines together or for bending a line to itself

SRB—selective reenlistment bonus

SRF—Shipboard Reaction Force

SSBN—nuclear-powered ballistic-missile submarine

SSGN—nuclear-powered guided-missile submarine

SSIC—Standard Subject Identification Code

SSN—nuclear-powered attack submarine

stack—shipboard chimney

stage—a platform rigged over the side of a ship from which maintenance (such as painting) can be performed on the hull

stanchion—vertical post for supporting decks; smaller, similar posts for supporting lifelines, awnings, and so on

standing rigging—see "rigging"

starboard—direction to the right of the centerline as one faces forward

state room—a living compartment for an officer or officers

station—an individual's place of duty; position of a ship in formation; location of persons and equipment with a specific purpose, as in "gun-control station"; order to assume stations, as in "station the special sea and anchor detail"

stay—see "rigging"

stem—extreme forward edge of a ship's bow

stern—the aftermost part of a vessel

stern light—white navigation light that can be seen only from astern

STOVL—short takeoff/vertical landing

stow—to store or pack articles or cargo in a space

STREAM—Standard Tensioned Replenishment Alongside Method

structural bulkhead—transverse strength bulkhead that forms a watertight boundary

SUBLANT—Naval Submarine Force, U.S. Atlantic Fleet

SUBPAC—Naval Submarine Force, U.S. Pacific Fleet

superstructure—the structure above a ship's main deck

SURF—Standard Underway Replenishment Fixture

SURFLANT—Naval Surface Force, U.S. Atlantic Fleet

SURFPAC—Naval Surface Force, U.S. Pacific Fleet

swab—a mop; to mop

SWCC—special warfare combat crewman

TA—tuition assistance

tackle—a combination of blocks and lines used either to change the direction of an applied force or to gain a mechanical advantage

TAD—temporary additional duty

tarpaulin—canvas used as a cover

taut—under tension; highly disciplined and efficient, as in "a taut ship"

TDY—temporary duty

tender—one who serves as a precautionary standby, as in "line tender for a diver"; a support vessel for other ships

TIR—time in rate

topside—weather decks; above (referring to the deck or decks above)

TRAMAN—training manual

trice up—to secure (older type) bunks by hauling them up and hanging them off (securing them) on their chains

truck—the uppermost tip of a mast

T&T—travel and transportation

turn in—to retire to bed; to return articles to the issue room

turn out—to get out of bed; to order out a working party or other group, as in "turn out the guard"

turn to—to start working

UA—unauthorized absence

UAV—unmanned aerial vehicle

UB—utility boat

UCMJ—Uniform Code of Military Justice

UD—undesirable discharge

UDT—underwater demolition team

under way—not moored

UNREP—underway replenishment

USHBP—Uniformed Services Health Benefit Program

USMTF—Uniformed Services Medical Treatment Facility

USW—undersea warfare

VA—Department of Veterans Affairs

VCNO—vice chief of Naval Operations

VERTREP—vertical replenishment

VFR—visual flight rules

VGLI—Veterans' Group Life Insurance

VLS—vertical launch system

void—an empty tank aboard ship

V/STOL—vertical/short takeoff and landing

waist—the amidships section of the main deck

wake—trail left by a vessel or other object moving through the water

wardroom—officers' messing compartment; collective term used to signify the officers assigned to a ship

watch—one of the periods, usually four hours, into which a day is divided; a particular duty, as in "life buoy watch"

watertight integrity—the degree or quality of watertightness

WB—workboat

weather deck—any deck exposed to the elements

weigh anchor—to hoist the anchor clear of the bottom

WFCOM—wire-free communication

wharf—structure similar to a quay but constructed like a pier

whipping—binding on the end of a line or wire to prevent unraveling

windward—in the direction of the wind

WQ&S—watch, quarter, and station

WTD—watertight door

XO—executive officer; second in command

yardarm—the port or starboard half of a spar set athwartships across the upper mast

yaw—(of a vessel) to have its heading thrown wide of its course as the result of a force, such as a heavy following sea

APPENDIX B
ONLINE RESOURCES

Listed below, by subject matter, are web addresses that may prove useful to you. Be aware that websites sometimes change their URLs (or addresses); if you find the address provided here does not work, try one of the popular search engines, such as Google or Yahoo, to locate the site you seek. Also, many Navy websites have current links to other Navy-related websites and web pages.

You should familiarize yourself with most or all of these websites. The content of many will be obvious by their names, but if in doubt, go to the website itself to see what is there.

Bluejacket's Manual (BJM) Website

www.usni.org/BlueAndGoldProfessionalBooks
/TheBluejacketsManual

This website is provided by the U.S. Naval Institute to keep this manual up to date and to provide supplementary material. Checking this site periodically will keep the information in your BJM up to date and accurate.

If you find errors in your *Bluejacket's Manual,* or if something needs to be updated, please notify us:

The Bluejacket's Manual
U.S. Naval Institute
291 Wood Road
Annapolis, Maryland 21409
-or-
BluejacketsManual@usni.org

After verification, we will make sure that your suggested modification or correction or update is posted on this website—with or without your name as you prefer.

GENERAL

All Hands Magazine: www.navy.mil/ah_online

All Instructions: doni.documentservices.dla.mil/allinstructions.aspx

All Notices: doni.documentservices.dla.mil/notices.aspx

Bureau of Personnel (BUPERS) Instructions: www.public.navy.mil/bupers
-npc/reference/instructions/BUPERSInstructions/Pages/default.aspx

Chief of Naval Operations (CNO) Instructions (OPNAV): doni.document
services.dla.mil

Command Directory: www.navy.mil/CommandDirectory.asp

Constitution of the United States: www.archives.gov/exhibits/charters
/constitution_transcript.html

Naval Vessel Register: www.nvr.navy.mil

Navy Correspondence Manual: doni.documentservices.dla.mil/SECNAV
%20Manuals1/5216.5%20(2015).pdf

Navy (General): www.navy.mil

Navy Regulations: doni.documentservices.dla.mil/navyregs.aspx

OPNAV (CNO) Instructions: doni.documentservices.dla.mil

Secretary of the Navy (SECNAV) Instructions: doni.documentservices.dla.mil

Standard Navy Distribution List (SNDL): doni.documentservices.dla.mil
/sndl.aspx

Standard Organization and Regulations Manual: www.usnwc.edu/getattach
ment/eed14d46-5a5a-4384-a008-52871a0057ae/3120-32D.aspx

CAREER

CNO Reading Program: navyreading.dodlive.mil

Enlisted Community Managers: www.public.navy.mil/bupers-npc/enlisted/community/Pages/default.aspx

Joint Ethics Regulation: www.dod.mil/dodgc/defense_ethics/ethics_regulation

Military Personnel Manual (MILPERSMAN): www.public.navy.mil/bupers-npc/reference/MILPERSMAN/Pages/default.aspx

My Education: myeducation.netc.navy.mil

Naval History and Heritage Command: www.history.navy.mil

Navy Advancement Center: www.nko.navy.mil/group/navy-advancement-center

Navy Awards: awards.navy.mil

Navy College Program: www.navycollege.navy.mil

Navy Commissioning Programs: www.public.navy.mil/bupers-npc/career/careercounseling/Pages/CommissioningPrograms.aspx

Navy Enlisted Manpower and Personnel Classifications and Occupational Standards: www.public.navy.mil/bupers-npc/reference/nec/Pages/default.aspx

Navy Equal Opportunity: www.public.navy.mil/bupers-npc/support/21st_Century_Sailor/equal_opportunity/Pages/default.aspx

Navy Knowledge Online: www.nko.navy.mil

Navy Personnel Command: www.public.navy.mil/bupers-npc

Navy Physical Fitness Program: www.public.navy.mil/bupers-npc/support/21st_century_sailor/physical/Pages/default2.aspx

Navy Sexual Assault Prevention & Response: www.navy.mil/local/sapr

Navy Uniform Support Center: www.mynavyexchange.com/nex/uniforms

Oath of enlistment: www.law.cornell.edu/uscode/text/10/502

Owners and Operators Manual (All Hands): www.navy.mil/ah_online/owners2016

Uniform Regulations: www.public.navy.mil/bupers-npc/support/uniforms/uniformregulations/Pages/default.aspx

U.S. Naval Institute: www.usni.org

EDUCATIONAL

CNO Reading Program: navyreading.dodlive.mil

Navy College Program: www.navycollege.navy.mil

Navy Knowledge Online: www.nko.navy.mil

My Education: myeducation.netc.navy.mil

Tuition Assistance: www.navycollege.navy.mil/ta_info.aspx

FINANCIAL

Government Travel Charge Card: www.defensetravel.dod.mil/site/govtravel
   card.cfm

myPay: mypay.dfas.mil

Navy Federal Credit Union (NFCU): www.navyfederal.org

Navy/Marine Corps Relief: www.nmcrs.org

Navy Mutual Aid: www.navymutual.org

Thrift Savings Plan (TSP): www.tsp.gov

United Services Automobile Association (USAA): www.usaa.com

HERITAGE

Naval History and Heritage Command: www.history.navy.mil

Naval Order of the United States: www.navalorder.org

Navy Hymn: www.history.navy.mil/browse-by-topic/heritage/customs-and
   -traditions/the-navy-hymn.html

U.S. Naval Institute: www.usni.org

LEGAL

Armed Forces Legal Assistance Locator: legalassistance.law.af.mil/content
   /locator.php

Joint Ethics Regulation: www.dod.mil/dodgc/defense_ethics/ethics_regulation

My Education: myeducation.netc.navy.mil

Naval Criminal Investigative Service (NCIS): www.ncis.navy.mil

Navy Judge Advocate General (JAG): www.jag.navy.mil

Navy Judge Advocate General Manual (JAGMAN): http://www.jag.navy
   .mil/library/instructions/JAGMAN2012.pdf

Navy Equal Opportunity: www.public.navy.mil/bupers-npc/support/21st
   _Century_Sailor/equal_opportunity/Pages/default.aspx

Navy Sexual Assault Prevention & Response: www.navy.mil/local/sapr

NONGOVERNMENTAL ORGANIZATIONS

Military Benefit Association: www.militarybenefit.org

Naval Order of the United States: www.navalorder.org

Navy Federal Credit Union (NFCU): www.navyfederal.org

Navy League: navyleague.org

U.S. Naval Institute: www.usni.org

Navy/Marine Corps Relief: www.nmcrs.org

Navy Mutual Aid: www.navymutual.org

NCIS Confidential Crime Tip Reporting: www.tipsubmit.com/webtips NAV.aspx?AgencyID=840

Together We Served: togetherweserved.com

United Services Automobile Association (USAA): www.usaa.com

PERSONAL

Armed Forces Insurance: www.afi.org

Armed Forces Legal Assistance Locator: legalassistance.law.af.mil/content /locator.php

Army & Air Force Exchange: www.shopmyexchange.com

Fleet and Family Support Program: www.cnic.navy.mil/ffr/family_readiness /fleet_and_family_support_program.html

Military Benefit Association: www.militarybenefit.org

Morale, Welfare, and Recreation (MWR): www.navymwr.org

myPay: mypay.dfas.mil

Navy Exchange: www.mynavyexchange.com

Navy Family Accountability and Assessment System (NFAAS): navyfamily .navy.mil

Navy Federal Credit Union (NFCU): www.navyfederal.org

Navy/Marine Corps Relief: www.nmcrs.org

Navy Mutual Aid: www.navymutual.org

Navy Uniform Support Center: www.mynavyexchange.com/nex/uniforms

Suicide Prevention: www.veteranscrisisline.net

Tricare: www.tricare.mil

Tuition Assistance: www.navycollege.navy.mil/ta_info.aspx

SOCIAL MEDIA

Chief of Naval Operations (CNO) Twitter Feed: twitter.com/cnorichardson

MCPON on Facebook: www.facebook.com/13MCPON

Secretary of the Navy (SECNAV) Facebook: www.facebook.com/Secretary oftheNavy

Secretary of the Navy (SECNAV) Twitter Feed: twitter.com/secnav

APPENDIX C
"ANCHORS AWEIGH"
OFFICIAL SONG OF THE NAVY

CURRENT LYRICS

Revised by MCPON John Hagen, USN (Ret.) in 1997
(It is Verse 2 that is most widely sung.)

[Verse 1]

Stand Navy out to sea,
Fight our battle cry;
We'll never change our course,
So vicious foe steer shy-y-y-y.
Roll out the TNT,
Anchors Aweigh.
Sail on to victory
And sink their bones to Davy Jones, hooray!

[Verse 2]

Anchors Aweigh, my boys,
Anchors Aweigh.
Farewell to foreign shores,
We sail at break of day-ay-ay-ay.
Through our last night ashore,
Drink to the foam,
Until we meet once more.
Here's wishing you a happy voyage home.

[Verse 3]

Blue of the mighty deep:
Gold of God's great sun.
Let these our colors be
Till all of time be done, done, done, done.
On seven seas we learn
Navy's stern call:
Faith, courage, service true,
With honor, over honor, over all.

HISTORY

LT Charles A. Zimmermann, USN, a graduate of the Peabody Conservatory in Baltimore, had been selected as the bandmaster of the Naval Academy Band in 1887 at age twenty-six. His father, Charles Z. Zimmermann, had played in the band during the Civil War years. Early in his career, Lieutenant Zimmermann started the practice of composing a march for each graduating class. By 1892 "Zimmy," as he was affectionately known by the midshipmen, had become so popular that he was presented with a gold medal by that year's class. More gold medals followed as Zimmermann wrote a march for each succeeding class.

In 1906 Lieutenant Zimmerman was approached by Midshipman First Class Alfred Hart Miles with a request for a new march. As a member of the Class of 1907, Miles and his classmates "were eager to have a piece of music that would be inspiring, one with a swing to it so it could be used as a football marching song, and one that would live forever."

Supposedly, with the two men seated at the Naval Academy Chapel organ, Zimmermann composed the tune and Miles set the title and wrote the first two stanzas in November 1906. This march was played by the band and sung by the brigade at the 1906 Army-Navy football game later that month, and for the first time in several seasons, Navy won. This march, "Anchors Aweigh," was subsequently dedicated to the Academy Class of 1907 and adopted as the official song of the U.S. Navy. The concluding stanza was written by Midshipman Royal Lovell, Class of 1926.

ORIGINAL LYRICS

[Verse 1]

Stand Navy down the field, sails set to the sky.

We'll never change our course, so Army you steer shy-y-y-y.

Roll up the score, Navy, Anchors Aweigh.

Sail Navy down the field and sink the Army, sink the Army Grey.

[Verse 2]

Get under way, Navy, Decks cleared for the fray,

We'll hoist true Navy Blue, So Army down your Grey-y-y-y.

Full speed ahead, Navy; Army heave to,

Furl Black and Grey and Gold and hoist the Navy, hoist the Navy Blue

[Verse 3]

Blue of the Seven Seas; Gold of God's great sun

Let these our colors be, Till all of time be done-n-n-ne,

By Severn shore we learn Navy's stern call:

Faith, courage, service true, With honor over, honor over all.

EPILOGUE

In the 1916 *Lucky Bag*, the Academy yearbook, the class prepared a surprise for Zimmermann. On page one was an impressive photo of the bandmaster in his full dress uniform, and on the next, a moving tribute to his devotion to the Naval Academy. Unfortunately, Zimmermann did not live to enjoy this tribute. He became ill and died suddenly on Sunday morning, 16 January 1916, of a brain hemorrhage. He was fifty-four years old. He was given a full military funeral, with midshipmen serving as pallbearers, and classes were suspended so the entire regiment could attend when he was buried in St. Mary's Cemetery on 19 January 1916. Later, his body was moved to the Naval Academy cemetery where a granite monument, a gift from the classes of 1916 and 1917, was erected, as says the inscription on the base, "by his Midshipmen Friends."

Alfred H. Miles, the original lyricist, continued his Navy career and retired as a captain.

Note: The word "weigh" in this sense comes from the archaic word meaning to heave, hoist, or raise. "Aweigh" means that that action has been completed. The anchor is aweigh when it is pulled from the bottom. This event is duly noted in the ship's log.

APPENDIX D
"THE NAVY HYMN"

Note: *The information provided here is derived from the Naval History and Heritage Command's website.*

The song known to United States Navy men and women as the "Navy Hymn" is a musical benediction that long has had a special appeal to seafaring men, particularly in the American Navy and the Royal Navies of the British Commonwealth and which, in more recent years, has become a part of French naval tradition.

The original words were written as a hymn by a schoolmaster and clergyman of the Church of England, the Rev. William Whiting. Reverend Whiting (1825–78) resided on the English coast near the sea and had once survived a furious storm in the Mediterranean. His experiences inspired him to pen the ode "Eternal Father, Strong to Save." In the following year, 1861, the words were adapted to music by another English clergyman, the Rev. John B. Dykes (1823–76), who had originally written the music as "Melita" (ancient name for the Mediterranean island of Malta). Reverend Dykes' name may be recognized as that of the composer given credit for the music to many other well-known hymns, including "Holy, Holy, Holy," "Lead, Kindly Light," "Jesus, Lover of My Soul," and "Nearer, My God to Thee."

In the United States in 1879, RADM Charles Jackson Train, an 1865 graduate of the United States Naval Academy at Annapolis, was a lieutenant commander stationed at the Academy in charge of the Midshipman Choir. In that year, Lieutenant Commander Train inaugurated the present practice of concluding each Sunday's divine services at the Academy with the singing of the first verse of this hymn.

The hymn, entitled "Eternal Father, Strong to Save," is found in most Protestant hymnals. It can be more easily located in these hymnals by consulting the "Index to First Lines" under "Eternal Father, Strong to Save." The words have been changed several times since the original hymn by Reverend Whiting was first published in 1860–61. One will find that the verses as now published differ from the original primarily in the choice of one or two words in several lines of each verse. However, inasmuch as it is not known whether the original words are now available in a hymnal, those original words are given below:

> Eternal Father, Strong to save,
> Whose arm hath bound the restless wave,
> Who bid'st the mighty Ocean deep
> Its own appointed limits keep;
> O hear us when we cry to thee,
> for those in peril on the sea.

> O Christ! Whose voice the waters heard
> And hushed their raging at Thy word,
> Who walked'st on the foaming deep,
> and calm amidst its rage didst sleep;
> Oh hear us when we cry to Thee
> For those in peril on the sea!

> Most Holy spirit! Who didst brood
> Upon the chaos dark and rude,
> And bid its angry tumult cease,
> And give, for wild confusion, peace;
> Oh, hear us when we cry to Thee
> For those in peril on the sea!

⚓ O Trinity of love and power!
Our brethren shield in danger's hour;
From rock and tempest, fire and foe,
Protect them wheresoe'er they go;
Thus evermore shall rise to Thee,
Glad hymns of praise from land and sea.

The best information available indicates that a new verse to "Eternal Father, Strong to Save" appeared in 1943 in a little booklet then entitled *A Book of Worship and Devotion for the Armed Forces*, published by the Board of Christian Education of the Presbyterian Church, U.S.A. All indications are that this new verse can be traced back to a completely separate hymn, "Lord, Guard and Guide the Men Who Fly," written by Mary C. D. Hamilton in 1915, during World War I. Apparently, during or shortly after World War II, someone adapted this verse to create what is often called the "Naval Aviation version."

⚓ Lord, guard and guide the men who fly
Through the great spaces in the sky,
Be with them always in the air,
In dark'ning storms or sunlight fair.
O, Hear us when we lift our prayer,
For those in peril in the air.

Research indicates that the above additions and alterations to Reverend Whiting's original ode are not the only changes that have been or will be made to the hymn. From time to time, individuals have been and will be inspired to write verses other than those that are indicated in this brief background. Here are some current alternates:

⚓ Eternal Father, grant, we pray
To all Marines, both night and day,
The courage, honor, strength, and skill
Their land to serve, thy law fulfill;
Be thou the shield forevermore
From every peril to the Corps.
—*J. E. Seim, 1966*

Lord, stand beside the men who build
And give them courage, strength, and skill.
O grant them peace of heart and mind,
And comfort loved ones left behind.
Lord, hear our prayer for all Seabees,
Where'er they be on land or sea.
—*R. J. Dietrich, 1960*

Lord God, our power evermore,
Whose arm doth reach the ocean floor,
Dive with our men beneath the sea;
Traverse the depths protectively.
O hear us when we pray, and keep
them safe from peril in the deep.
—*David B. Miller, 1965*

O God, protect the women who,
in service, faith in thee renew;
O guide devoted hands of skill
And bless their work within thy will;
Inspire their lives that they may be
Examples fair on land and sea.
—*Lines 1–4, Merle E. Strickland, 1972,*
and adapted by James D. Shannon, 1973
Lines 5–6, Beatrice M. Truitt, 1948

Creator, Father, who dost show
Thy splendor in the ice and snow,
Bless those who toil in summer light
And through the cold Antarctic night,
As they thy frozen wonders learn;
Bless those who wait for their return.
—*L. E. Vogel, 1965*

Eternal Father, Lord of hosts,
Watch o'er the men who guard our coasts.
Protect them from the raging seas

And give them light and life and peace.
Grant them from thy great throne above
The shield and shelter of thy love.

 —Author and date unknown

Eternal Father, King of birth,
Who didst create the heaven and earth,
And bid the planets and the sun
Their own appointed orbits run;
O hear us when we seek thy grace
For those who soar through outer space.

 — J. E. Volonte, 1961

Creator, Father, who first breathed
In us the life that we received,
By power of thy breath restore
The ill, and men with wounds of war.
Bless those who give their healing care,
That life and laughter all may share

 —Galen H. Meyer, 1969
  Adapted by James D. Shannon, 1970

God, who dost still the restless foam,
Protect the ones we love at home.
Provide that they should always be
By thine own grace both safe and free.
O Father, hear us when we pray
For those we love so far away.

 —Hugh Taylor, date unknown

Lord, guard and guide the men who fly
And those who on the ocean ply;
Be with our troops upon the land,
And all who for their country stand:
Be with these guardians day and night
And may their trust be in thy might.

 —Author unknown, about 1955

O Father, King of earth and sea,
We dedicate this ship to thee.
In faith we send her on her way;
In faith to thee we humbly pray:
O hear from heaven our sailor's cry
And watch and guard her from on high!

—Author and date unknown

And when at length her course is run,
Her work for home and country done,
Of all the souls that in her sailed
Let not one life in thee have failed;
But hear from heaven our sailor's cry,
And grant eternal life on high!

—Author and date unknown

Text extracted from a publication of the Bureau of Naval Personnel:

This hymn is often used at funerals for personnel who served in or were associated with the Navy. "Eternal Father" was the favorite hymn of President Franklin D. Roosevelt and was sung at his funeral at Hyde Park, New York, in April 1945. Roosevelt had served as Secretary of the Navy. This hymn was also played as President John F. Kennedy's body was carried up the steps of the U.S. Capitol to lie in state.

INDEX

118–19; information resources, 533–34; initial clothing issue, 9; name tags, 135; nicknames for, 118; optional items, 118; prescribes items, 118, 533; professionalism and wearing, 116, 144; rank or rate identification marks and devices, 104, 126–30, 534–43; rating insignia and devices, 107, 108, 127–28, 513, 514–29; regulations on, 116, 131, 144, 533; service stripes, 132; specialty marks, 107, 108, 513, 514–29; terminology, 117–19; training for folding and stowage of, 12; uniform of the day, 533; warfare and qualification insignia, 134, 547–48
union jack, 55, 63
unit bills, 246–51
United Services Organization (USO), 478
utilitiesman (UT), 107, 529, 531–32
utility boats, 300–301

vehicles: national anthem customs, 57; saluting customs, 47, 48
ventilation system, 233–34
vertical launch systems (VLSs), 400–401, 408
vertical replenishment (VERTREP), 293–94, 295, 344–45, 581
Vietnam War, 156, 157, 161–62
visitors, 13
visual signaling, 62, 67–68, 237, 450–54, 688–93
voice radio (radiotelephone) communications and prowords, 455–57, 694–95
voice tubes, 450
voids and tanks, 226–27, 346–47, 368

Walsh, Don, 159–60
War of 1812, 145, 150–52
warfare and qualification insignia, 134, 547–48
warfare specialty, 103
warhead, 401
warrant officers: application and appointments to, 468; commission as, 106; pay grades, ranks, rates, and forms of address, 504–5; promotion to, 16–17; terminology for, 17; uniform rank or rate identification marks and devices, 130, 542
wartime security, 206
Washington, George, 149
watch, quarter, and station (WQ&S) bill, 251, 353
watchstanding: armed sentries, 204, 313; armed watchstanding and use of small arms, 329, 660–64; conditions of readiness (cruising conditions), 313–14,

606–7; efficient and serious approach to, 308, 329, 605; information resources, 605; logs and log keeping duties, 324–25; lookouts, 317, 318–23; night vision and night-vision goggles, 326–28; purpose of, 308; on quarterdeck, 75; relieving the watch, 311, 325–26; sentry duty and general orders of a sentry, 204, 309–13, 606; shipboard watchstanding, 313–28; ship's bells, 315–16, 438, 608; traditional watch structure, 314–15, 607–8; watch section, 316; watch stations, 316–24, 329
watertight doors, hatches, and fittings, 226, 365–70, 610–12
watertight integrity, 225–27, 359, 364–70
weapon control systems, 414–15
weapons: ammunition handling safety regulations and precautions, 332–33, 334; designation systems, 401–2, 417, 649–52; guns, 412–14, 654–55; information resources, 648; joint electronics type designation system, 657–60; terminology and definitions, 397–401; types of, 652–57. *See also* firearms
Weapons Department, 195–96
Weapons-Repair Department, 198
website for BJM, xxvi, 2–3, 721–22
weight, 389–90
welding safety regulations and precautions, 347–48
West Virginia, 161
Whiting, William, 731, 732, 733
Wilkes, Charles, 159
Williams, James Elliott, 161–62
winds, 294, 297–98
wire rope, 269, 272, 276
wirefree communications (WFCOM), 364
workboats, 299
working over the side, 348
working uniforms, 120–24
World War I, 148, 156
World War II: effective damage control during, 386; exploration interests and chart used during, 159; leadership and courage during, 161, 162, 418–19; maritime power of U.S. during, 147, 148; Pearl Harbor attack, 161, 162, 201, 418–19; phonetic alphabet during, 688; power projection during, 156

X-47B aircraft, 639, 640

yeoman (YN), 108, 514, 529

Zimmerman, Charles A. "Zimmy," 728–29
zone inspections, 247–48, 266
Zumwalt-class destroyers, 571, 572

ABOUT THE AUTHOR

Thomas J. Cutler has been serving the U.S. Navy in various capacities for more than fifty years. The author of many articles and books, including several editions of *The Bluejacket's Manual* and *A Sailor's History of the U.S. Navy,* he is the Gordon England Chair of Professional Naval Literature at the U.S. Naval Institute and Fleet Professor of Strategy and Policy with the Naval War College. He has received the William P. Clements Award for Excellence in Education as military teacher of the year at the U.S. Naval Academy, the Alfred Thayer Mahan Award for Naval Literature, the U.S. Maritime Literature Award, the Naval Institute Press Author of the Year Award, and the Commodore Dudley Knox Lifetime Achievement Award in Naval History.

The **Naval Institute Press** is the book-publishing arm of the U.S. Naval Institute, a private, nonprofit, membership society for sea service professionals and others who share an interest in naval and maritime affairs. Established in 1873 at the U.S. Naval Academy in Annapolis, Maryland, where its offices remain today, the Naval Institute has members worldwide.

Members of the Naval Institute support the education programs of the society and receive the influential monthly magazine *Proceedings* or the colorful bimonthly magazine *Naval History* and discounts on fine nautical prints and on ship and aircraft photos. They also have access to the transcripts of the Institute's Oral History Program and get discounted admission to any of the Institute-sponsored seminars offered around the country.

The Naval Institute's book-publishing program, begun in 1898 with basic guides to naval practices, has broadened its scope to include books of more general interest. Now the Naval Institute Press publishes about seventy titles each year, ranging from how-to books on boating and navigation to battle histories, biographies, ship and aircraft guides, and novels. Institute members receive significant discounts on the Press' more than eight hundred books in print.

Full-time students are eligible for special half-price membership rates. Life memberships are also available.

For a free catalog describing Naval Institute Press books currently available, and for further information about joining the U.S. Naval Institute, please write to:

Member Services
U.S. NAVAL INSTITUTE
291 Wood Road
Annapolis, MD 21402-5034
Telephone: (800) 233-8764
Fax: (410) 571-1703
Web address: www.usni.org